REFERENCES TO HANDBOOK. The numbers below give
the heading and the page r ...
sections in the handbook.

D1314279

SENTENCE STRUCTURE	S1 Sentence Elements 370	S2 Phrases & Clauses 382	S3 Verbs & Verbals 383	Fragments (Period Fault) 386	S5 Fused Sentences 388	S6 Run-on Sentence 389
	S7 Comma Splice 390	S8 Faulty Parallelism 392	S9 Dangling Modifier 394	S10 Shifts in Subject-Verb 395	S11 Incomplete Construction 398	
WORD ORDER	WO1 Normal Order 400	WO2 Ambiguous Order 401	WO3 Awkward Separation 403	WO4 Unemphatic Order 404		
GRAMMATICAL FORMS	F1 Wrong Principal Part 407	F2 Tense Forms 407	F3 Case 411	F4 Agreement (Subject-Verb) 414	F5 Agreement (Pronouns) 420	F6 Vague Pronoun Reference 423
	F7 Faulty Complement 424	F8 Adjective Adverb 427				
PUNCTUATION	P1 Uses of Comma 429	P2 Misuse of Comma 437	P3 Uses of Semicolon 439	P4 Misuse of Semicolon 439	P5 Period 440	P6 Question & Exclamation Marks 441
	P7 Colon 441	P8 Quotation Marks 442	P9 Punctuation with Quotation Marks 444	P10 Apostrophe 446	P11 Ellipsis & Dash 446	P12 Parentheses & Brackets 448
MECHANICS	sp Spelling 452	abr Abbreviations 458	caps Capital Letters 459	hyph Hyphenation 462	ital Italics 464	no Numbers 464
	gloss Glossary 468					

A First Course in College Composition

Writing with a Purpose

Fourth Edition

JAMES M. McCRIMMON *The University of Illinois*

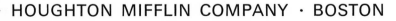 HOUGHTON MIFFLIN COMPANY · BOSTON

New York   Atlanta   Geneva, Ill.   Dallas   Palo Alto

ACKNOWLEDGMENT is made for permission to use material from the following sources.

From *The Forest and the Sea*, by Marston Bates. © Copyright 1960 by Marston Bates. Reprinted by permission of Random House, Inc.

From "The Secret of Life," by Loren Eiseley. Copyright 1953 by Loren Eiseley. Reprinted from *The Immense Journey*, by Loren Eiseley, by permission of Random House, Inc.

From *Storm*, by George R. Stewart. Copyright 1941 by George R. Stewart. Reprinted by permission of Random House, Inc.

From *Farewell to Sport*, by Paul Gallico. Copyright 1937, 1938 by Paul Gallico. Reprinted by permission of Alfred A. Knopf, Inc.

From "The Idealist" (*The Stories of Frank O'Connor*). Copyright 1950 by Frank O'Connor. Reprinted by permission of Alfred A. Knopf, Inc. Originally appeared in *The New Yorker*.

From *Not So Wild a Dream*, by Eric Sevareid. Copyright 1946 by Eric Sevareid. Reprinted by permission of Alfred A. Knopf, Inc.

From *The Necessary Angel*, by Wallace Stevens. Copyright 1951 by Wallace Stevens. Reprinted by permission of Alfred A. Knopf, Inc.

Extracts reprinted with permission of The Macmillan Company and Hutchinson & Co. Ltd. from *The Act of Creation* by Arthur Koestler. Copyright © Arthur Koestler 1964.

"Sailing to Byzantium," reprinted with permission of The Macmillan Company, Mr. M. B. Yeats, and Macmillan & Co. Ltd., from *Collected Poems* by William Butler Yeats. Copyright 1928 The Macmillan Company, renewed 1956 by Georgie Yeats.

From *The Italians*, by Luigi Barzini. Copyright © 1964 by Luigi Barzini. Reprinted by permission of Atheneum Publishers and Hamish Hamilton Ltd.

The following student essays, reprinted in whole or in part, from various issues of *The Green Caldron*; *A Magazine of Freshman Writing*, published at the University of Illinois, Urbana, Illinois: "Places of Pleasure," by Jane Lewis; "Why We Need More Westerns on Television," by Mary Louise Borgman; "Sugar and Spice and Stereotype," by Kathryn McAuliffe; "The Bullfight," by George M. Highsmith; "Seven Come Eleven," by Carol Stewart; "The Secret Life of Walter Mitty," by Philip G. Plotica; "Death of a Sad Man," by J. A. Sessler; "Age of Thunder," by Miriam Graham; "On 'Death'," by Tim Flynn; "Phonies and Phoniness," by David M. Klingel.

Photographs: p. 34, "Day and Night" (woodcut, 1938) by Maurits C. Escher, courtesy of Mickelson Gallery, Washington, D.C.; p. 51, courtesy of The American Museum of Natural History; p. 52, courtesy of the National Park Service.

CONTENTS

Contents

Part Four. **Handbook of Grammar and Usage**

PREFACE

The revisions embodied in this Fourth Edition of *Writing with a Purpose* are more comprehensive than those in earlier editions. They are designed to achieve the following results: to extend the concept of purpose as artistic control over the selection, arrangement, and presentation of material by more attention to prewriting; to emphasize the importance of content and to suggest means by which a student may obtain information and generate ideas for his writing; to provide more help with organization than exclusive attention to outlining permits; to relate examples and assignments more directly to literature than was done in earlier editions; and to provide many new models and exercises.

The three main divisions of the Third Edition have been increased to four in order to allow detailed attention to systematic prewriting, or planning, as an essential stage in the composition process. To provide space for new material on this topic, two chapters ("Synopses and Summaries" and "The Business Letter") have been dropped, and two others ("Using a Dictionary" and "Improving Vocabulary") have been reduced and incorporated in the chapter on "Right Words."

Within the present twelve chapters of Parts One through Three, the major revisions are as follows:

Chapter 1. The revision combines the content of former Chapters 1 and 2 on choosing and restricting a subject and determining and stating purpose.

Chapter 2. This new chapter aims to help students discover materials and generate ideas from observation, from reading, and through inferences drawn from these sources. The basic technique, illustrated by professional and student models, is the analysis of existing knowledge and its resynthesis into new forms by analogy, classification, and interpretation.

Chapter 3. This added chapter deals with the organization of papers which do not require formal outlines. Of the three informal patterns discussed — illustrative, analytical, and argumentative — the first two are expansions of a chapter which appeared in the Second Edition but was dropped from the Third. The material on the structure of argument has been brought forward from a later chapter to permit attention to informal argument during the first semester of the course.

Chapter 9. The former chapter on "The Critical Review" has been expanded to include the writing of critical essays other than reviews.

Chapter 12. The revision of this chapter, which in the Third Edition was entitled "Argument: Logical Persuasion," shifts the emphasis to the deliberative process employed in problem-solving. The material on logic and fallacies is retained as providing techniques for evaluating proposed solutions, but the chapter is now oriented toward decision-making rather than the structure of argument.

In general the effect of these revisions is to upgrade the content of the book to meet the changing needs of a student population which is coming to college better prepared and better motivated than ever before.

The emphasis on prewriting, invention, and organic structure reflects my concern with the content of compositions and my debt to much of what has recently been said and written about "the new rhetoric." Most of the specific revisions beginning with Chapter 3 are the result of suggestions made by instructors who have used earlier editions. I wish to acknowledge the helpful criticism provided by the following persons, without implying that they would necessarily approve of the changes I finally made. For a comprehensive review of the book as a whole I am especially indebted to Professors Richard L. Larson of the University of Hawaii, Ralph A. Loomis of the University of Michigan, Joseph F. Madden of St. Petersburg Junior College, Ted R. Spivey of Georgia State College, and Robert E. Wilkinson of Villanova University. I am also indebted for helpful criticism and suggestions about individual chapters to Professors Robert W. Cochran of the University of Vermont, Jack E. Conner of California State College at Hayward, Soren F. Cox of Brigham Young University, John B. Craven of Glendale College, California, James W. Culp of Abilene Christian College, Beth R. Dolan of Lackland Air Force Base, Marguerite W. Goodman of Millsaps College, G. O. Gunter of York Junior College, Pennsylvania, William C. Hamlin of the University of Missouri at St. Louis, Arno Hill of the University of Illinois, Grace King of Glendale College, John L. Kimmey of the University of South Carolina, Ruth G. Lewis of Washington University, W. E. Lindblad of Ball State University, Indiana, William C. Pratt and Claire J. Raeth, both of Miami University, Ohio, Robert Ian Scott of the University of Saskatchewan, Vernon Wanty of Towson State College, Maryland, Raymond E. Warden, Jr., of Indiana Central College, Robert Williams of Wisconsin State University at Superior, and Willson E. Wood of Western Kentucky State College.

To Mrs. Florence Trefethen of Tufts University I owe thanks not only for specific suggestions about revision but also for a number of student essays which I have used as models.

Finally, I am again much indebted to my wife, Barbara S. McCrimmon, for her revision of the chapter on the use of the library and for her help in proofreading at all stages.

JAMES M. McCRIMMON

Boston, Massachusetts

BIBLIOGRAPHY

The following works, organized under subject headings, form a short, selective bibliography of writings on language. Since many of these works contain their own bibliographies, they may be used as starting points for any student who wishes to investigate the subject further. The critical comments following the citation attempt to describe briefly the contribution of the work.

General. Works in this section are not limited to any of the subjects of the remaining sections but include several or all of them.

Allen, Harold B., ed. *Readings in Applied English Linguistics.* 2nd ed. New York: Appleton-Century-Crofts, 1964. An anthology of essays on linguistics and the application of linguistics to the teaching of composition and literature. A good introductory cross-section of the work being done in language by serious scholars.

Bloomfield, Leonard. *Language.* New York: Holt, Rinehart and Winston, 1933. The book which established the basic patterns of scientific investigation of language and which has served as a model for later linguists.

Bodmer, Frederick. *The Loom of Language,* edited by Lancelot Hogben. New York: Norton, 1944. A popular study of language, with special attention to the relation of English to other languages.

Carroll, John B. *The Study of Language.* Cambridge, Mass.: Harvard University Press, 1953. A comprehensive survey of the work in linguistics and related fields. Extensive bibliography.

Guth, Hans P. *English Today and Tomorrow.* Englewood Cliffs, N.J.: Prentice-Hall, 1964. A survey of English as a school subject and of the teaching of English as a profession. Although written as a guide for teachers and those who intend to become teachers of English, it is of general interest.

Laird, Charlton. *The Miracle of Language.* Cleveland: World Publishing Company, 1953. Because of its imaginative organization and presentation, this is perhaps the best introduction to the study of language available to a freshman.

Sapir, Edward. *Language.* New York: Harcourt, Brace, 1921. Also available in paperback edition as a Harvest Book. A book which has influenced the course of modern linguistics, especially important for its analysis of the relation between language and culture.

Saporta, Saul, ed. *Psycholinguistics: A Book of Readings.* New York: Holt, Rinehart and Winston, 1961. Although this book is too technical for undergraduates, some students may at least wish to scan it in order to see the interdisciplinary nature of modern studies of language.

History of the English Language

Alexander, Henry. *The Story of Our Language.* Toronto: Nelson, 1940. Revised edition available in paperback as a Doubleday Dolphin Book. A brief and very readable account of the evolution of English, with chapters on the major differences between British and American English.

Baugh, Albert C. *History of the English Language.* 2nd ed. New York: Appleton-Century-Crofts, 1957. The standard history of the English language.

Jesperson, Otto. *The Growth and Structure of the English Language.* New York: Appleton-Century-Crofts, 1923. Also available in paperback as a Doubleday Anchor Book. One of the major histories of the English language.

Robertson, Stuart. *The Development of Modern English,* revised by Frederic G. Cassidy. New York: Prentice-Hall, 1954. A series of studies in the historical backgrounds of modern English.

Grammar. At present three approaches to the study of grammar are available: *traditional, structural,* and *transformational.* The traditional approach, which is both the oldest and the most widely used, describes sentences in terms of traditional concepts (parts of speech) which have come down from Latin grammar. The structural approach, which was originally used by anthropologists to study primitive languages, describes statements in terms of "structures" of sound, form, and order. The transformational approach describes the way complex sentences may be generated from basic or "kernel" sentence patterns. Thus "The man at the door is sick" may be described as a transformation from two basic sentences, "The man is sick" and "The man is at the door."

These three methods of describing English sentences are not mutually exclusive. Traditional grammarians, for example, are also concerned with form and order, and transformational grammarians agree that the base from which they start is traditional grammar. Each method provides useful information about a sentence, but there is considerable agreement among linguists that transformational descriptions are often more discriminating and are therefore preferable, Meanwhile, still other methods are being investigated. Presumably the one that proves most efficient will someday become the standard method, but it is still too early to say which that will be. It could be a combination of methods.

In the following list, traditional, structural, and transformational grammars are represented.

Chomsky, Noam. *Aspects of the Theory of Syntax.* Cambridge, Mass.: M.I.T. Press, 1965. A review and reformulation of the theory of a transformational generative grammar which Chomsky had published in *Syntactic Structures* in 1957. Because of Chomsky's leadership in transformational grammar, this volume may be considered the basic text for the study of the transformational theory. It includes a bibliography which identifies other contributions. Students who wish to investigate the transformational method of analysis will find Owen Thomas's book (below) an easier introduction.

Curme, George O. *Syntax.* Boston: Heath, 1931. With *Parts of Speech and Accidence,* below, the most comprehensive grammar in this bibliography, and one of the best examples of the traditional approach.

Curme, George O. *Parts of Speech and Accidence.* Boston: Heath, 1935. See *Syntax,* above.

Francis, W. Nelson. *The Structure of American English.* New York: Ronald Press, 1958. An analysis of the means by which grammatical distinctions are made in English, with emphasis on sound structures. Written as a textbook for advanced undergraduates and graduates.

Fries, Charles C. *American English Grammar.* New York: Appleton-Century-Crofts, 1940. A description of the grammar of American English based on an analysis of more than 2000 letters written to a government agency. The result is both a helpful description of educated American language practices and an example of a scientific method applied to a description of grammar.

Fries, Charles C. *The Structure of English.* New York: Harcourt, Brace, 1952. A description of sentence structure based on an analysis of recorded conversations amounting to 250,000 words. Although the analysis has been criticized by other structural grammarians on the grounds that it does not pay sufficient attention to sound, the book is one of the influential documents of structural grammar.

Long, Ralph B. *The Sentence and Its Parts.* Chicago: University of Chicago Press, 1961. A traditional one-volume grammar of contemporary American English.

Sledd, James. *A Short Introduction to English Grammar.* Chicago: Scott, Foresman, 1959. The author himself calls his work a "transitional" grammar — that is, an attempt to provide a transition between traditional and structural grammar.

Thomas, Owen. *Transformational Grammar and the Teacher of English.* New York: Holt, Rinehart and Winston, 1965. A simplified account of transformational analysis designed as a textbook to be used by departments of English, schools of education, and secondary school teachers.

Usage. Whereas grammar is concerned with describing the grammatical system, usage consists of judgments about what language practices are acceptable among educated people.

Bernstein, Theodore M. *The Careful Writer: A Modern Guide to English Usage.* New York: Atheneum, 1965. This volume represents the conservative position with respect to usage, as Evans (below) represents the liberal position.

Bryant, Margaret M. *Current American Usage.* New York: Funk & Wagnalls, 1962. This is a scholarly study of usage rather than one based on subjective judgments. It is much less comprehensive than the books by Bernstein, Evans, and Fowler, but on matters on which it reports it may be said to be the standard reference.

Evans, Bergen and Cornelia. *A Dictionary of Contemporary American Usage.* New York: Random House, 1957. More comprehensive and detailed than Bernstein's book, partly because the print is smaller and the style is less anecdotal. More liberal than the Bernstein volume.

Fowler, H. W. *A Dictionary of Modern English Usage.* 2nd ed.; revised and edited by Sir Ernest Gowers. New York: Oxford University Press, 1965. This revision of an old favorite has been acclaimed as preserving the qualities that made the first edition so popular, while bringing it up to date. The usage is primarily British English.

Kennedy, Arthur G. *Current English.* Boston: Ginn, 1935. A comprehensive survey of the knowledge of modern English, containing a very useful bibliography.

Perrin, Porter G., and others. *Writer's Guide and Index to English.* 4th ed. Chicago: Scott, Foresman, 1965. Comprehensively applies the results of usage studies to the work in college composition.

Pooley, Robert C. *Teaching English Usage.* New York: Appleton-Century-Crofts, 1946. As the title suggests, this work is aimed primarily at teachers, but its discussion of common problems of usage is helpful generally.

Semantics. Books in this section are concerned with the study of meaning, especially with the symbolic nature of language and the factors that influence response to words.

Brown, Roger. *Words and Things.* New York: The Free Press of Glencoe (a division of The Macmillan Company), 1958. A readable synthesis of much of the scholarship in anthropology, linguistics, philosophy, and psychology having to do with the relation of words and things.

Hayakawa, S. I. *Language, Thought, and Action.* 2nd ed. New York: Harcourt, Brace & World, 1964. A second revision of an earlier edition, entitled *Language in Action,* a popularization of Alfred Korzybski's *Science and Sanity,* and probably the most popular book ever written on the subject of semantics.

Lee, Irving J. *Language Habits in Human Affairs.* New York: Harper, 1941. Another popularization of Korzybski's work, unusually rich in illustrative material.

Ogden, C. K., and I. A. Richards. *The Meaning of Meaning.* 3rd ed. New York: Harcourt, Brace, 1930. Also available in paperback as a Harvest Book. One of the earliest and most influential of the works on semantics.

Walpole, Hugh R. *Semantics: The Nature of Words and Their Meanings.* New York: Norton, 1941. A popular work on the subject, influenced by the work of Ogden and Richards.

PART ONE

Planning the Composition

PREWRITING: TOWARD PURPOSEFUL WRITING

SOURCES OF MATERIAL

PATTERNS OF ORGANIZATION

THE OUTLINE

1

Prewriting:

Toward Purposeful Writing

A perceptive student once said, "The trouble with Freshman English is you're supposed to know everything about writing before you get a chance to study any of it." In one sense, at least, he was right. In mathematics, foreign languages, and the sciences, you begin with the rudiments, and successive lessons build on what has gone before. But in composition all the skills required at the end of the term are also needed at the beginning. Even in his first essay, a student must choose a subject, limit it to manageable size, select pertinent material, organize it logically, develop his ideas in detail, and express them in orderly paragraphs and clear sentences with due regard for the conventions of usage.

If a student thinks of writing as a single operation, he must do most of these things at the same time. Unless his problem is a very simple one, he will be wise to think of composition as a process, and to break it into stages. The three principal stages are prewriting, writing, and revision. In *prewriting,* one tries to discover, as precisely as he can, just what he wants to do. He makes basic decisions that will direct and guide him when he begins to write, decisions that will define his subject and determine the attitudes he will take to both his subject and his reader. In *writing,* he carries out these decisions through a completed first draft. And in *revision,* he makes specific changes to improve the draft.

The divisions between these three main stages of composition are not clear-cut. Some parts of the process overlap two stages. For some essays, the selection and arrangement of material begins in prewriting, and often a writer makes extensive revisions even while writing his first draft. This overlapping is likely to be greater in short, informal essays, such as those

3

written impromptu in class. In longer, more formal compositions, such as research or term papers, the main stages are usually more deliberately separated. The following diagram illustrates both the separation and the overlapping.

Prewriting —————— Writing ————— Revision

Subject — restriction — purpose
      Selection and arrangement of material
          Paragraph and sentence structure
            Diction and mechanics
                Improvement and correction
                of first draft — proofreading

CHOOSING AND RESTRICTING A SUBJECT

The subjects of many of your essays will be at least partly determined for you by the wording of the assignment. But when you have a free choice, avoid the twin evils of sustained indecision and a nervous flitting back and forth between alternatives. You will generally write with more confidence if the subject lies close to your interests and experience. Otherwise, your choice of subject is less important than what you do with it. No amount of thinking will lead you to a subject that has never been treated before; but any subject, however commonplace, can yield a good essay if it is made to reflect the observations, ideas, and values of the author.

Often students overlook good subjects because they fail to see that what they think of as a single experience is really a series of experiences, any part of which might make an effective essay. For example, see how a visit to New York can be broken into many separate topics:

> The New York skyline
> Driving in New York
> My first subway ride
> The view from the Empire State Building
> Rockefeller Center
> Chinatown
> Harlem
> Eating in an automat
> The waterfront
> The Stock Exchange in action
> Shopping in New York
> Greenwich Village restaurants
> New York cabbies — fact and legend
> A visit to the United Nations

4

When a subject is thus broken down into subtopics, it is said to be *restricted*. The opposite of a restricted subject is a *general* one — for example, "My Visit to New York." Breaking a general subject into a number of restricted topics is useful in two ways. First, it exposes the inclusive nature of the general subject and shows that it contains more topics than can be dealt with thoroughly in one paper. How could anyone do justice to the United Nations in a single paragraph? Yet devoting even one paragraph to each topic in the list above would require a paper of fourteen paragraphs, something which no student has any intention of writing in a normal weekly essay. Anyone who begins to write on a subject so general as "My Visit to New York" is likely to finish with a list of the places he saw and little more than a sentence or two about each of them.

Restriction also helps to suggest an area of concentration. When one realizes that he cannot deal with fourteen topics, he may see that one of them — cabbies, for instance — can make a good essay by itself. This discovery will force him to concentrate, and the concentration will suggest interesting or significant incidents, examples, illustrations, and ideas.

As a first step toward finding a suitable subject, this kind of restriction by division helps, but it does not guarantee success. For example, students are often tempted to restrict an autobiographical subject by cutting the time it covers — by confining themselves to a single year or a particular summer vacation. This kind of restriction is more obvious than helpful. The goal of restriction is to get a topic that can be developed with satisfying completeness. Usually restriction in time or space alone is not enough, since an account of a whole summer vacation may still be only a general summary of the experience. On the other hand, an essay may deal with several years of the writer's life — if he selects from those years only experiences that clearly illustrate a theme or idea. Thus an essay on "My Struggle for Self-Confidence" can be more unified and detailed, even if it covers a dozen years, than one which records the unrelated events of a single day.

What efficient restriction provides is a unifying control. A general subject merely marks out an area in which the writer intends to look for something to say. A restricted subject narrows the range of investigation and thus increases the chances of the writer's finding what he wants to write about. To be truly useful, the restriction should guide the writer to an understanding of what he wants to do. For example, "College: A Conventional Pause Between High School and Marriage" and "College at Last!" not only specify the aspect of the general subject to be discussed but also suggest what materials to use and what to say about them. This kind of restriction limits the general subject by looking at it from a particular point of view, and thus rules out observations not pertinent to that point of view.

The following clock diagram illustrates the relation between a general subject and some useful restrictions.

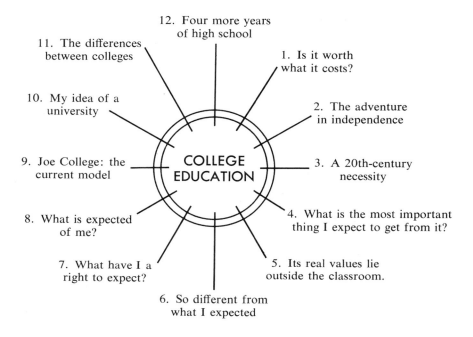

For each of these twelve restricted topics, here are some questions designed to encourage still further restriction. Thoughtfully asked and answered, such questions suggest the shape that the essay might take, and lead to some of the facts, observations, and opinions by which the subject may be developed.

1. What kind of costs — money, time, effort? What does a young man or woman give in exchange for a college education? How does one decide whether the investment is wise?
2. Independence from what? From parental control? From the limitations of home-town values? From adolescent confusions? How is it an adventure?
3. An economic necessity? A social necessity? A necessary challenge to the individual? Why is it a "necessity" at all?
4. What are the generally accepted advantages? Which of these means most to me? Why is this likely to be more obtainable in college than elsewhere?
5. What values — social, economic, intellectual, cultural? If none of these, what other? What is there about me that makes one of these sets of values more important than the others?
6. What did I expect? Why? In what ways different? Which of these deserves most emphasis?

7. From the faculty, the students, the library and laboratories, the total environment? What is meant by "right to expect"?
8. From whom — teachers, friends, parents? From myself?
9. Is there a "Joe College" nowadays? If so, what is he like? How does the current model differ from earlier ones? How significant are these differences?
10. What does the word "university" mean to me? If this were the University of Utopia, what would it be like? How would I spell out my concept of an ideal university?
11. Socially, academically, as preparation for graduate school? In terms of what?
12. How is college like high school? Is it chiefly in my relation to authority, or does the similarity lie in the conduct of the institutions?

The diagram suggests a dozen restrictions of one general subject, but it by no means exhausts the possibilities. The questions suggest ways in which each restricted topic might be further narrowed. They turn the writer's thoughts to particular aspects of the topic and so force him to define the topic and his relation to it. He now has a more limited area to investigate and clues that may lead him to investigate it in depth. Once he has thought out the possibilities of his general subject, as in this example, his purpose has begun to take shape and he has done a considerable amount of prewriting. All things being equal, he has now found a technique for directing his thoughts through a narrower channel.

▶ *As an exercise in restriction, prepare a clock diagram in which you show twelve restricted topics radiating from one general subject. Then select one of these restricted topics and write a memorandum to yourself showing by questions or comments ways in which you might explore a further definition of your subject.*

As a final illustration of limiting a subject, study the two essays that follow. Both were written to the same assignment: "Write an autobiographical essay." The first is specific and personal; it reports an actual experience and the author's changing reactions to it. The second is not limited to a single incident; it abstracts from a series of unspecified experiences the changing patterns that take shape as an individual matures. Yet, unlike as they are in content and style, both essays are excellent examples of how a thoughtful and sensitive student can restrict a general subject to a topic which he then views in his own unique way.

PLACES OF PLEASURE

One night, because we had nothing better to do, my roommate and another girl and I hopped in the car and set off for a grand tour of the campus "joints." On my journey I found neither dens of iniquity nor glimpses of a promised land, but merely the mildly amusing sequence of scenes I had

7

expected. I say amusing, for nothing is more a point of gentle laughter than a child; no one can help smiling when he sees a youngster mimicking the ludicrous actions of his elders in all seriousness; and at every place I went I saw children playing at being adults.

I saw children smoking in every way they had ever seen: in a nervous, endless chain; languidly as Cleopatra; in the fashion of underworld characters; or with a pseudo-sophisticated flick of the wrist.

I saw children talking in every tone imaginable: boisterously, pretentiously in earnest, in the manner of men and women of the world, or with an air of boredom.

I saw children drinking beer: they drank it from bottles, from glasses, from pitchers; they sipped it, they gulped it, they studied it; they adored it.

And all the time I felt I was in a land of Lilliputians with everything built to size: there were small rooms, cozy seats, tiny bottles, pint-sized ash trays, baby-faced proprietors, and little boy waiters. What could be more charming! And yet after a few moments of amusement I found myself becoming absolutely bored.

Not once did I see any one of these imitation cosmopolitans smoking for the sheer pleasure of it, talking because he had something to say, or drinking because he liked beer. Rather, they all gave me the impression that they had come, had sat, had smoked, had talked, had drunk, and were waiting for the enchanted words to be spoken and the magic dust sprinkled on their curly little heads and the wonderful miracle of "having a good time" to occur. I could see it running through their minds: "Adults can do what they want; this is what they do, so it must be fun."

My feeling of boredom melted to pity and I felt moved to cry out in a ringing voice with dramatic pauses — "Unhappy generation! You are right in your unhappiness. Your pleasures are not dictated to you. There is more joy to living than this. Rise up! Go forth!" — when suddenly it occurred to me that perhaps I was the odd personality, unable to enjoy standard entertainment. Maybe they were really having a good time.

In a cloud of uncertainty I followed my friends back to the dorm and got into the shower, the only place where my powers of reasoning function properly, and began to talk to myself.

"Jane," I said, "you have smoked L & M, Lucky Strike, Viceroy, Marlboro, Winston, Kentucky Brand, Camel, Chesterfield, and homemade cigarettes. You have talked to priests, psychiatrists, businessmen, teachers, teenagers, Chinese, Czechoslovakians, Japanese, Hawaiians, Germans, Hungarians, Swedish, English, and Americans about life, death, philosophy, sex, politics, morals, religion, and the future of America. You have drunk whiskey, vodka, rum, gin, vermouth, champagne, and your father's wine in bedrooms, barrooms, bathrooms, bowling alleys, basements, cocktail lounges, cars, and swimming pools. Have or have not all these things been fun?"

"Yes," I sighed, remembering.

"And have you or have you not enjoyed, along with smoking, jabbering, and drinking, the pleasures of reading, listening to music, watching plays, and praying on your knees to a hidden God?"

"I have," I replied, beginning to see the light.

"Then what right have you to laugh at, sneer at, pity, or judge the people you saw in the places you went to tonight?"

"No right at all," I whispered, scrubbing my ears.

But as I turned on the cold water all my confidence and defiance came back to me and "There was something sad and wrong in those places!" I cried to my departing self.

CHANGING PATTERNS

Experience does more than add to knowledge, it adds to the self as well. In a way, an individual accumulates personalities as he lives his life, personalities that form and shift and merge in response to different circumstances at different times. Every new situation creates a kind of vacuum around him; actions and reactions appropriate in familiar situations have to be modified in the new, and he is set free from old habits and attitudes. A person fills this vacuum with new habits and new attitudes stimulated by the new situation, with newly-discovered qualities which have found the necessary space in which to grow.

The process can be clearly seen in a girl who has left home for college. At home, long years of living in one context have imposed a certain pattern on her life, so that her family and friends see her, and she sees herself, only in terms of that pattern. Should she care more for books than for music, or more for clothes than for either, then those mark the boundaries of her world. Should she settle herself in a particular circle of friends, those friends and others like them become part of her pattern. She bases her life on the familiar, on what she had already been rather than on what she might yet be.

But life at college presents her with an entirely different situation. Circumstances, friends, activities, and ideas are all new, and demand new responses from her as she works out her place in these surroundings. She is not bound to the old pattern by assumptions and expectations based on it; she can see herself in different terms, so that this different kind of life allows her to change and grow, to depart from the old pattern toward new possibilities discovered in her contact with new experience. Eventually, as the new situation gradually becomes a familiar one, she will settle into a pattern again, and further growth will await for further experience. Proof that there has been a change shows up when a friend visits home, or when a parent visits college: the friend or parent may be surprised to discover a wit or an intensity, an apathy or an energy, that is foreign to the girl each knows on his own ground.

There is a related kind of flexibility at work in hundreds of other situations. A girl can behave in two very different ways on successive evenings, sometimes depending on the nature of the evening and the mood of her date. The laughing girl at a boisterous beach party will not be the same person on the evening that she discusses Shakespeare or Yeats until late in the night. But whether the changes are on a larger or a smaller scale, whether they are permanent and slow to evolve or temporary and quickly assumed, they are evidence of a fundamental characteristic of human nature. No individual is a single personality; his several selves develop and shift and mingle as he moves through experience, and each part contributes to the making of a whole.

9

In addition to what they show about restriction, these two essays illustrate how one's personality is reflected in his writing. Both girls are concerned with interpreting and evaluating their experience. Because they are quite different people, the materials they select and the uses they make of them are different. For the first girl, the specific and incidental is the stuff of thought; for the second, what controls thinking is an intellectual habit of clustering events and generalizing patterns from the clusters. But each girl is trying to understand herself more fully in the light of her response to experience, and each, in her own way, is so involved in what she is writing that finally she is reporting, thoughtfully and honestly, how she sees the bit of experience she is writing about. In this sense the second essay is as autobiographical as the first.

▶ *The following list of topics may be used in two ways. First, the topics may act as prompters for any student who feels that some kind of suggestion will get him off dead-center when he has a free choice of subject. Second, the list may be used as a common body of general subjects for whatever class exercises on prewriting your instructor thinks helpful. For this purpose, it is not expected that the subjects will actually be developed into essays. But there is something of value in a group of students discussing how certain general subjects might be restricted and what kinds of material would be required for different purposes. In such discussion, students may volunteer additional subjects.*

1. *Examples or anecdotes which illustrate a point.* Classic types are fables (the boy who cried "Wolf!"), the parables of the New Testament, and the kind of stories Abraham Lincoln told to make a point in a law case or political campaign. This mode of communication is popular in a wide range of discourse from social conversation to formal debate. The exercise requires two kinds of skill: the ability to understand clearly what point is to be made (purpose), and the ability to choose apt stories or examples to clinch that point (appropriate selection of material).
   a. Some people (or I) do not know how to respond to a compliment.
   b. Some people seem to have a genius for saying the right (wrong) thing at the right time.
   c. The only way to stop smoking is to stop.
   d. The greatest virtue a date can have is the ability to listen responsively.
   e. The essence of love is unselfishness.
   f. One way to prevent divorce is for married people to treat each other with the same courtesy they extend to strangers.

2. *Reminiscences* — recalling how things were or how you felt about them
   a. When you are five, a year is forever.
   b. Christmas used to be fun.
   c. That boy (girl) in the seventh grade
   d. Dad always bought me toys for himself.
   e. We don't have such storms nowadays.
   f. I remember the day President Kennedy was assassinated.

3. *Descriptions of people or places*
   a. The most self-sufficient person I ever met
   b. People I can't stand
   c. So sure of himself in public, so unsure in private
   d. The man (woman) I'd like to be
   e. The kind of girl who thinks the football players are talking about her when they go into a huddle
   f. My favorite view
   g. My home town
   h. The most interesting city I know

4. *Reports of events or actions*
   a. An accident
   b. A case of stage fright
   c. My moment of glory
   d. The stupidest thing I ever did
   e. A terrifying experience
   f. The most courageous act I ever saw
   g. I can laugh about it now, but then it was torture.
   h. The best laid plans of mice and men
   i. Cliff hangers in basketball or football

5. *Directions and processes* — showing someone how to do something
   a. What to watch at a football game
   b. How to cure a slice in golf
   c. Photography as an art
   d. How to make guests feel at ease
   e. Editing a high school paper
   f. Producing a play
   g. Skiing, surfing, or diving
   h. The new math
   i. How to moderate a discussion
   j. The best ways to get killed on a highway

6. *Reflections on your reading*
   a. My favorite poet, playwright, or novelist
   b. The inspiration of biographies
   c. The reality of fiction
   d. Why is violence so popular?
   e. Public opinion polls
   f. Cartoons
   g. The magazine I'd recommend to a college student

7. *Opinions and beliefs*
   a. Is burning a draft card a legitimate form of protest?
   b. Are student demonstrations a sign of something?
   c. Is our space program worth the cost?
   d. Is there a new morality?
   e. Should there be limits to freedom of expression?
   f. Is an honor system practicable?
   g. In what sense are all men born free and equal?

11

h. What do we mean by tolerance?
i. Are we overemphasizing education?
j. TV commercials — necessity or nuisance?
k. Do science and religion conflict?
l. Does compulsory attendance protect the student?
m. Is conformity always bad?
n. Loyalty to oneself
o. The courage of common people in their everyday lives

DETERMINING THE PURPOSE

You have seen how restricting a subject marks out an area of concentration and suggests what the writer should do in his paper. As restriction proceeds, these suggestions begin to provide a unifying control, so that an alert student knows pretty well what he wants to say by the time he begins to write his first draft. He may not — and probably will not — know every fact, example, and anecdote he will use; but he does know what kind of material will be pertinent and what will not, and he has a clear sense of what his essay is going to do and probably how it is going to do it. When he reaches this stage, he has determined his *purpose.*

The simplest way to define purpose is to say that it is the over-all design which controls what the writer is to do in the essay. By means of this decision he knows what he must do in the writing stage: what kind of materials he needs, possible ways in which they may be organized, perhaps even the tone he must take. When he determines his purpose he makes a basic decision about how his essay is to be written, and that decision directs and controls all the specific decisions he makes from then on.

A word of warning. We often describe a writer's purpose in terms of how he wants to affect his readers — to tell them what happened, to describe what something looks like, to explain to them how something works or is made, to persuade them to accept an opinion or a judgment, or even to amuse them. In this book we use the word not in this broad sense but with specific reference to how the writer is going to treat his subject in order to achieve this general effect. This restricted use does not mean that a writer can be unconcerned about his audience. On the contrary, an effective writer will be sensitive to the whole situation in which he is writing, including his audience, and that awareness will help him to shape and clarify his specific purpose. But here we assume that the writer knows whether he is trying to amuse, instruct, or persuade a particular audience in a particular situation, and that he is facing the problem of what he should do in his essay.

Imagine an expert golfer facing a twenty-foot putt on a rolling green. What is his purpose? To say that he wants to sink his putt tells us nothing useful. The important decision is *how* the shot is to be played. He studies the contour of the green, observes the grain and texture of the grass, and plans the path he wants his ball to follow. Only when he has thought out his problem in this way can he be said to know what he wants to do. His purpose, then, is to stroke his ball in such a way that it will follow the contour of the green in a *predetermined* path to the cup. The golfer makes a basic decision about how he is going to play the shot, and that decision controls the progress of the ball. Likewise the writer is trying to control the progress of his essay. His purpose, as the term is here used, is the cluster of basic decisions he makes about how his subject is to be treated.

An example of purposeful writing may make this explanation clearer. The student author of the following essay has set herself a difficult but interesting problem. With a free choice of subject, she has chosen to write an ironic criticism of TV westerns. That decision controls her whole approach to the assignment. Specifically, it forces her to make fun of westerns while pretending to admire them; to steer a narrow course between an obvious attack (which would not be funny) and a too-subtle criticism (which the audience might miss); to select examples and details that support her purpose at all times; and to use a style that will accentuate the humor. Read her essay and judge how well she has succeeded.

Why We Need More Westerns on Television

The other night I saw a wonderful western on television. It had just about everything you'd want — fast horses, handsome men, beautiful women, mean outlaws, sneaky Indians, waving grass, rolling plains, covered wagons, smoking pistols, hard liquor, torrid love, bitter tears, bloody death — just everything you could ask for, all packed together into one little hour, and early enough for the kids to see it, too. This program was really something and I think we need lots more just like it, because programs like that teach lots of things that everybody ought to know — things that help us in our everyday life, and at other times, too. I'll tell you what I mean.

Take making friends, for instance. Most people are pretty slow at this, but they don't have to be. This program showed that a person can make friends quickly if he really tries. There was a trail scout in this story and a Russian countess, and at the beginning, they didn't even know each other, but before the first commercial, which came about four minutes after they met, they were already lying in the grass and kissing, just as if they'd known each other for years. I think we should all take a lesson from this — it's sort of a symbol. A Russian and an American making love on the prairie under the sky. It has a lot of meaning to it.

Another thing about westerns is that they show the difference between good and bad people. After you watch a few westerns, it's pretty easy to tell which is which. The good men, for instance, seldom have beards or whiskers, and most of the bad men do. Also, the good man never shoots a person in the back — he waits until the person turns around to face him, which is the decent thing to do. On the other hand, bad men will shoot a man anywhere and will even shoot a woman or a dog sometimes. Speaking of women, there are good ones and bad ones, just like men. The good ones are usually married, while the bad ones usually aren't. The bad women usually wear real low-cut dresses or short ones, and the good women usually have on aprons; they might wear pretty tight dresses (the young good ones, that is; the old good women wear loose dresses), but they're hardly ever cut low. All these things are very helpful to people watching the program, because they know right away whose side to be on. And just like knowing how to make friends quickly, it's very helpful in life to know whose side to be on.

One of the best things westerns teach is our country's history. I'll bet people with television sets know lots more about history than people without television sets, because westerns on television are just crammed with history. They tell how we had to fight the pagan Indians every step of the way to get them to give us this land so that we could really make something out of it. (We let them go on living here, after we won the land fair and square, and we even gave them special areas called "reservations" to live on. They're real nice places — sort of like wild game preserves to keep animals from becoming what they call "extinct.")

When you start thinking about all the advantages of watching westerns, it's pretty plain to see that we ought to have more of them. There has been a lot of progress made toward getting more westerns on television, and you can see a good western almost any time except Sunday. Unfortunately, on Sunday afternoons there are things like symphony orchestras, documentary films, and panel discussions — real dull, long-hair stuff that most Americans wouldn't be interested in. The only good thing about Sunday is that before you know it, it's Monday again, and the beginning of a whole new week of interesting, educational, realistic, historical westerns. But friends, we've got to do something about Sunday afternoons.

▶ *The following questions concerning this essay may be discussed in class.*

1. What is usually the function of the opening paragraph of an essay? Does the opening paragraph of this essay perform that function? Can you point to any sentence that may be said to state the alleged purpose of the essay? Can you point to any sentence which suggests to the reader that the alleged purpose is not the real one? Considering the total purpose of the essay, how successful is this first paragraph?

2. What is usually the function of the final paragraph of an essay? Does the final paragraph of this essay perform that function? Comment on its effectiveness in terms of its purpose.

3. The three middle paragraphs carry the bulk of the ironic content. Does each deal with a separate part of the subject? If so, what? Comment on the appropriateness of the details in these paragraphs to the writer's purpose.

4. Does the author adopt any recognizable attitude toward the subject? If so, describe it. How is that attitude communicated?

5. Notice the many contractions (*I'll, don't, aren't, they're*) and colloquial expressions (*kids, lots of, sort of, pretty slow, real low-cut*). Is such diction appropriate in this essay? What would be the effect if we revised it to make it more formal? Is there any relation between the diction and the purpose?

6. Does the author of this essay achieve the purpose she set for herself? Do you feel that purpose controlled what she did at every step of the composition?

The control exerted by the purpose will be effective only if the writer understands what his basic decisions require of him and is dominated by that understanding. If he makes a mistake, he will be able to detect and correct it in revision. But a student who does not understand what his purpose requires may as well not have one. He may not even recognize serious organizational blunders when he has made them. Consider the following essay:

On Your Own

Before I came to this campus I knew things would be rough. I had heard from friends ahead of me in high school how big the U was and that a new freshman was sure to feel lost and lonely for a time. I had also been told that the work would be much harder than I was used to and that students got less help from the teachers. All this advice got summed up in the phrase, "At the U you're on your own." Now after three weeks here I know what the older fellows meant.

During Freshman Week I didn't know whether I was coming or going. I never had so many different activities crowded into one week. The first thing I did when I arrived on campus was to go to the dormitory and get my room. There I met my roommate, whom I had written a couple of times to during the summer. He introduced me to some of the other fellows in the dorm, and we compared notes about what we had done in high school and what we wanted to do here. It was a nice beginning for college, for I got to know several students who have been my good friends ever since.

During the next three or four days we had something scheduled every minute. We took physical examinations and scholastic tests and I had to take an extra math test because I did not have enough math in high school. After the tests we went to see our advisers, who told us what subjects we should take and helped us plan our programs. I didn't have too much trouble because one of the older boys in the dorm had briefed me on the courses I'd have to take, although the adviser almost refused to OK my program because I had forgotten to bring the slip showing I had taken my physical.

Registration wasn't as bad as I had been told. I came early in the alphabet, so I was able to get all of the classes my adviser had approved, except that I had to switch hours for my PE section. Those who came later were less lucky. By then classes were pretty well filled up and some students practically had to tear up their programs and start over again.

My real troubles began when classes started. Where my most difficulty was was the assignments. I thought I understood the work as it was being taken up in class, but it was a different story when I tried to do the assignments. Worst of all, every one of my instructors seemed to have the idea that his class was the only one I was taking. I had more homework for each course than I had for all my courses together in high school. Fortunately several of us in the dorm studied together and were able to help each other out.

There are good things to be said about this essay. It is a clear record of some of the boy's activities in the first weeks of school, and because these experiences are common the reader identifies with them. But the body of the essay does not develop the idea suggested in the title and the opening paragraph. The essay begins to veer away from that idea in the second paragraph and never gets back to it. Consequently there is an inconsistency in content which destroys its unity. This lack of unity shows up clearly when the five successive paragraphs are summarized:

1. This paragraph suggests that the writer will develop the idea that life at the U is "rough" because the new student is on his own.
2. The first two sentences introduce the confusion of Freshman Week, but the rest of the paragraph is about a pleasant association with other students. There is nothing "rough" about this experience.
3. The boy got through testing and program-planning easily, thanks to a briefing by the older boys. This paragraph shows no signs of confusion and presents no evidence that he is "on his own."
4. Registration was easier than he had expected; he missed most of the difficulties that other students encountered.
5. Class work and assignments were hard at first, but cooperative studying helped. There is some evidence of confusion here, but it does not last, and the boy does not have to face it alone.

What common idea runs through this essay and gives it unity? If the title and first paragraph are ignored, an idea emerges — that the first weeks of college were not as bad as the writer had been led to believe. But this is just the opposite of the idea suggested at the beginning. Such inconsistency suggests that the writer thought he had one purpose when he began the essay; the details that came to mind as he wrote, however, were connected with another purpose altogether, one he may not have recognized until it was implied on paper. If he had taken time to determine his purpose at the prewriting stage, the writer would have seen this inconsistency. Then he could have dropped the first paragraph and substituted something like this:

NOT AS BAD AS THEY SAID IT WOULD BE

Before I came to this campus I was told that a freshman should expect to feel lost and lonely during the first few weeks, because at the U a student gets little help from teachers or older students. He is on his own. I did not find it so. Instead, the whole experience of getting started in school seemed surprisingly easy.

This opening paragraph states the idea that the rest of the essay develops. To make sure that this purpose would be maintained throughout, the student might then summarize the content of the succeeding paragraphs as follows:

2. Far from being lonely, I soon met new friends in the dormitory.
3. Although the testing and program-planning were a bit hectic, the advice I got from older students was very helpful.
4. I had less difficulty with registration than I had expected.
5. Class assignments were difficult at first, but studying with other students in the dorm made the assignments clearer and easier.

This plan, if carefully followed, would have produced a consistent essay. But by the time the student had finished his original version, he evidently could not see what was wrong with it. The example shows that it is unwise for a beginner to count on removing organizational flaws during revision. The best time to avoid them is before the writing begins. A student who has got clear in his mind what he wants his essay to do has a standard which will guide him in deciding the appropriateness of particular sentences. If inappropriate material comes to mind as he writes, he will perceive that it does not fit and will edit it out.

You will now recognize that the function of prewriting is to discover and define the purpose of a projected essay. The sooner the purpose is determined, the better. A well-chosen title will often suggest the whole plan of the essay. For example, a student who restricts "College Education" to "Four More Years of High School" commits himself, if he understands the implications of his title, to the following procedure:

1. He is going to condemn college education in a specific way.

2. In doing so, he can use only examples and details which support the contention that college makes no significant advance over high school.

3. In organizing his material, his purpose requires him to apply the theme — no advance over high school — to whatever divisions of "college education" he chooses to discuss. These may include the curriculum, the faculty, the students and their organizations, homework, or any other topic which can be considered part of college education.

4. The tone of his essay will probably reflect disappointment or annoyance.

This kind of treatment is implied in the way he has restricted his subject in his title. In this example the restriction not only narrows the scope of the subject but also suggests a purpose, which, in turn, controls the choice of material and the way it can be organized and developed. In short, the restriction governs what the writer can do thereafter. But all this will be true only if the writer understands the kind of commitment he is making in the restriction. As the essay "On Your Own" showed, nothing is gained — and much is lost — by suggesting a purpose which the writer does not understand or intend to follow.

STATING THE PURPOSE

The purpose of an essay is often explicitly stated in one of two forms. In an essay to develop a dominant idea, the quickest way to indicate purpose is to state the idea at the beginning of the essay. Such a statement is called a *thesis*. In a paper which does not develop a dominant idea, the purpose may be stated as a brief introductory explanation of what the writer intends to do. This explanation is called a *statement of intent*.

Thesis: Public opinion polls have taken the suspense out of elections.
Statement of intent: This essay will explain how public opinion polls are conducted.

The first statement expresses an idea or judgment which the essay is to explain. The idea, therefore, will dominate the essay; it is what the essay is about. The statement of the idea is called a thesis. But the statement of intent does not express an idea. The writer intends to describe the process of conducting public opinion polls, not to express a judgment of them. His paper will have no thesis, but it will have a purpose, and that purpose is indicated in the statement of intent.

The Thesis

A thesis is usually a single sentence, *preferably a simple sentence,* and it is to the whole essay what a topic sentence is to a paragraph. The following might serve either as topic sentences for paragraphs or as theses for essays:

The first quality of a good speaker is a sense of confidence.
Final examinations encourage cramming.
All stories to the contrary, women drive as carefully as men.

The relation of the thesis to the rest of the essay may be quickly shown by an outline. Here is the thesis of an essay[1] to define the distinction between war and peace:

Thesis: The distinction between war and peace has three aspects: the legal distinction, which is deceptively clear; the political distinction, which is significantly vague; and the military distinction, which is clear only in retrospect.

This thesis informs a reader that the subject of the essay is the distinction between war and peace. It also tells him that the distinction is to be considered from three points of view — legal, political, and military

---

[1] The hypothetical example discussed here is based in part on passages from Chapter III, "The Distinction Between War and Peace," in Henry M. Wriston, *Strategy of Peace* (Boston: World Peace Foundation, 1944).

— and that the distinctions from these points of view differ in specified ways. Moreover, the thesis leads the reader to expect that the discussion of each distinction will be a major division of the essay. You would therefore expect the outline to have the following structure:

Thesis: As stated above.
  I. The legal distinction between war and peace is deceptively clear.
  II. The political distinction between war and peace is significantly vague.
  III. The military distinction between war and peace is clear only in retrospect.

From your knowledge of paragraph structure you will expect that, if each distinction is discussed in a paragraph, statements I, II, and III of the outline will become topic sentences, and each paragraph will explain its topic sentence. If the essay is a long one, the author may devote more than a single paragraph to each distinction. But the essay will still have the three main divisions shown in the outline.

The author's next step is also suggested by the thesis — to explain in detail each main point. By "deceptively clear," he means that, since a declaration of war is always a joint resolution adopted by Congress and signed by the President, there is never any doubt in law about when a state of peace changes to a state of war: it changes the moment the President signs the joint resolution. But that distinction is "deceptive" because, before the President makes the declaration effective with his signature, our troops and the enemy's may already have been engaged in battle — even for months or years — with heavy casualties on both sides. Having made this explanation, the author will want to support it with examples. He may cite the conflict in Vietnam, in which thousands of American troops fought the Viet Cong, bombed their bases and their transportation routes, killed and were killed, all without a declaration of war. He may cite many other examples — that most of our Pacific fleet was sunk at Pearl Harbor the day before war between Japan and the United States was declared by either side — and other instances of fighting between countries still technically at peace.

In his second main unit, the author will explain how the political distinction between war and peace is "significantly vague," and he will give examples to support his explanation. And he will follow a similar procedure for his third statement, that the military distinction is clear only in retrospect. He will do these things *because his thesis commits him to do them.* He has announced a purpose in the thesis, and that announcement delineates both the structure and the content of the essay.

This illustration shows three things. First, it shows why the thesis is called a statement of purpose: in announcing the main idea, the thesis implies that the purpose of the essay is to explain that idea. In effect, the thesis summarizes the content of the essay. Second, the illustration shows that the structure of the essay is inherent, whether stated or implied, in the thesis. Third, it shows that the kind of information needed is dictated by the thesis: the writer must cite examples of the three distinctions he discusses. In short, the purpose directs and guides the writer to what he must do. The great virtue of the thesis is that by committing him during the prewriting, it controls what he does in the writing.

Obviously this author did not begin with a thesis and then hunt material to support it. His study of the facts led him to his thesis, but having reached that conclusion, he then knew which facts to use and which to ignore. It is also obvious that his thesis had to be carefully worded, since carelessness or ambiguity in its statement might have distorted his purpose, and either committed him wrongly or left him unclear.

Because of the control a thesis exerts, confusion in the thesis can cause confusion in the writing. A good thesis forces a writer to resolve his difficulties before he begins to write. This can be an exacting discipline, and the inexperienced writer sometimes tries to escape it, in the hope that "things will come clear" in the writing. They seldom do. The protection that the thesis provides is worth the effort it costs.

Form of the Thesis. A good thesis is *restricted, unified,* and *precise.* To be restricted, it must indicate which of several approaches to the subject the writer will take. It thus limits the scope of the paper to what can be discussed in detail in the space available. Such a thesis as "There are serious objections to college grading systems" does not specify what objections the author will discuss. Like the unrestricted subjects discussed on page 4, it could be broken down into a number of purposes:

> The grading system is an inefficient way of evaluating student performance.
> The grading system emphasizes grades rather than learning.
> The grading system is abused by individual teachers.
> The grading system leads to cramming.
> The grading system leads to cheating.

Each of these objections, if developed with enough evidence to be convincing, would require a substantial essay. To discuss all of them in a single paper is to invite a superficial treatment which makes assertions without adequate proof. The unrestricted thesis gives no real clue to what the writer plans to do. Worse, it lulls him into thinking his purpose is clear when all he has is a general subject, and perhaps a general title — "Objections to the Grading System in Colleges."

An unrestricted thesis allows a student to write "about" a subject, without specifying what or how he is going to write about it. Such a thesis should be carefully reconsidered. If the writer has doubts, he can outline the main units he intends to discuss. If, as with college grading systems, these main units are either numerous or comprehensive, the thesis needs further restriction.

Apply this test to the following thesis and outline:

Thesis: John F. Kennedy will always be an inspiration to the American people.
  I. As a young naval officer Kennedy played a heroic role in the war.
  II. His *Profiles in Courage* is a great inspirational book.
  III. His handling of the Cuban missile problem was masterful.
  IV. He was the ideal of the new generation.
  V. His assassination was an international tragedy.
  VI. His memory will influence American politics for years.

The numbered statements explain the thesis. Are these six statements too many to develop with any thoroughness in a single paper? Would the writer be wiser to deal with only one and, in effect, make it his thesis? Here is what one writer does with an idea similar to IV above.

THE CONTEMPORARY MAN[2]

After Kennedy's death, Adlai Stevenson called him the "contemporary man." His youth, his vitality, his profound modernity — these were final elements in his power and potentiality as he stood on the brink of the Presidency. For Kennedy was not only the first President to be born in the twentieth century. More than that, he was the first representative in the White House of a distinctive generation, the generation which was born during the First World War, came of age during the depression, fought in the Second World War and began its public career in the atomic age.

This was the first generation to grow up as the age of American innocence was coming to an end. To have been born nearly a decade earlier, like Lyndon Johnson, or nearly two decades earlier, like Adlai Stevenson, was to be rooted in another and simpler America. Scott Fitzgerald had written that his contemporaries grew up "to find all Gods dead, all wars fought, all faiths in man shaken." But the generation which came back from the Second World War found that gods, wars and faiths in man had, after all, survived, if in queer and somber ways. The realities of the twentieth century which had shocked their fathers now wove the fabric of their own lives. Instead of reveling in being a lost generation, they set out in one mood or another to find, if not themselves, a still point in the turning world. The predicament was even worse for the generation which had been too young to fight the war, too young to recall the age of innocence, the generation which had experienced nothing but turbulence. So in the fifties some sought security at the expense of identity and became organization men. Others sought identity at the expense of security and became beatniks. Each course created only a partial man. There was need for a way of life, a way of autonomy, between past and present, the organization man and the anarchist, the square and the beat.

It was autonomy which this humane and self-sufficient man seemed to

[2] From Arthur M. Schlesinger, Jr., *A Thousand Days* (Boston: Houghton Mifflin Company, 1965).

embody. Kennedy simply could not be reduced to the usual complex of sociological generalizations. He was Irish, Catholic, New England, Harvard, Navy, Palm Beach, Democrat and so on; but no classification contained him. He had wrought an individuality which carried him beyond the definitions of class and race, region and religion. He was a free man, not just in the sense of the cold-war cliché, but in the sense that he was, as much as man can be, self-determined and not the servant of forces outside him.

This sense of wholeness and freedom gave him an extraordinary appeal not only to his own generation but even more to those who came after, the children of turbulence. Recent history had washed away the easy consolations and the old formulas. Only a few things remained on which contemporary man could rely, and most were part of himself — family, friendship, courage, reason, jokes, power, patriotism. Kennedy demonstrated the possibility of the new self-reliance. As he had liberated himself from the past, so he had liberated himself from the need to rebel against the past. He could insist on standards, admire physical courage, attend his church, love his father while disagreeing with him, love his country without self-doubt or self-consciousness. Yet, while absorbing so much of the traditional code, his sensibility was acutely contemporaneous. He voiced the disquietude of the postwar generation — the mistrust of rhetoric, the disdain for pomposity, the impatience with the postures and pieties of other days, the resignation to disappointment. And he also voiced the new generation's longings — for fulfillment in experience, for the subordination of selfish impulses to higher ideals, for a link between past and future, for adventure and valor and honor. What was forbidden were poses, histrionics, the heart on the sleeve and the tongue on the cliché. What was required was a tough, nonchalant acceptance of the harsh present and an open mind toward the unknown future.

This was Kennedy, with his deflationary wartime understatement (when asked how he became a hero, he said, "It was involuntary. They sank my boat"); his contempt for demagoguery (once during the campaign, after Kennedy had disappointed a Texas crowd by his New England restraint, Bill Attwood suggested that next time he wave his arms in the air like other politicians; Kennedy shook his head and wrote — he was saving his voice — "I always swore one thing I'd never do is — " and drew a picture of a man waving his arms in the air); his freedom from dogma, his appetite for responsibility, his instinct for novelty, his awareness and irony and control; his imperturbable sureness in his own powers, not because he considered himself infallible, but because, given the fallibility of all men, he supposed he could do the job as well as anyone else; his love of America and pride in its traditions and ideals.

This excerpt is the length of a substantial student essay, yet it deals with only one of the six points in the outline proposed on page 21. Restricting his thesis forces a writer to treat a limited topic in depth instead of a broad one superficially.

A good thesis is unified as well as restricted. To be unified, it must commit the writer to deal with only one dominant idea. Such a thesis as "The United Nations Organization has major weaknesses and cannot prevent a major war" requires the writer to do two things, not one. He must (1) demonstrate the weaknesses and (2) prove that the UN cannot prevent a major war. A paper with this double purpose will almost certainly fall into two parts having little connection with each other. If the writer believes that these two points are related — perhaps that one results from the other — he should show that relation in his thesis: "The organization of the UN makes it incapable of preventing a war between major powers." This thesis restricts the discussion to those features of organization which make the UN powerless to avert a major war and thus fuses the two parts into a unified purpose statement.

In the following theses the lack of unity at the left is removed in the revision at the right:

Printing has had a long and complex history, during which it has brought about social and cultural reforms.	The development of printing has brought about social and cultural reforms.
Mutual funds have grown rapidly in this country and offer advantages for the small investor.	Mutual funds have grown rapidly in this country because they offer advantages for the small investor.

In the first of these pairs, the thesis at the left requires the writer to do two things: first, to recount the history of printing — a big job in itself — and then to show the social and cultural reforms which have come from printing. The revision rules out much of the history and restricts the writer to the single task of showing how certain social and cultural improvements were made possible by advances in printing. Similarly, the first statement about mutual funds would make two papers — one a history, the other a justification. The revision requires the writer to select evidence from the history to argue that mutual funds have grown because of their uses to a particular group of people.

Note that the two revised statements express a logical relationship between two parts of a subject at first unrelated. In these examples the relationship is one of cause and effect. To find such a relationship is "to have an idea" — to perceive a truth or gain an understanding. This idea gives direction to your thinking and so shapes your writing.

▶ *For each of the following statements explain the lack of unity that might lead to trouble in the writing stage. Then revise the statement into a unified thesis, by separating or combining the ideas implied in the statement.*

1. Final examinations are an unsatisfactory instrument for evaluating a student's mastery of a course. They are often detrimental to student health.
2. The pressures to upgrade college education began after the Sputnik incident and exercised a considerable influence on the high school curriculum.
3. The regulations by which universities attempt to control the social conduct of students had their origins in the wishes of parents, but such

regulations have become increasingly difficult to enforce and are currently the source of much student discontent.

4. United States policy in Vietnam, which has evolved during the administrations of four Presidents, is dangerous to enforce and dangerous to abandon.

Finally, a thesis should be precise. It should be phrased in words which permit only one interpretation. Especially it should avoid words and phrases which are so general that they convey no exact meaning. For example, such statements as

My home town is one of the most interesting towns in the state.
Winston Churchill had a colorful career.

are useless as statements of purpose because the key words "interesting" and "colorful" could mean almost anything and hence exert no real control. A student who sets out to show that his home town is "interesting" is almost sure to end with an essay "about" his home town; one who intends to show that Churchill had a colorful career is likely to write "about" Churchill's life. Any student who intends to write "about" a subject has not yet established his purpose. He has merely lulled himself into a false sense of achievement.

▶ *To see how a vaguely worded thesis fails to control an essay, take the thesis "My home town is one of the most (or least) interesting towns in the state" and list all the major statements or topic sentences that might logically be made to support the thesis. Then suggest in parentheses what kind of material might be used to develop each such statement in the essay. Finally, suggest two or three specific theses which might be used for the general subject.*

Avoid figures of speech in a thesis. Metaphors and similes can be vivid and expressive within a composition, or even in a title, but in a thesis they can easily hide a confusion that might be exposed in a more literal statement. Consider this: "Where instructors are concerned, all that glitters is not gold." Does the sentence mean that the most entertaining instructors are not always the most helpful, or that the most accomplished scholars are not always the best teachers? Or does it merely mean that instructors are not always what they seem to be? The statement does not communicate a clear purpose. It may seem apt or clever, but in a thesis clarity is more important than effect.

▶ *Identify and explain any weaknesses you find in the following theses, and suggest revisions. Watch especially for vague words in key places. Number 10 illustrates an error not specifically described in the text, but you should be able to see what is wrong and make a satisfactory revision.*

24

1. The performance given by the concert pianist last night was sensational.
2. There is no more exciting game than football.
3. The Bay of Pigs incident was unfortunate.
4. Hawaii has a great future.
5. This essay will consider injuries in automobile racing.
6. The bonuses now being paid to persuade college football players to sign with professional teams are out of this world.
7. Arnold Palmer is the Babe Ruth of golf.
8. Whether to stay out of college and earn enough to see me through, or to work while I go to school? That is the question.
9. To achieve a superior record in college nowadays, one must keep his nose to the grindstone.
10. In the last forty years the world's record for the mile run has been reduced about sixteen seconds; the record for the pole vault has risen by more than three feet; in the same period at the Olympic Games the high jump record has increased by six inches, the broad jump more than a foot, the shot put fourteen feet, and the discus throw nearly fifty feet.

The Statement of Intent

Only essays developing a dominant idea have a thesis. Many other essays may be quite purposeful, but they do not develop an idea. There is no point in trying to force a thesis on such an essay. For example, if you want to explain the operation of a Diesel engine or to summarize the events leading to the Boston Tea Party, your paper will not have a dominant idea, although it will have a clear purpose. Any attempt to pretend it has a thesis by writing some such statement as "The operation of the Diesel engine is complex" or "The background of the Boston Tea Party is interesting" would waste time and distort your real intention. For you are concerned not with the complexity of the Diesel engine but with its mode of operation, and you have no intention of proving that the events leading up to the Boston Tea Party were "interesting" but only of showing what they were.

Although an essay may not have a dominant idea, it must have a purpose, and putting that purpose down on paper as a statement of intent will be helpful, even if that statement is omitted from the final draft of the essay. The following statements of intent make the purpose clear and help toward efficient development:

The purpose of this paper is to contrast efficient and inefficient methods of studying for an examination.

What are the alternatives to final examinations? I will suggest two and show their chief advantages and disadvantages.

This essay will identify and evaluate the most popular campus clichés.

I intend to illustrate the four most common kinds of changes in the meaning of words by tracing the evolution of *lady, gossip, boycott,* and *acorn.*

Notice that the last statement not only records the purpose but also suggests how the paper will be developed. A purpose statement of this type implies both the structure of the essay and the kind of material that will be used in filling out the structure.

SUMMARY

The content of this chapter may be summarized in eight pieces of advice:

1. To reduce the complexity of the composition process, break it into three stages: *prewriting, writing,* and *revision.* Even when these stages overlap, the division will emphasize prewriting and revision, both of which are sometimes neglected when composition is thought of as a single act.

2. The subject you choose is less important than what you do with it. Do not spend too much time choosing a general subject, and do not discard one subject for another at the first difficulty. Pick a likely subject and consider what you could do with it. This is the first step in prewriting. In your most efficient moments the whole prewriting process may be completed at this step.

3. What makes a composition interesting is not the uniqueness of the subject but the originality of the treatment. The only originality that a freshman, or almost anyone, has to offer is his own view of the subject — how he sees it and what he thinks about it. So unless the situation rules out the writer's personality, as it does in summaries and some reports, an essay should be a personal comment. The thing to worry about is whether it succeeds in presenting your view accurately, not whether that view is a conventional one. If your essay could have been written just as well by anyone in the class, it is probably presenting a stereotype of the subject.

4. Be wary of large subjects that map out more territory than you can cover. As a first step in restriction, break such subjects into subtopics; then see if one of the subtopics can be further restricted by discussing it from a particular point of view. The point of view defines your concept of the subject by suggesting your interest in it. For example, "As Philosophers, New York Cabbies Are Frauds" indicates one view of the subject; "The Taxi as a Schoolroom" suggests another.

5. As used in this book, the word *purpose* means the basic decision a writer makes about what he is going to do with his subject and how he is going to do it. In some essays the restriction and the discovery of purpose may occur simultaneously; in others, either may come first and suggest the other.

6. Establishing purpose sets up guidelines which will control progress through the essay. You cannot go outside these guidelines without destroying unity. If you understand the implications of your purpose, you will know what kind of material you need to develop your essay, and you will have a means of checking whether one pattern of organization is

better than others; at least you will know what kind of information you do *not* want and what patterns of organization are undesirable.

7. Purpose is best determined in prewriting. Indeed, the chief function of prewriting is to discover and define purpose. To take a general subject, restrict it to a subtopic, and decide how to treat that subtopic is to define purpose. In freshman courses, at least, the best way to reach that goal is through careful prewriting.

8. When an essay develops a dominant idea, the purpose should be stated as a thesis, usually a single sentence at or near the beginning of the essay. The thesis should be restricted, unified, and precise so that it clearly states the single idea which the essay is to develop. If the essay is not concerned with an idea, its purpose may be expressed as a statement of intent. Both kinds of purpose statements may also suggest the organization of the essay.

Exercises

Assume that the following essays have been selected in a contest in which each student in a class submitted the best essay he wrote during the term. From these three the winner is to be chosen. It must meet the following criteria:

1. It should have a subject sufficiently restricted to permit detailed development within the space of the essay.
2. It should have a clear purpose, whether stated or not, and everything in the essay should consistently develop that purpose.
3. It should be original in the sense that it reflects the personal point of view, attitudes, beliefs, or values of the writer.
4. It should say something worth saying, and say it in a style appropriate to the purpose.
5. It should be of interest to an audience of college freshmen.

You are one of the judges. Select the winner, and for each essay write a one-page judgment explaining in some detail why you rated it as you did. The judgments may be read in class and discussed.

SUGAR AND SPICE AND STEREOTYPE

Conformity in women's fashions is obvious on the campus. There is an "in" way of dressing for each occasion, and a coed finds this way just by taking a quick look at how the majority of girls dress. She then proceeds to make herself a very close copy of this majority.

Probably everyone has seen the typical Saturday afternoon coed shopper. Wearing a colorful knit headband and quilted ski jacket, she cashes her check at the currency exchange. She walks gracefully out the door and down Green

Street, her wool stretch pants tucked neatly into a pair of up-to-the-knee boots. The jacket is skimpy, the slacks are thin, and the boots have no lining. Only the coed's pride keeps her warm — and the fact that she's "in" with her fashionable wardrobe.

A day's shopping done, she returns to her room to get ready for her boyfriend's fraternity dance that evening. She combs her long straight hair, making sure that the bangs just cover her eyebrows for that provocative look. She dons a very plain black crepe dress that has a touch of lace here or there, and on her legs she wears black lace stockings, slipped into black, cut-away, low-heeled shoes.

Even when she returns to the dormitory and gets ready for bed, she puts on the same type of pajamas that all the other girls put on. Wearing a striped, ivy-league nightshirt, she shuffles from room to room and joins the others. They all greet her with smiling faces and striped, ivy-league night-shirts, and dance to the Beatles in their identical fluffy slippers.

What has become of individual creativity in clothing? Women have become lazy thinkers; they let Oleg Cassini and Bobbi Brooks decide for them what to wear and what to wear it to. Advertisements lure them into buying shoes they hate because the shoes are the season's latest fashion news. A short stumpy girl's admiration of famous fashion models forces her into a low-cut, frilly dress. It contributes nothing to her appearance but makes her feel better than ever because "Suzy Parker modeled this dress in *Vogue!*" Everywhere fat-legged girls wear fashionable knee sox despite the fact that the sox only emphasize their generously endowed limbs. Red-headed girls wear purple because it's the season's color.

Every place one looks — in the lecture room, on the crosswalks of the quadrangle, in the lounges of the women's residence halls — one sees women of all sizes and shapes dressed alike, not according to what flatters them, but according to what *Seventeen* says will flatter them. Our creativity is gone, along with our sensibility.

A FISHING TRIP? NO THANKS!

Although I had never been on a fishing trip, I had seen how much pleasure Dad always got from his annual fishing vacation and I had imagined that fishing, especially for muskies, must be thrilling. Therefore, when some friends invited me to accompany them on a two weeks' fishing trip to Sparrow Lake, Canada, Lair of the Big Muskies, I jumped at the chance. I was so eager to fish that the necessary preparations and the long, tedious car trip were severe tests of my patience. When we finally reached our cabin, late at night, I had difficulty getting to sleep. Visions of successful catches chased each other through my head. Had I known what I know now, I would have slept soundly — and late.

From the first day at the lake, most of our time was spent in the boat trying to catch muskies. We would get up before daylight, slosh some cold water on our faces, and prepare breakfast on a capricious kerosene stove. By the time it was light enough to bait a hook we would be pushing off from the wharf. Usually we would fish until noon, take an hour out for lunch, and try again until evening. Once we took sandwiches and a thermos of coffee with us and ate lunch in the boat, after rinsing our fishy hands in the lake. Once was enough. After that, we girls insisted on being put ashore to prepare lunch.

The prerequisite for comfortable fishing, I found, is the right kind of anatomy. I didn't have it. Even three cushions, piled one on top of another, only partially modified the hardness of the boat seat. I am sure that if God had intended the human frame to be subjected to five or six continuous hours on a narrow, wooden plank, He would have designed it differently. The slimy business of baiting the hook and of unhooking a fish when I was unfortunate enough to catch one, I could usually delegate to the men. But I never found a way of getting somebody to sit for me.

I admit that muskie-fishing has its exciting moments — the sudden thrill of a hard strike, those delicious seconds when you wait for the muskie to turn the bait in his mouth before you set the hook, his final desperate dive as you bring him near the boat, the first gleam of his greenish-white body as you pull him close to the surface, and the pistol shot that finally dispatches him. But those moments are paid for by hours of boredom and discomfort, when you sit, cold and wet, with nothing to do but fend off the persistent horse fly that is enamored of your knuckles. Even the thrill of landing a big one soon descends to an anticlimax as you spend a frustrating fifteen minutes trying to pry or cut the hooks from his vicious mouth or fumbling with numbed fingers to untangle the line, now hopelessly snarled in the contents of the spilled tackle box.

And when all this dreary routine is over, and your line is paying out freely from the side of the boat, what is there to look forward to? At best, the same thing over again — and all this for a fish which is hardly fit to eat. Do you blame me for deciding that if I had to be involved in such foolishness I would confine my efforts to steering the boat? That way I could save my disposition and what was left of my fingernails.

THE BULLFIGHT

In Spain, the bullfight is more than a sport: it is a part of the country's culture. The crises, the exciting moments in American sports, seem trivial compared to the Spanish contest between man and beast. In every bullfight, the matador faces death, pits his skill, strength, and knowledge against that of a bull whose only desire is to kill him.

Every Spanish bullfight fan is an afficionado; he can tell a dangerous pass from one which simply looks dangerous, and a good kill from a cowardly one. Most of the fans know about bullfighting from having tried it in an amateur fight. In fact, almost all Spanish boys have the desire to be a matador; and a great many try, some succeeding, others becoming banderillos or picadors, but most settling for a seat at as many bullfights as they can possibly attend. Because of their knowledge of the sport, the spectators are extremely critical, and a poor performance is always marked by the boos of the crowd and a barrage of seat cushions, wine bottles, and shoes. However, it is the same knowledge which makes the sport an impromptu art, a communication of emotion between matador and crowd.

The bullfight fan is like the American jazz fan who goes to hear the same group night after night, waiting for that one electrifying moment of the creative artist at his best; most of the time the music is mediocre, but when it's at its best, nothing else matters. And when the great matador, reaching his peak with a brave, strong bull, stands poised over those horns, hoping (but not knowing) that they won't come up and dig his very guts out, hoping that the sword doesn't hit a bone and break off in his hand, plunges his sword down into the back of the bull's neck and punctures the bull's lungs (he hopes), and when every man who ever saw an amateur bullfight or faced a bull or ran from one, knowing what it means to lean over a bull's horns and expose one's groin, holds his breath and, not saying a word, watches the matador in the hot, bright sun, on the white sand prove for the whole world to see his courage and strength and skill, sees him become one with the proud, noble, strong bull — this is the moment of truth.

So the bullfight is not a sport at all, but an art — not comparable to American baseball or American anything — the art of the matador who fights one day in Madrid, then sleeps in the back seat of a car filled with costumes, capes, sword, and manager's cigar smoke as it bounces over dirt roads, and despite T.B. or syphilis, or probably both, gets out of the car in time to eat, dress, and enter the arena to face two specially bred bulls in one afternoon, hoping to kill those bulls honorably, knowing that if he does, he will be a hero, and if he doesn't, he will be insulted verbally and physically.

2

Sources of Material

One of the definitions of the noun *material* given in *Webster's New World Dictionary* is "ideas, notes, observations, sketches, etc. that may be worked up or elaborated; data." It is in this general sense that the word is used here. A writer's material is the data he uses to carry out his purpose. The data may consist of examples, illustrative details, comparisons, case histories, cause and effect relationships, facts, figures, testimony, quotations, figures of speech, impressions, ideas, arguments, beliefs — anything that will help him to do what he wishes to do. The student who wrote "The Bullfight" (page 29) used three kinds of material: his knowledge of the action in a bullfight, his understanding of the relation between a matador and his fans, and his experience with American jazz.

Materials may be selected in either the prewriting or the writing stage. In short papers, especially those that draw mainly on memory, the materials usually come to mind during the writing. A writer with a clear sense of purpose has prepared a channel for his thoughts, and the appropriate facts, ideas, and examples flow through that channel almost of their own accord. In other papers the materials may have to be sought by "research," as a news reporter obtains material for a story by going out and looking for it. There is no one way of finding material, though for freshman essays the most common way is to reach into the mind.

Most of your material will come from two major sources: from your experience, and from the inferences you draw from that experience. Experience is knowledge already acquired, usually the sum of what you have observed, heard, and read. Inferences are the significance you give to the details of experience from these sources. Inferences in turn become part of experience, from which further inferences may be drawn. This cumulative pattern, variously described as "growth" or "education," is illustrated in the following paragraph:

In the Middle East, Americans usually have a difficult time with the Arabs. I remember an American agriculturalist who went to Egypt to teach modern agricultural methods to the Egyptian farmers. At one point in his work he asked his interpreter to ask a farmer how much he expected his field to yield that year. The farmer responded by becoming very excited and angry. In an obvious attempt to soften the reply the interpreter said, "He says he doesn't know." The American realized something had gone wrong, but he had no way of knowing what. Later I learned that the Arabs regard anyone who tries to look into the future as slightly insane. When the American asked him about his future yield, the Egyptian was highly insulted since he thought the American considered him crazy. To the Arab only God knows the future, and it is presumptuous even to talk about it.[1]

Notice how the American's inferences come from and lead to experience in this illustration:

1. He asks a question suggested by previous experience.
2. He meets an unexpected response and draws the inference, "Something is wrong here."
3. He seeks an answer for his problem. He does not get it from his interpreter, but if he finds out later why the farmer became angry, he will draw another inference, "In dealing with Arabs, don't ask questions about the future."
4. With this experience, he will hereafter estimate the yield of an Egyptian farm by asking what it was last year and the year before. Thus he will learn how to adapt to a new situation.

MATERIALS FROM OBSERVATION

Material derived from experience comes from two main sources, direct observation and reading. Observation is knowledge gained through sensory perception. The following selection is a humorous illustration of that knowledge:

THE CAMERA EYE[2]

By Newman Levy

We were seated in the lobby of the hotel as she walked swiftly by us, turned a corner sharply, and was gone.

"That's an uncommonly good-looking girl," I said to my wife, who was deep in a crossword puzzle.

"Do you mean the one in that imitation blue taffeta dress with the green and red flowered design?"

"The girl that just walked by."

"Yes," said my wife, "with that dowdy rayon dress on. It's a copy of

[1] From Edward T. Hall, *The Silent Language* (New York: Doubleday and Company, 1959).
[2] From *The Atlantic Monthly,* December, 1952. Copyright © 1952, by The Atlantic Monthly Company, Boston, Mass. 02116. Reprinted with permission.

one I saw at Hattie Carnegie's, and a poor copy at that. You'd think, though, that she'd have better taste than to wear a chartreuse hat with it, especially with her bleached hair."

"Bleached? I didn't notice her hair was bleached."

"Good heavens, you could almost smell the peroxide. I don't mind a bit of make-up provided it looks fairly natural. But you could scrape that rouge off with a knife. They ought to add a course in make-up to the curriculum at Smith."

"Smith? Why Smith?"

"From her class pin, of course. You must have noticed it hanging from her charm bracelet."

"I wasn't looking at her wrist."

"I'll bet you weren't. Nor at those fat legs of hers, either. A woman with legs like that shouldn't wear high-heeled patent-leather shoes."

"I thought she was a very pretty girl," I said apologetically.

"Well, you may be right," said my wife. "I was busy with my puzzle and I didn't notice her particularly. What's the name of a President of the United States in six letters, beginning with T?"

This passage suggests that women observe better than men do, but it would be possible to suggest the opposite by showing a man's response and a woman's to an intricate play in football. Probably people most effectively observe things and events that interest them or they already know something about. What you see in a Shakespearean sonnet or on a slide under a microscope depends on what you have previously seen on similar subjects (experience) and what you are looking for now (motivation).

Accurate observation can be learned, if the observer wants to learn and is willing to pay close attention. Most of us fail to observe accurately because we are not interested enough to exert the effort and concentration that efficient observation requires. But when our interest is aroused or when we feel a real need to observe, we can train ourselves to be expert. During World War II airplane spotters displayed almost incredible ability to distinguish between types of aircraft that were flashed on a screen for tiny fractions of a second. In that situation the need was strong enough to command the effort. So it is in painting. Anyone who has tried to draw or paint, say, a human hand, knows the continued and concentrated observation which the task requires. The artist trains himself to notice details of structure, color, and texture because he needs these materials for his work.

The greatest obstacle to accurate observation is the willingness to settle for a general impression. It is easier to say that the sky is blue than to identify shades of blue, and shades that are not blue. As a result we often cannot describe the sky in detail because we do not know what it looks like in detail. We have to fall back on generalities. Teachers are inclined to diagnose overgeneralization as a failure to use specific diction. But a student cannot know what specific diction to use unless he knows what specific image he wants to communicate. If he has only a general impres-

34

sion of his subject, he can describe it only generally. Often the trouble is not faulty diction but faulty observation.

A general impression is important, since it is the pattern into which all the specific details are finally organized. But the pattern should take shape in the observer's mind as a response to individual details; otherwise he may see only the obvious and have but a superficial knowledge of the subject. A simple illustration of the technique of holding off general impressions until they grow out of detailed information is provided in the following notes, which record a series of observations of a picture (see page opposite).

1. Most obvious are the flying birds, presumably geese. Asked to identify the subject at this stage, one would be tempted to say, "It's about flying geese."

2. The birds flying to the right are white; those to the left, black. There is no space between a white bird and the nearest black ones. Each becomes the background for the other, so that the black birds give shape to the white, and vice versa.

3. Both sets of birds become more sharply defined toward the front of their *V*'s. The first five birds show more detail than those that follow them: eyes, beaks, feathers, and curves of the body are more clearly defined. The birds in both sets degenerate into vague, ill-defined shapes the farther back they are from the leader, until they become indistinguishable from the fields below them.

4. In looking at the birds, the eyes of the observer shift alternately left-right-left, depending on whether he is watching the white birds or the black. At this stage the motion of the eyes and of the picture is lateral.

5. The fields are bounded by two rivers. On close inspection, the rivers are seen to be identical in all respects except shading. They have the same towns, bridges, roads, and landscapes, but — like the birds — one is light and one is dark, or perhaps we should say one is *in* the light and the other *in* the dark. Otherwise, each side of the picture seems to be a mirror-image of the other.

6. The whole picture now seems to emphasize light shading into dark. There is no sharp dividing line, as there would be in a mirror-image. Instead, there is a *range* from light to dark: the light gradually darkens.

7. The fields are clearly defined at the bottom of the picture, less clearly at the top. Indeed, as the eyes move up the picture the fields increasingly take the shape of birds.

8. As one observes all these details, the first general impression that the picture was about birds becomes less satisfying. The contrast between light and dark is now too dominant a theme to be subordinated to the birds.

9. As a result of this growing general impression, which of the following titles seems best to express the "meaning" of the picture: (1) Bird's-Eye View of a Landscape, (2) A Study in Black and White, (3) Day and Night? If none of these titles satisfies you, suggest one of your own.

▶ *As an exercise in observing a subject, do either 1 and 3 or 2 and 3 of the following:*

1. If you can draw, even poorly, draw a picture of any object in your room, or any object nearby (a tree, a car, a bridge). The attempt to draw the subject will do two things: it will force you to look closely at it and to see details of size, shape, texture, shading, etc., which you might otherwise miss; and it will force you to deal with details, since you cannot so easily escape into a general impression in a drawing.

2. If you cannot draw at all, examine the object *with the intent of drawing it,* and make notes on details that should appear in a drawing.

3. Describe your subject in writing from either your drawing (1) or your notes (2). Try to enable a reader to "see" the subject as you do.

The ability to see the specific details of a subject is essential to all description, and description of people, places, and things is a basic element in all composition. Just as a painter paints from a model, a writer must write from one, either a model he studies as he writes — as you were doing in the previous exercise — or one he can review ("see again") in his mind's eye. When Rachel Carson wrote the following description she was probably sitting at a typewriter in her study, not standing by the edge of the sea. But the evidence of her text clearly shows that she was recalling a series of detailed and careful observations. Indeed the passage is probably a composite of many observations made over a long period, from which she selected details to create just the picture she wanted.

Later, as I stood above the tide near the entrance to the pool, the promise of the rosy light was sustained. From the base of the steep wall of rock on which I stood, a moss-covered ledge jutted seaward into the deep water. In the surge at the rim of the ledge the dark fronds of oarweeds swayed, smooth and gleaming as leather. The projecting ledge was a path to the small hidden cave and its pool. Occasionally, a swell, stronger than the rest, rolled smoothly over the rim and broke in foam against the cliff. But the intervals between such swells were long enough to admit me to the ledge and long enough for a glimpse of that fairy pool, so seldom and so briefly exposed.

And so I knelt on the dark carpet of sea moss and looked back into the dark cavern that held the pool in a shallow basin. The floor of the cave was only a few inches below the roof, and a mirror had been created in which all that grew on the ceiling was reflected in the still water below.

Under water that was as clear as glass the pool was carpeted with green sponge. Gray patches of sea squirts glistened on the ceiling and colonies of soft coral were a pale apricot color. In the moment when I looked into the cave a little elfin starfish hung down, suspended by the merest thread, perhaps by only a single tube foot. It reached down to touch its own reflection, so perfectly delineated that there might have been, not one starfish, but two. The beauty of the reflected images and of the limpid pool itself was the poignant beauty of things that are ephemeral, existing only until the sea should return to fill the little cave.[3]

[3] From Rachel Carson, *The Edge of the Sea* (Boston: Houghton Mifflin Company, 1955).

If a writer has specific details in mind as he writes, his writing will reflect the accuracy and vividness of his observations and memory. In the following passage the author is explaining why there is a time lag between the onset of a rainstorm and the flooding of the rivers. His job is to spell out the process of absorption of rain by the earth. If he has not observed accurately, he can explain that process only in general terms: "The earth soaks up the rain," "The water sinks into the dry ground," "The rivers do not flood until the land is saturated." But notice that his diction is as much a sign of specific observation as it is of an extensive vocabulary — "punky dryness of rotting logs," "sodden," "porous mass," "shrunken" leaves and grasses that "uncurl" when they become "stiff" with moisture. As you go through the passage, underline those words or phrases which suggest that he has seen the things he is writing about.

By deep affinity, every grain of dust drew water to itself. The punky dryness of rotting logs grew slowly sodden. In the thickets of blackberry, and toyon, and poison oak, the dead leaves lay deep; beneath these rested the half rotted leaves and twigs of older years, and still deeper the mould of generations. This porous mass sucked moisture like a stiff sponge, and paradoxically the life-giving water even woke to new vigor the very processes of decay.

Still more, the living vegetation sucked in and held the rain. How many bucketfuls to change from black to green all the moss upon the rocks? How many tank-cars to wet all the pine-needles and all the oak leaves? How many trains of tank-cars to uncurl all the blades of grass upon all the hills? Leaves shrunken to conserve moisture expanded and grew heavy; drooping shoots stood up stiff and vigorous. The very cells expanded, and the protoplasm of its subtle chemistry absorbed to itself countless tons of water.

Even animal life drew in the water. Cattle and horses grew dark beneath the downpour. The fleeces of the sheep were heavy. Deer in the forest glades changed from dun to brown. Through the tunnels of ants and beetles the moisture seeped downward. The channels of earthworms were as millions of conduits. The myriad far-ranging burrows of gophers and ground-squirrels took the trickles deeper still. Then at last following the fissures of the earth itself the seeping moisture from the surface reached ground which was no longer dry, and began to join that great fluctuating reservoir of the waters which are beneath the earth.

Until all this should be fully achieved, the river was low. As well expect water to stand in a sieve as streams to run high before the land itself was satisfied.[4]

Students who feel that they have nothing to write about may be surprised at how much they have to say if they develop the habit of looking closely at the world about them and recording what they see. Specific observations are the stuff of which writing is made. And the first step in finding materials is to record what may be observed about the subject. The prerequisite for effective observation is the willingness to concentrate on details.

[4] From George R. Stewart, *Storm* (New York: Random House, 1941).

MATERIALS FROM INFERENCES

The materials you get from observation will often be reshaped in your mind by inferences you make about them. This reshaping will contain something of you and thus be your personal re-creation of the original materials. Usually this re-creation grows out of the way you combine existing materials. You discover a new relationship between *A* and *B,* and that discovery produces *C,* which is neither *A* nor *B* nor exactly their sum. Something has been added, and that something is an insight or an idea that you contributed.

You can observe this process at work when you "make sense" out of the following poem by E. E. Cummings[5]:

l(a

le
af
fa

ll

s)
one
l

iness

Because this is a strange pattern and looks only like a jumble of letters, you may be puzzled and jump to the conclusion that the poem makes no sense. But if you delay judgment and look more closely at the letters, you will see that some are inside and some outside parentheses. If you separate these two parts, you get

loneliness   aleaffalls.

Now if you look again at the second group, you will probably be able to break it into three words — *a leaf falls.* And you see that the poet is presenting the image of a falling leaf, which he associates with a mood of loneliness.

What you have done in interpreting the poem is first to take the pattern apart and then to rearrange the letters in a new pattern. In doing so, you have used two basic tools of thinking — analysis and synthesis. Analysis is the process of breaking something into its parts; synthesis is the process of recombining the parts into a new whole.

[5] © 1958 by E. E. Cummings. Reprinted from his volume *95 Poems* by permission of Harcourt, Brace & World, Inc.

In much of our thinking these two processes alternate. You have seen this alternation at work in some of the student essays you have read, most noticeably perhaps in the way the girl who wrote on TV westerns (page 13) combined quite separate bits of information to express and develop a new ironic idea of her own. Consider the sentences: "We let them [the Indians] go on living here, after we won the land fair and square, and we even gave them special areas called 'reservations' to live on. They're real nice places — sort of like wild game preserves to keep animals from becoming what they call 'extinct.' " In taking the notion of an Indian reservation from one context and the notion of a sanctuary for the preservation of wild animals from another, and combining them in a new ironic statement, she created a new image which was extremely effective for her purpose.

The way new ideas are born by bringing old ideas or old knowledge together into a new synthesis is dramatically illustrated by some famous scientific and technical discoveries. Archimedes discovered the principle of specific gravity by observing how the water rose in his bathtub when he immersed himself in it, and then relating that simple observation to his efforts to determine the gold content of a king's crown. The following example, related by Arthur Koestler, shows how Gutenberg finally transformed three bits of general knowledge into a plan for developing the printing press:

> At the dawn of the fifteenth century printing was no longer a novelty in Europe. Printing from wooden blocks on vellum, silk, and cloth apparently started in the twelfth century, and printing on paper was widely practised in the second half of the fourteenth. The blocks were engraved in relief with pictures or text or both, then thoroughly wetted with a brown distemper-like substance; a sheet of damp paper was laid on the block and the back of the paper was rubbed with a so-called *frotton* — a dabber or burnisher — until an impression of the carved relief was transferred to it. Each sheet could be printed on only one side by this method, but the blank backs of the sheets could be pasted together and then gathered into quires and bound in the same manner as manuscript-books. These "block books" or *xylographs* circulated already in considerable numbers during Gutenberg's youth. . . .
>
> Oddly enough, the starting point of Gutenberg's invention was not the block-books — he does not seem to have been acquainted with them — but playing-cards. In his first letter to Cordelier he wrote:
>
>> For a month my head has been working; a Minerva, fully armed, must issue from my brain. . . . You have seen, as I have, playing-cards and pictures of saints. . . . These cards and pictures are engraved on small pieces of wood, and below the pictures there are words and entire lines also engraved. . . . A thick ink is applied to the engraving; and upon this a leaf of paper, slightly damp, is placed; then this wood, this ink, this paper is rubbed and rubbed until the back of the paper is polished. This paper is then taken off and you see on it the picture just as if the design

had been traced upon it, and the words as if they had been written; the ink applied to the engraving has become attached to the paper, attracted by its softness and by its moisture. . . .

Well, what has been done for a few words, for a few lines, I must succeed in doing for large pages of writing, for large leaves covered entirely on both sides, for whole books, for the first of all books, the Bible. . . .

How? It is useless to think of engraving on pieces of wood the whole thirteen hundred pages. . . .

What am I to do? I do not know: but I know what I want to do: I wish to manifold the Bible, I wish to have the copies ready for the pilgrimage to Aix la Chapelle.

Here, then, we have matrix or skill No. 1: the printing from woodblocks by means of rubbing.

In the letters which follow we see him desperately searching for a simpler method to replace the laborious carving of letters in wood:

Every coin begins with a punch. The punch is a little rod of steel, one end of which is engraved with the shape of one letter, several letters, all the signs which are seen in relief on a coin. The punch is moistened and driven into a piece of steel, which becomes the "hollow" or "stamp." It is into these coin-stamps, moistened in their turn, that are placed the little discs of gold, to be converted into coins, by a powerful blow.

This is the first intimation of the method of type-casting. It leads Gutenberg, by way of analogy, to the *seal:* "When you apply to the vellum or paper the seal of your community, everything has been said, everything is done, everything is there. Do you not see that you can repeat as many times as necessary the seal covered with signs and characters?"

Yet all this is insufficient. He may cast letters in the form of coins, or seals, instead of engraving the wood, yet they will never make a clear print by the clumsy rubbing method; so long as his search remains confined to this one and only traditional method of making an "imprint," the problem remains blocked. To solve it, an entirely different kind of skill must be brought in. He tries this and that; he thinks of everything under the sun: it is the period of incubation. When the favourable opportunity at last offers itself he is ready for it:

I took part in the wine harvest. I watched the wine flowing, and going back from the effect to the cause, I studied the power of this press which nothing can resist. . . .

At this moment it occurs to him that the same, steady pressure might be applied by a seal or coin — preferably of lead, which is easy to cast — on paper, and that owing to the pressure, the lead would leave a trace on the paper — Eureka!

. . . A simple substitution which is a ray of light. . . . To work then! God has revealed to me the secret that I demanded of Him. . . . I have had a large quantity of lead brought to my house and that is the pen with which I shall write.

"The ray of light" was the bisociation of wine-press and seal — which, added together, become the letter-press. The wine-press has been lifted out of its context, the mushy pulp, the flowing red liquid, the jolly revelry . . . and connected with the stamping of vellum with a seal. From now onward these separate skills, which previously had been as different as the butcher's, the baker's, and the candlestick-maker's, will appear integrated in a single, complex matrix.[6]

There are several things to notice about this procedure of discovery. First, Gutenberg knew what he wanted. He was not trying to find out what he should do, but how he should do it. Clear knowledge of his final aim gave him a mental set which helped him to recognize the means even though he met them disguised by other contexts. Second, the materials he needed were at hand if he could recognize them. Without the right mental set he might never have recognized that a wine-press, or something like it, could be used to force paper down on type and thus cause the letters to be printed on the paper. Third, before he could combine his knowledge of the picture cards, the seals, and the wine-press into a new pattern, he had to break these objects out of the contexts in which he met them — that is, he had to analyze his existing knowledge before he could synthesize certain items to create a new pattern. This procedure is characteristic. Analysis always precedes synthesis, although the need for a synthesis may trigger the analysis.

The Gutenberg illustration shows a discovery made with difficulty after a great deal of deliberate searching. Some investigators report that the solution of their problem came quickly, sometimes in a flash. But in nearly every sudden discovery, the flash came only after the investigator had been seriously concerned with the problem for some time. Archimedes did not discover a method of determining the gold content of the king's crown just by taking a bath. Presumably he had been in his bathtub many times before without attaching any significance to the rise in the water level when he immersed himself. What happened was that his search for a solution to his problem had conditioned him to attach a new importance to something he had noticed on many other occasions. In that frame of mind he was able to see an analogy between the displacement of water by the weight of his own body and the displacement of water by metals of different weights.

The perception of an analogy between two otherwise unlike things is a powerful stimulus to discovering a new idea. The following excerpt shows how the sudden recognition that a sea and a forest are alike in ways significant to the investigator opened the door to a whole new approach to his subject.

[6] From Arthur Koestler, *The Act of Creation* (New York: The Macmillan Company, 1964).

41

Scientists visiting South America often came to see our laboratory and our forest stations. It was while showing the forest to one of these visitors, a botanist, that the idea of the biological similarity between the forest and the sea first occurred to me. We had lunch beside a little stream in a ravine where the forest was dark and quiet, singularly lifeless. Later I persuaded the botanist to climb the ladders on one of the trees, a dizzying experience avoided by many of our visitors. We rested at the 14-meter platform and then climbed on to the 24-meter platform, which was well up in the forest canopy at that particular point.

It was a sunny day, and the contrast between the forest floor and the forest canopy was striking. A nearby tree was in flower and humming with insect life. Mosquitoes, which had been scarce on the forest floor, began to annoy us. We had a good vantage point for bird watching and there were several birds about, including a large hawk perched on a nearby branch, completely indifferent to our presence.

In the course of our mosquito studies we had found that each different species had its characteristic flight habits. Some kinds were found only near the ground, others only high in the trees; some that were most common high in the trees in the morning or afternoon would come down near the ground during the midday hours, showing a sort of daily vertical migration.

While I was explaining this to my friend, it struck me, that this is just the way animals act in the sea. Most life is near the top, because that is where the sunlight strikes and everything below depends on this surface. Life in both the forest and the sea is distributed in horizontal layers.

The analogy, once thought of, was easily developed. The vocabulary for life in the sea could be transferred to the forest. In the treetops we were in what marine students call the pelagic zone — the zone of active photo-synthesis, where sunlight provides the energy to keep the whole complicated biological community going. Below, we had been in the benthos, the bottom zone, where organisms live entirely on second-hand materials that drift down from above — on fallen leaves, on fallen fruits, on roots and logs. Only a few special kinds of green plants were able to grow in the rather dim light that reached the forest floor.

My mosquitoes acted in some ways like the microscopic floating life of the sea, the plankton. Each species among the plankton organisms has a characteristic vertical distribution: some living only near the surface, others only at considerable depths, and so forth. The plankton organisms in general show a daily vertical migration, coming to the surface at night and sinking during the day: a migration to which my mosquitoes were only a feeble counterpart. But insects on land are only partially analogous with the plankton of the sea. A major portion of the plankton consists of micro-scopic plants, busy using the energy of the sun and the dissolved carbon dioxide of the water to build up starch and thus provide the basis for all the rest of the life of the sea. These microscopic plants would correspond not to the insects of the forest, but to the leaves of the trees. The forest insects would correspond only to the animal component of the plankton: to the copepods and tiny shrimp and larval fish which live directly on the plants or on each other at the very beginning of the endless chain of who eats whom in the biological community.

The real basis of the analogy is that both the forest and the sea are three-dimensional. The students of the sea have always been keenly aware of this, but the students of the forest have paid less attention to problems of depth. Of course the scale is utterly different. To compare the "gloomy depths of the forest" with the "gloomy depths of the sea" is so far-fetched as to be ludicrous — though each phrase is apt enough in its own context. The analogy is closest if we compare shallow tropical seas with tropical forests, especially with the great rain forests of the Amazon, the Congo and southeast Asia.[7]

In all such analogies the recognition of similarities is selective. There are more differences than similarities between seas and forests; but for the purpose of suggesting new ideas, what we ask is whether the similarities will yield a useful hypothesis. If we think of *A* as being similar to *B,* will our knowledge of *A* give us new insights into *B?* We can, of course, have bad analogies as well as good ones — analogies that will lead us astray. But if an analogy is considered as a possibility rather than a proof, it may offer a valuable hint toward discovery.

One of the commonest ways of constructing new knowledge from old is by regrouping items of information in a new classification. You can participate in this process by the following simple experiment. Suppose you are given the list of words below and asked to determine whether there are any regular patterns which describe how the meanings of these words change over a long period of time. At present the list is in alphabetical order. After each word two meanings are given, first an older meaning, and then a modern one. Your problem is to describe any regularities you discover in the changes from old to modern meanings.

1. *acorn* (various kinds of nuts — the seed or nut of oak trees)
2. *bonfire* (a fire for burning bones or corpses — any large outdoor fire)
3. *boor* (a farmer — an ill-mannered person)
4. *boycott* (an Irish captain who was ostracized by his neighbors — refusal to associate with any person or group)
5. *cad* (a younger son of an aristocratic family — an ill-mannered fellow)
6. *cattle* (property or wealth — cows, bulls, and steers)
7. *champagne* (wine from a French district — any wine resembling French champagne)
8. *corn* (a hard particle — the seed of a particular cereal crop)
9. *cunning* (knowing or skillful — tricky or meanly clever)
10. *dean* (an officer in charge of ten people — a major college administrator)
11. *deer* (any small animal — a particular animal with antlers)
12. *discard* (reject a card — throw something away)
13. *ferry* (travel — travel by boat)
14. *gossip* (a godparent — a spreader of rumors)
15. *hussy* (a housewife — a woman of low morals)
16. *knave* (a boy — a villainous man)

[7] From Marston Bates, *The Forest and the Sea* (New York: Random House, 1960).

17. *knight* (a young male servant — a titled person)
18. *lady* (a breadmaker — a woman of quality)
19. *martinet* (a French general who was a stickler for discipline — any rigid disciplinarian)
20. *minister* (a servant — a clergyman or statesman)
21. *pedagogue* (a slave — an educator)
22. *shibboleth* (a password used in the Bible — any word or phrase that identifies a particular group)
23. *shirt* (a loose outer garment worn by either sex — a garment worn by a man)
24. *skirt* (a loose outer garment worn by either sex — a garment worn by a woman)

As you study the material you notice that *acorn* has changed from a name for various kinds of nuts to a name for one kind: its meaning has become more specialized or restricted. Then you look at *bonfire* and decide that its meaning has changed in just the opposite way: once specialized, it has become broader or more general. This discovery, coupled with the previous one, suggests two possible kinds of change and two groupings — from broad to narrow and from narrow to broad, or restriction and extension.

You then note that *boor* does not fit into either of these groups, but seems to have acquired less pleasant connotations. You see that the same is true of *cad, cunning, gossip,* and some others. So you now have three groups, and you may guess that there will probably be another, one with *more* favorable connotations to contrast with the third group — a guess you find verified by *knight, lady,* and some others.

You find no other groups, and those you have discovered include all the words in your list:

1. toward narrower or more specialized meanings (*restriction*),
2. toward wider or more general meanings (*extension*),
3. toward less favorable connotations (*pejoration*),
4. toward more favorable connotations (*melioration*).

You will recognize this process as a combination of analysis and synthesis. The four groups were not explicit in the original list. In effect, you broke the list down into separate words and grouped all words like *acorn* in one category, all like *bonfire* in another, and so on till you exhausted the words and the categories. Each grouping constituted a new synthesis of words in the original list. Now you have not only a new way of looking at these particular words, but a pattern into which you can fit many others. For example, you can now classify these words, the early meanings of which are shown in parentheses: *campus* (field), *clerk* (cleric or clergyman), *cupboard* (a shelf for holding cups), *fowl* (any bird), *idiot* (a private person as contrasted with a public official), *nice* (foolish), *prude* (a modest person), *silly* (blessed), *starve* (to die in any manner), *steward* (a keeper of a pig sty).

Moreover, you now have the thesis and basic organization of an essay. Fill in the blanks below, and on notecards marked I, II, III, and IV write the examples that belong in each main division of the outline.

Thesis: _____

    I. _____

   II. _____

  III. _____

  IV. _____

At this point you may decide that you have enough material for a short essay, but that to write a longer one you need more examples. In any case, a plan that is complete in essentials emerges from the prewriting stage: (1) you have reshaped your material into new patterns by analysis and synthesis; (2) these patterns will determine the purpose statement of any essay that develops from your thinking, and will also suggest the organization of that essay; (3) the thesis and outline suggest what kinds of additional materials, if any, are needed.

This example illustrates the close interrelation among materials, purpose, and pattern of organization. Here the materials suggested a thesis and plan of organization, both of which then suggested additional material. The example also shows that when the basic thinking is done in the prewriting stage, the composition can sometimes be structured before the writing begins. Observation leads to a chain of prewriting activities.

MATERIALS FROM READING

In college writing much of your material will also come from reading. Here the process is more complex, for you will be concerned with two bodies of observations — the author's and those you make of his work. You will also be concerned with two bodies of inferences — those recorded in the literature and those you draw from or about it. Your actual subject is your response to what you read, and that response may be interpretive or critical. In an interpretive response you are dealing with what the work means; in a critical response you are concerned with evaluating the work. Both responses are possible sources of material for your own writing.

But both interpretive and critical responses depend on your own observations about the reading. You acquire material from the printed page in much the same way you acquire material from a picture or a personal experience, through careful observation. This acquisition always involves interpretation. The reader puts something of himself into the reading; the material he gleans is always a record of how *he* read the work, just as a viewer's impression of a painting is a record of how *he* saw the picture. Because of this subjective element, interpretation must be grounded on the object observed. In reading, this object is the text. A satisfactory interpretation must be consistent with the whole text. A reader is not free to ignore substantial parts of the text and to indulge in private interpretations which take off from the text and never return to it. But if what he says is consistent with the whole text, he has a right to emphasize what seems most important from his point of view.

Interpretation begins with a close examination of the text. The procedure is similar to that outlined for the detailed observation of a picture. Because some students want to rush into general impressions before they have studied the relations among details, they tend to make superficial interpretations of a piece of writing that seems "easy." And when writing seems "hard," they feel frustrated and too quickly decide that they don't know what it means or that it doesn't mean anything. The way to avoid either error is to examine the text piece by piece and let the observation of successive portions suggest the pattern of the whole. If we are content to begin with observations about individual words and gradually larger units, we may achieve a valid cumulative understanding of the whole.

On first reading the following poem by Emily Dickinson, many students assume that they grasp its meaning immediately, just as most viewers may at first suppose that the subject of the picture on page 34 is flying geese. Only through careful observation can a more satisfying interpretation be achieved.

> Apparently with no surprise
> To any happy flower,
> The frost beheads it at its play
> In accidental power.
>
> The blond assassin passes on,
> The sun proceeds unmoved
> To measure off another day
> For an approving God.

1. The first thing one notices is the simplicity of the poem's form — two quatrains which, when read aloud, have a sing-song rhythm found in some poetry written primarily for children. A reader might assume that the idea embodied in so simple a form must be equally simple.

2. The poem describes an action in which the frost nips off the head of a flower which has bloomed too early in the season or too late. At first reading, the poem seems merely to describe this natural event.

3. On closer observation, one expression emerges as unusual and arresting. Why is the frost personified as a "blond assassin?" "Assassin" suggests evil, and doers of evil are conventionally dark rather than blond. If the poet meant to provide merely a visual detail, why didn't she write "white assassin," since frost is more accurately white than blond? Perhaps

46

she intended some paradoxical fusion between the favorable connotations of "blond" and the evil connotations of "assassin."

4. Once this curious collision of impressions is observed, other words assume new interest. The frost's power is "accidental," which suggests that he is an unintentional murderer; he is merely playing. The happy flower seems to feel no surprise at becoming the victim of violence. In the world of human events, assassination is intentional, the victim is surprised, and a witness, in contrast to the "unmoved" sun, is shocked and horrified. The poet has described a violence in the natural world where none of the participants has human feelings; but because she has personified them, we think of human violence. This device emphasizes two points: (*a*) that violence in the rest of nature seems somewhat like human violence, (*b*) but that, for non-human nature, our normal reactions and values are inappropriate.

5. The last line suggests that God actually approves the violent event that the poem describes. Our theologies have predisposed us to think of God as gentle, or, if not gentle, at least just. Why, then, should God feel approval when a lovely flower is undeservedly killed, particularly a flower that is made to seem like an innocent human victim? It begins to seem that the poet is inviting the reader's attention to a discrepancy between what he thinks is right and what actually happens in nature. The poem is ironic.

6. Once this irony is sensed, the reader will have a more adequate idea of what the poet wishes him to observe. There is a wide gap between the world of man-made order based on morality and justice, and the world of raw nature, in which waste and violence are accepted as commonplace without value judgment. A question is suggested: Can these two contradictory systems both be valid? The reader is allowed to infer his own answer. He might interpret the poem to mean that man is not subject to the same indifferent waste and violence as the rest of nature, but lives according to a better set of values. Or he might make another interpretation — that man's confidence in a moral order is shown to be a delusion because of what happens in the uninhibited natural world.

7. By now, the reader has probably achieved an interpretation that is consistent with the text of the poem and does not neglect any of its details. If so, he has come to realize that the poem is no simple description of a natural event, but a brief expression of a complex philosophical question. He also realizes that the poem's simple form is deceptive and the burden of meaning is far greater than it suggests.

Whatever his interpretation, the student now has something to write about. He can show what the poem means to him, or he can respond to the judgment which the poem makes about life. If the latter, he may do one of several things: he may explain and comment on Emily Dickinson's view of nature; he may raise and explore the question whether man's ethical standards are contradicted by nature; he may discuss the sentimentality which personification encourages; he may attack the poem as trivial, or he may praise it for its insight into man's relation to nature. If he does any of these things, he should remember that his subject is not the poem itself, but his response to it.

The kinds of inferences discussed earlier apply also to reading. A poem, a play, or a story may suggest a comparison with another literary work. Huck Finn's journey down the river may be compared to Ulysses' long voyage home in the *Odyssey;* or the orations made over Caesar's body by Brutus and Antony in *Julius Caesar* may be contrasted for their motivation, structure, or effect. An idea taken from one source may be applied to others, as when Aristotle's concept of the tragic flaw is applied to Shakespeare's tragedies. Classifications or criticisms found in an essay may be evaluated or extended to other works.

In all these mental activities, the student is relating a new idea to previous knowledge much as Gutenberg related bits of knowledge to the concept of printing by movable type. The student writer relates ideas to each other, and the connection suggests something not previously known or thought of — at least by him.

As a final illustration of discovering materials, consider the evolution of the following student essay.

A class of twenty freshmen had been reading and discussing Sophocles' tragedy *Oedipus Rex*. One girl delivered an impassioned protest against the "injustice" of Greek religion, arguing that Oedipus never had a chance: it was ordained by the gods that he would kill his father and marry his mother, and nothing he could do would let him avoid that fate. The girl spoke so persuasively that many students in the class agreed with her.

But one student, though he took no part in the discussion, felt that she was being more emotional than critical, and was responding more to the myth on which the play was based than to Sophocles' treatment of the story. So he decided to refute her argument in his weekly essay.

As he thought about how this purpose might be carried out, it seemed to him that two main points should be made: first, that Oedipus' actions throughout the play were thoroughly consistent with his character as Sophocles had drawn it, so that Oedipus would have acted as he did even if there had been no prophecy; second, that the prophecy itself took into account Oedipus' character and was therefore a prediction of what a person like him would do in certain situations. In other words, the prophecy need not be evidence that the gods wanted the events to take place, but merely evidence that the gods knew they would take place.

The boy felt that he could clearly establish the first point from the facts of the text; he could show that Oedipus' actions were quite natural. The second point would be more difficult. It could be neither affirmed nor denied from the text, since Sophocles said nothing decisive on the matter. What was needed was some argument that would seem natural and would persuade the class that prophecy does not necessarily imply predestination.

Here is what he wrote:

The question arose in class whether Oedipus' actions were predestined. In my opinion, they were not. When Laius tried to kill him, he struck back. What else could a man of spirit do? When he solved the riddle and was offered the kingship by the grateful Thebans, he married the dead king's widow. This was politically expedient. By marrying Jocasta, Oedipus, then a stranger with no known family and no political connections, allied himself with the royal family and so reduced the possibility that any other claimant, including Creon, would attempt to seize the throne. By insisting that Teiresias and the old shepherd tell what they knew, Oedipus was acting in accordance with the prevailing moral code: it was both his religious and his civic duty to discover the murderer. Had he been a timid man, Oedipus might have retreated before Laius and taken the safe course when he sensed the drift of the witnesses' testimony, but then he would not have been Oedipus. He did what his character required him to do. I am sure that he would have acted as he did even if there had been no prophecy.

In my opinion, those who are rationalizing away the responsibility of Oedipus for his actions fail to distinguish between pre-knowledge and pre-destination. Of course Apollo knew what would happen to Oedipus. One of the many advantages of being a god is the ability to foretell the future. But the fact that Apollo knew what would happen does not prove that he made it happen. If I am sitting on a hilltop, looking down on a curving road on which two cars are speeding toward each other, I can see what the drivers of the cars cannot see. I can see that they are going to meet at that sharp curve and that, the way they are going, they will crash. But does my foreseeing the disaster prove that I caused it?

Apollo knew that Oedipus and his father would meet at a place where three roads come together. He also knew the characters of both men, and it took no great prophetic gift to foretell the result. It was clear to Apollo, as it was to Teiresias, that if the situation were right, Oedipus would ruin himself. He did not need divine help. He was perfectly capable of doing it by himself. To quote another dramatist,

> Our faults, dear Brutus, lie not in our stars,
> But in ourselves that we are underlings.

The material of the first paragraph comes directly from the play. The student's purpose governs the selection and organization of material, but nothing in the paragraph is invented. The information in it was familiar to everyone in the class, including the girl who was troubled by the injustice of the tragedy.

The material of the next two paragraphs was developed from an inference. Out of his wish to show that pre-knowledge need not imply predestination, the student brought together and connected in his mind two very different situations — a boy on a hilltop watching the course two cars are taking, and Apollo on Mount Olympus watching the course rash people are taking. This analogy was just the kind of argument he needed. He may not have thought of it before he started to work on his essay; but, like Gutenberg and the wine-press, his need and his earlier thinking prepared him for it, and the analogy came to meet his need. So also did the quotation from *Julius Caesar;* it was the right concluding detail.

SUMMARY

The content of this chapter is summarized below:

1. A writer's materials are the data he needs to develop the purpose of his work. These materials may be drawn from any useful source, but the chief source is the knowledge of the subject which the writer already possesses — a reservoir of information and ideas which has been filled from his experience. By recalling the material he needs, the writer can tap that reservoir selectively.

2. Another major source of material is observation of the subject. Observation is examination of the subject to notice specific details. Details are indispensable in description, and since all other forms of writing rest on description, the observation and recording of specific details is basic to every kind of writing.

3. The greatest obstacle to observing is the tendency to settle too soon for general impressions. General impressions are the final patterns which emerge from details, but observation of details should come first and the general impressions should be based on observation.

4. Still another major source of material is inferences drawn from observations. Inferring is relating observations or other knowledge in the mind and thus creating a new significance. The chief way to find new relationships is by a combination of analysis and synthesis. In analysis, elements in a situation or context are separated and examined individually. In synthesis, the elements separated are recombined into a new pattern.

5. Two of the most useful kinds of analyses and syntheses are analogy and classification. In analogy, things normally considered quite different are seen to be alike in some special way. An analogy may lead to a new view of one or both subjects and to a fusion of them into a new synthesis. In classification, elements are taken from their original context and grouped in new classes by selecting some characteristics and ignoring others. The new classes so formed become new concepts synthesized from old.

6. Especially in college, reading is a major source of experience and of materials for writing. Essays suggested by reading are *interpretive* when they explain what the literature means to the reader, and *critical* when they develop a judgment of the literature. The kinds of inferences drawn from observation can also be made from reading, the most common being comparison, contrast, analogy, and classification.

Exercises

A. For each of the two following pictures, first make notes recording your observations; then derive a general impression of the meaning of each picture from your specific observations; finally, write an essay contrasting the two cultures represented by the pictures.

B. Interpret the following difficult poem by answering the questions given below it.

SAILING TO BYZANTIUM[8]

By William Butler Yeats

1. That is no country for old men. The young
2. In one another's arms, birds in the trees,
3. — Those dying generations — at their song,
4. The salmon-falls, the mackerel-crowded seas,
5. Fish, flesh, or fowl, commend all summer long
6. Whatever is begotten, born, and dies.
7. Caught in that sensual music all neglect
8. Monuments of unageing intellect.

9. An aged man is but a paltry thing,
10. A tattered coat upon a stick, unless
11. Soul clap its hands and sing, and louder sing
12. For every tatter in its mortal dress,
13. Nor is there singing school but studying
14. Monuments of its own magnificence;
15. And therefore I have sailed the seas and come
16. To the holy city of Byzantium.

1. To identify Byzantium, refer to a dictionary. Since the speaker is sailing *to* Byzantium, he is sailing *from* somewhere else. The name of that place is not given, nor is it important, though the *nature* of the place is.

2. "*That* is no country . . ." To what place does *That* refer? It cannot be Byzantium, because that interpretation would not be consistent with lines 15 and 16.

3. Why is "that" no country for old men? Presumably lines 1–8 describe it in a series of images. What is the common subject of these images? What are the young concerned with? What is it that the birds, the salmon, and the mackerel — "fish, flesh, or fowl" — "commend"? Explain lines 5 and 6.

4. What does "all" in line 7 refer to? What is the "sensual music"? What contrast of values is suggested in lines 7 and 8? What is the significance of "unageing"?

5. Lines 9 and 10 present no problem, but perhaps 11 and 12 do. According to these lines, what makes an old man significant?

6. According to lines 13 and 14, there is only one way for a soul to learn to sing. What is it? What are the monuments of the soul's magnificence? Are these the same as the monuments mentioned in line 8?

7. Can you see now why the speaker is sailing to Byzantium and what he expects to find there?

Using the procedure you have been following, interpret the second half of the poem, given below. The meaning of "perne in a gyre" is obscure, but the phrase probably suggests a spiraling or whirling motion. In line 24 you will have to do some thinking about "the artifice of eternity." Could this phrase also be read as "the eternity of artifice"? What is the connection between "eternity" here and "unageing" in line 8?

17. O sages standing in God's holy fire
18. As in the gold mosaic of a wall,
19. Come from the holy fire, perne in a gyre,
20. And be the singing-masters of my soul.
21. Consume my heart away; sick with desire
22. And fastened to a dying animal
23. It knows not what it is; and gather me
24. Into the artifice of eternity.

25. Once out of nature I shall never take
26. My bodily form from any natural thing,
27. But such a form as Grecian goldsmiths make
28. Of hammered gold and gold enamelling
29. To keep a drowsy Emperor awake;
30. Or set upon a golden bough to sing
31. To lords and ladies of Byzantium
32. Of what is past, or passing, or to come.

When you have finished, answer the general question: What is the real subject of the poem, what is the poem about? Your answer will not say all about the poem, but it will at least show the "plain sense." It will provide the general impression that was difficult to state before the observation of individual details.

C. Compare or contrast the views of nature expressed in this poem and the one by Emily Dickinson which you studied earlier.

3

Patterns of Organization

We have seen that the way material is organized in an essay grows out of and is controlled by the writer's purpose. In a card game the way you arrange the cards in your hand depends on the game. There is one arrangement for bridge, but quite a different arrangement for poker. In any game the cards are arranged in the order that is most efficient for what the players intend to do.

So with writing: the purpose and the materials suggest the organization. Tentative decisions about organization are made as soon as the writer restricts his subject, and these decisions become firm as he defines his purpose. If the prewriting is efficient, the structure of the essay grows out of it.

But normally there comes a stage in prewriting when the writer uses a pen to help him think, and he jots down at least a rudimentary plan. This plan may begin as a simple enumeration of the points he wants to discuss — first, second, third, etc. — or as a series of topics, or even topic sentences, each of which he intends to develop into one or more paragraphs. For a writer who has his purpose clearly in mind, simple enumeration of points to be discussed may be enough to block out the parts of a short essay, and thus to establish the order of ideas or topics. More frequently, these are tentative gropings toward a structure, which may finally emerge as a more sophisticated outline. For example, the preliminary planning of the last chapter began with the following enumeration of topics:

1. Materials obtained from observation
2. Materials obtained from inference
3. Materials obtained from reading

Later these headings were expanded and revised into a simple topic outline:

55

SOURCES OF MATERIALS

I. Materials from observation
   A. Introductory illustration: *The Camera Eye*
   B. Prerequisites for observation
   C. Specific observation *vs.* general impressions
   D. The technique of observing: *Night and Day*
   E. Exercise in observation
   F. Relation of observation and specific diction: the Carson and Stewart examples

II. Materials from inference
   A. Analysis and synthesis: the Cummings poem
   B. The process of inference-making: the Gutenberg example
   C. Analogy: *The Forest and the Sea*
   D. Classification: Semantic Change

III. Materials from reading
   A. Observation as the basis for interpretation: the Dickinson poem
   B. Inferences from reading: the Oedipus essay

In its finished form the chapter follows the structure of this outline. The difference between the outline and the chapter is not one of organization, but of content. The outline has no content: it is a plan to determine and control the order in which the content will be presented. It is thus the last stage of prewriting. The discussion of each heading in the outline provides the content, and so develops the organizational pattern into a composition.

In general, patterns of organization are of three kinds: illustrative, analytical, and argumentative. The *illustrative pattern,* as its name implies, makes the meaning of a thesis or topic sentence clear by illustrating it. The movement within the pattern is from general to particular. The discussion moves toward a more and more specific statement of what is implied by the opening general statement. The *analytical pattern,* as *its* name implies, breaks the subject into parts and deals with each part in turn. The movement within the pattern is from the subject to its main divisions; the divisions are then subdivided and, if necessary, the subdivisions are further divided. These two patterns are often combined. In the outline above, all entries are analytical, since they break the subject into parts, but the additions following the colons are illustrative, since they provide examples and thus bring the discussion down to specific cases. Finally, the *argumentative pattern* arranges evidence in a logical order to prove a thesis or proposition. The movement within the pattern is from premise to conclusion.

THE ILLUSTRATIVE PATTERN

The structure of the illustrative pattern may be introduced by the following model:

THE METHOD OF SCIENTIFIC INVESTIGATION[1]

Thesis stated in first sentence and restated in second

[1] The method of scientific investigation is nothing but the expression of the necessary mode of working of the human mind. It is simply the mode at which all phenomena are reasoned about, rendered precise and exact.

Thesis clarified by an introductory comparison between mental operations of scientists and merchants

There is no more difference, but there is just the same kind of difference, between the mental operations of a man of science and those of an ordinary person, as there is between the operations and methods of a baker or of a butcher weighing out his goods in common scales, and the operations of a chemist in performing a difficult and complex analysis by means of his balance and finely-graduated weights. It is not that the action of the scales in the one case, and the balance in the other, differ in the principles of their construction or manner of working; but the beam of one is set on an infinitely finer axis than the other, and of course turns by the addition of a much smaller weight.

Main operations of scientific method identified. Thesis restated in light of this identification

[2] You will understand this better, perhaps, if I give you some familiar example. You have all heard it repeated, I dare say, that men of science work by means of induction and deduction, and that by the help of these operations, they, in a sort of sense, wring from Nature certain other things, which are called natural laws, and causes, and that out of these, by some cunning skill of their own, they build up hypotheses and theories. And it is imagined by many, that the operations of the common mind can be by no means compared with these processes, and that they have to be acquired by a sort of special apprenticeship to the craft. To hear all these large words, you would think that the mind of a man of science must be constituted differently from that of his fellow-men; but if you will not be frightened by terms, you will discover that you are quite wrong, and that all these terrible apparatus are being used by yourselves every day and every hour of your lives. . . .

Simple example introduced for sake of specific discussion to follow

[3] A very trivial circumstance will serve to exemplify this. Suppose you go into a fruiterer's shop, wanting an apple, — you take up one, and, on biting it, you find it sour; you look at it, and see that it is hard and green. You take up another one, and that too is hard, green, and sour. The shopman offers you a third; but, before biting it,

[1] By Thomas Henry Huxley.

57

you examine it, and find that it is hard and green, and you immediately say that you will not have it, as it must be sour, like those that you have already tried.

[4] Nothing can be more simple than that, you think; but if you will take the trouble to analyse and trace out into its logical elements what has been done by the mind, you will be greatly surprised. In the first place, you have performed the operation of induction. You found that, in two experiences, hardness and greenness in apples went together with sourness. It was so in the first case, and it was confirmed by the second. True, it is a very small basis, but still it is enough to make an induction from; you

Example analyzed to show it contains both induction and deduction, identified earlier as characteristic of the scientific method of investigation. The investigation of apples results in a "law" which resembles the natural laws in science

generalise the facts, and you expect to find sourness in apples where you get hardness and greenness. You found upon that a general law, that all hard green apples are sour; and that, so far as it goes, is a perfect induction. Well, having got your natural law in this way, when you are offered another apple which you find is hard and green, you say, "All hard and green apples are sour; this apple is hard and green, therefore this apple is sour." That train of reasoning is what logicians call a syllogism, and has all its various parts and terms, — its major premise, its minor premise, and its conclusion. And, by the help of further reasoning, which, if drawn out, would have to be exhibited in two or three other syllogisms, you arrive at your final determination, "I will not have that apple." So that, you see, you have, in the first place, established a law by induction, and upon that you have founded a deduction, and reasoned out the special conclusion of the particular case. Well now, suppose, having got your law, that at some time afterwards, you are discussing the qualities of apples with a friend: you will say to him, "It is a very curious thing, — but I find that all hard and green apples are sour!" Your friend says to you, "But how do you know that?" You at once reply, "Oh, because I have tried them over and over again, and have always found them to be so." Well, if we were talking science instead of common sense, we should call that an experimental verification.

Example extended to suggest analogy with process of verification in scientific investigation

And, if still opposed, you go further, and say, "I have heard from the people in Somersetshire and Devonshire, where a large number of apples are grown, that they have observed the same thing. It is also found to be the case in Normandy, and in North America. In short, I find it to be the universal experience of mankind wherever attention has been directed to the subject." Whereupon, your friend, unless he is a very unreasonable man, agrees with you, and is convinced that you are quite right in the conclusion you have drawn. He believes, although perhaps he does not know he believes it, that the more extensive verifications are, — that the more frequently experiments

have been made, and results of the same kind arrived at, —
that the more varied the conditions under which the same
results are attained, the more certain is the ultimate conclusion, and he disputes the question no further. He sees that
the experiment has been tried under all sorts of conditions,
as to time, place, and people, with the same result; and he
says with you, therefore, that the law you have laid down
must be a good one, and he must believe it.

Concluding para-
graph, which re-
states similarity of
procedures used in
example and those
used in scientific
investigation

[5] In science we do the same thing; — the philosopher
exercises precisely the same faculties, though in a much
more delicate manner. In scientific inquiry it becomes a
matter of duty to expose a supposed law to every possible
kind of verification, and to take care, moreover, that this is
done intentionally, and not left to a mere accident, as in
the case of the apples. And in science, as in common life,
our confidence in a law is in exact proportion to the absence of variation in the result of our experimental verifications. For instance, if you let go your grasp of an article
you may have in your hand, it will immediately fall to the
ground. That is a very common verification of one of the
best established laws of nature — that of gravitation. The

Final restatement
of thesis in light of
whole discussion

method by which men of science establish the existence of
that law is exactly the same as that by which we have
established the trivial proposition about the sourness of
hard and green apples. But we believe it in such an extensive, thorough, and unhesitating manner because the
universal experience of mankind verifies it, and we can
verify it ourselves at any time; and that is the strongest
possible foundation on which any natural law can rest.

The structure of this selection can be made clearer by the following summary of the paragraphs:

¶1. The thesis is stated and clarified.
¶2. The key term "method of scientific investigation" is explained in order
to advance the explanation of the thesis.
¶s 3–4. An example is given and analyzed to illustrate the meaning of the
thesis in a simple situation. *universalize a specific reference*
¶5. The concluding paragraph summarizes the discussion and makes a final
restatement of the thesis. *reinforce*

This is the illustrative pattern, though it does not always take precisely
this shape. Sometimes the concluding restatement is omitted, and usually
the thesis is not so frequently restated. Occasionally a number of short
illustrations are given, instead of a single extended one. But the core of
the pattern is statement of thesis, explanation of thesis, and illustration of
thesis: *statement — explanation — illustration.*

The three most common types of illustrations are *examples, comparisons,*
and *contrasts.* In "The Method of Scientific Investigation," the illustration

59

about tasting apples is a comparison; it compares the scientific method of the laboratory with the way we all approach generalizations on the basis of experience. Had Huxley wished to use an example, he would have described a laboratory experiment in detail, so that the reader might see how similar the experiment is to the way his own mind works. Had Huxley wished to use a contrast, he might have shown how scientific method and common sense differ from superstition.

Examples

An essay which illustrates a thesis solely by examples usually consists of an introductory paragraph followed by as many examples as the writer wishes or needs to give. The selection below shows how Konrad Z. Lorenz, a biologist, illustrates what is now called "imprinting" — the tendency of animals and birds to identify themselves as belonging to the species which they first encounter, either at birth or soon thereafter.[2]

Thesis stated and clarified

Birds reared in isolation from their kind do not generally know what species they belong to: that is to say, not only their social reactions but also their sexual desires are directed towards those beings with whom they have spent certain impressionable phases of their early youth. Consequently, birds raised singly by hand tend to regard human beings, and human beings only, as potential partners in all reproductive activities.

Example 1

A female barnyard goose which I now possess was the only survivor of a brood of six, of which the remainder all succumbed to avian tuberculosis. Consequently she grew up in the company of chickens and, in spite of the fact that we bought for her, in good time, a beautiful gander, she fell head over heels in love with our handsome Rhode Island cock, inundated him with proposals, jealously prevented him from making love to his hens, and remained absolutely insensible to the attentions of the gander.

Example 2

The hero of a similar tragi-comedy was a lovely white peacock of the Schönbrunn Zoo in Vienna. He too was the last survivor of an early-hatched brood which perished in a period of cold weather, and, to save him, the keeper put him in the warmest room to be found in the whole Zoo, which at that time, shortly after the first world war, was in the reptile house with the giant tortoises. For the rest of his life this unfortunate bird saw only in those huge reptiles the object of his desire and remained unresponsive to the charms of the prettiest peahens. . . .

Example 3

Another tame adult male jackdaw fell in love with me and treated me exactly as a female of his kind. By the

[2] Adapted from *King Solomon's Ring*, by Konrad Z. Lorenz. Copyright 1952 by Thomas Y. Crowell Company, New York, publishers.

hour, this bird tried to make me creep into the nesting cavity of his choice, a few inches in width. He became most importunate in that he continually wanted to feed me with what he considered the choicest delicacies. Remarkably enough, he recognized the human mouth as the orifice of ingestion and he was overjoyed if I opened my lips to him, uttering at the same time an adequate begging note. This must be considered as an act of self-sacrifice on my part, since even I cannot pretend to like the taste of finely minced worms, generously mixed with jackdaw saliva. You will understand that I found it difficult to cooperate with the bird in this manner every few minutes! But if I did not, I had to guard my ears against him, otherwise, before I knew what was happening, the passage of one of these organs would be filled right up to the drum with warm worm pulp, for jackdaws, when feeding their female or their young, push the food mass, with the aid of their tongue, deep down into the partner's pharynx. However, this bird only made use of my ears when I refused him my mouth, on which the first attempt was always made.

The structure of the illustrative pattern can be expressed by the formula: $T + E_1 + E_2$, etc., where T stands for *thesis* and E for *example*. When there is a concluding restatement, the formula is extended to: $T + E_1 + E_2 + \ldots R$. Had Lorenz ended with some such paragraph as the following, he would have followed this variation.

R These examples illustrate the general process of imprinting. A newborn bird identifies himself as a member of the species most immediate in his environment. He thinks he is a member of that race. This mistake in identity does not affect his inherited instincts. He still acts as geese, peacocks, or jackdaws have always done. When he becomes mature, he follows the patterns of courtship that are instinctual in his kind, and he expects his partner to follow them, too. He simply does not recognize that he and his partner are of different species.

The illustrative pattern is highly elastic. It can be extended to a long essay — 4000 to 5000 words — by choosing a number of examples and presenting each in detail. At the other extreme it can be restricted to a short paragraph, or even a sentence.

T Beauty is the quality which makes to endure. In a house that I know, I have noticed a block of spermaceti lying about closets and mantelpieces, for twenty years together, E_1 simply because the tallow-man gave it the form of a rabbit; and I suppose it may continue to be lugged about un-

E_2

E_3

changed for a century. Let an artist scrawl a few lines or figures on the back of a letter, and that scrap of paper is rescued from danger, is put in portfolio, is framed and glazed, and, in proportion to the beauty of the lines drawn, will be kept for centuries. Burns writes a copy of verses and sends them to a newspaper, and the human race take charge of them that they shall not perish.[3]

The structure of this four-sentence paragraph could hardly be simpler: a short topic sentence is followed by three illustrative sentences, each with an example of the topic idea.

A trunk in the attic is often a treasure chest of things that once were deeply meaningful to someone — pictures of relatives no longer identifiable by the family, faded newspaper clippings recording some triumph by one of the children on the athletic field or the high school theater, letters tied with ribbons or encased in boxes, old notebooks containing primitive stories or verses written in a child's hand, dresses that have been out of style for fifty years but are still lovely in a museum-like way.

Here a series of appositives — pictures, clippings, letters, etc. — illustrate "things that once were deeply meaningful" in the main clause of the sentence.

▶ *As practice in using the illustrative pattern, prewrite an essay consisting of a thesis and three examples, each of which will take a substantial paragraph. Jot down the thesis and the topic of each example, then* think out *the full development of each example. Finally,* write *the introductory paragraph and the first example of the essay.*

Comparison–Contrast *probably most efficient form of essay writing.*

Comparison and contrast are structurally so similar that we can consider them together. In the illustrative pattern the favorite type of comparison is *analogy,* the relating of two things — often otherwise quite unlike — to emphasize some significant similarity between them.

No one doubts that writing and speaking are active undertakings, in which the writer or speaker is clearly doing something. Many people seem to think, however, that reading and listening are entirely passive. No work need be done. They think of reading and listening as *receiving* communication from someone who is actually *giving* it. So far they are right, but then they make the error of supposing that receiving communication is like receiving a blow, or a legacy, or a judgment from the court.

Let me use the example of baseball. Catching the ball is just as much of an activity as pitching or hitting it. The pitcher or batter is the *giver* here in the sense that his activity initiates the motion of the ball. The catcher or

[3] From Ralph Waldo Emerson, "Beauty."

fielder is the *receiver* in the sense that his activity terminates it. Both are equally active, though the activities are distinctly different. If anything is passive here, it is the ball: it is pitched and caught. It is the inert thing which is put in motion or stopped, whereas the living men are active, moving to pitch, hit, or catch. The analogy with writing and reading is almost perfect. The thing which is written and read, like the ball, is the passive object in some way common to the two activities which begin and terminate the process.[4]

In this selection the author is meeting his need for an illustration which will show that *receiving* a communication is not a passive process. The analogy that comes to his mind is the work of the catcher in baseball. He can count on his audience to know that there is nothing passive about catching. He knows the reader understands how skillful and hard-working the catcher is, and he uses that knowledge to suggest that there is nothing passive about reading.

When two subjects, *A* and *B,* are being compared or contrasted, the contents of the essay will alternate between *A* and *B.* This alternation is best illustrated by two common patterns, or a combination of them: (1) the body of the essay may consist of two parts, each of one or more paragraphs, which describe *A* in the first part and *B* in the second; (2) related details of *A* and *B* may be presented in parallel form within each sentence, or in successive sentences, and each paragraph will contain a series of such pairs. These patterns are summarized and illustrated below.

$A + B$

Purpose:	A comparison to show significant differences between rugby and American football
A	A description of football in which the details are selected to set up a contrast with the details about rugby to be given in the second part of the essay.
B	A description of rugby to match that of football given in the first part.

$A/B + A/B$

Thesis:	Death is at all times solemn, but never so much as at sea.
A/B	A man dies on shore; his body remains with his friends, and "the mourners go about the streets"; but when a man falls overboard at sea and is lost, there is a suddenness in the event, and a difficulty in realizing it, which give to it an air of awful mystery. A man dies on shore — you follow
A/B	his body to the grave, and a stone marks the spot; . . . but at sea, the man is near you — at your side — you hear his voice, and in an instant he is gone, and nothing but a vacancy shows his loss.[5] . . . [And so on until the contrast has been completed.]

[4] From Mortimer J. Adler, *How to Read a Book* (New York: Simon and Schuster, 1940).
[5] From Richard Henry Dana, *Two Years Before the Mast.*

The following selection illustrates the thesis that only at a certain stage of its development does a people have the kind of faith in humanity which makes the production and appreciation of tragedy possible. The essay is developed through a contrast between an Elizabethan tragedy, *A,* and a modern tragedy, *B*.[6]

Statement of thesis. Explanation and expansion of the statement

[1] It is, indeed, only at a certain stage in the development of the realistic intelligence of a people that the tragic faith can exist. A naiver people may have, as the ancient men of the north had, a body of legends which are essentially tragic, or it may have only (and need only) its happy and childlike mythology which arrives inevitably at its happy end, where the only ones who suffer "deserve" to do so and in which, therefore, life is represented as directly and easily acceptable. A too sophisticated society on the other hand — one which, like ours, has outgrown not merely the simple optimism of the child but also that vigorous, one might almost say adolescent, faith in the nobility of man which marks a Sophocles or a Shakespeare — has neither fairy tales to assure it that all is always right in the end nor tragedies to make it believe that it rises superior in soul to the outward calamities which befall it.

Principally a discussion of B, but involves some A/B contrasts

[2] Distrusting its thought, despising its passions, realizing its impotent unimportance in the universe, it can tell itself no stories except those which make it still more acutely aware of its trivial miseries. When its heroes (sad misnomer for the pitiful creatures who people contemporary fiction) are struck down it is not, like Oedipus, by the gods that they are struck, but only, like Oswald Alving, by syphilis, for they know that the gods, even if they existed, would not trouble with them and they cannot attribute to themselves in art an importance in which they do not believe. Their so-called tragedies do not and cannot end with one of those splendid calamities which in Shakespeare seem to reverberate through the universe, because they cannot believe that the universe trembles when their love is, like Romeo's, cut off or when the place where they (small as they are) have gathered up their trivial treasure is, like Othello's sanctuary, defiled. Instead, mean misery piles on mean misery, petty misfortune follows petty misfortune, and despair becomes intolerable because it is no longer even significant or important.

More specific development of B

[3] Ibsen once made one of his characters say that he did not read much because he found reading "irrelevant," and the adjective was brilliantly chosen because it held implications even beyond those of which Ibsen was consciously aware. What is it that made the classics irrelevant

[6] From *The Modern Temper,* copyright, 1929, 1957, by Joseph Wood Krutch. Reprinted by permission of Harcourt, Brace & World, Inc.

to him and to us? Is it not just exactly those to him impossible premises which make tragedy what it is, those assumptions that the soul of man is great, that the universe (together with whatever gods may be) concerns itself with him and that he is, in a word, noble? Ibsen turned to village politics for exactly the same reason that his contemporaries and his successors have, each in his own way, sought out some aspect of the common man and his common life — because, that is to say, here was at least something small enough for him to be able to believe.

Transitional paragraph to introduce the detailed A + B *contrast to follow*

[4] Bearing this fact in mind, let us compare a modern "tragedy" with one of the great works of a happy age, not in order to judge of their relative technical merits but in order to determine to what extent the former deserves its name by achieving a tragic solution capable of purging the soul or of reconciling the emotions to the life which it pictures. And in order to make the comparison as fruitful as possible let us choose *Hamlet* on the one hand and on the other a play like *Ghosts* which was not only written by perhaps the most powerful as well as the most typical of modern writers but which is, in addition, the one of his works which seems most nearly to escape that triviality which cannot be entirely escaped by anyone who feels, as all contemporary minds do, that man is relatively trivial.

Description of A, *emphasizing those points which will later be contrasted with* B

[5] In *Hamlet* a prince ("in understanding, how like a god!") has thrust upon him from the unseen world a duty to redress a wrong which concerns not merely him, his mother, and his uncle, but the moral order of the universe. Erasing all trivial fond records from his mind, abandoning at once both his studies and his romance because it has been his good fortune to be called upon to take part in an action of cosmic importance, he plunges (at first) not into action but into thought, weighing the claims which are made upon him and contemplating the grandiose complexities of the universe. And when the time comes at last for him to die, he dies, not as a failure, but as a success. Not only has the universe regained the balance which had been upset by what *seemed* the monstrous crime of the guilty pair ("there is nothing either good or ill but thinking makes it so"), but in the process by which that readjustment is made a mighty mind has been given the opportunity, first to contemplate the magnificent scheme of which it is a part and then to demonstrate the greatness of its spirit by playing a role in the grand style which is called for. We do not need to despair in *such* a world if it has *such* creatures in it.

Description of B, *which contrasts with* A

[6] Turn now to *Ghosts* — look upon this picture and upon that. A young man has inherited syphilis from his father. Struck by a to him mysterious malady he returns to his northern village, learns the hopeless truth about

himself, and persuades his mother to poison him. The incidents prove, perhaps, that pastors should not endeavor to keep a husband and wife together unless they know what they are doing. But what a world is this in which a great writer can deduce nothing more than that from his greatest work and how are we to be purged or reconciled when we see it acted? Not only is the failure utter, but it is trivial and meaningless as well.

A conclusion which includes some further A/B contrasts

[7] Yet the journey from Elsinore to Skien is precisely the journey which the human spirit has made, exchanging in the process princes for invalids and gods for disease. We say, as Ibsen would say, that the problems of Oswald Alving are more "relevant" to our life than the problems of Hamlet, that the play in which he appears is more "real" than the other more glamorous one, but it is exactly because we find it so that we are condemned. We can believe in Oswald but we cannot believe in Hamlet, and a light has gone out in the universe. Shakespeare justifies the ways of God to man, but in Ibsen there is no such happy end and with him tragedy, so called, has become merely an expression of our despair at finding that such justification is no longer possible.

A paragraph summary of this selection will reveal the following structure:

1. A statement of the thesis that great tragedy is produced and appreciated by a people only at a certain stage of its development. This thesis is expanded by a contrast between an age of true tragedy and a more primitive people, on the one hand, and a more sophisticated people, on the other.
2. A description of what is missing in modern tragedy, *B,* with particular reference to Ibsen. This paragraph involves some *A/B + A/B* contrast in which details from ancient and Elizabethan tragedy are introduced.
3. A further description of modern tragedy, *B,* illustrated by a detail from an Ibsen drama.
4. A transitional paragraph to introduce a detailed contrast between *Hamlet* and *Ghosts.*
5. A detailed description of the view of man which *Hamlet* presents — *A.*
6. A detailed description of the view of man which *Ghosts* presents — *B.*
7. A concluding paragraph which introduces some further *A/B* contrasts and makes a value judgment.

▶ *Using the selection you have just studied as a model, choose one of the subjects listed below and illustrate it by comparison and contrast. In parentheses following each subject are possibilities for comparison and contrast. Select one for your development, and use both* A + B *and* A/B + A/B *in your essay.*

1. Modern American folk music (traditional folk music, modern English folk music, jazz)

2. Yankees (Southerners, Westerners, Europeans)
3. Small colleges (large universities)
4. The best TV commercials (the worst)
5. The dress of college students (older people's dress, high school dress, the dress of young people not in college)

THE ANALYTICAL PATTERN

The analytical pattern has been described as one that breaks a subject into its parts and discusses each part in turn. The three most common types of analysis are *classification, process,* and *causal relation.*

Classification

Classification was introduced in Chapter 2 with the exercise on the four types of semantic change (pages 43–45). In that exercise you selected from a list those words which could be grouped together in accordance with the kind of change they illustrated: changes toward wider meanings, narrower meanings, more favorable meanings, less favorable meanings.

Classification is the process of grouping together things which are perceived as being alike in some specific way. Draft boards classify as 1A young men who are considered to be alike in specified ways, and as 1Y, 2S, or 4F those who are alike in other specified ways. Classification both unites individuals into a group and separates them from other groups, so that it takes into account differences as well as similarities.

Classifications are man-made. Young men are not 1A or 4F until the draft board says so. When they are so described, their classification is an act of society, not of nature. Any individual may be, and usually is, classified in a number of ways: John Jones, college junior, honor student, chemistry major, 2S, Methodist, redhead, tenor, bachelor, halfback, and so on. None of these classifications is a complete description of John Jones, but each is a description of the classifier's interest in him at the moment. Each new classification of John Jones represents another way of looking at him.

When classification is used as a tool of thought, the categories impose a form on raw material that would otherwise be formless: for example, the list of words on pages 43–44 had no form until the words were arranged in four categories. Once the categories have been identified, the basic organization of the writing has been determined, and the content of the essay is chiefly a description of the characteristics of the items in each category.

▶ *The following selection illustrates both the organization imposed by the system of classification and the descriptive details by which each category is defined. Read the essay, then prepare a simple but accurate outline of it, and finally make notes on the characteristics of each category so that you can summarize the essay from your outline and notes.*

Body and Personality Types in Human Beings[7]

[1] The most striking fact about human beings is that, in many respects, they are very unlike one another. Their bodies vary enormously in size and shape. Their modes of thought and speech and feeling are startlingly different. Startlingly different, too, are their reactions to even such basic things as food, sex, money, and power. Between the most highly gifted and those of least ability, and between persons endowed with one particular kind of talent or temperament and persons endowed with another kind, the gulfs are so wide as to be bridgeable only by the most enlightened charity.

[2] These are facts which from time immemorial have been recognized, described in plays and stories, commented on in proverbs, aphorisms, and poems. And yet, in spite of their obviousness and their enormous practical importance, these facts are still, to a very great extent, outside the pale of systematic thought.

[3] The first and indispensable condition of systematic thought is classification. . . . Up to the present, all the systems in terms of which men have attempted to think about human differences have been unsatisfactory. . . . Does there exist a more adequate system? This is a question which it is now possible, I think, to answer with a decided yes. A classification system more adequate to the facts and more potentially fruitful than any other devised hitherto has been formulated by Dr. W. H. Sheldon in two recently published volumes, *The Varieties of Human Physique* and *The Varieties of Temperament*.

[4] Sheldon's classification system is the fruit of nearly fifteen years of research, during which he and his collaborators have made, measured, and arranged in order many thousands of standardized photographs of the male body, taken from in front, from behind, and in profile. A careful study of these photographs revealed that the most basic (first order) classification system in terms of which the continuous variations of human physique could adequately be described was based upon the discrimination of three factors, present to a varying degree in every individual. To these three factors Sheldon has given the names of *endomorphy, mesomorphy,* and *ectomorphy.**

[5] Endomorphy is the factor which, when predominant, . . . often results in soft and comfortable roundness of physique. At school the extreme endomorph is called Slob or Fatty. By middle life he or she may be so enormously heavy as to be practically incapable of walking. The endomorphic physique is dominated by its digestive tract. Autopsies show that the endomorphic gut is often more than twice as long and weighs more than twice as much as the intestine of a person in whom there is an extreme predominance of the ectomorphic constituent.

---

* These names are compounds of the Greek word "morph," meaning "form," and the prefixes *endo* (inner), *meso* (middle), and *ecto* (outer) to identify the relative positions of the layers of the embryo which develop respectively into the stomach, the muscles, and the nervous system.

[7] Adapted from Aldous Huxley, "Who Are You?" *Harper's Magazine,* November, 1944. Copyright © 1944, by Harper's Magazine, Inc. Reprinted by permission of Mrs. Laura A. Huxley.

[6] Predominant mesomorphy expresses itself in a physique that is hard and muscular. The body is built around strong heavy bones and is dominated by its extraordinarily powerful muscles. In youth, the extreme mesomorph tends to look older than his years, and his skin, instead of being soft, smooth, and unwrinkled, like that of the endomorph, is coarse and leathery, tans easily, and sets in deep folds and creases at a comparatively early age. It is from the ranks of extreme mesomorphs that successful boxers, football players, military leaders, and the central figures of the more heroic comic strips are drawn.

[7] The extreme ectomorph is neither comfortably round nor compactly hard. His is a linear physique with slender bones, stringy unemphatic muscles, a short and thin-walled gut. The ectomorph is a lightweight, has little muscular strength, needs to eat at frequent intervals, is often quick and highly sensitive. The ratio of skin surface to body mass is higher than in endomorphs or mesomorphs, and he is thus more vulnerable to outside influences, because more extensively in contact with them. His body is built, not around the endomorph's massively efficient intestine, not around the mesomorph's big bones and muscles, but around a relatively predominant and unprotected nervous system.

[8] Endomorphy, mesomorphy, and ectomorphy occur, as constituting components, in every human individual. In most persons the three components are combined fairly evenly, or at least harmoniously. Extreme and unbalanced predominance of any one factor is relatively uncommon. . . .

[9] In order to calculate the relative amounts of each component in the total individual mixture, Sheldon divides the body into five regions and proceeds to make a number of measurements in each zone. The records of these measurements are then subjected to certain mathematical procedures, which yield a three-digit formula. This formula expresses the amount of endomorphy, mesomorphy, and ectomorphy present within the organism, as measured on a seven-point scale of values. Thus the formula 7–1–1 indicates that the individual under consideration exhibits endomorphy in its highest possible degree, combined with the lowest degree of mesomorphy and ectomorphy. In practice, he would probably be extremely fat, gluttonous and comfort-loving, without drive or energy, almost sexless, and pathetically dependent on other people. How different from the well-balanced 4–4–4, the formidably powerful and aggressive 3–7–1, the thin, nervous "introverted" 1–2–7! . . .

[10] A question which naturally occurs to us is this: how closely is our fundamental psychological pattern related to our physical pattern? . . . What follows is a summing-up — necessarily rather crude and oversimplified — of the conclusions to which Sheldon's research has led.

[11] Endomorphy, mesomorphy, and ectomorphy are correlated very closely with specific patterns of temperament — endomorphy with the temperamental pattern to which Sheldon gives the name of *viscerotonia,* mesomorphy with *somatotonia,* and ectomorphy with *cerebrotonia.* Close and prolonged observation of many subjects, combined with an adaptation of the technique known as factor-analysis, resulted in the isolation of sixty descriptive or determinative traits — twenty for each of the main, first-order components of temperament. From these sixty, I select a smaller number of the more striking and easily recognizable traits.

[12] Conspicuous among the elements of the viscerotonic pattern of temperament are relaxation in posture and movement, slow reaction, profound sleep, love of physical comfort, and love of food. With this love of food for its own sake goes a great love of eating in company, an almost religious feeling for the social meal as a kind of sacrament. Another conspicuous viscerotonic trait is love of polite ceremony, with which goes a love of company, together with indiscriminate amiability and marked dependence on, and desire for, the affection and approval of other people. The viscerotonic does not inhibit his emotions, but tends to give expression to them as they arise, so that nobody is ever in doubt as to what he feels.

[13] Somatotonia, the temperament associated with the hard and powerful mesomorphic physique, is a patterning of very different elements. The somatotonic individual stands and moves in an assertive way, loves physical adventure, enjoys risk and loves to take a chance. He feels a strong need for physical exercise, which he hugely enjoys and often makes a fetish of, just as the viscerotonic enjoys and makes a fetish of eating. When in trouble, he seeks relief in physical action, whereas the viscerotonic turns in the same circumstances to people and the cerebrotonic retires, like a wounded animal, into solitude. The somatotonic is essentially energetic and quick to action. Procrastination is unknown to him; for he is neither excessively relaxed and comfort-loving, like the viscerotonic, nor inhibited and "sicklied o'er with the pale cast of thought," like the cerebrotonic. The social manner of the somatotonic is uninhibited and direct. The voice is normally unrestrained, and he coughs, laughs, snores and, when passion breaks through his veneer of civilization, speaks loudly. He is physically courageous in combat and enjoys every kind of competitive activity. . . .

[14] With cerebrotonia we pass from the world of Flash Gordon to that of Hamlet. The cerebrotonic is the over-alert, over-sensitive introvert, who is more concerned with the inner universe of his own thoughts and feelings and imagination than with the external world to which, in their different ways, the viscerotonic and the somatotonic pay their primary attention and allegiance. In posture and movements, the cerebrotonic person is tense and restrained. His reactions may be unduly rapid and his physiological responses uncomfortably intense. It is the cerebrotonic who suffers from nervous indigestion, who gets stage fright and feels nauseated with mere shyness, who suffers from the various skin eruptions often associated with emotional disturbances. . . .

[15] How do these temperamental assessments compare with the corresponding physical assessments of endomorphy, mesomorphy, and ectomorphy? The answer is that there is a high positive correlation. In some persons the correlation is complete, and the three-digit formula for temperament is identical with the three-digit formula for physique. More frequently, however, there is a slight deviation, as when a *four* in physical endomorphy is correlated with a *three* or a *five* in temperamental viscerotonia. Where there is a deviation, it is seldom of more than one point in any of the three components. Occasionally, however, the discrepancy between physique and temperament may be as much as two points; when this happens, the individual is under very considerable strain and has much difficulty in adapting himself to life. Deviations of more than two points do not seem to occur in the normal population, but are not uncommon among the insane.

The rules governing classification may be stated briefly:

1. Since classification requires division of the subject into categories, the division must be made on some clear and consistent basis. Thus classification by body types must use physical characteristics as the criteria; physical and personality types must not be confused in the same category.

2. If any class is divided into subclasses, there must be at least two subclasses, since it would be illogical to divide something into one part.

3. All classes on the same level of classification must be selected on the same basis. This requirement is a corollary of rule 1 above. Thus all subclasses under body types must represent divisions of the major body types: it would be illogical to divide body types into ectomorphs, mesomorphs, and viscerotonics, since the last is a personality type.

4. The system should take care of all items to be classified. Any system for classifying body types should classify all body types; any system for classifying personality types should include all personality types. If there are individuals who do not fit into the body or personality classes, the system is at fault.

Process

A process is a sequence of operations or actions by which something is done or made. The development of the human embryo from conception to birth is one process; the sequence of movements in driving a golf ball is another; the procedure by which the citizens of the United States elect a President is a third.

To describe a process, three steps are necessary. First, the writer must know the process in all its details and should preview it before describing it. Second, he must be able to divide the total process into its sequence or stages. Third, he must explain each stage in sufficient detail so that a reader can "see" the process in operation, or can perform it himself.

Following are the most common types of process essays:

1. The "how-to-do-it" essay, which gives directions for doing something, in the manner of a recipe.

2. The "how-it-works" essay, which shows an operation (often mechanical) in its successive stages. This type usually follows a time order and thus resembles narration. It may even be presented as a narrative by showing someone going through the process.

3. The "how-it-is-organized" essay, which shows how a complex organization (business, university, political party) functions by breaking it into departments and showing what each does. In this type the order is functional or spatial rather than chronological.

4. The "how-did-it-happen" essay, or causal process, which seeks a cause for a known effect. Such an essay usually shows *why* the event occurred by showing *how* it occurred. This type will be discussed under *Causal Analysis,* page 74.

The following essay is an example of type 2:

THE SPIDER AND THE WASP[8]

[0] In the adult stage the [Pepsis] wasp lives only a few months. The female produces but a few eggs, one at a time at intervals of two or three days. For each egg the mother must provide one adult tarantula, alive but paralyzed. The tarantula must be of the correct species to nourish the larva. The mother wasp attaches the egg to the paralyzed spider's abdomen. Upon hatching from the egg, the larva is many hundreds of times smaller than its living but helpless victim. It eats no other food and drinks no water. By the time it has finished its single gargantuan meal and become ready for wasphood, nothing remains of the tarantula but its indigestible chitinous skeleton.

[1] The mother wasp goes tarantula-hunting when the egg in her ovary is almost ready to be laid. Flying low over the ground late on a sunny afternoon, the wasp looks for its victim or for the mouth of a tarantula burrow, a round hole edged by a bit of silk. The sex of the spider makes no difference, but the mother is highly discriminating as to species. Each species of Pepsis [wasp] requires a certain species of tarantula, and the wasp will not attack the wrong species. In a cage with a tarantula which is not its normal prey the wasp avoids the spider, and is usually killed by it in the night.

[2] Yet when a wasp finds the correct species, it is the other way about. To identify the species the wasp apparently must explore the spider with her antennae. The tarantula shows an amazing tolerance to this exploration. The wasp crawls under it and walks over it without evoking any hostile response. The molestation is so great and so persistent that the tarantula often rises on all eight legs, as if it were on stilts. It may stand this way for several minutes.

[3] Meanwhile the wasp, having satisfied itself that the victim is of the right species, moves off a few inches to dig the spider's grave. Working vigorously with legs and jaws, it excavates a hole 8 to 10 inches deep with a diameter slightly larger than the spider's girth. Now and again the wasp pops out of the hole to make sure that the spider is still there.

[4] When the grave is finished the wasp returns to the tarantula to complete her ghastly enterprise. First she feels it all over once more with her antennae. Then her behavior becomes more aggressive. She bends her abdomen, protruding her sting, and searches for the soft membrane at the point where the spider's leg joins its body — the only spot where she can penetrate the horny skeleton. From time to time, as the exasperated spider slowly shifts ground, the wasp turns on her back and slides along with the aid of her wings, trying to get under the tarantula for a shot at the vital spot. During all this maneuvering, which can last for several minutes, the tarantula makes no move to save itself.

[8] From Alexander Petrunkevitch, "The Spider and the Wasp," *Scientific American,* August, 1952. Copyright © 1952 by Scientific American, Inc. All rights reserved.

[5] Finally the wasp corners it against some obstruction and grasps one of its legs in her powerful jaws. Now at last the harassed spider tries a desperate but vain defense. The two contestants roll over and over on the ground. It is a terrifying sight and the outcome is always the same. The wasp finally manages to thrust her sting into the soft spot and holds it there for a few seconds while she pumps in the poison. Almost immediately the tarantula falls paralyzed on its back. Its legs stop twitching; its heart stops beating. Yet it is not dead, as is shown by the fact that if taken from the wasp it can be restored to some sensitivity by being kept in a moist chamber for several months.

[6] After paralyzing the tarantula, the wasp cleans herself by dragging her body along the ground and rubbing her feet, sucks the drop of blood oozing from the wound in the spider's abdomen, then grabs a leg of the flabby, helpless animal in her jaws and drags it down to the bottom of the grave. She stays there for many minutes, sometimes for several hours, and what she does all that time in the dark we do not know. Eventually she lays her egg and attaches it to the side of the spider's abdomen with a sticky secretion. Then she emerges, fills the grave with soil carried bit by bit in her jaws, and finally tramples the ground all around to hide any trace of the grave from prowlers. Then she flies away, leaving her descendant safely started in life.

The selection begins with an introductory summary of the process, then each paragraph takes up a separate stage, so that, beginning with the first stage in the paragraph numbered 1, the six stages are described in six paragraphs, as follows:

Stage 1. The wasp flies over an area looking for the right kind of tarantula.

Stage 2. When she discovers one, she lands and examines it to be sure that it is the right kind.

Stage 3. When satisfied, she digs the hole in which she intends to bury the spider.

Stage 4. She re-examines the spider — this time more aggressively — looking for a vulnerable spot.

Stage 5. She attacks the spider and, after a struggle, succeeds in paralyzing it.

Stage 6. She drags the paralyzed spider into the hole, affixes her egg on its abdomen, fills the grave, and leaves.

This analysis by stages is a paragraph summary. The structure of the summary shows the structure of the essay, which could also be shown by short headings, if each heading described one of the stages:

  I. Looking for a victim

  II. Checking to be sure

  III. Digging the grave

  IV. Circling for an attack

  V. Paralyzing the spider

  VI. Burying the spider and the egg

Causal Analysis

A process broken into parts to establish a causal relation among the parts may be called a *causal process* or a *causal analysis*. Such a process may move from cause to effect or effect to cause. When the former, it begins with a known cause and shows the stages by which that cause will produce effects. For example, a doctor may predict the course of a disease once he has established that the disease (cause) is present.

When the process goes from effect to cause, it starts with the effect and seeks the cause, as when a doctor tries to identify the cause of a patient's symptoms. The process may include a chain of reasoning in which finding a cause leads to a prediction of other effects: if the lights have gone out (effect$_1$) because the power is off (cause), then the refrigerator won't work (effect$_2$) and the perishable food in the refrigerator will spoil (effect$_3$).

A common writing problem is to discover the causes of given effects. Such a problem is diagnostic: what's wrong with the car? why isn't she speaking to me? why didn't Hitler attempt to invade England? Sometimes a definitive answer can be given to such a question, but often we have to settle for an answer which cannot be proved beyond doubt.

The following selection, the conclusion to the essay about the spider and the wasp, illustrates the kind of causal analysis which seeks the most convincing answer. In the part you have already read, the author showed how the mother wasp provided for her offspring. As a result, we know how the operation was carried out. But we are still left with the puzzling question: why does the tarantula, which could kill the wasp, allow itself to be treated so? The following part shows the author's attempt to find a cause for the spider's strange conduct.

[1] In all this the behavior of the wasp is qualitatively different from that of the spider. The wasp acts like an intelligent animal. This is not to say that instinct plays no part or that she reasons as man does. But her actions are to the point; they are not automatic and can be modified to fit the situation. We do not know for certain how she identifies the tarantula — probably it is by some olfactory or chemo-tactile sense — but she does it purposefully and does not blindly tackle a wrong species.

[2] On the other hand, the tarantula's behavior shows only confusion. Evidently the wasp's pawing gives it no pleasure, for it tries to move away. . . . That the spider is not anesthetized by some odorless secretion is easily shown by blowing lightly at the tarantula and making it jump suddenly. What, then, makes the tarantula behave as stupidly as it does?

[3] No clear, simple answer is available. Possibly the stimulation by the wasp's antennae is masked by the heavier pressure on the spider's body. . . . But the explanation may be much more complex. Initiative in attack is not in the nature of tarantulas; most species fight only when cornered so that escape is impossible. Their inherited patterns of behavior apparently prompt them to avoid problems rather than attack them.

[4] For example, spiders always weave their webs in three dimensions, and when a spider finds that there is insufficient space to attach certain threads

74

in the third dimension, it leaves the place and seeks another, instead of finishing the web in a single plane. This urge to escape seems to arise under all circumstances, in all phases of life, and to take the place of reasoning. For a spider to change the pattern of its web is as impossible as for an inexperienced man to build a bridge across a chasm obstructing his way.

[5] In a way the instinctive urge to escape is not only easier but often more efficient than reasoning. The tarantula does exactly what is most efficient in all cases except in an encounter with a ruthless and determined attacker dependent for the existence of her own species on killing as many tarantulas as she can lay eggs. Perhaps in this case the spider follows its usual pattern of trying to escape, instead of seizing and killing the wasp, because it is not aware of its danger. In any case, the survival of the tarantula species as a whole is protected by the fact that the spider is much more fertile than the wasp.[9]

Here the author begins by stressing the intelligent conduct of the wasp in order to emphasize the apparent stupidity of the tarantula. He thus shows the need to discover why the spider acts as it does. Second, he shows two possible causes disproved by the facts. Third, he suggests a hypothesis — that the spider's actions reflect an instinctive behavior pattern. Fourth, he supports that hypothesis with supplementary evidence from the way spiders build their webs. Finally, he shows that the suggested cause is sufficient to explain the spider's behavior. The stages in his causal process can be summarized thus:

I. Introduction to provide contrast and thus pose the problem (¶1)
II. Refutation of possible but false causes (¶2)
III. Hypothesis suggesting the real cause (¶3)
IV. Support of hypothesis from web-building evidence (¶4)
V. Further support for hypothesis by showing that it offers a sufficient cause to explain the spider's actions (¶5)

This structure may be simplified still further:

I. Introduction to pose the question
II. Refutation of unsatisfactory answers
III. Discovery and support of a satisfactory cause

▶ *Analyze the structure of the following selection by first making a paragraph summary, then converting the summary to a simple outline, as was done with the causal process essay about the spider and the wasp. Then explain how the three paragraphs of the selection are related.*

What we know of prenatal development makes all this [attempts made by a mother to mold the character of her unborn child by studying poetry, art, or mathematics during pregnancy] seem utterly impossible. How could such extremely complex influences pass from the mother to the child? There is no connection between their nervous systems. Even the blood vessels of

[9] From Alexander Petrunkevitch, "The Spider and the Wasp," *Scientific American*, August, 1952. Copyright © 1952 by Scientific American, Inc. All rights reserved.

mother and child do not join directly. They lie side by side and the chemicals are interchanged through the walls by a process that we call osmosis. An emotional shock to the mother will affect her child, because it changes the activity of her glands and so the chemistry of her blood. Any chemical change in the mother's blood will affect the child — for better or worse. But we cannot see how a liking for mathematics or poetic genius can be dissolved in the blood and produce a similar liking or genius in the child.

In our discussion of instincts we saw that there was reason to believe that whatever we inherit must be of some very simple sort rather than any complicated or very definite kind of behavior. It is certain that no one inherits a knowledge of mathematics. It may be, however, that children inherit more or less of a rather general ability that we may call intelligence. If very intelligent children become deeply interested in mathematics, they will probably make a success of that study.

As for musical ability, it may be that what is inherited is an especially sensitive ear, a peculiar structure of the hands or of the vocal organs, connections between nerves and muscles that make it comparatively easy to learn the movements a musician must execute, and particularly vigorous emotions. If these factors are all organized around music, the child may become a musician. The same factors, in other circumstances, might be organized about some other center of interest. The rich emotional equipment might find expression in poetry. The capable fingers might develop skill in surgery. It is not the knowledge of music that is inherited, then, nor even the love of it, but a certain bodily structure that makes it comparatively easy to acquire musical knowledge and skill. Whether that ability shall be directed toward music or some other undertaking may be decided entirely by forces in the environment in which a child grows up.[10]

THE ARGUMENTATIVE PATTERN

Argument is often thought of as a means of persuading others to accept our opinions, but it is first of all a method by which we ourselves arrive at these opinions. We examine evidence and reach a conclusion from it, and the relation between the evidence and the conclusion is an *argument*. Argument, then, may be viewed as a form of thinking, and it is chiefly thus that it will be considered here. In its simplest form, an argument consists of two statements, one of which is a conclusion from the other.

> *Football is a dangerous sport.* Many injuries and deaths have resulted from football games in recent years.

These statements constitute an argument in which the *conclusion* (the italicized statement) is drawn from the other statement, called a *premise*. An argument always relates at least one premise and one conclusion.

The difference between statements that are so related and those that are not is illustrated by the following contrasts. Each pair at the left includes an italicized conclusion and a premise; it is an argument. For the pair at the right, no such premise-conclusion relationship exists.

[10] From William H. Roberts, *Psychology You Can Use* (New York: Harcourt, Brace & World, Inc., 1943).

P–C Relationship	*No P–C Relationship*
Final examinations cause unnecessary hardships for both students and instructors. *Final examinations should be abolished.*	Final examinations cause unnecessary hardships for both students and instructors. Final examinations encourage cramming.
John Jones is the most experienced candidate for the Senate. He has served in the House of Representatives and in his state legislature.	John Jones is the most experienced candidate for the Senate. He has five children.
The voting age should be lowered to eighteen. Eighteen-year-olds are asked to assume military responsibility and are therefore eligible to undertake political responsibility.	The voting age should be lowered to eighteen. Twenty-one as the age for voting is an arbitrary choice.

The arguments at the left are not necessarily convincing. Some readers may deny the premises; others may want additional premises ("evidence") before accepting the conclusion. But, whether generally acceptable or not, the paired statements at the left are related as those at the right are not. We may make that relationship more obvious by inserting "because" before the premise and "therefore" before the conclusion. No statement at the right can be inferred as a conclusion from the statement paired with it. Because twenty-one is an arbitrary choice for voting age, for example, we cannot conclude that the voting age should be lowered to any particular age — or, indeed, that it should not be raised.

So far we have been considering arguments of the simplest structure — a single premise and a single conclusion. Most arguments are more complex. They may consist of several premises from which a single conclusion is inferred — for example: Final examinations should be abolished because (1) they are detrimental to student health, (2) they place undue emphasis on memorizing facts, (3) they encourage last-minute cramming instead of daily preparation, (4) they penalize the nervous student. Or a conclusion from one or more premises may become a premise for another conclusion, as one unit of argument is built on another in the following:

1. If the thirteen-month calendar were adopted, all dates in existing books would have to be changed. (Premise for 3)
2. All contracts and leases would have to be redated. (Premise for 3)
3. The adoption would require large-scale conversions to the new system. (Conclusion from 1 and 2)
4. Monthly statements and payrolls would have to be prepared thirteen times a year instead of twelve times. (Premise for 5)
5. The adoption would be expensive. (Conclusion from 4)
6. The adoption of the thirteen-month calendar would require extensive and expensive changes. (Conclusions from 3 and 5)

This is how the argument would emerge in the writer's mind, but when he came to outline it, he would put the conclusions above their premises.

Below, the premise-conclusion relations are indicated by the *P–C* symbols at the left. These would not normally appear in a formal outline, but are given here to show the structure of the argument. For a while, at least, writing them out is a useful exercise in testing one's logic.

C   *Thesis:* The adoption of the thirteen-month calendar would require extensive and expensive changes. (*Conclusion from all statements*)

P–C   I. It would require large-scale conversions to the new system. (*Premise for thesis, and conclusion from A and B below, therefore marked both P and C at left*)

P   A. All dates in existing books would have to be changed. (*Premise for I*)

P   B. All contracts and leases would have to be redated. (*Premise for I*)

P–C   II. It would be expensive. (*Premise for thesis, and conclusion from A and B below, therefore marked both P and C*)

P   A. The cost of redating documents would be expensive. (*Premise for II*)

P–C   B. The cost of operating a business would increase. (*Premise for II, and conclusion from 1 below, therefore both P and C*)

P   1. Monthly statements and payrolls would have to be prepared thirteen times a year instead of twelve times. (*Premise for B above*)

The structure of an argument is a logical arrangement of premises and conclusions which attempts to "prove" a thesis (usually called the *proposition* in argument). The *P–C* symbols at the left distinguish between *C* (conclusion only), *P* (premise only), and *P–C* (both premise and conclusion). Notice that all statements are premises for the thesis, but some are also conclusions from other statements, and are thus both premise and conclusion. The thesis is the only statement which does not serve as a premise, and therefore the only one that can be marked *C,* conclusion only.

In argument, it is wise to establish the logical *P–C* structure in the prewriting stage, though this structure may not be strictly followed in the writing. One may begin with an example of one disadvantage of the thirteen-month calendar — say, an imaginary case of an office staff having to make out a payroll thirteen times a year instead of twelve. Once the reader's attention is caught by that example, the writer can return to the structure shown above.

Single subdivisions are not logical in classification, but they may be used in an argument, for sometimes a writer will base his conclusion on a single premise. A writer or speaker may show that an opponent has misquoted Secretary Rusk. The only way to do that is to provide the statement that Secretary Rusk actually made. Nothing else is necessary. The argument consists of a conclusion — The Secretary has been misquoted — and a single premise — the correct quotation. There is, therefore, no theoretical objection to a single premise. Of course, if a single premise is not enough to be persuasive, more should be given. Thus the single premise for II B in the outline is not an error, but additional premises would provide additional support for the conclusion.

► *The essay that follows is an argument written to show that Joyce Kilmer's popular "Trees" (here reprinted) is a bad poem. The main premise-conclusion structure has been worked out following the essay, but that structure is not complete. Read the poem and the essay carefully, then complete the structure by providing additional premises from the texts. As you do so, decide for yourself whether the argument of the essay is persuasive.*

TREES[11]

I think that I shall never see
A poem as lovely as a tree.

A tree whose hungry mouth is pressed
Against the earth's sweet flowing breast;

A tree that looks at God all day,
And lifts her leafy arms to pray;

A tree that may in summer wear
A nest of robins in her hair;

Upon whose bosom snow has lain;
Who intimately lives with rain.

Poems are made by fools like me,
But only God can make a tree.

WHY "TREES" IS A BAD POEM[12]

This poem has been greatly admired by a large number of people. The fact that it has been popular does not necessarily condemn it as a bad poem. But it is a bad poem.

First, let us look at it merely on the technical side, especially in regard to the use Kilmer makes of his imagery. Now the poet, in a poem of twelve

---

[11] The poem *Trees* by Joyce Kilmer; copyright 1913 and renewed 1941; copyright assigned to Jerry Vogel Music Co., Inc., 112 West 44th St., New York 36, N.Y. Used by permission of copyright owner.

[12] From *Understanding Poetry*, Revised Edition, by Cleanth Brooks and Robert Penn Warren. Copyright 1938, 1950, © 1960 by Holt, Rinehart and Winston, Inc. All rights reserved.

lines, only makes one fundamental comparison on which the other comparisons are based. . . . The comparison is that of a tree to a human being. If the tree is compared to a human being, the reader has a right to expect a consistent use to be made of the aspects of the human being which appear in the poem. But look at stanza two:

> A tree whose hungry mouth is pressed
> Against the earth's sweet flowing breast;

Here the tree is *metaphorically* treated as a sucking babe and the earth, therefore, as the mother — a perfectly good comparison that has been made for centuries — the earth as the "great mother," the "giver of life," etc.

But the third stanza introduces a confusion:

> A tree that looks at God all day,
> And lifts her leafy arms to pray;

Here the tree is no longer a sucking babe, but, without warning, is old enough to indulge in religious devotions. But that is not the worst part of the confusion. Remember that the tree is a human being and that in the first stanza the *mouth* of that human being was the *root* of the tree. But now, if the branches are "leafy arms" the tree is a strangely deformed human being.

The fourth and fifth stanzas maintain the same anatomical arrangement for the tree as does the third, but they make other unexpected changes: the tree that wears "a nest of robins in her hair" must be a grown-up person, a girl with jewels in her hair; the tree with snow on its bosom is a chaste and pure girl, for so the *associations* of snow with purity and chastity tell the reader; and the tree that "lives with rain" is a chaste and pure young woman who, although vain enough to wear jewels, is yet withdrawn from the complications of human relationships and lives alone with "nature," i.e., rain, or might be said to be nun-like, an implication made by the religious tone of the poem.

Now it would be quite legitimate for the poet to use any one of the thoughts he wishes to convey about the tree (1. the tree as a babe nursed by mother earth, 2. the tree as a devout person praying all day, 3. the tree as a girl with jewels in her hair, or 4. the tree as a chaste woman alone with nature and God) and to create a metaphor for it, but the trouble is that he tries to convey all of these features by a single basic comparison to a person, and therefore presents a picture thoroughly confused. The poet confuses his reader if the reader tries actually to *see* the images the poet uses or tries to think about their *implications;* and that is exactly what a good poet wants his readers to do, to *visualize* or *feel* or *hear* his images (for there are images of sight, touch, sound, etc.) and then to understand what those images imply, for that is one of the chief ways a poet *communicates* his meaning, a way more important in the long run to most poets than that of the actual flat prose statement of the idea.

It is possible to try to defend the poem by appealing to the title, "Trees," pointing out that no over-all consistency is called for: one tree is like the babe nursing at its mother's breast; another tree is a girl lifting her arms to pray, etc. But this defence is more damaging than the charge it seeks to meet; for the poem presents no real basis for seeing one tree as a babe and another as a devout young woman. Furthermore, such a defence calls attention to the general shallowness and superficiality of the imagery: the various comparisons reveal themselves as so many fanciful analogies, grounded in nothing deeper than a vague approval of the general loveliness of trees. (The student can easily determine how loosely decorative the images are by shifting some of the couplets about: the poem is so formless that its "structure" is not in the least disturbed thereby. . . .)

But in "Trees" there are other difficulties on the technical side. The rhythm is not well chosen. It is monotonous. Each stanza has the same rhythm, with a full pause at the end of a couplet and no pauses within the lines. The effect is sharp and pert, with no impression of thoughtfulness or of competent control on the part of the poet. This is especially inappropriate for a poem which pretends to treat a serious subject. . . . The rhythm does not contribute to a serious approach, nor does the treatment of imagery. But let us try to consider his *meaning* or *thought* as such.

The poet is expressing a highly romantic mood in which he pretends that the works of man's mind are not comparable in "loveliness" to the works of nature. What he wants to say is that he is tired of the works of man and takes refuge in the works of nature, which is quite different from comparing the two things on the basis of "loveliness." . . . But the two kinds of loveliness, that of art and that of nature, are not comparable; and in the second place, "loveliness" is not the word to apply to *Hamlet* by Shakespeare, "Lycidas" by Milton, *The Canterbury Tales* by Chaucer, etc. And the tree, as opposed to the poem, is lacking in *meaning* and *expressiveness;* it has those things only in so far as a man can give them to it. Kilmer writes:

> Poems are made by fools like me,
> But only God can make a tree.

That is perfectly true, but by the same line of reasoning God makes the poem too, through his agency in man. Or reversing the argument: Bad poems are made by bad poets like Kilmer and good poems are made by good poets like Yeats, Shakespeare, Landor, Milton, etc. Furthermore the paradox created by Kilmer breaks down, because it isn't justified in terms given in the poem; it will not stand inspection. . . .

But why has the poem been popular, if so bad? It appeals . . . to a stock response which has nothing to do, as such, with poetry. It praises God and appeals to a religious sentiment. Therefore people who do not stop to look at the poem itself or to study the images in the poem and think about what the poem really says, are inclined to accept the poem because of the pious sentiment, the prettified little pictures (which in themselves appeal to stock responses), and the mechanical rhythm.

*   *   *

C   *Thesis:* Joyce Kilmer's "Trees" is a bad poem.
P–C   I. It is technically bad.
P–C   A. The imagery is confused and superficial. (Provide the premises for this conclusion.)
P–C   B. The rhythm is monotonous. (Provide the premises.)
P–C   II. The poem lacks significant meaning. (Provide the premises.)

Notice that the explanation of why the poem is popular is not included. Technically it is not part of the argument, since it does not develop the thesis. It is a necessary part of the essay, because readers will want to know why a bad poem can remain popular; but that material does not prove that the poem is bad.

SUMMARY

1. The three major patterns discussed in this chapter are *illustration, analysis,* and *argument.*

2. The illustrative pattern clarifies a thesis by specific cases. It may give examples. The basic structure is $T + E_n + R$, where T stands for *thesis,* E for *example, n* for any number or series of numbers, and R for *restatement.* But variations are common: the restatement may be omitted; there may be frequent restatements; there may be explanatory material between thesis and example; and the number of examples will depend on the writer's needs. This pattern is also common for single paragraphs and even single sentences.

3. A second major form of the illustrative pattern is *comparison* or *contrast.* Here the thesis identifies the two subjects (A and B) as alike or unlike. Organization may be $A + B$, or $A/B + A/B$, etc. In the first, A is completed before B. In the second, A and B alternate, one trait or detail at a time, so that each pair helps build the comparison or contrast. The second form is harder to write, easier to read.

4. The analytical pattern proceeds by partition or division. The subject is broken into parts, and each part is discussed in turn. The chief kinds of analysis are *classification, process,* and *causal analysis.*

5. In *classification,* items are grouped into categories, which may be divided and if necessary subdivided through several levels, each a division of the one above it. At every level, the basis of classification must be clear and consistent. Main classes and subclasses cannot be placed on the same level. Usually the whole system of classification is thought out before writing, and the writing describes the categories previously established.

6. A *process* is a sequence of acts or operations which explain how to do something, how something works, how it is made or organized. The total sequence is broken into stages, each explained in turn. Many though not all processes follow a time order, and often the essay proceeds like a narrative.

7. *Causal analysis* breaks a sequence into *cause* and *effect,* and identifies whichever of these is the subject of inquiry. The procedure is investigative, and often the writer can establish only a possible cause. Causal analysis may be considered a kind of process, in which the writer is explaining *why,* not *how.*

8. In *argument,* the basic structure is a relation in which one statement is a *conclusion* drawn from another, called a *premise.* By using a con-

clusion as the premise in a new argument, a structure can be made more and more complex. The final conclusion (*C*) is the thesis; the main premises by which it is proved can be marked by Roman numerals; the premises for these statements can be marked by capital letters; the premises for these, in turn, by Arabic numerals; and so on as far as necessary.

9. All the informal patterns discussed in this chapter have an underlying similarity of structure, in that they all develop the implications of a thesis or general statement by providing support for it. The ultimate support is the illustrative, descriptive, or argumentative details which make the thesis clear or acceptable.

Exercises

A. The following selection establishes a contrast between Italians of the North (*A*) and those of the South (*B*). The predominant pattern is *A* + *B*, though *A/B* + *A/B* also appears. Using the essay about tragedy on pages 64–66 as a model, determine the organizational pattern of this selection, first by making notes for the structure of each paragraph, and second, by preparing a paragraph summary of the structure similar to that on page 66.

The application of some of the principles already outlined can, for instance, clarify the ancient and . . . profound difference between the Two Italies, the North and the South. There is no doubt that all Italians, observed from a distance, have a family resemblance. They all come more or less from the same stock, have predominantly dark hair, dark eyes and vivacious expressions. They have been shaped by similar historical vicissitudes and have developed or sharpened the same talents in order to survive. They all love life and enjoy a good show. They are all similarly wary of the law; they all pursue their type of happiness *alla* Guicciardini, the advancement of their private welfare, or *il particulare,* at the expense of society; they must defend themselves, their family and *consorteria* against the treachery, envy, hatred of men; they use the family as an ark to outlast natural calamities, historical convulsions, and political upheavals. Unlike the inhabitants of better organized nations, they have to rely on their private virtues and public vices, their adaptability, charm, intelligence, shrewdness, the use of their personal power.

All this is the same in the North as in the South. But there is a difference. The difference is important: it is one of the causes of the slower development of the southern economy, in the past century, and of the more rapid growth of the northern economy. It has so far defeated all attempts to bring the two standards of living more or less onto one level. It will always misdirect the spending of at least a part of the vast sums of money the government invests in the South. There is even a danger that the mutual mistrust and misunderstanding which separate the Two Italies may be strengthened and that national unity, which was always fragile at best, may become more unstable than in the past.

The private aims of southerners and northerners are, of course, more or less the same. The northerner, however, thinks that there is one practically sure way to achieve them: the acquisition of wealth, *la ricchezza*. Only wealth can, he believes, lastingly assure the defence and prosperity of the family. The southerner, on the other hand, knows that this can be done only with the acquisition of power, prestige, authority, fame. The northerner of whatever class, therefore, is perpetually trying to acquire wealth in its various forms. He wants a job, a good job, a better job; he wants land, capital, credit, industrial shares, houses, technical and scientific knowledge and expensive and rare university degrees, which assure him better-paid employment and advancement; he brings up his children with these aims in mind, educating them to become well-paid technicians, engineers, specialists. He undergoes any sacrifice in order to gain material advantages for himself and his family. He wants a rich wife, rich daughters- and sons-in-law, rich friends. He is similar to the French bourgeois, almost a pure *homo economicus*.

The southerner, on the other hand, wants above all to be obeyed, admired, respected, feared and envied. He wants wealth too, of course, but as an instrument to influence people, and, for that, the appearance of wealth is as useful as wealth itself. In the South, the little peasant, the illiterate day labourer, the olive-tree pruner, the sulphur miner, as well as the landed proprietor, the noble member of exclusive clubs, the *nouveau riche* owner of recently founded industries, all will cultivate the gratitude of powerful friends and relatives, the fear of their enemies, the respect of everybody, and the reputation of their families.

In Naples and in Milan there are, for example, wholesale fruit and vegetable merchants. They belong more or less to the same class of people. They have roughly the same education. They pay dues to a local association of *grossisti*, which belongs to a national confederation. They may meet at national congresses and even at European Market congresses. They probably know each other and nod when they meet. They consider themselves colleagues in a vague way. Here all similarities cease.

The Neapolitan usually tours the countryside with his henchmen, bullying and protecting peasants in his well-defined sector, and forcing them to sell their products only to him at the prices he fixes. He defends his territory and his vassal farmers from the encroachment of competitors. He carries a gun. He shoots straight. He can kill a man if necessary. He can command killers. As everybody knows that he can enforce his will and defend his power by killing his opponents, he never, or almost never, has the need to shoot. If the farmers were to refuse to sell at his price, he can leave their produce to rot in the field. The farmers never refuse because nobody else would dare buy their products in competition with him. A superficial observer, of course, would not know what exactly was going on, what were his real relations with the farmers and retailers, and would notice none of the invisible threats and fears. Farmers, dealers, henchmen, retailers, competitors, all smile, joke, exchange pleasantries, drink wine, shake hands. They appear to be the best of friends. Only rarely something goes wrong, and the police find an unexplained corpse in a country lane. The culprits are seldom identified. Nobody usually gets killed, however, in Naples, if he is careful and plays the game.

The Milanese is an entirely different kind of man. He resembles his foreign colleagues more than his Neapolitan or Sicilian competitors. He carries no gun, is followed by no henchmen, rarely sees the farmers he buys from, almost never tours the countryside. He sits in a modern office, surrounded by dictating machines, graphs on the wall, brisk secretaries. His business is carried on by telephone, with brokers and buyers in Germany, France or Switzerland, by the carload or the trainload, peaches from Verona, apricots from Naples, oranges from Sicily, grapes from Apulia, spring potatoes or cabbages from Tuscany. His only aim is to ship more and more refrigerated railway trucks abroad, filled with more and more of the fresh produce foreigners consume, at the highest possible prices. He naturally makes a lot of money, in good years one hundred or one thousand times more than his Neapolitan colleagues. But the Neapolitan does not mind. He is not unhappy about it. He wants other things than money, rarer and more satisfactory things. He wants to be well known (his sinister nickname must be recognized in the whole province); to be feared (policemen, at times, must forget they saw him go by); to be powerful (politicians must beg for his help at election time). He also wants to be loved (he will redress wrongs and protect unimportant people asking for his aid).

This, of course, is a didactic simplification, an example chosen to prove a point. Nothing is quite so simple in real life. There is no definite moral frontier between the two sections. Not all the South is purely southern, nor is all the North only northern. One finds men in northern Italy who apparently want to increase their power, authority, prestige and rank above anything else. Likewise, it is easy to find hundreds of people, in the South, who seemingly forgo all preoccupations of prestige in order to amass a lot of money. When observed closely, however, these exceptions usually confirm rather than confute the general rule. Frequently, in fact, the northerner who seems to pursue power does so only because power will generate more money, and the southerner who apparently seeks to increase his fortune really wants the added prestige which wealth brings him. There are, for instance, well-known politicians from the North, in Rome, who use their eminent position in the government in order to enrich their families; and southerners who amass possessions in order to become deputies, under-secretaries and cabinet ministers. Generally speaking, southerners tend to make money in order to rule, northerners to rule in order to make money.[13]

B. Select one of the following subjects. Do not write an essay on it, but prewrite by identifying the classes you would establish and by describing in note form the characteristics of each class. For the subject you choose, make whatever number of classes you think desirable.

1. The grading systems in high school and college are attempts to classify students according to their academic performance. There is considerable dissatisfaction with these systems. Devise a new system and be prepared to explain it in sufficient detail to make it clear.

2. Devise a system for classifying TV programs according to their content and the audience for which they would be suitable. Do not base the

[13] From Luigi Barzini, *The Italians* (New York: Atheneum Publishers, 1964).

system entirely on your own preferences, but try to get a system which considers various types of viewers.

3. In a functioning democracy people have a right to protest actions which they think are detrimental to the best interests of society. Classify the kinds of protests which you think are justifiable and those which you think are not.

4. If you don't like any of these choices, pose your own problem of classification, but make it a serious one.

C. Provide a causal answer to any one of the following questions. Begin by listing a number of possible causes, then select what seems to you to be the main cause and explain it in note form.

1. Why do students drop out of high school?
2. Why do adolescents rebel against parental control?
3. Why is it more difficult today than ever before for a high school senior to get into the college of his choice?
4. A causal explanation of your own choice.

D. Select one of the subjects below. For it write a restricted thesis as the conclusion for an argument. Then, using the outline on page 78 as a model, construct an outline of the argument.

1. The war in Vietnam
2. LSD
3. A modern trend in education
4. A subject of your own choosing

4

The Outline

For many of the essays you write, and nearly all the answers to essay-type examinations, the kind of planning shown in Chapter 3 will meet your needs. For long papers, however, especially for critical and research papers, you may be required to present an extensive outline at the end of the prewriting stage so that you and your instructor can check the plan before you begin to write the paper. It is with such outlines that this chapter is concerned.

TOPIC AND SENTENCE OUTLINES

A *topic outline* is one in which the entries are not complete sentences, but headings consisting of single words or phrases, which identify the topic to be discussed under each heading. You have seen such an outline on page 56, and you constructed one in the exercise on pages 43–45.

In a *sentence outline* each entry is a complete sentence. It not only identifies the topic to be dealt with; it also states what is to be said about the topic. Thus:

Topic entry: Endomorph
Sentence entry: The endomorph is dominated by his digestive tract.

The difference between topic and sentence outlines is as much one of use as one of form. The topic outline is convenient for setting down stages in a process — e.g., tee shots, fairway shots, approach shots, putting strokes. It allows the writer to block out his subject matter. But it does not tell him, or his reader, what is to be done with these parts. The sentence outline is the better form when the content is not a label but an idea. It is more restricting than the topic form, and — as we saw in studying the thesis — this restriction helps the writer by controlling him. The decision about which form to use depends on what the essay is to do. If it is going to develop an idea, the sentence outline will be safer; otherwise, the topic outline will be more convenient.

In fact, most sentence outlines emerge from preliminary topic outlines. The writer's first step is usually to block out the areas of the subject. He sets down the headings: I. Endomorphs; II. Mesomorphs; III. Ectomorphs. Then he asks himself what he wants to say about these topics, and his answers convert the topics into sentences:

    I. The endomorph is dominated by his digestive tract.
    II. The mesomorph is dominated by his muscles.
    III. The ectomorph is dominated by his nervous system.

Each of these sentences can become the topic sentence for a paragraph or a series of paragraphs comprising a larger unit of the composition. The writer then develops each paragraph or section, usually by illustration, and thus shows what it means to be dominated by the digestive tract, the muscular structure, or the nervous system.

SHAPING THE OUTLINE

If a writer begins to outline before he has clearly established the purpose of his essay, he will have to experiment with trial outlines in order to find out how his material should be shaped. He will be like the student trying to see what patterns of semantic change are illustrated by the list of words on pages 43–44. As long as he understands that he is groping for a plan, these trial outlines will help him discover what his essay should do. The danger is that he may settle too soon for an inefficient plan. It is always safer to postpone the formal outlining until the controlling decision about purpose has been firmly made. But if tentative or trial outlines are necessary, the final plan should be carefully checked before the writing is begun.

The following sequence will show an outline emerging through successive stages. It is assumed that the writer has made a serious study of the influence of heredity and environment on the individual and has concluded that neither can be proved to be more important than the other. This conclusion is the *thesis* of his essay; the *purpose* is to support that thesis.

Stage I

Simple topic outline establishes over-all organization by identifying major topic to be discussed

Thesis: It is not possible to prove that either heredity or environment is the more important influence on the individual.

    I. Difficulties of defining "heredity" and "environment"

    II. Difficulties of studying cases of the past

    III. Difficulties in experimental studies

Stage II

Major topics of earlier outline are further subdivided and entries begin to take shape as sentences. These are not always finished sentences, but they begin to convert topics into statements of ideas and thus indicate what is to be said about the topics.

Thesis: It is not possible to prove that either heredity or environment is the more important influence on the individual.

  I. Terms "heredity" and "environment" not definable.
    A. Heredity and environment cannot be separated.
    B. "Environment" too vague a term.
  II. Studies of famous and infamous people are not decisive.
    A. Famous people: Shakespeare, Newton, Lincoln.
    B. Infamous people: the Jukes family.
  III. Heredity and environment cannot be isolated in studies of children.
    A. Newborn babies have already had nine months of prenatal environment.
    B. Twins have different inheritances, and may or may not have significantly different environments.
    C. Identical twins do have the same inheritance, but we cannot be sure they have the same environment.

HEREDITY VS. ENVIRONMENT

Stage III

This final stage includes the following revisions:
1. The subdivision of previous entries is completed.
2. All entries are expressed as finished sentences and these are revised, if necessary, so that all sentences are as parallel in form as they can be made.
3. As a result of these revisions, each entry becomes a potential topic sentence for one or more paragraphs of the essay, and the outline also serves as a paragraph summary of the whole.

Thesis: It is not possible to prove that either heredity or environment is the more important influence on the individual.

  I. In practice we are not able to define "heredity" or "environment" with precision.
    A. We are not able to define "heredity" except in terms of characteristics which may have been influenced by environment.
      1. Some inherited characteristics of fruit flies appear only when the environment encourages their appearance.
      2. An acorn will never grow into anything but an oak tree, but whether it becomes an oak tree or not depends on soil, moisture, temperature, and other environmental conditions.
    B. We are not able to define "environment" with precision.
      1. The environment of individuals in a society is so complex that we cannot define it rigorously.
      2. Except in very limited laboratory experiments, the word "environment" is so vague that it is useless for disciplined discourse.
  II. We cannot reach any trustworthy conclusions about the relative influences of heredity and environment

by studying the histories of famous or infamous people.

A. A study of Shakespeare, Newton, and Lincoln provides us no answer.
   1. If their greatness was due to inheritance, why were other members of their families not distinguished?
   2. If their greatness was due to environment, why did others in the same environment not achieve greatness?
B. A study of the notorious Jukes family provides no conclusive answer.
   1. We know that the Jukes family had a bad inheritance and a record of delinquency, but we cannot be sure that the inheritance caused the delinquency.
   2. The Jukes family members had each other as part of their environment, and it is probable that any child brought up in that environment would have become a delinquent.

III. We cannot experimentally study heredity or environment apart from each other.
   A. We cannot do it by studying newborn babies.
      1. They have had nine months of prenatal environment before they were born.
      2. They may or may not later display characteristics which are assumed to be inherited.
   B. We cannot do it by studying ordinary twins.
      1. Such twins come from different eggs and have different inheritances.
      2. Such twins may have quite different environments; for example, a boy twin has a different environment than a girl twin, even when brought up in the same family.
   C. We cannot even do it by studying identical twins because, although they have the same inheritance, we cannot be sure about their environment.

Often an outline will go through more than three stages; an extensive outline will usually require at least that many. It is wise to lay out the main divisions of the outline before worrying about subdivisions. Establish all Roman-numeral headings first; then break each Roman-numeral heading into capital-letter entries, and so on, following the principle of completing one level of division before starting the next lower level. This way you remain in control of your outline: you will not be likely to distort the organization by developing some headings too much and others too little. Since any change in the content of the main headings (though not necessarily in the style) will probably require changes in the subheadings, too early attention to subheadings may be time wasted. Finally, when a careful outline is required, keep the purpose statement and main headings in your mind and reconsider them at convenient moments. Especially try to avoid finishing the outline at a single sitting. Second thoughts are often better than first, and you want to be sure about the over-all structure of your ideas before you begin to develop them in detail.

TESTING THE OUTLINE

As a check on the structure, it is usually wise to test the outline by asking the following questions:

1. Is the purpose statement (thesis) satisfactory?
2. Is the relation among the parts clear and consistent?
3. Does the order of the parts (sequence) provide a logical progression from the purpose statement?
4. Is the outline complete?
5. Can each entry be developed in detail?

Is the Purpose Statement (Thesis) Satisfactory?

Since the purpose statement controls the whole outline, a faulty statement invites trouble all along the way. As we have seen, the statement of purpose should be restricted, unified, and precise. A poor one can lead to a badly organized or a pointless paper. A rigorous checking of the purpose statement is therefore the first and most important step in testing the usefulness of a tentative outline.

As an additional illustration of what may develop from an unsatisfactory statement, consider the following:

> The purpose of this paper is to provide a better understanding of the American Indian by revealing a few facts about his everyday life and customs.

The author of this statement has not really clarified his purpose, and any paper he writes is likely to be superficial. Why does he think that "a few facts" about the everyday life and customs of the Indian will help us to understand him better? What kind of facts? What will be his criterion for using some facts and omitting others? When we look at his outline we see, as his purpose statement suggests, that he is going to write a pointless paper "about" the American Indian.

I. The Indian religion differs from the white man's.
   A. The Indian religion is complicated.
   B. His conception of the supernatural has a strong influence on his everyday life.
II. The Indian medicine man is one of the most important people in the tribe.
   A. The training of the medicine man begins at an early age.

   III. Dancing is of great importance in the life of the Indian.
      A. There are many classes of dancing.
      B. The instruments used to accompany the dancers are of a wide variation.
   IV. The education of the Indian was not very extensive.
      A. There were several Indian colleges built.
    V. The government of the Indian was simple.
      A. There were four divisions in the government.

The vagueness of the purpose statement encouraged the student to tack on anything that had any connection with his general subject. This example is an unusually bad one, but it shows what can happen when a student bases an outline on a fuzzy, pointless statement of purpose.

Is the Relationship Among the Parts Clear and Consistent?

In a good outline one can see how each main unit brings out an important aspect of the purpose statement and how each subdivision helps to develop its main heading. If there is any doubt about the relation of any heading to the purpose statement, that heading is either poorly stated or is a potential trouble spot in the outline. Whatever the reason, the difficulty should be removed before writing is begun.

Notice how clear is the relation among all parts of the following outline. Each Roman numeral shows a distinct relation to the thesis; each capital letter is a logical division of its Roman numeral. No entry in the outline fails to advance the purpose, and each introduces, at its proper place, a significant part of the argument. You can be confident that the paper written from this outline will be coherent and closely reasoned.

    Thesis: The age at which a citizen may vote should be reduced to 18.
     I. The present age limit has no logical justification.
       A. It has no relation to physical maturity.
       B. It has no relation to intellectual maturity.
       C. It has no relation to economic maturity.
     II. Whatever justification the present age limit once had has been removed by changed conditions.
       A. In the last war we were forced to draft 18-year-olds because they made the best soldiers.
       B. The draft necessitates a change in the voting age if we are to respect the political maxim that the responsibilities of citizenship presuppose the privileges of citizenship.
    III. The objections against reducing the age limit, like the objections against female suffrage, are based on unsupported assertions.
       A. It was asserted that women would use the vote foolishly, but the facts have disproved that assertion.
       B. It is asserted that 18-year-olds neither care about voting nor will take the trouble to make themselves politically informed, but the facts do not support that assertion.

IV. The argument that there has to be some minimum age begs the question, since reducing the age limit does not abolish it.

V. Reducing the age limit would broaden the base of our democracy, a consequence which has been traditionally desirable.

A good way to test an outline is to ask yourself, for every entry, whether it "points back" to the one it is developing. Do the Roman-numeral entries point back to the thesis or purpose statement? Do those with capital letters point back to the main headings? Notice below how A, B, and C all point back to I, the contention that the present age limit for voting has no logical justification.

I. The present age limit has no logical justification.

   A. It has no relation to physical maturity.

   B. It has no relation to intellectual maturity.

   C. It has no relation to economic maturity.

Notice also that any inconsistency in the form of the entries or parts will make their relationship less clear.

I. The present age limit has no logical justification.

   A. It has no relation to physical maturity.

   B. Intellectual maturity varies with individuals.

   C. The law does not require people to be economically independent before they can vote.

In this version the subdivisions A, B, C are no longer parallel in structure, and it is now more difficult to see how they point back to I. If we use these entries as topic sentences for successive paragraphs of an essay, we may, unless we are careful, distort the structure of the whole argument and throw an unnecessary burden both on ourselves, as writers, and on our readers. Consistent form in topics of equal rank is not just a matter of style; it emphasizes the relation of A, B, and C to each other and to the Roman-numeral statement which they develop. Consistent form thus provides tighter control over what we write and makes for more efficient planning.

Does the Order of the Parts Provide a Logical Progression?

Just as the sentences within a paragraph must follow a logical order, so must the parts of an outline. If any of the parts are out of order, the disorder will be magnified in the essay, and a reader will be confused or irritated. In the following outlines, compare the faulty version at the right with the more logical one at the left.

Purpose: To show Elizabeth's contribution to the development of the English navy

I. Condition of navy prior to Elizabeth's reign
   A. Its size compared with first-rate navies
   B. Its lack of government support
   C. Its inefficient use
II. Elizabeth's support of the "Sea Dogs" — Drake, Frobisher, Howard, Raleigh, and Grenville
   A. Political and economic reasons for her support
   B. Nature and extent of her support
III. Results of Elizabeth's support of Sea Dogs
   A. Economic rivalry with Spain
   B. Defeat of Armada and new prestige of English navy
   C. Extensive shipbuilding program to forestall Spanish retaliation
   D. More efficient design for ships
   E. Improved theory of naval warfare
   F. Foundation of English naval tradition
IV. Summary of condition of navy at end of Elizabeth's reign in contrast to condition described in I above

Purpose: To show Elizabeth's contribution to the development of the English navy

I. Condition of navy prior to Elizabeth's reign
   A. Navy relatively small in comparison with other first-rate powers
   B. Inadequate government attention to fleet
II. Development of naval warfare during the period
   A. Importance of battle with Spanish Armada
      1. Types of warfare used by both sides
      2. Defeat of Armada a turning point in English naval history
   B. Brief description of offensive and defensive forces of English navy
      1. Classification of ships as to size and armament
      2. Location of forces
   C. Work of Elizabethan Sea Dogs
      1. Influence upon Elizabeth
      2. Sea Dog fighting tactics
         a. Work of Drake
         b. Treatment of Spanish ships
III. Comparison of formation and battle tactics of Elizabethan and modern navies
   A. Factors of formation and battle tactics
   B. Closing paragraph

The outline at the left follows a *before-during-after* order. Part I describes the condition in which Elizabeth found the fleet, part II shows her support of the new naval leaders, part III deals with the immediate results of that support, and part IV summarizes all the results in a contrast with part I. Within these main units there is a logical progression of ideas. Within II the order goes from why Elizabeth acted (A) to what she did (B). In III the order is a succession of related consequences of her actions, which builds up to the contrast between I and IV. Throughout the outline the emphasis is on Elizabeth's contribution, as the purpose requires.

The order in the outline at the right follows no evident logical progression from the purpose statement. Elizabeth is mentioned only once, late in the outline in a minor heading (II C 1), and then without suggesting her contribution. In the main units the order seems to be haphazard. Part II — the largest unit — is limited to naval warfare, and part III is a wholly irrelevant comparison between Elizabethan and modern navies. Within the big central part II the organization is puzzling. What is the relation between types of warfare used by both sides (A 1) and the importance of the battle with the Armada? Does B 2 overlap A 1? Why does C shift the emphasis from Elizabeth to the Sea Dogs, when she is the subject of the paper? And if C is concerned with the Sea Dogs, why is only Drake mentioned?

The contrast between the logical order of these two outlines will be easier to see in the following simplification:

Logical Progression	*Illogical Progression*
I. Conditions existing before Elizabeth acted	I. Conditions existing before Elizabeth acted
II. What she did, and why	II. A collection of material, including types of warfare, significance of the Armada's defeat, the work of the Sea Dogs (chiefly Drake), treatment of the Spanish ships
III. The results of her action	
IV. Contrasted summary of the situation in I and III	III. Comparison of Elizabethan and modern navies

A careful comparison of these two outlines should suggest two conclusions. First, unless a writer seeks a logical progression, he can drift into a plan which does not organize, but merely ties material into bundles without regard to why things are put in one bundle rather than another, or even why the bundles were made up in the first place. Second, if the progression of ideas or materials is confused in the outline, it will be worse in the essay. The writer then simply passes his confusion along to the reader.

It will be obvious that the chief trouble in the outline at the right lies in the second main heading. The profitable question to consider is: How can a student detect such errors before they are allowed to give a faulty organization to his paper? Some general answers are possible. First, it will be easier to see the faults of an outline on the day after it has been constructed, when the student can approach the task with more objectivity. Second, when faced with what is possibly just a collection of material, the student can ask himself: What is the common subject of this material: What precise contribution to the navy did Elizabeth make here? Notice that a sentence outline might have saved the writer from trouble by restricting the things he could do under a sentence entry. Third, since this section is presumably dealing with Elizabeth's contribution, the writer could ask himself, at each subheading: Is this clearly a contribution that Elizabeth herself made? If it is a contribution, but the contribution is obscured by the heading, then the correction lies in revising the heading to make it show what it is intended to show. If this cannot be done, then the material is probably irrelevant to the purpose. Finally, these suggestions can be summed up in one piece of general advice: ask yourself, *What answer will I give the instructor if he thinks the progression of ideas here is not clear or not logical?* That question will force you to challenge the structure of the outline.

Is the Outline Complete?

This is really not one question but two: first, are all major units of the subject represented; second, is each major unit subdivided far enough to guide the development of the essay? In college essays, the second consideration is the more important. Obviously, if we are going to divide Gaul into three parts, we should deal with three parts. It is less obvious, but not less important, that if we are going to discuss the work of the Elizabethan Sea Dogs, we must not stop with Drake.

If you compare the two outlines we have just considered, you will see that part III of the left-hand outline provides a fuller subdivision of the material inadequately suggested in II C of the right-hand version. As a plan for a paper, the six headings under III at the left provide a fuller plan than the two headings under II C at the right. Of course, a writer may compensate for incomplete subdivision in the outline by complete development in the essay. But that requires him to do better planning while writing than he did when he was concerned only with planning. *In practice, students almost never correct the deficiencies of an outline during the composition of an essay.* Flaws in the outline are almost certain to be preserved.

Can Each Entry Be Developed in Detail?

Each entry in the outline should be fully developed when the essay is written. Every instructor has known students who construct outlines containing entries for which they have no material, so that all they have to say about these entries is what they have already said in the outline. *Every entry in an outline should be adequately developed, and no entry should appear unless the author has the material to develop it.* There can be no rigid rule about how much development each entry should receive. Sometimes a single entry will require two or three paragraphs in the essay; occasionally several minor entries may be dealt with in a single paragraph. For inexperienced writers, *a useful rule of thumb is that each entry will usually be developed into at least one paragraph.*

▶ *As a check on your ability to apply the tests you have just learned to a finished outline, apply each of the five tests listed on page 91 to the outline below. Make notes of your judgments at each step in the testing, including the evidence to support your judgment. Be prepared to use your notes as material for a class evaluation of the outline.*

THE BASIC STROKES — THE FRAMEWORK OF TENNIS

Thesis: The fundamental strokes of tennis, when correctly used, make the game an exact science.

I. The service, the drive, and the volley are classed as offensive strokes.
 A. The service — the opening stroke of the game — should be the opening for the attack.
  1. The service is taken from behind the baseline.
   a. At the start of the service the left side is facing the net with the right foot behind the left.
   b. The ball is tossed slightly higher than a fully extended arm.
   c. The racquet is brought up behind the head and with the whole weight of the body behind it, brought down hard on the ball.
  2. Speed and direction limit the possibility of one's opponent returning a good serve.
 B. The drive is the most important ground stroke in tennis.
  1. Most drives are taken from the baseline.
   a. The body must be at right angles with the net.
   b. The racquet should be lined up behind the ball.
   c. The ball should be carried forward with the racquet.
  2. Speed and direction often determine the better of two players.
 C. The use of the volley permits quick and decisive returns.
  1. The volley is taken close to the net.
   a. The volley is taken by stepping forward on the left foot and moving the body weight into the stroke.
   b. The ball is hit before it touches the ground.
   c. The racquet acts in a blocking manner.
  2. The possibility of one's opponent returning a deep well-angled volley is slight.
II. The lob and the smash are classed as defensive strokes.
 A. The lob is useful as a means of returning the volley.
  1. The lob is usually taken from the backcourt.
   a. The ball is hit from underneath and lifted high into the air.
   b. In the follow-through, there is a definite lift to the racquet.
  2. The lob is used in driving the volleyer back from the net.
 B. The smash is useful as a means of returning the lob.
  1. The smash is used to return a high ball lifted into the air by the opponent.
   a. The ball is met as high as possible in the air.
   b. The racquet is brought down upon the ball with the body weight coming forward with the swing.
  2. The speed and direction of the smash make a return difficult.

Testing an Argumentative Outline

The tests already given apply to any formal outline, including the outline of an argument. But there are some considerations so important in argument that they require special attention. These are discussed in detail in Chapter 12.

In addition to testing the structure of an argumentative outline, it is necessary to check its content. The basic test of content is: Will the argument convince the reader? The content of an argument is likely to be convincing on two conditions: that the premises are acceptable, and that the inferences are valid.

Are the premises acceptable? Premises may be statements of fact or testimonial statements. If they are statements of fact, they are true or false, depending on whether they do or do not correspond to the facts. Sometimes the truth or falsity of a statement of fact cannot be determined. We cannot, for example, say with certainty whether there is life on other planets. At present all we can say is that we do not know of such life, but a final answer — if one can ever be given — must await further knowledge. However, when it can be shown that a premise is false — for instance, that the sun revolves around the earth — whatever argument rests on that premise will be rejected.

Sometimes the premises are consistent with some of the facts, but not with all of them. For example, the statement that "Women are poor drivers" is true for some women, false for others — and therefore false for all women taken collectively. Sometimes premises accord with those facts that have been examined, but so few have been examined that we can have no confidence that they are typical of the whole class under discussion. We seldom have an opportunity to examine all the facts about anything, but whenever premises are so incomplete that they prove nothing, they cannot be accepted. An outline based on such premises would fail the test of completeness cited on page 96.

When premises consist of testimony by expert witnesses, they are not statements of fact, but expressions of the witnesses' judgment. In such cases, the acceptance of a statement depends on the acceptance of the witness. He must be an admitted authority on the question on which he is testifying, and there must be no significant reason for thinking that bias or self-interest disqualifies his testimony. Students sometimes want to quote the opinions of a prominent person — college president, scientist, senator, or successful businessman — whose views agrees with theirs. But prominence alone does not qualify a person as an expert. The only acceptable qualifications are demonstrable expertness on the question and freedom from bias.

Are the inferences valid? The word *valid* implies that the conclusion is inescapable because it follows logically from the premises. Tests of validity are often complex and technical, but this much can be said here: to be valid, a conclusion must follow demonstrably from the premises. From the premise that oxygen is necessary for combustion, it can be inferred that a candle in a vacuum will not burn, but it is not valid to infer that a lighted candle will burn simply because oxygen is present; other factors — a wet wick, for example — may prevent combustion. It is valid to infer that if a million pennies are tossed, about half of them will turn up tails; it is not valid to infer that, if a tossed penny turns up heads, it will necessarily come up tails on the next toss.

Because of the difficulty of proving that any effect will necessarily follow from a cause, we usually rely on probability. The probability is that a man of 70 has less time to live than a man of 35, all things else being equal. An insurance company will accept that inference as valid.

Inferences, therefore, are likely to be accepted as valid if there is a strong probability that the conclusions will follow from the premises. They are likely to be rejected if the conclusion seems only possible but not probable. Between these two extremes there may be considerable disagreement. It is the writer's duty to estimate this disagreement and to minimize it when he can.

It will be seen from this discussion that an argumentative outline should be tested for the acceptability of its premises and the validity of its inferences. This test takes the form of the question: *Will a reader accept this premise and will he share the conclusion drawn from it?* Much of the time, the best answer the writer can give to this question is, "Probably." But there is a great difference between carefully answering "Probably" and not asking the question at all.

If the writer doubts that the reader will be convinced, he should consider what he can do to strengthen his argument. Should he provide more premises? Should be modify the conclusion? Should he admit that the answer to the question is still so uncertain that a persuasive conclusion is not possible? These are all sound procedures. It is not sound procedure to assume that all a writer has to do is to *assert* a conclusion. Assertion is not argument, and no writer should assume that his unsupported assertions have any value.

Earlier in this chapter two argumentative outlines were presented. These were on heredity and environment (pages 89–90) and reduction of the voting age (pages 92–93). Test each of these outlines for its persuasiveness. You will not always be certain whether the premises are true, but you can at least get the consensus of your class on whether they are accepted. If you have any doubts about the validity of the inferences, explain and discuss your doubts.

SUMMARY

1. An outline is a formal plan for a projected essay. For short essays, the kind of planning shown in Chapter 3 will usually be sufficient; but for longer essays — especially critical papers, research papers, and extensive arguments — it will often be necessary to construct a plan in conventional outline form.

2. In a topic outline the entries are expressed in words or phrases; in a sentence outline each entry is a complete sentence. The topic outline is better for an essay which does not develop a dominant idea; for a paper that does develop an idea (thesis), the sentence outline is preferable. In practice, most sentence outlines evolve out of preliminary topic outlines.

3. The conventions of outlining require that all headings be given an appropriate symbol and be indented to show the degree of subdivision. They also require that the outline distinguish major and minor divisions and keep the grammatical structure of all headings parallel.

4. In preparing an outline, finish the major divisions before you touch minor ones. Do the Roman numerals before you begin the capital letters, and the capitals before the Arabic numerals. This will insure that you work out the outline in a series of stages.

5. When you think your outline is complete, test it by considering the following questions: (*a*) Is the purpose statement satisfactory? (*b*) Is there a clear and consistent relationship between the purpose statement and each main division, and between the main and minor entries? Do the Roman numerals point back to the thesis, and the capital letters to the Roman numerals? (*c*) Does the order of the parts provide a logical progression from the purpose statement? (*d*) Is the outline complete? Have all the major units been presented, and have the subdivisions been carried far enough to provide a reliable guide for the actual composition? (*e*) Can each entry be adequately developed in the final essay?

6. In addition to these tests, argumentative outlines should also be tested for the acceptability of the premises and the validity of the inferences.

Exercises

A. Prepare a sentence outline of the following selection. As preparation, first read over the whole essay to get an idea of its content. Then examine the first paragraph closely to see if it states the thesis or purpose of the essay. If it does, write down the purpose statement. If no purpose statement is explicitly given, can you frame one from the content of the paragraph? Next, examine each paragraph to see how it develops the purpose of the essay. Look especially for what seem to be topic sentences. If no topic sentence is explicitly stated, can you provide one? When you have finished the outline, check it against the text, partly to satisfy yourself that your outline is sound, and partly to notice how the paragraphs develop the outline entries.

Death is the great scandal in the experience of man; for death — as the destruction of the human person after a finite span of time — is the very negation of all man experiences as specifically human in his existence: the consciousness of himself and of his world, the remembrance of things past and the anticipation of things to come, a creativeness in thought and action which aspires to, and approximates, the eternal. Thus man has been compelled, for the sake of his existence as man, to bridge the gap between death and his specifically human attributes by transcending death. He has done so in three different ways: by making himself, within narrow limits, the master of death; by denying the reality of death through the belief in the immortality of his person; by conquering the reality of death through the immortality of the world he leaves behind.

Man can make himself the master of death by putting an end to his biological existence whenever he wishes. While he cannot live as long as he wants to, he can stop living whenever he wants to. While he cannot choose life over death when his life has reached its biological limits, he can choose death over life regardless of these limits. He can commit suicide; or he can commit what Nietzsche has called "suicide with a good conscience" by seeking out death, especially at the hand of someone else. He is capable of sacrificial death. In his self-chosen death for a cause in particular, on the battlefield or elsewhere, man triumphs over death, however incompletely. He triumphs because he does not wait until his body is ready to die, but he offers his life to death when his chosen purpose demands it. Yet that triumph is incomplete because it cannot overcome the inevitability of death but only controls its coming.

Man also denies the reality of death by believing in the immortality of his person. This belief can take two different forms. It may take the form of the assumption that the finiteness of man's biological existence is but apparent and that his body will live on in another world. It can also take the form of the assumption that what is specifically human in man will survive the destruction of his body and that man's soul will live on forever, either separated from any body or reincarnated in someone else's. This belief in personal immortality, in defiance of the empirical evidence of the finiteness of man's biological existence, is of course peculiar to the religious realm. It presupposes the existence of a world which is not only inaccessible to the senses but also superior to the world of the senses in that what is truly human in man is there preserved forever.

It is a distinctive characteristic of our secular age that it has replaced the belief in the immortality of the human person with the attempt to assure the immortality of the world he leaves behind. Man can transcend the finiteness of his biological existence either in his consciousness or in objective reality by adding to that existence four different dimensions which are in one way or another independent of that finiteness. They are different dimensions of immortality. He can extend his consciousness into the past by remembering it. He can extend his consciousness into the future by anticipating it. As *homo faber,* he embeds his biological existence within technological and social artifacts which survive that existence. His imagination creates new worlds of religion, art, and reason that live after their creator.

By thus bestowing immortality upon the past, man assures himself of immortality to be granted by future generations who will remember him. As the past lives on in his historic recollection, so will he continue to live in the memory of his successors. The continuity of history gives the individual at least a chance to survive himself in the collective memory of mankind.

101

Those who are eminent, or believe themselves to be so, aspire to posthumous fame which will enable them to live on, perhaps forever.

The ability to remember and the aspiration to be remembered call for deliberate action to assure that remembrance. The assurance of his life after death becomes one of man's main concerns here and now. Man on all levels of civilization is moved to create monuments which testify to his existence and will live after him. He founds a family and lives on in his sons, who bear his name as he bears his father's. He leaves an inheritance of visible things not to be consumed but to be preserved as tangible mementos of past generations. Over his grave he causes a monument of stone to be erected whose durability, as it were, compensates for the impermanence of what lies beneath. Or he may even refuse to accept that impermanence altogether and have his body preserved in the likeness of life. At the very least, he will have pictures made of himself to perpetuate his physical likeness.

This concern with immortality in this world manifests itself on the highest level of consciousness in the preparation of man's fame. He lives in such a way as to make sure that his fame will survive him. All of us, from the peasant and handicraft man to the founders of churches, the architects of empires, the builders of cities, the tamers of the forces of nature, seek to leave behind the works of our wills and hands to testify to our existence. *"Roma eterna,"* "the Reich of a thousand years" are but the most ambitious attempts to perpetuate man in his deeds. The tree that he has planted, the house that he has built, have been given a life likely to last longer than his own. At best, he as a person will live on in his works; at worst, he has the satisfaction of living on anonymously in what he has created.

It is, however, in the works of his imagination that man conquers the mortality of his body in the most specifically human way. The artists and poets, the philosophers and the writers, can point with different degrees of assurance to their work and say with Horace: "I have finished a monument more lasting than bronze and loftier than the Pyramids' royal pile, one that no wasting rain, no furious north wind can destroy, or the countless chain of years and the ages' flight. I shall not altogether die. . . ." In the works of his mind it is not just his physical existence, the bare fact that he once lived, that is remembered. Rather, what is remembered is the creative quality that sets him apart from all other creatures, that is peculiar to him as a man. What is remembered is not only the specifically human quality, but also and most importantly the quality in which he lives on as a unique individual, the like of whom has never existed before or since. In the works of his mind, man, the creator, survives.

Yet why are those works a "monument more lasting than bronze," and why can their creator be confident that "on and on shall I grow, ever fresh with the glory of after time"? Because the man endowed with a creative mind knows himself to be a member in an unbroken chain emerging from the past and reaching into the future, which is made of the same stuff his mind is made of and, hence, is capable of participating in, and perpetuating, his mind's creation. He may be mortal, but humanity is not, and so he will be immortal in his works. This is the triumphant message of Horace.

Our life, then, receives one of its meanings from the meaning we give to death. What we make of life is shaped by what we make of death; for we live in the presence of the inevitability of death and we dedicate our lives to the proof of the proposition that death is not what it seems to be: the irrevocable end of our existence. We search for immortality, and the kind of immortality we seek determines the kind of life we lead.[1]

B. Study the following introductory paragraph and do two things with it. First, prepare a sentence outline to show the structure of the essay that could be developed from this paragraph. Second, comment on the technique which the author is using in this paragraph.

ARE SOCIAL SCIENTISTS BACKWARD?

In discussing the relative difficulties of analysis which the exact and inexact sciences face, let me begin with an analogy. Would you agree that swimmers are less skillful athletes than runners because swimmers do not move as fast as runners? You probably would not. You would quickly point out that water offers greater resistance to swimmers than the air and ground do to runners. Agreed, that is just the point. In seeking to solve their problems, the social scientists encounter greater resistance than the physical scientists. By that I do not mean to belittle the great accomplishments of physical scientists who have been able, for example, to determine the structure of the atom without seeing it. That is a tremendous achievement; yet in many ways it is not so difficult as what the social scientists are expected to do. The conditions under which the social scientists must work would drive a physical scientist frantic. Here are five of those conditions. He can make few experiments; he cannot measure the results accurately; he cannot control the conditions surrounding the experiments; he is often expected to get quick results with slow-acting economic forces; and he must work with people, not with inanimate objects. Let us look at these conditions more closely.[2]

C. Using the following selection as a source of material and a stimulus, write an outline for a substantial argument about television. Your thesis may agree or disagree with all or any part of the author's argument. When you are finished, test your outline by the test of persuasiveness discussed near the end of this chapter.

Marxism notwithstanding, the profit motive is both legitimate and useful as a motive so long as it is not the *only* motive. Or to put it somewhat differently, the writer, the publisher, and the television company may quite properly want their respective enterprises to pay. In fact, the publisher and television company always, and the writer very often, would simply have to turn to some other activity if their enterprises didn't pay. And, on the whole, I think this economic pressure less unfortunate in its effects than the kind of bureaucratic pressure that, sooner or later, almost inevitably accompanies government-sponsored artistic projects, though I see no reason why such government-sponsored projects should not exist alongside of those that do have to make money. But to say this is not to say that the writer, the publisher, or even the TV official need assume that the *only* question he

[1] From Hans J. Morgenthau, "Death in the Nuclear Age," *Commentary,* September, 1961.

[2] From Donald L. Kemmerer, "Are Social Scientists Backward?" *American Association of University Professors Bulletin,* Autumn, 1948.

will ever ask is not merely, "Will this be profitable?" but, "Will this be more profitable than anything else I could possibly write, publish, or produce?"

It is discouraging to observe that the newest medium of communication comes nearest to accepting the profit motive as the *only* motive, and the great difference between television networks and publishers is simply that many publishers do take some pride in being responsible for things which they themselves, as well as the public, admire. The networks, on the other hand, despite occasional boasts about this or that sacrifice in the public interest, come much closer in profession as well as practice to saying simply, "We consider it our business to ask nothing except whether this or that program will win the largest possible audience and therefore most please the most profitable advertiser." Here, for example, is a pronouncement from Julius Babbathan, vice president and general manager of ABC, as quoted in *Newsweek,* November 11, 1963:

> What do you mean by "caliber programs"? I'll tell you what it means to me. It means a guy sitting there in front of a TV, with a hero sandwich in his hand and a glass of beer, saying, "That's a program I'd like to watch."

There is no free competition in commercial television. The national government has granted a few monopolies, which it protects. No one would protest more than these corporations if the government did not protect those who express horror at government interference with free enterprise or free expression — except when such interference protects their own monopoly.

Since the government *does* guarantee these fabulously profitable monopolies, would it be an unwarranted interference with what is actually a monopoly — not a business engaged in free competition — if a price were placed on this protection: That the monopoly, on pain of revocation of its license, should not operate on the assumption that the only criterion in preparing programs will be, "Will it produce a larger profit than any other?" After all, there is a sizable body of citizens with at least minority rights in the air waves who are not completely typified by "a guy with a hero sandwich in his hand and a glass of beer."

There is, moreover, a regulation which has often been proposed and which a government agency might impose without exercising any actual editorial control. It would certainly relieve the pressure of the advertisers and it opens no possible objections other than the fact that it might well make broadcasting somewhat less profitable — while leaving it quite profitable enough. That often proposed regulation is simply the requirement that the advertiser should sponsor the network program as a whole, not any one program of its choice.

Utopia? Perhaps it is, now that the sponsor has become so thoroughly accustomed to dictating and the broadcaster to so supinely accepting that dictation. But if this is true, it is simply another example of the way in which the newest commercial enterprises tend to be those which are the most crassly opportunist and the most abjectly determined to plan only in terms of what they believe to be the lowest common denominator — which, alas, the all-too-good rating systems enable them to do with what they regard as an adequate degree of accuracy.

Can you imagine a newspaper or a magazine run in this way, with each story, article, or editorial individually sponsored by the advertiser and not printed until such a sponsor could be found? Some magazines and some newspapers are accused (justly, no doubt) of being to some extent subservient to their advertisers. But no publication of any kind above the very lowest level has ever operated as the broadcasting industry does. Even news broadcasts and public service programs are likely to be sponsored if a sponsor can be found for them. But what newspaper would dare to interrupt both its news stories and editorials with the all too familiar "and now a word . . ."? Would any be willing either so to annoy its readers or so clearly advertise the fact that its advertisers are everywhere in control?

No one ever went broke by underestimating the taste of the American public, said H. L. Mencken, and this has been often quoted. If this is true, then it would be better for all of us if we didn't know just how low public taste actually is. If we didn't know, some chief of programing might overestimate that public taste just enough to raise the level of his network a bit and give his audience something a little better than what they would choose. Moreover, if there is anything in education, he might even raise the level of the public taste an equal amount.

Classical scholars have held different opinions concerning the question cynics sometimes ask: "Would the audience of fifth-century Athens really have liked less exalted dramas better than the works of Aeschylus, Sophocles, *et al.?*" Audiences certainly did flock to them, but then they had no choice, except to the extent that the satyr plays which followed the tragedies were an alternate choice. And even they, though they certainly were less exalted in sentiment, are still considered to have been, in their own way, no less admirable as literature. So far as I know, the question was never asked door-to-door in Athens.

And even if, as some scholars argue, the very exceptional audience of Periclean Athens would have turned up its nose at works offered by anyone who believes Mencken, the fact remains that a few centuries later the Roman emperors decided to try to keep the populace manageably docile by giving them precisely what they wanted, and then the drama gave way to musical vaudeville, and finally almost entirely to gladiatorial and wild beast combats.

John Stuart Mill (certainly not one to look with favor upon government interference with either business enterprise or free speech) once wrote in an essay an observation not sufficiently pondered by those who urge us to have unbounded faith in "the people," and who identify "the people" primarily with those who like to settle down in front of a TV set with a hero sandwich and a glass of beer:

Capacity for the nobler feelings is in most cases a very tender plant, easily killed, not only by hostile influences but by mere want of sustenance . . . Men lose their high aspirations as they lose their intellectual tastes, because they have not the time or the opportunity for indulging them; and they addict themselves to inferior pleasures, not because they deliberately prefer them, but because they are either the only ones to which they have access, or the only ones they are any longer capable of enjoying.

105

In any case, it is certain that if those who cater to the lowest possible public taste insist upon eagerly following its taste downward, then that taste will continue to descend as a sort of Gresham's law begins to operate.

Perhaps Mencken's statement was true in the past tense which he employed. No one ever has gone broke by underestimating the taste of the American public. But that doesn't prove that it can't be done or that nobody ever will go broke for exactly that reason. Given the attitudes and the methods of the television tycoons, someone may succeed in descending below the level of all but an ultimately unprofitable minority.

There is at least one hopeful sign, a discovery that the Nielsen Company itself recently made public: this year 1,000,000 fewer people were watching television than were watching it a year ago. That certainly is not because the quality of programs has been raised above their level.

It might just possibly mean that Mencken's pronouncement will have to be updated. Even the man with the hero sandwich and the glass of beer is beginning to get bored.[3]

[3] From Joseph Wood Krutch, "Man Is More Than a Statistic," *Saturday Review,* May 21, 1966.

PART TWO Expressing Ideas

5

Paragraphs:

Compositions in Miniature

A paragraph requires much the same process of composition as a whole essay, though in smaller scope. An essay must have a purpose; so must a paragraph. The purpose of an essay, if stated, is the *thesis;* that of a paragraph, if stated, is the *topic sentence.* An essay must have a clear structure and a reasonable progression of ideas; so must a paragraph. An essay must be developed in enough detail to make its general statements meaningful; so must a paragraph. In short, a paragraph is an essay in miniature.

FOUR REQUIREMENTS OF A GOOD PARAGRAPH

A good paragraph does its job thoroughly. If its function is to develop a unit of an outline, every sentence in the paragraph should clearly relate to that unit, and the sum of the sentences should make the reader feel that the unit has been efficiently developed. To create this impression a paragraph should have four qualities: *completeness, unity, order,* and *coherence.*

Completeness

A paragraph is complete when it does all it was intended to do. Consider the following:

> Too cold to snow? It never gets too cold to snow, but it frequently gets too cold for snow to fall in flakes, because at subzero temperatures the air is too dry to produce snowflakes.

This brief paragraph poses a question and provides an answer. Is it complete? Whether it is or not depends on how thoroughly the reader understands why dry subzero air will keep snowflakes from forming. This you may decide for yourself. Could you, on the evidence of this paragraph alone, explain to your classmates why dry, cold air reduces the formation of snowflakes? If your answer is no, see if the following version is more helpful.

> Too cold to snow? It never gets too cold to snow, but it frequently gets too cold for snow to fall in flakes. *Flakes fall when the air through which they pass is 32° Fahrenheit or slightly lower. At this temperature the air usually holds enough moisture to allow the flakes to become fat and mat together, and the fall is likely to be heavy. As the temperature sinks lower, the air becomes drier, the snowfall lighter and more powdery. At temperatures below zero a heavy fall of snow is rare. The snow that does fall takes the form of ice spicules, ice needles, or fills the air with fine, glittering, diamond-like dust.* The air at these subzero temperatures is usually too dry to produce flakes.[1]

Do you agree that this version gives a better explanation and that, by comparison, the first seems incomplete? The first answer is not detailed enough to meet the reader's needs; therefore it does not fully do what it was supposed to do. The explanatory details italicized in the second paragraph are needed to bring out the meaning of the general answer in the first version.

Supporting Details. Any details which help to make general statements more specific are said to *support* these statements. It is usual to classify such details as descriptive, narrative, expository, or persuasive, depending on the effect they are intended to achieve. But although narration often makes use of description, explanation may include both description and narration, and persuasion may include the other three. The italicized details in the second snowflake paragraph are expository, since they explain the process by which snow particles mat or fail to mat into flakes, even though "fine, glittering, diamond-like dust" describes the snow particles that fall at subzero temperatures.

Descriptive Details. Descriptive details tell what something looks, sounds, feels, tastes, or smells like — "fine, glittering, diamond-like dust," "the squeal of chalk on a blackboard," "the metallic aftertaste of canned orange juice." Descriptive details are the basic materials of writing, since all writing rests on observation, and descriptive details are the means by which observations are reported. Consequently narration, exposition, and argument all make use of description. You have seen such details used to classify body types, to compare the forest and the sea, to support the argument that "Trees" is a bad poem. In the following paragraph the

[1] From *The World Almanac, 1945.*

descriptive details are used to let a reader see what the "open range" of a Nebraska prairie looked like in frontier days.

> When the first courageous settlers came straggling out through the waste with their oxen and covered wagons, they found open range all the way from Lincoln to Denver; a continuous, undulating plateau, covered with long, red, shaggy grass. The prairie was green only where it had been burned off in the spring by the new settlers or by the Indians, and toward autumn even the new grass became a coppery brown. This sod, which had never been broken by the plow, was so tough and strong with the knotted grass roots of many years, that the home-seekers were able to peel it off the earth like peat, cut it up into bricks, and make of it warm, comfortable, durable houses. Some of these sod houses lingered on until the open range was gone and the grass was gone, and the whole face of the country had been changed.[2]

Most of the effective details in this paragraph are visual — the undulating plateau, the green grass from the burned-over areas, which later turned coppery brown, and the sod houses. Take away these details, and much less is communicated.

Narrative Details. Narrative details are specific bits of action which, when built into a sequence, show the reader what is happening in the narrative. Good examples from earlier pages are the jackdaw's stuffing Lorenz's ear with worm mash (page 61) and the actions of the wasp in finding, attacking, paralyzing, and burying the tarantula (page 72). The following paragraph is taken from a report on the sinking of the *Titanic*. The details report what people did and said in the scene with which the paragraph is concerned. Notice all the individual acts which, cumulatively, build a scene of disaster.

> A few men take up the refrain [of a hymn]; others kneel on the slanting decks to pray. Many run and scramble aft, where hundreds are clinging above the silent screws on the great uptilted stern. . . . The·hymn comes to its close. Bandmaster Hartley, Yorkshireman violinist, taps his bow against a bulkhead, calls for "Autumn" as the water curls about his feet, and the eight musicians brace themselves against the ship's slant. People are leaping from the decks into the nearby water — the icy water. A woman cries, "Oh, save me!" A man answers, "Good lady, save yourself. Only God can save you now." The band plays "Autumn":
>
> > "God of Mercy and Compassion!
> > Look with pity on my pain . . ."[3]

The paragraph alternates between panic and resignation. The core of the action is the quiet heroism and professional conduct of the band. Around that core are details of resignation (prayer) and panic. Then the paragraph is concluded with a detail from the music the band is playing.

[2] From Willa Cather, "Nebraska," *These United States,* ed. Ernest Gruening (New York: Liveright Publishing Corporation, 1924).
[3] From Hanson W. Baldwin, "R.M.S. Titanic," *Harper's Magazine,* January, 1934.

Expository (Explanatory) Details. Expository details have a wide range of uses — to illustrate a general statement, to compare or contrast two subjects, to explain a process, to define a word or a concept, to trace a causal relation, to interpret a statement or explain an idea. Most of these uses were illustrated in Chapter 3. In the following paragraph the term "hyperbole" is not explicitly defined, yet its meaning becomes quite clear from the short illustrative examples:

> *Hyperbole* is natural in unstudied speech: "I beg a *thousand* pardons," "scared to *death*," "I'd give the *world* to see him." Expressions of approval and disapproval are especially affected by hyperbole ("good for nothing," "a magnificent idea"), and the language of schoolgirls is proverbially made up of it: "thanks awfully," "extravagantly fond," "tremendously angry," "immensely obliged."[4]

Persuasive Details. These are the specific premises in arguments — what is often called "evidence" or "proof." In earlier pages such details were used to persuade readers that "Trees" is a bad poem, that artistic talent is not directly inherited, and that Oedipus was responsible for his own actions. In the paragraph below, the supporting details serve to persuade a reader of the harm done to our natural resources through the erosion of irreplaceable topsoil.

> The most obvious result of deforestation, overgrazing, and bad farming methods is soil erosion. American civilization, founded on nine inches of topsoil, has now lost one-third of this soil. Dr. Hugh H. Bennett, testifying before a Congressional committee in 1939, said, "In the short life of this country we have essentially destroyed 282,000,000 acres of land, crop and range-land. Erosion is destructively active on 775,000,000 additional acres. About 100,000,000 acres of cropland, much of it representing the best cropland we have, is finished in this country. We cannot restore it. It takes nature from 300 to 1000 years to bring back a single inch of topsoil and we sometimes lose that much topsoil as the result of a single rain, if it is an especially heavy torrential type of rain. . . ."[5]

The persuasion in this paragraph comes from the details — the facts and figures. Without their support, the argument would be too general to move a reader. If you drop out Dr. Bennett's testimony, you are left with nothing but an assertion that America has lost one-third of its topsoil through soil erosion. Such a statement will have no strong effect on a reader who is not an expert on that subject. He will feel that the situation is bad, but he will not see how bad. But if you tell him that we have already lost 100,000,000 acres of our best cropland, he is likely to be disturbed; and

---

[4] From James M. Greenough and George L. Kittredge, *Words and Their Ways in English Speech* (New York, 1900).

[5] From the book, *Road to Survival.* Reprinted by permission of William Sloane Associates. Copyright © 1948 by William Vogt.

if you add that it takes nature from 300 to 1000 years to replace a single inch of topsoil, he is likely to feel that something had better be done about the situation right away. That is the effect the paragraph is intended to have. The supporting details allow the writer to accomplish this purpose.

Unity

Since a paragraph develops a topic idea, stated or implied, there should be nothing in it which does not clearly serve that end. A unified paragraph makes clear reading. One which digresses or drifts away from the topic puts extra demands on the reader and sometimes thwarts him in his effort to follow the writer's thought.

A writer who sees clearly what he wants a paragraph to do is not likely to have much trouble with unity. Concentration on his purpose controls the sequence of his ideas, and he tends to grasp the paragraph idea and its development as a whole. He does not consciously plan the succession of sentences. He does not need to, because the sequence is part of his thought. It is when a writer is groping for ideas one sentence at a time that the unity of the paragraph is likely to suffer. A paragraph so written may reveal one of two flaws: (1) an obvious interruption in the sequence of ideas, caused by the introduction of irrelevant thoughts; (2) a gradual drift away from the stated purpose of the paragraph, as the author lets each succeeding sentence push him farther in the wrong direction. These flaws are illustrated in the following examples.

> It is a good thing that we learn to speak as children. If the learning were postponed until we were adults most of us would be too discouraged by the difficulties to persevere in the task. Perhaps, *in that event, our political campaigns would be conducted in sign language and our radio broadcasters would be required to learn the Morse code.* We take a child's learning to talk for granted, and not infrequently parents grow worried when their four-year-old stumbles over his consonants or becomes snarled in his syntax. Yet compared with the intellectual achievement of learning to talk, the discovery of the theory of relativity is a trifling accomplishment.

Clearly the author started with the idea that learning to speak is man's greatest intellectual achievement. But as he wrote he became interested in the possible consequences of our not learning to speak, and in an uncritical moment he introduced the italicized sentence. If he really wants to develop this idea — and it could be an entertaining one — he should save it for a new paragraph. But he should not let it intrude here, where it does not belong.

> In order to bring about harmony in our economy, Congress must force unions to become more responsible. This is no reactionary proposal. It is made in the interests of labor itself. Organized labor is an asset to the

economy of a nation. One has only to read of the conditions that prevailed in mills and mines and factories during the last century to understand what the lot of the workingman would be like if he were deprived of his right to unite with his fellow workers to force concessions from entrepreneurs whose short-sighted irresponsibility has been nourished on *laissez-faire.*

This writer drifts so steadily away from his topic sentence that he ends by saying the opposite of what he set out to say. If you study the paragraph carefully, you will see that he begins to go off the track in the second sentence. That sentence suggests to him that he must show that he is not a reactionary; so he begins to shift his point of view and to look at the labor movement historically. That viewpoint suggests the evils of management against which labor historically has fought. The reversal now becomes complete, and the writer ends by asserting the irresponsibility of management after starting out to assert the irresponsibility of labor.

The ability to see both sides of a question is valuable, but unless the topic sentence clearly implies that both sides are to be presented in the same paragraph, drifting from one side to the other frustrates the reader and produces a "broken-backed" paragraph. In revision this writer must go back to his topic sentence and develop the irresponsibility of unions throughout the paragraph. Then, if he wants to, he can point out in a second paragraph that he is sympathetic to unions and appreciates the role they have played in forcing management to be more responsible. There is nothing wrong with asserting that both unions and management should be responsible, but that assertion cannot be developed from the topic sentence this writer began with.

Orderly Movement (Sequence of Sentences)

If a paragraph is to be an organic unit, its movement should follow some clear order. There are various ways in which the material of paragraphs may be arranged. But certainly some orders will be more effective than others.

Consider the following:

[1] We all know that if we "burn" chalk the result is quick-lime. [2] There are a great many other ways of showing that chalk is essentially nothing but carbonic acid and quick-lime. [3] Chemists enunciate the result of all the experiments that prove this, by stating that chalk is almost wholly composed of "carbonate of lime." [4] By the procedure of burning we see the lime, but we do not see the carbonic acid. [5] If, on the other hand, you were to powder a little chalk and drop it into a good deal of strong vinegar, there would be a great bubbling and fizzing, and, finally, a clear liquid, in which no sign of chalk would appear. [6] Here you see the carbonic acid in the bubbles; the lime, dissolved in the vinegar, vanishes from sight. [7] Chalk, in fact, is a compound of carbonic acid gas, and lime, and when you make it very hot the carbonic acid flies away and the lime is left.

This paragraph is fully developed and unified. But a careful reader might notice a certain jerkiness in its development. Rereading, he would observe that the sequence of ideas in the paragraph is as follows:

1. A statement about a specific experiment — burning.
2. A statement about other experiments.
3. A conclusion drawn from all experiments.
4. A second statement about burning.
5. A statement about a specific experiment — dissolving.
6. A second statement about that experiment.
7. Another statement essentially about burning.

He would then understand what had bothered him on first reading: the author should have grouped the statements about burning in the first part of the paragraph, those about dissolving in the second part, and finally should have drawn the general conclusion about all such experiments. This is exactly what T. H. Huxley did in the paragraph from which our scrambled version was taken.

> We all know that if we "burn" chalk the result is quick-lime. Chalk, in fact, is a compound of carbonic acid gas, and lime, and when you make it very hot the carbonic acid flies away and the lime is left. By this method of procedure we see the lime, but we do not see the carbonic acid. If, on the other hand, you were to powder a little chalk and drop it into a good deal of strong vinegar, there would be a great bubbling and fizzing, and, finally, a clear liquid, in which no sign of chalk would appear. Here you see the carbonic acid in the bubbles; the lime, dissolved in the vinegar, vanishes from sight. There are a great many other ways of showing that chalk is essentially nothing but carbonic acid and quick-lime. Chemists enunciate the result of all the experiments that prove this, by stating that chalk is almost wholly composed of "carbonate of lime."[6]

Order in a paragraph is like organization in an essay, but because the paragraph is smaller in scope, it may be simpler to consider order as *direction*. We shall therefore discuss it in terms of five directional patterns: (1) from one time to the next, (2) from one space to an adjoining space, (3) from particular statements to a general statement or conclusion, (4) from a general statement to particular statements, and (5) from question to answer or from effect to cause.

Time. A time, or chronological, order is natural for narration and is commonly used in explaining the steps in a process. Events are recorded in the order in which they occur — first, second, next, and so on. Thus if you were telling a story, or giving directions on how to reach a certain destination or how to bake a cake, the natural order would be a time order. Here is an illustration:

[6] From Thomas Henry Huxley, "A Piece of Chalk."

Imagine, for a moment, that you have drunk from a magician's goblet. Reverse the irreversible stream of time. Go down the dark stairwell out of which the race has ascended. Find yourself at last on the bottommost steps of time, slipping, sliding, and wallowing by scale and fin down into the muck and ooze out of which you arose. Pass by grunts and voiceless hissings below the last tree ferns. Eyeless and earless, float in the primal waters, sense sunlight you cannot see and stretch absorbing tentacles toward vague tastes that float in water. Still, in your formless shiftings, the *you* remains: the sliding particles, the juices, the transformations are working in an exquisitely patterned rhythm which has no other purpose than your preservation — you, the entity, the ameboid being whose substance contains the unfathomable future. Even so does every man come upward from the waters of his birth.[7]

In this paragraph the normal chronological sequence is reversed, since the author is tracing the path of evolution backward from the present.

Space. A space order is useful when the writer wishes to report what he sees. The movement of the paragraph thus follows the movement of his eyes. That movement must have some continuity which a reader can recognize and follow. It need not start at the far left and move steadily to the far right, or vice versa, since in any view an observer's gaze is likely to be drawn quickly to the most conspicuous object. But there should be some logical or natural progression from one descriptive detail to the next. Notice that the following paragraph begins with a front view of the station buildings. Then, after describing their roofs and identifying the separate buildings, it focuses on the hut, and moves from the outside to the inside, which is the sequence a traveler would follow in approaching and entering the hut.

The station buildings were long, low huts, made of sun-dried, mud-colored bricks, laid up without mortar (*adobes,* the Spaniards call these bricks, and the Americans shorten it to *'dobies*). The roofs, which had no slant to them worth speaking of, were thatched and then sodded or covered with a thick layer of earth, and from this sprung a pretty rank growth of weeds and grass. It was the first time we had ever seen a man's front yard on top of his house. The buildings consisted of barns, stable-room for twelve or fifteen horses, and a hut for an eating-room for passengers. This latter had bunks in it for the station-keeper and a hostler or two. You could rest your elbows on its eaves, and you had to bend to get in at the door. In place of a window there was a square hole about large enough for a man to crawl through, but this had no glass in it. There was no flooring, but the ground was packed hard. There was no stove, but the fireplace served all needful purposes. There were no shelves, no cupboards, no closets. In the corner stood an open sack of flour, and nestling against its base were a couple of black and venerable tin coffee-pots, a tin tea-pot, a little bag of salt, and a side of bacon.[8]

7 From Loren Eiseley, *The Immense Journey* (New York: Random House, 1957).
8 From Samuel L. Clemens, *Roughing It.*

Particular to General. A common order in expository paragraphs is from a succession of particular statements to the general statement or conclusion to which the particulars lead. Huxley used this order (page 115) when he began a paragraph by describing an experiment which shows that chalk contains lime, related a second experiment to show that chalk also contains carbonic acid, and finally stated the conclusion that chalk is composed of carbonate of lime. By this order the reader is led to the conclusion through details of evidence or illustration.

A paragraph so organized will have the topic sentence at or near the end. Notice how the author of the following paragraph leads up to his topic sentence, "Logic is fun."

> If you enjoy working out the strategy of games, tit-tat-toe or poker or chess; if you are interested in the frog who jumped up three feet and fell back two in getting out of a well, or in the fly buzzing between the noses of two approaching cyclists, or in the farmer who left land to his three sons; if you have been captivated by codes and ciphers or are interested in crossword puzzles; if you like to fool around with numbers; if music appeals to you by the sense of form which it expresses — then you will enjoy logic. You ought to be warned, perhaps. Those who take up logic get glassy-eyed and absent-minded. They join a fanatical cult. But they have a good time. Theirs is one of the most durable, absorbing and inexpensive of pleasures. *Logic is fun.*[9]

General to Particular. The most popular order for expository paragraphs is just the reverse of the one above. It begins with a general statement, then moves to particulars which explain or illustrate, or persuade the reader to accept the generalization. In effect, the topic sentence at or near the beginning of the paragraph is an introductory summary of the content. That sentence may be followed by one or more explanatory statements which help to make its meaning clear. Then the paragraph proceeds with a number of specific examples or supporting details which illustrate the meaning of the topic sentence. This in small compass is the illustrative pattern you saw in Chapter 3 (pages 57–62). The following paragraph begins with a topic sentence, explains that sentence in general terms in the second sentence, and follows with a number of illustrations.

> Seven is supposedly one of the most powerful numbers. Wherever superstition involving numbers exists — and that includes the entire world — seven plays a prominent part. In East India, for instance, the natives refuse to work six days and rest the seventh. They believe that would be calamitous. Instead, they rest on the eighth day, missionaries notwithstanding. To the Hebrews seven was a sacred number. The Bible is full of the number seven. God made the earth in six days and rested on the seventh. Likewise, "there were seven years of plenty, and seven years of famine; Jacob served Laban seven years for Leah and seven for Rachael, and his

[9] From Roger W. Holmes, *The Rhyme of Reason* (New York: Appleton-Century, 1939).

children mourned for him seven days at his death. There was a whole complex of sevens involved in the fall of Jericho — on the seventh day the city was encompassed seven times by seven priests bearing seven trumpets. Balaam demanded seven altars, with seven bullocks and seven rams; Elijah sent his servant seven times to look for rain; and Elisha healed Naaman of leprosy by making him wash seven times in Jordan. Later we find Jesus casting out seven demons from Mary, speaking seven words from the cross, and commanding his followers to forgive their enemies, not seven times, but seventy times seven." The Greeks, too, considered seven lucky as did (and do) many other races. Our week is based on this same belief in the potency of the number seven.

For the reader, this general-to-particular order has the great advantage of announcing the topic at the beginning, making it easy to see the relation of each new sentence to the topic. For the writer, it has the advantage of holding his purpose clearly before him so that he is less likely to introduce irrelevant material or wander away from his point.

Two variations of this general-to-particular order deserve notice. The first is the paragraph that not only begins but also ends with a general statement. Until the last sentence, such a paragraph follows a general-to-particular order; then the topic idea is restated, usually in different words, as a concluding sentence.

> *Most disputes about whether or not men are stronger than women are meaningless because the disputants fail to consider that the word "stronger" may mean many things.* Most men can surpass most women in lifting heavy weights, in striking an object (say a baseball or an opponent's jaw), in running, jumping, or doing heavy physical labor. But the statistics indicate that most women live longer than most men, that they have a better chance of resisting disease, that they can beat men at operations requiring finger-dexterity and the ability to work accurately under monotonous conditions. On this kind of evidence it would be legitimate to argue that women are stronger than men. The truth is that each sex can surpass the other in certain kinds of activities. *To say that one is stronger than the other is to indulge in an argument which would not arise if the word "stronger" were more sharply defined.*

A second variation is the paragraph which deliberately reverses its movement. It usually begins with a topic sentence that states or implies a qualification or a contrast. The first half of the paragraph develops one phase of the idea, and the second half qualifies what has been said. Usually the point of reversal is indicated by a transitional connective such as *but, on the other hand, nevertheless, still,* or *yet.* For example:

> *The statement that the German people were ultimately responsible for the war is a half-truth which encourages a convenient oversimplification.* It is true that Hitler was the constitutionally appointed leader of the German nation and that, despite individual protests, his policies, as long as they were successful, had the approval, or at least the acquiescence, of the German voters. *But* in the world in which we live no man, no nation causes war.

To fix any ultimate responsibility for World War II we must go beyond Hitler and the Nazi ideology; we must look before Munich and the invasion of Poland. And the farther we look the more clearly we will see that the roots of war were world-wide, and that no nation was guiltless of nourishing them.

The italicized topic sentence suggests that (1) the German people were responsible for the war, (2) other people were also responsible. The next sentence supports the suggestion of German guilt. Then at the transitional *But* the paragraph reverses itself and moves toward the conclusion that all nations were responsible for the war.

A word of caution is necessary about this kind of paragraph movement. In the hands of an inexperienced writer, a reversed paragraph may easily become disunified, and may end, like the one on pages 113–114, by saying the opposite of what the author intended. To be successful, the reversal must be deliberate. The author must be aware at the outset that he intends to qualify his opening statement within the paragraph, and the topic sentence should be phrased to reveal that intention. Otherwise, it will often be safer to break the paragraph in two at the point of transition. For example:

> The statement that the German people were ultimately responsible for the war is a half-truth which encourages a convenient oversimplification. It is true that Hitler was the constitutionally appointed leader of the German nation and that, despite individual protests, his policies, as long as they were successful, had the approval, or at least the acquiescence, of the German voters.
>
> But in the world in which we live no man, no nation causes war. To fix any ultimate responsibility for World War II we must go beyond Hitler and the Nazi ideology; we must look before Munich and the invasion of Poland. And the farther we look the more clearly we will see that the roots of war were world-wide, and that no nation was guiltless of nourishing them.

Question to Answer, Effect to Cause. Less common is the paragraph that begins with a question and gives the answer, or begins with an effect and moves toward the cause. Such a paragraph may have no explicit topic sentence, since the answer or the cause is given by the paragraph as a whole. But the opening question, problem, or dilemma announces the purpose of the paragraph clearly if implicitly.

Here is a paragraph that moves from question to answer:

> Once while talking on this subject to a group of Americans who were going overseas, one very nice, exceedingly mild-mannered woman raised her hand and said, "You mean it's natural for me to feel irritated when another woman takes over my kitchen?" *Answer:* "Not only is it natural, but most American women have very strong feelings about their kitchens. Even a mother can't come in and wash the dishes in her daughter's kitchen without annoying her. The kitchen is the place where 'who will dominate?' is

settled. All women know this, and some can even talk about it. Daughters who can't keep control of their kitchen will be forever under the thumb of any woman who can move into this area."[10]

The following paragraph moves from effect to cause. The effect is the application by the bakers of London for an increase in the price of bread. The cause for this request is developed in the supporting details of their costs incurred.

In the year 1619 the bakers of London applied to the authorities for an increase in the price of bread. They sent in support of their claim a complete description of a bakery and an account of its weekly costs. There were thirteen or fourteen people in such an establishment: the baker and his wife, four paid employees who were called journeymen, two apprentices, two maidservants and the three or four children of the master baker himself. Six pounds ten shillings a week was reckoned to be the outgoings of this establishment of which only eleven shillings and eightpence went for wages: half a crown a week for each of the journeymen and tenpence for each of the maids. Far and away the greatest cost was for food: two pounds nine shillings out of the six pounds ten shillings, at five shillings a head for the baker and his wife, four shillings a head for their helpers and two shillings for their children. It cost much more in food to keep a journeyman than it cost in money; four times as much to keep a maid. Clothing was charged up too, not only for the man, wife and children, but for the apprentices as well. Even school fees were claimed as a justifiable charge on the price of bread for sale, and it cost sixpence a week for the teaching and clothing of a baker's child.[11]

The table on the opposite page summarizes the types of paragraph movement we have discussed.

Coherence

Literally, the word *cohere* means to hold together. A paragraph is said to have coherence when its sentences are woven together or flow into each other. If a paragraph is coherent, the reader moves easily from one sentence to the next without feeling that there are gaps in the thought, puzzling jumps, or points not made. If a paragraph lacks coherence, the reader will feel that the sentence, not the paragraph, is the unit of writing, and that he is reading a collection of separate statements rather than an integrated discussion.

Coherence Within the Paragraph. A paragraph which lacks unity or orderly movement will not be coherent, since a reader cannot move easily from one sentence to the next if the second sentence has no clear

[10] From Edward T. Hall, *The Silent Language* (New York: Doubleday and Company, 1959).
[11] From Peter Laslett, *The World We Have Lost* (London: Methuen, 1965).

SOME TYPES OF PARAGRAPH MOVEMENT

Time order

(A chain of events recorded in the order in which they occurred. Paragraph begins with the first event and ends with the last one. Usually no topic sentence.)

Event 1
Event 2
Event 3, and so on.

Space order

(Sentences in paragraph move from one area to the next as these are viewed, in turn, by the writer. Movement may be in any direction but must be easy to follow. Usually no topic sentence.)

Left-right, front-rear, up-down, or any logical movement from one space to the next.

Particular to general

(From a series of explanatory or illustrative statements to the conclusion drawn from them. Topic sentence at or near end of paragraph.)

Details leading up to concluding topic sentence.

General to particular

(From general statement to supporting details which explain, illustrate, or prove it. Topic sentence at or near beginning of paragraph.)

Conclusion or general statement followed by details of explanation or proof.

(*Variation 1.* Topic sentence restated as conclusion at end of paragraph.)

Details

(*Variation 2.* Topic sentence implies qualification or contrast which requires paragraph to develop first one phase then the other of topic sentence. Point of reversal indicated by transitional connective: *but, yet, still, on the other hand.*)

point of reversal

Question-answer, Effect-cause

(Paragraph begins with question or effect, then answers the question or shows the cause. Usually no topic sentence.)

Question or effect

Answer or cause

relation to the first. But coherence is not simply a matter of unity and consistent order. Consider the following paragraph:

[1] I was accepted and started work. [2] My experience had been derived chiefly from books. [3] I was not prepared for the difficult period of adjustment. [4] I soon became discouraged with myself and so dissatisfied with my job that I was on the point of quitting. [5] My employer must have sensed this. [6] He called me into his office and talked to me about the duties of my position and the opportunities for advancement. [7] I realized that there was nothing wrong with me or the job and I decided to stay.

This paragraph is fairly complete, it is unified, its development is orderly; yet it is a poor paragraph. The writer's ideas do not flow from one sentence to the next. Rather, they seem to come out in a series of jolts and jerks, because the connecting links between them are not expressed. The sentences are not knitted together; the reader is forced to tackle each one separately, and in hunting the connections he loses the flow and continuity which a more carefully constructed paragraph would provide.

Now look at the same paragraph slightly altered:

I was accepted, and started work. *Until that time* my experience had been derived chiefly from books, *and unfortunately* those books had not prepared me for the difficult period of adjustment *that every inexperienced secretary must face in a new position. Consequently* I soon became *so* discouraged with myself and so dissatisfied with the job that I was on the point of quitting. *I think* my employer must have sensed this, *for* he called me into his office and talked to me about *both* the duties of my position and the opportunities *it offered* for advancement. *That talk helped me considerably. From then on,* I realized that there was nothing wrong with me or the job *that experience could not cure,* and I decided to stay.

The second version is distinctly better than the first, and if you read both aloud, the difference between them will be still more obvious. Why? The content is substantially the same, the diction is scarcely changed, and the second version is only slightly more fully developed than the first. The general answer is that the second paragraph is more coherent because the author has provided transitions — bridges — between the thoughts expressed in the original sentences. These transitions are created by two means: sometimes by filling a small gap in the thought, thus providing better continuity of statement; sometimes by connecting words and phrases which tie sentences together.

Transition Through Continuity of Thought. A writer who thinks of a paragraph as a unit developing a single topic, who consequently composes a whole paragraph at a time, is not likely to write paragraphs seriously lacking in coherence. Most incoherent passages are a result of thinking in single sentences rather than whole paragraphs. When a writer works that way, he is likely to write one sentence, stop, think a minute, write a second sentence, stop, and continue in a series of spurts and pauses. Paragraphs written this way are almost sure to be weak in coherence, for the writer is starting afresh at every new sentence. He loses the feeling of continuity with the last sentence before he begins the next one. Consequently, he is likely to omit significant links or details of thought and thus leave gaps in his writing.

For example, when the author of the incoherent paragraph above stopped between sentences 1 and 2, she left out a small but important detail of her thought. She was contrasting her previous experience with her new one and she needed somewhere to make the point that *now* her experience was changing. In the revised version the phrase "Until that time" supplies the clue. Similarly, when she wrote that she was not prepared "for the difficult period of adjustment," she had in mind a particular adjustment, the kind that must be made "in a new position." But her original statement omitted that link in her thought. Again, she skipped a thought between sentences 6 and 7. She was helped by her talk with her employer. By failing to record that fact, she ran the talk and its result too closely together. In the revised paragraph the italicized sentence provides the missing detail and thus gives a fuller statement of what she meant. Finally, she omitted a necessary idea in her last sentence. There *was* something wrong with her, but nothing "that experience could not cure." The revision, by providing these omitted details, more thoroughly reflects all that was in the writer's mind.

, *Transition Through Connecting Words and Phrases. (1) Related Sentence Patterns.* A writer who thinks in sentences rather than in paragraphs often finds it hard to keep a consistent grammatical pattern running through a paragraph. In the first version of the example on page 122, the author herself is the subject of five sentences and her employer the subject of the other two. The following example is much less consistent:

> Although writing a research paper is a difficult assignment, many students make it more difficult than it need be because of inefficient work habits. The work on the paper is too often postponed until it is too late to do a decent job of it. Failure to find out at the beginning of the study whether sufficient material is available in the library often invites serious difficulty. Many students tackle the topic in detail before they have formed a general notion of the topic. It is unwise to begin reading the first book available and to plunge into fine points before the student has learned to understand the topic as a whole. The habit of taking notes too soon is inefficient. Students should postpone note-taking until they have decided what kind of information they need. It is also a mistake to quote a paragraph in its entirety. The notes should consist of the factual information taken from the paragraph.

Because this paragraph was obviously developed one sentence at a time, the writer failed to maintain any consistent point of view toward his material. He changes from active to passive voice, from a personal to an impersonal subject, and he uses seven different subjects for the nine sentences of his paragraph. As a result there is no grammatical consistency within the paragraph, and it reads as jerkily as it was composed.

Notice the improvement in this version:

> Although writing a research paper is a difficult assignment, many students make it more difficult than it need be because of inefficient working habits. Too often they postpone work on the paper until it is too late to do a respectable job of it. Often they invite avoidable difficulty by failure to find out at the beginning of their study whether sufficient material is available in the library. Instead of developing a general notion of the topic before tackling it in detail, they begin with the first convenient book and plunge into fine points before they see the topic as a whole. They take more notes than are necessary because they begin to take notes before they have decided what kind of information they need, and because they do not pick out the factual information in a paragraph but quote the paragraph in its entirety.

The biggest change here is that the noun *students* or its pronoun *they* has been made the subject of every sentence. This not only eliminates unnecessary and awkward shifting but allows the writer's purpose to develop easily and steadily through successive sentences.

It is of course not necessary that every sentence in a paragraph have the same subject. Changes of subject within a paragraph are often necessary or wise. But when arbitrary changes destroy coherence, revision to avoid these shifts will often greatly improve the paragraph.

Sentences with a repetitive pattern help bind a paragraph together. Once a reader senses the pattern, which he does from his knowledge of sentence structure, he follows that pattern until the punctuation signals that it is finished. The pattern becomes a kind of tune which the reader picks up and follows. This is especially true when the structure of the sentence consists of parallel parts. Notice the cohesiveness of the parallel structure running through the following paragraph.

Topic sentence	This failure to see the over-all pattern is also true of the first few weeks in college. Then everything is so new that
Clarifying statement	we are aware only of individual experiences, not of the pattern of these experiences. We move into a new home, live
Series of predicates with a common subject, "we"	with strangers, try to find our way around an unfamiliar campus, make decisions we never had to make before, plan academic programs we do not understand, go through a registration process that baffles and frustrates us at every step, listen to lectures which seemed logical as they moved from one sentence to the next but defy reconstruction from our notes, or struggle with assignments which seemed clear when announced but grow increasingly vague as we work on them. In all these activities we lack a sense of relation-
Restatement of topic sentence	ship; we do not see how things fit together; so for a few days or a few weeks we live in a world of unrelated events to which we cannot give any cohesive shape.

Here the opening sentence announces the topic idea of the paragraph. The second sentence explains the first, but still in a general way. The third consists of the subject "We" followed by a series of actions which specify the meaning of the first two sentences and illustrate the idea of the paragraph. The fourth sums up what has been said and thus completes the structure initiated in the first two. The whole paragraph is like a sandwich which enfolds the specific details of the third sentence between the sentences that precede and follow it. The parallelism of the elements in the third sentence holds the paragraph together.

(2) Pronoun Reference. Since a pronoun refers to an antecedent, the use of a pronoun in one sentence to point back to an antecedent in the sentence before is a simple and natural connecting device. Notice how the alternating use of pronoun and antecedent provides effective transitions in the following sentences:

There's more to a bluejay than any other creature. He has got more moods, and more different kinds of feelings than other creatures; and, mind you, whatever a bluejay feels, he can put into language.[12]

The use of pronouns often allows a writer to keep his subject running through the paragraph without falling into monotonous repetition. Notice how this is done in the following paragraph, in which nominative, possessive, and objective forms of the same pronoun bind the sentences together by inconspicuous repetition.

He was a monster of conceit. Never for one moment did he look at the world or at people, except in relation to himself. He was not only the most important person in the world, to himself; in his own eyes he was the only person who existed. He believed himself to be one of the greatest dramatists in the world, one of the greatest thinkers, and one of the greatest composers. To hear him talk, he was Shakespeare, and Beethoven, and Plato rolled into one. . . .[13]

(3) Transitional Markers. These are words or phrases placed at or near the beginning of a sentence or clause to signal the relationship between the new sentence and the one before it. The commonest markers are the simple connectives *and, or, nor, but, for,* which serve as bridges over which the reader may easily pass from one sentence or clause to the next. Others — sometimes called transitional connectives — indicate the direction which the new sentence is about to take and so prepare the reader for what is to follow. The commonest transitional connectives may be classified as follows:

1. To introduce an illustration: *thus, for example, for instance, to illustrate.*

[12] From Samuel L. Clemens, "Baker's Blue-jay Yarn."
[13] A description of Richard Wagner, from Deems Taylor, *Of Men and Music* (New York: Simon and Schuster, 1937).

2. To add another phase of the same idea: *secondly, in the second place, next, moreover, in addition, similarly, again, also, finally.*

3. To point a contrast or qualification: *on the other hand, nevertheless, despite this fact, on the contrary, still, however.*

4. To indicate a conclusion or result: *therefore, in conclusion, to sum up, consequently, as a result, accordingly, in other words.*

The following paragraph uses various transitional devices:

> The good educator is very serious but also very sensible. And somewhere in his soul there is a saving lightness. He understands, to begin with, the meaning of a recent remark: "Not everything can be learned." Some things are never taught; they are simply known. Other things cannot in the nature of things be known, either by student or by teacher. And then there is that endless series of knowable things only a few of which can be bestowed upon the student during the fragment of his life he spends in school.[14]

The transitional devices in this paragraph are the connectives *And* and *And then,* the pronouns *he* and *his* pointing back to the antecedent *educator,* and the connecting relationship between the words *everything, Some things,* and *Other things.* Still a subtler linking is achieved by the words *learned . . . taught . . . known . . . knowable.*

Here is another example:

	In a world in which the leaders of war democracies are the Daladiers and Chamberlains and Churchills, *we*
Deliberate repetition	*have reason to be proud of* Lincoln. *We have reason to be proud* that *with every opportunity* of setting up a dictatorship, he *did not succumb; with every opportunity*
Deliberate repetition	of betraying democratic values under the guise of war necessity, he *did not succumb. . . .* I have no intention of saying that Lincoln was wholly consistent in the strength of his humanism. . . . Yet there never was a time when
Interconnection of pronouns and antecedents	it was more important for us than now to know the capacity of a democracy to turn up *greatness* of Lincoln's sort from its humblest sons — a *greatness* that will survive the grime and savagery of war.[15]

All the transitional devices we have discussed are used in this paragraph. Lincoln, although his name is seldom the actual subject of a sentence, is referred to in almost every sentence and thus gives the paragraph a continuity of subject; the pronoun references help tie the

[14] From Mark Van Doren, *Liberal Education* (New York: Holt, 1943).

[15] From Max Lerner's review of Carl Sandburg's *Abraham Lincoln: The War Years,* in *New Republic,* December 6, 1939.

paragraph together; the purposeful repetition of similar phrasing in the first half of the paragraph strengthens the coherence; and the transitional connective *Yet* links the last sentence with the one preceding it.

Coherence Between Paragraphs. We have been thinking of the single paragraph as a unit. But it is, of course, only one of several units in the larger scheme of the whole paper. Just as there should be coherence *within* the paragraph, so there should be coherence *between* paragraphs.

In a well-organized essay developing a thesis, the relationship between paragraphs will be clear, for the reader will be following the thesis, and, especially if the topic sentence appears at the beginning of each paragraph, he will have no trouble seeing the relationship of each new paragraph to what has gone before. For example, each main unit of the outline on reducing the voting age (page 92) clearly referred to the thesis and so established the continuity of the essay.

Relating each topic sentence to the thesis creates the effect of "signposting" each paragraph, of informing the reader in advance what each is going to do, what part of the thesis it is going to develop. Such signposts serve the double purpose of setting off each paragraph as a structural unit of the essay and providing transitions between paragraphs.

The following selection illustrates the use of a variety of transitional devices: repetition of key words, pronoun references, references to events recorded in a preceding paragraph, keeping a common subject running through a paragraph, repetition of a significant idea either within a paragraph or among several paragraphs, and restatement of the thesis. All these devices tend to weave individual sentences into a unified composition.

Repetition of "city" keeps emphasis on Hamburg, which is the subject of this paragraph

[1] On three nights late in July and at the beginning of August 1943, the heavy planes of the RAF Bomber Command droned in from the North Sea and subjected the city of Hamburg to an ordeal such as Germans had not experienced since the Thirty Years' War. A third of the city was reduced to a wasteland. At least 60,000 and perhaps as many as 100,000 people were killed — about as many as at Hiroshima. A large number of these were lost one night when a ghastly "fire storm," which literally burned the asphalt pavements, swept a part of the city and swept everything into itself. Adolf Hitler heard the details of the attack and for the only known time during the war said it might be necessary to sue for peace. Hermann Goering visited the city with a retinue to survey the damage and was accorded so disconcerting a reception that he deemed it discreet to retire.

Points contrast with preceding paragraph

[2] Yet this terrible event taught a lesson about the economics of war which very few have learned and some, indeed, may have found it convenient to ignore. The in-

Reference to the bombing in previous paragraph

Pronoun references

Reference to "three nights" of first sentence in paragraph 1

Signals addition to what has been said

Reference to paragraph 1

Transition to content of paragraph 2

Pronoun references

Contrast with paragraphs 1 and 2

Repetition of "essential," a key term

dustrial plants of Hamburg were around the edge of the city or, as in the case of the submarine pens, on the harbor. They were not greatly damaged by the raids; these struck the center of the city and the working class residential areas and suburbs. In the days immediately following the raids production faltered; in the first weeks it was down by as much as 20 or 25 per cent. But thereafter it returned to normal. By then the workers had scanned the ruins of their former homes, satisfied themselves that their possessions and sometimes their families were irretrievable, had found some rude clothes and the shelter of a room or part of a room in a still habitable house, and had returned to work. On these three nights of terror their standard of living, measured by houseroom, furnishings, clothing, food and drink, recreation, schools, and social and cultural opportunities, had been reduced to a fraction of what it had been before. But the efficiency of the worker as a worker was unimpaired by this loss. After a slight period of readjustment, he labored as diligently and as skillfully as before.

[3] There is a further chapter to the story. Before the attacks, there had been a labor shortage in Hamburg. Afterward, despite the number killed and the number now engaged on indispensable repairs, there was no shortage. For, as a result of the attacks, thousands who were waiters in restaurants and cafés, attendants in garages, clerks in banks, salesmen in stores, shopkeepers, janitors, ticket takers, and employees in handicraft industries (which, being small and traditional, were more likely to be in the center of town) lost their places of employment. They had previously contributed nothing to war production. Their contribution to the standard of living proved dispensable. Now they turned to the war industries as the most plausible places to find employment.

[4] Even in the presumptively austere and dedicated world of the Third Reich, in the third year of a disastrous war, the average citizen had access to a wide range of comforts and amenities which habit had made to seem essential. And because they were believed to be essential they were essential. On such matters governments, even dictatorships, must bow to the convictions of the people even if — the exceptional case — they do not share them. The German standard of living was far above what was physically necessary for survival and efficiency. The RAF broke through the psychological encrustation and brought

"In doing so" connects last two sentences in paragraph

living standards down somewhere nearer to the physical minimum. (In doing so) it forced a wholesale conversion of Germany's scarcest resource, that of manpower, to war production.

Restatement of thesis which was first stated at beginning of paragraph 2

[5] In reducing, as nothing else could, the consumption of nonessentials and the employment of men in their supply, there is a distinct possibility that the (attacks on Hamburg) increased Germany's output of war material and thus her military effectiveness.[16]

Comb. of old + new

Transitional Paragraphs. Occasionally a whole short paragraph may serve as a transition. Such a paragraph always comes at a point where the author has finished one main unit of his composition and is about to start another. The transitional paragraph may be used in several ways. It may sum up what has been said before beginning the next unit. It may introduce one or more illustrations of a point already made. Or it may state what the writer intends to do next. The following paragraphs illustrate these uses.

To sum up before beginning the next unit:

Before we begin to analyze the merits of this proposal, let us review what we have already established. We have shown that the proposed program has several times been offered to the American people and has always been rejected. We have shown that its proponents have attempted to manufacture a need which does not exist. We have further shown that the program is being advocated by diverse groups which have nothing in common except a conviction that what is best for their special interests must also be best for the country.

To introduce a series of illustrations:

The point that I have been making is necessarily abstract. In order to make it more concrete, let me cite three illustrations, all of which are drawn from common experience.

To show what the writer intends to do next:

Now, you may admit all these things and yet inquire what can be done about them without sacrificing values that have become precious to us all. Since I realize that this question is a just one, I shall outline briefly the organization of the University of Utopia. It will be seen that not all the features of this university are new and original. At Wisconsin, Harvard, Swarthmore, and numerous other places, many phases of its plan have been tried and have succeeded. Much of the rest of the program has been under discussion at the University of Chicago and elsewhere for some years.[17]

[16] From John Kenneth Galbraith, *The Affluent Society* (Boston: Houghton Mifflin Company, 1958).

[17] From R. M. Hutchins, "The University of Utopia," *Yale Review,* March, 1931.

These transitional paragraphs connect what has gone before with what is to follow. Each is a sort of aside to the reader in which the writer shows the relations between parts of his work. The transitional paragraph, then, links larger units as a transitional word or phrase connects sentences or paragraphs.

CONSTRUCTING EFFECTIVE PARAGRAPHS

As a practical application of what we have been saying, let us take three assignments and work them out as finished paragraphs. For each we shall first state the problem, then analyze it, and finally present one possible solution.

A

A student is preparing a paper with the thesis that Thomas Jefferson's writings are characterized by habits of careful research and independent thinking. As one illustration of the thesis she wants to cite Jefferson's work, *The Life and Morals of Jesus of Nazareth*. Here is the material she has in her notes.

1. T. J. pasted Greek, Latin, French, and English texts of New Testament side by side.
2. T. J. thought the Bible should be read critically, like any other book.
3. T. J. accepted or rejected stories about Jesus on the basis of their agreement with natural laws. Thus the teachings of Jesus OK, but miracles out. Anything that had to be explained by revelation also out.
4. "I think that every Christian sect gives a great handle to atheism by their general dogma that, without revelation, there would not be sufficient proof of the being of God" — Letter to Adams
5. T. J. considered Christianity purest system of morality known.

If this student simply strings these notes together to look like a paragraph (as students sometimes do), this is the kind of product she will have:

Jefferson could read Greek, Latin, French, and English, so he pasted texts of the New Testament in these languages side by side. He thought that the Bible should be read critically, like any other book; so he accepted those stories about Jesus which agreed with natural laws, and rejected those that did not. He kept the teachings of Jesus but rejected the miracles. He also rejected anything that had to be explained by revelation. "I think," he wrote in a letter to Adams, "that every Christian sect gives a great handle to atheism by their general dogma that, without revelation, there would not be sufficient proof of the being of God." Jefferson considered Christianity the purest system of morality known.

Notice the weaknesses of this paragraph:

1. Although it discusses a book mentioned in a preceding paragraph, it does nothing to show a relation with that paragraph or any other. It needs some transitional sentence or phrase to tie it to what went before.

2. What is the purpose of the paragraph? We know from the description of the assignment that the writer wants to illustrate Jefferson's habits of careful research and independent thinking. The information does illustrate these habits, but its significance would be made clearer if stated in a topic sentence.

3. While the repetition of "He" provides some natural coherence within the paragraph, pronoun reference alone is not enough. The monotonous sentence structure and the lack of transition between the first two sentences and between the last two leave the paragraph merely a loose collection of sentences.

4. The last sentence seems to have no relation to the rest of the paragraph. If it is not a digression, its function should be indicated.

Now contrast the unsatisfactory paragraph with the one the student wrote:

> The actual writing of the book was controlled by two disciplines: careful collection and comparison of the evidence, and the acceptance or rejection of it on the basis of reason rather than authority. To compare the evidence, Jefferson pasted texts from the New Testament in Greek, Latin, French, and English in columns side by side. As he was proficient in all four languages he felt that he could come closer to the true meanings of the words by reading them in this way. To ensure that reason rather than the authority of tradition would guide him, he followed his own advice that the Bible should be read critically, like any other book. Accordingly, he accepted those stories which revealed the teachings of Jesus, and rejected stories of miracles, which, he felt, had no real relation to these teachings. He also rejected those passages which had to be supported by revelation. "I think," he wrote in a letter to Adams, "that every Christian sect gives a great handle to atheism by their general dogma that, without revelation, there would not be sufficient proof of the being of God." The result was a work which emphasized what Jefferson considered the purest system of morality known and toned down or omitted incidents which required a supernatural explanation.

Notice:

1. The topic sentence, which states the purpose of the paragraph (and so gives point to all that follows) and also refers to the preceding paragraph by the phrase "The actual writing of the book."

2. The explanation of why Jefferson pasted the four different texts side by side. This explanation is necessary to illustrate the thoroughness of his working habits.

3. The clearer explanation of his selection and rejection of material ("To ensure that reason rather than authority . . ."). This explanation helps to bind together four sentences which, in the unsatisfactory version, were connected only by a common subject.

4. The concluding sentence, which not only shows the pertinence of what previously looked like a digression but also, by showing Jefferson's emphasis, sums up the content of the whole paragraph.

5. The more pleasing effect obtained by slight but significant variations in the basic sentence pattern.

6. Finally, the fact that in shaping her notes into a paragraph the writer was doing a creative piece of composition. She was making something from her material, giving form to the information she had acquired, not just presenting it unedited.

B

A student has been asked to write a paragraph on democracy. In thinking about that subject he recognizes certain advantages of democracy and certain difficulties, which he jots down in contrasting columns.

Advantages	*Difficulties*
1. freedom of speech	1. responsibility to be well informed about all pertinent matters
2. freedom to think as he pleases	
3. freedom to worship (or not to worship) as he pleases	2. responsibility to evaluate conflicting policies and sense their effects on the future
4. the right and opportunity to engage in whatever work he chooses	3. distinction between interests of special groups and general welfare
	4. conflict between rights of majority and rights of minority

He wants to organize this material into a unified, coherent, and well-developed paragraph. How should he proceed?

One way would be to begin with a topic sentence which states that democracy has both advantages and difficulties and then list first the advantages and then the difficulties. If he does that, the paragraph will not advance beyond the notes. It will simply present the notes in paragraph form.

Another way would be to tie each advantage to a disadvantage under a topic sentence which says that, for every advantage it offers, democracy imposes a corresponding difficulty. The pattern of development in this method would be similar to the $A/B + A/B$ structure discussed in Chapter 3. This method will not prove to be practical, because the advantages and the difficulties do not *correspond* — that is, there is no clear relation between any one advantage and any one difficulty, and so the contrast would seem arbitrary.

A third way is to recognize that the opposite of "difficult" is "easy," and to organize the material under a topic sentence which says that democracy is both the easiest and most difficult form of government, and then to present the material which makes democracy seem easy before the material which makes it seem difficult. The student tries this method and writes the following paragraph.

Democracy is both the easiest and most difficult form of government for the citizen. It is the easiest because it allows people to speak and think and worship as they please and to engage in whatever occupations they think they are most fitted for. It is the most difficult because it requires them to be well informed about all political matters and to evaluate conflicting policies, not only for their immediate results but also for the effects they will produce in the future. It also requires people to be alert to the conflicts that arise between special interests and the general welfare and between the rights of the majority and the rights of the minority.

This paragraph is acceptable but not effective. Although it organizes the material of the notes in a straightforward manner, the result is not much better than what could have been achieved by the first method. But it will serve for a first draft. The student's problem now is to consider how it can be improved in revision. As he studies the paragraph, he makes the following notes to himself:

1. Change "people" to "the citizen" or "the individual" or "a man" so as to present the argument from the point of view of one person rather than of many and thus personalize the argument.
2. Get more contrast between the two parts of the paragraph by introducing the idea that the characteristics of democracy that make it easy for a man are not free; they have to be paid for by the difficulties.
3. Point up each half of the paragraph by a sentence that acts as a topic sentence for each half. This will tend to tie particular statements together.
4. Try to make more use of parallel structure in presenting particular difficulties. This will provide both greater coherence and greater emphasis.
5. The paragraph as now written is still pretty general. Try to provide more specific development in the revision, especially for the third sentence.

In accordance with his own directive to himself, he now revises the paragraph as follows:

From the point of view of the ordinary citizen, democracy is both the easiest and most difficult form of government. It is the easiest because it permits each citizen a high degree of freedom. In a democracy, more than in any other form of government, he remains his own man — free to think, talk, and worship as he pleases, and, within wide limits, free to engage in whatever kind of profession or career he is fitted for. Yet these privileges are not purchased without a price. For a democracy makes heavy demands on each citizen. It places upon him the responsibility of being continually informed of the needs not only of his own country but of the whole world. It requires him to weigh and decide which of several conflicting policies will best meet these needs. It demands that he distinguish between the interests of special groups and the general welfare, and between immediate and long-range interests. It insists that he learn to observe the will of the majority without ignoring the rights of minorities. And it constantly requires of him the difficult task of seeing the implications of economic, political, and social theories and of sensing the effect that these implications will have in the lives of his grandchildren.

One way to describe the difference between the two versions of this paragraph is to say that the style of the second has been improved. Another way is to say that the second provokes a more complete response from the reader and so has more meaning for him. For our purposes, the important thing to recognize is that the writer's job was not finished with the first draft. That draft was still an unfinished product, as most first drafts are.

C

In the play *Antigone,* Polynices, the brother of Antigone and Ismene, is killed while leading a rebellion against the state. Creon, the king, decrees that the corpse shall be denied the burial which the practices of religion require. Ismene accepts this decree but Antigone defies it and buries her brother at the cost of her own life. After reading the play, a student writes an essay containing the following paragraph.

> It is not surprising that Antigone and Ismene react quite differently to Creon's ban on the burial of their brother. Antigone has spent much of her life with death, misfortune, and hardship. It wasn't an easy task, I'm sure, for her to look after her blind father, Oedipus, during the wanderings of his exile, no matter how much she loved him, but during these years she learned a sense of responsibility to one's family which Ismene was not required to learn. Oedipus was constantly talking about the will of the gods and the importance of putting religious duties first. He talked frequently, too, about death as a release from pain. He had a temper that would fly up suddenly and cause him to act impulsively and rashly, without thinking about his own safety. And he despised Creon and his concern with only political considerations. It is only natural that some of this temperament would rub off on Antigone — like father, like daughter — and cause her to defy Creon's order. Ismene has been less influenced by Oedipus. She has been brought up by Creon and taught to obey him.

In a conference the instructor tells him:

> The point you are making is a good one, but this paragraph does not make it as clearly as it might, partly because the paragraph needs tightening up and partly because the structure of the contrast is blurred through making Oedipus the subject of four sentences in the middle of the paragraph. I suggest the following procedure for revision:
>
> 1. Before you begin to write, make two lists, one containing the attitudes or values that Antigone learned from Oedipus, the other containing the attitudes that Ismene learned from Creon. Use these lists as the basic material of your paragraph.
>
> 2. Explain Antigone's background in less space than you now use, without leaving out anything that helps develop your topic sentence. Keep Oedipus in the background. You want to focus on the Antigone-Ismene contrast, and the more attention you give to Oedipus, the more you blur that basic contrast.
>
> 3. Then develop the Ismene side of the contrast; her background can stand more detailed treatment.
>
> 4. It might be wise to work into your topic sentence the idea that the two girls had quite different backgrounds. That is the important point. It is

only because their backgrounds were different that their different reactions are not surprising.

5. Mark the transitional point in the contrast by some transitional device — *But, Yet, On the other hand,* etc.

6. Clinch the idea of the paragraph by restating the topic sentence in new form as a conclusion.

The student studies these directions and rewrites the paragraph as follows:

It is not surprising that Antigone and Ismene react quite differently to Creon's ban on the burial of their brother. The two sisters are products of different experiences. As the constant companion of Oedipus, Antigone has acquired from her father a strong sense of religious and family obligation and a conviction that divine laws take precedence over human laws. She has also learned to subordinate personal considerations of security and happiness to her religious duties. Perhaps she has also acquired something of her father's contempt for Creon as a person and for the narrow political values which he represents. It is natural, therefore, for her to reject Creon's authority when it clashes with her conviction that her brother must be given a burial service. Ismene, by contrast, has been little influenced by her father's religious values. She has grown up safely and securely in Thebes as a member of Creon's household. In her environment the values were political rather than religious, and the emphasis was on unquestioning obedience to political authority, to Creon as the ruler of the state and the ruler of the household. In accepting Creon's decree she merely did what she had been brought up to do. It is not necessary to assume that she loved Polynices less than Antigone did. Given their different backgrounds, it was as natural for Ismene to obey Creon as it was for Antigone to defy him.

Contrast the original and revised versions and decide: (1) whether you agree with the instructor's criticism of the original, (2) whether the student satisfied that criticism in his revision, (3) whether the revised version shows enough improvement to justify the efforts of both the instructor and the student.

Exercises

A. Study the structure of the following paragraphs carefully. Notice, especially, what the purpose of each paragraph is, how that purpose is expressed, what kinds of material are used to develop the purpose, what order the sentences follow, and what means the writer uses to obtain coherence.

(1)

On May 1, the *Nassau Lit* scheduled a banquet of old editors. It was a beautiful spring day, and Stanley Dell, Bishop, Wilson, and Fitzgerald drove down from New York for the occasion. All of them except Dell, who was driving, got a little drunk on the way down. They had set out with the idea of celebrating the spring, and had purchased in New York a supply of gilt laurel wreaths, lyres, and pipes of Pan. When they stopped for a moment outside Princeton on the old Lincoln Highway, Fitzgerald, having entered into the occasion with characteristic enthusiasm, made an ecstatic speech in praise of the spring, Princeton, and his friends. In this state of mind they arrived in Princeton, where they sought out Dean Gauss. They found him on his front lawn, and there crowned him with a laurel wreath, to the accompaniment of extempore verses on the occasion from Fitzgerald. They then separated to go to their various clubs until the banquet that night; the last anyone saw of Fitzgerald was when he went dancing up the walk of Cottage, a laurel wreath askew on his head and the pipes of Pan at his lips. It was, for all its innocence, precisely the image of him that was already in the mind's eye of respectable members of his club. He was quickly approached by the president and told that he was suspended from membership. He went straight to the station and back to New York, as hurt as he had been when, a child of six in Buffalo, he had approached a crowd of children and been told to go away, they did not want him around.[18]

(2)

The hobbits stood now on the brink of a tall cliff, bare and bleak, its feet wrapped in mist; and behind them rose the broken highlands crowned with drifting cloud. A chill wind blew from the East. Night was gathering over the shapeless lands before them; the sickly green of them was fading to a sullen brown. Far away to the right the Anduin, that had gleamed fitfully in sun-breaks during the day, was now hidden in shadow. But their eyes did not look beyond the River, back to Gondor, to their friends, to the lands of Men. South and east they stared to where, at the edge of the oncoming night, a dark line hung, like distant mountains of motionless smoke. Every now and again a tiny red gleam far away flickered upwards on the rim of earth and sky.[19]

(3)

By a strange perversity in the cosmic plan, the biologically good die young. Species are not destroyed for their shortcomings but for their achievements. The tribes that slumber in the graveyards of the past were not the most simple and undistinguished of their day, but the most complicated and conspicuous. The magnificent sharks of the Devonian period passed with the passing of the period, but certain contemporaneous genera of primitive shellfish are still on earth. Similarly, the lizards of the Mesozoic era have long outlived the dinosaurs who were immeasurably their biologic betters. Illustrations such as these could be endlessly increased. The price of distinction is death.[20]

[18] From Arthur Mizener, *The Far Side of Paradise: A Biography of F. Scott Fitzgerald* (Boston: Houghton Mifflin Company, 1951).

[19] From J. R. R. Tolkien, *The Two Towers* (Boston: Houghton Mifflin Company, 1955).

[20] From John Hodgdon Bradley, "Is Man an Absurdity?" *Harper's Magazine,* October, 1936.

(4)

In grading essay questions, I have found that the majority of students do not answer the questions asked. Instead the students try to reproduce everything the examiner has said in his lectures or twist the question to fit the parts of the course they studied for the exam. Each student walks into the exam with a mental set of what the questions will be, and answers accordingly. The answers read like Ponzo's soliloquy in *Waiting for Godot,* words piled on top of one another in a meaningless order, giving the impression of complete irrationality even though the individual words are meaningful. To some extent the student is not to blame for his reaction. He is placed in a stressful situation under pressure of time and in open competition with his fellow students. Often the student is in the dark about what the instructor is looking for. It makes a real difference just who is going to grade the paper. Professor X will be looking for one type of answer, Professor Y for another. Some students react to this with the shotgun approach, hoping that if they cover enough area, some of the shot is bound to hit the mark. The student assumes that he will not be penalized for correct but irrelevant answers. Somehow he feels that the instructor should be grateful for getting more than he asked for. The instructor, who has to *read* the answers, doesn't feel this way at all.[21]

(5)

The hopeful question is sometimes asked, "If insects can become resistant to chemicals, could human beings do the same thing?" Theoretically they could; but since this would take hundreds or even thousands of years, the comfort to those living now is slight. Resistance is not something that develops in an individual. If he possesses at birth some qualities that make him less susceptible than others to poisons he is more likely to survive and produce children. Resistance, therefore, is something that develops in a population after time measured in several or many generations. Human populations reproduce at the rate of roughly three generations per century, but new insect generations arise in a matter of days or weeks.[22]

(6)

The other day I was reading a note about an American artist who was said to have "turned his back on the aesthetic whims and theories of the day, and established headquarters in lower Manhattan." Accompanying this note was a reproduction of a painting called *Wooden Horses.* It is a painting of a merry-go-round, possibly of several of them. One of the horses seems to be prancing. The others are going lickety-split, each one struggling to get the bit in his teeth. The horse in the center of the picture, painted yellow, has two riders, one a man, dressed in a carnival costume, who is seated in the saddle, the other a blonde, who is seated well up the horse's neck. The man has his arms under the girl's arms. He holds himself stiffly in order to keep

[21] From Robert Sommer, *Expertland* (New York: Doubleday and Company, 1963).
[22] From Rachel Carson, *Silent Spring* (Boston: Houghton Mifflin Company, 1962).

137

his cigar out of the girl's hair. Her feet are in a second and shorter set of stirrups. She has the legs of a hammer-thrower. It is clear that the couple are accustomed to wooden horses and like them. A little behind them is a younger girl riding alone. She has a strong body and streaming hair. She wears a short-sleeved, red waist, a white skirt and an emphatic bracelet of pink coral. She has her eyes on the man's arms. Still farther behind, there is another girl. One does not see much more of her than her head. Her lips are painted bright red. It seems that it would be better if someone were to hold her on her horse. We, here, are not interested in any aspect of this picture except that it is a picture of ribald and hilarious reality. It is a picture wholly favorable to what is real. It is not without imagination and it is far from being without aesthetic theory.[23]

(7)

A distaste for all tragedy is sufficiently common among the vulgar. "Life is depressing enough," runs the platitude; "why go to the theater to be reminded of the fact? Give us Abbott and Costello or the Marx Brothers." Yet people of some sensitivity, while not necessarily eschewing low comedy, do find gratification in tragedy. They do not go to it to be depressed — that would be an idiotic exercise for anyone! — but because they find themselves, at the end of a good tragedy, emerging from the theater in a mood of chastened exaltation, a mood which makes life seem not less sad but more understandable and easier to bear — a mood which would be very difficult to define, had not Aristotle already so perfectly defined it.[24]

(8)

The major artist, the tragic realist who wishes to present the world common to all rather than a dream world, must temper his insight with detachment. Once he has created a fictional personage with a definite character or moral bent — a Romeo, a Hamlet, an Othello, a Captain Ahab — that character or moral bent becomes an antecedent from which certain consequences inevitably follow. The tragic realist cannot save his hero from the consequences of character, nor does he attempt to do so. He cannot rescue his hero from the universal tragic predicament of human beings, nor does he attempt to do so. The best he can do for his hero is to grant him (and us as spectators or readers) a flash of insight into the meaning of human destiny, an insight which reconciles him to his fate. At the end Captain Ahab must die, but he accepts his fate, content to be what he is. And we, as we view with insight the full unfolding of the inevitable consequences of individual character and of universal human nature, are content to be what we are, human beings who share a common fate which is both terrible and glorious.[25]

---

[23] From Wallace Stevens, *The Necessary Angel* (New York: Alfred A. Knopf, 1951).

[24] From Bernard Grebanier, *The Heart of Hamlet* (New York: Thomas Y. Crowell Company, 1960).

[25] From Henry Myers, "Literature, Science, and Democracy," *Pacific Spectator*, Autumn, 1954.

(9)

When I pulled the trigger I did not hear the bang or feel the kick — one never does when a shot goes home — but I heard the devilish roar of glee that went up from the crowd. In that instant, in too short a time, one would have thought, even for the bullet to get there, a mysterious, terrible change had come over the elephant. He neither stirred nor fell, but every line of his body had altered. He looked suddenly stricken, shrunken, immensely old, as though the frightful impact of the bullet had paralyzed him without knocking him down. At last, after what seemed a long time — it might have been five seconds, I dare say — he sagged flabbily to his knees. His mouth slobbered. An enormous senility seemed to have settled upon him. One could have imagined him thousands of years old. I fired again into the same spot. At the second shot he did not collapse but climbed with desperate slowness to his feet and stood weakly upright with legs sagging and head drooping. I fired a third time. That was the shot that did for him. You could see the agony of it jolt his whole body and knock the last remnant of strength from his legs. But in falling he seemed for a moment to rise, for as his hind legs collapsed beneath him he seemed to tower upward like a huge rock toppling, his trunk reaching skywards like a tree. He trumpeted, for the first and only time. And then down he came, his belly towards me, with a crash that seemed to shake the ground even where I lay.[26]

(10)

Whaling vessels never returned to New Bedford or Nantucket with the same crew that they shipped. Many whalemen deserted their floating hells in the Pacific Islands. Those who kept out of debt to the ship were encouraged to desert, or abandoned on frivolous pretexts, in defiance of the law, that their lays [shares in the profits of the voyage] might be forfeited. And once a Pacific beachcomber, a man seldom became anything better. A United States consul in the Pacific estimated in 1859 that three or four thousand young men were annually lost to their country through this channel. To replace them, Kanakas, Tongatabooars, Filipinos, and even Fiji cannibals like Melville's hero Queequeg, were signed on for a nominal wage or microscopic lay. Whaling vessels no longer returned as soon as their holds were full; a cargo would be shipped home by merchant vessels from Honolulu, and the voyage prolonged until the old hooker crawled around the Horn with a yard of weed on her bottom and a crew that looked like shipwrecked mariners.[27]

(11)

I think, too, that the way in which boys and girls differ is not what the masculine and feminine stereotypes have led us to expect. Boys, for example, seem to me usually more concerned with their appearance than girls and also to have more idea what they actually look like and how other people will

[26] From George Orwell, "Shooting an Elephant," *Shooting an Elephant and Other Essays* (New York: Harcourt, Brace & World, Inc., 1950).

[27] From Samuel Eliot Morison, *The Maritime History of Massachusetts* (Boston: Houghton Mifflin Company, 1921).

respond to the way they look. Our image of a beautiful girl is so rigidly defined and constantly reiterated by every medium of communication that it has become in a sense highly impersonal. Not every girl can be beautiful; but even a girl who is gets less credit for it than she deserves. It is always a little like seeing the Riviera; however breathtaking the effect, one's very first response is that it looks exactly the way it is supposed to, and that one has seen it before. Girls, therefore, are likely to approach beauty as if it were an effect to be achieved — not an *artificial* effect but still an *external* one — the invocation of a social norm which exists altogether independently of themselves. And their attitude toward the result is likely to be quite detached. A vain young woman is, in my experience, rare.

Boys, in contrast, are often very vain; and their vanity is very personal; if they are handsome, they think of their handsomeness as peculiarly their own. They dress for it specifically, not according to social norms; a well-built, sun-bronzed boy will fight like a tiger to keep his mother from getting him out of his torn T-shirt and Ivy League pants with the useful buckle in the back, and into a conservative suit designed to conceal his fearful symmetry. Boys seem to get a different kind of satisfaction than girls from response to their physical attractiveness. Girls, I believe, are likely to find admiration for their beauty stimulating — not in the erotic sense, but as an awareness that physical attraction may open avenues to a variety of interesting relationships and experiences; they become more alert. Boys seem to become less alert; they bask in physical regard like alligators on a log. Provided there is no seductive purpose behind the response they arouse — and this they are very quick to sense and resent — it seems to reassure them, and they get sleepy.[28]

B. Select any three of the following statements. Use each of them as the topic sentence of a substantial paragraph. Develop the paragraph so that it is complete, unified, and coherent. If you prefer to supply your own thesis, do so.

1. The transition from high school to college life is a difficult one.
2. *Mad Magazine* provides effective criticism of popular television programs.
3. Government censorship of literature should cease immediately.
4. What does it mean to be "in"?
5. In our educational system, there is too much emphasis on grades.
6. Knowledge and wisdom are not the same.
7. Teen-agers are both more cynical and more idealistic than their parents.

[28] From Edgar Z. Friedenberg, *The Vanishing Adolescent* (Boston: Beacon Press, 1959).

6

Effective Sentences

The sentences in a paragraph are not isolated statements but steps in a continuum. They are related to what has gone before and to what will follow. While it is traditional to call them units of thought, they cannot be considered as independent of the context of which they are a part. Though it is useful in a chapter like this to concentrate on the sentence as a unit of expression, that is an instructional convenience which is justified only if you remember that what you will be writing is not a collection of sentences but an integrated essay.

The Handbook (pages 363 ff.) deals with usage in sentence structure — that is, with the grammatical conventions. In this chapter we are concerned with rhetorical effectiveness, with the way sentences are constructed to provide the most efficient expression of the idea that the writer has in mind.

TYPES OF SENTENCES

A good writer uses a combination of three kinds of sentences: the *parallel* or balanced sentence, the climactic or *periodic* sentence, and, above all, what may be called the *common* sentence because it is the type most frequently used.

The Common Sentence

The common sentence, sometimes called the "loose" sentence as distinct from the periodic, is the favorite English sentence. It consists of some variation of the following subject-predicate structures:

> *A bell*   *rang.* [subject + intransitive verb]
>
> *Ted Jones*   *bought a car.* [subject + transitive verb + object]
>
> *The teacher* $\Big\{$ *is a woman.* [subject + linking verb + complement, which
> *became ill.* may be a noun (or pronoun), an adjective, or an
> *is here.*   adverb]

Variations of these basic sentence patterns are produced by making them more involved by the use of several processes, the chief of which for our purpose here are *coordination* and *modification*.

Coordination is the process of combining similar structures into pairs or series. Instead of saying

> The woman looked tired. Her children also looked tired.

we combine these two basic sentences into one —

> The woman and her children looked tired. —

retaining the common predicate, *looked tired,* and combining the two subjects into a compound subject. Similarly we can combine

> She looked tired. She looked frustrated. She looked unhappy.

into a single sentence

> She looked tired, frustrated, and unhappy.

by retaining the common subject and verb, and arranging the adjectives in a series. By this process we can combine a number of sentences (or pieces of information) into a single sentence.

Coordinate elements always have the same form. Literally, they are "of the same order." The compounds or series may consist of nouns, verbs, adjectives, adverbs, phrases, or clauses, but the two members of any compound, or the three or more elements of any series, must have the same grammatical form. We cannot compound nouns with adjectives or finite verbs with infinitives and still have coordinate elements. The requirement that coordinate elements have the same form will be important in our study of parallel constructions.

Modification, the second mode of expanding simple statements, can be described in different ways, depending on the descriptive system used. Here it will be considered as a technique for amplifying the meaning of a sentence and making it more specific by relating additional information to the words modified (called *headwords*). For example, to the sentence *The boy was found* the information can be added that the boy had been missing, that he was found in a gravel pit, that the finding occurred late this afternoon, and that he was unharmed. In the expanded sentence below, the underlined modifiers are related to their headwords by arrows:

> The *missing* boy was found *unharmed* *in a gravel pit*
> *late this afternoon.*

Some ways in which coordination and modification are used to build common sentences can be illustrated by two combinations of these five bits of information:

a. A signal was faulty.
b. An express plunged into the rear of a freight train.
c. Five people were killed.
d. Forty-seven people were injured.
e. The accident happened last night.

How that information is recorded in a sentence or two will depend on how the writer orders the events. If he is interested chiefly in establishing a causal sequence, he will follow a chronological order:

Last night a faulty signal caused an express to plunge into the rear of a freight train. Five people were killed and 47 were injured in the crash.

In this version *a, b,* and *e* are combined into one sentence, in which *a* becomes the subject and *b* the object of the main clause, and *e* becomes an adverbial phrase telling when the action of the sentence occurred. Then *c* and *d* are combined as coordinate clauses in the second sentence.

But if the writer is a newspaper reporter who wants to get down first the information that readers will think most important, he may present the sequence thus:

Five people were killed and 47 were injured last night when an express plunged into the rear of a freight train because of a faulty signal.

Here *c* and *d* are combined into a compound main clause, and the other items are expressed as modifiers of that clause — one adverbial phrase and two adverbial clauses.

The order of events in the accident itself was determined by cause and effect, but the order in these two reports of the accident is imposed by the writer's will. He makes his own sequence, and he makes it in accordance with what he wants to do. He cannot do anything he pleases. He cannot — if he wants to be read — write:

Five people were killed and a signal was faulty and 47 people were injured and last night an express plunged into the rear of a freight train.

He is bound by certain conventions which he and his reader learned by growing up using the language. But, within the limitations of these conventions, he has at his disposal a variety of ways of reporting the events, and, if he knows his business, he will make the sentence come out the way he wants it to. His chief tools are coordination and modification, by means of which he shapes five bits of information into one or two sentences.

The common sentence begins with a simple structure of subject-verb, subject-verb-object, or subject-verb-complement. Into that basic sentence are imbedded, as compounds or modifiers, additional pieces of information that make the original sentence more meaningful. As the sentence grows, it has more to communicate. If it grows too large, it may become so cumbersome that neither the writer nor the reader can handle it. If it does not grow enough, the information will have to be expressed in a number of sentences, and the writing may become wordy and tedious. The job of the writer is to decide which way of structuring the information into sentences allows him to make the most efficient combination of clarity, economy, and emphasis. Nobody who takes writing seriously thinks this is an easy job.

▶ *The following paragraph consists of ten common sentences. Study them individually to see what use they make of coordination and modification. The best way to begin is to pick out the main clause in each sentence and then see how other material is used to expand that clause. For example, notice especially the structure of the first sentence. Notice also the variations in the lengths of the sentences. Which is the longest, which the shortest? Why are Thurber's sentences shorter than those provided by the author of the paragraph?*

[1] Often the meditation continues while the writer is engaged in other occupations: gardening, driving his wife to town (as Walter Mitty did), or going out to dinner. [2] "I never quite know when I'm not writing," Thurber says. [3] "Sometimes my wife comes up to me at a dinner party and says, 'Dammit, Thurber, stop writing.' [4] She usually catches me in the middle of a paragraph. [5] Or my daughter will look up from the dinner table and ask, 'Is he sick?' [6] 'No,' my wife says, 'he's writing.' [7] I have to do it that way on account of my eyes." [8] When Thurber had better vision he used to do his meditating at the typewriter, as many other writers do. [9] Nelson Algren, for example, finds his plots simply by writing page after page, night after night. [10] "I always figured," he says, "the only way I could finish a book and get a plot was just to keep making it longer and longer until something happens." [1]

The Parallel Sentence

A parallel sentence is one which emphasizes coordinate structures. Strictly, any sentence in which elements are joined by coordinating conjunctions contains parallelism. But, as the term is used here, a parallel sentence is one in which the coordinate elements are so pronounced that rhetorically the effect of the sentence is very different from that of a common sentence.

The usual pattern of the parallel sentence is the *series*. In this construction three or more elements of the same grammatical pattern are linked together, as illustrated by the following examples:

[1] From Introduction by Malcolm Cowley to *Writers at Work: The Paris Review Interviews* (New York: The Viking Press, 1958).

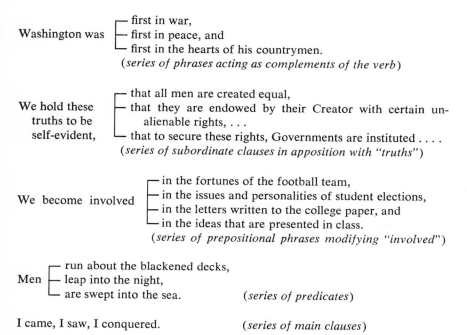

Washington was
- first in war,
- first in peace, and
- first in the hearts of his countrymen.
(*series of phrases acting as complements of the verb*)

We hold these truths to be self-evident,
- that all men are created equal,
- that they are endowed by their Creator with certain unalienable rights, . . .
- that to secure these rights, Governments are instituted . . . .
(*series of subordinate clauses in apposition with "truths"*)

We become involved
- in the fortunes of the football team,
- in the issues and personalities of student elections,
- in the letters written to the college paper, and
- in the ideas that are presented in class.
(*series of prepositional phrases modifying "involved"*)

Men
- run about the blackened decks,
- leap into the night,
- are swept into the sea.   (*series of predicates*)

I came, I saw, I conquered.   (*series of main clauses*)

As these examples illustrate, parallel constructions may be phrases, subordinate clauses, or main clauses; they may also be a series of single words, such as nouns, adjectives, or adverbs. The idea or information being presented in each element of the series is logically, grammatically, and stylistically similar to that of the other elements. For example, each element in the third series above identifies a particular kind of involvement; it is a prepositional phrase, and it is stylistically in balance with the other elements.

The chief use of the parallel sentence is to incorporate similar items in a coordinate structure. The most obvious example is the inclusion of a list of items in a sentence, but it is a natural structure to use whenever a writer wishes to present a sequence of similar ideas. Parallel sentences may also be effectively used to specify a general statement by providing examples of its meaning. Notice how the series of examples — *gardening, driving his wife to town,* or *going out to dinner* — illustrates the meaning of "engaged in other occupations" in the opening sentence of the paragraph which you analyzed in the exercise above:

Often the meditation continues while the writer is engaged in other occupations: gardening, driving his wife to town, . . . or going out to dinner.

This use of the parallel sentence is similar to the use of examples in the illustrative method of developing essays and paragraphs. Indeed, the long parallel sentence which provides a series of specific examples may easily grow into a paragraph. Notice it beginning to do so in the following sentence:

Muskie-fishing has its exciting moments — the sudden thrill of a hard strike, those delicious seconds when you wait for the muskie to turn the bait in his mouth before you set the hook, his final desperate dive as you bring him near the boat, the first gleam of his greenish-white body as you pull him close to the surface, and the pistol shot that finally dispatches him.

You can almost see the writer thinking his way through this sentence, going on from one example to another as he feels the need of making clear the meaning of his opening statement.

▶ *Identify the parallel structures in the following paragraphs. Are these structures whole sentences or parts of sentences? If parts, what parts? What role do these parallel structures play in developing the meaning or content of the paragraphs?*

Thus the Puritan was made up of two different men, the one all self-abasement, penitence, gratitude, passion, the other proud, calm, inflexible, sagacious. He prostrated himself in the dust before his Maker: but he set his foot on the neck of his king. In his devotional retirement, he prayed with convulsions, and groans, and tears. He was half-maddened by glorious or terrible illusions. He heard the lyres of angels or the tempting whispers of fiends. He caught a gleam of the Beatific Vision, or woke screaming from dreams of everlasting fire. Like Vane, he thought himself intrusted with the sceptre of the millennial year. Like Fleetwood, he cried in the bitterness of his soul that God had hid his face from him. But when he took his seat in the council, or girt on his sword for war, these tempestuous workings of the soul had left no perceptible trace behind them. People who saw nothing of the godly but their uncouth visages, and heard nothing from them but their groans and their whining hymns, might laugh at them. But those had little reason to laugh who encountered them in the hall of debate or in the field of battle. These fanatics brought to civil and military affairs a coolness of judgment and an immutability of purpose which some writers have thought inconsistent with their religious zeal, but which were in fact the necessary effects of it. The intensity of their feelings on one subject made them tranquil on every other. One overpowering sentiment had subjected to itself pity and hatred, ambition and fear. Death had lost its terrors and pleasure its charms. They had their smiles and their tears, their raptures and their sorrows, but not for the things of this world. Enthusiasm had made them Stoics, had cleared their minds from every vulgar passion and prejudice, and raised them above the influence of danger and of corruption. It sometimes might lead them to pursue unwise ends, but never to choose unwise means. They went through the world, like Sir Artegal's iron man Talus with his flail, crushing and trampling down oppressors, mingling with human beings, but having neither part nor lot in human infirmities, insensible to fatigue, to pleasure, and to pain, not to be pierced by any weapon, not to be withstood by any barrier.[2]

[2] From Thomas Babington Macaulay, *The Public Character of Milton.*

▶ *Using as a model one of the examples on pages 61–62, write a paragraph in which an opening general statement is made specific by a series of examples.*

The Balanced Sentence

When a parallel sentence consists of two contrasting major elements, often main clauses, we say that it is *balanced*. In such sentences the contrasted clauses are usually joined by a coordinating conjunction which serves as a fulcrum on which the two structures are balanced. Notice how the contrast in the following passage is developed in a series of balanced compound predicates.

> I felt myself in rebellion against the Greek concept of justice. That concept excused Laius for attacking Oedipus, but condemned Oedipus for defending himself. It tolerated a king's deliberate attempt to kill his baby son by piercing the infant's feet and abandoning it on a mountain, but later branded the son's unintentional killing of his father as murder. It held Oedipus responsible for his ignorance, but excused those, including Apollo, who contributed to that ignorance.

The structure of this paragraph can literally be diagramed as a scale, with the contrasted parts balanced on the fulcrum of the repeated conjunction *but*.

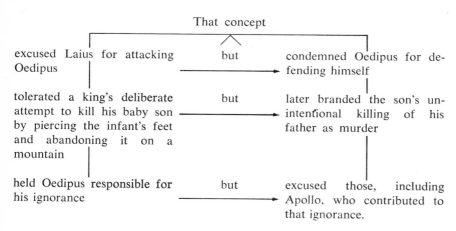

Such a balanced structure points up the contrast in the thought so that the rhetorical pattern reflects and supports the logical pattern. Moreover, the regular rhythm of the matching clauses is itself attractive to a reader. But notice it is the *repeated* contrast in the example that gives the sense of balance. If, instead of following the arrows across the scale, you read down the left side before reading the right, much of the balanced effect is lost. This experiment should suggest to you that when you are contrasting two things you will get better parallelism by contrasting them a part at a time. This was the technique used on page 63 in the balanced contrast between death at sea and death on land.

It should be emphasized that parallelism and balance are not mere stylistic ornaments. When such structures are used well, the similarities and differences expressed in the sentence patterns reflect similarities and differences which the writer has perceived. Parallel and balanced sentences owe much of their rhetorical force to the reader's recognition of this congruence between structure and thought. The balance in the Oedipus paragraph reflects a balance in the writer's judgment, and the reader learns from the sentence the discrimination which its structure suggests. Given the writer's purpose at that point, the balanced sentence was the most effective means of developing it.

The Periodic Sentence

A periodic sentence is one which builds through a series, usually of phrases or subordinate clauses, to a climactic statement of the main clause, as in the following:

> To this queer mixture of cultured and uneducated, of lowly and exalted, of those who came for love of drama and those who came to show their superiority, *the Elizabethan drama was shaped.*

Notice that the structure of this periodic sentence is almost the reverse of the parallel sentence about muskie-fishing on page 146. In that sentence the main clause came first and its meaning was made clear by the parallel details that followed. The reader learned what the main clause meant by seeing how it was illustrated. In the periodic sentence the parallel details are given first and prepare the reader for the main clause which is to follow. In both kinds of sentence the main clause says relatively little by itself. It is a generalized statement which is made meaningful by the concrete images which precede or follow it.

Because of the complexity of its structure, a sustained periodic sentence requires considerable skill, since the writer must clearly foresee the whole pattern before he begins to write. In a common sentence, he has much more freedom to continue or to stop. He can connect several main clauses or begin a succession of sentences with conjunctions. But the basic pattern of a periodic sentence has to be shaped in advance. For example, the writer of the following sentence is moving toward his main clause through a series of "if" clauses which successively deal with life, liberty, and the pursuit of happiness, and what he has to say about each of these subjects must be chosen for its contribution to the idea of the main clause.

> But if life hardly seems worth living, if liberty is used for subhuman purposes, if the pursuers of happiness know nothing about the nature of their quarry or the elementary techniques of hunting, *these constitutional rights will not be very meaningful.*

148

The longer a periodic sentence is, the more complex its pattern becomes. The following example, taken from the student paper on page 29, is very complex.

And when the great matador, reaching his peak with a brave strong bull, stands poised over those horns, hoping (but not knowing) that they won't come up and dig his very guts out, hoping that the sword doesn't hit a bone and break off in his hand, plunges his sword down into the back of the bull's neck and punctures the bull's lungs (he hopes), and when every man who ever saw an amateur bullfight or faced a bull or ran from one, knowing what it means to lean over a bull's horns and expose one's groin, holds his breath and, not saying a word, watches the matador in the hot, bright sun, on the white sand prove for the whole world to see his courage and strength and skill, and sees him become one with the proud, noble, strong bull — *this is the moment of truth.*

This sentence is so involved, contains so many ideas within ideas, that it defies clear diagraming. We can, however, see its dominant structure by omitting some of the material and reducing the sentence to its basic design.

And when the great matador . . . stands poised over those horns, ... [and]
   plunges his sword down into . . . the bull's neck and
   punctures the bull's lungs . . .
and when every man . . .
   holds his breath and . . .
   watches the matador . . . and
   sees him become one with the . . . bull —
this is the moment of truth.

A student needs to be very sure of himself to embark on a sentence as complex as that. Most would be well advised not to try. But if the writer can handle it, such a sentence is impressive. In addition to its cumulative effect, it gets a great deal said in its 150 words and is therefore, despite its length, an economical statement. If you think not, if you think it is wordy merely because it is long, try to present every idea and image it contains in your own words. You may be able to cut out a few adjectives, but you will not find it easy to say as much in the same space. This is a point to remember when we come later to talk of economy as a relation between the number of words and the meaning they convey.

The basic pattern of the periodic sentences we have looked at consists of two elements: a set of parallel structures followed by a main clause. The elements in parallel structure can be single words, though they are usually phrases or subordinate clauses. If we use *P* for phrase, *C* for subordinate clause, and *M* for main clause, we will have a convenient way of diagraming periodic sentences. After the following examples the diagrams are given in brackets. When a series consists of phrases within a clause, the phrases are placed in parentheses.

If we could retain the curiosity of our childhood and the idealism of our youth, and if we could combine both of these with the disciplined judgment of maturity, what men we might become! [C C M]

But when there is no hope of success, when every new effort is foreseen as another failure, and when each succeeding failure serves only to make frustration deeper and more acute, then surely no useful purpose is served by exhorting the poor fellow to try, try again. [C C C M]

If stories of sinking ships and burning towns, of killing cold and windlashed waves, of reckless men engaged in dangerous pursuits make up the warp of *The Long Ships Passing,* the woof is formed by the pressure of an expanding economy in an era becoming increasingly mechanized. [C (P P P) M]

> To die, to sleep; to sleep, perchance to dream;
> Aye, there's the rub . . . — *Hamlet* [P P P P M]

The habit of analyzing the structure of sentences is worth cultivating both for the knowledge it yields about rhetorical patterns and for the pleasure of recognizing and appreciating a writer's technique. You are not likely to have either the need or the desire to write in a freshman essay such a sentence as Lincoln's magnificent conclusion to his Second Inaugural Address, but just as you get pleasure from recognizing the design of a dress, a car, or a building, so you may get pleasure from seeing how the sentence was designed.

With malice toward none, with charity for all, with firmness in the right, as God gives us to see the right, let us strive on to finish the work we are in — to bind up the nation's wounds, to care for him who shall have borne the battle and for his widow and his orphan, to do all which may achieve and cherish a just and lasting peace among ourselves, and with all nations.

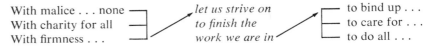

The diagram reveals the basic structure of the sentence: a series of three phrases preceding and three following the main clause. The opening phrases build up the periodic effect; but unlike the normal periodic pattern, the sentence does not end with the main clause. Instead it proceeds to a new climax as Lincoln uses the final series to define "the work we are in."

CHARACTERISTICS OF EFFECTIVE SENTENCES

An effective sentence is one that does for a reader what the writer meant it to do. Usually its purpose is to advance the development of the topic sentence of a paragraph. Except in a grammatical sense, it is not an independent unit of composition, and, at least in the first draft, a student's wisest course is to let his understanding of the purpose of the paragraph determine what he does in individual sentences. Revision is another matter.

Then he can consider the internal structure of his sentences and do whatever can be done to improve them.

Effective sentences have four qualities: *unity, economy, emphasis,* and *variety.* These are by no means independent of each other. Unified sentences are often economical and emphatic, and emphatic sentences are always unified and usually economical. But, despite some overlapping, it will be convenient in this chapter to deal separately with these four characteristics.

Unity

When we say that a sentence has unity we mean that everything in it has a logical relation to the purpose of the sentence as a whole and that nothing is omitted which is necessary to that purpose. For example, the sentence "If you like skiing, you will like Oregon" expresses a complete idea. If we try to express that idea in one of the following ways we destroy the unity of the sentence.

1. *If you like skiing.*   (This is only part of the idea, a fragment)

2. *If you like skiing, you will like Oregon, with its magnificent trout streams.*   (What relevance have the trout streams in a sentence about the winter attractions of Oregon?)

3. *You like skiing. You like Oregon.*   (The two ideas here are not joined into one as they were in the original statement)

These examples illustrate the chief causes of lack of unity. The first omits a necessary part of the thought, so that the sentence is logically as well as grammatically incomplete. So obvious an omission is usually a sign of carelessness, or even faulty proofreading, though it could reflect an almost complete ignorance of English sentence structure. If the latter is the explanation, the student needs remedial work; he must now learn what he should have learned in grade school — the mechanics of a written English sentence.

The second error is more common and more forgivable. As was pointed out in Chapter 1, unless a sense of purpose controls everything we do, we are in constant danger of letting irrelevant ideas creep into what we write. Even experienced writers have this trouble and often have to remove its effects in revision. Inexperienced writers, especially when feeling their way through a sentence, are often led away from their original purpose by new thoughts or associations which arise in their minds as they write. This tendency leads them to drift into confusion, as in the following sentence.

His mother, who has been living in Kansas, where she has been keeping house for her nephew who lost his wife in a car accident three years ago and needed help in bringing up his three small children, having been in poor

151

health since her husband died, because she suffered from chronic asthma, had to move to Colorado.

This sentence got out of control because the writer allowed all sorts of associations to get imbedded in it. The usual advice for his ailment is to write shorter sentences and be sure each deals with only one idea. And this is usually good advice, though in this instance little improvement would come from chopping the material into a series of short sentences — "His mother has been living in Kansas. She has been keeping house for her nephew. He lost his wife in a car accident, etc. . . ." What this writer needs is to get clear in his own mind what one idea he is trying to express, hold fast to it, and be sure in revision to delete all departures from it.

The third example on page 151 (*You like skiing. You like Oregon.*) illustrates an error best taken care of in revision. The two ideas are no doubt related in the writer's mind, but not in his sentences. The problem is to subordinate one idea (and one part of the statement) to the other. The writer has first to see that the skiing is one reason why he likes Oregon; and second, that evidence for a conclusion, though important, is subordinate to the conclusion itself.

Economy

Economy, the second main quality of effective sentences, is a relation between the number of words used and the amount of meaning conveyed. A sentence is not economical just because it is short, or wordy just because it is long. The test is not the number of words but the amount of work they do for the reader. Such classics of condensation as "Sighted sub, sank same," and "I came, I saw, I conquered" owe some of their effect to parallelism and alliteration and are probably a little too clever to be good models for freshman writing; but they do show that a person with a knack for concise statement can often say a great deal in few words.

The opposite of economy is wordiness, and again the test is qualitative, not quantitative. The long periodic sentence from "The Bullfight" (page 149) contains about 150 words, but it is not wordy. In contrast, the sentence at the left in the following example is wordy; it says no more in 54 words than is said in 16 words at the right.

Wordy	*Economical*
Although I cannot truthfully say that I was acclaimed during my high school career as a prodigy, being what is generally known as an average student, I was able to survive the rigors of four years of academic pursuits and to achieve graduation without ever having received a single failing grade in any subject.	Although I was only an average student in high school, I graduated without failing a course.

Wordiness is one of the worst weaknesses in writing. For the reader, it can often be worse than bad grammar, misspellings, and other lapses from educated usage. Bad grammar may irritate, but it will only occasionally confuse. But sustained wordiness obscures meaning and may baffle the reader completely.

In student writing the chief causes of wordiness are (1) misguided attempts at a literary style and (2) failure to eliminate useless words in revision.

Pretentious Diction. Good writing is first of all clear. "Literary" flourishes that make the reader's task harder are worse than useless; they are harmful. Consider this:

> It was fortunate, or unfortunate, depending on the circumstances and the evaluation thereof, that I had no formulated or precise conceptions when I left high school and commenced work as a telegraphist in the Public Service. While on duty one evening, a colleague, who was interested in weight-lifting, allowed me to peruse a book on the subject entitled *Big Arms,* by Bob Hoffman. Not yet having realized my latent interest in athletic endeavors, I was surprised at the manner in which the book held my interest. This I only realized after a while. It was that book which stimulated me to make a purchase of a weight-lifting set, and despite the inhibiting influences of long work hours, little sleep and irregular meals, to exercise in my free moments.

It would be hard to imagine a less successful paragraph, yet the student who wrote it has something to say: that his interest in weight-lifting stemmed from a book which a fellow worker in the telegraph office once lent him. That is not a difficult idea to express. Yet the student's inability — or unwillingness — to put it down in simple language traps him into a pretentious style and smothers his thought with words, many of them inappropriate and most of them unnecessary. The revision that follows has no special stylistic merit, except the greatest merit of all — it expresses a simple observation in suitable and concise language.

> I became interested in weight-lifting while I was working as a telegraphist. One of my office mates who was enthusiastic about the sport lent me a book called *Big Arms,* by Bob Hoffman. That book so stimulated me that I bought a weight-lifting set and began to exercise in every spare moment.

The second version has less than half as many words as the first; yet it includes everything that bears on the writer's purpose. It contains no distinguished diction, but none is required. The big words of the original version ("evaluation thereof," "formulated or precise conceptions," "commenced," "colleague," and "latent interest in athletic endeavors") are liabilities in such a paragraph. The second version is not only more concise; it is much more effective.

153

Useless Words. If you have ever composed a telegram you have had a valuable lesson in cutting out unnecessary words. Such ruthless pruning is neither necessary nor advisable in most college writing. But often a single word will do the work of two or three, and a short phrase may replace a long clause without hurting style or meaning.

The three most common means of reducing wordiness are excision, substitution, and direct statement.

Excision means pruning out useless words. Here are two examples.

1. Cutting out a purposeless introductory phrase:

    ~~With reference to the relationship between the laws of today and the laws of ancient times,~~ I think that the author is wrong in stating that the laws of today are based on ancient laws.

2. Cutting out useless words within the body of the sentence:

    I ~~only~~ hope I get as much ~~benefit~~ out of ~~my years of~~ college ~~work and study~~ as I got from ~~the four years I spent in~~ high school.

Substitution is the replacing of a wordy expression by an economical one.

1. Substituting one word for a phrase:

    I took an academic *course.* ~~line of subjects~~.

2. Substituting a phrase for a clause:

    She is the girl *in blue.* ~~who is wearing a blue dress~~.

3. Substituting a simple sentence for a compound or complex sentence:

    ~~He married~~ The former Jane Smith/ ~~she~~ is his third wife.

    They live in Eau Claire, ~~which is in~~ Wisconsin.

Direct statement is explicit statement. It says, rather than implies, what the author means, and it avoids *circumlocutions* — words or phrases which shy away from clear statement through timidity, false modesty, or literary affectation. Contrast the original and revised versions of the following.

    Officer, that man *stole* ~~appropriated~~ my purse.

He was ~~/ shall we say? / in an inebriated~~ *drunk.*
~~condition~~.

I *do* ~~find myself~~ not ~~in~~ complete*ly* ~~agreement~~ with
Dr. Jones.

▶ *In the following paragraph one minor and one major revision have been made to reduce wordiness. Explain specifically what has been done. How many words have been saved? Has any significant content been lost by the revision?*

Often, therefore, the first step in a writing
assignment is to analyze the situation. Sometimes
the analysis requires little more than a careful
reading of the directions and a decision about how
to interpret
the assignment. ~~is to be interpreted~~. At other
especially in persuasion,
times, the analysis will require careful consideration of many factors, including the attitudes of
the reader. ~~This kind of attention is likely to be especially important in essays which are designed to persuade someone to act or not to act in a certain way~~.

You may at this point be bothered by what may seem to be a contradiction. In Chapter 5 you were advised to expand your paragraphs by adding illustrative details; here you are being told to reduce wordiness. There is no contradiction. Details add substance; empty words do not, but take the same effort to read as if they did. The list of exciting moments in muskie-fishing (page 146) specifies the meaning of the topic sentence and is worth the space it takes. But the excised sentence in the example above says nothing that cannot be as well said by the inserted phrase, "especially in persuasion." The real test of wordiness is not the number of words alone, but the number of words in relation to the work they do.

Emphasis

Emphasis — the third main quality of effective sentences — is a relation between purpose and style. Within limits, a writer usually has available to him several ways of expressing an idea. If one way gives greater emphasis to what he wants emphasized, that is the one to be preferred. Both unity and economy affect emphasis, because clearness and brevity are emphatic; but here we shall deal with three other means of achieving desired emphasis — *emphatic repetition, emphatic voice,* and *emphatic order.*

Emphatic Repetition. We saw on page 126 that deliberate repetition can strengthen the coherence of a paragraph. It can also be used within a sentence to emphasize key words. Notice the force gained by the intentional repetitions in the following sentences:

> It was an act of senseless *brutality, brutally* planned and *brutally* executed, serving no purpose except to indulge a *brute* passion.

> The beatnik motivation is negative; they are *against* things — *against* the present and *against* the past, *against* materialism and *against* mysticism, *against* whatever has been considered valuable in literature, art, music, and philosophy, *against* anything associated with middle-class morality, and *against* all conventions but their own. With apologies to St. Paul: whatsoever things are of good repute, the beatnik is *against* them.

Emphatic Voice. It is common in composition courses to urge students to use verbs in the active rather than the passive voice. This advice is generally sound, because the active voice is usually more natural and the so-called "weak passive" sometimes leads to wordiness and to awkward shifts in structure.

Weak Passive	*More Emphatic Active*
A final examination was failed by both starting halfbacks.	Both starting halfbacks failed a final examination.
The instructor said that the papers would be graded by him in two or three days.	The instructor said he would grade the papers in two or three days.
He was not prepared for the test and so only half of the questions were answered.	Because he was not prepared for the test he answered only half of the questions.

But there are times when the passive is the more natural and the more emphatic form. In general, subject territory is a position of stress in a sentence, and putting a word there will tend to emphasize it, perhaps unwisely. For example, in *The legislature founded the University ninety years ago,* "the legislature" may not deserve the importance it is given in the sentence. If the writer is concerned with the founding of the University and not with the founding agency, he can get a more fitting emphasis by putting the sentence in the passive voice and dropping "the legislature" entirely: *The University was founded ninety years ago.* Whenever the agent of an active statement is obvious, or is unknown, or is unimportant, a better emphasis may be obtained by using the passive voice.

Active	*Explanation*	*Passive*
They re-elected the Labour Party.	"Labour Party" is the important term here, not "They." The passive gives the right emphasis.	The Labour Party was re-elected.
A man drove us around Old Quebec in an open carriage.	The driver here is not important and receives unnecessary emphasis in the subject position.	We were driven around Old Quebec in an open carriage.

Notice, however, that what we have assumed to be unimportant in these isolated statements might be made important by the context of the paragraph. If the last example occurred in a paragraph in which the writer was discussing the kindness of the people of Quebec, it could have been preceded by examples of such kindness — "One couple invited us to their home to taste French Canadian cooking. A lady took us on a tour of the cathedral. A man drove us around Old Quebec in an open carriage." In such a context, the agent of the action is important and is rightly made the subject. Because the choice between active and passive depends on the context and the writer's intention, an arbitrary rule "Never use the passive" would be unwise. A better rule would be, "Use the active voice, unless you are convinced that the passive will better provide the emphasis you need in a particular context."

Emphatic Word Order. The way a writer uses word order to obtain emphasis in a sentence depends on two considerations: What words does he wish to emphasize? What positions within a sentence provide the most emphasis?

Take the sequence: event — the shooting of Abraham Lincoln; place — Ford's Theater; time — the evening of April 14, 1865; assassin — John Wilkes Booth. Normally we would consider the name of the President the most important part of the sentence and would put it in the subject position. Then we would be required to follow with the verb. With that start, we could arrange the remaining three elements in any order we pleased, though there probably would be a normal preference for naming the assassin next. To indicate the flexibility of the last three elements, we shall arrange them vertically:

> | | by John Wilkes Booth |
> |---|---|
> | Abraham Lincoln was shot | in Ford's Theater |
> | | on the evening of April 14, 1865 |

But if the sentence occurred in a biography of the actor, he would probably be made the subject — *John Wilkes Booth shot Lincoln . . . .*

If the author were writing a history of Ford's Theater, he might order the sentence thus:

157

It was in Ford's Theater that Booth shot Lincoln on the evening of April 14, 1865.

And, if his purpose required it, he could begin with the date — *On the evening of April 14, 1865 . . . .*

In a longer sentence — whether compound or complex — both the beginning and the end are emphatic positions. The most important material is put in these positions, and less important material is placed in the middle. If unimportant details pile up at the end of a sentence, they may get more emphasis than they deserve, and the reader may feel that the sentence is "running down," because he expects important information at the end and does not get it. Notice the difference between the following versions:

Unemphatic Order	*Emphatic Order*
He was accused of cheating and was expelled from college by the Disciplinary Committee yesterday afternoon at a meeting.	He was accused of cheating and, at a meeting of the Disciplinary Committee yesterday afternoon, he was expelled from college.

In the sentence at the left the reader loses interest after the dramatic event, the expulsion, is announced. If the agent and time of expulsion are important enough to be included in the sentence, they should be placed in the middle, as they are in the version at the right.

Climactic order presents the material of the sentence so as to build up to a major idea. We have seen that the force of periodic sentences derives from this order, but climax may also be used in common sentences. The following examples contrast anticlimactic order (left) with climactic order (right). Study both versions and explain what changes were made in revision, and why.

Anticlimactic Order	*Climactic Order*
In a magnificent stretch run the favorite overtook six horses and won by a nose, thrilling the crowd.	The favorite thrilled the crowd by a magnificent stretch run in which he overtook six horses and won by a nose.
The prosecution asked in its summing up that the jury bring in a verdict of guilty, which was the only possible verdict considering the violence of the crime and the lack of provocation.	In summing up, the prosecution asked the jury to consider the lack of provocation and the violence of the crime and then bring in the only possible verdict — guilty.
He said that the UN had failed in its chief function, to preserve the peace of the world, although it had done much of which it could be proud and was still performing valuable services in many areas.	He said that, though the UN had done much of which it could be proud and was still performing valuable services in many areas, it had failed in its chief function, to preserve the peace of the world.

In general, any acceptable inversion of normal word order tends to emphasize the inverted word. In *Others he saved, himself he could not save,* the contrast is increased by putting the object of each clause ahead of its subject. In *Slowly and sadly we laid him down* and in *Right you are,* the modifiers are emphasized by being moved from the ends of the sentences to the beginnings. The following sentences would normally begin with *Time* as the subject — *Time is the leading idea* . . . . But notice the emphasis obtained by making it the complement and holding it till the very end of the sentence:

> The leading idea which is present in all our researches and which accompanies every fresh observation, the sound which to the ear of the student of Nature seems continually echoed from every part of her works, is — Time!

Variety

Logically, a discussion of variety in sentence structure belongs in a chapter on paragraphs. Variety is not a characteristic of single sentences but of a succession of sentences. We consider it in this chapter simply because it is convenient to discuss variety *after* we have considered parallel and periodic sentences, word order, and subordination.

Consider the following paragraph:

> Shakespeare's chronicle history of *Henry the Fifth* is a drama of kinghood and war. It is essentially a play about a young king's coming of age. Henry V had been an irresponsible young prince before his accession to the throne. He had to prove his worthiness as king by leading his army in war. He invaded France and captured Harfleur, and then tried to withdraw his troops to Calais. He and his men were confronted by a numerically superior French army at Agincourt. In a famous passage in Shakespeare's play, Henry urges his soldiers on to an incredible victory. The superior mobility and firepower of the English proved too much for the heavily armored French.

As you have probably noticed, all the sentences in this paragraph are similar in length and pattern. The number of words is respectively 14, 12, 14, 14, 15, 14, 16, 16; and, with one exception, the word order is subject, verb, and object or complement.

This much similarity may not become monotonous in a single paragraph, but a 500-word essay in this style could be quite tedious. A writer, like a baseball pitcher, is more effective with a change of pace, and varied sentences are more effective than those that plod along in constant lengths and patterns.

But a word of caution: *too much variety may be as bad as none at all.* The subject-verb-object pattern is the favorite order of English sentences, and a student who strives too hard to avoid it may end up with an affected and unnatural style or he may fall into awkward inversions. If you keep this caution in mind, the following discussion of ways to obtain variety will be helpful.

The best way to get variety of sentence structure is to be conscious of the need of it. Nothing that follows in this section will help a student unless he at least recognizes that his sentences are monotonous. Once he sees that they are too much alike in length and pattern, he can easily make specific revisions to break up monotony. Even one or two changes in a paragraph may produce a marked improvement.

Variation may be achieved by three methods: by inverting normal word order, by subordination, and by occasional use of periodic sentences. Usually these methods are used together. For example, when we revise the following passage at the left into the form at the right, we combine inversion, subordination, and periodic structure.

Monotony	*Variety*
I had only a single paddle and I was not used to handling a canoe in rough water. I could not hold its nose into the waves. The canoe tacked from side to side. I expected every moment to capsize.	Unaccustomed to handling a canoe in rough water with a single paddle, I could not hold its nose into the waves. As the canoe tacked from side to side, I expected every moment to capsize.

Here the first sentence of the original has been reduced to a phrase preceding the main clause in a short periodic sentence. The third sentence has been reduced to a subordinate clause preceding the main clause of another periodic sentence. The two subordinations and two inversions of the revised paragraph not only get rid of the monotony of the original but achieve better emphasis by giving greater grammatical importance to the two main ideas in the passage — *I could not hold its nose into the waves,* and *I expected every moment to capsize.*

Here is another illustration. For ease of reference, the sentences at the left are numbered.

1. John Stuart Mill was born in 1806 and died in 1873.	John Stuart Mill (1806–1873) was a child prodigy whose fame did not cease at maturity. As a logician, political economist, and man of letters, he was one of the most influential thinkers of the nineteenth century.
2. He was famous as a child prodigy.	
3. His fame continued through his life.	
4. He was a logician and a political economist and a man of letters.	
5. He was one of the most influential thinkers of the nineteenth century.	

In this example sentences 1–3 have been combined by reducing the dates to a parenthesis and making sentence 3 a subordinate clause. Sentence 4 has been reduced to a phrase and placed before the main clause (5) to form a periodic sentence.

▶ *As an exercise in achieving variety, study the sentence structure in the following paragraph. What variations do you find in length? Which sentences would you classify as predominantly common sentences, and which as periodic? Within both types, what kind of parallel structures do you find? When you have answered these questions, look back on your own high school years and write a paragraph in which you do for that subject what Sevareid does for his college experience in the 1930's. You need not imitate Sevareid; but try to get into your writing some of the variety he shows in this paragraph.*

[1] Now, when I read a novel of American campus life, or see a Hollywood version with its fair maidens in lovers' lane, dreamy-eyed youth in white flannels lolling under leafy boughs or lustily singing, arms about one another's shoulders, of their school's immortal glories and their own undying loyalty — when I come across all this, I am astonished and unbelieving, or I have a faint twinge of nostalgia for a beautiful something I never knew. [2] I remember only struggle, not so much the struggle of "working my way through" as the battle, in deadly earnest, with other students of different persuasion or of no persuasion, with the university authorities, with the American society of that time. [3] I remember emotional exhaustion, not from singing about the "dear old college" but from public debate. [4] I remember exhilarating triumphs and the most acute bitterness of my life. [5] A class reunion is something I have never experienced. [6] I would know few of the members of my class. [7] Our loyalties were not defined by such simple categories. [8] I remember only a small group of all the classes, of various ages, some from the college of liberal arts, others from law or medicine or agriculture — the small, intense group of my friends, cohesive by political conviction and solidified by struggle.[3]

Exercises

A. Check the following words, or any ten of your own choice, in your dictionary: *ambivalent, blatant, contrite, enigmatic, furbish, garrulous, jargon, myopic, punctilious, sanctuary.* For each word make brief notes on its source, original meaning, one present meaning, and an illustration of its use in that sense. Work all this information into a single sentence, as illustrated in the following example:

Synchronize, from the Greek words for "together" and "time," originally meant "contemporaneous," but now means "to cause to move at the same time," as in "The sound track was synchronized with the film."

B. Study the sentence structure in the following paragraphs. Pick out the best examples you find of parallel, balanced, and periodic sentences and describe their structures either verbally or by simple diagrams such as have been used in the text.

[3] From Eric Sevareid, *Not So Wild a Dream* (New York: Alfred A. Knopf, 1946).

(1)

The flag flying over the building to signify "a play is on" brought, indeed, a strange audience: a pit crowd of apprentices playing "hookey," town idlers, a few shameless women, travellers intent on seeing the sights, fighters off duty, seafarers ashore, etc.; and above in the balconies students and poets and a few shrewd burghers or minor court hangers-on (perhaps with ladies, who dared come only under masculine protection); and on the stage itself the fops and beaux and noblemen, as anxious to be seen as to see, interrupting the action if they willed, smoking and talking and displaying their figures and their finery. To this queer mixture of cultured and uneducated, of lowly and exalted, of those who came for love of drama and those who came to show their superiority, the Elizabethan drama was shaped. No doubt about its vociferous reaction if the lines or the action became too slow or too tame. Coarseness went down agreeably, but literary fineness might kill comedy or tragedy. If anything on the stage bored, the audience took to the dice or cards; and always there was much drinking of ale and widespread eating of fruits and sweets.[4]

(2)

The protagonist and antagonist are William Gibson, the author, and Henry Fonda, the star. Gibson is motivated by a conviction of the integrity of his characters. If his hero, Jerry, is a confused character, then Jerry's confusion must become explicit in the play, even though that confusion may, in turn, confuse the audience. If Gittel, his heroine, is a profane, promiscuous, but endearing little Brooklyn gamin, she has to be profane and promiscuous in the play, even at the risk of alienating the audience. Fonda is motivated by a sense of what an audience will accept, of what constitutes good theater. He wants the characters to be "likable"; therefore he wants potentially objectionable traits toned down. But there is an ironic twist to the conflict between these two points of view. Gibson and Fonda cannot simply slug it out to decide whose play is to be produced. They are committed to a two-million-dollar business enterprise, the success of which demands their complete cooperation.

Given the personalities of the two men, this cooperation cannot be achieved without considerable wear and tear on their nervous systems, even though both are honest, competent, and conscious of the importance of subordinating their personal preferences to the common good. Because Mr. Gibson has written the *Log* we know what he suffered: the constant frustration of seeing his play misunderstood by the one man without whom it could not be produced; the incessant demands for revision of the dialogue at every stage of production; the hours spent rewriting speeches which satisfied the star but were rejected by the director or which satisfied the director but were rejected by the star; the desperate decision to let Fonda improvise in rehearsals and copy his words verbatim, only to have the new version rejected by both star and director when it was written down; the physical and psychological exhaustion from working endlessly to satisfy demands that, to the

4 From Sheldon Cheney, *The Theatre* (New York: Longmans, Green, 1929).

author, were both unclear and artistically repugnant — in short, the soul-sapping despair of being caught in an unbearable yet inescapable situation. We do not know what Fonda suffered. There is no suggestion in the book that he is less sensitive than the author or less conscientious or less concerned about building a successful play. We do know, because Gibson tells us, that much of the time Fonda was morose and unhappy, that he wanted to escape from his contract as soon as he could honorably do so, and that he finally gave orders that Mr. Gibson was not to be admitted to his dressing room. From these facts we may infer that the actor, as well as the author, paid a price for his compromises.

C. Study the contrasted paragraphs below. First read both to get the general effect of the revision; then compare the two versions sentence by sentence. Be prepared to discuss the changes made or to suggest others that you think might be more effective.

Original	*Revised*
The Levenford of Dr. Cronin's book is really the town of Dumbarton. It is one of the oldest towns in Scotland. It was the most important town north of the Tweed at the time of the Anglo-Saxon invasion, and was called Alcluyd. The Pict chieftains gathered there when they were preparing to swoop down into England in search of plunder; and they always returned there to divide the spoils of victory. The town stands at the gateway to the highlands and has been the field of many battles. Its great island rock has served successively as a fortress for Picts, Romans, Northmen, Jacobites, and Royalists. It has often served as a refuge for the townspeople whenever they were attacked by superior forces. They would retreat to the rock, as the Athenians retreated to their ships, until an opportunity presented itself for overthrowing the invaders.	Dumbarton, the Levenford of Dr. Cronin's book, is one of the oldest towns in Scotland. At the time of the Saxon invasion, Alcluyd, as it was then called, was the only town of any importance north of the Tweed. It was there that the Pict chieftains gathered before swooping down into England in search of plunder, and there that they returned to divide the spoils of victory. Standing as it does at the gateway of the highlands, the town has been the field of many battles, and the great island rock of Dumbarton has served successively as the fortress of Picts, Romans, Northmen, Jacobites, and Royalists. When attacked by superior forces, the townspeople, like the Athenians deserting their city for the ships, would seek refuge in this great rock and bide their time until an opportunity for overthrowing the invaders should arise.

D. The following extract from a student paper could be considerably improved by revision. First study it to find its major weaknesses; then, using whatever means seem best to you, rewrite it.

There were new motives encouraging Benedict Arnold to commit treason. First, there were the repeated slights of Congress. In Philadelphia Arnold presented his accounts to Congress. They in turn appointed a committee to audit and investigate them. The committee took its time in reporting its findings and Congress failed to act. Arnold petitioned Congress a second time. They turned his petition down.

When Joseph Reed presented charges against Benedict Arnold, Congress took its time in settling them. The investigation dragged out over a period of several months. This began to cause Arnold to develop a persecution complex. It seemed whenever Congress was called upon to settle charges presented against Arnold it took them a long time to come to a decision.

Second, there was his need for ready cash with which to pay his debts. Arnold lived in a style of splendor and extravagance which was far beyond his means. He contracted more debts than he was able to pay. Rather than lower his standard of living he continued to go farther in debt. The people to whom he owed money finally asked him to pay up. This was of course impossible because he had no money. He petitioned Congress to settle his accounts, but they turned him down. He was confused and highly irritated. He finally resorted to all forms of acquiring money with which to pay his creditors. Some of the methods he resorted to were not in keeping with the rank he held.

7

Right Words

The English writer Jonathan Swift defined good writing as the art of putting "proper words in proper places." Although this definition tremendously oversimplifies, it does stress the fact that words are the units with which a writer works. Words are the medium of communication, even of communication to oneself. We think with words as we write with them, and neither thinking nor writing can be efficient unless the words are accurate. A concern with right words, therefore, is not just a matter of style. It is a matter of ordering experience, evaluating it, and communicating the results.

THE PRINCIPLE OF USAGE

The relation between a word and whatever it refers to (its *referent*) is a mental one. Words have no intrinsic meanings; their meanings are given by the people who use them. Therefore, when it is said that a word *has a meaning,* that statement should be understood as a short way of saying that the word *has acquired that meaning* or *is used in that sense.*

A word is always used in some situation or context, and we learn its meanings by observing the contexts in which it occurs. The meanings of "run" are what happens when a man runs for a bus, a child runs a temperature, a quarterback runs a team, a baseball player scores a run, a woman gets a run in her stocking, and so on. This is exactly how the writers of dictionaries (lexicographers) get their definitions. They gather sample contexts and write definitions to describe the meanings these convey, so that when a dictionary lists different meanings for the word "strike," it is recording the contexts in which the word "strike" occurs — to name an event in a baseball game, in bowling, in fishing, in a labor-management dispute, in prospecting for gold.

Many words have quite different meanings from those they once had. "Imp" once meant offspring and had no unpleasant associations; "buxom" was once complimentary, so much so that a fifteenth-century writer could use it to refer to the Virgin Mary; "manufacture" meant "to make by hand," but when goods came to be machine-made the old name continued to be used for the new process; "lingerie," when imported from France, meant "linen goods," but its most popular use today has nothing to do with linen; "quarantine" has long since lost its original Italian meaning of "forty days."

In addition, the language is steadily adding new words for new artifacts, processes, discoveries, and events. Quite apart from slang, which comes and goes with the seasons, what would Noah Webster make of such words as *airport, astronaut, auto, basketball, carburetor, dentifrice, gyroscope, launching pad, motel, movie star, nuclear fission, nylon, radar, scuba, television, world series,* and thousands of others? Yet these additions and changes are normal signs of growth. There is nothing static about the meanings of words in a living language.

This discussion can be summed up in the *principle of usage,* which is that the meanings of a word are determined by the ways in which speakers and writers *generally* use it. As people stop using a word in a particular way, that meaning becomes *obsolete,* and is so classified in unabridged dictionaries. If new meanings become generally accepted, they become *established* and are recorded in dictionaries.

DENOTATION AND CONNOTATION

The many meanings which a word may have may be described as of two main types. Consider these three sentences:

> Who is that *girl* with Bill?
> Who is that *wench* with Bill?
> Who is that *lass* with Bill?

All three italicized words point to the same referent — a relatively young human female. But, in addition, "wench" carries unpleasant associations; it not only points to a person but also expresses the speaker's attitude toward that person. Conversely, "lass" has poetic, picturesque, and rather pleasant associations. In contrast with "wench" and "lass," the word "girl" has neither pleasant nor unpleasant associations. We distinguish words which have strong associations from those which do not by saying that the former are *connotative* words and the latter are *denotative.* The meaning of "girl" is a *denotation* — the physical referent which the word denotes — whereas the meanings of "wench" and "lass" are *connotations* — compounds of the physical referent and an attitude which people associate with either the referent or the word. Such an attitude may be favorable or unfavorable. In "That is a cute hat" and "That is an absurd hat," the word "hat" is used denotatively in both sentences, but "cute" has favorable and "absurd" unfavorable connotations. Some words, such as *brave, efficient, fame, glory, hope,* and *valuable* usually have only favorable connotations. Others, such as *absurd, callous, hate, idiotic, lust, treason,* and *vicious* usually have only unfavorable connotations. Still others have favorable connotations in some contexts but unfavorable ones in others. Compare, for example, *free enterprise, free speech, free thinker, free love;* or a *fat check* and a *fat girl.*

The following verses aptly contrast favorable and unfavorable connotations:

> Call a woman a kitten, but never a cat;
> You can call her a mouse, cannot call her a rat;
> Call a woman a chicken, but never a hen;
> Or you surely will not be her caller again.
>
> You can call her a duck, cannot call her a goose;
> You can call her a deer, but never a moose;
> You can call her a lamb, but never a sheep;
> Economic she likes, but you can't call her cheap.
>
> You can say she's a vision, can't say she's a sight;
> And no woman is skinny, she's slender and slight;
> If she should burn you up, say she sets you afire,
> And you'll always be welcome, you tricky old liar.[1]

The denotative and connotative uses of words are sometimes referred to as *scientific* and *poetic* uses. These descriptions remind us that a writer's purpose determines his diction. A writer interested only in providing information will tend to use words at a denotative level. Since clear pointing to specific facts is his main aim, he cannot afford to let his readers make all sorts of private interpretations; therefore he tries to restrict interpretation by choosing words and contexts which are relatively free from connotations.

The following paragraph is a good example of scientific writing at a popular level. Notice that the words point to things, not to attitudes, and that the diction makes no attempt to create either favorable or unfavorable responses in the mind of the reader.

When a beam of sunlight enters a darkened room with dust in it, one can see the beam of light clearly defined as the light is scattered from the dust particles. The more dust particles in the room, the more the light is scattered; and if there is a real cloud of dust, the light is scattered so much that one can hardly see beyond it. The same thing happens to the beams from the headlights of a car in a fog. The small particles of water making up the fog in the air scatter the light that shines on them. The denser the fog, the more the light is scattered, the less of it gets through the fog, and the less one can see through a fog with even the most powerful beam of light. By measuring the fraction of the incident light that goes straight through the fog and the fraction that is scattered by the fog particles, one can estimate the number of

[1] John E. Donovan, "Semantics," *The Saturday Evening Post,* July 13, 1946. Reprinted by permission of Mrs. Gertrude D. Crane and *The Saturday Evening Post.*

water droplets in the fog — or the number of dust particles in the air. This method is accurate for determining the number of fine particles in a cloudy suspension in air or in water and is used frequently in analytical chemistry.[2]

The poet, in contrast with the scientist, is more concerned with creating emotional responses than with conveying information. His poetry may contain facts, may even be highly informative. But since his chief desire is to stimulate the imagination, he makes greater use of figurative language and of connotations which invite emotional responses. As the following passage illustrates, a poet who failed to do this would be most disappointing:

> The use of emotionally toned words is not, of course, always to be condemned. They are always harmful when we are trying to think clearly on a disputable point of fact. In poetry, on the other hand, they have a perfectly proper place, because in poetry (as in some kinds of prose) the arousing of suitable emotions is an important part of the purpose for which the words are used.
>
> In "The Eve of St. Agnes," Keats has written:
>
> > Full on this casement shone the wintry moon,
> > And threw warm gules on Madeline's fair breast.
>
> These are beautiful lines. Let us notice how much of their beauty follows from the proper choice of emotionally colored words and how completely it is lost if these words are replaced by neutral ones. The words with strikingly emotional meanings are *casement, gules, Madeline, fair,* and *breast. Casement* means simply a kind of window with emotional and romantic associations. *Gules* is the heraldic name for red, with the suggestion of romance which accompanies all heraldry. *Madeline* is simply a girl's name, but one calling out favorable emotions absent from a relatively plain and straightforward name. *Fair* simply means, in objective fact, that her skin was white or uncolored — a necessary condition for the colors of the window to show — but also *fair* implies warm emotional preference for an uncolored skin . . . . *Breast* has also similar emotional meanings, and the aim of scientific description might have been equally well obtained if it had been replaced by such a neutral word as *chest.*
>
> Let us now try the experiment of keeping these two lines in a metrical form, but replacing all the emotionally colored words by neutral ones, while making as few other changes as possible. We may write:
>
> > Full on this window shone the wintry moon,
> > Making red marks on Jane's uncolored chest.

No one will doubt that all of its poetic value has been knocked out of the passage by these changes. Yet the lines still mean the same in external fact; they still have the same objective meaning. It is only the emotional meaning which has been destroyed.[3]

[2] From Selig Hecht, *Explaining the Atom* (New York: The Viking Press, 1947).
[3] From Robert H. Thouless, *How to Think Straight* (New York: Simon and Schuster, 1939).

▶ *Decide from the context whether the italicized words in the following sentences and phrases are being used denotatively or connotatively. If connotatively, are the connotations favorable or unfavorable?*

1. I am *firm;* you are *stubborn;* he is *pig-headed.*
2. a *rubber* ball; a *rubber* check
3. a *dull* lecture; a *dull* knife
4. an *empty* glass; an *empty* life
5. The postman handed me a large, *square* envelope. Eric is handsome and attentive, but such a *square.*
6. The little girl had a *doll.* Her mother was quite a *doll,* too.
7. The difference between *a boyish prank* and *an act of vandalism* depends on whether it is your children or the neighbors' who do the mischief.
8. Would you describe this article as *scholarly* or *pedantic?*

THE ACCURATE WORD

Words are not right or wrong in themselves but as they succeed or fail to do what a writer wants them to do in a particular situation. If a word is to say what it was intended to say, it must have the right denotation and the right connotation. It must refer the reader accurately to the things and ideas which the writer wishes to communicate, and it must express only those attitudes which he intends to express.

Choosing the right denotation is usually easier than choosing the right connotation. Most student errors in denotation come from three sources: confusion of words with similar forms (*affect-effect, respectful-respective, stationary-stationery*); confusion of antonyms — words with opposite meanings (*antagonist-protagonist, port-starboard, urban-rural*); and the student's failure to be clear about what reference he wants made. The first of these mistakes is often considered an error in spelling. The second is usually a temporary confusion which will disappear as the student gets experience with the terms that cause trouble. The third error is the most difficult. More attention to specific diction will often help (page 179), but the only sure cure is to develop the habit of concern for accurate statement. There is no formula for developing that habit, but reading over your first draft slowly and challenging your diction is a constructive approach.

Most choices of diction are choices of connotation. When a word has obviously wrong connotations, as "skinny" for "slender" in an otherwise complimentary context, the fault is easy to spot and correct. Less obvious are the distinctions between words which are near synonyms (have similar meanings) but may have important differences in particular contexts. For example, "dawdle," "procrastinate," and "vacillate" all have the general meaning of not getting on with the job, but they suggest different kinds of inaction. Hamlet vacillates, and his vacillation leads to procrastination, but he does not dawdle.

169

▶ *In the following list, all the words in each line have roughly the same general meaning as the italicized word at the left; yet they cannot always be used interchangeably. Distinguish their differences by showing how they would affect the meaning of the phrase if they were substituted for the italicized word.*

An *angry* remark: annoyed, belligerent, indignant, irritable
A *careful* answer: cautious, circumspect, deliberate, painstaking
A *dirty* house: disorderly, filthy, messy, untidy
An *embarrassed* speaker: abashed, chagrined, flustered
An *odd* costume: bizarre, unmatched, unconventional, quaint
To *plead* for a favor: beg, coax, wheedle
To *reprimand* an offender: admonish, rebuke, scold, castigate
A *sharp* answer: clever, discriminating, unfriendly
A *tired* man: exhausted, sleepy, weary

THE APPROPRIATE WORD

Social Levels: Standard and Nonstandard English

Words not only point to things and to attitudes; they also reflect the social level of the person using them. Thus, "I have no money" and "I ain't got no money" refer to the same financial condition. One statement is just as clear as the other; but the connotations of the second invite the judgment that the speaker is not well educated. We distinguish between these two uses by saying that the first is *standard English* and the second is *nonstandard English*.

Standard English is a class dialect. It may be defined as the speech of those who enjoy a favored economic and social status in our society, and since this class may be roughly described as the educated class, we may say that standard dialect is the English that educated people speak and write. It is, therefore, the kind of English written and spoken by business executives, lawyers, doctors, ministers, teachers, writers, editors, artists, engineers, and other professional people, and, of course, by their families. All these comprise a small minority of those who use the language.

Nonstandard English is the language of those occupations which do not require what we call "higher education." It is essentially a spoken rather than a written language, but it is often imitated in writing by novelists, dramatists, and short-story writers when they are representing characters who would be expected to use nonstandard English. It is occasionally used by educated people when they are trying to be humorous, or sarcastic, or regional, or exaggeratedly humble.

Standard English is more expressive than nonstandard. The latter serves well enough the purposes for which it is commonly used, but its vocabulary is so limited that it can express many complex thoughts poorly if at all. Yet the strongest objection to it is social. Indeed, the use of nonstandard expressions is usually taken as a sure sign of inferior social background, and the unlucky speaker is handicapped in his struggle for economic and social advancement. This is one reason why teachers try so hard to weed nonstandard expressions out of student speech and writing. Colleges are preparing students to take their places on the economic and social levels at which standard English is spoken and written. College students, therefore, are committed to study and use it. Save in special assignments (chiefly fiction) in which the writer must represent uneducated speech, *nonstandard English has no place in college writing.*

The Range of Diction

• Within the standard dialect, writing styles may range from very formal to very informal. Before discussing this range, it will be useful to consider five classes of words into which the vocabularies of educated people can be divided.

Popular and Learned Words. In English, as in other languages, a great part of the total vocabulary consists of words which are common to the speech of educated and uneducated speakers alike. These words are the basic elements of our language. They are indispensable for everyday communication, and by means of them people from widely different social levels are able to speak a common language. These are called *popular words;* they belong to the whole populace.

Contrasted with these are words which we read more often than we hear, and write more often than we speak — words more widely used by educated than by uneducated people, and more likely to be used on formal than on informal occasions. These we call *learned words.* The distinction can be illustrated by contrasting some pairs which have roughly the same meaning.

Popular	Learned	Popular	Learned
agree	concur	lying	mendacious
beggar	mendicant	make easy	facilitate
behead	decapitate	near (in time)	imminent
break	fracture	prove	verify
clear	lucid	queer	eccentric
end	terminate	secret	cryptic, esoteric
fat	corpulent	surrender	capitulate
hair-do	coiffure	truth	veracity

Most learned words have been imported by educated people from a foreign language. At first these words retain their foreign pronunciations, meanings, and grammatical forms, but if they become so useful that they pass into the vocabulary of all classes, they lose their foreign characteristics and become Anglicized or naturalized — that is, treated as native words.

They lose their foreign pronunciations (*cottage, garage, lieutenant*), give up their foreign grammatical features (*gymnasia* and *indices* become *gymnasiums* and *indexes*), and acquire new meanings (*curfew, lingerie, quarantine*). In the process of being naturalized they usually pass through a transitional stage when both the foreign and the naturalized uses are common (*data are — data is; detoúr — détour; flair* meaning "capacity to detect" and also "having a knack for"). When the new uses begin to be popular they are often denounced as "mistakes," but when the process of naturalization is complete, the learned words in their new uses have become part of the popular vocabulary.

Idiomatic Diction. Every language contains many expressions which are not subject to logical analysis but are so characteristic that until one has learned to use them naturally he has not mastered the language. These are called idioms. Unless one has learned the language as a native, they are often troublesome to learn and use. For example, a foreigner who has learned what *hard* and *up* mean in English will still be puzzled by the phrase *hard up*. A Frenchman to whom the greeting "How do you carry yourself?" seems the most natural kind of expression will be puzzled by "How do you do?" Yet the only real difference between these two salutations is that one is the French way of talking and the other is the English way. Each is natural to the people who use it. Each is an idiomatic expression.

Because idioms are traditional rather than logical, they can be learned only by experience, not by rule. There is, for example, no rule that will tell us in advance what verbs will govern what prepositions. We say aim *at*, abide *by*, account *for*, arise *from*, and adhere *to*. The meaning of a verb may be no clue to its meaning in an idiomatic verb-adverb combination. A dictionary definition of *get* will be of little use in such phrases as *get ahead, get by, get over*. It is this arbitrary nature of idioms that causes trouble.

The following list illustrates common English idioms.

all in all	every now and then	mull over
be taken in	fight shy of	nice and cold
by and large	get away with	off and on
call off	get behind	pull through
call up	get on	put up with
catch fire	hard and fast	root out
come in handy	in any event	set about
do away with	keep up	set up
do up	look over	strike a bargain
down and out	make no bones about	tear up

You will notice that these idioms are mostly made up of popular words. They are used by all classes of people and are common to both standard and nonstandard speech. Often a particular idiom may be replaced by a more learned word. Thus "periodically" may be used for "every now and then" and "eradicate" for "root out." As we shall see later, whether such substitution is advisable will depend on the formality of the style.

Colloquialisms. The word *colloquial* is defined by the *American College Dictionary* as "characteristic of or appropriate to ordinary or familiar conversation rather than formal speech or writing." It does not mean here, as it is sometimes taken to mean, "incorrect," "slovenly," or "undesirable." Its closest synonym is "conversational." A colloquialism, therefore, is any word or expression in general use in the conversation of educated people.

This definition of *colloquial* makes it a broader term than *popular words* or *idioms.* Colloquialisms include popular words and idiomatic constructions; they also include learned words with popular meanings (the use of *alibi* to mean *excuse,* for example), and constructions which are not strictly idioms, especially the abbreviated or clipped forms of more formal words, such as *ad* for *advertisement.* The following are illustrations:

awfully (very)	fix (predicament)	over with (completed)
back of (behind)	it's me	party (person)
cute	kind (sort) of	peeve (annoy)
exam	lot(s) of	plenty (*adv.*)
expect (suppose)	mad (angry)	show (movie)
fellow	math	sure (certainly)

Slang. The *Oxford Dictionary* defines slang as "language of a highly colloquial type." Notice that the adjective is *colloquial* — that is, conversational — not *vulgar, incorrect,* or *nonstandard.* There may be specific slang words which are confined to standard or to nonstandard speakers, but slang is used at all social levels. Its use is less frequent and more discriminating among educated speakers, but, though a college president would usually avoid slang in a public address, he might well use it in many informal situations.

Slang has its origin in a desire to be vivid and original. People, especially young people, are constantly experimenting with language, using old words in unconventional ways (*kinky* = in high fashion, interesting) and, very rarely, coining new words (*groovy* = pleasant, wonderful, up-to-date). Many slang expressions are borrowed from the specialized vocabularies of particular occupations or recreations and put into general use —*zero in* (gunnery), *on the beam* (aeronautics), *behind the eight ball* (pool), *raise the ante* (poker), *pad* (rocketry), *offbeat* (music), *A-OK* (space flight). Most of them are figurative uses of expressions that have literal meanings in the general vocabulary — *no sweat, turned on, flipped, beat, cool, cat.*

If these adaptations serve a useful purpose, they may survive and in time be accepted as established usage. For example, the words *bus, cab, canter, hoax,* and *mob* were once slang but are now acceptable even in formal

English; the clipped forms *auto, phone, taxi,* and the words *enthuse, mad* (angry), and *shot* (hypodermic injection) were once slang but are now classified as colloquial; while such current slang terms as *sick* (morbid), *bugging* (electronic eavesdropping), and *kickback* are so common that their recognition as colloquialisms is already under way.

The great majority of slang terms, however, soon depreciate in value. The freshness that made them effective at first is soon worn off by overuse, and what was once creative becomes lazy borrowing. This is the chief reason why instructors often object to slang in college writing. If the slang words were carefully chosen and if they were appropriate to the purpose and style of the paper, they might be effective. But if slang were so chosen, there would be much less of it in student compositions.

Formal and Informal Styles

Formal English is primarily a written style, though it is occasionally used in public speeches of a serious or ceremonial nature. The following paragraph is an example of a formal style:

> There are, indeed, other objects of desire that if attained leave nothing but restlessness and dissatisfaction behind them. These are the objects pursued by fools. That such objects ever attract us is a proof of the disorganization of our nature, which drives us in contrary directions and is at war with itself. If we had attained anything like steadiness of thought or fixity of character, if we knew ourselves, we should know also our inalienable satisfactions. To say that all goods become worthless in possession is either a piece of superficial satire that intentionally denies the normal in order to make the abnormal seem more shocking, or else it is a confession of frivolity, a confession that, as an idiot never learns to distinguish reality amid the phantasms of his brain, so we have never learned to distinguish true goods amid our extravagances of whim and passion. That true goods exist is nevertheless a fact of moral experience. "A thing of beauty is a joy forever"; a great affection, a clear thought, a profound and well-tried faith are eternal possessions. And this is not merely a fact, to be asserted upon the authority of those who know it by experience. It is a psychological necessity. While we retain the same senses, we must get the same impressions from the same objects; while we keep our instincts and passions, we must pursue the same goods; while we have the same powers of imagination, we must experience the same delight in their exercise. Age brings about, of course, variation in all these particulars, and the susceptibility of two individuals is never exactly similar. But the eventual decay of our personal energies does not destroy the natural value of objects, so long as the same will embodies itself in other minds, and human nature subsists in the world. The sun is not now unreal because each one of us, in succession, and all of us in the end, must close our eyes upon it; and yet the sun exists for us only because we perceive it. The ideal has the same conditions of being, but has this advantage over the sun, that we cannot know if its light is ever destined to fail us.[4]

[4] From George Santayana, *The Sense of Beauty* (New York, 1896).

The tone of this passage is serious and dignified. The diction (*objects of desire, disorganization of our nature, inalienable satisfactions,* etc.) tends to be learned and elevated. The sentence structure makes frequent use of inverted word order, and many of the sentences tend to be long. Perhaps the quickest way to give some idea of the essential differences between formal and informal styles is to set up in parallel columns an excerpt from this passage and an informal rewriting of that excerpt:

Formal	*Informal*
There are, indeed, other objects of desire that if attained leave nothing but restlessness and dissatisfaction behind them. These are the objects pursued by fools. That such objects ever attract us is a proof of the disorganization of our nature, which drives us in contrary directions and is at war with itself. If we had attained anything like steadiness of thought or fixity of character, if we knew ourselves, we should know also our inalienable satisfactions.	We all have foolish desires. We want things which do not satisfy us when we get them. The fact that we want these things is evidence of our inconsistent nature. We are subject to conflicting desires and want to go in opposite directions at the same time. If we had a clearer understanding of our own needs and purposes, we would know what course was best for us.

The informal passage has a much more relaxed tone. The diction is simpler; the sentences are shorter (they average 13 words, in contrast to an average of 19 words in the formal version); the whole effect is less lofty. It should not be inferred that formal writing is "better" than informal, or vice versa. Ideally, the style should fit the situation in which it is used and should take into account the audience to whom the writing is addressed. For some audiences in some situations much is gained by the eloquence and dignity of a formal style. But for other audiences in other situations, ease and clarity may be what is most needed.

A Range of Styles. Between a very formal and a very informal style there is a wide range of shadings. That range may be suggested by the scale below, and the five examples that follow it. The scale is not intended to suggest that the whole stylistic range can be conveniently and clearly divided into five segments, or that any piece of writing can be precisely plotted on any point in the scale. The device illustrates the range of style; it does not define it.

Very Formal   *Very Informal*

1   2   3   4   5

175

1. I have, myself, full confidence that if all do their duty, if nothing is neglected, and if the best arrangements are made, as they are being made, we shall prove ourselves once again able to defend our island home, to ride out the storm of war, and to outlive the menace of tyranny, if necessary for years, if necessary alone. At any rate, that is what we are going to try to do. That is the resolve of His Majesty's Government — every man of them. That is the will of Parliament and the nation. The British Empire and the French Republic, linked together in their cause and in their need, will defend to the death their native soil, aiding each other like good comrades to the utmost of their strength. Even though large tracts of Europe and many old and famous States have fallen or may fall into the grip of the Gestapo and all the odious apparatus of Nazi rule, we shall not flag or fail. We shall go on to the end. We shall fight in France, we shall fight on the seas and oceans, we shall fight with growing confidence and growing strength in the air, we shall defend our island, whatever the cost may be. We shall fight on the beaches, we shall fight on the landing grounds, we shall fight in the fields and in the streets, we shall fight in the hills; we shall never surrender, and even if, which I do not for a moment believe, this island or a large part of it were subjugated and starving, then our Empire beyond the seas, armed and guarded by the British Fleet, would carry on the struggle, until, in God's good time, the new world, with all its power and might, steps forth to the rescue and the liberation of the old.[5]

2. Suppose it were perfectly certain that the life and fortune of every one of us would, one day or another, depend upon his winning or losing a game at chess. Don't you think that we should all consider it to be a primary duty to learn at least the names and the moves of the pieces; to have a notion of a gambit, and a keen eye for all the means of giving and getting out of check? Do you not think that we should look with a disapprobation amounting to scorn, upon the father who allowed his son, or the state which allowed its members, to grow up without knowing a pawn from a knight?

Yet it is a very plain and elementary truth that the life, the fortune, and the happiness of every one of us, and, more or less, of those who are connected with us, do depend upon our knowing something of the rules of a game infinitely more difficult and complicated than chess. It is a game which has been played for untold ages, every man and woman of us being one of the two players in a game of his or her own. The chessboard is the world, the pieces are the phenomena of the universe, the rules of the game are what we call the laws of nature. The player on the other side is hidden from us. We know that his play is always fair, just, and patient. But also we know, to our cost, that he never overlooks a mistake, or makes the smallest allowance for ignorance. To the man who plays well, the highest stakes are paid, with that sort of overflowing generosity with which the strong shows delight in strength. And one who plays ill is checkmated — without haste, but without remorse.[6]

[5] Winston Churchill addressing the House of Commons on June 4, 1949, after Dunkirk. Reprinted from his *Blood, Sweat, and Tears* (New York: G. P. Putnam's Sons, 1941).
[6] From Thomas Henry Huxley, "A Liberal Education and Where to Find It."

3. Frontier towns burned like tinder. The board streets and sidewalks, the open frame buildings, the lack of water pressure and of fire-fighting apparatus made them terribly vulnerable. Nearly every American city has had a great fire in its brief history. Often the lumber towns had a series of them. The very ground they rested on, built up of sawdust, slabs and refuse from the mills, was inflammable. The drying yards, with lumber stacked and open to the air, could quickly roar into acres of flame. There were always sparks from the big consumers and the straining boilers of the steam engines to start the disaster. Sawdust towns lived violently, with the rumble of logging, the snarl and scream of the buzz saw, and the tumult of the loading wharfs. And mostly they died violently. A sawmill town could not expect a peaceful end.[7]

4. Suppose my neighbor's house catches fire and I have a length of garden hose four or five hundred feet away. If he can take this garden hose and connect it up with his hydrant, I may help him to put out the fire. Now what do I do? I don't say to him before that operation, "Neighbor, my garden hose cost me fifteen dollars; you have to pay me fifteen dollars for it." No! What is the transaction that goes on? I don't want fifteen dollars — I want my garden hose back after the fire is over.[8]

5. You're going to paint that picturesque old barn. All right. One vertical line (better use charcoal) will place the corner of the barn, another line the base. A couple of lines for the trunk of the tree, and maybe a branch or two. Then a line to indicate the horizon — whatever divides the sky from whatever meets it (tree, barn, hill). That's all! No leaves, door-knobs, cats, mice, or daffodils. It's the painting that's fun, and any time wasted in getting into a mess of details is to be deplored. As we start to paint, anything resembling a real drawing on our canvas is purely accidental. . . .[9]

Of these five specimens along the range from formal to informal styles, the first and last lie outside the uses of normal freshman writing. The second, third, and fourth probably provide the best models for students to follow on most occasions. The Churchill paragraph is worth studying, not only for the historical importance of its subject matter, but also for the emphasis gained by the reiterated pattern of the parallel clauses beginning "We shall fight . . . ." The instructions for painting, although appropriate to the audience for which they were intended, would usually not be appropriate in the kind of writing with which freshman classes are concerned. But the differences in sentence structure, diction, and tone between very formal and very informal writing can best be seen in a contrast of the two extremes. For example, the average number of words in a sentence in the first passage is 36; in the fifth passage, 12 words.

[7] From Walter Havighurst, *The Long Ships Passing* (New York: The Macmillan Company, 1942).
[8] Franklin Delano Roosevelt introducing the Lend-Lease program at a press conference on December 17, 1940.
[9] From Joseph Alger, "Get In There and Paint," *Recreation,* November, 1944.

Confusion of Styles

A writer should choose the stylistic level most appropriate to his purpose, and he should stay with it. Words which are too formal or too colloquial for their context are discordant, or even ludicrous, and betray a lack of sureness. Notice the misfit diction in the following passage from an essay in which a student is relating how his service in the Marines helped to free him from the domination of his twin brother.

> I was never allowed to fight my own battles, for he was at my side and would step in and pound the hell out of my diabolical enemies. This, too, contributed to my shyness.
> During the terminating days of my high-school career I came to the conclusion that life in the Marine Corps would cure me of this bad attribute. I quickly told my brother. His eyes seemed to be glaring like a dragon's. He then told me, "I am going to join the army and you shall do such also."

The lapses here are clear enough. Except in some kinds of dialogue, profanity is almost never justifiable in college writing. If it is used at all, the whole style of the paper must be so obviously colloquial that the profanity does not call attention to itself. Yet here is profanity followed immediately by learned words like *diabolical, terminating,* and *attribute.* These two levels of usage, however justifiable either might be alone, are ludicrously inconsistent in the same paper. Other choices of diction are just as bad. The description of the brother's eyes "glaring like a dragon's" is a trite and far-fetched metaphor, and his words "you shall do such also" are comically unidiomatic. What the brother would probably say is, "I'm going to join the army, and so are you."

Incongruous diction is most conspicuous in writing which is clearly formal or clearly informal. The italicized substitutions shown below are obviously out of place in this paragraph (which is properly quoted on page 174):

> There are, indeed, other objects of desire that if *got* leave nothing but restlessness and *griping* behind them. These are the objects pursued by fools. That such objects ever attract us is a proof of the *cussedness* of our nature, which drives us in contrary directions and is at war with itself. If we had attained anything like steadiness of thought or fixity of character, if we knew ourselves, we should know also *what's good for us.* To say that all goods become worthless in possession is either a piece of *half-baked bunk* that intentionally denies the normal in order to make the abnormal seem more shocking, or else it is a confession of frivolity, a confession that, as an idiot never learns *what the score is,* so we have never learned to distinguish true goods amid our extravagances of whim and passion. That true goods exist is nevertheless a fact of moral experience. "A thing of beauty is a joy forever"; a great *yen,* a *bright idea,* a profound and well-tried faith, are eternal possessions. And this is not merely a fact, to be asserted upon the *say-so* of those who know it by experience. It is a psychological necessity.

There are contexts in which *got, griping, cussedness, what's good for us, half-baked, bunk, what the score is, yen, bright idea,* and *say-so* could be appropriate, but this is not one of them. These colloquial and slang expressions are as much out of place in a formal style as an electric guitar in a symphony orchestra.

Conversely, the italicized learned words in the following informal selection are hopelessly out of tone.

> Have you ever tried to quit smoking? It's quite simple. I know. I have *achieved abstinence* thousands of times already. In fact, I quit every day. I awaken in the morning — my nose and throat dry and parched. Then, I decide to *renounce all further association with the weed.* But it's a terrible vice over which I no longer have any control. I've got to have a smoke. Just one. Then I'll *refrain from further indulgence* the rest of the day. Just one to take care of my terrible longing. I can go without food, without drink. But I must have a cigarette. Just one.
>
> So I smoke one before going to school. Only that one. I promise myself, I'm not going to smoke any more today. I'll leave my cigarettes home today. Yeh, that's what I'll do. And since I have no cigarettes, I *shall be unable to make even a momentary concession to appetite.*

THE SPECIFIC WORD

In this context "specific" is the opposite of "general." A specific word points to a particular referent — a particular person, object, or event; a general word points to a group or class of referents. Thus "Arnold Palmer," "Mickey Mantle," "the present heavyweight champion," "the apple tree beside my garage," and "last night's rain" indicate particular referents. But "golfer," "baseball player," "pugilist," "tree," and "rain" indicate group referents. The general term, therefore, includes a number of specific terms, as "red" includes carmine, coral, crimson, maroon, rose, scarlet, vermilion, and so on, and as "Midwest" includes Michigan, Minnesota, Illinois, Indiana, Iowa, and several other states.

Actually the contrast between "specific" and "general" is relative. A term may be specific in contrast to one word, but general in contrast to another. We can show this relativity by the following table.

Very General	*Less General*	*More Specific*	*Quite Specific*
athlete	baseball player	Dodger pitcher	Sandy Koufax
college student	freshman	member of Dr. Jones's composition section	Bill Mason
vegetation	tree	apple tree	the apple tree beside my garage
criminal	thief	pickpocket	the man who stole my wallet

As you see, the words in the middle columns are more specific than those at the left but more general than those at the right.

The more general words are, the harder it will be for a reader to see precisely what a writer intends them to mean. For example, "The man was making preparations for a journey" is such a general statement that we get almost no picture of what the man was actually doing. He may have been making hotel reservations, buying a railroad ticket, having his car tuned up, arranging for someone to handle his business affairs, or packing a suitcase.

Notice below how the specific diction at the right communicates meaning which is not conveyed by the general diction at the left.

General	*Specific*
He is an accomplished athlete.	He is a top-flight golfer.
He drives an old car.	He drives a 1960 Buick.
The boy has a serious disease.	George Travers has diphtheria.
I have been reading a Shakespearean play.	I have been reading *Macbeth*.
Her grades at midsemester were unsatisfactory.	She received two F's and a D at midsemester.
After the strenuous activities of the day, I did not feel like dancing.	After playing 36 holes of golf, I did not feel like doing the watusi.

To find the most telling specific word or phrase requires thought, and too many students are willing to take the easy way out and use "utility words" instead. Of these words, Professor A. G. Kennedy says, "Any long-used and well-developed language accumulates ultimately a supply of general utility words which have such broad meaning and general application that they can be utilized in a great many different ways with no special change of meaning."[10] These, as their name implies, are useful words. In conversation, their general meaning is often sharpened by tone of voice, facial expression, or gesture. Their discreet use in writing needs no defense, but when a writer uses them to excess, his work is likely to be colorless and inexact, as the following sentences show.

1. It gave me a *funny feeling* to hear him say that another war was inevitable. (Precisely what is a "funny feeling" in this context — a feeling of despair, of panic, of hopelessness, of shock, of disgust, of revulsion?)

2. His wife is always a *good dresser*. Today she wore a *lovely outfit*. It was a *nice shade of blue*. She also wore a *cute* little hat with a matching blue ribbon. ("Good" in what sense — chic, tasteful, glamorous? What was the "outfit" — a suit, a blouse and skirt, a sweater and skirt, a one-piece dress? Precisely what shade of blue was it? Can you imagine a fashion reporter describing a woman's costume as "an outfit in a nice shade of blue"? Does "cute" give you a clear picture of the hat?)

[10] *Current English* (Boston: Ginn and Company, 1935), p. 552.

3. That kind of publicity is always *bad business* for *an organization,* and the boys in our chapter house felt *pretty bad* about it. (What is meant by "bad business" here? Does it cause the fraternity to lose prestige on campus? Does it make it more difficult to get dates? Does it hurt pledging? Does it invite administrative interference in fraternity management? If the organization is a fraternity, why not say so? When the boys feel "pretty bad," how do they feel? Angry? Ashamed? Disgusted? Embarrassed? Resentful? Indignant?)

The italicized words in these sentences are so vague, could mean so many different things, that the sentences fail to communicate precise meaning. They reveal either fuzzy or lazy thinking and should never be allowed to get beyond the first draft. The way to revise them is, first, to sharpen the idea to be expressed and, second, to choose words specific enough to express it exactly.

Sensory Words. A number of specific words refer to sensory experiences, to what we see, hear, touch, taste, and smell. Because these words call up sensory images, they are particularly effective in description. In the following list, some words could fit into more than one sensory category.

Touch: chill, clammy, cold, corrugated, grainy, gritty, harsh, jarring, knobby, moist, nubby, numb, plushy, rough, satiny, slimy, slithering, smooth, sting, tingle, tickly, velvety.

Taste: bland, biting, bitter, brackish, briny, metallic, minty, nutty, peppery, salty, sour, spicy, sweet, tainted, vinegary, yeasty.

Smell: acrid, fetid, greasy, mouldy, musky, musty, pungent, putrid, rancid, rank, reek, stench, sulphurous, woodsy.

Sound: bellow, blare, buzz, chatter, chime, clang, clatter, clink, crackle, crash, creak, gurgle, hiss, hum, murmur, pop, purr, rattle, rustle, screech, snap, splash, squeak, swish, tinkle, whine, whisper.

Sight: blaze, bleary, bloody, burnished, chalky, dappled, ebony, flame, flash, flicker, florid, foggy, gaudy, glare, glitter, glossy, glow, golden, grimy, haze, inky, leaden, lurid, muddy, roiled, sallow, shadow, smudged, spark, streak, tawny, turbid.

Sensory words help the reader feel the experience that the writer is recording. Notice how the following description makes the reader feel, hear, see, and smell the details of ploughing.

The ploughing, now in full swing, enveloped him in a vague, slow-moving whirl of things. Underneath him was the jarring, jolting, trembling machine; not a clod was turned, not an obstacle encountered, that he did not receive the swift impression of it through all his body; the very friction of the damp soil, sliding incessantly from the shiny surface of the shears, seemed to reproduce itself in his finger-tips and along the back of his head. He heard the horse-hoofs by the myriads crushing down easily, deeply, into the loam, the prolonged clinking of trace-chains, the working of the smooth brown flanks in the harness, the clatter of wooden hames, the champing of bits, the click of iron shoes against pebbles, the brittle stubble of the surface ground crackling and snapping as the furrows turned, the sonorous, steady breaths wrenched from the deep, laboring chests, strap-bound, shining with sweat, and all along the line the voices of the men talking to the horses. Everywhere there were visions of glossy brown backs, straining, heaving, swollen with muscle; harness streaked with specks of froth, broad, cup-shaped hoofs, heavy with brown loam; men's faces red with tan, blue overalls spotted with axle-grease; muscled hands, the knuckles whitened in their grip on the reins, and through it all the ammoniacal smell of the horses, the bitter reek of perspiration of beasts and men, the aroma of warm leather, the scent of dead stubble — and stronger and more penetrating than everything else, the heavy, enervating odor of the upturned, living earth.[11]

This stress on the value of specific words should not imply that general diction is never desirable. For example, when you are asked to summarize a 5000-word essay in 500 words, your purpose is to state the central thought of the essay, not its illustrative detail, and your summary has to be more general than the original. Moreover, a writer will not always intend to be specific. His statement may depend not on a set of particular facts but on a broad or universal truth. Whether a subject should be treated generally or specifically is part of the decision about purpose. An excellent illustration is the writing of the Declaration of Independence.

The committee appointed to write the Declaration had a double duty to perform. It had, in the same document, to make a general statement of the relationship between free people and their governors and a particular statement of the abuses which George III had committed against the Colonies. The first part of the Declaration is necessarily, and wisely, general:

> We hold these truths to be self-evident, that all men are created equal, that they are endowed by their Creator with certain unalienable rights. . . . That to secure these rights, Governments are instituted among Men, deriving their just powers from the consent of the governed. . . .

These remarks could apply to any nation, and have been interpreted by other nations as applying to themselves. The second part is more specific:

> For quartering large bodies of troops among us. . . .
> For cutting off our Trade with all parts of the world:
> For imposing taxes on us without our Consent:
> For depriving us in many cases of the benefit of Trial by Jury. . . .

These charges refer to particular acts of a particular monarch. This part of the Declaration is less valuable as a universal inspiration but more informative as a statement of why the Colonies renounced their allegiance to George III.

[11] From Frank Norris, *The Octopus.*

182

The contrast between the two parts of the Declaration shows that there is a time to be general and a time to be specific. Your own analysis of the assignment should guide your choice, but you should know that college instructors emphasize specific diction mainly because much college writing is more general than it need be.

FIGURATIVE LANGUAGE

Figurative language communicates by analogy. One thing is likened to another, usually familiar, and the comparison invites the imagination to visualize the similarities or the differences.

> An aged man is but a paltry thing,
> A tattered coat upon a stick . . .

combines a literal statement in the first line with a vivid and emotionally charged figure in the second. To call an old man "a paltry thing" — a literal statement — indicates what the poet thinks of age. But to compare him to a scarecrow, "a tattered coat upon a stick," suggests a hollow, empty quality in old age, a feeble helplessness that arouses pity and compassion. Good figures of speech grow out of active thought and strong feeling in the writer, and they arouse similar responses in a reader.

The commonest figures of speech are metaphors, similes, allusions, and personification.

Metaphors and Similes

Both metaphor and simile compare two things, but the former says they are the same, whereas the latter merely says they are similar. Metaphor says an old man *is* a scarecrow; simile says he is *like* one. Here are other examples:

Metaphors	*Similes*
The sky was a vast black blanket riddled with tiny star holes.	The star-dotted sky was like a vast black blanket riddled with tiny holes.
The moon was a ghostly galleon tossed upon cloudy seas.	As fresh he was as is the month of May.
Marriage had modified his conception of her. Once she had been his lovely wild rose; now she was the thorn in his flesh.	The judge's head oscillated from one side of the net to the other, for all the world like the pendulum of a grandfather clock.

The effectiveness of metaphors and similes lies in their power to evoke images, emotions, even the very flavors of experience, which are difficult if not impossible to communicate in literal terms. They picture vividly in a few words what would be less effectively described in many. Consider how the following metaphors describe an abstract, complex, and emotional attitude toward life in terms which allow a reader to share the mood and emotions of the speaker:

> Life's but a walking shadow, a poor player
> That struts and frets his hour upon the stage
> And then is heard no more. It is a tale
> Told by an idiot, full of sound and fury,
> Signifying nothing.

A long essay on life's insignificance could evoke a particular state of mind no more forcefully than Shakespeare did in this triple metaphor in which Macbeth sees his life as unsubstantial as a shadow, as ephemeral as an actor's performance, and as meaningless as an idiot's babbling.

To move to something still more difficult, consider these lines from T. S. Eliot's *The Love Song of J. Alfred Prufrock:*

> When the evening is spread out against the sky
> Like a patient etherized upon a table. . . .

The presence of *like* signals a simile, though an evening and an etherized patient seem, at first, so different that we wonder why they are compared at all. Presumably the patient is motionless and quiet, unconscious, between life and death, in a waiting phase which will be terminated by something dramatic. He is possibly pale, surrounded by the colorless sterility of an operating theater. So the evening is a still, relaxed time between light and darkness, a suspension which will be terminated by night. There is a sense of danger in the night to come, just as there is danger in the operation the patient will undergo. The comparison is unique and satisfying.

Many words and phrases seldom thought of as figures of speech are metaphors or similes. Thus *foil* and *parry* come from fencing; *checkmate* is a metaphor from chess; *rosy red* and *sapphire blue* were once similes, as were *dirt cheap* and *silver hair. At bay* describes a hunted animal when it finally turns to face the baying hounds; a *crestfallen* cock is one whose comb no longer stands erect because of an injury in a fight; and an *alarm* was a call to arms. Many other expressions retain their metaphorical appearance, but are so common that we no longer think of them as figures of speech — expressions such as the mouth of a river, the face of a clock, the front (originally "forehead") of a house, the brow of a hill, the top of the morning.

Allusions

Allusions are figures of speech which suggest a similarity between people, places, or events — real or imaginary — as in "the Babe Ruth of Bowling," "the Athens of the Midwest," "a dog-in-the-manger attitude."

The suggested comparison depends on the reader's having certain pieces of knowledge and predictable attitudes toward the subjects of that knowledge.

> Though I have seen my head (grown slightly bald) brought in upon a platter
> I am no prophet . . .

expects the reader to recall the death of John the Baptist and to compare him in his heroism with T. S. Eliot's speaker, J. Alfred Prufrock. To be understood, allusions must draw upon a general body of knowledge, such as myth or history or literature. All of us have ideas about certain personalities — Atlas, Helen of Troy, Joan of Arc, Henry VIII, Sir Walter Raleigh, Pocahontas, Abraham Lincoln — and about certain events — the stratagem of the Trojan Horse, the suicide of Cleopatra, the Crucifixion, the Crusades, Columbus's first voyage, the California gold rush, the assassination of John F. Kennedy. It is from such reservoirs of information that allusions are drawn.

Like metaphors and similes, allusions are vivid and memorable, but they must be used with care. Allusions which are overused become trite and stale. Conversely, an allusion which a reader does not recognize will mean nothing and may annoy him. Rather than blame his own ignorance, he will label the allusion "pedantic." A suitable allusion not only communicates effectively but gives the pleasure of recognition. The choice of an allusion, like any choice of diction, is determined by its appropriateness to the idea, its freshness, and its aptness for the intended reader.

Personification

Personification is the device of endowing animals, inanimate objects, abstractions, and events with human qualities and abilities:

> The eagle, perched on his mountain throne, surveyed the far reaches of his kingdom.
> The flames ate hungrily at the wooden foundations.
> The once proud trees bent meekly before the storm.
> All around, the forest united in a conspiracy against them.
> Her clothes not only invited attention, they commanded it.

Personification, like metaphor, simile, and allusion, implies and pictures a similarity. But whereas metaphor may compare any two things, one of the elements of a personification must be a human characteristic. The subject must be described in terms of human appearance, actions, attitudes, feelings, or responses. As with other figures of speech, the effective personification is the unhackneyed one. Consider, for example, these famous lines of Andrew Marvell:

> But at my back I always hear
> Time's wingèd chariot hurrying near.

The personification of time as Father Time is common enough, but here Time becomes a more distinctive and interesting figure, a charioteer relentlessly pursuing the speaker.

Inappropriate Figures

The power of figures of speech to call up vivid images sometimes leads an uncritical writer into trouble. For if the figures are inappropriate, they may suggest no reference at all, or they may call up images which are incongruous or incredible. The student who described his brother's eyes as "glaring like a dragon's" (page 178) was writing without thinking. If he had asked himself, "Is this really the way he looked?" he might have realized that his simile was neither fresh nor appropriate. Obviously he did not "see" what he was saying. The habit of using figurative language without visualizing its probable effect often results in confused imagery:

> When spring comes, the face of old Mother Earth is arrayed in garments of breath-taking beauty.
>
> Efforts to help the veterans were sidetracked by a bog of red tape.
>
> The President's ill-advised action has thrown the ship of state into low gear, and unless congressmen wipe out party lines and carry the ball as a team, it may take the country months to get back on an even keel.

The beauty of spring has often been compared to that of a woman's face, or to a woman's clothes; but telescoping the two images suggests a face wearing clothes, and is ludicrous. Sidetracked effort is a common enough metaphor, but to mix this railroad image with that of a bog and then with red tape, shows that the writer was not visualizing. The third sentence, more chaotic still, mixes images of a ship, a car, some lines that can be erased (chalk or pencil lines?), a football team, and a ship again — all in one blurred comparison. Mixed images, like shifts in sentence structure, show what comes of changing the structure halfway through a sentence. They also show what comes of using words because they "sound good," not because of what a reader will get from them.

Similes, too, may go wrong if images are mixed or inappropriate:

> He felt as uncomfortable and out of place in a room full of women as a wolf in a sheepfold.
>
> The huge rock went crashing down the hill like a lover rushing to meet his lass.

Far-fetched similes like these invite the reader to see unlikely similarities which are incongruous or strained. It is hard, for instance, to think of a wolf being uncomfortable in a sheepfold, or to picture a rock crashing downhill in the same mood and manner as a young man going to meet his girl. A reader is more likely to laugh at such a comparison than to accept it sympathetically.

▶ *Identify the following figures of speech. If you consider any of them inappropriate, explain why.*

1. Life like a dome of many-colored glass
   Stains the white radiance of eternity.
2. Drivers who drink keep Charon working overtime.
3. Into this great forest the hand of man had never set foot.
4. His words fanned the flame of her indignation and caused it to boil over.
5. Along the river bank the willows were whispering in the wind.
6. I cannot praise a fugitive and cloistered virtue . . . that never sallies out and sees her adversary, but slinks out of the race, where that immortal garland is to be run for, not without dust and heat.
7. Like the foolish virgins in the Bible, the politicians have been asleep at the switch and have allowed a glorious opportunity to go down the drain.
8. The trouble with arguing with your wife is that, even if you win, it's a Pyrrhic victory.
9. Can Honour's voice provoke the silent dust,
   Or Flattery soothe the dull cold ear of death?
10. For anyone who has slept in one of those hammocks the bed of Procrustes would have no terrors.
11. The hydrogen bomb may yet prove to be another Frankenstein.
12. You shall not press down upon the brow of labor this crown of thorns. You shall not crucify mankind upon a cross of gold.
13. Even as a young man, this colossus of industry, this Napoleon of finance, was recognized as a budding business genius.
14. Such appears to me, king, this present life of man on earth in comparison with the time which is unknown to us, as though you were sitting at the banquet with your leaders and thanes in winter and the fire was lighted and the hall warmed, and it rained and snowed and stormed outside; and there would come a sparrow and quickly fly through the house, come in through one door and go out through the other. Now in the time that he is inside he is not touched by the storm of winter; but that is only the twinkling of an eye and the least interval, and at once he comes from winter back to winter again. So this life of man appears save for but a little while; what goes before or what follows after we do not know.

THE UNSPOILED WORD

The terms *trite, hackneyed, shopworn, threadbare,* and *cliché* are used to characterize expressions which have been spoiled by overuse. Just as cloth loses its luster and fruit its texture by excessive and careless handling, so words and phrases in special senses lose interest and force by too much use. Such expressions as "a calculated risk," "a moral victory," "a near miss," "frame of reference," "escalation," and such figures of speech as "blind as a bat," "busy as a bee," "cool as a cucumber," "safe as the bank" were once vigorous and crisp, but they have lost the freshness which made them effective and are now little more than conspicuous utility words, common in casual conversation, but undesirable in any writing in which the choice of diction is important.

The worst thing about trite diction is the way it blocks thought. A writer who uses a ready-made phrase instead of fashioning his own thought into words soon has no thought beyond the stereotyped comment which his trite diction suggests. Consequently his ideas and observations follow set patterns: any change in personnel becomes a "shakeup"; all hopes become "fond," "foolish," or "forlorn"; standard procedure for making a suggestion is to "drop a hint"; defeats are "crushing"; changes in the existing system are "noble experiments" or "dangerous departures"; unexpected occurrences are "bolts from the blue"; and people who "sow wild oats" always have to "pay the piper" even though they are "as poor as churchmice." The result is a kind of automat-thinking in which the writer puts in a trite phrase and pulls out a platitude.

Triteness can be cut out in revision, and should be. But the best way to keep it out of your writing is to keep your diction specific. As long as you are thinking about what you want your writing to do, you are likely to use clear, fresh words. Triteness is usually a sign that the writer has stopped thinking. Notice how the following essay fails to provide the illustrative detail and specific diction necessary to make the thoughts clear, and resorts instead to trite statements which serve as escapes from thinking. Underline every trite expression you detect in it.

> To be taken out of a little world, high school, and placed on a large university campus was a big step in my life. From the first day I arrived at the University, I changed. I could no longer be "mother's little girl" and run to her for advice on what to do about this and how to do that. I had to change.
>
> I am, from all outward appearances, the same person I was when I left home in September and yet, I'm not. Being with people who are more mature has helped me grow up. I've developed a more grown-up idea of life. I've had to make decisions and judgments I've never before been faced with. I've had to give my own opinions and as the old saying goes, "fend for myself." Life isn't a bower of roses, and I've learned it. I've learned to think more seriously of why I'm at school and what I'm deriving from it. Am I doing my best down here? If not, I'd better get busy. People depend on me and I've had to shoulder responsibility. I've grown up a lot. I'm on my own. I have to be able to prove to myself and my parents I can take my place in the world.
>
> Money doesn't grow on trees and how well I've learned that. What a rude awakening, when I finally realized all the odd change I used to ask for at home wasn't with me at school. I had thought my allowance was an enormous amount and, before I knew it, it was gone. College has taught me "a penny saved is a penny earned." I've learned to live within my allowance and have some left to store in my bank for a rainy day.

College has helped me to become a more mature person who has the ability to make decisions for herself. It's not all in the books, what you learn at college. It's your everyday existence with different people and situations that gives you something more, perhaps helps you grow up a little. It's made me a better person and more able to cope with any situation which is to come.

IMPROVING VOCABULARY

The major consideration in any attempt to improve one's vocabulary should not be quantity but usefulness. The size of one's vocabulary is more important in reading than in writing, not only because all of us read much more than we write, but also because as readers we cannot control the author's choice of diction but must respond to whatever words he chooses. As writers, we decide what words to use, and our choice will be determined by selecting from the words we already know the ones which best express the thought and fit the context of the particular sentence we are writing.

It is useful to distinguish two kinds of vocabulary: *recognition* and *active*. The recognition vocabulary is the total stock of words a person knows well enough to understand when he meets them in context. He may not be able to define all these words, and there are many that he will never use in his own speech or writing, but if he can interpret them correctly when he meets them in context, they are part of his recognition vocabulary. The active vocabulary, on the other hand, is the stock of words that a person actually uses in his own speech or writing. It is, of course, a much smaller stock — perhaps a quarter the size of the recognition vocabulary.

Improving Your Recognition Vocabulary

Attempts to improve one's recognition vocabulary should be selective. A college freshman does not have the young child's need to learn additional words as quickly as he can. The freshman starts from a very considerable base. Estimates of the average size of a college freshman's vocabulary now suggest a figure upwards of 100,000 words. Statistical averages are not reliable for individuals, but it seems reasonable to believe that the most useful additions to your recognition vocabulary are words you are likely to encounter in your college reading. The more you read, the more new words you will encounter. If you make it a habit to assimilate new words into your vocabulary, you will make significant additions without further effort.

The best prerequisite for increasing vocabulary is a desire to learn — not just to learn words, but to know more about any subject that comes one's way. It has been said that a first course in biology introduces students to more new words than a first course in a foreign language. These words not only name animals and plants and their parts but also express concepts, processes, and relationships. So learning the words is part of learning the subject. There is a good case for the argument that a person's vocabulary is a product of his intellectual growth. Attempts to increase vocabulary apart from that growth are often artificial and short-lived.

Recognition by Context. For a number of reasons, the best way to improve your recognition vocabulary is to watch context. This is the method you must use in understanding speech, since you cannot usually stop a speaker while you look up a word in a dictionary. Second, it is the method used by lexicographers (makers of dictionaries); far from being a "lazy" or "guessing" method, it is the only way to become sensitive to educated usage. Third, it is the method you have been using for the last sixteen or seventeen years, and by it you have learned most of the words now in your recognition vocabulary.

As you acquire skill and confidence in interpreting words from context, you will learn to spot the ways in which a speaker or writer helps to make clear the meanings of unusual words. Sometimes he will actually define a new word, as we did with *lexicographers* above. Sometimes he will explain the word by showing it in operation, as when we are told that a *scribe* makes and preserves books. Sometimes he will repeat the meaning in other words of similar meaning, as when a writer couples the learned words *symbols and referents* with their popular equivalents *words and things*. Sometimes he will use a practical illustration to make the meaning clear. By learning to look for such aids you will not only become a better reader and listener, but you will begin to use these explanatory techniques yourself and so become a better speaker and writer.

▶ *Each of the following passages contains an italicized word, the meaning of which may be obtained from the context. Can you tell without consulting a dictionary what each of these words must mean?*

1. The lawyer said that such newspaper stories were *prejudicial* because they encouraged the public to judge the defendant guilty before he had been tried.

2. The *pediatrician* examined the baby carefully and recommended a change in formula.

3. There was an obvious *disparity* in their ages; he looked old enough to be her father.

4. An Englishman who says that he finds American women homely may not be *disparaging* them. He may just mean they make him feel at home.

5. We are often uncertain what punishment to inflict for such offenses. If we are too harsh, we may seem to be seeking vengeance rather than justice; if we show too much *clemency,* we may give the impression that we do not consider the offense a serious one.

Discovery by Dictionary Reference. When you look up a word in your dictionary[12] you should try to find out as much as you can about it. You know that when you are introduced to someone your chances of remembering his name or even recognizing him again are influenced by the extent of your first experience with him. If all you learn is his name, you may forget that quickly; but if you talk with him and find out what he does for a living, where he comes from, what his background is, and what his chief interests and hobbies are, you may remember him well months or even years later. The same thing is true of your introduction to new words. The more you find out about them from your dictionary, the better you will remember them; and the better you remember them, the more likely you are to transfer them to your active vocabulary.

The kinds of information provided in a college-level desk dictionary are illustrated in the following entry:

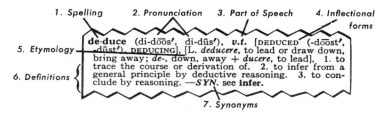

1. Spelling   2. Pronunciation   3. Part of Speech   4. Inflectional forms

5. Etymology

6. Definitions

de·duce (di-dōos′, di-dūs′), *v.t.* [DEDUCED (-dōost′, -dūst′), DEDUCING], [L. *deducere*, to lead or draw down, bring away; *de-*, down, away + *ducere*, to lead], 1. to trace the course or derivation of. 2. to infer from a general principle by deductive reasoning. 3. to conclude by reasoning. —*SYN.* see **infer**.

7. Synonyms

From *Webster's New World Dictionary of the American Language,* College Edition. Copyright © 1966 by The World Publishing Company, Cleveland, Ohio.

This information consists of (1) the spelling, including the way a word is broken into parts if it has to be hyphenated; (2) the pronunciation; (3) the part of speech in which the word is used; (4) its principal parts, if it is a verb (or its plural form if it is a noun with an irregular plural); (5) its etymology, or the form and meaning it had in the language from which it came; (6) the definitions; and (7) sometimes synonyms or antonyms. In some entries there may be subject labels to identify the special field in which a particular definition is used, as *astronomy* or *physics.* In other entries usage labels may identify a word as *archaic, slang, colloquial,* or *dialectal.* Because different dictionaries use slightly different systems for recording all this information, you should read the introductory matter in your dictionary and be sure you know how to read the word entries.

---

[12] For the college student, the best all-purpose dictionary is a desk dictionary. Although the best of these contain less than a quarter of the entries in an unabridged dictionary (see page 242), they are so well edited that they provide nearly all the information one is likely to need about words. Among the most widely used are the following (alphabetically listed): *The American College Dictionary,* Random House, New York (*ACD*); the Funk and Wagnalls *Standard College Dictionary,* text edition, Harcourt, Brace & World, New York (*SCD*); *Webster's New World Dictionary,* World Publishing Company, Cleveland (*NWD*); *Webster's Seventh New Collegiate Dictionary,* G. & C. Merriam Co., Springfield, Mass. (*NCD*).

▶ *The following quiz will test your knowledge of your own dictionary. Check your answers by the introductory pages and selected entries.*

1. How does your dictionary record variant spellings of the same word: in one entry or in different entries? Is the preferred spelling necessarily "more correct" than an alternate spelling?

2. How is pronunciation indicated in your dictionary? Is there a key to the symbols at the bottom of the page, or only in the introductory matter?

3. Where are the etymologies shown: after the inflectional forms, or at the end of the entry? In the entry shown above, *L* is the symbol for Latin. Other common origins are *Gr* (Greek), *F* (French), *N* (Norse), *O* for *Old*, as in *Old English, Old French,* etc. If you are not sure how to interpret these symbols, where in your dictionary can you find out?

4. In what order are the definitions given: in historical order, or in order of most frequent use? If you are not sure, where can you find out?

5. How are foreign words identified — that is, words that are still considered foreign rather than English, and so have to be underlined in manuscript or italicized in print? If you are not sure, how can you find out? (Hint: Check *Gestalt, bon voyage, in absentia.*)

6. For which of the following entries are synonyms or antonyms given: *ambition, deface, fiendish, luster, restive, voracious?*

7. How are the following words pronounced: *acclimate, alias, banal, data, ennui, impious, impotent, joust, schism, Wagnerian?*

The things you most need to know about a new word are its pronunciation, etymology, and meanings. The pronunciation not only helps you to pronounce it conventionally in reading aloud or in speech, but also helps you fix the word in your memory. Since the appearance of a word is often no safe clue to its sound, we have all had the embarrassing experience of making a very obvious mispronunciation when called upon to read an unfamiliar word aloud. Even such fairly common words as *abyss, blatant, caprice, decade, echelon, façade, gauge,* and *ribald* can be troublesome for a person who has met them only in his reading and has never heard them spoken.

The etymology of a word gives you its family history and thus makes your knowledge of it more complete. When you know, for example, that *crucial* comes from the Latin word for *cross,* you can see that in a crucial decision, we figuratively stand at a crossroads and decide which way we will go, and you may discover a hitherto unsuspected relationship among *crucial, crucify, crusade,* and *crux.*

Apart from its usefulness in making you a more discerning or more critical user of words, the study of etymology can be a pleasant hobby. It may not make the study of the *calculus* any easier to know that its name came from the Latin word for a pebble and goes back to the days when the Romans used pebbles to help them with their arithmetic; but it is interesting to be reminded from what primitive origins modern calculating machines have come. It is a testimony to human intolerance that *sinister* originally meant *left-handed* and a *barbarian* was once a *stranger*. And it is amusing to discover that our slang phrase *in the coop* perpetuates the original meaning of *jail,* a cage or coop. Some people find it as much fun to collect etymologies as to collect stamps, and much less expensive.

Recognition by Word Analysis. Looking up an etymology inevitably leads to word analysis, the breaking down of a word into its parts and the recognition of the original meaning of each part. Thus we are analyzing *docile* when we see that it is made up of the root *docere,* "to teach," and the suffix *-ile,* "capable of," so that a docile person is literally one who is capable of being taught.

Because so many Latin and Greek words have been borrowed and assimilated by English, a knowledge of the most common Latin and Greek prefixes and roots (the suffixes are less important for our purposes) helps us to recognize, at least in a general way, the meanings of many words. For example, the ability to recognize *-cede (-ceed)* and *-cess* as forms of the Latin *cedere,* "to yield" or "go," gives us a partial clue to the meanings of the English words *cede, cessation, cession, accede, access, accession, accessory, antecedent, ancestor, concede, concession, concessionaire, exceed, excess, incessant, intercede, intercessor, precede, precedence, predecessor, procedure, proceed, process, procession, recede, recess, recessive, secede, succeed, succession,* and their inflectional forms. One writer has estimated that a knowledge of fourteen Latin and Greek roots will help us to recognize over 14,000 words.[13]

Common Latin prefixes and roots, their original meanings, and illustrative English words derived from them are given in the following list:

ab (away from, down): abase, abate, abdicate, abduct, abhor, abnormal
ad (to, toward): adapt, addict, adduce, adequate, adhere, adjacent, admit
ante (before): ante-bellum, antecedent, antedate, antemeridian, anterior
bellum (war): bellicose, belligerent, rebel, rebellion
bene (well): benediction, benefactor, beneficent, benefit, benevolent, benign
bi (two): biannual, biaxial, biceps, bicuspid, bifocal, bigamist, bilabial
cap, cept (take): capable, captivate, capture, concept, deception, intercept
cide, cis (cut, kill): decide, matricide, suicide, concise, incision
circum (around): circumference, circumlocution, circumspect
cogni (know): cognition, cognizance, connoisseur, incognito, recognize
com (with): command, commence, commission, compact, compare
contra (against): contraband, contradict, contrapuntal, contrary, contrast
cor (heart): cardiac, core, cordial, courage, discord, encourage, record
cult (care for): cult, cultivate, culture, agriculture, horticulture
curr, curs (run): currency, current, curriculum, courier, course, excursion
de (off, down, wholly): debase, decapitate, decay, deceive, decline, deduce
dent (tooth): dental, dentifrice, dentoid, denture, indent, trident

[13] James I. Brown, *Efficient Reading* (Boston: D. C. Heath and Company, 1952), p. 117.

dict (say): dictate, diction, edict, indicate, indict, predict, verdict
duc, duct (lead): conduct, deduce, duct, duke, educate, induct, product
ex (beyond, from, out): examine, exceed, excel, except, excite, extend
extra (outside): extracurricular, extradite, extraneous, extrapolate
fac, fect (make): facile, fact, factory, faculty, manufacture, affect, effect
fin (end): confine, define, final, finale, finish, infinite, refine
in (on, in, toward): inaugurate, incarcerate, incipient, incline, include
in (not): inactive, inane, inarticulate, incest, infamous, insensible
inter (among, between): interaction, intercede, intercept, interfere
ject (throw): abject, dejected, eject, interject, projectile, reject, trajectory
loqui, locut (talk): colloquial, eloquent, loquacious, ventriloquist, elocution
luc (light): elucidate, illustrate, lucid, pellucid, translucent
mal (bad): malady, malcontent, malefactor, malice, malignant, malpractice
mit, miss (send): admit, commit, intermittent, remit, transmit, missile
mor (dead): morbid, moribund, mortal, mortify, mortuary
ped (foot): biped, impediment, pedal, pedestrian, pedicure, pedometer
pel, puls (drive): compel, dispel, expel, propel, repel, impulse, pulse
pon, posit (place): component, exponent, postpone, preposition, transpose
port (carry): deport, export, import, portable, report, support, transport
post (after): postdate, posterity, postgraduate, posthumous, postmortem
pre (before): preamble, precaution, precede, predict, preface, prefer
pro (forward): proceed, procession, produce, profane, profess, proficient
re (again, back): react, rearm, reassure, recall, recede, recreate, return
rupt (break): abrupt, bankrupt, disrupt, erupt, interrupt, rupture
scrib, script (write): circumscribe, inscribe, script, scripture, transcription
spect (look): aspect, inspect, perspective, retrospect, spectator, spectrum
sub (under): subaltern, subconscious, subject, submerge, subside
super (above): superb, supercilious, superfluous, superior, supersede
tain, ten (hold): abstain, contain, detain, retain, tenable, tenacious, tenet
tang, tact (touch): tangent, tangible, contact, tact, tactical, tactual
trans (across, over): transcend, transcribe, transfer, transfuse, transgress
uni (one): unicorn, uniform, unify, unilateral, union, Unitarian, unity
vene, vent (come): convene, intervene, revenue, adventure, invent
vers, vert (turn): verse, version, avert, convert, extrovert, invert, vertical
vid, vis (see): evident, provident, revise, supervise, vision, visor, vista
voc (call): advocate, avocation, convocation, evoke, provoke, vocabulary

Common Greek forms and their derivatives are shown below:

anthropo (man): anthropoid, anthropology, misanthrope, philanthropy
auto (self): autobiography, autocracy, autogamy, automobile, autotoxin
bio (life): biochemistry, biogenesis, biography, biology, biometry, biotic
chrono (time): anachronism, chronic, chronicle, chronological, synchronize
gen (birth, race): eugenics, genealogy, genesis, genetics, homogeneous
gram, graph (write): diagram, epigram, telegram, graphic, phonograph
homo (same): homocentric, homogenize, homograph, homonym
hydr (water): hydrant, hydraulic, hydrogen, hydrophobia, hydroplane
log (science, speech): biology, cosmology, etymology, epilogue, eulogy
micro (small): microbe, microfilm, micrometer, microphone, microscope

mono (one): monocle, monogamy, monograph, monolith, monologue
morph (form): amorphous, anthropomorphic, metamorphosis, morphology
pan (all): panacea, Pan-American, pancreas, pandemonium, panorama
phil (friend): Anglophile, bibliophile, Philadelphia, philharmonic
phon (sound): euphony, gramophone, phoneme, phonetic, symphony
poly (many): polyandry, polychromatic, polygamy, polyglot, polysyllabic
syn (together): synonym, syntax, synthesis, sympathy, symposium
tele (far): telegraph, telepathic, telephone, telescope, television

Improving Your Active Vocabulary

Although your active vocabulary is the stock of words you actually use in speaking and writing, we have considered the recognition vocabulary first because we almost always recognize words others use before we begin to use them ourselves. The active vocabulary is expanded chiefly by converting words from the recognition vocabulary. Usually this conversion takes place naturally as we become more and more familiar with a word. For example, some of the words you have met in this book have probably passed over into your active vocabulary — such as *analogy, colloquial, context, etymology, idiom, synonym, thesis,* and *transition.*

This natural conversion can be extended and accelerated. Practice using a word as you look it up in your dictionary. When you revise your writing, consider what other words you know that might fit the context. Make a note of words you are quite familiar with but never use, and begin deliberately to introduce them into your writing and speaking.

A second method of conversion is to sharpen your understanding of certain words by distinguishing their meanings from those of similar words — for example, to distinguish among *quick, prompt, ready, apt* — so that you may confidently use them in context. To differentiate clearly among such words, consult a dictionary of synonyms, or, if none is handy, a general dictionary. This kind of exercise not only makes you aware of shades of meaning but at the same time helps you to convert the words into your active vocabulary.

A third method — and the best as far as your writing is concerned — is to discipline yourself to seek specific words whenever anything you have written is unnecessarily general. The effort to find the specific word will require you to search your recognition vocabulary for appropriate terms. For example, in trying to specify "lacking order," you may think of many words referring to some kind of disorder — *bedraggled, chaotic, confused, dislocated, disoriented, entangled, irregular, jumbled, lawless, muddled, mussed, scrambled, shapeless, slovenly, unsystematic, untidy.* As you turn these words over in your mind, looking for the one that best conveys your thought, you are bringing all of them, not just the one you finally choose, into your active vocabulary.

If you own or have access to a *thesaurus,* you will find it helpful in the kind of conversion just mentioned. A thesaurus is a special kind of word

Expressing Ideas

book which records under a single entry all words expressing the general notion of that entry. The most popular of such works is *Roget's* (pronounced Rozhay's) *Thesaurus,* published in a number of editions. The simplest way to use this work is to look up the general word in the index, note the section number under which it is entered, and consult that section in the main part of the book. Thus if you want to find words referring to the ideas of *obedience* and *disobedience,* you look in the index for these words, find that they are listed under section numbers 764–765, turn to these sections, and this is what you find:[14]

764. OBEDIENCE

NOUNS 1. obedience *or* obediency, compliance, acquiescence; submission 763; dutifulness, duteousness; observance, attentiveness; law-abidingness.

VERBS 2. obey, mind, heed, keep, observe, regard, listen to; comply, yield obedience; do what one is told, do as one says, do the will of, do one's bidding, come at one's call, lie down and roll over [slang]; take orders, attend to orders, do suit and service, follow the lead of; answer the helm; submit 763.6.

ADJS. 3. obedient, compliant, complying, acquiescent; submissive 763.12; dutiful, duteous; loyal, faithful, devoted; lawabiding.

4. at one's command, at one's pleasure, at one's disposal, at one's nod, at one's call, at one's beck and call.

5. henpecked, tied to one's apron strings, on a string, on a leash, in leading strings.

ADVS. 6. obediently, compliantly, acquiescently; submissively 763.17; dutifully, duteously; loyally, faithfully, devotedly; in obedience to, in compliance with.

7. obediently yours, at your service, ∼ command *or* orders, as you please.

765. DISOBEDIENCE

NOUNS 1. disobedience, nonobedience; undutifulness, unduteousness; insubordination, unsubmissiveness, indocility, noncompliance, unresignedness; lawlessness, waywardness, frowardness; intractability 624.4.

2. refractoriness, recalcitrance, contumacy, contumaciousness, obstreperousness, unruliness, restiveness, fractiousness, orneriness [coll. or dial.]; breachiness.

3. rebelliousness, mutinousness, riotousness; insurrectionism, insurgentism; seditiousness.

4. revolt, rebellion; mutiny, mutineering; insurrection, insurgence, riot, *Putsch* [Ger.], *emeute* [F.]; uprising, rising, outbreak; general uprising, *levée en masse* [F.]; *Jacquerie* [F., peasant revolt]; sedition; revolution 147; strike 787.7.

5. rebel, revolter; insurgent, insurrectionist; mutineer; rioter, brawler; malcontent, *frondeur* [F.]; agitator 646.11; revolutionist 147.3; insubordinate.

VERBS 6. disobey, not mind, not heed, not keep *or* observe, not listen to, pay no attention to, ignore, disregard, defy, fly in the face of, go counter to, set at naught.

7. violate, transgress 767.4.

8. revolt, rebel, kick over the traces; rise up, rise, arise, rise up in arms; mutiny, mutineer; insurrect [coll.]; riot, run riot; revolutionize 147.4; strike 787.9.

ADJS. 9. disobedient, transgressive, violative, lawless, wayward, froward; undutiful, unduteous.

10. insubordinate, unsubmissive, indocile, uncompliant, uncomplying, unresigned; intractable 624.12.

11. refractory, recalcitrant, contumacious, obstreperous, unruly, restive, resty [dial.], fractious, ornery [coll. or dial.]; breachy.

12. rebellious, rebel, rebelly [coll.]; mutinous, mutineering; insurgent, insurrectionary, insurrectional, riotous; seditious, seditionary; revolutionary 147.5

ADVS. 13. disobediently, insubordinately, unsubmissively, indocilely, uncompliantly, unresignedly; intractably 624.17; obstreperously, contumaciously, restively, fractiously; rebelliously, mutinously.

14 From *Roget's International Thesaurus,* Third Edition. Copyright © 1962, by Thomas Y. Crowell Company, New York, publishers. Reprinted by permission.

Two words of caution. First, new words must be chosen for their use-fulness, not for their impressiveness. The real purpose of increasing your vocabulary is to increase your ability to communicate, and communication is not improved by calling a daily newspaper "a diurnal publication" or a sick friend "an incapacitated colleague." Second, the new words must fit the contexts in which they are to be used. Although *glib* means *smooth* in such phrases as *a glib speaker* and *a glib argument,* we cannot talk about *a glib surface* or *a glib texture.* It is better not to use a word at all than to use it in the wrong context. For this reason, it is usually safer to introduce new words in writing rather than in impromptu speech, since the written word may be more easily checked and reconsidered. If these two cautions are observed, deliberate conversion from the recognition to the active vocabulary can be a profitable exercise.

Exercises

As a review of all that has been said about diction in this chapter, study the following passages, and for each write a report which classifies the style as (1) decidedly formal, (2) informal, (3) distinctly informal. In each case explain why you classify the passage as you do.

(1)

The dictum that the style is the man is well known. It is one of those aphorisms that say too much to mean a great deal. Where is the man in Goethe, in his birdlike lyrics or in his clumsy prose? And Hazlitt? But I suppose that if a man has a confused mind he will write in a confused way, if his temper is capricious his prose will be fantastical, and if he has a quick, darting intelligence that is reminded by the matter in hand of a hundred things, he will, unless he has great self-control, load his pages with metaphor and simile. There is a great difference between the magniloquence of the Jacobean writers, who were intoxicated with the new wealth that had lately been brought into the language, and the turgidity of Gibbon and Dr. Johnson, who were the victims of bad theories. I can read every word that Dr. Johnson wrote with delight, for he had good sense, charm and wit. No one could have written better if he had not willfully set himself to write in the grand style. He knew good English when he saw it. No critic has praised Dryden's prose more aptly. He said of him that he appeared to have no art other than that of expressing with clearness what he thought with vigor. And one of his Lives he finished with the words: "Whoever wishes to attain an English style, familiar but not coarse, and elegant but not ostentatious, must give his days and nights to the volumes of Addison." But when he himself sat down to write it was with a very different aim. He mistook the orotund for the dignified. He had not the good breeding to see that simplicity and naturalness are the truest marks of distinction.[15]

[15] From W. Somerset Maugham, *The Summing Up* (New York: Doubleday and Company, 1943).

197

(2)

The Gothic cathedrals of England had soared in a way to fill worshippers with awe and wonder. The classical work of Wren in his rebuilding of St. Paul's and more than fifty City churches made less appeal to emotion and more to a tempered intellectual respect. He and his successors made religion seem reasonable. With their calm authority they struck more at the mind than at the heart while graciously serving the eye. They searched for a civilized utility in their concept of a holy place; the sense of a celestial mystery belonged to the Middle Ages. In the same way, when we now see one of the palaces which Wren created or altered as at Kensington or at Hampton Court, we realize that he was creating a habitable home and not a fortress or a fantastication. The old palaces had been erected to impress; they were monstrously and majestically planned for persons who were Majesties.[16]

(3)

The scullery was a mine of all the minerals of living. Here I discovered water — a very different element from the green crawling scum that stank in the garden tub. You could pump it in pure blue gulps out of the ground; you could swing on the pump handle and it came out sparkling like liquid sky. And it broke and ran and shone on the tiled floor, or quivered in a jug, or weighted your clothes with cold. You could drink it, draw with it, froth it with soap, swim beetles across it, or fly it in bubbles in the air. You could put your head in it, and open your eyes, and see the sides of the bucket buckle, and hear your caught breath roar, and work your mouth like a fish, and smell the lime from the ground. Substance of magic — which you could tear or wear, confine or scatter, or send down holes, but never burn or break or destroy.[17]

(4)

Well, sir, we started going around together that very day, and we went together for the rest of the semester, and we kept on going together all summer long, and I got to admit it was pretty horrible. The trouble was, Totsi was always taking pictures. Like we'd be out picking up tin foil or playing kick-the-can or like that, and all of a sudden, right in the middle of everything, Totsi would see a man or a dog or a cloud or a building or you name it, and she would whip out her Leica and put on all kinds of lenses and filters and start shooting pictures like a maniac.[18]

(5)

From those high storied shelves of dense rich bindings the great voices of eternity, the tongues of mighty poets dead and gone, now seemed to speak to him out of the living and animate silence of the room. But in that living

[16] From Ivor Brown, *London, An Illustrated History* (New York: London House and Maxwell, 1966).

[17] From Laurie Lee, *The Edge of Day* (New York: William Morrow and Company, 1959).

[18] From Max Shulman, "Love Among the Shutterbugs."

silence, in the vast and quiet spirit of sleep which filled the great house, amid the grand and overwhelming stillness of that proud power of wealth and the impregnable security of its position, even the voices of those mighty poets dead and gone now seemed somehow lonely, small, lost and pitiful. Each in his little niche of shelf securely stored — all of the genius, richness, and whole compacted treasure of a poet's life within a foot of space, within the limits of six small dense richly-garnished volumes — all of the great poets of the earth were there, unread, unopened, and forgotten, and were somehow, terribly, the mute small symbols of a rich man's power, of the power of wealth to own everything, to take everything, to triumph over everything — even over the power and genius of the mightiest poet — to keep him there upon his little foot of shelf, unopened and forgotten, but possessed.[19]

(6)

What always gets me about these scholarly excursions into the language of the underworld, so to speak, is how they smell of the dictionary. The so-called experts in this line have their ear to the library, very seldom to the ground. They do not realize what a large proportion of these cant terms (using cant a bit too broadly) is of literary origin, how many of them crooks and cops use *after* writers have invented them. It is very difficult for the literary man to distinguish between a genuine crook term and an invented one. How do you tell a man to go away in hard language? Scram, beat it, take off, take the air, on your way, dangle, hit the road, and so forth. All good enough. But give me the classic expression actually used by Spike O'Donnell (of the O'Donnell brothers of Chicago, the only small outfit to tell the Capone mob to go to hell and live). What he said was: "Be missing." The restraint of it is deadly.

Throughout his play *The Iceman Cometh,* ONeill used "the big sleep" as a synonym for death. He used it, so far as one can judge from the context, as a matter of course, apparently in the belief that it was an accepted underworld expression. If so, I'd like to see whence it comes, because I invented the expression. It is quite possible that I reinvented it, but I never saw it in print before I used it, and until I get the evidence I shall continue to believe that O'Neill took it from me, directly or indirectly, and thought I was using a standard term.

Those who investigate cant, underworld or sports jargon etc. at the source are always surprised by how little of the picturesque lingo is used by the very people who are supposed to use nothing else . . . Some invented slang, not all, becomes current among the people it is invented for. If you are sensitive to this sort of thing, I believe you could often, not always, distinguish between the colored-up lingo that writers produce, and the hard simplicity of the terms that originate in the circle where they are actually used. I don't think any writer could think up an expression like "mainliner" for a narcotic addict who shoots the stuff into a vein. It's too exact, too *pure*.[20]

---

[19] From Thomas Wolfe, *Of Time and the River* (New York: Charles Scribner's Sons, 1935).

[20] From *Raymond Chandler Speaking,* edited by Dorothy Gardiner and Kathrine Sorley Walker (Boston: Houghton Mifflin Company, 1962). Copyright © 1962 by the Helga Greene Literary Agency.

(7)

Adventure stories weren't so bad, but as a kid I was very serious and always preferred realism to romance. School stories were what I liked best. The trouble was that even they seemed to be a bit far-fetched, judging by our standards. The schools were English and quite different to the one I attended. They were always called "the venerable pile," and there was usually a ghost in them; they were built in a square that was called the "quad," and, to judge by the pictures, were all clock-towers, spires and pinnacles like the lunatic asylum with us. The fellows in the stories were all good climbers, and used to get in and out of the school at night on ropes made of knotted sheets. They dressed queerly; they wore long trousers, short black jackets and top-hats. When they did anything wrong they were given "lines." When it was a bad case they were flogged, and never showed any sign of pain, only the bad fellows, and they always said "Ow! Ow!"

Mostly, they were grand chaps who always stuck together and were great at football and cricket. They never told lies, and anyone who did, they wouldn't talk to him. If they were caught out and asked a point-blank question, they always told the truth, unless someone else was in it along with them, and then wild horses wouldn't get them to split, even if the other fellow was a thief, which, as a matter of fact, he frequently was. It was surprising in such good schools, with fathers who never gave them less than five quid, the number of thieves there were. The fellows I knew hardly ever stole, even though they only got a penny a week, and sometimes not even that when their fathers were on the booze and their mothers had to go to the pawn.[21]

(8)

Much can be said, of course, about the confusion of styles in modern writing. Perhaps distinctions among styles are now indeed less clear and stable than they were in a less troubled age; perhaps the clumsier writers do ignore the existing distinctions while the sophisticated use them to play sophisticated tunes; perhaps the scrupulously objective lexicographer cannot establish those distinctions from his quotation slips alone. For all that, distinctions do exist. They exist in good writing, and they exist in the linguistic consciousness of the educated. Dr. Gove's definers prove they exist when they give *egghead* as a synonym for *double-dome* but then define *egghead* in impeccably formal terms of "one with intellectual interests or pretensions" or as "a highly educated person." Such opposition between theory and practice strikes even a timid and generally admiring reviewer as rather odd, as though some notion of scientific objectivity should require the scientist to deny that he knows what he knows because he may not know how he knows it.

In the absence, then, of convincing argument to the contrary, a simple reader is left with the uneasy feeling that the abandonment of *"Colloq."* was a mistake which the introduction of more quotations does not quite rectify and that as a teacher he must now provide foreigners and inexperienced students both with some general principles of linguistic choice and with

[21] From Frank O'Connor, "The Idealist," *Traveller's Samples: Stories and Tales* (New York: Alfred A. Knopf, 1951).

specific instruction in instances where the new dictionary does not discriminate finely enough among stylistic variants. The dictionary leaves unlabeled many expressions which this teacher would not allow a beginning writer to use in serious exposition or argument except for clearly intended and rather special effects: (*to be caught*) *with one's pants down, dollarwise, stylewise* (*s.v. -wise*), (*to give one*) *the bird, dog* "something inferior of its kind," *to enthuse, to level* "deal frankly," *schmaltz, chintzy, the catbird seat, to roll* "rob," *to send* "delight," *shindig, shook-up, square* "an unsophisticated person," *squirrelly, to goof,* and the like. Enforcing such modest niceties will now be more difficult; for classroom lawyers and irate parents will be able to cite the dictionary which the teacher has taught Johnny how to read but which has collapsed the distinction between formal and informal Standard English. Similar difficulties could occur with various mild obscenities . . . which should be marked not only as slang but with some one of the warning labels that the dictionary attaches to the almost quite adequately recorded four-letter words; and the label *slang* itself might well be more freely used with the various synonyms for *drunk* — *stewed, stinko, stoned, tight, tanked, sozzled, potted, pie-eyed, feeling no pain, blind, looped, squiffed, boiled, fried, high,* etc. Odzooks![22]

(9)

Facing a big-league pitcher with a bat on your shoulder and trying to hit his delivery is another vital experience in gaining an understanding of the game about which you are trying to write vividly. It is one thing to sit in the stands and scream at a batsman, "Oh, you bum!" for striking out in a pinch, and another to stand twenty yards from that big pitcher and try to make up your mind in a hundredth of a second whether to hit at the offering or not, where to swing and when, not to mention worrying about protecting yourself from the consequences of being struck by the ball that seems to be heading straight for your skull at an appalling rate of speed. Because, if you are a big-league player, you cannot very well afford to be gun-shy and duck away in panic from a ball that swerves in the last moment and breaks perfectly over the plate, while the umpire calls: "Strike!" and the fans jeer. Nor can you afford to take a crack on the temple from the ball. Men have died from that. It calls for undreamed-of niceties of nerve and judgment, but you don't find that out until you have stepped to the plate cold a few times during batting practice or in training quarters, with nothing at stake but the acquisition of experience, and have seen what a fine case of the jumping jitters you get. Later on, when you are writing your story, your imagination, backed by the experience, will be able to supply a picture of what the batter is going through as he stands at the plate in the closing innings of an important game, with two or three men on base, two out, and his team behind in the scoring, and fifty thousand people screaming at him.[23]

[22] From James Sledd, "The Lexicographers' Uneasy Chair," *College English,* May, 1962. Reprinted with the permission of the National Council of Teachers of English and James Sledd. (The dictionary under discussion is *Webster's Third New International Dictionary.*)

[23] From Paul Gallico, *Farewell to Sport* (New York: Alfred A. Knopf, 1938).

(10)

Knowledge is one thing, virtue is another; good sense is not conscience, refinement is not humility, nor is largeness and justness of view faith. Philosophy, however enlightened, however profound, gives no command over the passions, no influential motives, no vivifying principles. Liberal Education makes not the Christian, not the Catholic, but the gentleman. It is well to be a gentleman, it is well to have a cultivated intellect, a delicate taste, a candid, equitable, dispassionate mind, a noble and courteous bearing in the conduct of life — these are the connatural qualities of a large knowledge; they are the objects of a University; I am advocating, I shall illustrate and insist upon them; but still, I repeat, they are no guarantee for sanctity or even for conscientiousness, they may attach to the man of the world, to the profligate, to the heartless, pleasant, alas, and attractive as he shows when decked out in them. Taken by themselves, they do but seem to be what they are not; they look like virtue at a distance, but they are detected by close observers, and on the long run; and hence it is that they are popularly accused of pretense and hypocrisy, not, I repeat, from their own fault, but because their professors and their admirers persist in taking them for what they are not, and are officious in arrogating for them a praise to which they have no claim. Quarry the granite rock with razors, or moor the vessel with a thread of silk; then may you hope with such keen and delicate instruments as human knowledge and human reason to contend against those giants, the passion and the pride of man.[24]

[24] From John Henry Newman, *The Idea of a University.*

PART THREE  # Special
Assignments

8

The Essay-Type Examination

The essay-type examination is one of the most practical of all composition assignments. By requiring a student to compose in one or more paragraphs an answer to a specific problem, it calls forth most of the skills which the composition course tries to develop. It tests the student's ability to read accurately and to write purposefully within a rigid time limit. It is thus as much a test of thinking and writing ability as of knowledge.

Failure to recognize this fact usually leads to unsatisfactory answers and poor grades. Instructors frequently complain that the worst student writing is done on essay-type examinations. Of course the pressure under which examinations are written is not conducive to stylistic finish. But the chief weaknesses of examination answers are not that they are ungrammatical or awkward but that they are not *composed* at all. The student does not first plan what he wants to say and then develop his intention into an adequate answer; too often he begins to write without any clear purpose and assumes that as long as he is writing he is answering the question. The result is frequently an answer which is irrelevant, inadequate, unclear, and even self-contradictory.

This chapter attempts to improve the quality of essay examinations by a practical application of the principles of purposeful writing which were discussed in Parts One and Two of this book. The treatment of the subject is organized under the following recommendations:

1. Before beginning to answer any part of an examination, read the question carefully to see what it requires of you. If you misinterpret the question, your whole answer may be off the point, even if it shows detailed knowledge of the subject and is otherwise well written. For this reason, it is wise to ask yourself before you begin to write: "What does this question require me to do?" Notice, especially, whether the question asks you to *explain, summarize, discuss, evaluate,* or *compare.* These are often key words in an essay examination. If you are asked to evaluate a paragraph or a poem, a summary or explanation of the paragraph or a paraphrase of the poem will not satisfy the requirement. If you are asked to compare two characters in a play, a description of each character may not develop a comparison. Presumably the wording of the question has been carefully thought out, and you will be expected to follow the directions which the wording implies. There is no point in beginning to write until you have a clear idea of what kind of answer is required.

To see how a competent student can drift into an unfortunate answer because of failure to read the instructions carefully and to be clear about what they require, consider the following contrasted essays. The directions were: "Illustrate the differences between early and late Renaissance painting by contrasting Fra Filippo Lippi's *Madonna and Child* with Raphael's *Sistine Madonna."* These directions clearly indicate that the answer must show how early and late Renaissance painting differed; the evidence of the difference is to be drawn from two paintings, each of which is to be taken as typical of its period. Of the contrasted answers below, the one at the left received a grade of C, the one at the right a grade of A.

C Answer	*A Answer*
Filippo's picture is simply designed, and the figures are naturalistic. The Madonna is sweet, gracious, and human, dressed in the mode of the times. The Bambino is a natural, playful child. He is being lifted up by two older boys — undoubtedly Fra Filippo's family posed for the picture. The background is a stylized landscape of rocks and streams, bounded by a frame. The Madonna is seated in a chair with an elaborately carved arm which stands out in the foreground.	Fra Filippo's picture is a good example of early Renaissance naturalism. The Madonna — his own wife — is wearing a stylish gown, which is painted in faithful detail. Her hair is dressed in the mode of the time. She is seated — as though in her own home — on an elaborately carved chair, with a framed painting of a landscape serving as the background. Her pose and expression are calm, perhaps devout, but neither exalted nor humble. She is an ordinary worldly mother with a chubby baby,
Raphael designed the *Sistine Madonna* in a pyramid with the Madonna herself at the apex. She carries the curly-haired Child, and although she is standing still, her garments swirl as in a strong wind. One's eye is first caught by the figure of Pope Sixtus at the lower left, and through the folds of his garment and his uplifted eyes, drawn toward the central figure of the Virgin. Her garments, billowing to the right, draw the eye downward	who is being lifted to her rather ungracefully by a saucy angel. The entire scene is intimate, personal, and joyous, but hardly reverent. Filippo, pleased with the new-found technical mastery of his age, is content to paint what he sees.
	Raphael was able to get above his technique and make it expressive of lofty emotion. The figures in the *Sistine Madonna* are monumental and stand out against a subdued back-

again to the figure of St. Barbara, kneeling on a cloud. Her eyes are cast down, and the glance follows hers to discover two jaunty cherubs leaning on the lower frame. They look upward, thus deflecting the eyes of the beholder up again, completing the movement of the design. This painting is one of the high points of the development of Renaissance art.

ground. The Madonna, her feet resting weightlessly on a cloud, wears an expression of sublime dignity. She holds with graceful ease the Child, whose sober eyes reveal the portent of His future. The figures wear classic robes, whose flowing lines give a wonderful, circling movement to the painting. A cloud of tiny cherubs' heads, peeping through the effulgence surrounding the Virgin, completes the heavenly setting. Where Filippo's work is mere copying, Raphael's is imaginative and spiritual. This loftiness of conception combined with grace of design and beauty of execution is the flower of the High Renaissance.

Why did one answer receive an average and the other an excellent grade? Both are roughly the same length; both are well written; both show an intimate knowledge of the pictures they are contrasting. What is the difference between them? The difference is essentially in the selection of details. The answer at the left is unsatisfactory because it ignored a significant part of the question. What the student actually wrote was a description of the *Madonna and Child* and another description of the *Sistine Madonna*. The details she presents describe the pictures effectively, but they do nothing to show the differences between early and late Renaissance painting. Therefore her answer does not satisfy the question. The answer at the right selects details which do illustrate the differences between the two periods, and thus gives purpose to the contrast between the pictures. The author is not merely describing two pictures; she is describing the characteristics which make them represent their two different periods. That is what the question required.

2. *Think out your general answer before you begin to develop it.* Since there is almost no opportunity for rewriting in an essay examination, your answer must be satisfactory as it is put on paper. If a student has the purpose or topic sentence of his answer clearly in mind, explanatory and illustrative details will suggest themselves as he writes. But a student who has not determined what he wants to say before he begins may veer away from the question or may write a series of unrelated sentences which do not add up to a unified answer. On some questions, it may be advisable to jot down on the back of the blue book or the mimeographed examination sheet the information you want to work into your answer; on others, framing the topic sentence will be preparation enough. This advice repeats what was said in Chapters 1 and 3, but the advice becomes even more im-

portant in an examination because of the very limited opportunity for revision.

The answer given below shows a carefully planned response to the following question:

> Just before he dies, Laertes says to Hamlet, "Mine and my father's death come not on thee, nor thine on me." In view of the facts of the play, how do you interpret this statement?

The student thinks over the statement and the facts of the play and frames his general answer thus:

> Laertes' statement fits some of the facts but not all of them and is best understood as a request to let bygones be bygones.

This is the topic sentence or thesis of his answer. It requires the student to do three things: (1) to show that Laertes' statement fits some of the facts, (2) to show that it does not fit other facts, and (3) to explain what he means by interpreting the statement as a request to let bygones be bygones. Notice how he satisfies the requirements of his own purpose statement and therefore the requirements of the question.

> Laertes' statement fits some of the facts but not all of them and is best understood as a request to let bygones be bygones. True, Hamlet is not responsible for Laertes' death, because Hamlet thought he was engaging in a friendly bout with blunted swords. When he picked up Laertes' sword in the mix-up he did not know it was poisoned. Since Laertes deliberately put the poison there, he was responsible for both Hamlet's death and his own. Hamlet killed Polonius by mistake, thinking that the person behind the curtain was the king. To that extent it was an accidental killing, but a killing nevertheless. I think Laertes' statement is not intended as a literal description of the facts but as a reconciliation speech. I interpret the statement as meaning: "We have both been the victims of the king's treachery. Forgive me for your death, as I forgive you for mine and my father's."

This answer is an excellent example of purposeful writing in a paragraph: topic sentence, followed by supporting details, followed by a restatement of the topic idea in a concluding statement. The structure of the paragraph is implied in the topic sentence. Since the student has thought out his whole answer before beginning to write, he has control of the paragraph's content. He knows that what he must do is to document his topic sentence from the facts of the play.

Contrast that answer with one given by a student who has not thought out his general answer to the question and begins immediately to recount the facts, without considering how these facts relate to the question he is supposed to be answering.

> Laertes returns from France and learns that his father has been killed by Hamlet. He is almost mad with grief and rage and in a stormy scene with the king he demands revenge. He and the king conspire to arrange a duel

between Laertes and Hamlet in which Laertes will use a poisoned sword. The duel takes place after Ophelia's funeral, and Laertes cuts Hamlet with the poisoned sword. Then, in a scuffle, their swords are knocked from their hands and Hamlet picks up Laertes' sword and wounds him. Meanwhile the king has put poison in a goblet of wine he intended for Hamlet, but the queen drinks it instead. When Hamlet sees she is dying he kills the king; then both Hamlet and Laertes die.

The statements in this paragraph do not add up to any satisfactory answer to the question that was asked. The student has not interpreted Laertes' final speech; he has not even shown its inconsistency with the facts. He has simply summarized the action of the play from the time of Laertes' return from France until his death in the duel. Since the facts of the play are known to everyone in the class, this student gives himself no chance to make a contribution through his answer. No doubt he thought he was answering the question, but it is obvious that he has not done so.

Failure to read the question carefully enough to see what it requires and failure to prewrite an answer to that question are interrelated. To a student who knows the subject, careful reading of the question suggests an answer, and a prewritten answer invites a check against the wording of the question. A student who misses on the first step will probably miss on the second also. The sensible thing to do is postpone the writing until one knows what he is trying to say, and why. Hurrying into an unformed answer merely substitutes writing for thinking, always a costly replacement on an examination.

3. Remember that nothing so annoys a grader as a series of unsupported, unexplained generalizations. Next to irrelevance, vagueness is the chief sin of examination answers. One can understand vagueness when a student has such an uncertain knowledge of the subject that anything he says is likely to be vague. Here we are concerned with the kind of vagueness that comes not from ignorance but from faulty habits of composition.

A common cause of vagueness is the kind of incomplete statement which presents the answer at a general or abstract level and leaves it there without any explanatory or illustrative detail. For example, had the student who wrote the excellent paragraph on Laertes' speech written instead —

Laertes' statement distorts the facts. It is not an accurate report of what happened. He is rationalizing away his own guilt and that of Hamlet by blaming Claudius. —

the grader would have had to guess what the student had in mind. He would want to know: Why is it not an accurate report? In what sense is it a rationalization? For what, specifically, is Laertes blaming Claudius? The answer scarcely goes beyond the topic sentence and remains so general that it does not make its meaning clear. Students sometimes shrug off criticism of generality in such answers by saying, "Oh, you know what

I mean." But no student has a right to ask the grader to fill in omitted information for him. It is not the examiner's responsibility to complete a student's answer. So far as time permits, a student should always make general answers specific by examples or illustrative details.

The amount of time available for answering a question will, of course, affect the amount of detail that can be given. But much can be done even in a very limited time if the student appreciates the need to be specific. In the following example, students had ten minutes to answer the question: "Compare and contrast Wordsworth and Byron on their attitudes toward the French Revolution and Napoleon." The general answer is

> Both men at first welcomed the French Revolution and the rise of Napoleon; both later turned against them.

But a student who stops with that general answer makes three mistakes. First, he mistakenly assumes that what is required is just a conclusion, not the facts and reasoning on which it is based. Had the instructor wanted short, unexplained answers, he could have designed the examination as a short-answer quiz and allowed about a minute for each answer. An essay-type examination requires an essay for an answer. That requirement is part of the context in which the student is being examined. Second, the student who gives such a general answer does not use the full time allotted to the question, and therefore places himself at a disadvantage in competition with students who do use the full time. Third, the student loses an opportunity to show the depth of his knowledge. If he can go beyond the general answer given above, he owes it to himself to do so. Even in the limited time available, much more could have been done with the question, as the following answer shows.

> Both men at first welcomed the French Revolution and the rise of Napoleon; both later turned against them. Wordsworth changed first. He was ready at one time to throw in his lot with the revolutionists (*Prelude*), but their excesses and his own conservative inclinations made him increasingly unsympathetic. Byron seems to have been less shocked by the terror of the Revolution than by Napoleon's change from a liberator to a conqueror. His attack on Napoleon in *Childe Harold* is bitter, all the more bitter because of Byron's appreciation of what Napoleon might have done for Europe.

The difference between these two answers is not only the difference between an undeveloped topic sentence and a fully developed paragraph; it is also the difference between a grade of A and a grade of D. The second answer demonstrates the ability to see what is needed, to select the information which meets that need, and to organize the information into the comparison and contrast which the question requires.

We have stressed the kind of vagueness that comes from incomplete statement because, for a student who knows the subject on which he is being tested, it can be easily corrected. Vagueness that comes from ignorance of the subject cannot be remedied during the examination; its causes go back to poor study habits. Vagueness that comes from the inability to express oneself clearly requires sustained remedial attention to diction and sentence structure, and the examination room is no place for remedial exercises. But specification by illustration and reference to the text can be achieved by an act of will. A student who knows his subject can easily provide the illustration once he clearly understands the need for it.

4. Padding an answer to make it look like an essay is more likely to hurt than help. A student who pads his answer by wordiness, repetition, or irrelevant comment draws attention to the fact that he has little to say and is trying to conceal his ignorance. The student is naive who thinks that a grader will accept obvious padding as a contribution to the answer. There is a relationship between length and content, because presenting content takes space. For example, the effective answers in preceding pages could not have been reduced in length without losing significant content. But no experienced grader equates mere length with content. He is not easily persuaded that an answer is good just because it is long. He is more likely to be indignant at having to take time in one of the busiest weeks of the school year to separate a few kernels of wheat from a bushel of chaff.

The answer on page 212 is a padded response to the question on the French Revolution and Napoleon given on page 210. The grader's marginal comments are included. When the padding in this answer is removed, the pertinent comment is reduced to two sentences. These sentences do not constitute an adequate answer, but they are not made more adequate by the irrelevant comments, which merely introduce new errors.

When the padding is not deliberate, it is a sign that the student is not thinking efficiently. He does not see what is needed, he is not controlled by a sense of the purpose of his answer, and so he writes one sentence at a time and drifts into repetitions and digressions. Given a knowledge of the subject, the best cure for inefficient thinking is purposeful prewriting.

SUMMARY

The advice given in this chapter may be summarized very briefly:
1. Before writing, study the question to see what it requires.
2. Before writing, frame the general answer which will satisfy the requirements which you identified in step 1 above. This general answer will define the purpose of your essay, as a topic sentence defines the purpose of a paragraph.
3. Be specific. Do not leave your answer at the general level of step 2 above, but provide the specific details, illustrations, and textual references needed to support your general answer and give it meaning.
4. Remember that padding an answer will not improve it and may lower rather than raise your grade.

The French Revolution was one of
the great events of the ~~nineteenth century.~~
~~It brought to an end the government of the~~
~~aristrocrats and the king and their oppression~~
~~of the common people.~~ It was a New Deal
for the French people, and liberals in Europe and America ~~supported it,~~ especially
~~since one of its heroes was Lafayette who was~~
~~also one of the heroes of the American Revolu-~~
~~tion, which also overthrew the government~~
~~of a king and his aristrocratic generals.~~ Because of their interest in the common man,
Wordsworth and Byron supported the Revolution, which put an end to the tyranny of
the aristrocrats and the oppression of the
common people.

~~Their attitude toward Napoleon was~~
~~somewhat different. For years England lived~~
~~in fear of a French invasion and Englishmen~~
~~were united in their opposition to Napoleon~~
~~and his wars of conquest. It was largely~~
~~through their efforts that Napoleon was~~
~~finally defeated at Waterloo by the Duke of~~
~~Wellington.~~ Wordsworth and Byron were against
Napoleon's wars of conquest, and they were glad when
he was finally defeated by Wellington at Waterloo.

It began in 1789

Declared a traitor
by the National
Assembly and
forced to flee the
country

Partly true, but
inadequate

Partly true, but
inadequate

Nothing to do
with the quest

sp!

useless
repetition

Nothing to do
with the ques

useless
repetition

There is nothing in this answer that suggests you have even
read the assigned material. The crossed-out parts show irreleve
padding. The two sentences which deal with the question do not
differentiate between Wordsworth and Byron, and distort the
attitudes of both.

A Padded Answer with the grader's comm

Exercises

Each of the following lettered exercises consists of three answers to a given question. Since some of the questions may require information which you do not already have, the first essay is always an A answer which can be used as a standard for judging the other two. For each set, write a specific criticism of the second and third answers by contrasting them with the first.

A

In the Sermon on the Mount, Jesus calls the attention of his listeners to the "fowls of the air" and the "lilies of the field." Contrast this use of references to details in nature with Plato's use or non-use of similar references in the Myth of the Cave.

(1)

Although not principally a nature lover, Jesus freely used examples from the world of nature as allusions and analogies to introduce or support a moral lesson. In showing that the fowls of the air were fed by God without sowing or reaping, he meant to explain that men should have faith that God would provide for them. In asking his listeners to consider the lilies of the field, which, without weaving or spinning, were beautifully arrayed, he was advising his audience to be more concerned about spiritual values than about material possessions and outward signs of success.

Plato used the myth of the cave to illustrate that the natural world is imperfect, a world of shadows. Those who rely on evidence from their senses are trapped in the natural world as in a badly lighted cave. To seek truth, a man has to realize that sensations are imperfect reflections of the world of ideas, which is the only *real* world. Man has to approach the world of ideas through his intellect, not through sensory experience. Therefore, the world of nature is a distraction which has to be put aside before man can acquire pure wisdom. One would not expect, then, allusions to nature as a teaching device in Plato's work. His appeal is not to experience but to reason. He often uses analogies — the cave itself is one — but they are sophisticated analogies for a sophisticated audience, and they require concentrated thought to be understood. Both Plato and Jesus were teachers who exalted the world of the spirit over the natural world, but their teaching methods were quite different. Jesus used natural analogies to call on the everyday experiences of simple people; Plato invited his educated listeners to reason with him. These differences made allusions to nature appropriate for Jesus, but less appropriate for Plato.

(2)

Jesus said in the Sermon on the Mount that the fowls of the air were fed by God and did not have to labor on their own behalf. The lilies of the field were more glorious than Solomon without exerting themselves to make their own clothes, another indication of God's design. Jesus often used examples of this kind to make His sermons more vivid. "Ye are the salt of the earth" is a further example, together with the good trees bringing forth good fruit, and evil trees bringing evil fruit. "By their fruits ye shall know them." Jesus' sermons might be called poetic in this respect.

Plato, as we can see in *The Republic,* where the myth of the cave appears, was not favorably disposed towards poets and lacked a true poetic quality in his writings. His arguments were usually exercises in pure reasoning, in which some less-informed person was led by Socrates to accept some point. These arguments are often verbally tricky, and running through them all was the thought that nature could not teach a man anything really useful. For Plato, each individual lily would have been only an imperfect example of some invisible lily which was not in the world of nature but in the world of ideas.

(3)

It is always interesting to compare Christian philosophy with what preceded it. In all the ancient world, Socrates, as portrayed in the works of Plato, seems most definitely the predecessor of Jesus. Both were effective teachers. Both strove to live moral lives and to provide examples of right action for others. Both became victims of public opinion and finally died for their beliefs.

There were, however, some differences in their teachings. Socrates was interested in climbing to the pinnacle of intellect where the good, the true, and the beautiful all converge. He recommended reason as the method for doing this. If a man thought clearly, he would also be a good man and a person with a sense of what was truly beautiful. In his concern with accurate, logical thinking, Socrates neglected the beauties of nature. In fact, he often found them a hindrance, as in the myth of the cave. But Jesus often mentioned natural details to his followers, as in the Sermon on the Mount. He thought that faith was more important than reason. He offered, as Plato did not, the hope of an after-life which common people could understand, and which they needed. It was the promise of this after-life which made Christianity so attractive that it finally prevailed over the might of Rome. Compared with this promise, Plato's ideal world appeals only to thinkers, and only to some of them. There are many intellectuals who do not agree with Plato.

B

Early in *Huckleberry Finn,* Huck contrives his own "murder." How does this episode illustrate the theme of the novel and the development of Huck's character?

(1)

A search for freedom, whether Huck's wish to be free of "sivilization" or Jim's wish to be free from slavery, is an important theme in *Huckleberry Finn.* Freedom involves a clean break with the past, an escape from the familiar and reappearance in a new environment. Huck tries to make this clean break by simulating his own "murder." The scene he contrives by scattering pig's blood on the ground and wrecking the cabin in which he has been held prisoner will prevent a search for him and will enable him to begin a new life. There is symbolic significance in this contrived "murder." Huck often seems to have a death wish, trying to cancel out the old Huck to be born again in some new place with some new family. Throughout the novel, though, these new identities are cut short by some violence or catastrophe on land, and Huck is lured back to the peacefulness of life on the river.

Besides its psychological significance, this contrived "murder" shows the reader something about Huck's character in contrast to Tom Sawyer. Tom's plans are always elaborate, influenced by the romantic books he has read. In operation, they become silly and usually ineffective, just as the "pirate" raid really becomes a raid on a Sunday School picnic. Huck, on the other hand, while admiring Tom's methods, contrives a plan that is orderly, practical, and successful. It is not surprising that, by the end of the novel, when Tom is master-minding Jim's escape in his typically silly fashion, Huck seems critical of his former idol. Although he still thinks of himself as a lesser person than Tom, he cannot but observe that he has succeeded in achieving an escape, something that Tom never quite manages.

(2)

Huck's contrivance of his own "murder" affirms Mark Twain's admiration for realism, as opposed to his contempt for romanticism. This preference is obvious throughout the novel. Huck's plotting is rather imaginative, but, more important, it is realistic. Huck has a definite purpose in his scheme — to escape from his drunken father. He is not inventing a murder just for the sake of adventure, as Tom Sawyer might do. This incident is one of several which is directed toward the support of realism. Another of Mark Twain's novels, *A Connecticut Yankee in King Arthur's Court,* also includes this theme. The practical hero succeeds because he is realistic, while those around him are infected with a romantic view of life. Mark Twain was always annoyed by romantic fiction, particularly the works of Sir Walter Scott and James Fenimore Cooper.

Realism is the key to Huck's character. When other boys are excited by forming a pirate band, Huck has doubts. He is down-to-earth and practical. Huck always has a matter-of-fact view of life, which makes him a pleasant companion for the King and the Duke, two unsavory characters he meets on the river. Huck is not fooled by them, but acts congenial. He goes along with their schemes just to be agreeable. This ability to get along with people is part of Huck's realistic nature.

(3)

From the moment Huck sees those crossed nails in that heel print, he knows that evil is approaching. The evil is his father, who has always been jealous of his son. Huck has received beatings for doing nothing more than knowing how to read. This time when his father reclaims him, Huck firmly decides that he cannot put up with any more of Pap's cruel treatment. When the proper moment arrives and his father is away, Huck makes his escape. He contrives a "murder" scene which is realistic enough to be convincing. He kills a hog and scatters its blood at the scene of the "crime." He sets a scene of struggle and violence in Pap's cabin, thereby demonstrating his intelligence and attention to detail.

Huck desires freedom more than anything else in life. Jim, Huck's friend and companion, also desires freedom. Even Tom Sawyer, with his swashbuckling ideas, seems to desire freedom from the simple life of the small town in which he lives. But Huck needs freedom most because of his abusive father and his own innate dislike for the Widow Douglas's civilized way of life. Huck is always restless in town, but finds his true happiness and freedom on the river.

C

Thoreau said, "A man is rich in proportion to the number of things which he can afford to let alone." In a paragraph, explain the meaning of this statement with reference to Thoreau's life at Walden.

(1)

This apparently paradoxical statement reflects Thoreau's values in his simple life at Lake Walden, uninvolved by the petty demands which harassed his neighbors. He deplored the fact that many men were not free, but were dominated by their acceptance of conventional needs. All around him in Concord he saw people distracted from a complete life by their efforts to pay off mortgages on their farms, by their wishes to travel, by trying to keep up appearances in dress, by a series of self-imposed duties to the community. Thoreau wished to be free to read, to observe nature, and to think. He obtained this freedom by restricting his material needs and reducing to a minimum the amount of time spent in maintaining a living. Judged by the norms of his society, his life at Walden was frugal, but by his own standards it was rich in time and tranquillity.

(2)

During his time at Walden, Thoreau deliberately practiced letting things alone. He built himself a simple cabin with just enough space for his needs. Into this he put a minimum of furniture, and even abandoned some pieces of limestone on his desk because they needed to be dusted each day. He lived on a plain but nourishing diet. Whenever friends walked out to visit him, he entertained them simply and informally, not becoming trapped by the demands of conventional standards of hospitality. From this vantage point in the woods, he criticized the townsmen of Concord for their excesses in food, clothing, shelter, and social obligations.

(3)

At a time when people spend so much of their time in order to "keep up with the Joneses," one has to admire Thoreau for his willingness to be different. All of his life was marked by actions which seemed right to him. One example is his going to prison rather than paying taxes to support a system which he despised — slavery. He wanted to be let alone, to do as he pleased, without worrying about what his neighbors thought of him. Removing himself to Walden Pond was just another example of his originality. He wanted to be let alone, so for two years he maintained himself in a little cabin, enjoying the companionship of woodsmen and farmers who happened by and who shared his appreciation of the beauties of nature. Some people might think this a dreary life. Most of us, if we were given an acre of country and our own company, would find ourselves bored because we have lost the habit of solitary thought. But it was what Thoreau wanted, and he did not care what other people thought about it.

D

In Shakespearean tragedy, knowledge is the root of evil. Discuss this generalization briefly with reference to *King Lear* and *Macbeth*.

(1)

Ever since Eden, the Judaeo-Christian tradition has linked knowledge with evil. This linkage is sometimes suggested in Shakespeare's tragedies, but not in all plays and certainly not definitely enough to stand as a generalization. Perhaps *Macbeth* best illustrates the pairing of knowledge and evil. The Weird Sisters prophesy two increases in Macbeth's political power, the first of which is almost immediately verified when he is made Thane of Cawdor. One might say that his knowledge of the future impels him towards killing the king, that, if he had never heard the Weird Sisters, he might have remained a loyal, useful subject instead of becoming a tyrant and perpetrator of horrors. Yet the reader senses in Macbeth and his wife, even from the start, a latent ambition merely waiting to be touched off by some outside influence. The knowledge he receives is that influence and thus contributes to eventual evil. His knowledge, though, is neither complete nor solely responsible; given to a patient and gentle man like Banquo, it produces no evil at all.

King Lear presents a different relationship. Evil seems to spring from the absence of knowledge. The king, unable to evaluate his daughters accurately, lacking knowledge of their real qualities, divides his kingdom unfairly. Secondly, he lacks self-knowledge in his autocratic rashness. Even an evil daughter perceives, quite accurately, that he has "only slenderly known himself." Lear's humiliation, his suffering in the storm, and his temporary madness bring him to a more accurate understanding of himself and others. The final act of the play, though bleak indeed, is lightened by this better understanding. Knowledge is there associated with good, not with evil. One cannot, therefore, make the sweeping generalization that Shakespeare's tragedies present knowledge as the root of evil.

(2)

Knowledge is indeed the root of all evil. The reason for this is that one cannot imagine things without knowledge, but, once he knows a few things, he can combine them with others and imagine all sorts of possibilities, many of them evil. This is clearly shown in *Macbeth*. Macbeth is happy and successful until the Weird Sisters give him a vision of what his life might be. Then he becomes moody and dissatisfied, troubled to the point where he sees a dagger in empty air and sees the ghost of Banquo, whom he has unjustly murdered. The same knowledge works upon Lady Macbeth's personality and causes her to encourage the murder of the king. Later in the play, she too becomes psychologically disturbed and, while sleep-walking, relives the horrible, evil moments of her career.

King Lear provides additional evidence that knowledge is the root of evil. When the play begins, the king does not have a true knowledge of his daughters' characters and cannot see evil in Goneril and Regan when they make hypocritical protestations of their love for him. He is soon brought to realize how little these "dog-hearted daughters" love him, and this terrible realization brings him grief, suffering, and even insanity. Had he remained blind to their true characters, he might have lived out his remaining years in peace and happiness.

(3)

Like most generalizations, this one is false. *King Lear* includes some good characters who gain knowledge in the course of the play and some evil characters who make the good suffer. The evil characters seem to have more knowledge than the good at the opening of the first act, but, as the play goes on, the good characters acquire knowledge. This play seems to belie the generalization.

In *Macbeth,* the situation is somewhat different. Knowledge is more definitely at the root of evil. Macbeth gains more and more knowledge as the play develops, but his moral quality declines steadily, until he is finally like a vicious animal. An increase in knowledge seems to be closely related to an enlargement of evil in his character and the disintegration of his personality.

9

The Critical Essay

A critical essay is one which evaluates its subject. The subject may be a literary work, a motion picture, a television program, a painting or an exhibition of paintings. The subject may be the whole contribution made by someone over several years — for example, an actor's career or a President's administration; it may be an activity or a trend, such as pop art or the civil rights movement. Whatever the subject, the writer is concerned with explaining and evaluating it, in order to give his readers a wider and deeper understanding of it.

Because the subjects of most critical essays in an English class are literary, this chapter will reflect that emphasis. A student writing such a critical essay is evaluating a novel, play, poem, short story, essay, or a collection of such pieces. He is concerned with four questions: (1) What does the work set out to do? (2) How does it go about doing this? (3) How effective is the achievement? (4) How significant is the total work in its purpose and achievement? The student must, therefore, identify the author's purpose, analyze his methods, and appraise the success and significance of the work. His judgment may be favorable, unfavorable, or balanced. But, if his criticism is an effective one, it should give a reader fresh and valuable insight into the subject.

THREE STAGES OF CRITICISM

The following discussion will divide the process of criticism into three phases: *interpretation, technical analysis,* and *judgment.* Interpretation is concerned with showing what the work means, and answers the first of the four questions. Technical analysis deals with the techniques by which the author selects, shapes, and presents his material; it provides answers to the second question. Judgment shows the critic's appraisal of the effectiveness and general purpose of the work, in answer to questions 3 and 4. These three stages are separated here to make the explanation clear. Actually, they often overlap or proceed simultaneously.

Interpretation

A critic who interprets a work is showing how he reads it, what it means to him. He may say, "This is what the work means" or "This is its meaning," but the interpretation does not lie in the work; it lies in the mind of the interpreter. This distinction is not a quibble. Here are eight interpretations of Shakespeare's *Hamlet,* each advanced and supported by a critic with considerable claim to being an authority on the subject:

1. *Hamlet* is a play about a man who could not make up his mind.
2. *Hamlet* is Shakespeare's refinement of a traditional revenge play.
3. *Hamlet* is the tragedy of a charming and accomplished prince who is a victim of melancholia.
4. *Hamlet* is the tragedy of a moral man corrupted by the evil standards and pressures of an evil environment.
5. *Hamlet* is a dramatic illustration of an Oedipus complex, of a young man who loves his mother and resents his father and stepfather as rivals.
6. Hamlet is an ambassador of death who brings ruin to all with whom he is intimately associated.
7. *Hamlet* is a study of the ruthlessness required of kings, and of the trouble that ensues in the state when the leader's sense of political responsibility is weakened by conscientious misgivings.
8. *Hamlet* is a spectacle play, the appeal of which lies in a series of spectacular scenes presented on the stage.

Each of these interpretations can be supported by evidence in the text, but since the interpretations are in obvious disagreement, it may be inferred that each emphasizes certain aspects of the text and ignores or de-emphasizes others. Each interpretation may be valuable for the insight it gives, but they cannot all state the "real meaning" of the play. They are best understood as partly autobiographical statements in which the critic testifies how *he* reads the play.

It is obvious that, in writing a critical essay, we cannot achieve the kind of objective accuracy we would seek in factually describing a simple event. Each critic interprets a work of literature in the light of his own reading, his own experience, his own principles of selection. An interpretation cannot, then, be "right" or "wrong" in the conventional sense. But there is a standard of reliability which requires that the interpretation contradict neither the text being examined nor those facts about the author and his work that have been firmly established by scholarly researches.

Interpretation is never mere summary. Telling the story of a play or a novel, or paraphrasing a poem, is not an act of criticism. Criticism requires that the critic give meaning to the work, and this a summary does not do. For example, a summary of William Golding's *Lord of the Flies* would tell what happened in the novel, each incident in the order in which it occurred. The following discussion of the book does not tell what happened, except in a very general way. Rather it attempts to describe the significance of what happened, as the critic determines that significance. This is his interpretation.

The book is an allegory. The boys are presented as typical of human nature as it is essentially. Their isolation on an island is a device whereby the author is able to transcend what he would consider the façade of civilization in order to reach man as he truly is. The book prescinds entirely from anything of the supernatural and, even more so, from anything derived from revelation.

The theme of the book is that the human condition is irrational. Man has no nature, but rather is an excrescence from chaotic, cruel and blind forces which are violent and yet meaningless. Man springs forth from these forces and regresses into them. The violence which develops on the island only reflects in microcosm the violence of the rest of the world: the boys appear on the island as the result of some atomic catastrophe; the sole intruder on the island is the dead pilot who is shot down from the firmament overhead, and the boys leave the island in the company of armed men traveling in a warship. When all is said and done, man's condition is represented as something hateful. Thus the novel is representative of the spirit of much of modern thought and art.

Ralph's obsession with maintaining a fire is symbolic of man's illusion that civilization will bring salvation. The usage of fire to symbolize the arts and sciences of civilization was canonized in the Prometheus legend, and a reflection of that myth is found in the book when the forces of chaos plan to steal back the fire. Civilization, however, is merely a momentary veneer which ill conceals man's essential nature. Under pressure, even Ralph, the protagonist of civilization, begins to revert to his primal condition, forgetting the importance of the fire.

Almost immediately after the boys' arrival on the island, the forces of violence, blind power and cruelty, typified by Jack, Roger and their associates, begin to struggle to attain ascendency over the values of civilization and traditional authority, represented by the fire and Ralph with his conch. These boys hanker for violence and a return to the primordial chaos, typified by the hunt. Soon their antagonism becomes hostility, as the hunt and blood-lust become responsible for the fire dying out and the chance for a return to civilization being missed. It is at this time, significantly, that the specter of some mysterious beast begins to loom up before the boys. The beast becomes a source of terror and division among them as fear grows of some unchained and superior force in their midst.

What is the beast? It is man himself. Piggy intimates this. "I know there isn't no beast — not with claws and all that, I mean. But I know it isn't fear either — unless we get frightened of people." But it is Simon, the seer, who spells out the truth explicitly. " 'Maybe there is a beast. . . . What I mean is — maybe it's only us. We could be sort of. . . .' Simon became

221

inarticulate in his effort to express mankind's essential illness. Inspiration came to him. 'What's the dirtiest thing there is?' As an answer, Jack dropped into the uncomprehending silence that followed it the one crude, expressive syllable."

This paragraph is critical. The vilest of human things is used as a symbol of man himself. This is not a random remark, for an underlying concern with human excrement runs throughout the book. Any doubt as to the correctness of this interpretation is dissipated when the beast appears to Simon and confirms Simon's insight. "Fancy thinking that the Beast was something you could hunt and kill! You knew, didn't you? I'm part of you? Close, close, close! I'm the reason why it's no go? Why things are what they are?" And what name is given to this beast? He is the "lord of the flies." This is a cryptogram for the reader because the Aramaic word in question, "beelzebub," is not always translated thus. Another meaning given for this word is "lord of dung." The beast then is human nature itself — vile and hateful, worthy to be symbolized by human excrement. It is this hateful power which Jack apotheosizes and begins to worship.

Man, however, is merely part of a larger chaos from which he has come and toward which he regresses. The murder of Simon takes place when the boys are in an orgy of frenzied dancing, a frenzy which reflects in microcosm the tearing wind, jagged lightning and powerful rain of the universe. And where do the dead return? Simon, the aviator and Piggy, the book explicitly states, all are carried out to sea, to the sea which in its ineluctable movement reflects the vast and meaningless movement of the universe. This is the significance of the last paragraph of chapter nine. "Only two dead," Ralph later informs his rescuers, and then he adds significantly, "and they've gone."

The book, then, presents man and the universe as a cruel and irrational chaos. This artistic vision, typical of modern art, induces a sense of despair and even hatred of what is human. One joins with Satan himself in the devil's loathing of man. This is why certain critics have termed some aspects of modern art diabolic. There is supreme irony in the title of the book itself. The term "lord of the flies" is, as has been mentioned, a translation of the word "beelzebub." And Beelzebub is Satan.[1]

Mr. Egan's purpose in writing this critique was to illustrate what the novel means to him, to interpret it in a way which invites the reader to share his idea of its meaning. To do this, he has selected and arranged some of the incidents from the novel which support his interpretation. His selection and arrangement are subjective, guided by his individual view of the book. But his interpretation is reliable because it does not contradict the text or anything we know about Golding's intentions in writing the book. Had he distorted the meaning of events to make them conform to a personal idea which was alien to Golding's apparent purposes, the interpretation would not be reliable.

[1] From John M. Egan, "Golding's View of Man," *America,* January 26, 1963. Reprinted with permission from *America,* The National Catholic Weekly Review, 106 W. 56th Street, New York, N.Y. 10019.

Technical Analysis

Technical analysis comments on the language and structure of the work, on the techniques used by the author to convey his meaning. For example, another critic points out that each of Golding's novels is based on a metaphor, but that Golding undercuts the metaphor with a concluding "gimmick," as he prevents the murder of Ralph and the complete triumph of Jack's savagery by the sudden appearance of the cruiser which "rescues" the boys. The gimmick is not something inherent in the material; it is a technical device used to stop or modify actions which are implied by the theme of the book, as the complete triumph of the forces of savagery is implied in the preceding pages of *Lord of the Flies*. The critic's analysis continues with further discussion of how the author manages his material.

The following extract from a student essay makes a technical analysis by showing how James Thurber handles contrasts and transitions in "The Secret Life of Walter Mitty":

> What makes "The Secret Life of Walter Mitty" more than just another amusing short story is Thurber's unique and effective use of contrasts. Consider, for example, the first three paragraphs. Here the Walter Mitty of imagination is placed side by side with the Walter Mitty of reality. The contrast between the iron-hearted Naval Commander, bravely giving orders to his men, and the chicken-hearted Walter Mitty, timidly taking orders from his wife, is quite apparent. But the use of contrasts is by no means restricted to the beginning of the story. On the contrary, it is employed all the way through to the very last word. Compare the quick-thinking Doctor Mitty, famous surgeon, to the Walter Mitty who cannot park his car, remove his tire chains, nor readily remember to buy a box of puppy biscuits. Compare also the "greatest shot in the world" or the daring Captain Mitty, or the "erect and motionless, proud and disdainful, Walter Mitty the Undefeated" with the Walter Mitty who seeks the quiet refuge of a big leather chair in a hotel lobby. Contrasts are effective tools for any writer, but the straightforward manner in which Thurber employs them enhances their effectiveness considerably.
>
> After briefly skimming through the collection of contrasts that makes up "The Secret Life of Walter Mitty," one might feel that there is little connection between the paragraphs describing the imagined Walter Mitty and the Mitty of reality. However, closer observation reveals that Thurber does, by the use of suggestive words and phrases, cleverly establish links between the Mitty of fact and the Mitty of fancy. Examine the following lines taken from the end of paragraph one and the beginning of paragraph two of "The Secret Life of Walter Mitty":
>
> ". . . The Old Man'll get us through," they said to one another. "The Old Man ain't afraid of Hell!" . . .
>
> "Not so fast! You're driving too fast!" said Mrs. Mitty. "What are you driving so fast for?"
>
> We shudder to think that there might be a connection between Hell and life with Mrs. Mitty, but, unfortunately, such could be the case. Consider how Mrs. Mitty's mention of Doctor Renshaw and the event of driving by a

hospital lead to a daydream in which Walter Mitty, a distinguished surgeon, assists Doctor Renshaw in a difficult operation. Take note also of how a newsboy's shout about the Waterbury trial initiates the trial of Walter Mitty in the following paragraph. Such skillful employment of transitions, by which an event in reality triggers an event in the imagination, is sound not only from the literary standpoint, but also from the psychological point of view.

This critic has not concerned himself with interpretation, for the meaning of Thurber's story — that a timid, insecure, and weak character can take refuge in heroic fantasies — is easily grasped by any perceptive reader. The critic has instead analyzed Thurber's method of conveying this meaning. First he treats the repeated use of contrasts in moving back and forth between the "real" world of Walter Mitty and the more satisfying life of his daydreams, and gives illustrations of this movement. Next he demonstrates that the opposing elements in any contrast have a subtle connection in thought or language.

Judgment

In interpretation the critic discusses what the work has done; in technical analysis he discusses how it is done; in judgment he discusses the effectiveness and the significance of what is done. At this stage, more clearly than at the others, the critic evaluates the work by expressing an opinion of it as a whole. In order to support that opinion, he cites evidence from the text, and that evidence usually includes some technical analysis. This procedure was demonstrated in Chapter 3 in the judgment that "Trees" is a bad poem. There the critic pointed to the inconsistency of the metaphors to support his judgment that the poem is artistically bad.

The following student essay illustrates an adverse judgment not of a poem's artistry but its significance. The poem is given first in order to allow you to check the student's comments against the text.

A Noiseless Patient Spider

A noiseless patient spider,
I mark'd where on a little promontory it stood isolated,
Mark'd how to explore the vacant vast surrounding,
It launch'd forth filament, filament, filament, out of itself,
Ever unreeling them, ever tirelessly speeding them.

And you O my soul where you stand,
Surrounded, detached, in measureless oceans of space,
Ceaselessly musing, venturing, throwing, seeking the spheres to connect them,
Till the bridge you will need be form'd, till the ductile anchor hold,
Till the gossamer thread you fling catch somewhere, O my soul.

— Walt Whitman

This is what the student wrote:

"A Noiseless Patient Spider" illustrates that what is *avant-garde* for one generation may become trite for another. In his own time, Whitman was an innovator, breaking loose from prescribed forms into free verse, substituting a passionate outpouring of responses for the more restrained observations of conventional poets. This poem provides a representative example of his achievement.

The whole poem rests on a comparison between the attempts of a spider to fasten the first thread for his web and the attempts of the human soul to find its security. In each action, the one real and specific, the other abstract and more vague, the process is one of continual trial and error. Within the poem, neither the spider nor the soul actually achieves success, but one feels that the process of trying will continue.

In order to express this continuity, Whitman uses appropriate devices of diction, syntax, and meter. The inclusion of several words ending in "ing" in both stanzas, the repetition of "filament" in the first stanza and "O my soul" in the second, and the long lines of the second stanza tend to elongate the action. All of the first stanza is a single sentence, which also conveys an impression of length. The second stanza suggests endlessness because it is an incomplete sentence.

Since the two stanzas compare such very different things as a spider and a soul, the poet has connected them with a common body of metaphor, using images of a boat in a vast ocean trying to get an anchor hold on some solid ground. The poem includes, then, three major images: the spider, the soul, and the boat unreeling its anchor rope.

If Whitman uses an accepted poetic device of comparing a specific item from nature with something more abstract, and follows the standard for good poetry by making his form appropriate to his meaning, why isn't this poem really interesting? I think it is because his idea is trite. Everyone knows the old story of Robert Bruce's watching the spider and making its patient aspiration the model for his own behavior. The poem seems to say almost the same thing, but in a more artificial way. Perhaps, too, poetry has progressed beyond Whitman to the point where we no longer appreciate such a simple comparison as this one. The reader can see the meaning easily, and will probably accept it with boredom and no argument. In our time, it is scarcely news to learn that each individual is isolated in a vast world and must try to establish lines of communication with someone or something outside himself. An excellent poem will outlast its own time, but this one, after the passage of a century, is very old-fashioned.

Notice that the judgment refers to both interpretation and technical analysis. Since the student author admits that interpretation is not difficult and since his adverse judgment of the poem is based not on technical defects but on triteness of idea, he could legitimately have ignored both interpretation and technical analysis, but his inclusion of them tends to establish him as competent by showing that he understands the structure of the poem and that his judgment does not proceed from ignorance.

▶ *Now contrast the foregoing criticism with that given below by another student on the same poem. You may wish to consider the following questions:*

> 1. *Has the critic offered any interpretation of the poem? If he has, is his interpretation clear? If he has not, why do you suppose he neglected it?*
> 2. *What kinds of technical analysis does the critic present? Does he establish any relationship between the meaning and the technique of the poem?*
> 3. *On what kinds of evidence does the critic find the poem ineffective? Is this evidence clear and well supported?*
> 4. *On what kinds of evidence does the critic find the poem trivial or purposeless? Do you agree?*
> 5. *Does the critic seem to be treating the poem fairly?*

Write a paragraph or two in which you compare the two criticisms and evaluate both.

Walt Whitman is usually considered one of America's greatest poets. In my opinion, his reputation is unwarranted. "A Noiseless Patient Spider" offers evidence of some of the things which baffle the reader in Whitman's poems and raises a serious question whether this is really good poetry.

The poem is divided into two stanzas, each with five lines. The lines within stanzas are of unequal lengths and employ various metrical patterns, in the manner of free verse. The free-verse writer has poetic license to use this variety, but it is difficult to remember a poem when there is so little regularity in its pattern. I always feel that a poem like this isn't really finished, that the poet has stopped work before he was able to bring his idea into a more organized form.

The inadequate form in this poem conveys meaning that is also somewhat defective. The first stanza sets out to describe a spider's actions in beginning to make its web. Anyone who has ever watched a spider will immediately recognize that Whitman's description is inaccurate. The thread is actually extruded from a spider's body in a kind of slow, squeezing motion, which makes such words as "launch'd," "unreeling," and "speeding" seem inappropriate. The poet should have observed more carefully before setting out to write his descriptive verses.

In the second stanza, the poet turns to another idea and directly addresses his soul. Since the activities of a soul are not observable, one cannot complain of inaccuracy here. Yet it seems awkward to think of a human soul as throwing an anchor or flinging a gossamer thread. The poet has obviously tried to make the abstract idea of the soul more concrete, but, in my opinion, he has made it ridiculous.

One may well ask why Whitman wrote this poem. He ventures into the world of nature and comes out with a description which is neither accurate nor beautiful. He makes an impassioned plea to his soul, but it is impossible to discover what he is asking or what his final conclusion is about the soul. To be good, a poem, like any other communication, should have a purpose beyond the mere putting of words on paper.

THE CRITICAL BOOK REVIEW

The reviewing of a book, a typical assignment for college freshmen, is the application of what has already been said about criticism to a single work. Properly written, a review is an evaluation, never a mere digest, though in some cases the content may be summarized in the introductory paragraph. The body of the review is an evaluation in which the reviewer is answering the critical questions already mentioned: What does the book do? How does it do it? How effective is the treatment? How significant is the total work?

This reference to critical questions should not be interpreted as meaning that the reviewer must take up each of these questions in order and treat them all at equal length. If he feels that the book is so difficult that it requires an extended explanation, he may devote most of his effort to interpretation. Or he may spend most of his time developing the judgment he has made of the book, and include interpretation and technical analysis only incidentally. Deciding how to organize the review is part of the obligation of authorship. The best organization will be the one that most efficiently allows the reviewer to develop whatever purpose he has established for the review during the prewriting stage.

As an illustration of the way an able student rises above a formula and makes his essay do what he wants it to do, consider the following review of *Death of a Salesman.*

Death of a Sad Man

It may be difficult to determine whether or not *Death of a Salesman* fits the classical definition of tragedy, but there is no difficulty in seeing that it is one of the most moving and important contributions to the realm of modern theater. The problem which confronts Willy Loman is one which almost every human being must face at one time or another during his life. What do you do when you find that your dreams will never be anything more than dreams? What do you do when your self image is tarnished and dented and finally destroyed by reality? What do you do when you fail?

Willy Loman suffers from his ineptness more than the average person because he has made success the basis for his whole life, and success is one thing which Willy has never achieved. Most people discover failure early in their lives and are able to make the necessary adjustments to keep their personal world and goals in perspective. Sooner or later we all realize that only a gifted few will ever conquer their environment and that the rest of us will have to be content with an uneasy compromise. Happiness can be found within the confines of a family. The bond of love can be the basis for any life. Unfortunately, Willy Loman has always frosted over his defeats and failures; he has never come to grips with himself and his problem. Because of this, he has never really been able to appreciate Linda, the wife who has loved him so faithfully despite all his faults. Through his constant deification of success, he has warped the values of his two sons until they hold the same views which have been Willy's downfall.

The strongest bond which Willy has been able to build between himself and another person is the one with his oldest son Biff. As Willy starts to grow older, he subconsciously begins to realize that the goals he has set for himself are unattainable. But, he tells himself, there is still one way open. Through Biff, Willy feels he can accomplish the things which up to now he has only dreamed of. Now the world will see what a Loman is made of. It almost seems possible, for Biff idolizes his father, but Willy's relationship with his son carries the seed of its own destruction. It is inevitable that Biff will realize that his father and everything his father believes in constitute nothing more than one lie piled on top of another. When Biff finds his father in a cheap hotel with a strange woman seeking the low and common pleasures which ill befit a man of success and character, he is lost and betrayed. The father whom he had idolized never really existed. His father's principles, in which he had believed, are nothing but lies and falsehoods. What can he do but reject his father and everything he stands for? Everything which had motivated him to love and admire his father before now fosters hatred and disgust.

And where does this leave Willy? It leaves him without any hope of making his mark upon the world. Now the failures, and defeats, and trivialities of a lifetime, which the intricacies of the human mind had so mercifully spared Willy, come back to him and he is forced to accept them for the realities which they are. It is a slow process, one which can last years. It is also a tragic process, especially for a man whose life has had a basis the like of Willy Loman's. Can any man look back on a life of failure when he knows that his failures have destroyed not only himself but the son for whom he had wanted so much? If there is such a man, it is not Willy Loman.

There is almost no technical analysis here. The student is not concerned with how the playwright achieves his effects. There is a judgment, which is most clearly expressed in the last two sentences, but it is a judgment more of the hero than of the play. The whole essay is concerned with how the student responds to the work. Since that response shows how the student reads the play, it may be classified as interpretation. Yet the student is not really interested in explaining what the play means. He is concerned with the human problem it dramatizes, and he takes the meaning and the significance for granted. What he wants to write about is the moral weakness of Willy Loman, and the consequences of that weakness. The strength of his criticism is the sureness with which he relates Willy's fate to his false standards of values. It is that idea that controls the sequence and content of the paragraphs. The student knows what he wants to say, because he knows what he thinks about the play — and what he thinks about it is a result of his total involvement in reading it.

Reading for the Review

The preparation of a good review requires careful reading as well as careful writing. Lazy or uncritical reading will nearly always result in a poor review; therefore, you should begin to read the book *with the intention of reviewing it.* An awareness of this intention will help to point your reading, just as the intention of outlining or writing an essay examination helps you to read purposefully. This does not mean that one should make up his mind about a book in the first thirty pages and then skim the rest merely to find additional evidence to support a hasty judgment. Quite the opposite. Except in rare cases, an honest reviewer will not make a final judgment until he has read the whole book. But if he reads alertly, he will formulate tentative judgments as he goes along.

In beginning to read, always pay special attention to the introductory or prefatory material. The opening paragraphs usually reveal the purpose and may even summarize the organization. The preface of a book is often the clearest statement of what its author proposes to do. It may also contain explanations which will affect your review. For example, if the author of a biography of John F. Kennedy states in his preface that he has limited himself to a study of Kennedy's political life, it would be embarrassing to miss that statement and condemn the book on the ground that it failed to present an adequate picture of Kennedy's personal life. A reviewer has a right to point out, even regret, the limitations an author imposed on himself. But he does not have the right to condemn a writer for not doing what he never intended to do.

For most books it will be wise to take notes as you read. These notes should contain at least a clear statement of the purpose of the book, some hints about its structure and technique, and specific references to pages and passages which illustrate special qualities of concern to your interpretation, analysis, or judgment. These notes will serve a double purpose: they will help to keep your reading alert and so give you a keener insight into the success or failure of the work, and they will reduce or eliminate the time required to go back and find what you remember as good evidence to support your observations.

Writing the Review

The writing of a critical review presents no special problems of composition. As long as you satisfy the requirements discussed earlier, you are free to organize and present your material in whatever way best suits your purpose. The writing of a critical review, therefore, is merely the application to a particular assignment of the principles of composition discussed in Parts One and Two of this book.

As always, the first step is a concern with purpose. Before you begin to write, you must be clear about two things: your obligations to your readers and your over-all judgment of the book. If you are sure of these things, the organization of your paper should present no unusual difficulty. But if you begin without understanding what is expected of you or what you want to do, your review may be hard to write and even harder to read.

Therefore, if you have no clear understanding or judgment of the work when you finish reading it, you should review your notes and analyze your impressions in order to clarify your thinking.

For many students the most difficult part of a critical paper is the opening paragraph. It is quite reasonable, of course, to plunge at once into your final judgment of a book and then devote succeeding paragraphs to developing the reasons for that judgment. But if you feel that this is too abrupt — and it often is — there are various other ways of beginning, such as:

1. With an introduction of the author, telling the reader who he is, what other books he has written, or how he came to write this one.

2. With a summary of the problem or a statement of the theme which the author is discussing. Thus, a review of a book on psychedelics might begin with an explanation of the subject and of the concern which it has created.

3. With an anecdote or an illustration, either to suggest the mood of the review or to introduce the author's attitude toward his subject.

4. With a quotation that sums up the purpose of the book.

5. With a description of the book in general terms to give the reader a brief, comprehensive picture of it.

6. With a classification of the book to show how it resembles or differs from others of the same kind.

7. With a combination of two or more of these openings.

As you develop your review be on guard against these common weaknesses:

1. Taking up a disproportionate space to explain the action or content of the book so that the review is essentially a digest instead of a criticism.

2. Picking out parts for discussion instead of reviewing the book as a whole. It is justifiable to criticize particular parts in relation to the whole, but a student who concentrates on particular sections is likely to produce a distorted impression of the book as a whole.

3. Drifting into digressions which better illustrate the ideas of the critic than the merits or demerits of the book.

4. Allowing the tone of the review to suggest exaggeration or bias and thus giving the reader the impression that the critique is not a fair one.

5. Keeping the review at too general a level by failing to provide specific illustrations of general statements.

The first four of these weaknesses result from failing to keep the purpose of the review clearly in mind. The last comes from a failure to remember that the reader cannot see into the reviewer's mind and hence can never be quite clear about what his general judgments mean unless these are made explicit. In the critical review, as in all writing, the writer must illustrate his general observations to make them convincing.

The following student review illustrates both merits and weaknesses:

AGE OF THUNDER

Frederic Prokosch's *Age of Thunder* is ample evidence that beautiful writing is not enough. Few living writers can handle the English language with more distinction than this poet turned novelist. Even Thomas Mann has paid tribute to the Prokosch prose. But, I think Prokosch's isolated talent of turning exquisite sentences or fashioning fabulously beautiful passages (sometimes several pages in length) actually destroys his chances of achieving greatness. His character development, plot construction, and even intellectual honesty tend to disappear in a purple mist of liquid syllables.

Prokosch's novel pictures the life and death struggles of the maquis in the Haute-Savoie during the years of French underground resistance. Jean-Nicolas, a loyal parachutist spy, dropped for vague reasons of collecting information, dreams his way toward the Swiss border on a magic carpet of Prokosch philosophizing. Later, Jean-Nicolas is betrayed to a German officer by a shadowy caricature named Robinson. That this Robinson or the German commandant would entertain and edify this obvious spy with long and rather juvenile philosophical essays sounded unreal to me.

I do not believe that three mountain gangsters who waylay Allied sympathizers would talk like three versions of Prokosch while planning the murder of Jean-Nicolas. And I do not believe that Susanna, the convenient virgin who tosses the conventions aside like the "winter garment of repentance" upon meeting Jean-Nicolas, would talk or act as she did. In fact, the whole novel is Prokosch any way you cut it.

Incidentally, logical readers who have an eye for detail will want to know why the Swiss border was always a line of hills as these poetic escapists approached it, and how it suddenly became a river when they reached it. But Prokosch, in his illogically slap-happy approach to the problem, undoubtedly thinks such matters are beneath his attention. Personally, I think Prokosch had better stick to poetry.

The only good points I can see about the whole book are the beautifully written passages and the romantic backdrops. However, the reader wants to know how the maquis operated, how the Germans and the collaborationists countered their efforts, and what men would do, think, and say under such circumstances. It is here that Prokosch evades the issue and covers it up with his philosophizing.

As freshman work, this review has many good qualities. It describes the book, makes a clear judgment, and supports it with some evidence. But there are some things in the review that may bother a reader. First, judgments about style usually need illustration. A few sentences, even a phrase or two, showing Prokosch's style would lend meaning to the reviewer's judgment. Second, a little more restraint would make the review more convincing, for such expressions as "even intellectual honesty tends to disappear," "illogically slap-happy approach," "the whole novel is Prokosch any way you cut it," and "Prokosch had better stick to poetry" may strike a reader as intemperate condemnation, if not arrogance. Third, a reader may reasonably ask why it is illogical to describe a boundary from a distance as a line of hills and later define it from close up as a river — lines of hills are visible from a distance; rivers are less visible. Finally, in a context of such unsympathetic comment, a reader may wonder if, in condemning Prokosch's work for its lack of realism and its failure to explain how the resistance movement actually operated, the reviewer has not missed the author's purpose. As these doubts accumulate, a reader is likely to lose confidence in the reviewer.

THE LONG CRITICAL ESSAY

In some courses a long critical essay is a major assignment. The student chooses an area of concentration, carries out a program of independent reading in that area, identifies the specific problem he wishes to investigate, and finally writes an essay of some 2000 words or more expressing the results of that study. The organization and documentation of such an essay are no different from those for a research paper, as discussed in Chapter 11. The present treatment of the long critical essay is limited to its subject matter.

The long critical essay may develop an interpretation, an analysis, a judgment, or all three combined, but it is never a mere summary of the reading. It is a unified essay organized to develop whatever purpose the student has determined. It may be a study of a single work and possibly the scholarly articles available on that work. It may deal with several works by the same author, or with similar or contrasted works by different authors. It may trace the development of a work or the critical reputation of its author. It may develop a single idea (thesis), or it may discuss the subject under a succession of major headings without developing a thesis. The following six descriptive titles of student essays are given merely to suggest something of the variety of subject and treatment in such an essay.

"How 'Noble' Does a Tragic Hero Have to Be?" A contrast of *Oedipus Rex, Ghosts, Death of a Salesman,* and *Sweet Bird of Youth* to show that the social status of the hero is not decisive in creating a tragic response to his ruin.

"Is the Ending of *Huckleberry Finn* an Artistic Failure?" A study of the novel and the criticism of it, leading to the conclusion that Tom Sawyer's romantic stratagems for freeing Jim seriously weaken the novel.

"Primitive Influences in Three Modern Novels." A comparison of *Lord of the Flies, Diary of a Simple Man,* and *The Old Man and the Sea* to show symbols of primitivism in each of them.

"The Indifference of Nature in Crane's 'The Open Boat.'" A study of the structural elements by which Stephen Crane develops his theme that nature is neither friendly nor hostile, but merely indifferent to man.

"The Vindication of D. H. Lawrence." A study of the history of censorship of D. H. Lawrence's novels.

"Two Views of Man." A contrast between T. S. Eliot's and William Golding's views of man.

Topics such as these can be successfully developed from a close reading of texts supplemented by a study of relevant critical writings and other scholarly materials that will assist the student in formulating his own critical judgment.

Exercises

A. First study the poem that precedes the student essay below, and formulate your own critical judgment. Then read the essay and write a substantial paragraph of comment on it.

ON "DEATH"

Death

Death, be not proud, though some have called thee
Mighty and dreadful, for thou art not so;
For those whom thou think'st thou dost overthrow
Die not, poor Death; nor yet canst thou kill me.
From Rest and Sleep, which but thy picture be,
Much pleasure; then from thee much more must flow;
And soonest our best men with thee do go —
Rest of their bones and souls' delivery!
Thou'rt slave to Fate, chance, kings, and desperate men,
And dost with poison, war, and sickness dwell;
And poppy or charms can make us sleep as well
And better than thy stroke. Why swell'st thou then?
One short sleep past, we wake eternally,
And Death shall be no more; Death, thou shalt die!

On one's first reading of John Donne's Holy Sonnet "Death," the reader is apt to say, "It's different." It is this difference which serves as the beginning of the poem's originality. Donne's approach to his material takes a point of view which is opposite in nature to that which is generally held; his opening words deride Death, maintaining that he is not powerful and ought not to be proud. Instead of treating his subject with dignity and respect, instead of looking at it from a distance, Donne is colloquial and direct, as if he were engaging Death in a very familiar conversation. Such a beginning catches the reader off guard and, by the surprise of its directness, is an excellent attention-securing device. After this beginning there are no more stunts; the poet is in earnest. This earnestness is essential to the poem's conviction, which, emotionally at least, convinces the reader.

Superficially, this poem is quite commonplace. It is an assertion of man's ultimate defeat of Death in immortality. However, there is far more value in this poem as a work of art than in the mere message, ideas, or thoughts

233

of the author. It is true that thoughts are proper constituents of the totality which is a poem. Other things being equal, the more profound the thought, the greater the poem. By "other things being equal," I simply mean that thought does not of itself make the poem; it is only one element in the ultimate fusion which is poetry, not prose. Often poets are deliberately obscure, forgetting or ignoring the obligation to be as clear as possible so that communication between them and their audience may take place. But this can be decided only after every effort has been made to understand. It is well to remember that genuinely complex thought usually requires a complementary complexity of expression.

Although Donne's poem abounds in this complexity of thought and expression, it is a logical, reasoned argument in support of a thesis announced in the opening lines. Such a reasoned argument would suggest prose; Donne turns prose to poetry by dramatizing his material. Although Death is given no opportunity to talk back, the poem is a debate, one side of a debate, rationally worked out point by point.

Let us now make a rather brief analytical critique of the poem's message. John Donne is trying to remove fear from death. The poem is based on the Christian view that an eternal afterlife follows death, that death is merely a transition period, a temporary pause between the two "lives." Since "rest" and "sleep," which are images of Death, give men pleasure, Death, the reality, must give men more. Therefore, there is nothing to be dreaded about Death. Since the best men go with death most readily, an idea which is possibly an intentional variation of the popular saying, "The good die young," there can be nothing terrible about Death. Since Death is a slave to "Fate, chance, kings, and desperate men" and is associated with unpleasant things like poison, war, and sickness, it has nothing to be proud of in the company it regularly keeps. Since drugs can produce sleep as well as Death, there is nothing in particular to be dreaded in Death, nothing peculiar to its power.

After a brief elaboration on the general sonnet form which Donne has followed, it will become evident that this form is essential to the development and theme of this poem. A sonnet is a fourteen-line poem in which a conventional pattern is used to give added weight to the thought and feeling. Donne's "Death" is a characteristic example of the English sonnet. The general form is three quatrains followed by a couplet with the major division in emphasis coming at the end of the twelfth line. The concluding couplet is a dramatic climax, an intense and concentrated statement of the "point" of the whole poem, a summing-up of the consequences of what has been presented. Here the poet focuses the application of the experience developed in the three quatrains, criticizes, modifies, or expands it, and at once unifies and evaluates the experience out of which the sonnet is made.

Looking back, one begins to see the unique relation of this sonnet structure to the thematic content. First the dogmatic statement, "Death, be not proud"; secondly, an enumeration of reasons why Death has small ground for pride; finally, the last lines themselves rise to a climax of their own in the paradoxical phrase, "Death, thou shalt die," the final word on the whole matter. The entire poem is a figure, basically a metaphor, with Death compared to a person. It is this extended personification of Death which makes this caricature, this exaggeration of the mildness of Death, extremely realistic.

B. Make a paragraph analysis of the following review and see what it reveals about the relative proportions of the introduction and the body of the review. If you are familiar with *The Catcher in the Rye,* do you agree that "Mr. Salinger's main purpose was to expose the shocking 'phoniness' that exists in our society and to demonstrate the disastrous effect that such 'phoniness' can wreak in the delicate, formative years of adolescence"? Whether or not you know the novel, judge this review according to how well it satisfies the criteria discussed in the chapter.

Psychologists use a very interesting type of test in studying the human mind. I believe they call it a "word association" test. As the psychologist reads a certain word, the patient answers with whatever word he first thinks of. This immediate response indicates to the psychologist the feeling or meaning which the first word evokes in the patient's mind. After many tests of this type, psychologists have learned that many people respond with exactly the same word to the first mention of a given word; whenever "Civil War" is mentioned, the majority of patients respond with "Gettysburg" or "Gettysburg Address."

Selecting a word to cover and explain so varied and controversial a book as J. D. Salinger's *The Catcher in the Rye* is a very difficult task, if not an impossible one. But if *The Catcher in the Rye* were given as the first word in a word association test, I feel that the majority of the people who had read the book would respond with either "phony" or "phoniness." By "phoniness" is meant a conscious or unconscious attempt to make the observed appearance seem different from the actual reality. A simple, concrete example would be the wearing of old, ragged underwear beneath a good-looking, new suit of clothes. A "phony" then would be any person who attempts to perpetrate "phoniness" — anything which is insincere, hypocritical, or counterfeit. In the light of these definitions, I think that *The Catcher in the Rye* is primarily a study of "phonies" and "phoniness." I think that Mr. Salinger's main purpose in writing this book was to expose the shocking "phoniness" that exists in our society and to demonstrate the disastrous effect that such "phoniness" can wreak in the delicate, formative years of adolescence.

Mr. Salinger attempts to accomplish his difficult, yet extremely worthwhile purpose by presenting a succession of "phonies" for us to consider, and by showing their continued effect upon a single person, Holden Caulfield. The adjective which best describes Holden is "confused." He is confused and puzzled about life and its essential purposes, about morals, religion, education, and — not least of all — about "phoniness." It is the concern about "phoniness" which aggravates Holden's confusion and eventually causes him to become self-destructive. As Holden comes in contact with more and more "phonies," each exhibiting subtler and subtler types of "phoniness," the trend becomes unmistakable. Holden becomes more suspicious and distrustful of people, and he becomes "phony" himself in his confusion. Eventually he becomes completely unbalanced and cannot be sure whether "phoniness" really does exist, or whether his distorted mind is producing "phoniness" where none really does exist. This end is, indeed, not "pretty," but I think it does accomplish the purpose which Mr. Salinger intended.

10

Using the Library

The library is indispensable to higher education because it provides the literature of all areas of study and research. As you progress through college, your courses will require the use of an ever-wider variety of library materials. It will be to your advantage to learn, as early as possible, the titles and location in your library of the chief works of general reference and the standard specialized sources in your chosen field of study. Although this chapter will give you an introduction to these, several full-length guides to reference work are available — for example, *How to Do Library Research*[1] by Robert B. Downs.

THE CARD CATALOG

A card catalog is a register of all the materials held by a library. It consists of cases of trays in which 3 × 5 inch cards, marked with information, are filed alphabetically. Several types of cards are filed together according to the first significant word on the topmost line of the card: an "author card" has the author's surname first on the top line; a "title card" has the title on the top line; and a "subject card" has a subject heading at the top. There should be at least one of each kind of card for every book.

A typical author card is shown on the opposite page. This is a facsimile (reduced) of an author card manufactured by the Library of Congress for use in all libraries. It contains the basic and authentic information about the book. The call number is added by the individual library. A duplicate of this card becomes a title card when *The heathens* is typed above the author's name. Another duplicate becomes a subject card when *Religion, Primitive* is typed across the top, in capitals or in red ink. There will then be three

[1] Urbana, Illinois: University of Illinois Press, 1966.

cards in the catalog for this book, each filed in its alphabetical place — two in H-trays and one in an R-tray.

In this subject heading, *religion* is the dominant word, so the normal word order is inverted. In the heading *Religious education,* however, the word *education* is not considered dominant, and so comes last. Subject headings can be confusing to the student until he has become familiar with library terminology. Remember that subject headings are made as specific as possible, and that you will save time by looking first for the precise topic you have in mind. For example, if you want to read about St. Paul's Cathedral in London, you would look for *St. Paul's Cathedral,* not for *Churches – England* or *Cathedrals – England* or *London – Churches.*

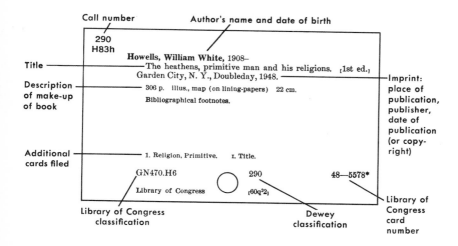

The card catalog will help you to find the proper headings by means of "cross-reference cards." A "see" reference gives a heading that is not used and tells which related term can be found in the catalog:

Farming   Humor

See   *See*

Agriculture   Wit and humor

"See also" cards refer to headings under which similar materials are placed, and come at the end of the filing sequence:

Cocoa   Pessimism

See also   *See also*

Chocolate   Optimism

Classification Systems

Most American academic libraries use either the Dewey Decimal System or the Library of Congress System for identifying and arranging materials on the shelves. Printed descriptions of these systems will be found at the main desk of the library, and brief versions may be posted in certain places.

The main divisions of the Dewey subject classification are as follows:

000–099	General Works	600–699	Applied Sciences
100–199	Philosophy and Psychology	700–799	Fine Arts and Recreation
200–299	Religion	800–899	Literature
300–399	Social Sciences	F	Fiction in English
400–499	Languages	900–999	History, Travel, Collected Biography
500–599	Pure Sciences	B	Individual Biography

These numbers are expanded by adding decimal places, each with a meaning: 998.2 — history of Greenland. You will need to know the numbers pertaining to your fields of special interest.

The main divisions of the Library of Congress classification are:

A	General Works	L	Education
B	Philosophy, Psychology, Religion	M	Music
		N	Fine Arts
C–D	History and Topography (except America)	P	Language and Literature
		Q	Science
E–F	America	R	Medicine
G	Geography, Anthropology, Sports and Games	S	Agriculture, Forestry
		T	Engineering and Technology
H	Social Sciences	U	Military Science
J	Political Science	V	Naval Science
K	Law	Z	Bibliography

This system is expanded by adding letters (QA — mathematics) and numbers.

Each published item is given a "call number" (see the facsimile card above) which consists of a subject designation from the classification scheme (290 for *The Heathens*) and a "book number" identifying the individual publication (H83h for the Howells book). A year may be added below for a later edition of a book or for the date of a serial publication. Taken as a whole, the call number is the only complete designation of a particular item in the library and therefore must be copied in full if one is to get the publication referred to by the card. The call number is always in the upper left-hand corner of the card.

Filing Rules

The following are widely accepted rules or conventions practiced by libraries in filing cards alphabetically, and a knowledge of them will help you make thorough and efficient use of the card catalog.

1. Filing is done word-by-word, or short-before-long, rather than letter-by-letter.

> North America
> North Sea
> Northanger Abbey
> Northern Ireland
> Northern Rhodesia
> The Northerners

2. Abbreviations and numbers are filed as though they were spelled out — *Dr. Faustus* will be found under *doctor, St. Lawrence* under *saint, U.S. News* under *United States, 19th Century Authors* under *nineteenth*.

3. In personal names *Mac, Mc,* and *M'* are filed as though they were all *Mac.* The foreign prefixes *de, van,* and *von* are ignored — *Hindenburg, Paul von.*

4. Cards for books *by* an author are filed before those *about* him, and in between will be books of which he is a "joint author," that is, one whose name does not appear first on the title page.

5. For the same word or name, the filing order is person, place, title.

> Hudson, William Henry
> Hudson, N. J.
> The Hudson and its Moods

6. Titles are filed according to the first significant word, ignoring *a, an,* and *the* and their foreign equivalents.

7. Subjects are usually subdivided in alphabetical order, but history is divided chronologically.

Printing — Exhibitions	Italy — History — To 1559
Printing — Specimens	Italy — History — 1559–1789
Printing — Style manuals	Italy — History — 1789–1815

The Shelf List

In addition to the main alphabetical card catalog, every library maintains a "shelf list," or catalog of the books in the order in which they stand on the shelves. The shelf list consists of one card for each book in the library collection, the cards being arranged in trays in the order of the call numbers. This is the subject catalog of the library, where you can find in one compact group of cards the titles of the books the library has on any subject. You may not use the shelf list often, but you should know that it is possible by this means to check the library holdings in your special field of interest. In some instances, too, you may be referred to the shelf list to learn what issues of a periodical the library has, or in what location on campus a certain work can be found.

THE REFERENCE COLLECTION

When you need to get information for your themes and research papers, you will go first to the reference room. There you will find dictionaries, encyclopedias, indexes, directories, handbooks, yearbooks, guides, and atlases covering almost every area of human knowledge. You should know what kinds of reference works are available and should become acquainted with the most important works of each kind.

Printed Catalogs

Catalogs in book form supplement the card catalog of the library by showing what books are available elsewhere. Most academic libraries have the two great printed library catalogs, those of the British Museum·and the Library of Congress. The latter is now called the *National Union Catalog,* and contains titles reported from other libraries in addition to those for which Library of Congress cards have been printed. It appears in monthly installments, in two sections, one arranged by author, the second by subject. Music, phonograph records, motion pictures, and filmstrips are cited as well as printed materials.

The main current publication lists for the United States are these:

Cumulative Book Index. A monthly list of books published in the English language, except government documents. It is "cumulated" periodically, that is, several issues are combined into one volume.

Publishers' Trade List Annual. A collection of publishers' catalogs bound together.

Books in Print. The annual author-title index to the *Publishers' Trade List Annual.*

Subject Guide to Books in Print. Also published annually.

The main lists of periodicals and newspapers are the following:

Union List of Serials in Libraries of the United States and Canada.

New Serial Titles. A monthly supplement to the *Union List.*

N. W. Ayer & Son's Directory of Newspapers and Periodicals. The best source of information about newspapers of the United States and its territories, Canada, Bermuda, Panama and the Philippines.

Ulrich's Periodicals Directory. Covers foreign as well as domestic periodicals.

Indexes to Periodical Literature

Since much of your writing will be based on periodical articles, and since these articles are not included in the card catalog, you will need to make use of periodical indexes. The most widely used index of general periodicals is the *Readers' Guide to Periodical Literature,* which lists the articles in a selected group of American periodicals of a nontechnical nature.

It is published semimonthly, except monthly in July and August, and is cumulated annually. At the front of each issue and of each bound volume is a list of the periodicals indexed, the abbreviations used for their titles, and a key to other abbreviations used. Articles are indexed mostly by subject, but some titles and authors are used as entries. Here are some sample entries[2]:

DAY, Richard
    Clean up your driveway. Pop Sci 188:145 Mr '66

Author entry for an article in *Popular Science Monthly,* Volume 188, page 145 of the issue for March, 1966.

DAY lilies
    Daylilies make you look good. il Sunset 136:253 Mr '66

Subject entry for an illustrated article in *Sunset* magazine.

DAY of absence; drama. See Ward, D. T.

Title entry referring the reader to the author entry for the citation.

DAYLILIES. See Day lilies.

Reference from a heading not used to the one used.

DEAFNESS
    Stubborn husband. il Good H 162:12+ Mr '66

Subject entry for an article about deafness in *Good Housekeeping,* Volume 162, page 12 and continued on subsequent pages not following consecutively.

DEBT
    See also
    Credit

Reference to a related subject heading under which articles on debt may be found.

For research on a technical or highly specialized topic, you will need to consult a specialized periodical index, such as:

Air University Library Index to Military Periodicals
Applied Science and Technology Index
Art Index
Bibliographic Index
Biography Index
Biological and Agricultural Index
Book Review Index
Bulletin of the Public Affairs Information Service
Business Periodicals Index
Education Index
Engineering Index
Essay and General Literature Index
Index Medicus
Index to Legal Periodicals
Social Sciences and Humanities Index
United Nations Document Index

The *Bulletin of the Public Affairs Information Service* is an index to American social science publications, including books and pamphlets. The *Bibliographic Index* cites bibliographies appended to foreign and American periodical articles and also those published separately. The *Air University Library Index* refers to articles, news items, and editorials in military and aeronautical periodicals.

[2] From *Readers' Guide to Periodical Literature,* April 10, 1966 (New York: H. W. Wilson Company, 1966).

The standard newspaper index for the United States is the *New York Times Index*. Published semimonthly and cumulated annually since 1913, this index will help you find the date of an event, so that you can consult the *Times,* or another newspaper of that date, for the comments of the press.

For quick reference and brief accounts of important news, the weekly world news digest, *Facts on File,* is useful. Published since 1940, it records events day by day, and has quarterly and annual indexes.

In addition to indexes, major fields have abstracting services to indicate the contents of periodical articles. Examples of these are:

Biological Abstracts
Chemical Abstracts
Economic Abstracts
History Abstracts
International Political Science Abstracts

Meteorological and Geoastrophysical Abstracts
Psychological Abstracts
Science Abstracts: A. Physics; B. Electrical Engineering
Sociological Abstracts

Government Documents

The bulk of government documents are neither cataloged nor indexed in periodical indexes; but two lists of documents are published by the United States government, and these lists are bound and kept in libraries — the *Monthly Catalog of United States Government Publications* and the *Monthly Checklist of State Publications.*

General Dictionaries (Unabridged)

Unabridged dictionaries, because of their completeness, are the best sources of information about words in the general vocabulary, and should be used as supplements to the student's own desk dictionary. The best known are:

A Dictionary of American English, 4 vols., University of Chicago Press.
New Standard Dictionary of the English Language, Funk and Wagnalls.
The Oxford English Dictionary, 12 vols. and supplement, Clarendon Press, Oxford. (A corrected reissue, in 1933, of *A New English Dictionary on Historical Principles,* 10 vols. and supplement, 1888–1928.)
The Random House Dictionary of the English Language.
Webster's Third New International Dictionary of the English Language, G. & C. Merriam Co. (The Second Edition of *Webster's New International Dictionary* is also still in general use.)

The Oxford English Dictionary is a particularly valuable resource for tracing the history of words and their meanings.

General Encyclopedias

The chief general encyclopedias for the college level are the *Encyclopaedia Britannica* and the *Encyclopedia Americana.* The *Britannica* is no longer published in England, but the influence of its distinguished British contributors since its beginning, in 1771, remains. The *Americana* is the second-oldest of the general encyclopedias.

Collier's Encyclopedia is an attractive American work, more recently compiled; *Chambers'* is an old English encyclopedia, re-edited in 1950. The *Columbia Encyclopedia* is a good one-volume reference work. There are also, of course, encyclopedias for many nations in other languages.

Yearbooks

Yearbooks are devoted to the chief occurrences of the preceding year and are published as quickly as possible after its close. Each of the major encyclopedias publishes an annual supplement as a means of keeping its material up to date, and these you will find shelved with the parent sets.

There are three "almanacs," compilations of miscellaneous statistics, records, events, and information not otherwise gathered together, any one of which would make a useful addition to a student's personal library. Each contains some material not included in the others. They are:

World Almanac and Book of Facts. Published by the New York *World-Telegram* and the *Sun,* a source of data for nearly a century.

Information Please Almanac, Atlas and Yearbook. Named for a former radio program and first published in 1947.

Reader's Digest Almanac. A new publication of 1966, with illustrations.

The designation "yearbook" is used for various publications, some appearing every few years, and some, like the *Yearbook of Agriculture,* providing thorough coverage of one topic each year.

For information on governmental matters, there are several valuable annual or biennial publications.

Book of the States. A biennial compilation of data on state governments.

Congressional Directory. Annual. Gives detailed information about Congress.

Municipal Year Book. Gives statistical data for American cities.

Statesman's Year-book. A British publication covering the nations of the world. Gives political and economic data.

Statistical Abstract of the United States. Published by the Bureau of the Census. Gives data on political, economic, and social institutions.

United States Government Organization Manual. Describes the departments of government, lists key personnel, and prints the Constitution of the United States.

Yearbook of the United Nations. Has résumés of the sessions of the General Assembly, and reports on the other activities of the UN.

Specialized Sources

The multiplication of specialized reference books in recent years makes any brief list of them inadequate, but a selection indicating the broad scope of factual material available may be useful as a preliminary guide. For subject matter not indicated here, ask your librarian. For complete bibliographic details of the titles in the following list, check the standard source, *Winchell's Guide to Reference Books*.[3]

Arts

In the field of the arts some of the most famous reference works are of foreign origin, particularly French, German, and Italian. Numerous one-volume guides to individual arts complement the larger sets.

American Art Directory. A source for information on museums, art schools, art associations of the U.S. and Canada. One of several such guides.

Concise Encyclopedia of Antiques. Signed articles on furnishings, prints, drawings, crafts of all kinds, with many illustrations. In five volumes.

Dance Encyclopedia. All forms of dance are discussed in articles by specialists.

Dictionary of Architecture and Building. By Russell Sturgis. Although old, the standard dictionary in this field in English.

Encyclopedia of Jazz. One volume with definitions, history, biography, discography.

Encyclopedia of Painting. Covers the world from prehistoric times; includes appraisals of paintings.

Encyclopedia of World Art. An ambitious projected fifteen-volume set, begun in 1959, issued simultaneously in Italian and in English by the Istituto per la Collaborazione Culturale. Authoritative monographic studies of topics including art by areas and individual artists of the world.

Focal Encyclopedia of Photography. One volume on a newly recognized art form.

Grove's Dictionary of Music and Musicians. A classic multivolume British work, kept up to date by supplements.

History of American Sculpture. Edited by Lorado Taft.

History of Architecture. By Sir Banister Fletcher. A standard work with a new edition in 1961.

History of Theatrical Art in Ancient and Modern Times. By Karl Mantzius. In six volumes; the pioneer work in the field, and still a useful source of information.

Variety Music Cavalcade. A two-volume chronology of popular music from 1620 to 1961.

Biography

Chambers's Biographical Dictionary. An English publication of general scope, with commentaries on people and events, and with an unusually good subject index.

---

[3] Constance M. Winchell, *Guide to Reference Books,* 7th ed. (Chicago: American Library Association, 1951). *Supplements,* 1950–1952; 1953–1955; 1956–1958; 1959– June, 1962. 8th edition in process.

Current Biography. Sketches about contemporary American celebrities, with photographs.

Dictionary of American Biography. A multivolume set containing scholarly articles about important Americans no longer living.

Dictionary of National Biography. The British equivalent of the above. These two are the classic biographical works.

National Cyclopaedia of American Biography. More than fifty volumes to date, containing a broad coverage of American historical biography.

New Century Cyclopedia of Names. Includes literary characters, names from myths and legends, places, and events, in one volume.

Webster's Biographical Dictionary. One volume of brief factual data and pronunciation of names of famous persons of history.

Who's Who. An annual listing of prominent living British persons, with abbreviated biographical data. *Who Was Who* is a separate list of the biographees now deceased, with date of death.

Who's Who in America. A biennial equivalent of the British work, with the companion volume *Who Was Who in America.*

Who's Who in ———. Besides those of other nations, there are many specialized publications using this general title, such as *Who's Who in Space* and *Who's Who in New England.* Other similar lists of living persons can be found under different titles, as *American Men of Medicine* and *Directory of American Scholars.*

Education

American Universities and Colleges. Published by the American Council on Education. Gives detailed basic information on each institution.

Dictionary of Education. Definitions of educational and related terms.

Education Directory. Published by the U.S. Office of Education in four sections, listing institutions, educational officers, government officials, and educational associations at all levels, from city to federal.

Encyclopedia of Educational Research. A most important source, although only published about every ten years. Contains articles by educational leaders on developments in various aspects of education.

Guide to Graduate Study: Programs Leading to the Ph.D. Degree. By the American Council on Education.

International Guide to Educational Documentation, 1955–1960. By UNESCO. Arranged by countries, it gives sources, publications, reference works, research, statistics, biographies of leaders.

Mental Measurements Yearbook. Appears every four or five years. Reviews tests and refers to reviews published elsewhere.

Study Abroad. An annual publication of UNESCO.

World of Learning. An annual list of educational, scientific, and cultural organizations of the world.

World Survey of Education. A three-volume publication of UNESCO. The first volume deals with education in general, the second with primary education, the third with secondary education, arranged by countries.

History

Cambridge Histories: Ancient, Medieval, and *Modern.* The greatest multi-volume histories, published by the Cambridge University Press. The oldest of these, the *Cambridge Modern History,* is currently being replaced by an entirely new publication based on recent scholarship, called the *New Cambridge Modern History.*

Dictionary of American History. A multivolume work edited by James Truslow Adams, with short articles. A companion volume is the *Atlas of American History.*

Dictionary of Dates. A chronology of historical events.

Encyclopedia of American History. A one-volume compendium of events, facts, and biographies.

Encyclopedia of World History. One volume, chronologically arranged.

Guide to Historical Literature. A bibliography of selected works in history.

Guide to the Study of the United States of America. A source book of the literature, published by the Library of Congress.

Oxford History of the American People. By Samuel Eliot Morison. A recent example of the valuable one-volume Oxford histories.

Shepherd's Historical Atlas. First published in 1911 and frequently re-issued, this book of maps covers world history with emphasis on Europe.

West Point Atlas of American Wars. Two volumes: *1689–1900;* and *1900–1953.* Gives battle maps and commentary.

Literature

Reference books in literature abound. There are indexes to various literary forms, encyclopedias, critical works, selected lists of good reading, and concordances to the works of great authors. A sample of other kinds of material is given here.

American Authors 1600–1900; British Authors Before 1800; British Authors of the Nineteenth Century; Junior Book of Authors; Twentieth Century Authors. A series edited by Stanley Kunitz and Howard Haycraft.

Annual Bibliography of English Language and Literature. A source for studies of these topics, arranged by centuries of literature and types of language study.

Bartlett's Familiar Quotations. The most popular of several books of quotations from poetry and prose, identifying authors and works.

Bibliography of American Literature. A four-volume work valuable as a historical guide.

Cambridge Bibliography of English Literature. A major work in four volumes and supplement.

Cambridge Histories of American and *English Literature.* Standard sets covering literature into the twenties.

Columbia Dictionary of Modern European Literature. Begins just before the turn of the century; gives critical comment.

Contemporary Authors. A "bio-bibliographical" guide to present-day writers and their works, in several volumes, 1962 to date.

History of English Drama, 1660–1900. By Allardyce Nicoll, a work of five volumes, with detailed articles, and also lists of theaters and plays.

Literary History of England. Edited by Albert C. Baugh. A four-volume work, also available in one volume.

Literary History of the United States. Sometimes identified by the name of one of its editors, R. E. Spiller, this is an evaluative two-volume work, the second volume a bibliography.

Masterplots. A multivolume cyclopedia of world authors, with critical biographies and plots of their literary works. Annual since 1957; two volumes indexing literary characters were published in 1963.

Oxford Companions to: *American Literature, English Literature, Classical Literature, French Literature, the Theatre.* Useful volumes for quick reference.

Oxford History of English Literature. A new compilation begun in 1947, with twelve volumes projected.

Reader's Encyclopedia. A second edition was published in 1965 of this favorite volume of brief reference to world literature from antiquity to the present.

Mythology and Classics

Atlas of the Classical World. An English publication of 1959.

Dictionary of Greek and Roman Biography and Mythology. One of three classical dictionaries by Sir William Smith, a great nineteenth-century editor.

Dictionary of Non-Classical Mythology. A source for material on non-Western cultures.

Gayley's *Classic Myths in English Literature and in Art.* A famous old multivolume work, known by its editor's name. Also in a one-volume edition.

The Golden Bough. By Sir James Fraser. A great exhaustive study of mythology in twelve volumes, also condensed into one volume.

Harper's Dictionary of Classical Literature and Antiquities. An older work of broad coverage.

Larousse World of Mythology. One of a new series of lavishly illustrated encyclopedic volumes bearing the name of a great French encyclopedist.

Mythology of All Races. The standard multivolume set in the field.

New Century Classical Handbook. A recent compilation embodying the latest archaeological research, with many photographs.

Oxford Classical Dictionary and *Oxford Companion to Classical Literature.* More of Oxford University's contributions to the field of reference.

Philosophy and Psychology

Annual Survey of Psychoanalysis. A source for recent developments.

Comprehensive Dictionary of Psychological and Psychoanalytical Terms: A Guide to Usage. Published in 1958.

Dictionary of Philosophy and Psychology. Edited by J. M. Baldwin; a classic older work.

247

Dictionary of Psychology. One volume, which includes foreign terms.

Harvard List of Books in Psychology. Added to by supplements.

History of American Philosophy. By Herbert W. Schneider.

History of Psychology in Autobiography. A four-volume compilation of "intellectual histories" written by great psychologists about themselves.

History of Western Philosophy. By Bertrand Russell; one of several works on the history of philosophy.

Professional Problems in Psychology. A valuable guide for the literature of the field, as well as information on the profession.

Religion

Besides dictionaries, histories, concordances of the Bible, and other types of reference book in the area of religion, there are several encyclopedias of individual faiths. The chief of these are the multivolume Catholic and Jewish encyclopedias, both older works, the former in process of being re-edited. Other one-volume encyclopedias of both of these faiths have more recently been published, and there are also encyclopedias of various Protestant sects. Among the more general works are the following:

Atlas of the Bible; Atlas of the Early Christian World. Recent British publications.

Book of Saints. A dictionary of canonized saints with brief biographies and a calendar.

Cambridge History of the Bible: in the West from the Reformation to the Present Day. Long articles on the history of the Bible in Europe and the United States, with full-page photographs of pages from famous Bibles.

Concise Encyclopedia of Living Faiths. Long, detailed articles on religions of the world make this British publication valuable.

Encyclopedia of Religion and Ethics. A multivolume standard work edited by James Hastings, who also edited a classic *Dictionary of the Bible*.

History of Religions. In two volumes, this work gives detailed accounts of the religions of the civilized peoples of Asia, the Near East, and Europe.

Interpreter's Bible. Twelve volumes containing the King James and Revised Standard texts in large print, accompanied by an exegesis.

New Schaff-Herzog Encyclopedia of Religious Knowledge. A standard work recently re-edited, in thirteen volumes and two supplements.

Religions, Mythologies, Folklore: an Annotated Bibliography. Includes periodicals, and is arranged both by subject areas and by type of book.

Science and Technology

The constant multiplication of reference books in scientific and technological fields insures that information even on very new branches is available. There are handbooks and dictionaries of terms for nearly all fields. There are encyclopedias of the classic sciences and of such specialties as Electronics, X rays and Gamma Rays, Space Science, and Polymer Science and Technology. Multilingual glossaries of scientific terms are also growing in number. Some other samples are:

Atlas of the Universe. A well-illustrated volume by Ernst and DeVries.

Bibliography of North American Geology. An annual publication of the U.S. Geological Survey.

Compendium of Meteorology. Published by the American Meteorological Society, one volume of articles by authorities in the rapidly developing atmospheric sciences. It has been supplemented by *Meteorological Monographs,* Volume 3, Nos. 12–20.

Famous First Facts. A record of first happenings, discoveries, and inventions in the United States, with dates and descriptions of patented devices.

Geography of Commodity Production. Treats commodities of the world by their derivations: agriculture, the forest, the sea, mining, and manufacturing.

Gray's *Anatomy of the Human Body.* A classic which is still re-edited.

Guide to the History of Science. One of three works by George Sarton elucidating the early development of science. Has an extensive bibliography.

Guide to the Literature of Mathematics and Physics. An excellent bibliographical aid.

Harper Encyclopedia of Science. A new multivolume work of broad scope.

McGraw-Hill Encyclopedia of Science and Technology. A fifteen-volume set of 1960, supplemented by yearbooks.

Scientific, Medical, and Technical Books Published in the United States of America. Edited by R. R. Hawkins, a standard annotated bibliography.

Van Nostrand's Scientific Encyclopedia. A one-volume compendium on science in general.

Social Sciences

In addition to dictionaries of politics, economics, and the social sciences, and the classic *Palgrave's Dictionary of Political Economy,* there are a number of one-volume encyclopedias in this field. Some other references are:

American Negro Reference Book. One volume giving history, statistics, economic and legal status of Negro people in the United States.

Biographical Directory of the American Congress, 1774–1961. Information not easy to find elsewhere.

Black's Law Dictionary. Defines terms and phrases in legal use in America and England, ancient and modern.

Cambridge Economic History of Europe. In six volumes; covers the time from the Middle Ages to the current era.

Commercial Atlas and Marketing Guide. One of Rand McNally's specialized atlases of the United States.

Encyclopedia of the Social Sciences. In fifteen volumes, the main comprehensive reference work in the field.

Encyclopedia of Social Work. An extension of the former *Social Work Yearbook,* in its fifteenth issue in 1965.

International Bibliography of Economics; of Sociology. Annual publications of UNESCO.

London Bibliography of the Social Sciences. The most famous bibliography in the field, listing the holdings of nine London libraries.

Political Handbook of the World. An annual publication of the Council on Foreign Relations.

Sources of Information in the Social Sciences: A Guide to the Literature. A good recent bibliography.

Worldmark Encyclopedia of the Nations. A comprehensive five-volume work.

Exercises

A. Suppose that you were going to write a paper on one of the following subjects. Choose the sources named in this chapter that you would consult for general preliminary information and the indexes you would search for periodical articles on the subject.

Leonardo da Vinci	Saint Matthew
The Peace Corps	Arthur Miller's plays
Race relations	Viet Nam
Volcanoes	Computer languages
The Rohrschach test	Atlantis
Weather modification	Hybrid corn
The Battle of Shiloh	*Oliver Twist*

B. Choose a famous person and compile a bibliography for an essay about that person. Consult all the possible sources suggested here, your library's card catalog, and your librarian. Try to find at least twenty books, periodical articles, and sources of biographical data to read.

11

The Research Paper

The research paper is a standard assignment in college classes. It goes under various names, but whether it is called a "research paper," a "documented paper," a "library paper," a "term paper," or a "reading report," it is written to present the results of a student's reading on a subject. The student selects a topic, reads about it in books and periodicals, takes notes, and writes a long paper based on the information he has uncovered.

There are four reasons for the prevalence of this assignment. First, because it combines reading, note-taking, organization, and development at a mature level, it provides the student with a worthwhile experience in using many of the skills cultivated in the English course. Second, it gives him a practical introduction to his college library and helps him to use it efficiently thereafter. Third, it makes him familiar with research procedures and conventions that he will use increasingly in college. Fourth, it gives a conscientious student the intellectual satisfaction of becoming, at least by freshman standards, something of an expert on a particular subject. It is for this reason that good students finish their research papers with a sense of achievement. They have been given a chance to show what they can do on their own, and they have the satisfaction of knowing that they have proved themselves.

But if the research paper is to have the educational value it is intended to have, it must be an honest job. Any student who perverts the assignment by deliberately plagiarizing the paper not only convicts himself of dishonesty but raises the question whether the money and effort being expended for his education are justified.[1] Few college students will deliberately plagiarize, but some drift into unintentional plagiarism because of careless habits of note-taking which may have been tolerated in high

[1] Plagiarism is the presentation of another's writing or another's ideas as one's own. Legally, socially, and academically it is considered a form of theft, and is usually punished in college by automatic failure in the course or by expulsion.

school. For this reason, no student should assume from his high school experience that he knows how to write a college research paper. Before he begins work on the assignment, he should make a careful study of what it requires of him. It is the purpose of this chapter to make these requirements clear.

In general, undergraduate research papers are of two kinds: *reports* and *theses*. The chief differences between these types come from the author's intent. The writer of a report wishes to find out the facts of his subject and present them in a clear, orderly, and detailed account. The writer of a thesis research paper is studying the facts to draw a conclusion from them; this conclusion becomes the thesis of his essay; and he selects and organizes his material to develop his thesis. Because it usually presents a more difficult problem, the thesis paper will be emphasized in this chapter, but the kind of paper you write will be determined by your instructor's directions for the assignment. Most of the advice in this chapter applies to both types of papers.

PREVIEW OF RESEARCH PROCEDURE

Before we consider the separate steps in preparing a research paper, let us first preview the whole procedure. Suppose you have been asked to choose a topic, study it, and write a 2000-word, documented paper which shows the results of your study.

Because you are interested in Mark Twain you decide to take him as your general subject. When you check the card catalog in your library you discover that so much has been written on him that you hardly know where to begin. You feel that the safest thing to do is to start with a general source — perhaps the *Dictionary of American Biography,* the *Cambridge History of American Literature,* or Spiller's *Literary History of the United States.* These sources make you generally acquainted with Twain's life and writings and suggest useful bibliographies which you can consult.

After some preliminary reading, you begin to see some specific fields of investigation; you could deal with Twain's private life, with his career as a lecturer or as a humorist, with his critical reputation during his lifetime and later, or with any of his chief works. At this stage you are ready to make a major restriction of your subject. You decide that you want to investigate what the critics have said about his masterpiece, *Adventures of Huckleberry Finn.* This decision is a turning point in your study, because you now turn away from other areas and restrict yourself to this one. You do this because you recognize that only by restricting the scope of your investigation can you hope to get a subject which you can treat with thoroughness within the time and space available to you.

Until now you have not taken notes or made a bibliography of the works you think you should consult. You have felt a need to familiarize yourself with the general subject, and you saw no point in making notes until you had settled on a restricted subject. But now you begin to check your references and the card catalog for titles that seem to be pertinent to a study of the criticisms of *Huckleberry Finn*. You make a preliminary bibliography and begin to read some of the works. As you read, you take notes on note cards. You use a separate card for each note and are careful to identify the exact source of your note on each card.

As your reading progresses and your pile of notes grows, you are thinking about the kind of paper you might write. You see three distinct possibilities:

An essay tracing the critics' reactions to *Huckleberry Finn* from the date of its publication to the present. Such an essay would probably be organized chronologically. It would probably not be dominated by any one idea and would therefore not have a thesis. But it might make a good research report.

An essay developing an answer to the question, "Is *Huckleberry Finn* a picaresque novel?" In your reading you have met several assertions that it is a picaresque novel. You have checked the characteristics of such a novel and are inclined to think that Huck's character is significantly different from that of the typical picaresque hero. Your answer to the question with which you began would give you your thesis and a tentative organization of the material. I. A definition of the picaresque novel; II. Identification of the picaresque elements in Twain's novel; III. A detailed explanation of the differences between *Huckleberry Finn* and the characteristics which you defined in part I.

An essay expressing your final judgment of the merits of the novel. Your judgment would be based on your knowledge of both the novel and the critical opinions about it, but you would be evaluating these opinions, not just summarizing them. Your judgment would be the thesis of the essay.

Depending on which possibility you choose, you will now revise your bibliography and your notes, discarding items which are no longer pertinent and adding new material from reading which is now concentrated on your newly defined purpose. As you proceed with this specialized study, you will begin prewriting the paper by making tentative outlines of your material and seeing where the notes fit the outline and where additional information is needed. When you are fully satisfied with your plan and your notes, you will prepare a final outline and be ready to start writing the essay.

The imaginary assignment we have been considering illustrates the recommended procedure for writing a research paper. That procedure may be summarized as follows:

1. Make a survey of the material available on your general subject.
2. Become familiar with the general subject through introductory sources, but postpone note-taking.
3. Restrict the general subject as quickly as you can. Remember that your reading does not become fully pertinent until you have decided the question you wish to answer or the specific phase of the subject that you wish to develop.

4. When you feel that your subject is becoming specialized, prepare a preliminary bibliography and begin to take notes.

5. Continue to restrict your subject as soon as the results of your specialized reading suggest further restriction.

6. When you feel that restriction of the subject is complete, decide what precisely you intend to do with that subject.

7. Begin the preliminary outlining of the paper. You have probably already begun to plan the organization in your head or by means of scratch outlines, but you are now ready for more formal outlines.

8. Fill in by additional investigation the blank spots that remain.

9. When the research is complete, make a final outline and write the first draft of your paper.

Most of the steps summarized above are preparatory. The total process would be considerably shortened if you knew at the beginning what you know by the time you have reached step 6. The more quickly you arrive at step 6, therefore, the more profitable your investigations will be and the less time they will require. Under favorable conditions you may be able to skip some of the preliminary stages, but even if you cannot, a clear realization that you are looking for a phase of the subject that may be dealt with completely within the limits of your paper will help you to speed up the first steps.

We may now profitably consider the separate stages of carrying out the research assignment.

CHOOSING A SUBJECT

Ideally, the subject should arise out of the student's own need to find an answer to some question. If, as a result of previous reading or of some experience in an English, history, or social science course, you want an answer to such questions as

What was behind the abdication of Edward VIII?
How did Greek Tragedy develop?
Why were the public opinion polls wrong in the 1948 elections?
How did the United States become involved in Vietnam?

you have a specific subject, the answer to which may give you the thesis of a research paper. If you have no such question in mind, you will have to choose some area of investigation and restrict it as was done in the illustrative example of the paper on Mark Twain.

The four reasons for the assignment of the research paper are given on page 251. Any subject which satisfies these requirements will be a satisfactory one; any subject which does not will be unsatisfactory. Especially to be avoided are the following kinds of subjects: those which would be developed from personal experience and therefore require no research; those which are so subjective that they cannot be significantly affected by research (such as "Who was the greater poet — Chaucer or Milton?"); those that could be adequately discussed from a single source, such as the explanation of a process; and those that are so comprehensive that they could be treated only superficially in a 2000-word essay. Among the last of these are controversial questions concerning national policy, such as "Is the policy of containing Communism all over the world feasible?" An answer could be provided for such a question, but not in a 2000-word essay.

PREPARING A BIBLIOGRAPHY

In the sense in which you will be using the term in your college work a *bibliography* is a list of books, articles, and other publications. A *preliminary* bibliography lists the works you expect to use for a paper. A *final* bibliography lists the works you actually did use. A preliminary bibliography is made on 3 × 5 inch cards, with each title on a separate card. A final bibliography is typed or handwritten as a solid list. Both contain the same basic information for each item included — author's name, title of work, and facts of publication (place, publisher, and date).

The Preliminary Bibliography

In preparing a bibliography, as in other tasks, a few minutes' careful consideration of the problem may save hours of needless work and result in a better product. Many students rush uncritically to the card catalog. Before you begin your actual search for titles, ask yourself two questions: What kind of material do I want? What are the most likely places to find it?

It is wise to ask these questions, because different subjects require different approaches to the preparation of a bibliography. If you are dealing with a subject recently developed, the card catalog will be of little use to you. It records only books, and the very latest material in a book is usually at least a year old. For a current topic you must get most of your information from newspapers and recent magazine articles. On the other hand, many subjects — the development of the alphabet, for example — have been thoroughly treated in books, and little of significance will be found about them in current periodicals. The best general sources of information are the card catalog and the *Readers' Guide to Periodical Literature.* For some subjects the best approach will be through an index to technical publications; for others, *The New York Times Index* may yield the required information most readily. Before beginning the bibliography, you should check the appropriate lists of reference works in Chapter 10.

Once you have started to prepare your bibliography, the following advice may be helpful:

1. Try to make your bibliography selective as you prepare it. There is no point in listing three titles which contain the same information, or

books which have little to say on your subject. Develop the habit of guessing intelligently whether a book will be useful to you. In some subjects — space exploration, for example — an old book is likely to be dated. Usually the best way to guess at a book's usefulness is to draw it out of the library and look at it quickly. Read the preface, or part of it; check the table of contents; see how much space it gives to your subject. With a little practice you will usually be able to tell within three minutes whether the book will be of use to you.

2. Watch for critical bibliographies, which evaluate the works they list and thus tell you what sources are best and for what topics. Many serious studies contain such bibliographies, at the ends of chapters or the end of the whole work, and so give you valuable leads to other sources.

3. Study the indexes of books on related subjects. A book on psychotherapy may contain a pertinent discussion of hypnotism. But do not begin to read it through merely in the hope that it *may* contain such information. Instead, turn to the index and see how many references are given under hypnotism or related headings. Sample the most likely of these references. Similarly, if your study is biographical, check the indexes of memoirs and letters by people acquainted with your subject.

All this advice may be summed up in two words: *act purposefully.* You will save much time, and work with more confidence and enjoyment, if you feel that you are not just drifting around in a library hoping to pick up useful information but are following a calculated plan for discovering it.

The Form of the Bibliography

Each bibliographical card should contain three essential pieces of information: *(1) the name of the author, (2) the title of the work, (3) the facts of publication.* In addition, a card may contain, for the convenience of the student, the library call number and a note concerning the contents of the work. The following card is typical for a book.

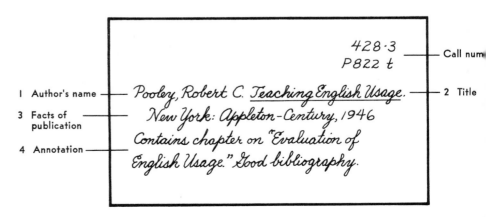

The form of the entry varies with the kind of publication being cited, and the major variations are illustrated in the sample bibliographical entries shown below.

1. A Book by a Single Author or Agency

Gulley, Halbert E. <u>Essentials</u> <u>of</u> <u>Discussion</u> <u>and</u>
<u>Debate</u>. New York: Henry Holt and Company,
1955.

a. The author's surname comes before his given name or initials for ease in alphabetizing.
b. If the book is the work of an agency, committee, organization, or department, rather than of an individual, the name of the agency takes the place of the author's name.
c. If no author is given, the citation begins with the title.
d. The title of the book is italicized (represented in manuscript by underlining each word separately).
e. The facts of publication are the place of publication, the publisher, and the date of publication, in that order.
f. If more than one place is given on the title page, use only the first.
g. If no date of publication is given, use the latest copyright date, usually found on the reverse of the title page.
h. The punctuation in the sample above is the preferred form.

2. A Book by Two Authors

Wellek, René, and Austin Warren. <u>Theory</u> <u>of</u> <u>Lit-</u>
<u>erature</u>. New York: Harcourt, Brace and Com-
pany, 1949.

a. The name of the second author is not inverted; otherwise the form is the same as that of Example 1.
b. The order of the authors' names is the same as that on the title page; hence Wellek comes first, even though Warren would be alphabetically earlier.

3. A Book by Several Authors

Murray, Elwood, and others. <u>Integrative</u> <u>Speech</u>.
New York: The Dryden Press, 1953.

a. The Latin abbreviation *et al.* is a common variation of "and others" and may be used if preferred:

Murray, Elwood, <u>et al</u>.

b. When there are three authors, but not more than three, it is a common practice to give all three names. Thus the first part of the entry shown above could have been listed:

```
Murray, Elwood, Raymond H. Barnard, and J. V.
    Garland.
```

4. An Edition Other Than the First

```
Bailey, Sydney D. British Parliamentary Democ-
    racy. 2nd ed. Boston: Houghton Mifflin
    Company, 1962.
```

a. If the work is a revised or later edition, the appropriate abbreviated designation (Rev. ed., 2nd ed., 3rd ed., 7th ed.) is placed immediately after the title and separated from it by a period.
b. Only the date of the edition being cited is given.

5. A Work of More Than One Volume

```
Johnson, Edgar. Charles Dickens: His Tragedy and
    Triumph. 2 vols. New York: Simon and Schuster,
    1952.
```

a. The number of volumes follows the title, is separated from it by a period, and is always abbreviated as shown.
b. If the volumes of a multivolume work were published over a period of years, the inclusive dates are given, as shown in the next entry.

6. An Edition of an Author's Work

```
Haight, Gordon S., ed. The George Eliot Letters.
    7 vols. New Haven: Yale University Press,
    1954-55.
```

a. If the edition is by more than one person, the names of the editors are arranged as in Example 2 or 3, whichever form is appropriate.
b. In *A Manual of Style* (University of Chicago Press) the abbreviation for "editor" or "editors" is enclosed in parentheses — (ed.) or (eds.). The form used above for the Haight volumes is preferred by the *MLA Style Sheet*.

7. An Edited Collection or Anthology

```
Thomas, Wright, and Stuart Gerry Brown, eds.
    Reading Prose. New York: Oxford University
    Press, 1952.
```

8. A Translation

Gouzenko, Igor. The Fall of a Titan, trans.
Mervyn Black. New York: W. W. Norton & Company, 1954.

9. A Pamphlet

Because there is considerable variation in the bibliographical information given in pamphlets, they are sometimes difficult to cite. Whenever possible, treat them like books, with or without an author (Example 1). If the bibliographical information is so incomplete that you cannot confidently describe the pamphlet, show it to your instructor and get his advice. Following are three variant forms:

Chafee, Zechariah, Jr. Freedom of Speech and
Press. New York: Carrie Chapman Catt Memorial
Fund, 1955.

Bureau of the Budget. The Federal Budget in
Brief: Fiscal Year 1954. Washington, D.C.:
U.S. Government Printing Office, 1953.

Your Library: A Guide for Undergraduate Students,
University of Illinois [n.d.].

a. The last example is intended to show a difficult pamphlet, since the only bibliographical information given is the title.
b. The symbol [n.d.], meaning "no date," is used to show that no date of publication or copyright is given and that the omission is not your oversight. If your typewriter does not have brackets, put them in by hand.

10. An Essay in an Edited Collection

Highet, Gilbert. "The American Student as I See
Him," Patterns in Writing, ed. Robert B. Doremus and others. New York: William Sloane
Associates, 1950.

a. This entry requires two titles and both an author and an editor.
b. The title of the essay (or story or poem) is in quotation marks, and the title of the book is italicized.
c. The comma separating the two titles comes *inside* the final quotation marks.

11. An Article in an Encyclopedia

Macaulay, Thomas Babington. "Samuel Johnson,"
Encyclopaedia Britannica, 11th ed., XV, 463–471.

"Navigation Acts," The Columbia Encyclopedia,
1950, pp. 1367–68.

a. Some encyclopedia articles are initialed, and the authors are identified in a list at the beginning of the volume. The article on Johnson is signed *M*, Macaulay's initial.
b. The British spelling *Encyclopaedia* is often bothersome to American students. Copy the title exactly as it is given on the title page.
c. Either the edition number *or* the date of publication may be used. Thus "1911" could have been used instead of "11th ed." in the first example, and "2nd ed." instead of "1950" in the second.

12. A Magazine Article

McCall, Raymond G. "H. L. Mencken and the Glass
of Satire," College English, XXIII (May, 1962),
633–636.

Hammond, E. Cuyler. "The Effects of Smoking,"
Scientific American, 207:39–51 (July, 1962).

Hacker, Andrew. "The Boy Who Doesn't Go to College," The New York Times Magazine, June 24,
1962, pp. 11, 14–18.

a. Two titles are separated and differentiated, as in Example 10.
b. No place of publication or publisher is given, but volume, date, and page numbers are shown. The first entry shows the preferred form in nonscientific fields, with Roman numerals for volume and Arabic numerals for pages and a parenthetical date between the two number systems. The second entry shows the preferred form in scientific fields, with the volume number preceding the colon and the page numbers following it. The third entry shows the form for magazines included as newspaper supplements.
c. The words "volume" and "page" (or their abbreviations "vol." and "p.") are not used when, as in the first two entries above, both volume and page numbers are given.

13. A Newspaper Article

Reston, James. "Washington: A Trial Balance Sheet
at the Mid-Year," The New York Times, June 29,
1962, p. 26.

Editorial, The [Champaign–Urbana] News–Gazette,
June 14, 1962, p. 12.

"Dublin ReJoyces," Newsweek, July 2, 1962, p. 80.

a. The examples successively illustrate a signed article, an untitled editorial, and a titled but unsigned story.
b. The name of the city is italicized if it appears on the newspaper as part of the title. If not, it is inserted without italics in square brackets, as shown above. The definite article is italicized only if it is part of the title.
c. News magazines, such as *Newsweek* and *Time,* are treated as newspapers rather than as magazines.

▶ *In order to get practice as quickly as possible with the various forms illustrated in this discussion, convert the following information into conventional bibliographical form. Since the number of each item corresponds to the number of a preceding illustration, you can check your answer against the appropriate illustration.*

1. A book by John R. Reinhard called Medieval Pageant, copyrighted in 1939 and published by Harcourt, Brace and Company in New York.

2. A book called The Reader Over Your Shoulder, written by Robert Graves and Alan Hodge, and published in New York by The Macmillan Company in 1944.

3. A book published by the University of Illinois Press at Urbana, Illinois, in 1952. The book was written by Gordon N. Ray, Carl J. Weber, and John Carter and is called Nineteenth Century English Books.

4. The second edition of a book entitled A Browning Handbook, written by William Clyde DeVane and published by Appleton-Century-Crofts of New York. This second edition was published in 1955.

5. A two-volume edition of Selected Works of Stephen Vincent Benét, prepared by the author and published by Farrar and Rinehart of New York in 1942.

6. John M. Manley's edition of Chaucer's Canterbury Tales, copyrighted in 1928 and published in New York by Henry Holt and Company.

7. Masters of American Literature, a two-volume work edited by Leon Edel, Thomas H. Johnson, Sherman Paul, and Claude Simpson, and published in Boston by Houghton Mifflin Company in 1959.

8. A translation by Dorothy Bussy of a novel by André Gide. The translation, called Lafcadio's Adventures, was published by Alfred A. Knopf, Inc. of New York in 1928.

9. A pamphlet entitled Memo: The Citizen and International Trade prepared by the League of Women Voters and printed in Washington, D.C. in 1952.

10. Charles Lamb's essay on Old China, reprinted in Literary Masters of England, which was edited by Nelson S. Bushnell, Paul M. Fulcher, and

Warner Taylor and was published in 1950 by Rinehart & Company, New York, as a revised edition.

11. An article by M. S. Fisher on pages 573–576 of volume XI of the Encyclopedia of the Social Sciences. The article is entitled Parent Education.

12. An article entitled, Present Status of Advanced Composition and Rhetoric, on pages 177–179 of volume 16 of College English. The article was written by Tyrus Hillway and appeared in December, 1954.

13. A newspaper story headed Spanish Students Opposed to Franco in the St. Louis Post-Dispatch. The story was written by Camille M. Cianfarra and appeared on page 13A of the issue for January 5, 1956.

The Final Bibliography

The final bibliography will be typed from the bibliographical cards and will follow the forms already discussed. It should contain a citation for each work mentioned in the footnotes. It may also contain a few works which you found to be useful background references, even though you neither cited nor quoted them in your paper. But padding a bibliography to make it look imposing is more likely to annoy than to impress an instructor. If your instructor prefers, your bibliography may be annotated — that is, it may contain a brief statement explaining the significance of each item or of selected items.

In typing or writing your bibliography, observe the following conventions unless your instructor recommends modifications.

1. If the bibliography is long, group the publications according to type: books, magazine articles, newspaper articles, etc. When the bibliography consists of a single page, this grouping is less necessary. If in doubt whether grouping is desirable, consult your instructor.

2. Within each group, list items alphabetically by author's surname or, if the author is not given, by the first letter of the title (not counting "A," "An," or "The").

3. If more than one book by the same author is being listed, you may substitute a 7-space line for the author's name after you have once given it:

        Baldwin, T. W. <u>William Shakespeare's Five-Act Structure</u>. . . .

        ———. <u>William Shakespeare's Petty School</u>. . . .

4. Single-space each item and double-space between items.

5. In each item, indent two spaces for all lines after the first.

The bibliography of the sample research paper on pages 324–325 illustrates some of these conventions.

INTRODUCTORY READING

For most research studies the reading may be divided into three stages — introductory, intensive, and supplementary. The introductory reading gives the background needed in order to begin the investigation intelligently. The intensive reading provides the bulk of the information from which the paper will be written. The supplementary reading fills in gaps and provides added information needed to make the paper complete.

Once the function of the introductory reading is understood, it will be clear that note-taking at this stage is not profitable. The information obtained from this reading is probably not going to appear in your paper, or if it does, it will probably be so general that notes are not needed. This reading should therefore be done quickly. Indeed, the early accumulation of miscellaneous notes may actually be confusing, since a student who has notes on every aspect of his subject is likely to have a harder time deciding which phase of it to concentrate on.

Usually the best sources for introductory reading are general works — articles in encyclopedias, chapters in elementary textbooks, histories, biographical references, and specialized dictionaries. For example, a student setting out to answer the question, "How Did English Spelling Become So Illogical?" might profitably begin with the article on the English Language in a good unabridged dictionary, the *Encyclopaedia Britannica,* or such textbooks as Baugh's *History of the English Language* or Jesperson's *Growth and Structure of the English Language.* These works would not only refer him to more specialized studies but would also provide him with the background necessary to profit from such studies.

NOTE-TAKING

When you begin intensive reading, you should also begin taking notes. The results of your preliminary reading may be carried in your head, but you are now beginning to collect the actual evidence from which your paper will be written, and it is important to the success of all the rest of your work that both the form and the content of your notes be satisfactory.

The Form of the Notes

All notes should be written on cards[2] and should contain two kinds of information: (1) the fact or opinion being noted, and (2) the exact source from which you took it. This second item is absolutely necessary, since you will be required to identify the sources of your material in the footnotes

---

[2] Some instructors prefer 4 × 6 inch cards in contrast with the 3 × 5 inch bibliographical cards.

to your paper. Usually that means you must identify the author, title, and page of the book or article from which the note was taken. Here is a typical note made from a book:

> *Morison, Samuel E.*
>
> <u>*Admiral of the Ocean Sea,*</u> *p. 7*
>
> *Columbus born in Genoa, 1451, between Aug. 25 and October, of family of woolen weavers who had lived in Genoese Republic for at least 3 generations.*

If you are making a number of notes from the same source, the complete identification given above may be abbreviated. Thus, if you are using no other work by this author, "Morison, p. 7" would be enough, since your bibliographical card would provide the full title. Or you may give each of your bibliography cards a separate identification symbol and use that symbol and the page number on every note card made from that work. But no matter what system is used, each card must be accurately identified. To avoid any possibility of a slip, *always write the identification before you begin the note.*

The practice of using note cards instead of notebooks has grown out of the experience of thousands of research workers. To be really useful your notes must be so flexible that you can shuffle them to suit whatever order you finally decide upon and can discard useless notes easily. Notes written solid in a notebook cannot conveniently be rearranged or edited. They are fixed in the order they had in the source from which they were taken, whereas the order which suits your final purpose may be entirely different. Recording information in a notebook is therefore inefficient, no matter how easy it may seem at first glance.

Only one note should be placed on a card. Two notes on one card are inseparably bound together. Since you must be free to shuffle your notes, to discard useless ones and add supplementary ones, the only satisfactory method is to use a separate card for each.

It is wise to leave enough space at the top of each card so that you may write in a subject heading when you group your cards and develop your outline, thus:

> *Learned Superstitions*
>
> *Danzig, p. 40*
> *Pythagoreans identified numbers with human qualities. Odd numbers male, even numbers female.*
>
> *1 = reason*   *2 = opinion*
> *3 = justice*   *4 = marriage*

Because these subject headings may be changed as your organization develops, it is wise to enter them in pencil.

The Content of Notes

Your notes may contain statements of fact or of opinion, in your own words or in the words of the author from whose work they came. The cards shown below contrast a quoted opinion and the same opinion stated

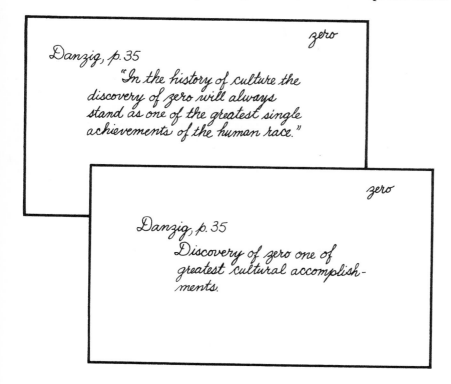

> *zero*
>
> *Danzig, p. 35*
> *"In the history of culture the discovery of zero will always stand as one of the greatest single achievements of the human race."*

> *zero*
>
> *Danzig, p. 35*
> *Discovery of zero one of greatest cultural accomplishments.*

in the student's words. *If the wording as well as the content is taken from a source, be extremely careful to use quotation marks, both on your note card and, later, in your paper.* Failure to use quotation marks on the note card may later lead you to think that the information is expressed in your own words and thus may trap you into unintentional plagiarism.

Whenever possible, your notes should be summaries of the source material, not direct quotations. Too many quotations result in wordiness and give the impression that the student has merely strung together statements made by others without digesting these statements or doing any thinking about them. The following contrast also shows the economy achieved by summarizing the material before putting it on the note card.

Original	*Summary*
When comparing the financial success of two business firms of the same kind, we do not simply say that the firm making the greater profit is the more successful. What we compare is not profits alone, but profits relative to total investment. That is, if p and i represent profit and investment, respectively, the value of the quotient p/i (that is, the percentage of profit) serves to measure relative financial success.	Comparative financial success of two firms not measured by profits alone, but by formula p/i, when $p =$ profit, and $i =$ investment.

But in summarizing material, care must be taken to be sure that the summary accurately represents the content of the original source. The summary should be checked against the original before it is placed on the note card. If this is done, and the student is satisfied that he has not distorted the information in summarizing it, the economy of the summary will be reflected not only in the note card but also in the part of the essay written from it. The summary helps to make both the note-taking and the writing more efficient. The following note, for example, is an accurate summary of a five-paragraph passage containing about 500 words:

Danzig, pp 1-3

Number sense

Says number sense not to be confused with counting. Counting confined to humans, but some animals, birds, insects — crows and "solitary wasps", for example — have remarkable sense of number.

Notice that such cards are identified just as carefully as if they contained direct quotations. The material is taken from the work of another and must be acknowledged in footnotes.

There are two exceptions to this advice to summarize informational content whenever possible. If the student is going to criticize a passage, he should quote it directly and he should be careful that he has not distorted the meaning of even a direct quotation by presenting it out of context. If the context is so long that it cannot conveniently be given in full, the student is under a special obligation to be sure that the quotation faithfully represents the author's meaning. The second exception is statements that are so apt, dramatic, or forceful that they would lose some of their effect in a summary.

What has been said about note-taking may be summarized as follows:

1. Put notes on cards, not in notebooks, with one note to a card.

2. On each card identify the exact source of the note, including the page number. Abbreviations may be used only when there is no danger of ambiguity.

3. The actual words of an author must be placed in quotation marks, whether the notes are statements of fact or of opinion.

4. Summarize extensive quotations if possible, but still identify the source.

5. Use direct quotation whenever you intend to attack or criticize a statement in your source.

6. Be careful that your notes — whether direct quotations or summaries — do not distort the meaning when taken out of their original context.

7. Finally, remember that these conventions governing note-taking are designed to teach you good research habits as well as to protect you from beginners' mistakes. Follow the conventions at all times, even when a home-made system might seem more convenient.[3]

STATING AND OUTLINING THE THESIS

Before you formulate your thesis, be sure to review pages 20–24. The following observations supplement that discussion and are confined to four kinds of difficulties that students encounter at the thesis-writing stage.

The most serious difficulties have their origin in faults which occurred long before the writing of the thesis. If a student has chosen a subject about which no thesis can be formulated, or if he has failed to restrict his general subject and so has gathered only a miscellany of information, he cannot write a satisfactory thesis, and there is nothing at this late date that his instructor can do to help him. The only solution is to start over from the beginning, and there is not time for that. The student simply has to accept the consequences of his failure to understand the assignment and to work purposefully toward carrying it out.

[3] It might be wise at this point to study the set of student notes provided with the research paper on pages 281–325.

Many students create trouble by trying to avoid the discipline of writing a thesis. Faced with the task of expressing a controlling idea in a single sentence, they take one of two escapes: they write a thesis so general that it exerts no control over the development of the paper, or they write one which looks good but has no relation to the material in their notes and therefore does not represent the idea they intend to develop. Faulty theses are usually exposed if there is time to discuss them in class, through the collective criticism of twenty students exploring the meaning of a sentence on the blackboard.

Since the research paper is usually one of the longest and most complex papers written by college students, it nearly always requires a careful outline. Indeed, many instructors make the writing of a detailed outline a critical stage in the preparation of the paper and do not allow students to begin actual composition until the outline is approved.

The best preparation for outlining your research paper is a careful review of Chapter 4, with special attention to pages 88–96, which discuss shaping and testing the organization. Most good students begin to develop the outline mentally while they are doing their intensive reading. From time to time they spread their notes on a table and study ways of grouping them. When they find them falling into logical groups, they begin to write the subject label on each card in the group. Students who work this way actually tackle outlining in three stages: (1) classifying information by subject groups while the information is still in the notes, with periodic attempts to work the groups into a running outline; (2) preliminary outlining to discover a thesis or to test one which is beginning to take shape in the mind; (3) final outlining, in which the structural pattern which has been developing through the two earlier stages is given its finished form.

The final outline, then, is merely a refinement of the organization already suggested by the study of your notes. But observe that the notes will suggest a pattern only if they have been efficiently made — that is, if each note is on a separate card, if useless cards are discarded with each restriction of the subject, if the content of the note cards is economically stated so that you can see at a glance what information each card contains. If the notes have not been efficiently taken — if they are long, undigested excerpts crowded together on both sides of the pages of a notebook — they will suggest neither a thesis nor an outline. The student who makes such notes must expect to have a hard time with his outline.

▶ *Each of the following numbered excerpts contains the thesis and the main statements of a student outline. To be satisfactory, an excerpt should give you at least a clear hint of what the student proposes to do in his paper and how he proposes to do it. In each excerpt, study the thesis and the relation of the main statements to that thesis. If the excerpt is satisfactory in both respects, mark it OK. If it is not satisfactory, explain why.*

1. Quaker education is essentially a religious education.
    I. Family life is oriented to the belief that parents must set a moral example for the children.
    II. The school program, in its curriculum, conduct, choice of teachers, and texts, emphasizes religious instruction.
    III. The Meeting, to which children are admitted at an early age, establishes a pattern of silent worship.

2. Adolf Hitler's rejection as an artist led him to develop psychological complexes which resulted in the destruction of his beloved Germany.
    I. As a boy Hitler rebelled against his father's wish to make him a civil servant.
    II. Hitler's failure to graduate from high school kept him from being admitted to art school in Vienna.
    III. During his Vienna years, opera was Hitler's chief passion.
    IV. While in Vienna, Hitler first conceived of himself as a political leader.

3. The plot and sub-plot of *King Lear* are interrelated by situation and language.
    I. Both stories involve parents whose faulty evaluations of their children bring them humiliation and suffering.
    II. Images about animals, violence, and eyesight appear in both stories.
    III. A greater emphasis is given to the story of Lear than to the story of Gloucester.

4. Witch-hunting in seventeenth-century England was the product of Puritan anxieties about evil.
    I. A serious interest in witches as the devil's agents was largely confined to Puritan clergymen and writers.
    II. Most prosecutions against witches occurred during the Interregnum, when Puritans held political and judicial power.
    III. The last large outbreak of witch-hunting occurred among English Puritans in Salem, Massachusetts.

5. Utopian literature has, in the twentieth century, become anti-Utopian literature.
    I. Earlier models of Utopia were postulated on radical social and economic improvements.
    II. The actual achievement of such improvements has focused the attention of writers upon the losses of individuality and privacy which have resulted.
    III. Modern literary models of the future deal with the individual's insignificance and helplessness within an efficiently run new order.

6. The popular conception of a schizophrenic as a person with a "split personality" is inaccurate.
    I. The "split personality," as popularly conceived, is a symptom of amnesia, not schizophrenia.
    II. The split which actually is present in schizophrenia is the separation of a person from his social and physical environment.

COMPOSING THE PAPER

All that has been said about composition in Part Two of this book applies to the research paper. In addition the research assignment has its special problem — the relationship between borrowed material and the use that is made of it. The research paper is admittedly and necessarily written from information derived from printed sources. But that information has to be woven into an essay which is essentially the student's own work. A student who has worked purposefully will not have too much difficulty reconciling these two conditions, for he will have selected his material with a view to using it in support of a purpose he has been forming as he reads. In a sense he is like a man who is building a house with bricks obtained from others. The bricks are not his, but the design and construction of the house are. *Writing a research paper, then, is not just stringing together statements from books and magazines. It is a complete reorganization and reworking of the source material into an original composition.*

Failure to recognize this sometimes results in a paper which is merely a transcription of the information in the note cards. The following excerpt from a student research paper reveals this weakness:

Article 123 of the Mexican Constitution has the sole purpose of solving the labor problem. It is looked upon as the declaration of the rights of the workmen.[10]

The workers' hours have a maximum limit of eight hours for a day's work. At least one day's rest for every six days' work is to be enjoyed by everyone.[11]

Children over twelve and under sixteen years of age can work only six hours a day, and children under twelve are not permitted to be made the subject of a contract.[12]

The minimum wage that can be received by a workman should be considered sufficient according to the conditions of life prevailing in the workman's particular region of the country. This same compensation is to be paid without regard to the sex of the worker.[13]

Wages are required to be paid in legal currency

rather than by any other representative token with which it is sought to substitute money.[14]

---

[10]Tannenbaum, p. 529
[11]Ibid.
[12]Ibid.
[13]Ibid.
[14]Ibid., p. 530.

Obviously, all this student is doing is setting down the contents of five note cards, all from the same source and four from the same page. He has not organized his material to develop any judgment of his own. The noticeable inequalities of style suggest to a reader that he has occasionally copied the actual wording of his source without using quotation marks. At any rate, there is nothing in the excerpt to suggest any contribution of the student's own. The same facts built into a paragraph which the student has actually created himself might come out like this:

Article 123 of the Mexican Constitution attempts to standardize labor conditions by setting up basic principles governing hours and salaries. It provides a maximum work-week of six eight-hour days, prohibits the contractual hiring of children under twelve years of age, and limits the employment of children between twelve and sixteen to six hours a day. It requires that all wages be paid in legal currency, thus eliminating company scrip and other cash substitutes. It provides for a minimum wage scale which takes into account differences in the standard and cost of living in various parts of the country. It abolishes discrimination against women by making the wage rate the same for both sexes. In general, therefore, it seeks to establish a uniform code which will provide the general pattern of labor-management relations throughout the country.[10]

---

[10]Tannenbaum, pp. 529-530.

The first of these two versions is a series of raw notes; the second is a unified paragraph created by the student. Both contain exactly the same facts, but the revised version rearranges and rewords the facts to make them develop the idea stated in the opening sentence. It also avoids the over-documentation of the first version by acknowledging the two pages of Tannenbaum's book as the source for all the information in the paragraph. If an instructor were to compare the second version with the notes from which it was written, he would clearly see that the writer had mastered the information he was using and had shaped it to suit his own purpose. This point has already been illustrated by an assignment in paragraphing on pages 130–132. It is further illustrated by the comparison of notes and text of the sample research paper on pages 281–325.

Because of the importance of the research paper, the composition should usually be done in three stages: writing the rough draft, preparing the final revision, and proofreading the finished paper. No two of these stages should be completed at a single sitting; indeed, it is best to allow at least a day between the completion of one and the beginning of the next.

How a student should compose the rough draft will depend partly on his work habits and partly on the nature of his material. For the average student the best advice is to break the total job into the main units of the outline and to tackle these units in order. The first draft of a paper so developed is likely to be a bit stiff, to proceed rather mechanically from one step to the next, and to lack the qualities that make for an interesting or effective style. But these are not serious weaknesses if careful revision is to follow.

Footnotes and any graphic illustration being used should be written into the rough draft so as to avoid difficulties with spacing in the final version. Even though footnotes are finally placed at the foot of the page, some students find it convenient in the first draft to insert them between ruled lines within the text immediately after the line containing the footnote marker. Not all research papers need or are suited to graphic illustrations — tables, graphs, charts — but since these aids present complex or cumbersome data compactly and thus make the reader's task easier, they should be used when they are appropriate.

The revision should turn the rough draft into a finished essay. It should provide smooth transitions between units — a more difficult task in a long composition than in a short one. It should polish the diction and sentence structure and remove any awkward constructions. It should check the relationship of detailed information to the topic idea. It should make sure that direct quotations are clearly marked and that indirect quotations and summaries actually serve the purpose of a paragraph and are not merely strung together without any purpose other than to get *something* written.

When the paper has been revised, the final bibliography should be added. This will be a list of the sources actually used in preparing the paper. It should include all sources cited in the footnotes and may contain one or two works which were valuable as background material even though not actually cited in the paper. The form of this bibliography was discussed on page 262.

Finally, the paper should be proofread at least twice to detect any errors which survived the revision. These readings should be mainly concerned with mechanical matters — doubtful spellings, punctuation, usage, and typographical errors. The proofreadings should include both the footnotes and the bibliography, and it is wise at this stage to check these against the recommended forms. Proofreading should be done slowly — more slowly than reading for content. Some students find it helpful to read the paper aloud slowly so as to concentrate on the appearance of each word.

DOCUMENTING THE EVIDENCE

As we have said, all information taken from a specific source must be identified in a footnote.[4] That is, the evidence must be *documented*. The purpose of this convention is twofold: (1) to avoid the appearance of representing somebody else's work as yours; (2) to let the interested reader consult your sources and so check the accuracy of your investigation or carry on his own. This convention is so important in research writing that inaccurate documentation — or none at all — is regarded as a serious offense. For the research writer it is both good manners and good morals to acknowledge sources fairly and accurately.

When to Footnote

Inexperienced research writers often have difficulty in deciding what statements require documenting. The general principle is that you should cite the source of any statement for which you are indebted to the work of another. For most student research this general principle can be broken down into six conditions. You should provide a footnote whenever:

1. You use a direct quotation.
2. You copy a table, chart, or other diagram.
3. You summarize a discussion in your own words.
4. You construct a diagram from data provided by others.
5. You paraphrase an opinion which you have read rather than reached independently.
6. You present specific evidence which cannot reasonably be considered common knowledge.

[4] The kind of footnote discussed here is called a "reference footnote." Footnotes may also qualify, explain, or comment on statements made in the text when it would be awkward to include such matters in the main discussion. Such footnotes may be called "explanatory footnotes." This footnote is explanatory. It provides an explanation which, though necessary, would be awkward to include in the body of the text.

The first four of these conditions are sufficiently definite to require no discussion. Difficulties, if any, will come from the last two, and these difficulties are better resolved by experience than by definition. By the time you have got well into any research project, you will have reached conclusions you did not have when you began your study. Unless these conclusions came specifically from one of your sources, they need not be documented. They are products of your total reading, not borrowings from any specific source.

Similarly, as you become familiar with a subject, you will find that facts of which you at first were ignorant are so well known that they must be considered common knowledge. For example, you probably do not now know the dates of Matthew Arnold's life. But if you were writing a research paper on Arnold you would find them common knowledge to all the writers you were reading. It would be unnecessary, and a little naïve, to footnote these dates. This does not mean that no factual information need be footnoted. If you were recording the number of fatalities at Gettysburg, the tonnage and dimensions of the *Santa Maria,* or the population of London in 1450, you would be expected to cite your source in a footnote. The question of what can legitimately be considered common knowledge is difficult to answer in the abstract, except by the general advice, *When in doubt, footnote it.* Since one function of the freshman research paper is to give experience in using footnotes, your instructor will probably prefer too many rather than too few.

How to Footnote

A footnote consists of two parts: the footnote marker, a number placed in the text at the end of the statement to be documented and slightly above the level of the typed or handwritten line; and the footnote proper, which usually comes at the foot of the page and is numbered to correspond with the marker. Footnotes are separated from the text by a triple space and from each other by a double space. The first line of a footnote is indented, and footnote numbers do not start afresh on each page but run consecutively throughout the paper. These conventions are illustrated in the sample paper on pages 281–325.

The purpose of the footnote is to identify as precisely as possible the source to which the statement in the text is indebted. Although no one form is universally preferred, the minimum information required is a clear reference to the author, title, and page. The first reference to a source needs to give fuller information than do subsequent references to that source.

In general, a footnote reference is similar in form to a bibliographical citation, *but there are noteworthy differences.* The following summary presents the most important conventions of footnoting.

1. **Author**

   a. In a footnote the author's name is given in its normal order — John Smith — not inverted as in a bibliography.

   b. When more than one author is to be named, the form is the same as that used in a bibliography (page 257) except that the first author's name is not inverted.

   c. In a reference to an edited work, the editor's name, in normal order, goes in place of the author's name and is followed by "ed." — with or without parentheses as in the bibliographical form.

   d. After the first reference to a work in a footnote, the author's or editor's name is usually shortened to surname only in subsequent footnotes.

   e. If there is no author's or editor's name, the footnote begins with the title.

2. **Title**

   All titles follow the forms used in bibliography, but after the first footnote reference, the author's surname and the page number are enough — for example: Gulley, p. 11 — provided that only one author is being cited by that name and only one book by that author. Unless both these conditions are true, a short form of the title is commonly used — Gulley, *Essentials,* p. 11. After the first reference to a magazine or newspaper article, the title of the magazine or the newspaper may be used without the title of the article — *Life,* p. 17, or *The New York Times,* p. 23. Obviously these short forms cannot be used if more than one issue is being cited. For the use of "ibid.," see pages 276–277.

3. **Facts of Publication**

   a. The place and date of publication are given in the first reference to a book. After that they are omitted. When given, both are enclosed in parentheses and separated by a comma — (Boston, 1967). The name of the publisher, which is also a fact of publication, is often omitted in the first footnote reference, particularly if there is a bibliography which gives this information. If the publisher is given in the first footnote reference, the style is as follows — (Boston: Houghton Mifflin Company, 1967).

   b. The facts of publication for a magazine article do not include place and publisher, but do include the volume and page numbers (see heading 4 below), and the date of issue — month (not abbreviated), day (if the magazine is published oftener than once a month), and year. The date is enclosed in parentheses.

   c. The facts of publication of a newspaper article consist of the month, day, and year, *not in parentheses,* and the page.

4. **Volume and Page Numbers**

   a. In references to a one-volume work, the abbreviation "p." is used for *page* and "pp." for *pages.*

b. When the reference is to a work of more than one volume, both the volume number and the page number must be given.

c. When both volume and page numbers are given, the abbreviations "vol." and "p." (or "pp.") are *not* used. Instead, use Roman numerals for the volume number and Arabic numerals for the page number for both books and magazines — X, 48. One major exception to this form is the practice in scientific studies of using Arabic numerals for both volume and page in citing magazines. In this form the volume number comes first and is separated from the page number by a colon — 10:58.

5. Use of "Ibid."

As noted above (see under heading 2, page 275), a short form is commonly used for a footnote reference after the first, which is given in full. "Ibid." (an abbreviation for *ibidem,* "in the same place") is used to refer to a work cited in the *immediately preceding* footnote. If the second reference is to the same volume and page of the work, "ibid." alone is sufficient. If the second reference is to a different volume or page of the work, then "ibid." must be followed by a comma and the new volume and page numbers.

"Ibid." cannot be used to refer to a preceding footnote if a reference to another source intervenes. The following examples illustrate correct and incorrect uses of "ibid."

Correct Uses of "Ibid."

[1]Edgar Johnson, <u>Charles</u> <u>Dickens</u>: <u>His</u> <u>Tragedy</u> <u>and</u> <u>Triumph</u> (New York, 1952), I, 24.

[2]<u>Ibid</u>. (This is a reference to the same volume and page as the preceding.)

[3]<u>Ibid</u>., p. 27. (Still referring to Volume I, but to a different page.)

[4]<u>Ibid</u>., II, 95.

[5]<u>Ibid</u>., I, 28.

Incorrect Uses of "Ibid."

[1]Edgar Johnson, <u>Charles</u> <u>Dickens</u>: <u>His</u> <u>Tragedy</u> <u>and</u> <u>Triumph</u> (New York, 1952), I, 24.

[2]<u>Ibid</u>., I, 24. (Omit I, 24.)

[3]<u>Ibid</u>., II. (Page number required.)

[4]George Orwell, <u>Dickens</u>, <u>Dali</u>, <u>and</u> <u>Others</u> (New York, 1946), p. 68.

[5]Ibid., p. 26. (This is correct if it refers to Orwell's work, but not if it refers to Johnson's, because of the intervening reference to Orwell.)

Notice that "ibid." is followed by a period. It is capitalized when it begins a footnote. Since usage varies with respect to italicizing "ibid.," follow your instructor's preference.

6. Punctuation

The punctuation of the footnote need present no problem, since, except for periods after abbreviations and at the end, commas may be used throughout. Even the period at the end is optional, though its use or omission should be consistent.

The following footnotes illustrate the preceding discussion and may be used as models against which to check your own footnotes.

First Reference to a Book

[1]René Wellek and Austin Warren, Theory of Literature (New York, 1949), p. 5.

SUBSEQUENT REFERENCE: *Ibid.*, p. 22; OR, Wellek and Warren, p. 22; whichever is applicable.

Reference to an Essay in an Anthology

[2]George Santayana, "Lovers of Illusion," Reading Prose, ed. Wright Thomas and Stuart Gerry Brown (New York, 1952), p. 486.

SUBSEQUENT REFERENCE: *Ibid.*, p. 489; OR Santayana, p. 489; whichever is applicable.

Reference to a Magazine Article

[3]Hugh L. Dryden, "The International Geophysical Year," The National Geographic Magazine, CIX (February, 1956), 289. OR 109:289 (February, 1956).

SUBSEQUENT REFERENCE: *Ibid.;* OR Dryden, p. 289; whichever is applicable.

Reference to an Article in a Single-Volume Encyclopedia

⁴"Mississippi Scheme," The Columbia Encyclopedia, 2nd ed., p. 1294.

> As noted on page 260, the year — in this citation, 1950 — may be substituted for the edition number.

Reference to an Article in a Multivolume Encyclopedia

⁵"Traquair, Sir John Stewart," Encyclopaedia Britannica, 11th ed., XXVII, 214.

> This article is unsigned. In a signed article, the author's name would precede the title of the article. As noted on page 260, the year of publication — in this citation, 1911 — may be substituted for the edition number.

Reference to a Newspaper Article

⁶Lloyd E. Millegan, "Advice to Overweight: Try Karate," The New York Times, June 12, 1966, p. S7.

⁷"Salt Treatment of Trees Described," St. Louis Post–Dispatch, January 5, 1956, p. 4C.

7. Miscellaneous Abbreviations

In addition to those already used, the following abbreviations are in common use in footnotes:

cf., "compare."

chap(s)., "chapter(s)."

f., ff., "and the following page(s)." (pp. 17 f.: "page 17 and the following page"; pp. 17 ff.: "page 17 and the following pages")

l., "line." (l. 10).

ll., "lines." (ll. 6–12).

passim, "in various places in the text." Used to indicate a number of scattered references to a subject.

[*sic*], "thus." Used in brackets to indicate that an apparent error is not a miscopying but appeared thus in the source.

PRESENTING THE FINISHED ASSIGNMENT

The assignment has not been fully met until the paper has been presented to the instructor in the form which he has stipulated. A typical student research paper consists of the following parts:

1. A title page containing at least the title of the paper and the student's name and section number.

2. A detailed sentence outline of the paper.

3. The body of the paper, typed if possible, each page numbered and adequately footnoted. Only one side of the page is used, of course. If the paper is typed, the text should be double-spaced. Quotations of five or more lines should be indented and single-spaced without quotation marks.

4. Conventional footnotes with corresponding footnote markers at appropriate points in the text.

5. A bibliography of works used in preparing the paper.

6. The note cards used in writing the paper, arranged in the order in which they were used, labeled with outline symbols to show their relation to the outline, and tied together or sealed in an envelope. The purpose of handing in the notes is to allow the instructor to trace the development of your paper from outline and notes to finished composition.

If your instructor wishes to modify these requirements, he will notify you. Make sure that you understand clearly what is wanted. If you are uncertain, consult your instructor well in advance of the deadline.

Exercise

The following student research paper, complete with outline, notes, text, footnotes, and bibliography, is presented as an exhibit for detailed study. It is not offered here as a perfect paper but as a fair sample of what a superior freshman student will do with a research project. If you analyze it according to the following directions, you will have a useful review of the process of writing a research paper.

First, study the outline, paying particular attention to the relationships among the sentences. Do the Roman numeral statements show a clear relation to the thesis? Do the subordinate parts clearly relate to the main units? Challenge every statement to test its relation to the idea it is being used to develop.

Second, study the text for structure alone. Is there a clear relation between successive parts of the paper and the outline? Does every paragraph play a part in advancing the purpose of the thesis, or are there any irrelevant paragraphs? Is there adequate transition between the paragraphs? Check the relation of text and outline by inserting the outline symbols in the margin opposite appropriate units of the text. If you find paragraphs which do not relate directly to the outline headings, consider whether they are legitimate transitions or are mistakes. Comment on the opening paragraph, and especially the first sentence, as an introduction to the paper and as a statement of purpose; can you suggest how this introductory paragraph might be improved?

Third, study the notes as notes, to see what kind of material they contain. Is each note accurately identified as to source? Is the content of the note pertinent to the student's purpose? Is the student digesting material as he makes the notes, or is he mostly copying material without digesting it?

Fourth, study the relation of notes and text. Are the paragraphs merely strings of notes in the same form they had in the note cards or is the author *composing* from the notes? If the author is more successful sometimes than others, notice where he is successful and why. If there are paragraphs which contain information not in the notes, try to determine whether such information would normally be part of the background a student would build during such a study. If there are notes that were not used, should they have been used, or was the author wise in omitting them? Try to see the development of the paper from the notes so that you will be better prepared to handle this problem when you come to it in your own paper.

Fifth, check the footnotes and bibliography. Do the forms used in this paper agree with your understanding of the conventions?

Finally, evaluate the whole paper in terms of: (1) the purposefulness of the author's procedure as it is revealed in notes, outline, and text, (2) the thoroughness of the development of the paper within the limits of a 2000-word assignment, (3) the success of the author in communicating to you, as a reader, the results of his study.

The following student research paper is printed by permission of the author, Charles Derber.

Not all instructors require a title page, but if one is required, the form shown here may be used as a model.

The format, or physical appearance, of this paper illustrates general principles of good usage. The text is double-spaced. Long quotations are single-spaced and indented from the left margin. Footnotes are single-spaced, but a blank line between footnotes allows for raising the footnote number. As shown here, following the MLA *Style Sheet recommendations for Masters' and Doctors' theses, the first footnote on each page is separated from the last line of text by triple-spacing (that is, two blank lines), not by a typewritten or hand-ruled line. A ruled line of separation is entirely permissible, however, and the instructor's preference in this respect should be followed. Each footnote begins on a new line (with regular paragraph indention).*

White typewriter paper of standard size (8½ × 11 inches) should be used, on one side only. Pages should be numbered, and margins should be generous.

WINGATE'S RAIDERS: THE NUCLEUS OF A NATIONAL ARMY

by

Charles Derber

English 111, Section C

Mr. Draperson

May 25, 1962

Wingate's Raiders: The Nucleus of a National Army

Thesis: The Jewish concept and conduct of defense
against Arab guerrilla warfare were modified
significantly by Orde Wingate's military
innovations.

I. Before Wingate's military operations in 1938, the
concept and conduct of Jewish defense proved favorable to the Arabs in their peculiar guerrilla
offensive.
  A. The organization and tactics of the Arab guer-
     rilla fighters enabled them to wage a devastat-
     ing hit-and-run warfare from 1936 to 1938.
  B. The Jewish defensive strategy did not meet the
     military challenges of Arab warfare.

II. Wingate's study of the warfare in Palestine from
1936 to 1938 convinced him that basic changes in
the Jewish defense were necessary.
  A. His experience in Jewish settlements convinced
     him that Haganah's strategy of limited defense
     was suicidal.
     1. He believed that it was militarily unsound
        to defend against Arab attacks from the
        inside of the settlements.
     2. He believed it necessary to track the move-
        ment of Arab gangs and supplies by penetra-
        tion of small patrols into Arab territory
        at night.
  B. His study convinced him that the Jewish fight-
     ing force must reorganize into a national army
     and adopt the discipline and duty procedure of
     a regular army.

III. By carrying through his plans in the establishment and operation of the Special Night Squads,
Wingate implemented his theories of defense.
   A. His Special Night Squads adopted the strategy
that a defense must be offensive.
      1. The S.N.S. operated at night in small
patrols outside of the settlements in
defense of the Haifa pipeline.
      2. They perfected the use of the surprise
attack to destroy Arab gangs and supplies
whose movements they had charted.
   B. The Special Night Squads became the core of a
national army and adopted a severe discipline
and duty procedure.
      1. In his training courses, drill exercises,
and military operations, Wingate inflicted
the discipline of a regular army on his
men.
      2. In the duty procedure that he enforced,
Wingate imbued his men with the regularity
of standard army routine.

On the pages opposite the text are shown the notes from which this paper was written. No notes were required for the introductory first paragraph, or for the transitional paragraph on page 12. As the paper was developed, some notes were combined; others were not used; still others were used in the first draft but deleted in revision. These notes do not include background material which the author collected before he decided on his thesis. Note cards containing information actually footnoted are identified here by a number corresponding to the footnote.

WINGATE'S RAIDERS:

THE NUCLEUS OF A NATIONAL ARMY

This paper deals with the contribution that
Captain Orde Wingate made to the Jewish defense
against Arab attacks during the years 1936-1939.
When Wingate arrived in Palestine as a British intelligence officer, the Jews were meeting these attacks
with strictly defensive measures inherited from the
Haganah, an underground resistance organization.
When he left three years later, the Jews had learned
to defend by preventive guerrilla attack. In bringing about this change Wingate provided a pattern for
the creation of a unified Jewish national army.

The historical background of the Arab-Jewish
conflicts with which this study is concerned may be
summarized briefly. After World War I Palestine
became the scene of a conflict between the Jewish
drive for a national home and the Arab opposition
to that drive. The conflict began with the Balfour
Declaration of 1917 in which the British government
supported the Zionist movement; it increased in

1 Jewish immigration

Enc. Brit., XVII, 134
    Jewish immigration 1920-38
1920-24 42,784
1925-29 57,022
1930-34 91,258
1935 61,854
1936 29,727
1937 10,536
1938 12,868

Arab objectives

Wells, p. 25
    In 1930's Arabs fighting for:
1. Stop Jewish immigration
2. Arab nat'l gov't in Pal.
3. British withdrawal of Balf. Decl.
4. End Br. mandate
5. Stop sale of land to Jews
6. Treaty with Brit. recognizing Arab sov'ty in Pal.

Start of Arab revolt

3

Royal Inst., p. 76
    April 15, 1936 — First sign of revolt when Arabs held up Jews, killed 1, on road from Nablus to Tulham. False report of this affair led to several conflicts betw. Arabs + Jews.

Arab terrorism – org.

4

Viton, p. 321
    Arab terrorists in countryside well organized in bands of 80-150 under some experienced leaders — replaced local govts in places they controlled, even taxed the people.

5 Arab arms

Royal Inst., p. 76
    Prohibition of sale of arms did not affect Arabs because they had rifles from pre-war and war years, also smuggled arms from Trans-Jordan.

Haj Amin el Husseini

Collins, p. 175
    Prominent Arab trouble maker, Haj Amin el Husseini, the Grand Mufti, religious head of the Sunni Sect of Moslem faith in Pal. Had power to inflame local Arabs and initiate indirectly most Arab attacks on Brit. and Jews. Was allied with Hitler.

intensity as Arabs rioted against the immigration

of 100,000 Jews in the 1920's and another 150,000

between 1930 and 1935.[1] In 1935 the Arabs demanded

that Britain end its mandate over Palestine and

recognize Arab sovereignty in that area.[2] When

this demand was refused, the Arabs, in 1936, began

a series of attacks on the Jews which were to last

four years and be known as the Arab Revolt.[3]

The Revolt quickly expanded into a guerrilla

war. Organized into bands of 80 to 150 men,[4] well

armed with rifles left over from World War I or

smuggled from Trans-Jordan,[5] and led by men experi-

[1]Hans Kohn, "Palestine: V. Post-World War I Developments," Encyclopaedia Britannica, 1959, XVII, 134.

[2]Linton Wells, "Holy Terror in Palestine," Current History, XLIX (December, 1938), 25.

[3]Royal Institute of International Affairs, Great Britain and Palestine, 1915-1939 (London, 1939), p. 76.

[4]Albert Viton, "It's War in Palestine," Nation, CXLVII (October 1, 1938), 321.

[5]Royal Institute, p. 76.

Arab leader – Kaukji

Royal Inst., p. 80
    Sept. 3, 1936 – Fawzi Kaukji – famous Syrian revolutionary transferred his activities to Pal. and became head of guerrilla offensive

Arab terrorism

Royal Inst., p. 77
    By June-July, 1936, revolt raging. Typical action: acts of violence against Jews; destruction of crops and property; cutting of telegraph lines; blowing up railway tracks and bridges; ambushing of trains and car convoys

Arab terrorism

Brit. Reports (1937), p. 6
    Terrorist campaign in 1937: isolated murder; armed attacks on military, police, and civilian road transport; attacks on Jewish settlements and Arab and Jewish private property

Arab terrorism

N.Y. Times, Mar. 15, 1937, p. 12
    3 Jews slain by Arabs hiding in ditch – 1 Jew stabbed by Arab – 2 Jews injured by Arab bombs – numerous shootings of Jews by Arabs.

1937 terrorism - statistics

Brit. Reports (1937), pp. 11-12

1937 Statistical Terrorist Record

(p. 11) Bomb + firearm attacks against:		(p. 12) Total Casualties	Killed	Wounded
Police	109	Police		
Jewish Settlements	143	British	4	2
Jewish transports	38	Arab	10	4
Arab transports	23	Jewish	2	2
British houses	2	Officials		
Arab houses	109	Civil	2	–
Shepherds	11	Mil.	5	5
Ploughmen	3	Civilians		
		Arabs	44	53
		Jews	32	83

Mosley, p. 40
    Arabs led by guerrilla fighter named Kaukji from Syria – purely hit + run tactics – waged a running campaign almost impossible to counter by normal military methods. Thus British efforts fairly unsuccessful.

enced in guerrilla tactics, the Arabs destroyed crops and property, cut telegraph lines, dynamited railway tracks and bridges, and ambushed trains and convoys.[6] In 1937 alone they made 143 attacks on Jewish settlements, killing 32 civilians and wounding 83.[7] In conducting this guerrilla war the Arabs had two great advantages. First, they were mobile and hence could wage a hit-and-run campaign extremely difficult to oppose with ordinary military procedures.[8] Second, the bands could dissolve quickly when seriously threatened and mix with the civilian Arab population, who would hide them and their weapons. The members of the guerrilla bands were thus personally protected and their arms and supplies were easily

[6] Royal Institute, p. 77.

[7] League of Nations Mandates. British Reports on Palestine and Trans-Jordan, 1937-1938, Report for 1937 (London, 1939), p. 12.

[8] Leonard Mosley, Gideon Goes to War (New York, 1955), p. 40.

9

Arab terrorist tactics

Royal Inst., p. 104

Rebels mixed with sympathetic population which wouldn't expose them or their weapons. Thus difficult to capture.

Haganah – origin

Koestler, p. 67

Origin of Haganah in "Watchmen" – defended selves and families before World War I – romantic figures – rode horseback, wore Arab headgear, spoke Arabic fluently, knew Arab customs.

10

Haganah

Koestler, pp. 69-71

After W. W. I, Watchmen disappeared, re-placed by Haganah – illegal, semi-underground group which rose to meet Arab terrorism in 1929.

10

concealed.[9]

In attempting to defend themselves against Arab attacks, the Jews were limited both in organization and in strategy. They were not permitted by the British to have any organized fighting force or even to possess firearms. The nucleus of their defense was a semi-underground organization called the Haganah, which in Hebrew means "defense." The Haganah had its origin in pre-war Jewish settlers known as "watchmen," who protected themselves from Arab attack by patrolling their lands on horseback. After the Balfour Declaration, in response to the increasing Arab hostility, these watchmen were unofficially replaced by the Haganah, which operated relatively independently in each Jewish settlement.[10] Its function was to defend the settlement against attack. To do this it smuggled in weapons and supplies, but its policy was limited to defense; it did not engage in

[9]Royal Institute, p. 104.

[10]Arthur Koestler, _Promise_ _and_ _Fulfilment_ (New York, 1949), pp. 67-71.

Haganah—Havlagah

Syrkin, p. 314

1936-39, Haganah adopted principle of Havlagah, meaning self-restraint. Arab acts of terrorism not met by similar acts, but arms and supplies smuggled in for defense of individual settlements.

Supernumeraries

N.Y. Times, Sept. 12, 1938, p. 4

British could not handle Arab terrorism and thus forced to give Jews some measure of self-defense, so created supernumeraries.

Supernumeraries

Koestler, p. 73

Certain number of Haganah men made into supernumerary police force. First time some aspect of Haganah organization became legal.

Supernumeraries

Brit Reports (1937), p. 13

Training of Jewish supernumeraries:
1. recruits given course in weapon training under military instructors - given rank of lance corporal and sent back to settlements.
2. supernumeraries trained other supers in each settlement
3. supers armed with rifles & Greener guns

counter or preventive attacks. Its own description
of its policy was "Havlagah" or self-restraint.[11]

Because the British were unable to protect Jewish settlements and because they respected the
policy of Havlagah, they established a Jewish Supernumerary Police Force.[12] Haganah sent certain of its
members to be trained as supernumeraries. These
recruits were given military instruction, rifles,
and Greener guns, and sent back to train other
supernumerary police.[13] This police force was the
only legal part of the Haganah. It strengthened
the Haganah, but it did not change its basic organization or concept of operation.

In September of 1936, while the Revolt was in
full force, Orde Wingate, a new intelligence officer
of the British Headquarters, arrived in Palestine.

[11]Marie Syrkin, Blessed Is the Match (Philadelphia, 1947), p. 314.

[12]The New York Times, September 12, 1938, p. 4.

[13]British Reports, Report for 1937, p. 13.

Wingate - to Pal.

Mosley, p. 34

Sept. 1936 – Wingate and wife sailed for
Pal. – Appointment as Intelligence Officer on staff
of H. Q. British Forces, Jerusalem – worked first
in Haifa under Brigadier Evetts

14

Wingate - background

Dict. of Nat. Biog., p. 962

Wingate born in India – Feb. 26, 1903 –
military ancestry, both father and grandfather
were well known military men – brought up in
strict Puritan atmosphere

15

Wingate - char.

Weizmann, II, 398

Wingate's two passions - military science and
Bible - an amazing combination of student and
man of action.

6

Wingate's thinking and action were to have a profound influence on the conduct of the Jewish defense
during the next three years. Born in India in 1903,
he had been brought up in a stern Puritan atmosphere
which deeply affected his perspective on affairs in
Palestine.[14] He was described by his friend, Chaim
Weizmann, as having two passions--the Bible and
military science.[15]

An incident reported by David Hacohen, a prominent contractor and an influential Zionist, illustrates the combination of these two passions. One
day, as Hacohen and Wingate were driving through the
valley of Jezreel, Hacohen noticed Wingate scanning
the valley in a state of obvious excitement.

> Suddenly Wingate cried out: "But why was he
> defeated? He ought to have won this battle!
> The man was a fool!"

[14]Dictionary of National Biography, 1941-1950,
p. 962.

[15]Chaim Weizmann, Trial and Error, The Autobiography of Chaim Weizmann (Philadelphia, 1949), II,
398.

16

Wingate - char.

Sykes, p. 117

   Wingate's two passions - military sci. and
Bible - illustrated in incident reported by David
Hacohen (contractor and Zionist). Driving with
Hacohen through valley of Jezrul, Wingate burst
into a long tirade at Saul's "incompetence" in losing
the crucial battle of Mt. Gilboa. (For verbatim
account from Sykes, see separate sheet.)

7

"Who do you mean?" asked Hacohen, trying to think back to the Allenby campaigns.

"I mean Saul!" cried Wingate, and then he went on somewhat in this style: "That man Saul had all his army <u>there</u> (pointing). I mean up there on the heights on Gilboa, south of his water supply, which was there (pointing to the water course)--imagine the folly of that when his enemy was to the north <u>there</u>, in Shunem (pointing again), and why did he do it? He could have brought his army over--he had freedom of movement--how do I know, because the night before the battle he went nearly all the way to Tabor to visit the witch of Endor--<u>there</u> (pointing to Ein-Dor). Do you know why he did it-- the damned fool!-- because he had brought all his women and all his furniture and his tents and his household with him. He didn't know how to travel light. He was a bad soldier."

"But do you think," asked Hacohen, "that it matters much now?"

"What!" shouted Wingate. "Matter! Of course it matters! By his folly, by his incompetence, Saul threw away his position, and he held the greatest position a man has ever occupied or could ever occupy in history. He was King of the Jews! He had been elected to rule over the most wonderful people in the whole world, the only people who had discovered God--and he threw it all away by his sheer damned silly incompetence! Matter! Of course it matters!" And so on for a long time.[16]

Wingate's knowledge of the Bible convinced him

that the Jewish drive for a homeland in Palestine

[16]Christopher Sykes, <u>Orde Wingate</u> (Cleveland, 1959), p. 117.

17

Wingate - Zionist

Sykes, pp. 109-10

Wingate arrived in Pal. sympathetic with Arabs. In less than month, he became extreme Zionist. This caused by seeing reality of land situation, seeing determination and restraint of Jews, and influence of Bible.

18

Wingate in Jerusalem

Sykes, p.127

1937 - Wingate in Jerusalem - spent time in study of land and on reports of all recent military activity - familiarized self with Hebrew and met more Jews in Haganah and Jewish political leaders.

was divinely sanctioned, and within a month of his
arrival he was converted to Zionism.[17] His passion
for military science led him to make a thorough
study of the warfare in Palestine and convinced him
that basic changes in the Jewish defense were necessary.

During the next two years Wingate devoted his
time to a study of the geography of the land and the
military activities of the Jews and Arabs.[18] He
conducted this study by personally making long ex-
ploratory journeys throughout Palestine and certain
neighboring countries where rebels were based. He
observed the defense activities of many Jewish settlements, studying in detail the settlements at
Afikim, Hanita, and Tirat Tsevi.

The major conclusion that Wingate drew from his
observations was that Haganah's concept of limited
defense was suicidal. The Jews must not wait for

[17]Sykes, pp. 109-110.
[18]Ibid., p. 127.

19

Wingate on tactics

Mosley, p. 53

Wingate tells Hanita settlers that new tactics must be adopted. "You Jews of the settlements have been fighting a defensive war against the Arabs for too long. It will not save your lives or your settlements.... We must try a new kind of war."

20

Wingate on tactics

Sykes, p. 145

Wingate arrived at Hanita where 40 supernumeraries were stationed—observed defense was from inside of settlement—Argued that Jews must defend from the outside and organize patrols to operate outside

9

Arab attacks and meet them within the settlements but must meet the enemy near the Arab villages and adopt their guerrilla tactics. He first reached this conclusion at Afikim and developed it more fully during his stay at Hanita. One night, after several weeks at Hanita, he called the settlers together and told them, "You Jews of the settlements have been fighting a defensive war against the Arabs for too long. It will not save your lives or your settlements. . . . We must try a new kind of war."[19] He told the forty supernumeraries stationed at Hanita that they must organize patrols to defend the settlement from the outside rather than the interior.[20]

Wingate's concept of the use of these patrols soon changed from defensive to offensive. He proposed to the Haganah General Staff the formation of Special Night Squads which would penetrate enemy territory, spy out the location of supply depots and

[19]Mosley, p. 53.
[20]Sykes, p. 145.

21

Wingate on tactics

Sugrue, p. 70

Wingate's proposition to Haganah staff of what the S.N.S. would involve: operate on the basis of reliable info; strike at night; hit the bands in their hide-outs or at villages where they are quartered

22

Wingate preparations

Mosley, p. 51

At Hanita, Wingate would make long trips at night into Arab territory. Discovered routes and depots and planned attacks.

23

Wingate preparations

Sykes, p. 140

Wingate first put his months of study to use at Tirat Tsevi — worked out paths of entry for arms smuggling and organized supernumeraries into small patrols which guarded these paths and discovered many of the Arab supply routes

routes, and observe concentrations of guerrillas.[21]
With this information the patrols could better defend their settlements by launching preventive
attacks and thus destroying Arab potential for new
raids. Wingate himself demonstrated both the operation and the value of this policy. From Hanita he
took small groups of men across the Syrian border
under cover of night and showed them Arab supply
bases and how to attack them.[22] At Tirat Tsevi he
organized the supernumeraries into small patrols
which scouted supply routes and then guarded the
paths by which the Arabs were smuggling their
weapons.[23]

The changes that Wingate believed necessary in
the Jewish defense were not confined to military
strategy. From the beginning of his stay in Pales-

[21]Thomas Sugrue, Watch for the Morning (New
York, 1950), p. 70.

[22]Mosley, p. 51.

[23]Sykes, p. 140.

24

Wingate on offensive policy

Sykes, p. 113

Wingate meets Wilenski. At first meeting tells him that policy of self restraint was out of date – situation now required an offensive on the part of Jews. "The need was for the formation of an army, and he declared in all seriousness that it was his ambition to lead a Jewish army into battle."

Wingate on Jewish fighting

Mosley, p. 36

In conversation with Wilenski – Chief Intell. Offic. of Haganah – Wingate declared Jews would have to fight to win independence. Said "There will be no free Palestine for the Jews unless you fight and win. And you will not win, my friend, unless I teach you how to fight and lead you into battle."

2

Wingate on mil. sit.

Sykes, pp. 120-24

After four months in Pal. Wingate wrote letter to cousin with following observations about military situation: military strength of Arabs is negligible; potential strength of Jews equivalent to two Brit. Army Corps; in case of war, essential to have Jewish trained fighting force. He concluded that he wants to raise Jewish brigade in Pal.

tine he was convinced that the Haganah had to be replaced by a Jewish national army, and that he was the man to develop that army and lead it. After only a month in the country, he insisted to Emanuel Wilenski, chief intelligence officer of the Haganah, that a Jewish army must be formed.[24] During a long discussion with Wilenski, on whom he made a deep and lasting impression, he said, "There will be no free Palestine for the Jews unless you fight and win. And you will not win, my friend, unless I teach you how to fight and lead you into battle."[25] Three months later, he wrote to his cousin analyzing the potential strength of a Jewish brigade and expressing his desire to stay in Palestine and organize such a force.[26] In 1937 he wrote to Weizmann, then in England negotiating with British officials, urging him to persuade the British to permit the organ-

[24]Sykes, p. 113.

[25]Mosley, p. 36.

[26]Sykes, pp. 120-124.

27

Wingate to Weizmann

Sykes, pp. 130-1

    Wingate in late 1937 wrote letter to Weizmann saying:

1. Weizmann must obtain for Jews right of self-defense
2. Jews must be permitted to raise "Jewish Palestine Defense Force"
3. Wingate offers services to assist in formation of this force

28

SNS

Sykes, p. 141

    In Haifa, Wingate asked permission to form SNS from Jewish supers and Brit. soldiers - said these patrols working at night were only way to counter Arab terrorist activities

ization of a Jewish Palestine Defense Force, which
Wingate offered to train.[27]

By the end of 1937 Wingate had thus reached
certain definite conclusions about necessary changes
in Jewish military strategy and organization. His
establishment and operation of the Special Night
Squads in his remaining years in Palestine brought
about many of these changes and significantly modified the Jewish defensive efforts.

Early in 1938 Wingate requested permission to
organize from Jewish supernumeraries and British
volunteers small patrols which could effectively
stop the night raids and arms-smuggling of the
Arabs.[28] At this time Arab gangs were making repeated night attacks on the main oil pipeline which
extended from Trans-Jordan across the northern half
of Palestine to Haifa. Wingate was given permission
to organize Special Night Squads to protect the

[27] Sykes, pp. 130-131.

[28] Ibid., p. 141.

SNS

Mosley, p. 61
     Wingate sent to patrol pipeline to
Haifa. Officially was Intell. Offic. in Nazareth, but let second in command do work
and established self in Ein-Harod where
Haganah sent him their best men to be
trained for SNS.

SNS

Sykes, p. 149
     Original S.N.S. organization: two platoons
at each of four settlements including Ein-
Harod — working originally with 39 Br. soldiers
and 80 Haganah men — eventually more supers
so that he formed nine patrols.

pipeline. He was officially given the new position of intelligence officer of Nazareth, but he ordered his second-in-command to take full charge in Nazareth, while he established himself in the small community of Ein Harod, where he spent all his time constructing the Special Night Squads, the S.N.S.[29]

As organized by Wingate, the S.N.S. consisted of eight small patrols--two stationed at each of four settlements including Ein Harod.[30] These patrols operated exclusively at night, and their function was twofold: to protect the pipeline and to wipe out in surprise raids supply bases and gang hideouts which had been located by reconnaissance. The procedure of carrying out the first function is illustrated by the first major S.N.S. attack on June 11, 1938. That night two squads left the settlement in civilian cars and were dropped off at intervals, so that Arab tracking of their movements

[29] Mosley, p. 61.

[30] Sykes, p. 149.

SNS – 1st operation

Sykes, p. 150

June 3, 1938 – first operation of SNS.
Wingate with 7 others went out and successfully defeated gang of saboteurs: adventure
outside settlement, at night, offensive and
successful.

SNS tactics

Mosley, pp. 62-3

Wingate taught deception in transportation – men start in mil trucks and jump
off sides into ditches and hide – Arab spies
followed trucks while men reassembled and
began raids

31

SNS – 1st big operation

Sykes, p. 151

First real battle for SNS – June 11 – 2 patrols
left in civilian cars in eve. – dropped off at
intervals so spies couldn't track them –
patrols led by 2 outposts 20 yds. apart with
grenades, then 2 scouts 20 yds. apart, then
main body of patrol in single file – moved in wide
arcs across pipeline – met raiders at Danna whom
outposts with grenades chased into the village –
patrols surrounded gang and captured men
& weapons.

3

SNS effectiveness

Brit. Reports (1938), p. 11

July 1938 – pipeline damaged only once due
to intensive defensive patrolling. In previous
months damaged 10, 7, and 18 times.

would be extremely difficult. Reassembled, the
patrols organized in the strict formation Wingate
had taught them--two outposts in front, armed with
grenades and marching twenty yards apart, followed
by two scouts also twenty yards apart, followed by
the main body marching single file. In this fashion
the patrol crisscrossed the pipeline area in large
sweeping arcs and came across a gang of saboteurs
near the village of Danna. Under cover of the rest
of the squad, the outposts, using their grenades,
chased the gang into Danna, where the entire patrol
surrounded and captured it.[31] This type of operation in defense of the pipeline proved so efficient
that in July of 1938 the Arabs were able to damage
the pipeline only once, as contrasted with an average of twelve successful attacks during each of the
three preceding months.[32]

The second function of the S.N.S.--surprise

[31]Sykes, p. 151.

[32]British Reports, Report for 1938, p. 11.

An SNS operation

Sykes, p. 176
Most successful venture of SNS - perfect
use of surprise - surrounded at night large
gang of raiders planning to sabotage pipeline
- 5 SNS surrounded Khirbet Beit Lidd - attack
totally successful, all men & weapons captured

An SNS operation

Sykes, p. 168
Wingate leads SNS across miles of difficult land to surprise gang of smugglers -
perfect timing and marching lead them to
hideout at 3 AM as planned - 11 smugglers
killed and 4 wounded - SNS confiscated arms
& drugs.

attacks on gang and supply locations previously charted by reconnaissance squads--is illustrated by the raid on Khirbet Beit Lidd, in which Wingate with several squads surrounded the village and then launched an attack which totally destroyed a large gang and all its supplies.[33] In attacks of this kind, Wingate's long study of the Arab routes of supply and infiltration enabled him to find his way to Arab hideouts over the most difficult terrain late at night and to surprise the rebels. On one such venture he led a small patrol for many miles over rough countryside to a smugglers' hideout. The surprise was complete when the patrol reached its destination at 3 A.M. as planned. Eleven smugglers were killed and needed supplies and arms were con-fiscated by the patrol.[34]

During his work with the S.N.S. Wingate was dominated by the thought that he was building the

[33] Sykes, p. 176

[34] Ibid., p. 168.

35

Wingate : SNS → Jewish Army

Sugrue, p. 72

Wingate tells Hag. Gen. Staff after they accepted his plan for SNS that this was beginning of a Jewish Army.

36

Wingate : SNS → Jewish Army

Sykes, p. 175

Wingate made clear to corpsmen he considered them to be the core of a Jewish army - his opening address in training courses was: "Our purpose here is to found the Jewish Army."

37

Wingate's SNS training courses

Mosley, p. 69

At SNS along with courses in discipline & strategy were rigorous exercises in marching & drilling and frequent operations against Arab gangs.

Wingate's training course

Mosley, pp. 66-7

Wingate taught course at training school entitled "A Course for Jewish Sergeants" - now part of training handbook for Israeli Army.

core of a Jewish national army. His opening words
to his Haganah recruits were, "Our purpose here is
to found the Jewish Army," and he and his men then
worked with a mutual appreciation of this purpose.[35]
There were three phases of training: first, rigorous
courses in discipline and strategy; second, exacting
exercises in marching and drilling; third, experience in actual night raids.[36] In all of these
phases Wingate inflicted the discipline of a regular
army on his men.

The basic training course, entitled "A Course
for Jewish Sergeants," has become a part of the
training handbook for the modern Israeli Army.[37]
Notes from eight of the lectures in this course are
extant. The subjects of these lectures are the
functions of various army units in war, particularly
those of the infantry, and the duties and conduct of

[35]Sykes, p. 175.

[36]Mosley, p. 69.

[37]Ibid., pp. 66-67.

Wingate's training course

Sykes, p. 174

Notes on 8 lectures have survived: 1. Nature of war; 2. infantry platoon in battle; 3. infantry in defense; 4. infantry in attack; 5. leadership and military vices; 6. tasks of different forces; 7. field artillery in support of field infantry; 8. tasks of engineers and cavalry.

"Soldiers' 10 Commandments"

Mosley, p. 67

"Soldiers' Ten Commandments" –
1. Know and love what you fight for; 2. Carry out every proper order of your commander; 3. Use your equipment sparingly and only for your duty; 4. Abstain from brutality & cruelty; 5. Keep body & equip. in good condition; 6. Be able to endure physical hardships; 7. Place welfare of comrades before your own; 8. Increase technical ability whenever possible; 9. Carry out entrusted tasks speedily; 10. Submit complaints to commander thru proper channels.

Wingate's training course

Mosley, p. 69

Wingate taught Jews to avoid worst vices of soldier: "quarrelsomeness, laziness, indulgence." It is the bad soldier who loses self control under arduous physical strain.

the soldier.[38] Wingate was especially concerned
with the latter topic and delivered long lectures on
proper soldierly conduct and the virtues of leadership. He wrote a code, labeled "The Soldiers' Ten
Commandments," which enumerated the obligations and
values of the virtuous soldier.[39] He taught his men
that the worst vices of the soldier are quarrelsomeness, laziness, and indulgence, and that the best
soldier is the one who can keep his restraint and
control under any physical or mental strain.[40]

During the operations of the S.N.S., Wingate
carried out the discipline that he preached in his
training courses. Numerous examples can be cited of
his ruthlessness towards men who refused or failed
to execute orders during operations. On his first
raid, he forced a young Jewish soldier to shoot in
cold blood an Arab who refused to give information

[38]Sykes, p. 174.

[39]Mosley, p. 67.

[40]Ibid., p. 69.

41

Wingate's discipline

Mosley, pp. 58-9

On first raid – Wingate teaches discipline.
Makes a Jewish soldier shoot an Arab who refused to identify location of supply base – this
taught soldiers necessity of obedience and cold-
ness in war. Strikes a soldier who accidentally
made noise by kicking stone when silence was
imperative.

Wingate's discipline

Sugrue, pp. 72-3

Jewish soldier on night march had new
boots which squeaked – Wingate told him
to keep them quiet but it was impossible
although he tried – Wingate struck him
with butt of pistol – boy took boots off and
walked barefoot.

on the location of Arab armaments. Later when returning from that same raid, Wingate struck a soldier who accidentally disturbed a stone which made
a slight noise when Wingate had ordered complete
silence.[41] Another example of Wingate's severity
occurred during a night march when a Jewish soldier
who was wearing new boots found that he could not
keep them from squeaking. Wingate ordered him to
stop the noise, and when the squeaking continued
despite the desperate efforts of the soldier, Wingate struck him with the butt of his pistol. The
boy then took off his boots and walked barefoot over
the rough terrain, only in this fashion being able
to appease Wingate.[42]

In addition to teaching army discipline, Wingate accustomed his men to the regularity of standard army procedure through the duty routine that he
enforced. The regular schedule of operation for a

[41]Mosley, pp. 58-59.
[42]Sugrue, pp. 72-73.

43

SNS. schedule

Sykes, pp. 151-2

SNS schedule of duty: (1) few days of day
instruction, then beginning of service with
regular SNS at night. (2) duty for fortnight —
patrol on 9 or 10 nights – week's leave. (3) 2 wks.
duty. After 3 wks. recruit was veteran
soldier.

new Haganah recruit was several days of instruction
followed by the beginning of service with the squads
at night. They were on active duty for two weeks,
nine or ten nights of which they engaged in night
patrol. They were then given a week's leave, after
which they returned for another two weeks of duty.
It was generally acknowledged that after three weeks
of this kind of training, the green recruit with no
previous military experience became a veteran soldier.[43] When the S.N.S. expanded with the arrival
of an additional 100 men, Wingate revised his former
schedule into an eleven-day cycle, but maintained
the regularity of the procedure. The men thus
became accustomed to a routine characteristic of an
organized army.

Thus, in organization, strategy, and tactics,
Wingate achieved definite modifications in the
concept and conduct of Jewish defense. Although the
S.N.S. was dissolved by command of the British in

[43]Sykes, pp. 151-152.

44

Wingate's contribution

Dict. Nat. Biog., p. 963

Wingate in his SNS taught that reprisals to Arab terrorism should and could be better done by Jews from the settlements than organized British soldiers.

Wingate's contribution

Koestler, p. 74

Wingate taught Jews to counter Arab hit & run raids — in particular to move and fight at night.

45

Wingate's contribution

Sugrue, p. 74

Wingate taught Jews that Jews could win in Arab-Jew war, that intelligence, equipment, and skill, not numbers, count, and that Arab disturbances could be quelled at initial stage of rioting.

4

SNS → Jewish army

Sykes, p. 155

Thru leadership of Wingate, SNS became "beginnings of Jewish army." He gave them confidence in their fighting ability and instilled in them a unity and an esprit de corps which provides the core for an army.

1939, and Wingate left Palestine in that same year, the successes of his S.N.S. had proved certain things to the Jews that permanently altered their perspective. They had learned that Jewish soldiers operating in small groups from the settlements were more capable of carrying out reprisals to Arab acts of terrorism than were the British soldiers.[44] More generally, they had learned that they could preserve their own security and were not dependent on the British. They had learned that, despite their inferiority in numbers, they were capable of winning a full-scale war with the Arabs.[45] Perhaps most important, they had acquired a sense of unity which provided a basis for the creation of a unified Jewish National Army.[46]

[44]*Dictionary of National Biography*, p. 963.

[45]Sugrue, p. 74.

[46]Sykes, p. 155.

Bibliography

Collins, R. J. Lord Wavell: A Military Biography. London: Hodder and Stoughton, 1948.

Koestler, Arthur. Promise and Fulfilment. New York: The Macmillan Company, 1949.

Kohn, Hans. "Palestine: V. Post-World War I Developments," Encyclopaedia Britannica, 1959, XVII, 134.

League of Nations Mandates. British Reports on Palestine and Trans-Jordan, 1937-1938. London: H. M. Stationery Office, 1939.

Mosley, Leonard. Gideon Goes to War. New York: Charles Scribner's Sons, 1955.

The New York Times, March 15, 1937, p. 12.

The New York Times, September 12, 1938, p. 4.

Royal Institute of International Affairs. Great Britain and Palestine, 1915-1939. London: Oxford University Press, 1939.

Sugrue, Thomas. Watch for the Morning. New York: Harper and Brothers, 1950.

Sykes, Christopher. Orde Wingate. Cleveland: The World Publishing Company, 1959.

Syrkin, Marie. Blessed Is the Match. Philadelphia: The Jewish Publication Society of America, 1947.

Viton, Albert. "It's War in Palestine," Nation, CXLVII (October 1, 1938), 320-323.

Weizmann, Chaim. Trial and Error, The Autobiography of Chaim Weizmann. 2 vols. Philadelphia: The Jewish Publication Society of America, 1949.

Wells, Linton. "Holy Terror in Palestine," Current History, XLIX (December, 1938), 24-26.

"Wingate, Orde Charles," Dictionary of National Biography, 1941-1950. London: Oxford University Press, 1959.

12

Deliberation:

Problem-Solving

Deliberation is the process of thinking one's way through to the solution of a problem. The stages of the process can be illustrated by the following imaginary example.

Suppose your car suddenly develops a loud knock in the engine. At first you think it is a temporary condition caused by impurities in the gasoline, so you change brands, but to no avail. You then recognize that the problem is more complicated. You wonder what to do about it.

You begin by asking the attendant at a service station to listen to the knock. He says the trouble comes from one of two sources: either the elevators are sticking, or the rings are worn out. If the elevators are sticking, the sound can be removed by adding a lubricant to the gasoline; but if the rings are worn out, they will have to be replaced, and that is an expensive operation.

You try the lubricant, but it does no good. After a few days you take your car to a garage and ask the mechanic to check it. He says the rings do need to be replaced, and he estimates the cost at $450. He then points out that some minor repairs are also needed, and that these will add another $75 to the bill.

You now begin to wonder whether the car is worth such an investment. It is six years old and has been driven at least 120,000 miles. The repair costs have increased noticeably in the last six months, and you will soon need new tires. You begin to think of replacing the car itself. Helpful salesmen suggest a number of possibilities: you can select from some twenty late-model used cars ranging in price from $900 to $2500. You inspect several of these and your choice narrows down to three: a $1200

Volkswagen, a $1500 Falcon, and a $2000 Impala. You now have five choices: to repair your old car, to buy any one of the three you have selected, or to continue to drive the old car without repairs.

You reject the first and last of these solutions almost at once. You now weigh the advantages and disadvantages of the three remaining solutions — the condition of the cars, their mileage, operating costs, future trade-in values, ease of handling, added features (such as a radio), and appearance. You consult knowledgeable friends and finally decide that, all things considered, the Falcon is your best buy.

Now if you can afford to finance the purchase by yourself, your problem is solved. But if you need help from home, you will have to persuade your father that your decision is the wisest one. He may raise questions you have not considered, or he may suggest new possibilities. Not until all these considerations are met will your problem be solved.

This example shows the six principal stages in problem-solving:

1. *Becoming aware of the problem.* Awareness of a problem grows out of a felt need. When you realized that you had to do something about the knock in your engine, you became aware of your problem. As long as things go smoothly, there is no problem — at least none that is recognized.

2. *Gathering information.* When you reached the stage of consulting the service station attendant and the garage mechanic, you were seeking information about your problem. This stage is common to all problem-solving. People want to know how the problem arose, what caused it, what can be done about it. This is a continuing stage. Everything is done in the light of the information available; and as new information is discovered, decisions may have to be revised or rejected. In our example, the need for more information continued through the final stage of persuading Dad to finance the purchase of the car. We may sometimes have to act without complete information, but generally it is foolish to make an important decision without a conscientious effort to gather and consider as much information as possible.

3. *Identifying possible solutions.* This stage is closely related to gathering information, but now the information gathered is restricted to identifying and understanding proposed solutions. Besides repairing the old car, what other possibilities are there? At this stage the investigator is not evaluating possible solutions; he is merely identifying them and understanding their provisions.

4. *Evaluating possible solutions.* Once the possible solutions are known, the next stage is to evaluate them. Evaluation may be defined as a process of argument in which one examines premises and the conclusions drawn from them. The investigator is not yet trying to persuade anyone, even himself, that he has made a wise decision. Indeed, he has not yet made a decision, but is still trying to choose among alternatives. So for each argument he checks the premises (evidence) and the reasoning to find out whether the conclusion of the argument is reliable.

Evaluation is often difficult, because many disruptive elements can enter into the argumentative process. The investigator may be emotionally committed to one solution. He may be motivated by a desire to prove a point. He may have a mind-set which makes him ignore or fail to appreciate certain information. He may not be informed about the facts. He may be unable to distinguish between valid and invalid inferences. In evaluating alternatives, then, it is necessary to be aware of these pitfalls and to resist hasty conclusions. The more you can view argument as a mode of thinking, the more skill you will gain in evaluation. Above all, avoid the notion that argument is a contest to be won by overpowering or outmaneuvering one's opponents.

5. *Reaching a decision.* Reaching a decision is often the final stage in solving a problem. What follows is to implement the decision through action. From then on, the test of the decision is empirical — how well does it work? If it turns out badly, the whole question may have to be reconsidered. In fact, most decisions are temporary. Changing conditions and new evidence constantly require fresh deliberation, which may lead to very different decisions or, more often, refinements of old ones.

6. *Persuasion.* Many solutions require an additional stage, persuasion: someone else has to be persuaded that the decision is wise. In this discussion we are purposely separating persuasion from the other stages of deliberation because students often think of argument as synonymous with persuasion. The two processes overlap, but they do not coincide. Argument is the process of reaching conclusions; persuasion is the process of getting others to accept them. Persuasion includes argument, because one way of gaining acceptance is to show how our conclusions are reached — how the premises lead to them. But beyond that, persuasion is concerned with the most effective means of presenting the argument, and this requires analysis of the audience and of the whole situation.

TYPES OF PERSUASION

One can persuade by the logic of his argument, the trust or confidence he inspires, or the skill with which he arouses the emotions of others. These appeals are often interrelated. A person who presents a reliable argument is more readily thought trustworthy than one whose reasoning is obviously fallacious, and the strongest argument is at once logically and psychologically persuasive.

Trustworthiness

In general, the proponent of an argument will be considered trustworthy if he is well informed, reasons logically, shows no self-interest or bias, seems genuinely concerned with the welfare of his audience, is fair to his opponents and their arguments, and is frank in answering questions or criticisms of his own views. Conversely, he will be judged untrustworthy if he seems to have no real grasp of his subject, makes obvious errors in reasoning, seems motivated at least in part by self-interest, seems more interested in exploiting than enlightening others, abuses his opponents and distorts their arguments in order to refute them, is evasive in answering questions and angry at challenge or criticism, and generally seems more concerned with refuting others than with reaching a wise decision.

Trust is gained or lost by the response to a person's character as a whole. One man may win confidence even though the audience feels that he should be better informed on some points or is not as full or clear in his presentation as he should be. Another man who is obviously biased or unfair may forfeit confidence even though he is trustworthy in all other ways.

Psychological Persuasion (Emotional Appeal)

Psychological persuasion appeals mainly to the emotions. Such appeals may rightly be condemned when they constitute the whole persuasion, especially when the emotions are aroused to keep the reader from thinking. But if an argument is logical, an additional appeal to the emotions gives it added force. Contrast the following arguments, in both of which the same person is trying to persuade his readers that something should be done to ensure safety in the design of automobiles:[1]

(1)

A transportation specialist, Wilfred Owen, wrote in 1946, "There is little question that the public will not tolerate for long an annual traffic toll of forty to fifty thousand fatalities." Time has shown Owen to be wrong. Unlike aviation, marine, or rail transportation, the highway transport system can inflict tremendous casualties and property damage without in the least affecting the viability of the system. Plane crashes, for example, jeopardize the attraction of flying for potential passengers and therefore strike at the heart of the air transport economy. They motivate preventative efforts. The situation is different on the roads.

Highway accidents were estimated to have cost this country in 1964, $8.3 billion in property damage, medical expenses, lost wages, and insurance overhead expenses. Add an equivalent sum to comprise roughly the indirect costs and the total amounts to over two per cent of the gross national product. But these are not the kind of costs which fall on the builders of motor vehicles (excepting a few successful law suits for negligent construction of the vehicle) and thus do not pinch the proper foot. Instead the costs fall to users of vehicles, who are in no position to dictate safer automobile designs.

[1] Both passages from Ralph Nader, *Unsafe at Any Speed* (New York: Grossman Publishers, 1965).

(2)

As described by a California Highway Patrol officer, John Bortolozzo, who witnessed the flip-over while motoring in the opposite direction, the Pierini vehicle was traveling about thirty-five miles an hour in a thirty-five mph zone in the right lane headed towards Goleta. He saw the car move towards the right side of the road near the shoulder and then "all of a sudden the vehicle made a sharp cut to the left and swerved over." Bortolozzo testified at the trial that he rushed over to the wreck and saw an arm with a wedding band and wristwatch lying on the ground. Two other men came over quickly and began to help Mrs. Pierini out of the vehicle while trying to stop the torrent of blood gushing forth from the stub of her arm. She was very calm, observed Bortolozzo, only saying that "something went wrong with my steering."

The appeal in the first passage is largely statistical. It is logically persuasive, but 50,000 fatalities, $8.3 billion, and two per cent of the gross national product are abstractions which many readers cannot translate into anything they see or feel. If the argument remained thus abstract throughout, some readers would soon tire of it, and few would be roused to action.

The second argument appeals to the emotions. Logically it is less persuasive than the first, because it deals only with a single case, and there is no evidence that the case is typical. But the second passage makes the argument personal, as the first does not. The detail of the severed arm with a wedding ring and a wristwatch is something the reader can see and respond to. If the situation is bad, and if this is a representative example, the author is justified in using it.

The most successful emotional appeals engage sympathy or indignation by means of specific details. Such appeals are most useful in stimulating the feeling of need for action. To anyone who wants to bring about a change, this is probably the most important stage in an argument, since few proposals are considered seriously until the present situation is shown to be intolerable.

Statistical arguments alone seldom lead to action. First, they are usually so abstract that a reader has difficulty translating them into something concrete. Second, complicated figures are hard to keep in mind and hence are less persuasive than their users suppose. In general, statistics are impressive only when their meaning has been rubbed into the consciousness and emotions of the reader.

Psychological persuasion operates by making the reader *feel* the impact of a logical argument. The most useful device is the example. Is LSD dangerous? Tell what actually happened to someone who used it, and then give the statistical, testimonial, and scientific evidence that keeps the example from being dismissed as an isolated case. The example will gain attention for the logical persuasion to come. It may also follow and give color to a logical argument which might otherwise seem too abstract.

▶ *The following excerpt represents about one per cent (three pages out of nearly three hundred) of a comprehensive attempt to persuade readers that something must be done — and soon — to stop the waste of our natural resources. This excerpt is concerned with one unit of the total argument, with persuasion to preserve our wild life. Read the selection and answer the questions that follow it.*

A love of the outdoors and its creatures has been an important part of our heritage from the time when Catesby made the first paintings of American wildlife . . . . Thoreau, Emerson, Whitman, Melville, Cooper, Jeffers, Beebe, and a host of other writers have been profoundly influenced by our forests, our birds, our surrounding seas. Painters from Audubon to Benson, Rungius, and Jaques have sought the beauty of our wildlife. A consciousness of nature has influenced our culture more than that of any other people except, possibly, the British. Today, as we are caught in the grinding mesh of a mechanized civilization and the monotony of unrewarding tasks, we need as never before to turn to the healing hills and forests, with their rich company of plants and animals.

Yet we have neglected and abused and destroyed that company. The last of the innumerable hosts of passenger pigeons died in a cage in 1914. The heath hen has not been seen since 1932. The Eskimo curlew that heaped the wagons of market gunners was last taken in Argentina during its winter migration in 1924. The eastern puma, which controlled deer populations as an escapement keeps a watch from running away, was destroyed over fifty years ago. The grizzly bear, leading character in much of our folklore, survives in pathetic and precarious remnants. The magnificent bighorn sheep clings on in only a few isolated outposts.

The list of species whose existence hangs by a thread is a long one; it includes the glacier bear, fisher, marten, wolverine, kit fox, timber wolf, Florida cougar, several seals, key deer, woodland caribou, Florida manatee, several whales, great white heron, trumpeter swan, California condor, the magnificent whooping crane, and the ivory-billed woodpecker — largest and most spectacular of its family in North America. Whether our wild ducks can survive the hammering they get from two million hunters is far from certain.

During thousands of years, nature evolved a reproduction rate, among these birds and mammals, that would provide enough replacements to ensure perpetuation of the species, despite normal, natural losses that evolved along with the animals. These included predation, disease, parasitism, the hazards of weather and migration. Most of these checks are still effective. But to them man has added his own destruction of the animals — and vast desolation of the swamps, forests, rivers, and fields that are the only places in which these creatures can live. Small wonder their survival depends on eternal human vigilance in their behalf!

That we have not lost more of them we may attribute to the size and richness of our country, and — compared to the Old World — the relatively low human pressures on the environment. But now, with the stockmen seeking the ultimate blade of grass, the sawyer the last great tree, and the engineer sites for enormous reservoirs, protection for our wildlife requires constantly increasing thought and effort.

Because we have not lost more of them, because we still are possessed of a considerable wealth of wildlife, many of us have remained unconcerned. This is a good deal like the attitude of the small boy who didn't want to earn a quarter because he had a quarter. Or, on a higher plane, like melting down Cellini vessels with the justification that those of Leonardo remained.

Indeed, the vandalism that wipes out the last whooping crane, the last ivory-bill, seems far worse. Vessels are dead things, contrived by man in a few weeks or months. The condor that rides the winds over the California hills, the curlew that spanned two continents with its crying, were millions of years in the making. The very forces that shaped the earth molded their form, determined their destiny. Through thousands and tens of thousands of generations, the wind and the cold, the march of the seasons, the changes on the land, the failure and success of plants, and the craftiness of enemies hammered at the malleable substance of these creatures. Endless sorting, endless discarding, endless change brought them to ultimate perfection for the world in which they live. Can man, like some blundering sorcerer's apprentice, afford to smash the crucible in which they have been refined, reduce them to a mere memory, a bunch of stuffed feathers in a museum? Not, it seems to me, without pitifully impoverishing himself!

Fortunately, for those who are unimpressed by any value not backed up by a gold reserve, it is possible to show that the worth of our birds and mammals and reptiles and even many insects can be measured in terms of cash-on-the-barrelhead. Our game birds, mammals, and fishes support a two-billion-dollar a year industry — hunting, fishing, and associated activities. Our fur bearers are worth probably a quarter as much. The value of wild creatures in maintaining a balanced, healthy ecology in which man can thrive is unquestionably far greater than any figure that has been assigned to their direct exploitation. They add incalculably to the health — psychosomatic health — of those who turn to them for outdoor enjoyment, with or without gun and rod. The basic training their pursuit gave our young men contributed significantly to the speed with which we were able to turn a group of non-militaristic citizens into a superb corps of jungle fighters. The appreciation and defense of our wildlife need no apology. But they do require a constant renewing; we must keep on reminding ourselves that this treasure is unequaled, and that only positive actions can preserve it for our enjoyment.[2]

*

1. Do you find the selection persuasive? If not, why not?
2. Does the author seem trustworthy? On what do you base your opinion?
3. Do you find any effective use of emotional appeal in the selection? If so, identify it.
4. Is the communication abstract or concrete? Is your answer related to your judgment of the persuasiveness of the selection?

Persuasion by Logical Argument

We saw in Chapter 3 that an argument is a premise-conclusion structure. When two or more statements are so related that one is a conclusion drawn from the others, the group constitutes an argument. The mental act of going from the premise to the conclusion, of drawing or inferring the conclusion from the premise, is called *inference*. Thus the structure of a simple argument may be diagramed thus:

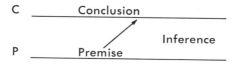

We also saw in Chapter 3 that simple arguments can be built into more and more complex ones by using the conclusion of one as the premise of another (page 77).

An argument is *reliable* if both premises and conclusion are acceptable — that is, if the premises are true and the conclusion follows logically from them. In so far as an argument can be persuasive, reliable arguments are persuasive. But we have seen that even a reliable argument may fail to persuade if its proponent does not inspire confidence or if the argument itself is too abstract to engage attention and interest.

TYPES OF PREMISES

The most common types of premises are statements of fact, judgments, and expert testimony. *Statements of fact* may be verified by checking against the facts they report. If a statement corresponds to the facts, it is "true"; if it does not, it is "false." Since the facts lie outside the mind of the person making the statement and are assumed to be the same for all people, the truth or falsity of a factual statement does not depend on opinion.

Statements of fact make the most reliable premises. Among intelligent people the authority of facts is often decisive. Even though different conclusions can sometimes be drawn from the same factual premise, controversies tend to dissolve when they are reduced to questions of fact. For this reason, the best preparation for argument is a diligent search for the facts.

Judgments are conclusions inferred from facts. An inference may be so obvious that the judgment hardly differs from a statement of fact, or the judgment may go so far beyond the facts that we have trouble seeing what they were. For example, consider these judgments:

The cost of a new car in 1967 is more than double what it was in 1942.

All things considered, a new car in 1967 is a better buy for the money than a new car was in 1942.

The first statement is a conclusion drawn from a contrast of the prices, and the inference involves nothing more than a simple computation. The inference of the second statement includes a consideration of the relative purchasing power of the dollar in 1942 and 1967, a consideration of the improvements in modern cars, and a decision that the increase in value more than offsets the increase in cost. This kind of value judgment depends as much on *evaluation* of the facts as on the facts themselves, and since evaluation may differ with different people, such a judgment will often be less reliable than a statement of fact. In the example used at the beginning of this chapter, the decision that the Falcon was the best buy was a value judgment.

Expert testimony is a statement by a person presumed to be an authority on the subject. It may be factual, as when a doctor describes the conditions revealed by an autopsy; or it may be a judgment, as when a psychiatrist testifies that in his opinion the defendant is insane. Expert testimony is frequently necessary, although it is often overused in student arguments; when it is used, it is subject to the tests for trustworthiness described earlier.

TYPES OF INFERENCES

Inferences are traditionally classified as *inductive* and *deductive,* and the processes as *induction* and *deduction.* In induction we start with specific information and try to see some pattern in it. In deduction we start with a general statement and try to discover more specific implications or particular instances of it. For example, if we polled a number of Iowa voters and inferred from their answers that Iowa would vote Republican in the next election, we would be making an inductive inference — reasoning from individual responses to a general conclusion. But if we began with the premise that farm states vote Republican and reasoned that since Iowa is a farm state it will vote Republican, we would be making a deductive inference — reasoning from a general statement to a particular implication of it. Although induction and deduction are often combined, it will be convenient to discuss them separately.

Induction

Induction is of three types: *generalization, causal relation,* and *analogy.*

Generalization. A generalization is a conclusion about a whole class or group based on a study of some of its members. If we measured 2000 American and 2000 British soldiers and found that the average height of the Americans was greater, we might infer that American soldiers as a group are taller than British soldiers. We would be studying a sample of each group and, from the sample, drawing a conclusion about each class.

Obviously a generalization based on a few samples, all things else being equal, is riskier than one based on many samples. The measurements of twenty American and twenty British soldiers would be too few to warrant any conclusion. But the mere size of a sample is not by itself a trustworthy test of generalization. If we measured 10,000 British soldiers, all members of crack regiments with minimum height requirements of six feet, we could draw no reliable conclusions about the average height of British soldiers, since we would have no reason to assume that the sample was representative — indeed, we might conclude that it was not. The members of the crack regiments are not *typical* in height.

It is important to understand this distinction, because hasty assumption that samples are typical is the chief cause of unsound generalization. It is often difficult — sometimes impossible — to be sure a sample is typical, and much useful reasoning is based on samples which can only be presumed so. But for any serious generalization, all possible care should be taken to see that the samples probably are typical. Any sample which tends to be "loaded" — that is, more likely true for part of a class than for all of it — should be rejected. The following samples are all loaded.

> A study of college hospital records to determine how many days a semester a student is likely to be sick. (The sample will exaggerate because it ignores the healthiest part of the student population — those who did not need hospitalization.)

> A contrast of unemployment figures in Michigan in June and January to determine whether unemployment is increasing. (A comparison between two Junes would be safer, since the January figures may be increased by seasonal unemployment.)

> An analysis of all automobile accidents reported in a state during a year to determine whether men or women are the safer drivers. (If there are more men drivers than women drivers, or if men drive more frequently for longer distances or under adverse conditions, one would expect more men to be involved in accidents. The sample is likely to be loaded.)

The commonest safeguard against loading is to choose samples at random. A random sample is one in which the items are selected entirely by chance, as in a lottery, or by some other procedure so arbitrary that it is almost the same as a chance selection — for example, choosing the first word on every twentieth page of a dictionary. The assumption behind random selection is that any inference made from a sample so selected would be equally valid for any other sample selected at random.

Another method of sampling is the *stratified sample,* in which the whole class being studied is divided into significant subgroups, and samples are chosen from each subgroup in proportion to its size. In a college population which contained twice as many men as women, two-thirds of the sample would be men; if the class populations showed a ratio of five freshmen, four sophomores, and three juniors to two seniors, that ratio would be observed in the sampling. In a stratified sample, the samples in each subgroup are chosen by random selection.

Any answer obtained by sampling expresses a probability, not a certainty. The better the sampling technique, the higher the probability of correct prediction. In the 1964 Presidential election, the Vote Profile Analysis used by one of the broadcasting companies predicted the results with 100 per cent accuracy from a sample of 2000 out of the nations 175,000 precincts — a sample of little more than one per cent! In contrast to such accurate sampling is the *hasty generalization,* which draws a conclusion about a large group from a few samples, without regard to how typical the samples are. Many generalizations about racial or national groups, about men as contrasted with women, about teen-agers, about college students and faculty members, are the kind described as hasty.

Causal Relation. Probably the most common kind of inductive reasoning is that which relates two events and concludes that one is the cause of the other. Such a conclusion reflects an underlying assumption called the *principle of causation.* According to this principle, every event has a cause, so that, whenever we discover that event *B* must follow event *A,* we may say that *A* is the cause of *B* and *B* the effect of *A.*

Causal reasoning may go from cause to effect or from effect to cause. Either way, we reason from what we know to what we are trying to determine. Sometimes we reason from an effect to a cause and then on to another effect. Thus, if we reason that because the lights have gone out the refrigerator won't work, we first relate the effect (lights out) to the cause (power off) and then relate that cause to another effect (refrigerator not working). This kind of reasoning is called, for short, *effect to effect.* It is quite common to reason through an extensive chain of causal relations. If when the lights go out we take the milk out of the refrigerator, we reason in the following causal chain: lights out — power off — refrigerator not working — temperature will rise — milk will sour. In other words, we diagnose a succession of effects from the power failure, each becoming the cause of the next.

Causes are classified as necessary, sufficient, or contributory. A *necessary cause* is one which must be present for the effect to occur, as combustion is necessary to drive a gasoline engine. A *sufficient cause* is one which can produce an effect unaided, but there may be more than one sufficient cause: a dead battery is enough to keep a car from starting, but faulty spark plugs or an empty tank will produce the same effect. A *contributory cause* is one which helps to produce an effect but cannot do so by itself, as running through a red light may help cause an accident, though other factors — the presence of pedestrians or other cars in the intersection — must also be present.

Most of our concern with causal relations arises from a need to discover causes. Something happens, and immediately we ask "Why?" In attempting to answer that question — to find the cause — we usually go through one or more of the following stages in our thinking:

1. Whatever the cause is, it must exist in the situation and it must be sufficient to produce the effect. This assumption requires us: (1) to check the situation carefully in order to identify possible causes, and (2) to consider which of the possible causes is sufficient to produce the effect. In making this analysis we are influenced by our past experience with similar situations. If we have repeatedly observed that event *B* follows event *A,* we incline to infer that *A* is the cause of *B.* But we should remember that, although a cause always precedes an effect, one event can regularly precede another without being its cause. Eight o'clock classes always come before nine o'clock classes, but the first do not cause the second.

2. If a sufficient cause is eliminated from the situation, the effect will be eliminated, unless other causes are also operating. At this stage in our reasoning we are ready to test the possible causes to see if there is any connection between them and the effect. If the effect ceases when we remove a possible cause, this possible cause is the actual one. If we suspect that a light failure is caused by a faulty bulb, we can substitute a new bulb and see whether the effect (no light) is removed. If it is, we need look no further for the cause. But if the new bulb does not give light, we cannot infer that the original bulb was all right, since the effect could have been produced by any of several sufficient causes or a combination of them — for example, a defect in the bulb, the wiring, the outlet, or in more than one of these.

3. If the cause is introduced into a similar situation it will produce a similar effect. This is an additional way to test possible causes. If we suspect that a light failure is due to a faulty bulb, we can predict that the bulb will not light when placed in a socket where another bulb has been burning. If the bulb does light, we must reject the hypothesis that it was faulty and caused the light failure. If the bulb does not light, we have additional support for our belief that it is the cause we are seeking.

Whether we go through all three of these stages to discover a cause will probably depend on how important finding the cause is to us. To find our faulty bulb we need not go beyond the second stage, once we find that changing bulbs removes the difficulty; but a laboratory scientist attempting to establish the cause of a disease would perform every experiment he could think of before reaching a final conclusion.

The most common errors in causal reasoning are:

1. Assuming that *A* causes *B* because *A* always precedes *B,* as in assuming that the setting of the sun causes moonlight.

2. Mistaking an effect for a cause, as in blaming the car's inefficiency on the knocking in the engine.

3. Mistaking a contributory cause for a sufficient cause, as when a tail-

gating driver explains a crash by saying that the car ahead stopped suddenly.

4. Failing to recognize that the cause may be not a single event but a complex: for example, ignoring the function of a catalyst in some chemical reactions.

Two common ways to discover a probable cause are *the method of agreement* and *the method of difference*. The method of agreement assumes that if all possible causes of an effect are identified and only one of these always precedes the effect, then that possible cause is the probable cause. The method of difference assumes that if all possible causes of an effect are identified and only one of these is missing when the effect fails to occur, then that missing possible cause is the probable cause. Both methods are reliable only when all possible factors have been identified.

▶ *Suppose you are running a series of experiments to discover under what conditions the effect* E *will appear. Your experiments yield the following data, in which each letter represents a possible cause of* E. *Use the methods of agreement and disagreement to discover the only conditions under which* E *will appear. Assume that all possible causes have been identified. If you find that no single letter is the cause of* E, *consider whether two letters acting in conjunction may be identified as the cause.*

A	D	O	R	V	————	E
A	D	Q	S	T	————	No E
R	S	T	U	V	————	No E
M	O	R	T	V	————	E
O	K	L	M	N	————	No E
B	C	K	O	R	————	E
B	F	R	W	O	————	No E

Causal Generalization. The kind of causal analysis we have been considering works best with events in which all possible causes can be isolated and tested independently. But many problems do not permit such a procedure. We cannot, for instance, test the hypothesis that fluorides prevent tooth decay by eliminating all other possible factors affecting tooth decay — hereditary factors, prenatal environment, diet, etc. All we can do is to contrast the amount of tooth decay in people who use fluoridated tooth paste or drink fluoridated water with the amount in people who do neither. Basically, we are generalizing from contrasted samples and making a causal-relation inference from the generalization. We are thus combining two types of inductive reasoning in what is called a *causal generalization.*

Causal generalizations are useful for suggesting causes that cannot otherwise be identified, but we should be careful to recognize that, like all generalizations, what they establish is a *probability*. How reliable that probability is will depend on how reliable the reasoning is. If the generalization is sound — if enough typical samples have been examined — and if care is taken to ensure that other possible causes have not been ignored or underestimated, the probability revealed by the causal generalization may be sufficient for practical purposes. Thus the causal generalization that doctors can reduce infection in surgery cases by scrubbing their hands and sterilizing their instruments before operating has yielded great practical benefits. But if the generalization is a hasty one and if the alleged cause is not sufficient to produce the effect, a causal generalization may lead to nothing more than a superstition, such as the belief that breaking a mirror brings seven years of bad luck.

▶ *The following extract from a long article[3] illustrates a causal generalization. When you have finished reading it, answer the questions that follow.*

After designing and pretesting a questionnaire in the fall of 1951, we trained more than 22,000 American Cancer Society volunteers as researchers for the study. Between January 1 and May 31 of 1952 they enrolled subjects in 394 counties in nine states. The subjects, all men between the ages of 50 and 69, answered a simple confidential questionnaire on their smoking habits, both past and present. A total of 187,783 men were enrolled, filled out usable questionnaires and were successfully kept track of for the next 44 months. Death certificates were obtained for all who died, and additional medical information was gathered for those who were reported to have died of cancer. All together 11,870 deaths were reported, of which 2,249 were attributed to cancer.

The most important finding was that the total death rate (from all causes of death combined) is far higher among men with a history of regular cigarette smoking than among men who never smoked, but only slightly higher among pipe and cigar smokers than among men who never smoked. . . .

Men who had smoked cigarettes regularly and exclusively were classified according to their cigarette consumption at the time they were enrolled in the study. It was found that death rates rose progressively with increasing number of cigarettes smoked per day. The death rate of those who smoked two or more packs of cigarettes a day was approximately two and a quarter times higher than the death rate of men who never smoked. . . .

During the course of the study 7,316 deaths occurred among subjects with a history of regular cigarette smoking (some of whom smoked pipes and/or cigars as well as cigarettes). We divided these deaths according to primary cause as reported on death certificates. Only 4,651 of these cigarette smokers would have died during the course of the study if their death rates had exactly matched those of men of the same age who had never smoked. The difference of 2,665 deaths (7,316 minus 4,651) can be considered the "Excess deaths" associated with a history of regular cigarette smoking. Of these excess deaths 52.1 per cent were attributed to coronary artery disease of the heart, 13.5 per cent to lung cancer and the remainder to other diseases. From this it is apparent that as a cause of death coronary artery disease is by far the most important disease associated with cigarette smoking. . . .

[3] From E. Cuyler Hammond, "The Effects of Smoking," *Scientific American,* July, 1962. Copyright © 1962 by Scientific American, Inc. All rights reserved.

All together 127 deaths were attributed to cancer of other tissues (mouth, tongue, lip, larynx, pharynx and esophagus) that are directly exposed to tobacco smoke and material condensed from tobacco smoke. In 114 of these cases the diagnosis was confirmed by microscopic examination. Of these 114 men, 110 were smokers and only four had never smoked. The figures suggest that pipe and cigar smoking may be more important than cigarette smoking in relation to cancer of one or more sites included in this group, but the number of cases was not sufficient for a reliable evaluation of this point. Nevertheless, these cancers were the only causes of death for which the death rate of pipe and cigar smokers was found to be far higher than the death rate of nonsmokers.

Other reported causes of death showing a fairly high degree of association with cigarette smoking were gastric and duodenal ulcers, certain diseases of the arteries, pulmonary diseases (including pneumonia and influenza), cancer of the bladder and cirrhosis of the liver. Many other diseases appeared to be somewhat associated with cigarette smoking. . . .

After reviewing the evidence, the mildest statement I can make is that, in my opinion, the inhalation of tobacco smoke produces a number of very harmful effects and shortens the life span of human beings. The simplest way to avoid these possible consequences is not to smoke at all. But one can avoid the most serious of them by smoking cigars or a pipe instead of cigarettes, provided that one does not inhale the smoke. An individual who chooses to smoke cigarettes can minimize the risks by restricting his consumption and by not inhaling.

*

1. Do you consider the article trustworthy? Explain your judgment with specific illustrations.

2. Is there any psychological persuasion in the article? Illustrate your answer by reference to the text.

3. What is the thesis or general conclusion of the article?

4. Make a sentence outline of the argument. In doing so, you will have to distinguish between explanatory and argumentative sections. For example, the first paragraph, which explains how the study was conducted, is not part of the argument. You may wish to begin with a preliminary topic outline, but your final outline should be in sentence form and should show the premises and conclusions.

5. Evaluate the reasoning both as causal relation and generalization. Support all judgments by specific reference to the text.

Analogy. Analogy is the type of reasoning in which we infer that if two things are alike in several important respects they will also be alike in certain other respects. The following selection shows how this inference develops.

We often wonder whether or not Mars is inhabited. . . . Did you ever ask yourself why it is *Mars* that interests us so much in this connection? It is because Mars is so similar to the earth in major respects. It has a similar history, a comparable temperature, an atmosphere, is subject to similar solar seasons; it revolves around the sun, it gets light from the sun, it is subject to the law of gravitation, etc. May it not also be similar in respect to harboring life? If Mars were without water, like the moon, or experienced great extremes of temperature, like Mercury, we should not be so much interested in it. But we entertain the idea because Mars is so similar in many respects to the earth *and life has evolved on the earth!*[4]

In exposition and description, analogy can often make abstract ideas concrete or explain the unfamiliar by likening it to the familiar. In argument, analogy can be useful but it can also be misleading. It is helpful in suggesting hypotheses for further investigation. For example, if we have found that the best protection against one virus disease is to isolate the virus and prepare an immunizing serum from it, we can predict that the same method will work with another virus disease. If the prediction proves true, the analogy has helped to solve our problem. If the prediction proves false, the suggested solution will be quickly rejected and no great harm will have been done.

Analogy is also useful when we have no other means of reaching a conclusion. For example, we cannot descend to the bottom of the ocean and collect evidence about the kinds of life, if any, existing there, but we can infer by analogy that the characteristics we observe in the depths we can penetrate will hold true in those we cannot. But such inferences are, at best, tentative, and we replace them by more reliable evidence where possible.

Analogy may be more persuasive than it should be and lead us to a conclusion which is not true. For a single difference can render a whole analogy false. The test of an analogy is the question, *Are the two things analogous for the purpose for which the analogy is being used?* They may have many differences which are unimportant to the inference based on the analogy. But they must not be different in any detail essential to that inference. Thus the analogy that a motherless baby ape could be reared by feeding it as if it were a human baby would be sound because, despite many differences, young apes and human babies have similar digestive systems. But to reason that because two varieties of mushrooms look much alike, both will be good to eat, is a dangerous analogy, since edible and poisonous mushrooms often look much alike — except to the expert.

▶ *In the following analogy the eighteenth-century philosopher David Hume compares the universe to a machine and uses that comparison to infer the existence of a Divine Intelligence. Comment on the structure and persuasiveness of the argument.*

Look round the world, contemplate the whole and every part of it: you will find it to be nothing but one great machine, subdivided into an infinite

[4] From Roger W. Holmes, *The Rhyme of Reason* (New York: Appleton-Century, 1939).

number of lesser machines, which again admit of subdivisions to a degree beyond what human senses and faculties can trace and explain. All these various machines, and even their most minute parts, are adjusted to each other with an accuracy which ravishes into admiration all men who have ever contemplated them. The curious adapting of means to ends, throughout all nature, resembles exactly, though it much exceeds, the productions of human contrivance — of human design, thought, wisdom, and intelligence. Since therefore the effects resemble each other, we are led to infer, by all the rules of analogy, that the causes also resemble, and that the Author of nature is somewhat similar to the mind of man, though possessed of much larger faculties, proportioned to the grandeur of the work which he has executed. By this argument . . . do we prove at once the existence of a Deity and his similarity to human mind and intelligence.

Deduction

Deduction starts with a given statement as a premise and draws conclusions from it. The conclusions are implied in the given statement. For example, the following conclusions are implied in the statement: *A square is a rectangle with equilateral sides:*

1. A rectangle with the horizontal sides either larger or smaller than the vertical sides is not a square.
2. Squares are necessarily rectangles, but rectangles are not necessarily squares.
3. The sum of the angles within a square is 360 degrees.
4. If a square is divided into two triangles by a diagonal line, each of the triangles so formed is a right-angle triangle.
5. The triangles so formed are congruent.
6. The sum of the angles in each of these triangles is 180 degrees.
7. Each of the triangles has two acute angles.

In drawing these conclusions we do not need to measure lines or angles. We simply recognize that 1 above is another way of expressing the given statement, that 2 is another way of stating 1, and so on through successive conclusions. This is not the way we work when using induction. Then we select and study specific samples and draw conclusions from the data so obtained. In deduction we study statements and draw conclusions from what they imply. We are, in effect, saying, "Given statement *A,* statement *B* follows." Deduction is "thinking out" the implications of statements. The following illustrates the process.

In College X each academic department has an advisory committee to advise the head of the department on matters of policy. For one department, the first of the following statements is permanently true; the others are true of the current committee.

1. All full professors in the department are always members of the committee by virtue of their rank.
2. All members of the committee are married.

3. No woman is a member of the committee.
4. Every member of the committee has the Ph.D. degree.

It is possible to draw conclusions by using some of these statements as premises, thus:

> *P1* All full professors in the department are members of the committee by virtue of their rank.
>
> *P2* All members of the committee are Ph.D.'s.
>
> ---
>
> *C* All full professors in the department are Ph.D.'s.

This conclusion necessarily follows from the premises. It is another way of saying what is implied in the premises. But these premises do not imply that it is necessary to have the Ph.D. degree to become a full professor, or to serve on the committee; nor do they imply that membership on the committee is restricted to full professors. In checking these implications, remember that statements 2, 3, and 4 refer to members of the current committee and that only statement 1 refers to any advisory committee appointed in this department.

▶ *Which of the following conclusions can validly be drawn from any combination of the premises above? Justify your answers.*

1. No woman in the department is a full professor.
2. No woman in the department has the Ph.D. degree.
3. The department discriminates against women.
4. All full professors in the department are married.
5. To be a full professor in the department, one must be married.
6. To become a full professor, one must be in the department for at least five years.
7. If a woman in the department is promoted to a full professorship, she will become a member of the advisory committee.

A deduction is said to be *reliable* when, and only when, it fulfills two conditions: that the premises are *true,* and that the inference leading to the conclusion is *valid.* In this context, "true" means "in accordance with the facts." If some members of the current advisory committee are not Ph.D.'s, then the second premise of our model deduction above will be false, and no argument based on that premise will be reliable. An inference is valid if it necessarily follows from the premises, even if one of the premises is false. For example, if we are given the premise that not all points on the circumference of a circle are equidistant from the center, then we must conclude that the radii in a circle may be of unequal length. This, of course, is absurd, but it is absurd because the information we have been given is false; the inference drawn from that information is valid, since there is no error in the reasoning. The argument is not reliable, because the premise is false, but the inference is nevertheless valid. The relation among truth, validity, and reliability is illustrated by the following chart:

Valid inference from true premises. The argument is RELIABLE.

   P1   Boston is in Massachusetts.
   P2   Massachusetts is in New England.
   C   Boston is in New England.

Valid inference from false premises. The argument is NOT RELIABLE.

   P1   Chicago is in Virginia.
   P2   Virginia is in New England.
   C   Chicago is in New England.

Invalid inference from true premises. The argument is NOT RELIABLE.

   P1   Boston is smaller than Chicago.
   P2   Philadelphia is smaller than Chicago.
   C   Boston and Philadelphia are the same size.

Invalid inference from false premises. The argument is NOT RELIABLE.

   P1   All industrial cities have skyscrapers.
   P2   All state capitals have skyscrapers.
   C   All state capitals are industrial cities.

▶ *In the following exercise assume that all premises are true, even though you know from experience that at least some of them are false. Then mark the italicized conclusions Valid or Invalid and explain your answers.*

   1. All blondes are beautiful. Mary is a blonde. Therefore *Mary is beautiful.*

   2. No blonde is beautiful. Susan is not a blonde. Therefore *Susan is not beautiful.*

   3. All college professors are wise. Her father is not a college professor. Therefore *her father is not wise.*

   4. Some football players are All-Americans. He is a football player. Therefore *he is an All-American.*

   5. Anyone with an IQ of 140 or more is classified as a genius. He has an IQ of 160. Therefore *he is a genius.*

The form of deduction used in the exercise above is called a *syllogism*. A syllogism is a three-sentence argument, consisting of a *major premise,* a *minor premise,* and a *conclusion* drawn from both premises. There are many types of syllogisms, but the four discussed below are the major types. Since we are primarily concerned here with validity, we shall not consider the truth of the premises.

Type 1: The Categorical Syllogism

In this type each statement consists of two terms connected by a verb. There are three terms in all, each used twice. In the following example the terms have been underlined and lettered to make the example more clearly reveal the structure of the model. (For convenient reference we shall abbreviate major premise, minor premise, and conclusion to *MP, mp,* and *c* respectively.)

Model	*Example*
MP. All *A* are *B.*	All college students are high school graduates.
mp. *C* is *A.*	Joe Smith is a college student.
c. *C* is *B.*	Joe Smith is a high school graduate.

A categorical syllogism begins with a statement about all members of a class, a statement which identifies some characteristic that all members of the class share. It then proceeds to identify one member of the class and to infer that he has the class characteristic. Notice that, except for the necessary change from plural to singular in *A* and *B,* each term has precisely the same meaning each time it is used. This is important, because a term used in two meanings is actually two terms, and we then have more than three terms. As the model shows, this syllogism cannot have more or less than three terms. The following example illustrates a violation of this rule.

MP. All college students are high school graduates.

mp. Joe Smith is an honor student.

In these premises, "honor student" and "college students" are not synonyms, since there may be honor students in high and elementary schools. The syllogism has four terms and we can draw no conclusion from the premises.

Now let us gain some experience with validity in the categorical syllogism by taking a series of premises and seeing what conclusions may be validly derived from them. Remember that we are chiefly concerned with seeing what the premises imply. We cannot draw any conclusion which is not necessarily implied in the premises.

MP. All college professors are absent-minded.
mp. Father is absent-minded.

We can draw no conclusion from these premises. The major premise is a statement about college professors, not about absent-minded people; therefore we cannot infer that father is a college professor. But if the major premise read, "Only college professors are absent-minded," we could infer that father is a college professor. Or if the minor premise said, "Father is a college professor," we could conclude that he is absent-minded.

MP. All college professors are absent-minded.
mp. Father is not absent-minded.

We can conclude that father is not a college professor. If he is not absent-minded he does not qualify as a college professor according to the major premise. In this syllogism, saying that father is not absent-minded is another way of saying that he is not a college professor.

> *MP.* No college professor is absent-minded.
> *mp.* Father is absent-minded.

We conclude that father is not a college professor, since his absent-mindedness rules him out of the class according to the major premise. Notice that although this major premise does not start with "All," it is still a statement about all college professors, since to say that none of them has a certain characteristic is the same as to say that all of them lack that characteristic.

> *MP.* No college professor is absent-minded.
> *mp.* Father is not absent-minded.

We can draw no conclusion. The major premise does not say that *only* college professors are free of absent-mindedness. If it did, we could conclude that father is a college professor. But, as stated, the major premise does not imply that freedom from absent-mindedness is a sure sign of being a college professor.

Quite frequently a categorical syllogism lies half-concealed in a shortened form called an *enthymeme,* a form not easy to recognize without practice:

(1) Father is a college professor; therefore he is absent-minded.
(2) Father must be absent-minded, because he is a college professor.
(3) Since all college professors are absent-minded, father must be absent-minded.

To test the validity of the shortened form, first rewrite the syllogism in its full form. In doing this, certain connectives can be important clues: *because, since,* and *for* introduce premises, and *therefore, so,* and *then* introduce conclusions. When these words appear it is not hard to reconstruct the syllogism. In (1) above, *therefore* identifies the second statement as the conclusion, and you can work backward from the conclusion to provide the missing major premise:

> *MP.*
> *mp.* Father is a college professor.
> *c.* Father is absent-minded.

By checking the clue words you should be able to identify the missing part of (2) also as the major premise, and the missing part of (3) as the minor premise.

When these clue words are not present, an enthymeme is more difficult to detect:

Father must be absent-minded! He's a college professor, isn't he?

Here, with major premise missing, is a classic example of "jumping to a conclusion" — from minor premise only. This is the danger of the unexamined enthymeme.

The three most common errors with categorical syllogisms are hasty generalization in the major premise, ambiguous terms, and misinterpretation of the major premise.

Hasty Generalization in the Major Premise. In the categorical syllogism the major premise refers to all members of a class and is therefore a generalization. If that generalization is unacceptable, the syllogism is not reliable. If not all college professors are absent-minded, any syllogism based on the premise that they are will be unreliable, no matter how valid the rest of the reasoning. Of course, the syllogism will be just as unreliable if the minor premise is false, but the most common error is a faulty major premise.

Ambiguous Terms. Unless the terms are precise, we cannot be sure they are consistently used with the same meaning. What do "radicals" and "un-American" mean in the following premise?

All radicals are un-American.

We cannot derive reliable syllogisms from such loose terms, for they can have many meanings and we can never be sure what precisely they mean in any part of the syllogism. Again, what does "superior" mean in the following premises?

MP. All superior students receive better-than-average grades.
mp. Three-letter men are superior students.

Before we can draw a conclusion, we must be satisfied that "superior" means the same in both these premises. If it means "academically superior" in the major premise and "athletically superior" in the minor premise, it is ambiguous. But if in both premises it means "having better-than-average grades," it is not ambiguous. The premises would then better be written:

MP. All students with better-than-average grades are classified as superior students.
mp. Three-letter men have better-than-average grades.

From these premises it is valid to infer that "Three-letter men are classified as superior students." Whether the syllogism is reliable will then depend on the truth of the premises, not on their logic.

Misinterpretation of the Major Premise. The major premise "All full professors are members of the advisory committee" does not mean the same as "All members of the advisory committee are full professors." Yet this kind of misinterpretation is frequent:

347

All Communists oppose U.S. policy in Vietnam.
He opposes U.S. policy in Vietnam.
He is a Communist.

This inference would be valid only if the major premise were reversed:

All who oppose U.S. policy in Vietnam are Communists.

But in its first form we must consider that the major premise is misinterpreted. "All Communists oppose U.S. policy in Vietnam" does not mean "All who oppose U.S. policy in Vietnam are Communists."

A helpful clue to a misinterpreted major premise of a categorical syllogism is the relative position of term *A* in the major and minor premises. In the major premise, term *A* occupies the subject position, but in the minor premise it occupies the complement position.

$$MP.\ \text{All } A \text{ are } B.$$
$$mp.\ \ C \text{ is } A.$$

But in the misinterpretation, *A* does not appear in the minor premise, and *B* is the complement in both premises:

$$MP.\ \text{All } A \text{ are } B.$$
$$mp.\ \ C \text{ is } B.$$

Remember that in the erroneous form both premises end with the *B* term.

Type 2: The Conditional or Hypothetical Syllogism

Here the major premise asserts that, if a certain condition is satisfied, a certain consequence will follow:

Model	*Example*
MP. If *A*, then *B*	^A If he fails the final exam, ^B he will fail the course.
mp. A	He failed the final exam.
c. B	He failed the course.

In this example the conclusion necessarily follows from the premises. But what happens if he passed the final exam? The major premise does not say. Conceivably he could get an A on the final and still fail the course. Had the major premise stated "If, *and only if,* he fails the final exam, he will fail the course," then it would be valid to infer that a passing grade on the exam would guarantee passing the course. The consequence stated in *B* of the major premise can be predicted only if the condition in *A* is met. If *A*, then *B;* but if not *A,* no conclusion can be drawn.

There is a vast difference between *if* and *only if*. Thus, "If she is wearing the red dress, I will ask her for a date" does not rule out asking her if she is wearing blue. But that possibility would be ruled out by the wording "If, and only if, she is wearing the red dress."

What conclusion can we infer from the following premises?

A   B

MP. If she is wearing the red dress, I will ask her for a date.
mp. I asked her for a date.

Can we infer that she wore the red dress? We cannot. We have just seen that this major premise does not rule out the possibility of asking her even if she wears blue. That the consequence stated in *B* has occurred does not prove that the condition stated in *A* was met. Logicians state this as a rule by saying that in a hypothetical syllogism *affirming a consequent (B) does not permit a conclusion.* We can draw no conclusion from these premises. Again, if *A* had read "If, and only if, she is wearing the red dress," then we could infer that the boy could not have asked the girl for a date unless she was wearing the red dress.

Now, in

A   B

MP. If she is wearing the red dress, I will ask her for a date.
mp. I did not ask her for a date.

can we infer that the girl did *not* wear the red dress? Yes, because the major premise commits the boy to ask for a date if the girl is wearing the red dress. He *must* ask her if she is wearing red. Therefore, if he did not ask her, she could not have been wearing the red dress. If the consequence in *B* does not occur, we can infer that the condition in *A* was not met. Logicians state this as a rule by saying that *the denial of a consequent (B) requires a corresponding denial of an antecedent (A).*

The four possibilities for the hypothetical syllogism may be summarized thus:

1. If *A* happens, *B* must happen; the inference that *B* will happen if *A* does is valid.
2. If *A* does not happen, no valid inference is possible.
3. If the consequent, *B,* occurs, we cannot be sure why it occurred; therefore we cannot infer from *B* that the condition in *A* was met.
4. If the consequent, *B,* does *not* occur, we can reason that since *B* has to occur if the condition, *A,* was met, the non-occurrence of *B* is proof that the condition, *A,* was not met.

We can affirm the consequent if the condition is met, and we can be sure the condition was not met if we know the consequent did not occur. These are the only valid inferences we can make with this kind of major premise.

▶ *If a conclusion can be validly inferred from each of the minor premises below, state it. If no conclusion can be inferred, write "None."*

> *MP.* If the team wins the game, it will win the title.
> *mp 1.* The team won the game.
> *mp 2.* The team did not win the game.

349

mp 3. The team won the title.
mp 4. The team did not win the title.

Repeat the same minor premises with the following major premise.

If, and only if, the team wins the game, it will win the title.

What valid inferences may now be made?
Repeat the same minor premises with the following major premise:

Unless the team wins the game, it will lose the title.

What valid inferences may now be made? Notice that "Unless the team wins" has the same meaning as "If the team does not win."

Type 3: The Alternative Syllogism

This type pairs two statements and says that if one is not true, the other is.

Model	*Example*
	A B
MP. Either *A* or *B*.	Either the power is off or the tubes are defective.
mp. Not *A* (OR Not *B*).	The power is not off.
c. *B* (OR *A*).	The tubes are defective.

The model shows that we can draw a valid inference only if the minor premise is negative. If either of the two statements in the major premise is not applicable, the other one must be. But what can we infer if the minor premise is affirmative: if the power is off or if the tubes are defective? We can make no valid inference from an affirmative minor premise because, although the major premise asserts that one of the two statements must describe the situation, it does not exclude the possibility that both are true. Therefore if the power is off we can conclude nothing about the tubes: they may or may not be defective. And if we know that the tubes are defective, it does not necessarily follow that the power is on.

This kind of syllogism bothers students who interpret "either *A* or *B*" as meaning "only one." That interpretation would be justified if the major premise read, "Either *A* or *B*, but not both at the same time." Without such a qualification, the major premise must be interpreted as meaning "at least one of the two." For example, when a college course has as a prerequisite "either algebra or physics," that prerequisite does not exclude the student who has had both algebra and physics. The prerequisite requires at least one of the two; so does the alternative syllogism. *In an alternative syllogism "either . . . or" does not imply that the alternatives are mutually exclusive.*

▶ *For the major premise "Either the train is late or he missed it," what valid inferences may be drawn from the following minor premises?*

> mp 1. The train is late.
> mp 2. The train is not late.
> mp 3. He missed the train.
> mp 4. He did not miss the train.

If the major premise reads "Either the train is late or he missed it, but not both at the same time," what valid inferences may be drawn from the minor premises given above?

One danger in using the alternative syllogism is that the two possibilities in the *either-or* choice of the major premise do not exhaust all the possibilities. Thus in the example used as a model, there may be a third explanation of the trouble: the wiring may be faulty. In the example of the train, the person seeking an explanation may have forgotten that his watch shows daylight-saving time but trains run on standard time. If there are more than two possibilities, the alternative syllogism cannot be used. If it is used when other conditions are possible, it results in the *either-or fallacy,* an error which oversimplifies the problem by ignoring other possibilities. The opportunities for this fallacy are so plentiful that the alternative syllogism may do more harm than good.

Type 4: The Disjunctive Syllogism

This type sets up two mutually exclusive statements and says that if one is true, the other must be false.

Model	*Example*
	A B
MP. Not both *A* and *B*.	She cannot <u>love me</u> and <u>tell lies about me.</u>
mp. *A* (OR *B*).	She does tell lies about me.
c. Not *B* (OR Not *A*).	She cannot love me.

In the example the mutually exclusive statements are "love me" and "tell lies about me." The major premise tells us that if she does either, she cannot do the other; so we could infer the conclusion "She does not tell lies about me" if the minor premise were "She loves me." But what conclusion could we draw from a minor premise "She does not love me" or from "She does not tell lies about me"? We could draw no conclusion from either of these premises. The syllogism implies that if one statement is so, the other must not be so; but it does not rule out the possibility that neither is so — that the girl neither loves the man nor tells lies about him. This distinction you know from experience. You know that a statement in the college catalog that "Students cannot take physics and chemistry in

351

the same year" does not imply that a student who does not take physics must take chemistry. He may take neither. *The disjunctive syllogism permits a conclusion only when one of the two statements is affirmed in the minor premise.*

▶   *For the major premise, "You cannot have your cake and eat it too,"*
what conclusions may be validly inferred from each of these minor premises?

> mp 1. You have eaten your cake.
> mp 2. You have not eaten your cake.
> mp 3. You do not have your cake.
> mp 4. You have your cake.

▶   *As a review of the four types of syllogisms studied, state any conclusions that may validly be inferred from these premises:*

1. All psychiatrists are M.D.'s.
   All surgeons are M.D.'s.
2. All widows have deceased husbands.
   Mrs. Jones is a widow.
3. No Canadian citizen may vote in the U.S. elections.
   Robert Kennedy is not a Canadian citizen.
4. Either he returned the book on time or he paid a fine.
   He did not pay a fine.
5. Either I have the wrong number or she is not at home.
   I have the wrong number.
6. He will either be fined or sent to jail.
   He paid a fine.
7. If you send that letter you will be sorry.
   You do not send the letter.
8. If you send that letter you will be sorry.
   You are not sorry.
9. You cannot vote at home and use an absentee ballot.
   You did not vote at home.
10. She cannot be in New York and Chicago at the same time.
    She is not in New York.
11. All Republicans voted for Watson.
    Mr. Anders voted for Watson.
12. No Democrat voted for Holmes.
    My history teacher is a Democrat.
13. If you study with me you will pass the exam.
    You did not pass the exam.
14. Unless you pay him he will be nasty.
    You pay him.
15. Unless you pay him he will be nasty.
    You do not pay him.
16. All *A* are *B*.
    C is *B*.

17. If *A*, then *B*.
    Not *A*.
18. Either *A* or *B*.
    B.

Combined Induction and Deduction

In most deliberation, induction and deduction are not so separate as our treatment of them might suggest. It might be more accurate to say that induction and deduction are not two kinds of thinking but two points of view from which we can describe the act of thinking. Sometimes the distinction we make between them is determined by what part of the activity we wish to emphasize. We have seen, for example, that the major premise of a categorical syllogism is a generalization which is a result of induction, and that we can say "either-or" in an alternative syllogism only when we have learned inductively that no other possibility exists.

Consider the reasoning process that goes on when a physician is making a diagnosis of a patient's illness:

1. He observes the symptoms (facts). This is an inductive operation. In some illnesses the observations may be extensive and varied and may require the use of such observational aids as X rays and laboratory tests.

2. He frames a series of tentative hypotheses (diagnoses) to explain the facts already observed. At this stage he is seeking possible causes, an inductive procedure; but even these tentative hypotheses are conditioned by deductions made from previous experience — "Appendicitis produces certain symptoms; this patient has these symptoms; therefore he may have appendicitis."

3. For each hypothesis he makes a deduction that allows him to predict a way of testing or verifying the hypothesis. At this stage he is using deduction to suggest an inductive procedure.

4. He tests inductively to see if the conditions predicted by the deduction are true. If they are, the truth of the hypothesis becomes more probable, though several tests may be required. If the tests do not support the hypothesis, he returns to stage 2 and repeats through 4 with another hypothesis; again he uses induction and deduction in combination. He may have to repeat the process from hypothesis to verification many times.

5. When he is satisfied that all possible tests support a hypothesis, he makes a final decision or diagnosis, though this diagnosis may have to be confirmed by surgery.

The procedure followed by the physician is a practical example of problem-solving. Except that the consequences are more serious and the operations more complex, it is not radically different as a process from the example given at the opening of this chapter — the decision to buy a new car. The physician, like the car owner, goes through the following stages: he gathers information; he identifies possible solutions; he evaluates these solutions; he reaches a decision. The physician can skip the first stage, becoming aware of the problem, because the patient has established that a problem exists by consulting him. But like the car owner, he finds that the need for information continues until the final decision has been made.

▶ *Recall the process you went through in making some major decision, perhaps in choosing your college. Trace the steps leading to your decision. Did you go through a deliberative sequence? Can you identify inductive and deductive reasoning in the making of that decision?*

FALLACIES

A *fallacy* is an error which makes an argument unreliable. The following discussion will group fallacies in two general classes: those that distort an argument, and those that oversimplify it.

Fallacies of Distortion

Literally, the word *distort* means "to twist out of shape." Any error which misrepresents all or part of an argument by twisting its meaning is a fallacy of distortion. The following types are the most common.

Begging the Question. A question is "begged" when one or more of the premises by which it should be proved are assumed to be true without proof. The best defense against this fallacy is to show how the begging takes place. The following examples illustrate such arguments:

Examples	*Analysis*
Dad, you don't need to worry about lending me the money for this business. Just as soon as the profits come in I can pay you back with interest.	*This argument assumes that the profits will be sufficient to pay off the debt. That, however, is a major part of dad's doubt, and needs to be proved.*
Much of this talk about spending millions for slum clearance is based on the fallacy that if we provide fine homes for people who live in the slums they will suddenly become responsible and productive citizens. This argument puts the cart before the horse. The basic trouble is with the people who live in the slums. These people are thoroughly shiftless and irresponsible. The conditions under which they live prove this. If they had any initiative or industry they would not be living under slum conditions.	*This is an argument in a circle. The thesis that slum-dwellers are responsible for slum conditions is supported by asserting that if they were not responsible they would not be living in slums. The writer assumes that what he has to prove is true, and his argument goes round in the following circle: Slums are caused by shiftless tenants; this is true because shiftless tenants cause slums.*

"There is bound to be life on other planets." "Can you prove it?" "Well, can you prove there isn't?"	*This example shifts the burden of proof. In arguments both inside and outside law courts, "He who asserts must prove." We cannot prove an assertion by defying the opposition to disprove it.*

Ignoring Context. Words have specific meaning in context. If the context is changed, or — as more often happens — if part of it is ignored, the whole statement may be misrepresented. If an instructor says, "You will pass the course if your grades for the rest of the term are consistently above C," a student who ignores the conditional clause ignores a significant part of the instructor's statement. If such a student later complains that he ought to have received a passing grade ("But you told me I would pass!"), he should be prepared to prove that he met the condition which the instructor established in the context of the complete statement.

Distortion by ignoring context is not always deliberate. People sometimes read or hear what they want to be told, and through some emotional need misinterpret what is said. Whether distortion is deliberate or not, the way to correct it is to re-examine the whole context and show how omission misinterprets the original.

Extension. This is the device of distorting an argument by extending or exaggerating it. Often it is a special case of ignoring context. Someone states that some high school graduates enter college inadequately prepared in English and mathematics. An opponent thereupon charges that the statement belittles high school teaching. This charge greatly extends and exaggerates the original remark. First, the original concerned only *some* students, not all; second, it concerned only *two* high school subjects, not all; third, it did not place the blame on the teachers of the deficient students. Again the best defense is to return to the original statement and show what it meant in its context. If the extension is not deliberate, the charge will be withdrawn. If the distortion is deliberate and is not withdrawn, it will be exposed and will damage the accuser more than the accused.

Red Herring. The scent of a red herring dragged across a trail which hounds are following may be stronger than the original scent and so divert the hounds from their quarry. In rhetoric, a red herring is a false issue introduced to lead attention away from a real one. Usually the false issue arouses an emotional response which creates a digression. If in a discussion of the draft system someone asks, "Do those of you who want to change the draft believe that young men have no obligation to their country?" he has introduced a red herring. In the heat of emotional responses to that question, it may be hard to focus on the practical question whether specific changes in the draft would be wise or not. As this example shows, a red herring may be introduced by extension. The best defense is the defense against extension: a restatement of the issue originally under consideration, to show that the red herring is a false issue.

Name-Calling. Name-calling presents an issue in loaded terms, thereby making it difficult for some persons to consider that issue objectively. They are, in effect, led into prejudging at a level of emotional associations. They are less willing to seek the evidence on which a rational judgment might be made when a proposal is branded, for example, as "communist-inspired" or "beatnik agitation." If the charges implied in these names can be supported by evidence, the evidence should be presented. When that is done, the audience is given the facts before it is asked to make the judgment. There is nothing wrong with calling an event "communist-inspired" if the speaker proves the charge. The fallacy of name-calling is that the judgment is made without evidence.

Argumentum ad Hominem. This is the fallacy of attacking the man instead of his argument. Such an attack is legitimate when the man presents no argument except his own unsupported testimony. The device is frequently used in law courts to discredit a witness who is testifying as an expert. If it can be shown that he is not expert or that his testimony cannot be relied on because of his character, then his trustworthiness as a witness is seriously challenged. But if his argument rests on evidence and reasoning, it should be evaluated at these levels. The real fallacy in *argumentum ad hominem* is that it substitutes an attack on the man for an attack on his argument.

The fallacies so far mentioned are merely the most common types of distortion. The chief defense against any distortion is the ability to detect it and to explain how it works. The major risk a person runs in distorting an argument is that, if exposed, he forfeits confidence — and with it the chance of persuading others.

Fallacies of Oversimplification

Any argument that allows us to reach a conclusion without considering all pertinent factors tends to oversimplify. The most common fallacies of oversimplification are *hasty generalizations, stereotypes, inadequate causal relationships, either-or fallacies,* and *trivial analogies.*

Hasty Generalization. A hasty generalization jumps to a conclusion from insufficient evidence. Unless the samples are clearly typical, a small number proves nothing, or at least much less than is claimed. Here is a representative case.

Example	*Analysis*
Girls just aren't any good at logic. Although there are twelve girls to ten men in our logic section, the four highest scores on the final exams were made by men and the four lowest by girls.	*In the first place, what would make us believe that what is true of twelve girls in one class will be true of all girls? In the second, are the top four and bottom four scores typical of the scores in the class? Even as a comparison for this class alone, the sample is faulty. It would be better to take the median score of the girls and compare it with the median score of the men. If the comparison favored the men, it would justify the conclusion that girls in this class do less well than men in this class on an examination in logic. That is a less impressive conclusion than the one offered in the original argument.*

Stereotype. A stereotype is a description or standardized mental image which pays too much attention to characteristics supposedly common to a group and not enough to individual differences. We begin with a number of individuals who have one thing in common (let us say that they all have married children); we group them into a class (mothers-in-law); we develop an attitude towards that class (mothers-in-law are interfering) based on a hasty generalization; then we apply that attitude to individual mothers-in-law without waiting to see whether or not they actually are interfering. The reasoning behind the stereotype can be set up as a syllogism: *All mothers-in-law are interfering; she is a mother-in-law; she is interfering.* This syllogism is unreliable because the major premise is not universally true.

To help us avoid this fallacy some students of language advise us to use index numbers after the class names to remind us that each member of a group has his own personal characteristics — that $German_1$ is not $German_2$ that $college professor_A$ is not $college professor_B$, that $freshman_{1967}$ is not $freshman_{1957}$. Whether we write these index numbers or merely think them, they are useful reminders not to assume that individuals with a common class name will be alike in all respects.

Inadequate Causal Relations. As superstitions illustrate, it is easy to find a cause, even for complex events, if we just pick a convenient item and call it the cause. Such a procedure, however, does not advance our understanding of the event. Two ways to oversimplify a causal relation are to accept a contributory cause as a sufficient cause and to accept another effect as the cause. An example of each type of oversimplification follows.

Examples	*Analysis*
I know my spelling is terrible. All the members of my family are poor spellers.	*Family environment may contribute to poor spelling, but it is not the sole cause. The student has oversimplified by failing to consider other causes, about which he could do something.*
I failed the course because the instructor had a prejudice against me.	*Even if we assume that the prejudice existed, it must be the effect of some cause. This reasoning mistakes a possible effect for a cause. A more probable reason is that the student's conduct caused both the alleged prejudice and the failure.*

The Either-Or Fallacy. In deciding on a course of action we often choose between alternatives. Sometimes there are only two alternatives, but if there are more than two, we oversimplify the choice by limiting it to two possibilities.

Example	*Analysis*
On the question whether the husband should be the boss in the household, there are only two alternatives: either the man will be the boss or the woman will. Any man who lets himself be dictated to by a woman is a sorry specimen and probably deserves what he will get. But most of us will not make that mistake. We will make it known at the start, gently but firmly, that we intend to be masters in our own homes. The sooner the little lady gets that idea through her head, the better for everybody.	*There are three possible positions to take on this question: the husband should be boss; the wife should be boss; nobody should be boss. This argument overlooks the third possibility; therefore it is not true that if the husband does not dominate, the wife will. Essentially the example oversimplifies the question by unnecessarily limiting the alternatives.*

Trivial Analogies. Although an analogy is always suspect when it is not supported by other kinds of reasoning, a carefully planned analogy is often persuasive. But, except possibly for hasty generalizations, there is no more common fallacy than the use of impromptu, ill-considered, and trivial analogies, based on a superficial resemblance between two events or conditions. Often these are mere clichés — *You can't teach an old dog new tricks.* In any controversy analogies come easily — usually too easily — to mind. It is wise not to accept them until they have been carefully examined to see if there is a significant difference between the things being compared.

Example	*Analysis*

A French Minister of Education is reported to have told a visitor that at that moment every fourth-grade pupil in all France was studying exactly the same lesson. In France the national government controls education. If we adopt the proposed federal aid to education bill, we will bring about federal control of our schools and get the same kind of regimentation that exists in France.

A student using this analogy should first satisfy himself that there are no essential differences in the governmental structures of the two countries. When he tries to do so he will discover that France does not have a federal form of government and that the educational control in France more nearly resembles our state control. That discovery would make the student question the worth of the analogy in a question primarily concerned with federal control. If he still wants to use the analogy he will at least feel an obligation to show in detail that, despite this difference, the two countries are analogous where education is concerned.

All these fallacies — *hasty generalizations, stereotypes, inadequate causal relations, either-or fallacies,* and *trivial analogies* — oversimplify the problem by allowing us to reach conclusions more easily and more quickly than is possible in disciplined deliberation.

▶ *The following arguments contain various types of fallacies. Evaluate each and explain clearly what is wrong with it. Do not be content with naming the fallacy. The skill you are trying to develop is not identification but analysis; it is more important to explain the errors than to name them.*

1. I don't know what the colleges are teaching nowadays. I have just had a letter of application from a young man who graduated from the state university last June. It was a wretched letter — badly written, with elementary errors in spelling, punctuation, and grammar. If that is the kind of product State is turning out, it does not deserve the tax support it is getting.

2. There are two kinds of rattlers, those whose bite is fatal, and those that cause swelling and discomfort but not death. That is why some people die from rattler bites and some don't. If we kept accurate records on snake bites we would find that people who recover were bitten by the non-fatal rattler; those who do not recover have been bitten by the fatal type.

3. It comes down to this: either NATO should require the European countries to finance and man the European part of the program or we should pull out of the organization.

4. We would not have all these strikes and riots and demonstrations if people would only practice the Golden Rule.

5. All right-thinking people will support the police chief's efforts to clean out the pornographic literature which is being openly sold to our young people. If there were an epidemic of typhoid, the health authorities would

359

be expected to do everything in their power to wipe it out. Pornography is worse than typhoid, since it corrupts the minds and morals of the young, not just their bodies. The city should take as vigorous action to wipe out this moral disease as it would take to wipe out the physical one.

6. In taking the position that men accused of crimes cannot be interrogated without their lawyers being present, the Supreme Court is showing more concern for the protection of the criminal than for the protection of society. The laws were made to protect law-abiding citizens, not those who defy the law. The truth is that a criminal loses his rights as a citizen when he commits a crime. It is the duty of the police to get at the truth, and they have a right to question him, as long as they don't use force in the process.

7. MR. A: With all the things that have to be taught in English, there is not much point in devoting a great deal of class time to questions of disputed usage. The distinction between *shall* and *will,* the use of *like* as a conjunction, saying *data is* for *data are* — these are not choices between educated and uneducated speech, since both forms are used by educated people. A teacher may prefer one form to the other. He may encourage his students to follow his preference. But he should not use valuable class time to teach over and over again a distinction which, whatever its historical justification, is no longer a fact of English usage. We have more important things to do.

MR. B: The difference between Mr. A. and myself is that I respect the purity of the English language, and he does not. If we permit *will* instead of *shall* and *data is* for *data are,* where do we draw the line? Mr. A. says that the incorrect forms become correct because educated people use them. I say that no one who says *data is* is an educated man. But Mr. A. is advocating the philosophy of "anything goes." Many of our troubles come from the adoption of that philosophy in various walks of life — in business, in government, in personal morality. It is a philosophy which reduces the conventions of educated speech to the level of gutter talk, and I think anyone who has any regard for the purity of his native tongue should stand up against the corruptive effects of this false philosophy.

8. College students, at least American college students, are different from all other people on this planet; they are the only people who try to get as little as possible for their money. They will spend the most valuable years of their lives and upwards of $10,000 in trying to derive as little as possible out of their college courses, provided only that they will receive their coveted diplomas at the end of four years of such effort.

9. If the University allows men to live in unsupervised houses and to keep whatever hours they please, it should extend the same privileges to coeds.

10. That's the kind of remark you'd expect from a college professor. They're all alike — a bunch of long-haired visionaries, none of whom ever met a payroll.

11. The old Biblical injunction, "By their fruits ye shall know them," is still a pretty good test. The Communists are interested in stirring up trouble wherever and whenever they can; so if you find strikes and riots and rowdy demonstrations, you can be pretty sure that there's a Communist somewhere in the background.

12. Careful research shows that the most successful men have the largest vocabularies. This proves that the development of an extensive vocabulary is a cause of success.

13. The professor says that two negatives do not make an affirmative in English, but the facts are against him. Any high school freshman could tell him that when you multiply minus *a* by minus *b*, the result is a plus or positive quantity. That is not just the freshman's opinion, or my opinion, or the opinion of educated people everywhere. It is a mathematical law. And it holds true whether it is written in English, Latin, Greek, or Hindustani.

14. In America the law is supposed to be the same for all men. The present draft law grants favored treatment to the rich and the educated. Therefore it is un-American.

15. The argument that football is a dangerous sport is disproved very simply by showing that the death rate — not total deaths, but deaths per thousand — among high school, college, and professional players combined is much less than the death rate of the total population.

16. In reviewing a play the critic wrote: "The plot of this play is fascinating in a strange way: you keep looking for something to happen, but nothing does. The characters never come close to greatness, and the few witty lines seem out of place among the platitudes of the dialogue." The advertisements read: "Fascinating plot — characters close to greatness — witty lines."

17. No, I have not read the bill. No, I have not thought about it. I don't need to. It is being supported by Congressman Blank, and there isn't a worse scoundrel in the country. When I see Blank in favor of something, I'm against it.

18. The reason that Japan produces so many good marathon runners is that the Japanese have fewer automobiles than we do. The Japanese learn to use their legs instead of riding around in cars. That's why they win.

19. More people die of cancer than ever before. That's what comes from living in cities and breathing polluted air. Fifty years ago there was much less cancer. The air was cleaner then.

20. Dad says that high schools today do not prepare boys adequately for college. When he graduated from high school all his classmates who were going on to college could get into any college in the country. Now most of the graduates of our high school have to settle for their second or third choices.

21. It is a waste of public funds to send a girl to a state university. All a girl wants from college is a husband. A good matrimonial agency would meet her needs at less cost to the taxpayers.

22. I don't think it's fair that teen-age drivers should have to pay an extra premium for car insurance. Most teen-agers I know drive better than their parents. On the other hand, women don't have to pay an extra premium, and everybody knows what women drivers are like!

23. A nation, like an individual, must live within its income. Either may justifiably go into debt for limited sums for limited periods, especially if the means of retiring the debt are provided for when the debt is contracted. But neither a nation nor an individual can stay solvent by following a policy of contracting a permanent debt, which cannot be repaid and is never intended to be repaid.

24. The fundamental problem in a democratic society is education. In a democracy the citizens are continually faced with alternatives. Whether they choose wisely or not will depend on how well educated they are. It is for this reason that each state must support public education generously. The better that support, the better the educational system, and the better the educational system, the wiser the citizens and thus the state.

25. I dined in a London restaurant last summer, and the filet of sole was nearly inedible. What's more, a friend of mine traveled on a British ocean liner, and she said the menus were boring — too much roast beef and potatoes. The English seem to have no talent for cooking.

PART FOUR

Handbook of
Grammar and Usage

A POINT OF VIEW TOWARD GRAMMAR

SENTENCE STRUCTURE

WORD ORDER

FORMS OF WORDS

PUNCTUATION

MECHANICS

GLOSSARY OF TERMS AND USAGE

A Point of View
Toward Grammar

English, like all languages, has developed a great many conventions popularly and generally known as "the rules of grammar." The nature of these rules is widely misunderstood, and because of this misunderstanding, the study of the conventions of educated usage is often less profitable than it might be. The first step toward using your native language with confidence is to acquire a sensible attitude toward these rules. We shall attempt to foster such an attitude by showing you what is meant when we talk about rules of grammar, how these rules have grown up and are still growing, and how you can use this knowledge to solve your own language problems. A point of view from which you can see particular questions of usage in perspective will help you to judge for yourself which usages are acceptable, and when.

THE EVOLUTION OF ENGLISH

The language that Americans speak and write is descended from the language spoken by the English, Scottish, and Irish immigrants who founded the British colonies in America. Their language, in turn, was descended from the dialects of Germanic tribes which, during the fifth and sixth centuries, invaded Britain and settled there. One of these tribes, the Angles, later became known as the Englisc (English) and thus gave their name to a country and a language, both of which they shared with other peoples — the Saxons, the Jutes, and, later, the Danes and the Normans.

These ethnic groups were the Founding Fathers of the English language, but other peoples too have made their contribution to its development. As England grew in political, economic, and cultural importance, the language borrowed from various sources the words it needed to name the things and ideas that Englishmen were acquiring. Today the vocabulary of the English language is international in origin, and to talk, as some people do, of "pure" English is to use a word as inappropriate as it is misleading.

The language which has come down to us through some fifteen centuries has undergone great changes. A modern college student would find the English of Chaucer something of a puzzle. And before Chaucer — well, judge for yourself. Here are the opening lines of the Lord's Prayer in the English of nearly a thousand years ago:

Fæder ūre,
þu þe eart on heofonum,
sī þīn nama gehālgod.
Tōbecume þīn rīce.
Gewurþe ðīn willa on eorðan swā swā on heofonum.

A contrast of this form of the Lord's Prayer with the modern version offers a brief but revealing impression of the changes that have occurred in the language during its development from an insignificant Germanic dialect to one of the most widely spoken languages the world has known. These changes were the product of evolution rather than of revolution. True, there were times when so many basic changes occurred so rapidly that they seem revolutionary in retrospect. But by and large, the language changed slowly as it reflected gradual shifts in the speech habits of those who spoke English.

This evolutionary process is still going on. Any one of us can notice hundreds of examples of it in our own experience. We can hear the older pronunciations of *penalize* (peenalize), *status* (staytus) and *detour* (detoor) being challenged by pronunciations which were at first labeled "uneducated" but which have gradually become more common, even in the speech of educated people. We can observe words acquiring new meanings. And we can watch grammatical distinctions which once were generally observed falling more and more into disuse as substitutes take over their work.

THE RULES OF GRAMMAR

Contrary to popular belief, the rules of grammar do not determine how the language should be spoken and written. Grammar is a science, and it follows the general scientific method of reporting not what *ought to be* but what *is*. Except for differences of subject matter, the rules of grammar are much like the laws of physics and chemistry: they are scientific generalizations about the facts. In grammar, as in physics, these generalizations must be verifiable. If the rule does not fit the facts, or if it ceases to fit them, it must be revised or discarded.

Ideally, the grammar of a language is a description of the speaking and writing habits of the people who use it. Since there are some 300,000,000 users of English, widely separated geographically, politically, economically, and socially, the task of drawing a picture of their common linguistic habits is not easy. The grammarian simplifies his task by confining himself to the basic patterns of speech intonation (pitch, pause, and stress), morphology (the forms of words), and syntax (the relations of words within a sentence). He collects samples, analyzes them, finds patterns in them, and generalizes the patterns into a system. By these means he describes the very elaborate set of signals by which English conveys grammatical meaning. But he is describing how the language works, not how he thinks it ought to work. The only "rules of grammar" he recognizes are those statements which most accurately describe the system.

What most people mean by "rules of grammar" are statements about preferred usage. In addition to studies of grammar, we have studies of how educated people speak and write English. Since the schools are committed to preparing their students to become members of the educated class, they have accepted the usage of educated people as their standard, and they do what they can to help students observe that standard in their speech and writing. For this reason teachers insist that, in spelling, punctuation, sentence structure, grammatical agreement, and diction, students follow the conventions of standard usage. Some of these conventions include grammatical details, but others are not part of grammar as it has been described above.

Decisions about usage are sometimes difficult for two reasons. First, in an ever-changing language, usage is not constant. Spellings, pronunciations, styles of punctuation, meanings, and grammatical constructions which were not recognized by one generation may be accepted by another, and there is likely to be a "usage gap" between what people think educated usage is and what it has in fact become. Second, many people have strong opinions about usage and approve or condemn certain uses no matter what the facts are. These two conditions make it difficult in particular constructions to get an authoritative description of usage which is acceptable to everyone. Fortunately, such constructions are relatively few. For the most part, the conventions of educated usage are clearly established and can be accurately described. If we want to call these descriptive statements "rules of grammar," we may do so, but it would be wise to remember in what sense we are using "rules" and "grammar."

The rules of grammar, then, are not "Thou-shalt-not's"; they say, "This is how it is done." They are explanations of conventions that have grown up between writers and readers. Learning to use one's language is learning to use these conventions. A writer who ignores them will find his work rejected or discredited. The penalty he pays for his ignorance is not just a failing grade in an English course. The real penalty is that he cuts himself off from economic, social, and intellectual opportunities that he will later value. The testimony of business and professional leaders on the importance of effective writing and speaking in an industrial society is almost unanimous.

ON BEING YOUR OWN AUTHORITY

Socially, a sophisticated person is one who is familiar with social conventions and observes them naturally and comfortably. Linguistically, a sophisticated person is one who observes language conventions naturally and comfortably. One aim of the composition course is to encourage the student to develop linguistic sophistication, to make him aware how things are done in English, and to help him do them habitually without having to stop and puzzle over them.

There are two reasons why this aim cannot be met by viewing grammar as a set of arbitrary rules which must be learned and practiced. First, this view distorts the relationship between purpose and technique. Just as the Sabbath was made for man, not man for the Sabbath, so the conventions of usage should serve, not be served by, the writer's purpose. A student whose main thought is to get his spelling, punctuation, and grammatical forms "correct" is in no condition to communicate. For him, writing will be a frustrating exercise, to be done only under compulsion and to be avoided whenever the compulsion is removed. This is why some students believe that all their linguistic worries will be over as soon as they "pass" the composition course.

Second, memorizing the conventions of usage is at best a poor substitute for working with them. All we know about learning tells us that memorized facts are soon forgotten unless they are clearly related to life goals and put to use outside the classroom. A student who conscientiously learns the rules of spelling or punctuation *in order to please or pacify his instructor* will soon forget them, and the progress that he and his instructor worked so hard to achieve will largely be lost. This is one reason why student writing so often deteriorates after completion of the composition course.

To accomplish the purpose of the course, at least with respect to the conventions of usage, a student must realize two things: he must recognize that following the conventions of language may help him communicate better and so make him a more powerful person; and he must understand that, while dictionaries and handbooks are helpful reference works, he must often make his own decisions about usage when these books are not available or are not decisive.

This second requirement may seem like a tall order, since, in effect, it asks the student to become his own authority on language. But there is no alternative. To use a language well, one must use it confidently. No one can speak or write with confidence if he continually depends on the crutch of a handbook. It is only a temporary aid, useful for those linguistic questions which cannot yet be answered from experience, but to be dispensed with as soon as possible.

How is this confidence to be won? In the long run, it is gained, as are so many things, by observation. That is how the grammarian learns grammar and how the editors of dictionaries learn the meanings of words — by observing how educated people use their language. An intelligent curiosity about language is therefore the first requirement for using it well. A student who has or develops that curiosity will seldom be seriously bothered by the "rules," because he has discovered them through his own observation of language practices.

The handbook that follows is a temporary substitute for your own experience. It presumes to tell you what the conventions are. If you know what they are, you do not need the advice. If you do not know, the advice will provide you with information to solve some of your immediate writing problems. It is assumed that your instructor will decide from your writing which conventions you need to study and will refer you to the section or sections dealing with them. It is hoped that you yourself will care enough about your own writing to make a special point of mastering, by observation as well as by handbook exercises, whatever conventions are now conspicuously ignored in your writing.

The material of the handbook is organized under six main headings, the first four of which are marked by an identifying letter: *sentence structure* **(S)**, *word order* **(WO)**, *forms of words* **(F)**, *punctuation* **(P)**, *mechanics* (spelling, capitalization, italics, etc.), and a *glossary* of grammatical terms and usage. Under each lettered heading, the numbered sections deal with specific parts of the subject. Thus, **S1–S3** review the basic grammar of sentences and so provide the apparatus for analyzing sentence structure; **S4–S7** deal with the distinction between sentences and non-sentences; **S8–S11** deal with inconsistencies in sentence patterns. If you have occasion to use the handbook, it might be wise to familiarize yourself with at least its over-all organization.

S ▶ Sentence Structure

S 1 *Sentence Elements*

The elements of English sentences can be considered from two points of view, their forms and their functions. Many words change in form as they change in use, and the study of these form changes is called *morphology.* The classes into which such words are placed may be called *form units.* These are five: nouns, pronouns, verbs, adjectives, and adverbs. The study of the functions of sentence elements is called *syntax,* and the elements may be called *function units.* These are: subjects, verbs, objects, complements, modifiers, connectives, and absolutes.

FORM UNITS

Of the traditional eight parts of speech, three — prepositions, conjunctions, interjections — have no inflected forms and are therefore not form units.

Nouns

Words such as *boy, girl, man, woman, child, dog, car, garage, house, flower, tree, kindness, faith,* and thousands of others belong to a class which usually has different forms for singular and plural and for the possessive case. These words are **nouns.** The great majority of English nouns form the plural by adding *-s* or *-es* to the singular. About five per cent are irregular and form their plurals in one of the following ways:

a. **-en Plurals** (*children, oxen*).

b. **Vowel-Changing Plurals** (*foot-feet, goose-geese, louse-lice, man-men, mouse-mice, tooth-teeth, woman-women*).

c. **Unchanged Plurals** (*deer, sheep, swine*).

All these irregular plurals are relics of Old English plural inflections which once were common but, during the evolution of the language, were generally superseded by the *-s* plural.

d. **Foreign Plurals** (*agenda, alumnae, bacilli, data, synopses*).

Words borrowed from foreign languages bring with them foreign methods of forming the plural. If these words pass into popular speech there is a strong tendency to ignore the foreign plurals and to treat them as English nouns. Until that change has become accepted, the foreign plural is used.

As used in sentences, nouns serve as subjects, objects, complements, modifiers, or objects of prepositions, as in the following examples:

That *man* was here again. (Noun as subject.)
Our *neighbors* bought a new *car.* (Nouns as subject and object.)
Her *uncle* is a *physicist.* (Nouns as subject and complement.)
His *mother's* health is bad. (Nouns used as modifiers usually have the possessive case form shown here. Otherwise, nouns are not inflected for case.)
At the *door,* behind the *desk,* on the *table,* for *dinner,* with *cream.* (In each phrase the first word is a preposition, the last a noun.)

Pronouns

Personal Pronouns. Words such as *he, she, we, them, you, it,* etc., belong to a class called **personal pronouns** and are inflected for gender, number, case, and person. The complete inflection of the personal pronouns follows.

NUMBER	CASE	1ST PERSON	2ND PERSON	3RD PERSON		
				mas.	*fem.*	*neut.*
Singular	*Subjective*	I	you	he	she	it
	Possessive	my (mine)	your(s)	his	her(s)	its
	Objective	me	you	him	her	it
Plural	*Subjective*	we	you	they	all	
	Possessive	our(s)	your(s)	their(s)	genders	
	Objective	us	you	them		

Case forms indicate the function of a pronoun in its clause, whether subject, modifier, or object. The forms for person indicate the person speaking (first), the person spoken to (second), and the person spoken about (third). The word "pronoun" means "for a noun," and pronouns can be substituted for nouns in a sentence. That is, they serve as subjects, objects, complements, modifiers, or objects of prepositions, thus:

He was here again. (Subject.)
I saw *him* yesterday. (Subject and object.)
Who put the dent in *your* fender? (Subject and modifier.)
The black hat is *mine.* (Complement.)
For *him,* to *me,* with *her,* behind *them.* (Objects of prepositions.)

Relative Pronouns. The pronouns *who, which, that, what,* with their compounds, *whoever, whosoever, whichever, whatever,* and *whatsoever,* are often used to relate a subordinate clause to its main clause. When so used, they are called **relative pronouns.** The only relative fully inflected for case is *who,* which has the forms: *who* (subjective), *whose* (possessive), *whom* (objective). This pronoun is not inflected for number or gender. The compounds *whoever* and *whosoever* have no distinct forms for the possessive, but become *whomever* and *whomsoever* respectively in the objective case — thus:

Whoever did this should be horsewhipped.
I'll take *whomever* I can get.
Whosoever believeth in me shall not perish.
To *whomsoever* it may concern.

Demonstrative Pronouns. When *this* and *that* are used as pointing words they are called **demonstrative pronouns.** When so used, they are inflected for number. Their plural forms are *these* and *those* respectively — thus:

This is mine; *these* are yours.
That was the seventeenth; *those* records were lost.

Reflexive Pronouns. In such sentences as *He corrected himself, You will hurt yourself, They are deceiving themselves,* we call *himself, yourself,* and *themselves* **reflexive pronouns** because the object refers to the same individual or group as the subject. Reflexive pronouns are inflected as follows:

	Singular	*Plural*
1st person	myself	ourselves
2nd person	yourself	yourselves
3rd person	himself, herself, itself	themselves

Verbs

Such words as *be, do, walked, told, have been, was, wrote, said, will try, shouting, scolded, to expect* belong to a class of words inflected to show number, person, voice mood, and tense. These words are **verbs.**

Principal Parts. All tenses are made from certain forms of the verb used either alone or in combination with other verbs. Thus, all tenses of the verb *to talk* are made from the forms: *talk, talking, talked* (I *talk,* I am *talking,* I do *talk,* I *talked,* I have *talked,* I have been *talking,* I will *talk,* etc.). Similarly, all tenses of the verb *to speak* are made from the forms: *speak, speaking, spoke, spoken.* These forms are called the **principal parts.**

The vast majority, known as **regular** verbs, are like *talk* and form both the past tense and the past participle by adding *-ed* or *-d* to the first principal part (*talk, talked, talked; blame, blamed, blamed*). Such verbs have two characteristics: the vowel remains unchanged in all principal parts; and the forms for the past tense and the past participle are identical.

Verbs which do not have both these characteristics are said to be **irregular.** The difference between regular and irregular verbs may be illustrated by contrasting the principal parts of *conquer* (regular) and *see* (irregular):

Present Tense	*Present Participle*	*Past Tense*	*Past Participle*
conquer	conquering	conquered	conquered
see	seeing	saw	seen

Tense. Although it is possible to recognize some thirty different tenses, not counting idioms which do the work of tenses, six tenses are considered basic. These are

Simple present: They object	*Present perfect:* They have objected
Simple past: They objected	*Past perfect:* They had objected
Simple future: They will object	*Future perfect:* They will have objected

Mood. Of the three moods of English verbs — the **indicative, imperative,** and **subjunctive** — the indicative is by far the most common. A verb is in the indicative mood unless:

1. It expresses a command or entreaty (*Sit down! Please listen to me!*), in which case it is in the imperative mood.

2. It is used in one of the following ways, in which case it is in the subjunctive mood:

    a. To express a condition contrary to fact (If I *were* you, I would go).

    b. To grant a concession (*Be* it as you say).

    c. To state an improbability (If this *were* the end of the matter, I'd be happy).

    d. To conduct certain parliamentary proceedings (I move that the committee *go* on record; it is moved and seconded that this measure *be* adopted).

The form used for the imperative mood is always the same as the first principal part. The subjunctive, once fully inflected, is so little used in modern English that we need consider only the forms for the simple present and past tenses of the verb *to be*. These are *be* for all persons in the singular and plural of the simple present and *were* for all persons in the singular and plural of the simple past.

Voice. English verbs have two voices: **active** and **passive.**

    Active. A girl *opened* the door.
    Passive. The door *was opened* by a girl.

When a verb is changed from active to passive, the object of the active verb becomes the subject of the passive verb. The passive voice is formed by adding the past participle to the appropriate tense form of the verb *to be* (The door *is opened, was opened, will be opened,* etc.).[1]

Adjectives and Adverbs

Adjectives and adverbs cannot always be distinguished by their form. Most adverbs end in *-ly*, but so do some adjectives (*silly, lively,* and *manly,* for example). Some adverbs (*clean, far, fast, straight,* etc.) do not have *-ly,* and some have two forms, one with and one without that ending (*late-lately,*

[1] For the use of the passive voice, see pages 156–157.

loud-loudly, slow-slowly, etc.). For these reasons, adjectives and adverbs are best recognized by their function in a sentence: adjectives modify nouns or pronouns; adverbs modify verbs, adjectives, or other adverbs.

When an adjective precedes the noun or pronoun it modifies (a *blue* gown), it is called an **attributive adjective.** When it both completes a verb and modifies its subject (The man is *lazy*), it is called a **predicate adjective.**

Adverbs, in addition to their chief function of modifying verbs, adjectives, and adverbs, are frequently used in the following ways:

1. As interrogative adverbs to introduce a question (*Where* were you? *When* did he go? *Why* did you say that?).

2. As sentence modifiers to modify a whole sentence rather than a single element (*Maybe* he is ill. *Incidentally,* that answer is wrong).

3. As conjunctive adverbs (or transitional connectives) to join two sentences and modify the second one (The men did not complain; they were, *however,* rather sullen for the rest of the evening. His wife was not hostile; *on the contrary,* she seemed most friendly).

Comparison. Modern English adjectives and adverbs have lost the inflectional endings they had in Old English except those which show **degree of comparison.** There are three such degrees: positive, comparative, and superlative.

There are three methods of indicating comparison in adjectives and adverbs: (1) by adding *-er* for the comparative and *-est* for the superlative; (2) by prefixing *more* for the comparative and *most* for the superlative; (3) by using different words for each degree:

Positive	Comparative	Superlative
(1) strong	stronger	strongest
(2) beautiful	more beautiful	most beautiful
(3) good	better	best

Of the three methods, the first two are considered regular. In general, words of one syllable take the *-er -est* endings, and words of more than two syllables use *more* and *most.* The usage in two-syllable words is divided, though words common in popular speech tend to retain *-er -est.*

The third method is called irregular comparison. Several words that are irregularly compared have the same form for adjective and adverb. Here are the most common irregular comparisons:

Positive	Comparative	Superlative
bad, ill	worse	worst
far	farther, further	farthest, furthest
good, well	better	best
little	less, lesser	least
much, many	more	most

FUNCTION UNITS

If we use the letters *S* (Subject), *V* (Verb), *O* (Object), *M* (Modifier), and *K* (Connective) to label the function units of the following sentence, we can readily see the nature of their relationships:

$$S \quad K \quad S \quad V \quad O \quad M$$
Dad and Mother liked Alice at once.

The words in this sentence are related chiefly through word order or position. We saw in Chapter 6 (page 142) that two of the basic patterns of English sentences are Subject-Verb (S-V) and Subject-Verb-Object (S-V-O). These patterns are so dominant in English sentences that even in meaningless sentences, such as *The X's elled,* and *The X's elled the Y's,* we want to interpret the first as a S-V and the second as a S-V-O pattern. This illustration suggests that the relative positions of the function units in a sentence largely define the subject-verb-object relations. The other units are defined by their positions with respect to the subjects, verbs, and objects.

Subject–Verb–Object

The S-V-O sentence pattern, a favorite in English, is called the **actor-action sequence.** In such a sentence the subject identifies the actor, the verb the action, and the object the recipient of the action. If all English sentences followed this sequence, we could define our chief function units by saying that the subject tells us who or what performed the action suggested by the verb, and the object tells us who or what was acted upon. But this method of explaining subject-verb relationships works only with actor-action sequences. It does not work in the following sentences, which also follow established English patterns.

1. *She* was accepted by Dad and Mother at once. (Passive)
2. Our English *instructor* is Mr. Wesley. (Subject-verb-complement)
3. *He* seems older. (Subject-verb-modifier)
4. There is a *hole* in my sock. (Expletive)

Because of such exceptions as these, the subject cannot be defined as the performer of the action, except in an actor-action sequence. It can better be defined in terms of word order or position, if the special order of the expletive pattern is kept in mind. It is still better not to define it at all, but to recognize it through experience. After all, this is how you recognize all language patterns.

It is traditional to use the term "verb" to name both a form and a function unit. It is a form unit by virtue of its various forms for tense, mood, number, etc. It is a function unit by virtue of its relation to subjects, objects, and complements. Confusion between the form and function of verbs often leads students to mistake infinitives, participles, and gerunds for finite verbs. If you have this trouble, see *Verbs and Verbals,* page 383.

Verbs are usually classified as **transitive, intransitive,** or **linking.** A **transitive verb** is followed by an object, which completes the predicate:

> She *asked* an embarrassing *question.*
> He *wants sympathy.*
> I *wrote* a *letter.*

An **intransitive verb** is not followed by an object but makes a complete predicate by itself:

> The girls *have left.*
> Tomorrow our vacation *begins.*

A **linking verb** connects the subject to a complement, a noun or an adjective:

> Smith *is* a sophomore.
> They *were* ill.
> He *felt* sick.
> The audience *became* restless.

The most common linking verb is the verb *to be.*

The objects we have considered so far are called **direct objects.** In the actor-action sequence they designate the receiver of the action. In sentences such as

> I gave *him* the book.
> We asked the *teacher* a difficult question.

the italicized words are called **indirect objects.**

▶ *Identify subjects, verbs, direct and indirect objects in the following sentences.*

1. Somebody took my hat.
2. I called, but nobody answered.
3. The girls are giving a party; we have been invited.
4. The family bought Dad a new radio.
5. Nothing has been done. The material has not arrived.
6. Give the boy another chance. He deserves it.
7. Try this one. It may fit you better.
8. We have not received your application; it may come in today's mail.
9. The test contained five questions. I finished early and gave the instructor my paper.

Complements. Verbs such as *be, become, get, feel, look, seem, smell, taste,* and others often serve as "linking verbs" — that is, they link a completing construction to the subject, as in *Bill is a junior.* The unit that follows and completes a linking verb is called its **complement.** When the complement is a noun it looks exactly like a direct object. For example, in

He consulted a doctor.
He became a doctor.

we call the first "doctor" an object and the second a complement. The only formal difference between them is that the first follows a transitive verb, and the second follows a linking verb.

In some sentences, the complement of a linking verb is an adjective:

We felt sleepy.   She seems happy.
He looked sick.   This tastes good.

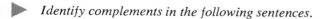 *Identify complements in the following sentences.*

1. These nails look rusty. Throw them away.
2. Your watch is slow. You will be late.
3. That girl is Ted Norton's daughter.
4. This is my raincoat; that one is yours.
5. His story was a strange one, but it sounded true.
6. The child remains stubborn. Perhaps he is scared.
7. The man they want must have a college degree and some practical experience in industry.

Modifiers

In general, a **modifier** describes a subject, object, complement, or another modifier, or tells how, where, when, why, or under what conditions the action of a verb took place. The italicized modifiers in the following sentences illustrate these uses:

We took a *second* look. (Modifies object.)
Old soldiers never die. (Modifies subject.)
Honesty is the *best* policy. (Modifies complement.)
It was a *most* unlikely story. (Modifies the modifier *unlikely*.)
He arrived *later*. (Modifies the verb — tells when.)
He arrived *at the party*. (Modifies the verb — tells where.)
He went *for my sake*. (Modifies the verb — tells why.)
I will go, *if you pay my way*. (Modifies the verb — tells under what conditions.)
I will go, *even if I'm not invited*. (Modifies the verb — tells despite what conditions.)

The word being modified is called the **headword.** If the headword is a noun, the modifier consists of one or more adjectives preceding the noun, as in our first three examples, or of a phrase following the noun, as in *A man from the office called you,* or of a subordinate clause following the noun, as in *A man who works in your office called you.* If the headword is a verb, the modifier may be a single adverb, a phrase, or a subordinate clause, and may come either before or after the verb. For example, the italicized clauses in the last two items of the list above could be placed at

377

the beginning of the sentence. If the headword is another modifier, the new modifier is usually an adverb preceding the headword, as in the fourth item on our list.

▶ *Identify the modifiers in the following sentences.*

1. My bicycle is a black one with white trim.
2. It was an oppressively hot day.
3. There is something strangely familiar about his face.
4. She lives in the brick house at the end of the block.
5. The new car was damaged beyond repair.
6. Go sit under that tree while I change the tire.
7. I'll go if you will wait till I get back.
8. Worried by his failure to write, his mother telephoned him.
9. Unless we get there by noon we won't have time for shopping.
10. Having studied the map at the last gas station, I knew we were on the wrong road.

Connectives

Connectives join other units in a sentence and usually come between these units. The three most common types are **coordinating, subordinating,** and **transitional** connectives.

A **coordinating connective** joins two similar, or coordinate, elements:

Tom *and* I will go. (Connects two subjects.)
Bill grumbled *and* sulked for days. (Connects two verbs.)
He fought cleverly *and* courageously. (Connects two modifiers.)
I'll do it *but* I won't like it. (Connects two main clauses.)
Either Bert *or* I will do it. (*Either — or* connects two subjects.)
We have *neither* the money *nor* the time. (Connects two objects.)
You pretend to be her friend, *yet* you gossip about her. (Connects two main clauses.)

A **subordinating connective** does two things: it joins two clauses and subordinates one to the other. If we take two main clauses

He is cross. He is tired.

and join them with *because* — *He is cross because he is tired* — we not only connect the two clauses but we subordinate the second to the first. In this example *because* is a subordinating connective. In the following examples the subordinate clauses are in parentheses and the connectives in italics:

I don't know (*why* he did it).
He did not say (*when* he would return).
I won't do it (*if* you seriously object).
You may go (*whenever* you please).

In these examples the subordinating connective comes between the clauses it joins. But a subordinate clause may precede the main one, and the connective may come at the beginning of the sentence:

(*If* you seriously object), I won't do it.
(*Because* I flatter him), he likes me.
(*Since* you are in a hurry), I won't bother you about it.

Relative pronouns (page 371) also serve as subordinating connectives.

The man (*who* was here) left his phone number.
I can't find the book (*that* you want).

A **transitional connective** joins two main clauses or relates two sentences by providing a transition between them. See "Transitional Markers," pages 125–126.

▶ *In the following sentences, identify coordinating and subordinating connectives.*

1. Smile when you say that.
2. I have no idea what he wants.
3. When the right time comes, I will tell you.
4. I would do it if I could, but I cannot.
5. His only faults are that he has neither looks nor money.
6. She has had nothing to eat or drink since she came home.
7. Although he is taller, he weighs less.
8. While I want to be pleasant and agreeable, I cannot do what you ask.
9. Neither Helen nor Jean has the book you want.
10. Although he brings me nothing but trouble, I must do what I can for him.

Prepositions as Connectives. Such words as *after, around, at, behind, beside, for, in, into, of, on, to, with* are called **prepositions** when they precede a noun or pronoun and show its relation to some other word in the sentence, usually a verb, adjective, or noun:

He is good *at* tennis. (Relates the noun *tennis* to the adjective *good.*)
They live *in* Detroit. (Relates the noun *Detroit* to the verb *live.*)
I am the head *of* the house. (Relates the nouns *head* and *house.*)

Absolutes

Occasionally a unit in a sentence has no specific grammatical relationship to any other unit, yet clearly belongs. We call it an **absolute construction.**

Consider the following sentences:

Nonsense, it is all a hoax!
Good heavens, is it that late?
Mr. Hughes, may I talk to you for a moment?

No, I won't do it!

She said — *as if I cared* — that she was through with me.

The italicized expressions serve useful purposes, but they are not grammatically related to other sentence elements. They are absolute constructions.

SUMMARY OF SENTENCE ELEMENTS

Sentences can be studied in terms of two kinds of units: *form* units, which show inflectional changes in a word, and *function* units, which show how words are related in a sentence, chiefly through word order.

Form Units

Nouns. The largest class of words in English. These words are inflected for number and possessive case. The prevalent pattern for forming plurals is the addition of *-s* or *-es* to the singular, but some nouns, like *children, mice, sheep,* and foreign plurals (*bacteria, vertebrae, alumni, parentheses*) are irregular. Chief uses: subjects, objects, complements, modifiers (in possessive case), and objects of prepositions.

Pronouns. A class of words inflected for number, case, person, and gender. Personal pronouns are the most highly inflected class in English. Other pronouns (relative, demonstrative, reflexive) show only partial inflection. Chief uses: the same as nouns.

Verbs. A class of words inflected chiefly for tense, but also for number, person, mood, and voice. Verbs are the key words in sentences. They form the predicate, with or without object or complement.

Adjectives, Adverbs. Two classes of words inflected to show comparative and superlative degree. Chief uses: adjectives modify nouns; adverbs modify verbs, adjectives, and other adverbs.

Function Units

Subjects. The starting point in the subject-verb-object relationship. In the actor-action sequence, the subject identifies the performer of the action, but its relationship with the verb is predominantly one of position or word order. Any construction which can fill the subject position may act as the subject of a sentence, but most subjects are nouns or pronouns.

Verbs. Three classes: transitive (with object), intransitive (without object), linking (with complement). Verbs are both form and function units. As function units they should not be confused with verbals (infinitives, participles, gerunds).

Objects. Used to complete the predicate when the verb is transitive. Two types: direct and indirect. Complements perform a similar function by completing linking verbs.

Modifiers. Single words, phrases, or clauses which make the meaning of a headword more specific by describing or limiting it. Single-word modifiers are adjectives or adverbs and usually precede their headword. Phrase or clause modifiers usually follow their headwords, but the position of modifiers of verbs is quite variable.

Connectives. Three types: coordinating, subordinating, transitional. Coordinating connectives, also called *conjunctions,* join similar functions — two subjects, two verbs, two modifiers, etc. Subordinating connectives join subordinate clauses to main clauses; transitional connectives tie sentences together by providing a transition between them.

Prepositions, which relate nouns or pronouns to other words, also serve a kind of connecting function, although they are not usually classified as connectives.

Absolutes. Any unit which does not serve as subject, verb, object, complement, connective, preposition, or modifier in a sentence. It may at times be a loose modifier of the whole sentence, but it is usually grammatically independent of any specific sentence element.

Review Exercise

Using the symbols, *S*–Subject, *V*–Verb, *O*–Object, *C*–Complement, *M*–Modifier, *K*–Connective, and *A*–Absolute, identify the underlined elements in the following sentences. For your convenience, subordinate clauses have been placed in parentheses. Occasionally an element and its modifier have been underlined as a single element.

1. The woman offered no explanation.
2. Henry, you are impossible!
3. Bill's father will retire next year.
4. My parents are moving tomorrow.
5. Mother wore a blue skirt and a white blouse.
6. She is irritable (when she is tired).
7. (When she feels well) she is a pleasant person.
8. He likes to wrestle and he wrestles well.
9. The governor was re-elected by a narrow margin.
10. The defeated candidate resumed his law practice.
11. Because of the wind, the mountain climbers abandoned the attempt.
12. He will try to speak (whenever he gets a chance).
13. Everyone hopes (that the worst is past).
14. The answer to that question is unknown.
15. The doctor will see you now, Mr. Brown.

S 2   *Phrases and Clauses*

a. A phrase is a group of two or more words acting as a single function unit in a sentence but not having a subject and verb of its own.

In the following sentences the phrases are italicized.

She stood *by the door.* (Phrase modifies verb.)
He *has been calling* you. (Phrase is verb.)
Hunting big game is expensive. (Phrase is subject.)
A page *near the end* is missing. (Phrase modifies subject.)
Her brother is *a medical student.* (Phrase is complement of verb.)
My dear woman, I never said that! (Phrase is absolute.)

b. A subordinate clause is a group of words acting as subject, object, complement, or modifier, but having a subject and verb of its own.

In the following sentences the subordinate clauses are italicized.

Whoever did that is foolish. (Clause is subject of verb *is.*)
You may ask *whatever you want.* (Clause is object of verb *may ask.*)
The people *who lived there* have moved. (Clause modifies subject.)
I will go *wherever you send me.* (Clause modifies verb.)
This is the book *that I want.* (Clause modifies complement.)

In each of these sentences the subordinate clause is introduced by a subordinating connective. This connective may sometimes be omitted without changing the subordinate nature of the clause:

This is the book *I want.*
The plumber *you sent for* is here.

c. A main clause has a subject and verb but does not act as a subject, complement, or modifier.

It may be a complete sentence in itself; it may be part of a compound sentence; or it may be an absolute in a larger sentence.

I cut the lawn. (Main clause in a simple sentence.)
I cut the lawn, and *Joe raked it.* (Two main clauses forming a compound sentence.)
He said — *wasn't it mean of him?* — that I was an irresponsible adolescent. (Italicized main clause is an absolute in a complex sentence.)

▶ *Distinguish between main and subordinate clauses in the following sentences by underlining main clauses once and subordinate clauses twice.*

1. I will do whatever you say.
2. What he said is nobody's business.
3. The book that I bought cost a dollar.
4. The dress I bought is too tight.

5. If that is how you feel, you go your way and I'll go mine.
6. The man who is wearing the plaid shirt is his brother-in-law.
7. We don't want your advice; we just ask to be left alone.
8. Get a good night's sleep. This is the best preparation I know for the examination.
9. He said that he was terribly embarrassed. If I had been he, I would have been sick.
10. He said there was nothing he could do.

Review Exercise

In the following passages certain constructions have been underlined and numbered. Copy the numbers and opposite each write *Main Clause, Subordinate Clause,* or *Phrase,* whichever is appropriate.

A (1) It was a bright sunny day (2) when we left Columbus (3) in a tightly packed car (4) for Sparrow Lake, Canada. (5) Along the way (6) we stopped at Niagara Falls (7) to see one of nature's beautiful creations, and then (8) continued to drive (9) what seemed to be an endless distance. (10) At last (11) we arrived in Orillia, Canada, (12) bought a few necessary supplies, and (13) drove down a typical washboard road (14) till we arrived (15) at our destination.

B The relationship (1) between a writer and a reader may be illustrated (2) by an analogy with dancing. Anybody (3) who has danced knows (4) that both partners move (5) in accordance with patterns (6) which both understand and take for granted. The man, (7) by his leading, indicates which pattern (8) he wishes to set; (9) the girl follows. (10) If the man leads his partner (11) to expect one kind of movement and then switches to another, (12) the girl will have difficulty following.

(13) The relationship between the writer and reader is similar. Each assumes (14) that the other is familiar with the basic patterns of sentence structure. The reader, (15) like the girl in the dance, must follow the writer's lead, and (16) as long as the writer follows an accepted pattern (17) the reader has no trouble. But (18) if the writer sets one pattern in the first half of a sentence and (19) then shifts to another, (20) the reader is likely to be confused.

S 3   Verbs and Verbals

Much trouble with verbs comes from failing to distinguish verbs from verbals. A **verbal** is derived from a verb but does not act as a verb in a sentence. For example, in the sentences

> *Wrestling* IS a body-building sport.
> *To wait* IS not easy.
> He SPOKE in *threatening* terms.

the verbs are in small capital letters. The words *wrestling, to wait,* and *threatening* may look like verbs but they do not act as verbs. *Wrestling* and *To wait* are the subjects of their sentences; *threatening* modifies *terms.* These words are verbals, not verbs.

Verbals are of three types: **infinitives, participles,** and **gerunds.**

a. Such verbals as *to do, to choose, to be seeking, to have said,* and *to have been invited* are called infinitives.

Usually, but not always, they have the infinitive marker *to.* They often serve as subjects (*To do* that is not easy; *to be excused* from class is a rare treat) or as complements (They asked *to go;* we expected *to be called*), but they occasionally act as modifiers (I bought it *to read;* we have no time *to spare*).

▶ *Identify the infinitives in the following sentences.*

1. Nobody wants to tell him.
2. He is said to have refused an offer to settle out of court.
3. I'd like to do good work and have fun, too.
4. We tried to call them and explain the difficulty.
5. To play as well as he does takes more time than I can afford to give.
6. You should be able to analyze and evaluate the information and reach sound conclusions from it.
7. She seems to be looking for an excuse to pick a quarrel with him.
8. He is said to have done the same thing in several states and to be wanted by the police in Texas.
9. Not to have invited her would have caused trouble.
10. He is thought to be willing to sell at a low price in order to settle the estate quickly.

b. A participle is a word or phrase which is derived from a verb but acts as a modifier.

The present participle ends in *-ing* (*crying, smiling, sulking*). The past participle most frequently ends in *-ed* (*disgusted, excused, inspired*), but many are irregular (*chosen, grown, kept, slung*). The following sentences illustrate forms and uses of participles.

His *fighting* days are over. (Present participle modifies subject.)
He is a *fighting* fool. (Present participle modifies complement.)
Having fought all challengers, he retired. (Past participle modifies subject *he.*)
Goldsmith wrote a poem about a *deserted* village. (Past participle modifies the object of *about.*)
Having been deserted by her husband, she supported the family. (Passive form of past participle modifies subject *she.*)

▶ *Identify the participles in the following sentences.*

1. She is a clinging vine.
2. A broken watch is of little use.
3. The metal is now near the breaking point.
4. This is a thrilling story.
5. Thrilled by the movie, we stayed up too late.
6. A drunken man is usually a bore.
7. Disappointed by the results, he gave up the experiment.
8. With screeching brakes the car came to a jarring stop.
9. They have forgotten that they called him the forgotten man.
10. The play having been called back, it was now third down and seven.

c. Gerunds, or verbal nouns, have the same form as the present participle but are used as subjects and objects in a sentence, not as modifiers.

The only difference between a gerund and a present participle is one of function.

Thinking is hard work. (Gerund is subject of verb *is.*)
That will take some *thinking.* (Gerund is object of verb *will take.*)
Looking innocent won't help you. (Gerund is subject of *won't help.*)
She can't stop *crying.* (Gerund is object of *can't stop.*)

▶ *Distinguish between the participles and gerunds in the following sentences by identifying each verbal and explaining its function in the sentence.*

1. Bacon said that reading makes a wise man.
2. During the semester his reading speed increased significantly.
3. This course requires too much reading.
4. They were looking for an abandoned mine.
5. Abandoned by her allies, Czechoslovakia was forced to yield.
6. Tired by the long hike, we took a nap before dinner.
7. Looking for trouble is the quickest way to find it.
8. Becoming angry will not help; try smiling for a change.

Review Exercise

Distinguish between verbs and verbals in the following sentences by underlining verbs once and verbals twice.

1. Swimming is fun. I would like to swim well. I was swimming yesterday. My brother has been swimming since he was four.
2. They say that a rolling stone gathers no moss; they could just as truthfully say that a stone that is rolling isn't gathering anything but momentum.
3. It is easier to win a letter in college than to receive a Phi Beta Kappa key. That is a point worth remembering when we are tempted to make fun of serious students.

385

4. The statement that a watched kettle never boils is not true. Water in a kettle boils just as quickly watched or unwatched. But you are more conscious of time when you are watching the kettle and therefore the time seems to be longer.

5. I am tired of having to be told what I may and may not do. My parents seem to have forgotten how they resented too much supervision when they were my age.

6. Discouraged by his grades, he was thinking of quitting school. But the dean persuaded him to revise his habits of studying and finish the semester before making a decision.

7. Leave him alone! Let him do it his own way. He has to learn some day to discover his own mistakes and correct them, and he might as well make a beginning now.

8. Having tried everything to get good grades without studying, we reluctantly decided to give that method a try.

9. Weakened by hunger and exposure, the old couple were in serious condition.

10. He said nothing would interfere with his ambitions, but he has found that it is easier to profess ambitions than to achieve them.

S 4   *Fragmentary Sentence and Period Fault*

Use complete sentences, not sentence fragments. Avoid especially separating a subordinate clause or a phrase from its main clause by the use of a period.

Sentence Fragment	*Explanation*	*Full Sentence*
He is always complaining about his grades. *Although he does nothing to improve them.*	*The italicized clause is a modifying clause, not an independent statement.*	He is always complaining about his grades, although he does nothing to improve them.
The Tigers made two runs in the ninth. *Thus tying* the score.	Tying *is not a verb, but a present participle modifying the main clause.*	The Tigers made two runs in the ninth, thus tying the score.
It was difficult to decide which choice to make. *To return* to school or *to accept* the job.	*The italicized infinitives modify* choice; *therefore they do not act as verbs.*	It was difficult to decide whether to return to school or to accept the job.
It was a wonderful week. *Fishing* and *swimming* every day and *dancing* every night.	*The italicized words are gerunds. They are changed to verbs at the right.*	. . . We fished and swam every day and danced every night.

386

The use of a period between a main clause and a subordinate clause or phrase is called a **period fault.** As the revisions above indicate, period faults may be corrected either by changing the faulty period to a comma, thus incorporating the separated phrase or subordinate clause within the sentence to which it belongs, or by expanding the fragment into a main clause so that it can stand as an independent sentence.

In dialogue and in informal writing which imitates conversation, fragmentary sentences are more common than they are in exposition. The fragment may simply be an exclamation: *Oh! Nonsense! Wonderful! Good Heavens!* It may serve as a question: *Cigarette? Lemon or sugar? Anything else?* It may be a phrase or clause uttered in response to a question: *Maybe. Not at all. If you wish. Whenever it is convenient.* Or it may be a stereotyped expression, such as: *The more, the merrier. First come, first served. Like father, like son. Easy come, easy go.* When it is used in these ways, the fragmentary sentence is sometimes called a **minor sentence.**

In general, college writing does not lend itself to the use of minor sentences, though they may be used when they are appropriate to the context. If your instructor has referred you to this section of the handbook, it is because he feels that your sentence fragments are not justified by the context of your essay.

▶ *In the following sentences correct the period faults.*

1. He refused to answer the question. Despite the fact that he knew his silence would be interpreted as guilt.

2. The author of such books or magazine articles writes to appeal to the general public. Not just to a few.

3. The judge said that the court was not inclined to show mercy. This being the third time the defendant had been convicted of that offense.

4. I refused the job. Although I could have used the money.

5. I think I would do as I did then. Conditions remaining the same.

6. The same procedure is used in the running of wind sprints as was used in the long runs. Twenty minutes of exercises. Two warm-up turns around a quarter-mile track. Followed by several fast sprints of 220 yards.

7. The technique of the Communists was to publicize every act of oppression and intolerance and at the same time to assure minority groups that the Communists were concerned about their plight. Thus exaggerating the failures of Democracy and implying that Communism was a philosophy of brotherly love.

8. He died alone and in poverty. Deserted by those who had once sung his praise and borrowed his money.

9. This has been one of those days that we all have once in a while. When, no matter how careful we are, everything seems to go wrong.

10. He said that all this talk about security puzzled him. That he knew no way of guaranteeing that his investments would turn out as he had planned them. Or even of being sure that he would live to know how they did turn out.

11. After filling out the necessary papers and making a deposit. I was assigned to my room.

12. This spring my father had to make a very difficult decision. Whether to sell his business and move to California. Or to remain here where all his friends are. He finally decided to go to California. Which pleases me very much.

13. Two of the most unforgettable characters in my life are my parents. Unforgettable not only because of our common bond but also because of the striking differences in their personalities.

14. You should take into consideration whether such a marriage would force John into a type of work he dislikes. Instead of giving him the opportunity to look around for the kind of work he really likes.

15. The possible solution to the problem of juvenile delinquency could be more and better recreational facilities. Facilities that would fill the spare time of the teen-ager and keep him occupied.

S 5 *Fused Sentences*

Do not fuse two sentences by omitting necessary punctuation.

Fused Sentences	*Separated Sentences*
I knocked on the door when the lady came I gave her my most ingratiating smile.	I knocked on the door. When the lady came I gave her my most ingratiating smile.
Why should I apologize when he insulted me he did not apologize.	Why should I apologize? When he insulted me he did not apologize.
It is difficult to believe that he said that what could he have been thinking of?	It is difficult to believe that he said that. What could he have been thinking of?
Why do you ask what concern is it of yours?	Why do you ask? What concern is it of yours?

► *Separate the following fused sentences.*

1. I will not object on the other hand don't expect me to contribute.

2. It could have been anyone I know of no way of finding out who did it.

3. The first couple of years will be difficult after that much of the work will be routine.

4. The northern pike is the gamest fish in these waters pound for pound he will outfight a walleye every time.

5. The sheriff's office is not willing to carry out the ruling of the court even though the evictions are legal they are afraid of public sympathy with the tenants.

6. Because of its involved forms for case and gender German is a difficult language for most students it is the most difficult language in college.

7. I wrote to Mother when she answered I knew that the story had been exaggerated since then I have learned that the newspaper printed a retraction.

8. Informative lectures bore me when information is available in books I would rather read it than listen to it.

9. In situations such as this one there is no way of reaching a compromise unless both sides are willing to make concessions the dispute will become a stalemate.

10. At Roosevelt's death Truman succeeded to the Presidency without any real executive experience, without previous training, and without a unified party to direct him, he was called on to fill the most exacting job in the world.

S 6 *Run-on Sentence*

Avoid the excessive use of "and" and "so" to string together a number of main clauses.

Sentences so formed are called **run-on sentences.** The best way to remove the run-on effect is to subordinate part of the material to the rest.

Run-on Sentence	*Revision*
I did not know how Mother would feel about my accepting the invitation, *so* I called her on the phone *and* she said it was all right, *so* I accepted.	Because I did not know how Mother would feel about the invitation, I called her on the phone. When she said it was all right, I accepted.

Remove the run-on effect in the following examples.

1. The game went into extra innings and we had to go home and get dressed or we would be late for the party, so we had to leave at the end of the ninth.

2. I was standing by the window and looking into the street and two cars suddenly crashed together. So I ran down the stairs and joined the crowd that was beginning to collect.

3. He said that thousands of draftees could not pass the army physical tests and were rejected and that most of their deficiencies could have been cured by proper medical attention and that this proved that the health of the nation was bad and something should be done about it.

4. Final examinations are not a good way to find out what a student knows about his courses and they cause students to stay up most of the night before an exam and drink too much coffee and smoke too many cigarettes, and this causes eyestrain and headaches, so it is not good for their health, so I would think that somebody around this university could think up a better system.

5. I believe the most valuable quality a woman can have is the ability to be a good cook. Meals are a very important part of everyday life, and a man's whole day may depend on the kind of breakfast he has and the way it

is served. So every girl should be taught to cook a good meal and serve it attractively and her chances of making a successful marriage will be increased.

S 7   *Comma Splice*

Do not confuse the structure of a sentence by the misuse of a comma where an end mark of punctuation ought to be.

The use of a comma instead of a period or a semicolon between two main clauses not joined by a connective is called a **comma splice.** Since a reader assumes, rightly, that a comma is an internal mark of punctuation, a comma splice will suggest to him that the sentence is not finished. He will therefore read through the comma and may become confused by the unclear structure of the sentence — for example:

> He has never before been suspected of theft, *to the best of my knowledge,* he has been employed by his present firm since he graduated from high school.

To which main clause does the italicized modifier belong? Which statement is the writer qualifying: that the man has never before been suspected of theft, or that he has always worked for the same company? The reader is free to guess, but he will get no help from the sentence. This comma splice brings about a real failure of communication, the worst kind of sentence error.

Because the comma splice sometimes causes this kind of confusion, many teachers strongly condemn all comma splices, even though some cause no real break in communication, and even though comma splices are not rare in the writings of some competent professional writers. It would better accord with the facts to say that, at its best, the comma splice is unconventional and, at its worst, it makes communication impossible. The sometimes indiscriminate condemnation of comma splices by college instructors is a result of painful experience with the latter type.

Comma splices may be corrected by one of three methods.

1. The simplest way is to change the faulty comma to a period or a semicolon, whichever is more appropriate:

Comma Splice	*Revision*
His chances of election are not good, because the independents do not like him, it would be safer to nominate another candidate.	His chances of election are not good, because the independents do not like him. It would be safer to nominate another candidate.
This is the best book I have ever read, it kept me up all night.	This is the best book I have ever read; it kept me up all night.

2. A second method of revision is to provide a coordinating connective between the two main clauses, thus making the comma conventional punctuation:

Comma Splice	*Revision*
She says she does not like football, I doubt that she has seen two games in her whole life.	She says that she does not like football, but I doubt that she has seen two games in her whole life.
It will cost a great deal of money, there is no guarantee that the plan will succeed.	It will cost a great deal of money, and there is no guarantee that the plan will succeed.

3. The third method is to subordinate one main clause to the other:

Comma Splice	*Revision*
He is discouraged about flunking, I think he will quit school.	He is so discouraged about flunking that I think he will quit school.

When two main clauses are joined by a transitional connective — *consequently, however, moreover, nevertheless, therefore* — the conventional punctuation between them is a semicolon, though a period is not unusual:

I admit that he is honest and conscientious; nevertheless, I will not vote for him.

When two short main clauses are felt to be closely related, informal usage sometimes prefers a comma to a semicolon:

I passed, Mary doubled.
The women like him, the men don't.

▶ *Using whatever method seems best, revise the comma splices in the following sentences.*

1. The two days preceding the Spring Carnival are filled with much excitement, all the houses and organizations try to create interest in their floats.
2. There is still plenty of opportunity in this country, if a young man really cares about building a career, his chances of success are as good today as ever.
3. There are two wires sticking out from two small holes in the center of the dash, they have to be crossed to turn on the ignition.
4. The school had an attendance of 1500 students, this number included night school enrollment.
5. Do you believe that children should never be spanked, or do you believe that moderate spanking helps them to develop self-discipline, this is a question on which many parents disagree.

6. The difficulties are great, but not insuperable, although the answer is not in sight, it can be obtained by patient and persistent work.

7. There are too many students for each teacher, no one receives any direct help or attention.

8. In all three of these bills there is free choice of doctors, dentists, and hospitals, the only requirement is that they must be participants in the plan.

9. I remember how I used to spend hours living in a dream world as I sat in my room and followed the adventures of men who had superhuman powers, some of them stopped bullets which bounced off their bodies, others jumped over buildings and flew through space under their own power.

10. Their vocabularies seem to be made up of twenty-letter words, their sense of humor, if they have one, is very dry.

11. I had to fight temptations which led me away from my music, much to my dismay, the temptations quite often won.

12. The wages are low and the work is monotonous, moreover, the job offers little chance of promotion.

S 8 *Faulty Parallelism*

Keep the elements in a parallel construction parallel in grammatical form.

Faulty Parallelism	*Explanation*	*Acceptable Structures*
Few people understood the full extent of his disappointment or *how angry* he really was.	*Compound object of* understood. *The first object is a phrase, the second a subordinate clause. The two should be in parallel form.*	Few people understood the full extent of his disappointment or *the degree of his anger.*
Because he has always been wealthy *and with indulgent parents,* he has never been forced to accept responsibility.	*Compound modifier consists of a subordinate clause and a phrase. Should be two clauses or two phrases.*	Because he has always been wealthy and *has been protected by indulgent parents,* . . . (or) Because of *his wealth* and *his indulgent parents,* . . .

Sentence elements arranged in a series should have the same form: a phrase should be followed by a phrase, a clause by a clause, a noun by a noun, and a verb by a verb. The following sentence contains a series which enumerates the powers of a commission:

The Commission has the power *to investigate, to conciliate, to hold* hear-ings, *to subpoena* witnesses, *to issue* cease-and-desist commands, *to order* rein-statement of a discharged employee, and *to direct* the hiring of a qualified applicant.

Notice that, grammatically, most of the sentence is a series of infinitive phrases, each identifying one of the powers of the commission and therefore modifying the noun *power*. Since each element in the series has the same modifying function, it is given the same infinitive form. It would have been possible to use a form other than the infinitive, as long as the same form was used throughout — (The Commission has the power *of investigating, of conciliating, of holding,* etc.). What is not acceptable is to mix forms. Notice how the following student sentence shifts from nouns to verbs and thus disrupts the parallel structure which the series demands.

The Commission has the power of investigation, conciliation, holding hear-ings, subpoena witnesses, issue cease-and-desist commands, order the re-instatement of a discharged employee, and direct the hiring of a qualified applicant.

▶ *Rewrite the following sentences to revise faulty parallelism.*

1. Many of our laws are descended from old Roman laws, but being changed to fit our modern needs.
2. A decision must be made as to whether the acres of grass surrounding the university buildings are more important from a standpoint of land-scaping or to be converted into practical parking lots open to all personnel, staff, and students.
3. For a settlement I will accept either twelve new blinds or having the old ones perfectly repaired.
4. She is inclined to be giggly and always embarrassing her escort.
5. My two ambitions are to have my own business, thus being my own boss, and having enough money to provide my children with a good home and education.
6. There is no happy ending such as occurs in most novels, but rather how people that sin usually do not have a happy life as they grow older.
7. These discoveries may have been thought of back in the seventeenth century and being used now.
8. Speak softly and you should carry a big stick.
9. He was encouraged to go on by the hopes of his parents, because his teachers advised him to continue, and for the sake of his own future.
10. His chief weaknesses are that he expects too much, being unwilling to put forth the necessary effort, and not accepting criticism.
11. Uncle John taught me such things as honesty, faith in God, to be considerate, and making progress but never at the expense of others.
12. My requirements for an ideal wife are honesty, intelligence, pleasant-ness, being able to cook and do housework, and to have confidence in me.

S 9 *Dangling Modifiers*

Avoid introductory modifying phrases which are left dangling because they have been given nothing to modify in the main clause.

Dangling Modifier	Explanation	Revised Version
Walking downtown, a streetcar jumped the tracks.	*In the absence of anything else to modify,* walking *seems to modify* streetcar. *The revised version contains a subject which the participle can logically modify.*	Walking downtown, I saw a streetcar jump the tracks.
Impressed by the newspaper stories, war seemed inevitable.	*Who was impressed? The opening phrase needs something to modify. The revised version gets rid of this difficulty by making* we *the subject of the main clause.*	Impressed by the newspaper stories, we felt that war was inevitable.

Errors such as these are the result of making a shift in the subject of the main clause while the sentence is being written. Presumably the writer meant to make *I* the subject of the main clause in the first sentence and *we* the subject in the second, but he inadvertently switched subjects to *streetcar* and *war,* and thus left the modifiers dangling. The best way to correct the error is to revise the main clause so that it has a subject which can be modified by the introductory phrase, as shown in the revised versions. Another way is to recast the opening phrase as a subordinate clause:

When I was walking downtown, a streetcar jumped the tracks.
Because we were impressed by the newspaper stories we felt that war was inevitable. (This revision combines both methods suggested above.)

Sometimes a dangling modifier begins with an **elliptical clause** — a subordinate clause, some elements of which are not expressed. The simplest revision of a dangling elliptical clause is to supply the necessary elements and complete the clause.

Dangling Modifier	Revised Version
When only five years old, my mother died.	When I was only five years old, my mother died.
While still of preschool age, my father began daily batting practice with me.	While I was still of preschool age, my father began daily batting practice with me.
Although working full time on an outside job, my grades remained good.	Although I was working full time on an outside job, my grades remained good.

As all these examples suggest, the most troublesome dangling modifiers are those beginning with an introductory verbal phrase or an elliptical clause. A dangling modifier at the end of a sentence is more likely to be awkward or unemphatic than ambiguous.

Dangling Modifier	*Explanation*	*Revised Version*
He took a full program of studies during each summer session, *thus graduating in three years.*	*The main idea in this sentence is that the student graduated in three years. The revision expresses that idea as a main clause at the end of the sentence and thus gives it greater emphasis.*	By taking a full program of studies during each summer session he was able to graduate in three years.

Improve the following sentences by revising the dangling modifiers.

1. Upon hearing a sharp click the suds subsided and the dial on the top of the washing machine read "drain."
2. Working in a drugstore, several professors chat with me every day.
3. After signing for all your classes, the next place to go is the finance office.
4. When in high school, classes were dull and monotonous.
5. When placing these men under arrest, comic books were usually found in their possession.
6. By getting your purpose clearly in mind at the beginning, the actual writing will be easier.
7. Without expecting a reply, a letter was written to the President.
8. Being very tired, the walk home took much too long.
9. By improving the English Department a student would not only be prepared for college English but for any subject.
10. After rushing to get to the station on time the information clerk said that the train would be more than an hour late.
11. Completely unaware that the landing gear had been damaged and that a crash landing at the end of the flight was inevitable, the plane, with its carefree passengers, sailed confidently through the night.
12. The car failed to observe the curve sign, thus losing control and going over the embankment.
13. Oddly enough, school was no more a drudgery, resulting in better grades.
14. I believe that, by delaying marriage until after your college graduation, the chances of happiness are much better.

S 10   *Shifts in Subjects and Verbs*

Unintentionally shifting a sentence from one pattern to another results in awkward, inconsistent structures. Such inconsistencies may arise from awkward shifts in the form of the subject or verb.

a. Avoid unnecessary shifts of subject within a sentence or paragraph, especially shifts between personal and impersonal pronoun subjects.

In the examples below, the grammatical subjects are italicized.

Shifted Subjects	Explanation	Revised Version
When *one* gets through with a three-hour examination *you* are exhausted.	*The subject shifts from the impersonal pronoun* one *to the second personal pronoun* you. *A shift from* one *to* he *is conventional but the shift to* you *is not. Any of the three revisions at the right would be an improvement.*	When *one* gets through . . . *one* is exhausted. When one gets through . . . *he* is exhausted. When *you* get through . . . *you* are exhausted.
The *worries* about entrance examinations leave the minds of the students before *they* leave for the campus. The last *days* are spent shopping for clothes during the day and gallivanting with friends at night. Their *families* receive little attention, and entrance *examinations* are no longer thought of.	*Although these three sentences all deal with the same logical subject (the students' activities before leaving for college), the paragraph has five grammatical subjects. This unnecessary shifting of the subject weakens the unity of the paragraph. The revision at the right reduces the subjects to two forms: the noun* students *and the pronoun* they.	During the last week before leaving for campus, *students* spend their days shopping for clothes and their nights attending farewell parties with their friends. *They* have little time to spend with their families and no longer worry about entrance examinations.
I did not like to refuse his invitation, but a *person* can't spend all their time going to shows.	*Although the writer is the logical subject of both clauses, the grammatical subject shifts from* I *to* person, *and the pronoun* their *shifts in the second clause from singular to plural. The author would have been wiser to use the first personal pronoun throughout.*	*I* did not like to refuse his invitation, but *I* can't spend all my time going to shows.

b. Avoid unnecessary shifts in the forms of the verbs. Keep the tenses consistent and especially avoid shifting from active to passive voice.

In the following examples the verb forms are in italics.

Shifted Verb Forms	*Explanation*	*Consistent Verb Forms*
The older girls *had* a coke party to get us acquainted and it *was* deeply *appreciated* by me.	*The shift from active voice in the first clause to passive in the second is unnecessary and awkward. The revision subordinates the second clause and keeps both verbs in the active voice.*	I *appreciated* the coke party which the older girls *gave* to get us acquainted.
As centuries *passed*, the dress patterns *become* more and more complicated.	*The tense changes from past to present. Since the changes in dress were taking place while the centuries were passing, the verbs in both clauses should be in the same tense.*	As centuries *passed*, the dress patterns *became* more and more complicated.
He *said* he *will call* for me at eight.	*The author is confusing the tenses for direct and indirect discourse. Either form at the right will serve.*	He *said* he *would call* for me at eight. He *said*, "I will call for you at eight."

▶ *Revise the following student sentences to remove the awkward shifts in subjects or verbs.*

1. It often makes one shudder at the sights you see.
2. You know it's really very odd how a person can have so many different feelings about something they plan to do.
3. I have experienced the strange sensation of losing one's wallet. When something like this happens you do not know what to do.
4. Upon completion of my program I'm informed that all the sections I wanted have been closed.
5. I was told to hurry over to Civil Engineering Hall or I may not get what I wanted.
6. My high school days taught me the value of learning to get along with others. As you worked with others you learned to accept responsibilities and to be a good follower. We were supposed to learn to be both followers and leaders.
7. There I was with a stack of papers, cards, envelopes, a time table, and a catalog, and he wants me to stop and sign my name.
8. I asked Dad if I may borrow the car for the evening.
9. They had known hardship at first hand, for the dangers and misery of war had been experienced by them.
10. To do the author justice, a good job of exposing the foolishness of the English aristocracy was done in several instances in the book.
11. Faith means to have complete confidence in someone, even if they are under suspicion.
12. He said that we would be late anyway, so let's go ahead and not worry.

13. We talked over the problem thoroughly for an hour, but no decision was reached.

14. One way of judging the maturity of a person is to find out how well they are able to govern themselves.

15. I have been making these medallions since I was a junior in high school and I found it a satisfying hobby.

16. In choosing a mate for the rest of one's life certain qualities are searched for according to your individual preferences and standards of what a wife should be.

17. There are a great many socially timid students on the campus. The University tries to help them. They are urged to join a group with similar interests. With the variety of possibilities offered, success is inevitable. An adjustment of this kind is every bit as important as academic success.

18. After paying my tuition and having my picture taken, an invitation to subscribe to the *Daily* was extended to me.

19. After an hour we came up with what my roommate called the perfect program. It looked awfully difficult to me, but if she said it was good what can a new freshman do but accept it?

20. To me dependability means simply what the word itself says — being able to depend on a person, whether it be simply to remember to pick up a loaf of bread at the grocery store, or whether it is depending on them to provide a home and love for your children.

S 11   *Incomplete Constructions*

Do not omit words necessary to the structure of a sentence.

Careless omissions often occur in making a clean copy of a paper, since copying is a mechanical task which takes little attention to meaning. For this reason, the final copy should be carefully reread before it is turned in.

Other omissions are the result of confusion about the structure of a sentence. The constructions most likely to be incompletely written are illustrated below.

Incomplete	*Explanation*	*Complete*
We searched through all our pockets, but no money.	*Incomplete main clause. The conjunction* but *requires a main clause to balance the sentence. The verb* found *cannot be omitted.*	We searched through all our pockets, but *found* no money.
I don't like the crowd which he associates.	*Omitted preposition. With a choice of two forms of the subordinate clause —* with which he associates *or* he associates with — *the writer has failed to supply* with *in either position.*	I don't like the crowd *with* which he associates. (or) I don't like the crowd he associates *with*.

Incomplete	*Explanation*	*Complete*
Statistics show that college men like their studies better than women.	*Omitted verb resulting in a possible ambiguity. What is being compared is not* studies *and* women, *but* men *and* women. *To avoid ambiguous comparison, the clause having* women *as the subject must be given a verb.*	Statistics show that college men like their studies better than women do.
Their hope is the child has wandered off with some older companions who will take care of him.	*Omitted subordinating connective. While such connectives may often be omitted without causing difficulty, an omission which allows the subject of the subordinate clause to be misread as the complement or object of the verb in the main clause should be avoided.*	Their hope is *that* the child has wandered off with some older companions who will take care of him.
Today is as hot, if not hotter, than any day this summer.	*Confused comparison. This construction confuses two idioms* — as hot as *and* hotter than. *Since these idioms take different prepositions,* than *will not serve for both. Possibly the best way to express this comparison is to avoid this construction entirely by using one of the substitutes shown at the right.*	Today is one of the hottest days of the summer. Today is at least as hot as any day we have had this summer. Today may be the hottest day of the summer.

▶ *Revise the following sentences to complete the incomplete constructions.*

1. He is as old, if not older, than I.
2. He understands German better than his brother.
3. She is as proud of the choir as the students.
4. I advertised my car in the papers, but no response.
5. I have and always will say that he is innocent.
6. The state he wants to live in his old age is California.
7. The trouble was the fuel pipe was clogged.
8. He was patient and tolerant of the children's bickering.
9. It made her mother from a girl to an old woman in twelve short years.
10. Nowadays glasses often add rather than detract from a girl's looks.
11. He is as good, if not better, than any guard in the conference.
12. Having eaten and my schedule again altered, I finished registration.
13. She would rather live in a large city than the country.
14. When at a party a man should show respect and attention to his wife.
15. Azaleas are easier to grow in the South than the Midwest.

WO ▶ Word Order

WO 1 *Normal Order and Accepted Inversions*

Normal Order

The normal order of words in English sentences may be summarized as follows:

1. Except in questions and expletive-type sentences (*There is a ray of hope*), the standard order of the main function units is subject-verb-object or complement.

2. Single adjectives precede, and adjective phrases follow, their head-words (*a trusted* man *of the people*).

3. Adverbs usually follow verbs, but may come elsewhere. Adverbs modifying adjectives or other adverbs precede the headword (He is *very* old. They dance *remarkably* well).

4. Main clauses usually precede subordinate clauses, but the following exceptions are common:

    a. Adjective clauses follow their headwords immediately (The man *who did it* should be punished).

    b. Adverbial clauses, especially conditional clauses, often precede the main clause (*If you do that,* you'll be sorry).

    c. Noun clauses acting as subjects or objects occupy the subject or object position (*That he will accept* is taken for granted. He says *that you are afraid*).

5. Closely related elements are kept as close together as possible. Thus a preposition immediately precedes the object and its modifiers (the top *of the highest mountain*); modifiers remain close to their headwords; and subject-verb, verb-object, and pronoun-antecedent combinations are not separated unless the special needs of the sentence require. In short, the order of the elements in a sentence should reveal their relationship.

Accepted Inversions

Any inversion of normal word order tends to attract attention and to emphasize the inverted expression. If this emphasis is desirable and if the departure from normal order is not outlandish or unidiomatic, a writer may gain interesting variety in sentence structure by moderate use of inversion. The commonest inversions for emphasis are as follows:

a. If it does not create misinterpretation or awkwardness, an element may be transposed from its normal order for emphasis.

Normal Order	*Emphatic Inversion*
The skies cleared *slowly*.	*Slowly* the skies cleared.
No leaf stirred *in all the forest*.	*In all the forest* no leaf stirred.
He threw *out* the runner.	He threw the runner *out*.
That is a good country *from* which to come.	That is a good country to come *from*.
There is no excuse *for him*.	*For him* there is no excuse.

b. For stylistic reasons, a normal sentence may be inverted into a periodic sentence.

Normal	*Periodic*
Think only this of me *if I should die*.	*If I should die*, think only this of me.
I broke the window *in order to unlock the car door*.	*In order to unlock the car door*, I broke the window.

For a more detailed discussion of the periodic sentence see page 148.

c. If no vagueness or awkwardness results, related elements, which normally would not be separated, may be interrupted by absolute or modifying constructions.

Interruption	*Explanation*
These, *I am told*, were his last words.	*Absolute between subject and verb.*
Their conduct *in this situation* was heroic.	*Modifying phrase between subject and verb.*
Related elements, *which normally would not be separated*, may be interrupted.	*Nonrestrictive modifying clause between subject and verb. This particular interruption is normal order.*
He answered, *with obvious annoyance*, that the story was false.	*Modifying phrase between verb and complement.*
Don't *under any conditions* make such a promise.	*Modifying phrase between parts of a verb.*

WO 2 *Ambiguous Order*

Be sure that the relationship between modifying words, phrases, or clauses and the elements they modify is clear.

If a modifier is so placed that it could modify either of two elements, its reference will be ambiguous. If the ambiguity is complete, the reader will be unable to tell which meaning was intended. More frequently he will be able to make the correct interpretation but will be conscious of the writer's ineptitude.

Ambiguous Order	*Explanation*	*Revised Order*
They talked about going on a second honeymoon *frequently,* but they never did.	Frequently *is closer to* going *than to* talked *and could modify either. It thus looks both ways, or "squints." Placing it immediately before or after* talked *removes the ambiguity.*	They talked *frequently* about going on a second honeymoon, but they never did.
The car is in the garage *which he smashed.*	*Since conventional order places adjective clauses after the nouns they modify, a reader is tempted to take* garage *as the antecedent of* which. *Putting the modifying clause immediately after* car *removes this possibility.*	The car *which he smashed* is in the garage.
There is a lecture tonight about juvenile delinquency *in the student lounge.*	*The italicized phrase was intended to modify the main clause but its position suggests that it locates the scene of the delinquency rather than of the lecture.*	Tonight there is a lecture *in the student lounge* about juvenile delinquency.

▶ *Remove possible ambiguities in the following sentences by changing the position of faulty modifiers.*

1. Fortunately, the fire was put out before any serious damage was done by the volunteer firemen.
2. A car came down the street decked with ribbons.
3. I listened while he talked attentively.
4. Everyone stared at the girl who was dancing with the dean in the low-cut gown.
5. There was a noisy disturbance when the speaker said that at the back of the hall.
6. Humphrey Bogart played the part of the man who was corrupted by gold superbly.
7. He looked at the boy with sad eyes.
8. My roommate brought me the book from the library that I wanted.
9. At one time his neighbors said he had been in jail.
10. No one would treat his father like that unless he was irresponsible.

WO 3 *Awkward Separation of Elements*

Related elements in a sentence may be separated (see page 401), but there should usually be no unnecessary separation of subject and verb, verb and object or complement, modifier and its headword, or preposition and its object.

Unnecessary separation of such closely related elements distorts the sentence pattern and interferes with ease of reading.

Awkward Separation	Explanation	Revised Order
My *father*, after considering what the trip would cost and how long it would take, *refused* to go.	*Awkward separation of subject and verb. The unnecessary interruption of the main clause by a phrase and two subordinate clauses distorts the structure of the main clause.*	After considering what the trip would cost and how long it would take, my father refused to go.
The evidence *shows*, if you examine it carefully and impartially, *that the best baseball is played in the National League.*	*Awkward separation of verb and its object. The reader has to leap over the if-clause to find the object of* shows.	A careful and impartial examination of the evidence shows that the best baseball is played in the National League.
He gave the *sweater* to his girl *that he had won in track*.	*Awkward separation of noun and its modifying clause. This kind of separation resembles the ambiguous modifiers discussed on page 402.*	He gave the sweater that he had won in track to his girl. (or) He gave his girl the sweater that he had won in track.
We *have* since then *had* no more trouble.	*Awkward separation of two parts of verb by modifying phrase.*	Since then, we have had no more trouble.
I am neither in support *of* nor opposed to *the bill.*	*Awkward separation of preposition* of *and its object. The revision at the right is the best way of expressing the idea.*	I neither support nor oppose the bill.

The **split infinitive** often provokes criticism in college writing. An infinitive phrase is "split" when an adverb separates its parts (*to* almost *laugh, to have* never *tried*). In some sentences (I decided *to* almost *quit*) the split infinitive gives a wrong emphasis and is awkward. In others (The prosecution failed *to* completely *demolish* the alibi), the intervening modifier gives a more precise emphasis or is more idiomatic than if the position of the modifier were changed. Although neither the facts of usage nor the judgment of grammarians justifies blanket condemnation of split infinitives, the safest practice for a college student is to place the modifier before or after the infinitive, whichever position gives the emphasis he wishes. For example:

Split Infinitive	*Revision*
He tried *to* quickly *retreat*.	Quickly he tried *to retreat*.
	(or)
	He tried *to retreat* quickly.

▶ *Revise the following sentences to eliminate any unnecessary separation.*

1. Her father, even, admits that she is extravagant.
2. Dad promised that he would in plenty of time get the tickets.
3. I was until yesterday of that opinion.
4. Herself more than others she will hurt by her conduct.
5. He is reported to recently have denied the story.
6. He had no desire to or expectation of getting married.
7. Every one of my instructors, I am firmly of the opinion, acts as though his course was the only one I am taking.
8. Although some kinds of extracurricular activities are overrated for some students, those are often socially valuable that give a shy girl experience in working with both men and women.
9. I was so surprised that I forgot what I intended to say to her when she smiled.
10. He said while he did not object to our going that he would like to stay home.

WO 4 *Unemphatic Order*

Since the emphasis on any sentence element often depends on its position, a writer must be careful not to give too much or too little emphasis by placing an element in a wrong position. The following precautions should help you to avoid the most frequent faults of emphasis in student writing. See also the discussion of *Emphasis* on pages 155–159.

a. Do not place minor ideas at the ends of sentences.

The most emphatic position in an English sentence is the end; the next most emphatic position is the beginning; the least emphatic is the middle. Unimportant ideas coming at the end of a sentence will be made unduly conspicuous by their position, and the sentence will seem to run down hill.

Notice the contrast in effectiveness in the following sentences.

Unemphatic Order	*Emphatic Order*
Last night someone stole our car while we were in the theater.	Last night, while we were in the theater, someone stole our car.
She is innocent in my opinion.	In my opinion she is innocent.
Nothing can be done, however.	Nothing, however, can be done.
He is going to propose, I think.	I think he is going to propose.

b. Do not weaken the force of an important concluding statement by reducing it to a participial phrase.

Many a good sentence ends with a participial phrase, but to use such a phrase for an idea which is important enough to deserve a main clause often creates a lame ending. For example, in

He fell from the roof, *thus breaking his neck.*

the italicized phrase is at least as important as the main clause, yet it is grammatically subordinate and trails off weakly. The idea in the phrase is important enough to come at the end of the sentence, but it deserves the dignity of a stronger grammatical form:

He fell from the roof and *broke his neck.*

c. Do not place a conjunctive adverb at the beginning of a sentence unless you deliberately wish to emphasize it.

Conjunctive adverbs — *however, moreover, nevertheless, therefore,* etc. — serve in a double capacity. As conjunctions they connect; as adverbs they modify. But they are relatively weak modifiers referring to the whole sentence rather than any element of it, and consistently placing them at the start of the sentence may give them too much emphasis. If they deserve emphasis, as the third example below may do, they may be used to start the sentence; but they are usually better near, not at, the beginning.

I am willing to advise you. I will not, *however,* accept responsibility for what you do.

He thinks she deceived him deliberately; he is *therefore* in no mood for a reconciliation.

We have repeatedly tried to make friends with them and have been consistently repulsed; *nevertheless,* I shall try again.

d. Do not misrepresent meaning by putting a modifier in the wrong position.

Since a modifier usually seems to refer to the nearest referent, be careful that the position of modifiers gives the meaning you want to convey. The following sentence can mean quite different things depending on the position of the adverb.

They *secretly* intend to be married.   They intend to be married *secretly*.

In the first sentence the position of the modifier emphasizes the intention; in the second, it emphasizes the nature of the ceremony. Either meaning is possible, but the one expressed depends on the position of the modifier.

The following contrasts also show how much the position of a modifier can affect meaning.

John *just* made it.	*Just* John made it.
Mary knows *only* the date.	*Only* Mary knows the date.
Until today they promised to stay.	They promised to stay *until today*.

e. Do not overuse inverted word order as a short cut to a "literary" style.

Inexperienced but ambitious writers sometimes try to create a literary style by using a great many self-conscious inversions. While unusual word order is arresting, strained or distorted inversion that does little but call attention to itself is more a vice than a virtue. Inverted order is exceptional order. It should be used deliberately and with restraint.

Affected	*Natural*
Pleasant were those days.	Those were pleasant days.
Little cared I what my parents said.	I cared little what my parents said.
Learn he must to appreciate his own deficiencies.	He must learn to appreciate his own deficiencies.

▶ *Revise the following sentences to avoid misplaced emphasis.*

1. The chairman said that the committee would continue in session until all business had been dispensed with, if there was no objection.

2. He scored through center after two unsuccessful plunges, thus tying the game.

3. I would have liked to take her to a movie but I did not even have a dollar; moreover, my only decent suit was at the cleaners'.

4. I almost read the whole novel last night. I could have finished it had I started an hour earlier, I believe.

5. Time for my assignments I never seem to find, thus being always behind.

6. Neither of the candidates intends to speak here, as far as I know.

7. He said that I could come over and listen to his records tonight, if I had time.

8. She graduated in three years with highest honors from the University.

F ▶ Forms of Words

F 1 *Wrong Principal Part*

a. Use the accepted principal part.

The use of the wrong principal part (*blowed* for *blew* or *seen* for *saw*) is often an advertisement of nonstandard speech habits. As we pointed out on page 372, the great majority of English verbs form the past tense and past participle by adding *-ed* to the first principal part. All exceptions are specifically listed in a good dictionary (see page 191). If you are uncertain about the accepted principal parts of a particular verb, consult your dictionary.

b. Distinguish between the forms for the past tense and the past participle.

In verb phrases the past participle, not the past tense form, should follow an auxiliary verb (is *done,* has *been*). Except when the verb is acting as an auxiliary (*had* gone, *was* crying), its past tense form is not used in combination with another verb.

Confusion of Forms	*Conventional Forms*
It is *broke*.	It is *broken*.
These tires are *wore* out.	These tires are *worn* out.
He has *began* all over again.	He has *begun* all over again.
The river is *froze* solid.	The river is *frozen* solid.
Everybody has *went* home.	Everybody has *gone* home.
Have you *wrote* to him?	Have you *written* to him?

F 2 *Tense Forms*

a. Avoid illogical sequence of tenses.

1. Keep the tenses of main clauses consistent.

Do not shift needlessly from present to past or from historical present to simple past.

Inconsistent	*Explanation*	*Consistent*
She laughed, and I asked her what she knew about him. She *laughs* again, this time much louder.	*In the first sentence all verbs are in the past tense; but in the second sentence* laughs *is present. There is no reason for the shift.*	She laughed, and I asked her what she knew about him. She *laughed* again, this time much louder.
For five rounds the young challenger danced and ducked and jabbed and piled up points. Then the champion found an opening – and Bam! The fight *is* over.	*All the verbs except the last are in the past tense. The last sentence shifts to historical present tense. Either that tense or the simple past should have been used throughout.*	For five rounds the young challenger danced and ducked and jabbed and piled up points. Then the champion found an opening – and Bam! The fight *was* over.

2. Keep the tense of a subordinate clause in logical sequence with that of the main clause.

Illogical Sequence	*Explanation*	*Logical Sequence*
They *have made* so much money last year that they bought a second store.	*The present perfect* (have made) *suggests a more recent action than the simple past* (bought); *it is illogical to use the present perfect for the earlier action.*	They *made* so much money last year that they *have bought* a second store.
Before I was introduced to her I *heard* rumors of her unsavory reputation.	*Since the rumors came before the introduction, the past perfect tense should be used in the main clause.*	Before I was introduced to her I *had heard* rumors of her unsavory reputation.

b. In converting direct discourse to indirect discourse observe the conventional change in tense.

Direct discourse reports the actual words of the speaker, and quoted verbs should be in the tense the speaker used. When direct discourse is converted to indirect discourse, the tenses of the original quotation are, whenever possible, pushed one stage further into the past. Thus an original present tense form becomes past and an original past becomes past perfect. Since there is no tense more past than past perfect, an original verb in that tense does not change.

Direct Discourse	*Explanation*	*Indirect Discourse*
He said, "I *want* to read that novel."	*Change simple present to simple past.*	He said that he *wanted* to read that novel.

Direct Discourse	Explanation	Indirect Discourse
He said, "I *wanted* to read that novel yesterday."	*Change simple past to past perfect.*	He said that he *had wanted* to read that novel yesterday.
He said, "I *had wanted* to read that novel until I *saw* the movie."	*Leave the verbs as they are. There is no way to make* had wanted *more past than it is, and to change* saw *to* had seen *would destroy the sequence of tenses.*	He said that he *had wanted* to read that novel until he *saw* the movie.

The following examples contrast faulty and accepted conversion from direct to indirect discourse.

Direct Discourse	Faulty Conversion	Accepted Conversion
I said, "He *is* a good financial risk."	I said he *is* a good financial risk.	I said he *was* a good financial risk.
I asked, *"Have* you *consulted* your physician?"	I asked if he *consulted* his physician.	I asked if he *had consulted* his physician.

c. Observe the conventional tense relationships between verbs and verbals.

The tense of a verbal is not determined by the tense of the verb in the main clause. Regardless of the tense of the verb, a present participle is used to express an action occurring at the same time as that of the verb. A perfect participle expresses time before that of the verb. A present infinitive indicates the same time or a time later than that of the verb. A perfect infinitive suggests time before that of the verb.

Rounding the last turn he *was* ahead by two yards.	The present participle (*rounding*) and the past tense verb refer to simultaneous actions.
Having finished housecleaning she *washed* her hair.	The perfect participle (*having finished*) refers to an action before that of the verb (*washed*).
I *tried to telephone* you.	The verb (*tried*) and the present infinitive (*to telephone*) refer to actions occurring at the same time.
I *expect to hear* from him tomorrow.	The expectation is now; the hearing has yet to occur. Therefore the present infinitive refers to a time later than that of the verb.
They *are reported to have adopted* a child.	The perfect infinitive points to a time before the reporting.

Unconventional Sequence	Explanation	Conventional Sequence
Asking the blessing, we began to eat.	*Since the blessing was asked before the eating began, the perfect participle is required.*	*Having asked* the blessing, we began to eat.
Having faced the spectators, the referee signaled a holding penalty.	*Since both actions took place at the same time, the present participle is required.*	*Facing* the spectators, the referee signaled a holding penalty.
We meant to *have told* you earlier.	*The perfect infinitive suggests that the telling occurred before the intention. The present infinitive is the required form.*	We meant *to tell* you earlier.
I am sorry *to overlook* that fact.	*Since the overlooking occurred before the regret, the perfect infinitive should be used.*	I am sorry *to have overlooked* that fact.

▶ *Revise the following sentences to correct any illogical or unconventional sequence of tenses.*

1. There is little chance of promotion in that job unless you had a college degree.
2. While the outlook wasn't hopeless, it is discouraging.
3. We wanted to have reported the robbery earlier, but we thought we had better wait until we are sure.
4. Before I arrived they had a serious quarrel.
5. I asked if she has seen him recently.
6. She answered, "I had not seen him for more than a year."
7. We wondered what they are thinking now.
8. Finishing the job, he put away his tools.
9. For years now they had been good friends but they disagree more and more frequently.
10. He asked if I consider him a good teacher.
11. I said that I thought he is better than average.
12. Meeting Bill's wife, I have asked her when he would be home.
13. She said that he had been coming next Saturday.
14. I intended to have ignored the gossip, but I could not.
15. They sat up all night studying, having hoped to get at least a B on the final examination.
16. I would have liked to have seen that movie.

F 3   *Case*

Case is a system of inflection to show the relation of nouns and pronouns to other words in the sentence. English has three cases: **subjective** (or nominative), **possessive** (or genitive), and **objective** (or accusative). In general, a word is in the subjective case when it acts as a subject, in the objective case when it acts as an object, and in the possessive case when it modifies a noun (*his* bicycle, the *boy's* dog).

English nouns, pronouns, and adjectives were once fully inflected to show case, but word order and idiomatic constructions have largely replaced case endings in modern English. Adjectives are no longer inflected; nouns are inflected only in the possessive case (the *boy's* cap); only pronouns (and chiefly the personal pronouns) still make any considerable use of case forms. The study of case in modern English, therefore, is pretty much restricted to the case of pronouns.

a. The case of a pronoun is determined by its function in its own clause.

If a pronoun is the subject of its clause, it takes the subjective case; if it is an object, it takes the objective case; if it is a modifier, it takes the possessive case. There are two modifications of this practice: (1) a pronoun subject of an infinitive takes the objective case (I want *him to see* it); and (2) the complement of the verb *to be* takes the subjective case in formal usage (It was not *I* who said that).

The general convention stated above may be broken down as follows:

Pronouns take the subjective case when:
   1. They are subjects of verbs (*I think* that *he missed*).
   2. They are in apposition with subjects (Three men — Fred, Roy, and *I* — were elected delegates).
   3. They are complements of the verb *to be* (I am sure it *was he*).

Pronouns take the objective case when:
   1. They are objects of verbs (Mother *likes her*).
   2. They are objects of prepositions (They pointed *at me*).
   3. They are in apposition with objects (They gave *us* — Dave and *me* — the money).
   4. They are subjects or objects (or complements) of infinitives (I want *her to go*. We didn't expect *to see him*. Wouldn't you like *to be me?*).

Pronouns take the possessive case when:
   1. They modify a noun or a pronoun (Those are *my* six *children;* this is *his one*).
   2. They precede and modify a gerund (What's wrong with *his swimming? His winning* was a surprise).

b. Most errors in case occur in a few constructions.

In general, errors in case occur for two reasons: (1) because the construction is such that the student does not readily see the function of a pronoun; and (2) because the case which is inappropriate in writing is so often used in speech that the colloquial form seems more natural than the more formal one. Often these two reasons merge. That is, the construction requires more deliberate analysis than speakers have time to give it and so begets a colloquial usage which competes with the formal one.

The following constructions create most of the "case" troubles in college composition:

1. **Parenthetical constructions.** Any construction which interrupts the normal pattern of a clause is likely to obscure the function of a pronoun in the clause. In the following sentence it is quite clear that *who* is the subject of *won* and takes the subjective case:

> That is the man *who* won the prize.

But if we introduce a parenthetical clause — *they say* — into the original sentence, the function of *who* becomes less clear:

> That is the man who they say won the prize.

There is now a tendency to assume that *who* is the object of *say* and to put it in the objective case. But grammatically its function has not changed. The parenthetical clause is an absolute and has no grammatical relationship to any element in the sentence. Yet the faulty analysis suggested by the interrupting construction often leads to the selection of the wrong case.

Wrong Case	*Explanation*	*Correct Case*
The man *whom* they think did it has been arrested.	*Pronoun is subject of* did *and should be subjective.*	The man *who* they think did it has been arrested.
She introduced me to a man *whom* she said was her employer.	*Pronoun is subject of* was *and should be subjective.*	She introduced me to a man *who* she said was her employer.
He is the general *whom* the reporters agree was most popular with the troops.	*Pronoun is subject of* was *and should be subjective.*	He is the general *who* the reporters agree was most popular with the troops.

2. **Complement of "to be."** (See page 477 in Glossary).

3. **"Whoever" and "whomever."** These two relative pronouns follow the rule that the case of a pronoun is determined by its function in its own

clause, but because they often follow a transitive verb or the preposition *to,* they are often mistaken as objects when they are not.

Confused	*Explanation*	*Revised*
Invite *whomever* will come.	*Pronoun is subject of* will come; *whole clause is object of* invite.	Invite *whoever* will come.
Send it to *whom-ever* you think would like it.	*Relative pronoun is subject of* would like. *The preposition* to *and the absolute* you think *do not affect its case.*	Send it to *who-ever* you think would like it.

4. **Comparative with "than" or "as."** The case of a pronoun following *than* or *as* in a comparison often causes difficulty. Such comparisons as

> He is at least as old as *she.*
> I am about twenty pounds lighter than *he.*
> The judge liked us better than *them.*

are considered as contracted statements which in full would be

> He is at least as old as *she is.*
> I am about twenty pounds lighter than *he is.*
> The judge liked us better than *he liked them.*

In the expanded form *than* and *as* are connectives joining two clauses, and the pronouns are the subjects of the italicized clauses. The convention is that the pronoun in the contracted comparison takes the case it would have if the comparisons were fully expanded. That is, it takes the subjective case if it is the subject of the unexpressed verb, and the objective case if it is the object of that verb.

5. **Possessive with a gerund.** A pronoun preceding and modifying a gerund takes the possessive case (I am opposed to *his going*). In a formal style, a noun modifying a gerund also takes the possessive case (Imagine *John's saying* that!). Colloquial usage, which usually ignores this convention and puts the modifier in the objective case (Imagine *John saying* that!), has influenced both speech and informal writing.

The following sentences further illustrate the use of the possessive case when a noun or a pronoun modifies a gerund:

> There is really no excuse for *his failing* the course.
> I resent *David's trying* to influence her.
> We are embarrassed by *their* continual *begging.*
> They object to *my having dated* you.
> *Mary's interrupting* annoys him.
> *Their believing* that doesn't surprise me.

413

▶ *In the following sentences some of the italicized case forms are conventionally acceptable in college writing and some are not. If the acceptable case has been used, place a check (√) opposite the number of the sentence. If the wrong form has been used, write the acceptable form opposite the number of the sentence.*

1. Between you and *I,* she is asking for trouble.
2. I think I am a little older than *he.*
3. Was it really for my mother and *I?*
4. I am as much to blame as *her.*
5. All the men went fishing, *him* along with the others.
6. I want *him* to be notified.
7. I would like to catch *him* doing that.
8. The instructor was disappointed by *us* doing so badly.
9. Helen, *who* I dislike, is coming with her.
10. *Whom* can you imagine did such a thing?
11. He was the kind of man *whom* everybody said would have made a wonderful father.
12. There is a girl *whom* I admire.
13. *Whoever* you are, come out.
14. Tell it to *whoever* will listen.
15. I shall marry *whoever* I please.
16. We can play as well as *them.*
17. *His* refusing our offer was a serious disappointment.
18. He means *us* two, you and *I.*
19. The prize should go to *whoever* has the highest score.
20. There are few men more capable than *he.*
21. That was the last of *me* running for office.
22. Select *whomever* you wish.
23. I don't know whether I can do it as well as *him.*
24. Let's keep this a secret between *we* two.

F 4 *Agreement (Subject — Verb)*

In grammar the term **agreement** is used to describe the relationship between the inflectional forms of different elements within a sentence. When two related elements (subject and verb, pronoun and antecedent) show the same kind of inflection, they are said to agree. Thus a verb agrees with its subject if its form shows the same number and person as the subject. A pronoun agrees with its antecedent if both show the same gender, number, and person.

The fundamental convention of agreement is that the inflectional endings of two related elements should agree as far as possible. Since different parts of speech are inflected for different purposes (verbs for person, number, and tense, not for gender or case; nouns for number and possessive case, not for person or tense), related elements can agree only in those qualities which they have in common. If they agree in these, complete agreement is taken for granted. Therefore, the general rule might be more usefully stated in the negative: *There should be no grammatical disagreement between the inflectional endings of related elements within a sentence.*

Verbs agree with their subjects in number and person.

A singular subject requires a singular form of the verb, a plural subject a plural form. If the subject is a personal pronoun, inflected for person, the verb agrees in person. If the subject is a noun it is always considered to be in the third person, and takes the third person form of the verb. The following sentences illustrate this agreement:

> *I am* late. (Subject first person singular; verb first person singular.)
> *He is* sorry. (Subject third person singular; verb third person singular.)
> The *man works* slowly. (*Works* is third person singular to agree with *man.*)

Troublesome Constructions

The following constructions cause most of the difficulties in subject-verb agreement:

1. When two or more singular subjects are connected by *and*, a plural form of the verb is required.

> He and his brother *are* identical twins.
> Tom, Joe, Griff, and I *make* a good foursome.
> Both the bull and the calf *have won* prizes.
> A fool and his money *are* soon *parted.*

There are three modifications of this convention. First, when each of the singular subjects is considered individually, the singular form of the verb is used. This usage is most frequent after *each* or *every:*

> Here, every man and woman *works* for the good of the organization.
> Each boy and girl *makes* a separate report.

Second, when the two singular subjects refer to the same person or thing, the singular verb is used.

> My wife and boss *has* something to say about that.
> Grape juice and ginger ale *is* a good drink.

Third, mathematical computations may take either a singular or a plural verb.

> Five and five *is* ten.   Two times three *is* six.
> Five and five *are* ten.   Two times three *are* six.

2. When two or more singular subjects are connected by or, nor, or but, a singular form of the verb is required.

Mason or Dixon *is* to be elected.
Neither Bill nor Hugh *has* a chance.
Not Sue but Betty *was invited*.
Neither the Giants nor the Dodgers *is* going to win.
Not only his wife but even his mother *finds* him selfish.

3. When one of two subjects connected by or, nor, or but is singular and the other is plural, the verb agrees in number with the nearer one.

Neither Lewis nor his lawyers *were* there.
Not only the boys but also their father *encourages* it.

4. When two subjects connected by or or nor differ in person, the verb agrees with the nearer.

Jean or you *are* to go.
Either Red or I *have won*.

When conforming to this rule creates an awkward sentence, we usually restate the idea in a form which is both correct and natural. For example, rather than write

Neither Mary nor I am to blame.
You or he is the leading contender.

we would restate these sentences as follows:

Mary is not to blame; neither am I.
You and he are the leading contenders.

5. A singular subject followed immediately by as well as, in addition to, including, no less than, with, together with, or a similar construction, requires a singular verb.

The husband as well as the wife *needs* advice.
The coach together with his assistants *was praised*.
The president no less than the secretary *is* responsible.
The store in addition to the farm *was sold*.

Because this convention sometimes seems illogical (since more than one person or thing is included in the subject phrase), there is a tendency to avoid the construction altogether and to write:

Both the husband and the wife *need* advice.
The coach and his assistants *were praised*.
The president *is* just as responsible as the secretary.
The store and the farm *were sold*.

416

6. A singular subject followed by a plural modifier requires a singular verb.

> The *attitude* of these men *is* definitely hostile.
> The *leader* of the rebel forces *has* been captured.
> *One* of the women in the back row *looks* sick.
> A *list* of the names of all survivors *is* available.

In conversation, a plural modifier immediately before a verb often leads to a plural verb. This is particularly true in a sentence like the fourth above, in which the subject is followed by a long modifier containing two plural nouns. This colloquial usage has less justification in writing, since the more deliberate nature of writing and revision makes it easier to use the conventional form.

7. Such indefinite pronouns as *anybody, anyone, each, either, everybody, neither, nobody, no one,* and *somebody* generally require a singular verb.

> *Anybody* who does that *is* just reckless.
> *Does anyone* want to split this with me?
> *Each* of them *makes* fifty dollars a week.
> *Somebody has been using* my shaving soap.
> *Nobody* in town *admits* seeing him.
> *Everybody does* as he pleases.

8. The pronouns *any* and *none* take either singular or plural verbs.

> *Are any* of you *going* to the show?
> *Any* of these times *is* satisfactory.
> *None works* so faithfully as he.
> *None are expected* from that district.

9. When the subject is a relative pronoun, the verb agrees with the antecedent of that pronoun.

> He is one of the *men who act* as advisers.
> This is one of those *problems which have* two solutions.

10. When a sentence is introduced by the expletive *There* or the adverb *Here,* the verb agrees with the following subject.

> Here *is* your *money*.
> Here *are* the *receipts*.
> There *are* no second *chances*.
> There *are* a *man* and a *boy* in that boat.
> *Is* there a *chance* of his winning?
> *Were* there many *people* present?

417

This convention is not strictly observed in spoken usage, because we often begin a sentence with an expletive followed by a single subject and then add more subjects before we finish the sentence. For example:

> Did you see anyone there that I know?
> Well, there was Joe Botts, and Ray Carroll, and Dan Snader.

In speech, we cannot conveniently revise the verb to take care of these additional subjects. But we do have such an opportunity in writing, and hence a plural verb is more common in such sentences.

11. **When a sentence is introduced by the expletive** *It,* **the verb is always singular, regardless of the number of the subject.**

> It *is* the *Johnsons.*
> It *is we* whom they want.

12. **The complement of the verb** *to be* **does not affect the number of the verb.**

> *Books are* her chief source of enjoyment.
> The one *thing* you must be ready for *is* their attempts to disguise the play.
> *What annoys me* about them *is* their constant complaints.

If the demands of this convention result in an awkward sentence, the wisest thing to do is to recast it.

Conventional but Awkward	*Revised*
The amusing *thing* about campaign speeches *is* the attempts that both sides make to represent themselves as the only friends of the people.	In campaign speeches, it is amusing to see how both sides attempt to represent themselves as the only friends of the people.

13. **A collective noun takes a singular verb when the class it names is considered as a unit, a plural verb when the members of the class are considered individually.**

Singular	*Plural*
The jury *is* finally complete.	The jury *were* divided in their opinions.
The family *holds* an annual reunion.	My family *have* never been able to agree.
The clergy *is* wretchedly underpaid.	The clergy *are* supporting this proposal from their pulpits.

This convention also applies to such nouns as *number, part,* and *rest.*

A large number *is* expected.

A number of errors *have* been found.

Only part of the order *was* delivered.

A great part of the people *have* no opinion on the question.

The rest of the page *is* illegible.

The rest of the votes *are* about equally divided among the three candidates.

14. Titles of books, magazines, movies, newspapers, plays, and the like take a singular verb.

> *The Good Companions* is a fine novel.
> *The Outcasts* was not a success at the box office.
> *The New York Times* is his bible.

15. Plural numbers take a singular verb when they are used in a phrase to indicate a sum or a unit.

> A million dollars *is* a great deal of money.
> Ten years *is* too long to wait.
> Five per cent *is* good interest.
> Forty hours *is* the regular work week.

16. Certain nouns which are plural in form but singular in meaning generally take a singular verb. The most common of these are *dynamics, economics, electronics, ethics, mathematics, news, physics, semantics, statics, whereabouts.*

> Economics *has* been called the dismal science.
> No news *is* good news.
> Semantics *is* the study of meanings.

▶ *Indicate the form in parentheses which would be preferred in college writing:*

1. All hope of finding the victims alive (has, have) been abandoned.
2. One of the two girls (is, are) going.
3. Neither of my uncles (have, has) any children.
4. There (is, are) plenty to go around.
5. There (is, are) two mistakes in your work.
6. There (is, are) an apple and an orange for each child.
7. Five hundred dollars (is, are) more than I can afford.
8. Either Mary or Jean (was, were) here.
9. Neither Roy nor his dad (have, has) seen it.

10. The gangster, with all his henchmen, (were, was) arrested.
11. The father no less than the children (is, are) to blame.
12. The parents no less than the children (is, are) to blame.
13. Every one of the group (are, is) here.
14. Here (is, are) a piece of cake and a glass of milk.
15. (Is, are) there two pictures like that?
16. Two hundred pounds (were, was) his best weight.
17. The engine in addition to the body (was, were) in bad shape.
18. Bacon and eggs (are, is) the favorite breakfast.
19. It (is, are) the Thompsons.
20. There (is, are) one for each couple.

F 5 *Agreement (Pronoun — Antecedent)*

Pronouns agree with their antecedents in gender, number, and person.

If the antecedent is a masculine singular noun, the pronoun should be the masculine singular third person pronoun (*he, his,* or *him*). A pronoun does not necessarily agree with its antecedent in case, since its case is determined by its function in its own clause (see page 411).

Examples	*Explanation*
The *men* got *their* wages.	*Their* is third person plural to agree with *men*. The plural form of the pronoun is the same for all genders.
The *girl* found *her* watch.	*Her* is third person feminine singular to agree with *girl*.
The *boy* misses *his* dog.	*His* is third person masculine singular to agree with *boy*.
The *plane* changed *its* course.	*Its* is third person neuter singular to agree with *plane*.

Troublesome Constructions

Most troubles with agreement of pronouns occur in a half-dozen constructions, and arise because of conflict between formal and colloquial usage. In general, formal usage insists that the *form* of the antecedent, not its *meaning,* determines the number of the pronoun, whereas colloquial usage tends to be governed by *meaning.* For example, *everybody* is singular in form but plural in meaning, since it refers to more than one person. Formally, *everybody* requires the singular form *his;* colloquially, it often is followed by the plural form *their.* In general, this colloquial usage is discouraged in college writing, so that *his* rather than *their* is the safer form.

1. When two or more antecedents are connected by *and,* a pronoun referring to them is plural.

> *Bill* and *Ted* are looking for *their* girls.
> *Helen* and *I* are buying *our* tickets today.
> That *man* and his *partner* have ruined *themselves.*

2. When the antecedent is *each, either,* or *neither,* followed by a plural modifier, a singular pronoun is preferred.

> *Each* of the girls is sure *she* is going to win.
> *Neither* of the men would admit *his* mistake.
> *Either* of these women may lose *her* temper at any time.

3. When the antecedent is *everybody, each, either, everyone, neither, nobody,* or *a person,* a singular pronoun is preferred.

> *Each* has *his* own group of supporters.
> *Everybody* had *his* work in good shape.
> *Nobody* had *his* speech ready today.
> *Everyone* was keeping *his* fingers crossed.
> *A person* finds *himself* in trouble if he begins to cut classes.

Notice that the masculine form of the pronoun is generally used when the sex of the antecedent is unknown or when the antecedent refers to both sexes, thus:

> *Everyone* should vote for the candidate of *his* choice.
> The boys and girls have been told that *everybody* must do *his* share of the work.

But if the context clearly shows that the antecedent is feminine, the feminine pronoun is used:

> When we girls have a picnic *everyone* brings *her* own utensils.

4. When the antecedent is the impersonal *one,* the third person pronoun is generally used, unless the style is very formal.

> *One* must watch *his* step with that girl.
> *One* can't really blame *himself* for that.
> If *one* had a second chance, how much wiser *he* might be.

In a very formal style the impersonal pronoun is sometimes used throughout.

> Under such conditions *one* laments *one's* utter incapacity to be of any genuine service.
> *One* finds *oneself* wishing that the evidence were more convincing.

5. When the antecedent is a collective noun, the pronoun may be either singular or plural, depending on whether the group is considered as a unit or as a number of individuals.

Singular	*Plural*
The *family* keeps pretty much to *itself*.	The *family* may have *their* private quarrels but *they* always agree in public.
The judge reprimanded the *jury* for *its* disregard of the evidence.	At the request of the defense attorney, the *jury* were polled and *their* individual verdicts recorded.
The *team* had *its* back to the wall.	The *team* are electing *their* captain.

6. The relative pronoun *who* is used when the antecedent is a person; *which* is used when the antecedent is a thing; *that* is used to refer to persons, animals, or things.

> This is the *man who* drove the car.
> The *girl who* found it is here.
> The *woman that* I mean had brown hair.
> Here is the *parcel which* (or *that*) she left.
> This is the *cow that* jumped the fence.

The possessive form *whose* is theoretically confined to persons, but in practice is often used when the more formal *of which* seems awkward.

> The *nation whose* conscience is clear on that score is exceptional.
> The newspaper *whose* reporters are most alert gets the most scoops.

▶ *Indicate the form in parentheses which would be preferred in college writing:*

1. A person has to decide for (himself, themselves).
2. Neither of them will promise (their, his) support.
3. Everyone must bring (his, their) own food.
4. A person must do (one's, his) best.
5. Each of the boys tried as hard as (they, he) could.
6. One must do (one's, their) utmost.
7. The team was cheered for (its, their) courage.
8. Nobody in the room (were, was) willing to give up (their, his) (seat, seats).
9. He would just as soon insult a person as look at (them, him).
10. One must work twenty years to be eligible for (their, one's, your) pension.
11. There is the man (which, that) lost the money.
12. Each girl must contribute (their, her) share of the expenses.

13. Every boy and girl in the class (were, was) awarded a certificate for (their, his, her) work.

14. The car (with the broken fender, whose fender is broken) is mine.

15. Give this to the lady (which, who) lost it.

16. The committee (has, have) always voted according to (its, their) consciences.

17. Has everyone got (his, their) own coat?

18. After Ohio State won the title (they, it) went on to play in the Rose Bowl.

19. He is the instructor (which, who) told me my English was weak.

20. The nation to (whom, which) I am referring is not Russia.

F 6 *Vague Pronoun Reference*

A pronoun which refers to a whole clause rather than to an explicit antecedent sometimes puts an additional strain on the reader by requiring him to do something which is really the writer's responsibility. The following examples illustrate pronoun references which, because they are unnecessarily vague, make the writing less precise than it should be.

Vague Reference	*Explanation*	*Revision*
They have agreed to have a formal church wedding, *which* pleases their parents.	*The pronoun* which *has no explicit antecedent but refers to the whole idea expressed in the main clause. The vague reference may be improved by supplying an antecedent as in the first revision or, better, by recasting the sentence as in the second revision.*	They have agreed to have a formal church wedding, *a decision* which pleases their parents. (or better) Their decision to have a formal church wedding pleases their parents.
The bigger car will be expensive to operate. Not only will its repairs cost more but its gasoline consumption will be greater. You should take *this* into account.	*The demonstrative pronoun* this *has no explicit antecedent, is singular in form, and refers to two different costs. In the revised version, the phrase* these added costs *removes the difficulties.*	The bigger car will be expensive to operate. Not only will its repairs cost more but its gasoline consumption will be greater. You should take *these added costs* into account.
The crash is being investigated. At present *they* think that the planes must have collided.	*The antecedent of* they *is not identified. The writer, of course, is thinking of the investigators. The statement would be improved by dropping the pronoun.*	At present the investigators think that the planes must have collided.

Vague Reference	*Explanation*	*Revision*
If he does not get to work on his research assignment pretty soon *it* is going to be difficult for him to get it finished on time.	*The first* it *is impersonal but looks at first glance as if it should refer to* research assignment — *particularly unfortunate because the second* it *does have this reference. The sentence would be improved by keeping* he *the subject of both clauses.*	If he does not get to work on his research assignment pretty soon he may not get it finished on time.

▶ *Revise the following sentences if necessary to make the pronoun references clear.*

1. When you advance to the upper grades — fifth, sixth, seventh, and eighth — there are two grades in each room, which allows you to become acquainted with more pupils.

2. She hasn't a good word to say for anybody. Her parents are old-fashioned, her girl friends are catty, her boy friends are conceited, and her instructors are sarcastic. This makes me discount anything she tells me about a person.

3. I expect to receive a D in History and, at best, another D in Accounting, which means that I will be on probation next semester.

4. In high school they always told us exactly what we were to do and how we were to do it.

5. In the book it says that the meanings of words are determined by the ways people use them, which surprised me.

6. In college I like the way they treat you as an adult and call you Mister and Miss. This is a pleasant change from the way it was in high school.

F 7 *Faulty Complement*

a. Avoid an illogical or awkward construction as the complement of the verb *to be*.

The verb *to be* is most frequently used either as an auxiliary verb (I *am* learning) or as a linking verb (Honesty *is* the best policy). When used as a linking verb, it links its complement to its subject and thus acts as a kind of equals sign (Honesty = best policy). A reader who is familiar with the conventions of English sentence structure expects two things of this linking verb: (1) that it will be followed by a complement, (2) that the complement will be such that it can be logically equated with the subject. If either of these expectations is denied him, he will be bothered. Thus, if he encounters the sentence, "Honesty is in the little details of everyday life," he will feel that the promised linking relationship has not been provided.

He will want to revise the sentence to read, "Honesty is best expressed in the little details of everyday life," thus changing *is* from a linking to an auxiliary verb (*is* expressed).

Similarly, a reader who meets the sentence, "Honesty is what you do in such a situation," will feel that the complement throws the equation out of balance, since it equates the abstract noun "Honesty" with a statement of action. He will want to revise the sentence to read, "What to do in such a situation is to tell the truth," so that both sides of the equation refer to an action (*to do* and *to tell*).

In order to avoid such annoying constructions, a writer should make sure that the complement of *to be* can be logically equated with the subject. If it cannot, or if the equation results in a wordy or awkward sentence, the writer should either revise the form of the complement or rewrite the sentence to get rid of the misleading linking verb.

Illogical or Awkward Complement	Explanation	Revised Sentence
Before I built the house all I had learned about carpentry was *watching my dad.*	*The equation requires some statement of knowledge, not a statement of how the knowledge was obtained. Of the various possible revisions, perhaps the best is to substitute a more active verb which does not promise an equation.*	Before I built the house all that I knew about carpentry I had learned from watching my dad.
The chief disadvantage of weeping willows is the branches are brittle and break easily.	*The sentence has two faults. Logically, it is the brittleness that constitutes the disadvantage, not the branches; grammatically, the plural noun* branches *following* is *sounds like a subject-verb disagreement. The sentence may be saved very simply, by providing a subordinating conjunction so that the final clause is revealed as a complement.*	The chief disadvantage of weeping willows is that the branches are brittle and break easily.
The most unusual food I ever had was when I ate a serving of boiled snails.	*The reader expects the food to be identified immediately after the linking verb. The adverbial clause stresses time, instead, and is wordy.*	The most unusual food I ever ate was a serving of boiled snails.

425

b. Avoid the use of *is when, is where,* and *is if* when the complement of *to be* is intended to describe or define the subject.

This advice is a special application of the more general statement given in **a.** The use of an adverbial clause instead of a noun or noun phrase is one kind of illogical complement which occurs frequently in student definitions. This error and its revision are illustrated by the following examples.

Faulty Complement	*Explanation*	*Revision*
Plagiarism is *when you represent another person's writing as your own.*	*The reader expects to find what plagiarism is, not when it is. The construction calls for a noun phrase similar to the italicized phrase at the right.*	Plagiarism is *the representation of another's writing as one's own.*
Manslaughter is *where a person is killed deliberately but without premeditation.*	*Again, the construction requires a statement of what manslaughter is, not where it is.*	Manslaughter is *the deliberate but unpremeditated killing of a person.*
A comma splice is *if a comma is used to separate two independent sentences which are not connected by a coordinating conjuncion.*	*The complement should tell what a comma splice is, not how a comma splice is made. Use a noun such as* use *at the right.*	A comma splice is *the use of a comma to separate two independent sentences which are not connected by a coordinating conjunction.*

c. Use the adjective form for the complements of sensory verbs.

A **sensory verb** is one which identifies some action of the senses — seeing, hearing, feeling, etc. Since the complements of these verbs usually describe the subject rather than the action of the verb, they are adjectives, not adverbs. Their adjectival function can be illustrated by expressing the complement as an attributive adjective, as in the parenthetical phrases at the ends of the following sentences:

> Your hands feel rough. (rough-feeling hands)
> This tire looks good. (good-looking tire)
> That dog smells awful. (awful-smelling dog)
> This water tastes bitter. (bitter-tasting water)

To use an adverb after these verbs would suggest that the writer was describing the manner in which the feeling, looking, smelling, and tasting were performed. Unless the modifier completing a sensory verb is clearly intended to describe the action suggested by the verb, an adjective is the correct form.

Revise the following sentences to remove the faulty complements.

1. The source of his fortune was from real estate.
2. The reason I failed the course was missing a third of the lectures.
3. A hybrid is when you cross two different types of plants.
4. Whatever is in the oven smells deliciously.
5. The chief merit of the play was in its humor.
6. I read in this morning's paper where there has been another airplane crash.
7. Technically, a sophomore is having 26 hours of credit.
8. What annoys me about him is he plays practical jokes.
9. Conduct unbecoming a student is if you do something you shouldn't and get caught.
10. Half an hour after dinner he became quite sickly.
11. One of his greatest assets is how well he can tell a story.
12. The thing I most regret about working my way through college was the dates I never had time for.
13. After that kind of experience I can't help feeling bitterly about her.
14. The most embarrassing thing that can happen to you on a trip is when you run short of money and try to cash a personal check at a gas station.
15. The reason they were divorced was not supporting his family.
16. The thing that troubled me most was cats all over the place.
17. An Act of God is when something happens, like a flood, which nobody is really to blame for.
18. The difference between an amateur and a professional is when an athlete is paid for playing a sport.
19. An honor student is if you have a straight B average.
20. The only money he has is his grandfather left him a small inheritance.

F 8   *Confusion of Adjective — Adverb*

Faulty modifiers which are a result of word order are discussed in **WO 2.** This section is limited to errors in the form of the modifier.

a. Do not use an adjective to modify a verb.

Adjective Misused for Adverb	*Correct Form*
The old car still runs *good*.	The old car still runs *well*.
Do it as *careful* as you can.	Do it as *carefully* as you can.
Listen *close* to what I tell you.	Listen *closely* to what I tell you.

b. Do not use an adjective to modify an adverb or another adjective.

Adjective Misused for Adverb	*Correct Form*
He is *considerable* better today.	He is *considerably* better today.
It will *sure* be a difficult decision.	It will *surely* be a difficult decision.

c. Do not use an adverb as the complement of a sensory verb unless you clearly intend to modify the verb, not the subject. (See F 7)

d. When a modifier could modify either a noun or a verb, indicate by the form which you intend.

Adverb	*Adjective*
Tie the knot *tightly* and *securely*.	Tie the boat *tight* to the dock.
Her husband held her *firmly*.	He kept his resolutions *firm*.
John spoke out *forthrightly*.	His answers seemed *forthright*.

► *Rewrite the following sentences to revise or delete faulty modifiers.*

1. He plays every shot so easy that it looks simple.
2. The way you put it, it sounds pretty well.
3. She near fainted when he told her.
4. We ought to treat everybody fair and square.
5. It was obviously a cheap made dress.
6. Let's divide the work equal among the three of us.
7. The night watchman had been gagged and tied tight in a chair.
8. After I had explained the problem as good as I could, she was real nice to me.
9. The work had been done so sloppy that I spoke real sharp to him.
10. We were considerable wiser after that experience.

P ▶ Punctuation

P 1　*Uses of the Comma*

The common marks of punctuation are the *period* [.], *comma* [,], *semicolon* [;], *colon* [:], *question mark* [?], *exclamation mark* [!], *quotation marks* [" " or ' '], *apostrophe* ['], *dash* [—], *parentheses* [( )], and *brackets* [ ]. Most of these marks have highly specialized functions, and once these are understood, it is easy enough to use them conventionally. The chief exception, perhaps, is the comma, which is at once the most common mark of punctuation and the one with the most complex uses.

The comma is used to make the internal structure of the sentence clear. It does so in three general ways: (1) by separating elements which might otherwise be confused, (2) by setting off interrupting constructions, and (3) by marking words out of normal order. This section will specify and illustrate these three uses.

a. Use commas to separate elements which might otherwise seem to run together.

1. To prevent a confused, ambiguous, or awkward reading.

The most important use of the comma is to prevent a confused, ambiguous, or awkward reading. All other uses are subordinate to this one. Notice how the confused sentences at the left are made clear at the right by the use of commas.

Confused	*Explanation*	*Clear*
Mr. Smith our milk-man has been hurt.	*Is this a statement to or about Mr. Smith?*	Mr. Smith, our milkman has been hurt. (or) Mr. Smith, our milkman, has been hurt.
I do not care for money isn't everything.	*Lest* money *seem to complete* care for, *a* comma *should be inserted after* care.	I do not care, for (*or* because) money isn't everything.

Confused	*Explanation*	*Clear*
A hundred yards below the bridge was flooded.	*Comma necessary to avoid misreading of* bridge *as the object of* below.	A hundred yards below, the bridge was flooded.
When we had finished eating the cigarettes were passed around.	*Comma necessary to show that* cigarettes *is not the object of* eating.	When we had finished eating, the cigarettes were passed around.

2. To separate two main clauses joined by a coordinating conjunction (*and, or, nor, but*).

The real purpose of this convention is to prevent possible misinterpretation on first reading, specifically to keep the subject of the second main clause from being misread as a second object in the first clause. Consider the following sentences:

> He sprained his ankle and his temper was ruined.
> He traded his car and his wife was angry.

In both these sentences the noun following the conjunction appears, at first reading, to be part of a compound object of the first verb. The comma before the conjunction shows clearly that the two nouns are in different clauses:

> He sprained his ankle, and his temper was ruined.
> He traded his car, and his wife was angry.

When there is no possibility of a confused reading, the comma becomes less necessary and is often omitted. But even when it is not functionally necessary, careful writers insert a comma between two connected main clauses if the subject of the second differs from that of the first, as in the following examples:

> I tried to sleep, but my neighbor's radio made that impossible.
> The huge elm had been cut down, and a garage now covered the spot where it once stood.

But notice that a comma is generally not used when the subject of the first clause is understood as the subject of the second:

> I discussed the question with the family and then made my decision.

3. To separate elements in a series.

> He promised them only *blood, sweat, toil,* and *tears.*
> *Reading, swimming,* and *dancing* are my favorite recreations.

It was said of Washington that he was *first in war, first in peace,* and *first in the hearts of his countrymen.*

North passed, East bid two spades, South bid three hearts, and *West doubled.*

We were *tired, hungry,* and *disconsolate.*

As these illustrations show, the series may consist of single words, phrases, or clauses. The items in the series may be nouns, pronouns, verbs, verbals, adverbs, or adjectives, though within a single series they must not shift from one part of speech to another. The comma before the conjunction joining the last two items is optional. Its use is largely a matter of personal preference, though it is more likely to be omitted in an informal style than in a formal one.

She is small, dark, and vivacious.
        (or)
She is small, dark and vivacious.

4. To separate contrasted elements in a *this, not that,* construction.

He is sick, not drunk.
We are disgusted, not angry.
The German schools became institutes of propaganda, not of education.
This is a problem which must be handled with sympathy, not harshness.

5. To separate direct quotation from such constructions as *He said, She answered, We replied,* etc.

He said, "You are only half right."
"This," I said, "is the last straw."
"Nobody asked you, sir," she said.
"But," he asked, "what if they refuse?"

Since the quotation marks themselves set off the quoted material, no confusion would result if the comma were omitted; but convention requires the comma. Whether the punctuation should come *inside* or *outside* the quotation marks is discussed in **P 9.**

6. To separate elements in dates, addresses, and place names.

January 1, 1960; Dec. 25, 1910. (Comma between day and year.)
875 Main Street, Galesburg, Illinois. (Comma between street and city and between city and state.)
Chicago, Illinois, is the second-largest city in the country. (Notice the comma before and after the state.)
He was born in London, England. (Comma between city and country.)

7. In the following miscellaneous constructions:

In figures — 22,745; 1,000,000; 150,743,290.
In names followed by titles — R. W. Leeds, M.D.
At the end of the salutation in informal letters — Dear Joe,
After an introductory *Yes* or *No* — Yes, I'll do it.

▶ *In the following sentences insert commas where they are needed for ease of reading or are conventionally required. Some of the sentences may be satisfactory as they are.*

1. This summer our family tried a split vacation. Dad went fishing in Minnesota with Bill and me and Mother took my sister to New York.
2. Below the town glittered with a million lights.
3. My roommate learned about the deal and wrote a story about it for the *Daily*.
4. The correct quotation is "And malt does more than Milton can / To justify God's ways to man."
5. The author was Housman not Pope. He was born on March 26 1859.
6. Will you please forward my mail to 1620 Third Avenue Anoka Minnesota?
7. I expect to be there as long as the fishing is good.
8. The correct sum is 14530 not 14350.
9. I'll take orange juice ham and eggs and coffee.
10. He praised the food and the waitress seemed pleased.
11. He married Helen and her sister served as bridesmaid.
12. "I wonder" he said "if she still lives in Geneva Illinois."
13. "I think not" I answered. "She was living in Kansas City Missouri when I last heard of her."
14. Throughout the ceremony was inspiringly conducted.
15. The room was a clutter of discarded clothing strewn books and newspapers overflowing ash trays and dirty dishes.
16. After all their hopes were too ambitious.
17. We tried to look in the cellar windows but someone had placed cardboard rectangles against them on the inside.
18. I cannot stay longer for Susan will be expecting me to meet her at the station.
19. The students sat tensely while the test papers were being distributed and then began to write feverishly.
20. The letter should be addressed to A. D. Jones M.D. Christie Clinic Champaign Illinois.

b. Use commas to set off an interrupting construction.

Any construction which comes between subject and verb, verb and object or complement, or any two elements not normally separated, may be called an interrupting construction. If the interruption is awkward, it should be avoided; but many interrupters are necessary and conventional. These should be set off by commas, so that a reader can recognize them and still see the basic pattern of the sentence.

We must distinguish, however, between constructions which actually interrupt and those which come between related elements without interrupting them. For example, in

The girl, *you say,* has gone.

the italicized clause comes between subject (*girl*) and verb (*has gone*). The interrupter need not occupy this position. The sentence could have been written:

You say that the girl has gone.
The girl has gone, you say.

But in the sentence

The girl *you want* has gone.

the italicized clause identifies the particular girl and cannot be moved without weakening the sentence. Although the clause modifies the subject, it so closely identifies it that we consider *The girl you want* as the "whole subject" of *has gone.* A modifying phrase or clause which is so closely related to another element that it is felt to be a part of that element should not be set off with commas, since the commas would distort the relationship, not clarify it. The italicized modifiers in the following sentences are so necessary that they are not considered interrupting constructions:

The man *with him* is his brother.
The girl *at the piano* is his wife.
The leader *of the revolt* has been captured.

As you study the following uses of commas to set off interrupting constructions, notice this about all of them: *an interrupting construction between subject and verb or verb and complement requires two commas to enclose it.* These commas act like mild parentheses and are always used in pairs.

1. To set off an appositive.

An **appositive** is an identifying word or phrase (a noun or pronoun and its modifiers) which is considered grammatically equivalent to the noun or pronoun it identifies:

His father, *the president of the company,* will be responsible.
They want us, *you and me,* to go.
I want to see Dr. Roberts, *the English professor.*

The first two examples show that the appositive is often a particular kind of interrupter. The third appositive does not interrupt the main clause, but is conventionally separated from the rest of the sentence by a comma.

2. To set off nouns of address.

A **noun of address** is a proper or common noun used to name the listener when we are speaking to him directly (I wish, *Dad,* you would reconsider your decision. I understand, *Mrs. Ellison,* that you are now a grandmother). Such nouns may occupy the beginning, middle, or end of a sentence, so that strictly speaking they are not always interrupters. But they are always set off from the rest of the sentence by commas.

> I would like to ask you, *Mr. Jones,* for your opinion.
> *Sir,* I'd like to ask a question.
> Listen, *chum,* I've had enough of you!
> I wish I were going with you, *Ted.*

3. To set off conjunctive adverbs and other transitional markers.

Conjunctive adverbs (*however, moreover, therefore,* etc.) are adverbs which double as connectives between sentences. Usually they provide a transition between two sentences and they come *near,* and occasionally *at,* the beginning of the second sentence.

> We thought, moreover, that we could get away with it.
> On the other hand, there was a chance that prices would go up.
> You must try, first of all, to consider it objectively.

The commas around *therefore* are sometimes omitted:

> I am therefore canceling the order.

4. To set off a nonrestrictive modifier.

A modifier is said to be **restrictive** when it specifies a particular member or members of a group. Thus in "The President *who said that* was Lincoln," the italicized modifier selects from the whole class of Presidents a particular one. When a modifier does not limit a class to a particular group or individual but modifies the whole class, it is said to be **nonrestrictive.** Thus in "The President of the United States, *who is both the chief of state and the leader of his party,* holds one of the most powerful offices in the world," the italicized modifier refers to all Presidents of the United States and does not restrict the statement to any particular one. It is a nonrestrictive modifier.

The following examples include restrictive and nonrestrictive modifiers. We should recognize that context often determines how a modifier is to be interpreted and that it might be possible to place the sentences at the right in contexts which would make the modifiers restrictive.

Restrictive	*Nonrestrictive*

    All students *who were absent* will be required to do an additional assignment.

    College students, *who represent a superior intellectual group,* must be asked to accept the responsibility of leadership.

    Soldiers *who have flat feet* had better stay out of the infantry.

Soldiers, *who are selected by physical fitness tests,* should show a lower sickness rate than that of the total population.

Restrictive modifiers are so much a part of the whole subject that they cannot be omitted without changing the basic meaning of the sentence. Nonrestrictive modifiers, on the other hand, can be omitted without significant change in basic meaning. Compare the following revisions with the originals which we just read.

    All students . . . will be required to do an additional assignment. (This is not what the original statement meant.)
    College students . . . must be asked to accept the responsibility of leadership. (This is substantially what the original statement meant.)
    Soldiers . . . had better stay out of the infantry. (Not the original meaning.)
    Soldiers . . . should show a lower sickness rate than that of the total population. (The original meaning has not been substantially changed.)

Nonrestrictive modifiers are set off by commas; restrictive modifiers are not. The examples already given illustrate this difference in punctuation.

▶ *In the following sentences, provide commas to set off appositives, nouns of address, conjunctive adverbs, and nonrestrictive modifiers. Some sentences may require no additional punctuation.*

    1. Mr. Ludovic the new German instructor was born in Berlin.
    2. The man wearing the Stetson is his uncle.
    3. The tall man who happened to be wearing a Stetson said he had never been west of Chicago in his life.
    4. Do you think Bill that we could play a round after work?
    5. Are these your gloves Mrs. Davidson?
    6. The suit that he bought two years ago fits him better than the one he bought last winter.
    7. The doctor looking very grave came towards us.
    8. I thought however that things would be different this time.
    9. The girl evidently on the edge of tears could hardly finish her story.
    10. Sir may I trouble you for a light?
    11. My girl's mother who used to be an English teacher helps me with my themes.
    12. The dog which had evidently been trained sat beside the table and begged charmingly for food.
    13. First turn on the gas and oil; second set the choke; third pull the rope.

14. I had a talk with her father who is not so crotchety as you led me to believe.

15. I had a talk with the man who witnessed the accident.

16. The elm tree disease is killing off most of the old elms; consequently the people in our neighborhood are planting maples.

17. No, I mean the Mr. Brown who lives over on Florida Avenue.

18. I hear that Abelson the fire marshal was badly hurt last night.

19. A scientist called Fermi was chiefly responsible for the success of the Chicago experiment.

20. Mr. Welch our next-door neighbor has a daughter who placed second in a national beauty contest. There is some talk that she will be given a movie contract. That however may be merely rumor.

c. Use commas to mark an inversion.

1. To emphasize an inverted element.

Any word, phrase, or clause transposed from its normal position is said to be inverted.

> *Myself,* I will vote in favor of it.
> *Except for physics,* my courses are not difficult.

But if the inversion is so common as to seem normal, the comma is usually omitted. No commas would be used in the following inversions:

> *Yesterday* I had a bad time of it.
> *In 1913* the concept of total war was unknown.
> *In the following sentences* the verbs are underlined.

2. To set off a long introductory phrase or an adverbial clause preceding the main clause.

When a sentence opens with a long phrase or adverbial clause, it is conventional to use a comma between this element and the main clause:

> *Pulling over to the curb at the first opportunity,* I waited for the fire engines to pass.
> *If there is going to be any difficulty about this request,* I would rather withdraw it.
> *Being ignorant of the facts of the situation,* I could say nothing.
> *If I go,* you'll be sorry.
> *To be sure of getting up in time to catch the train,* I left a call with the switchboard operator.
> *When you say that,* smile.

This convention is not universal. The comma is generally used when, as in the last example, the introductory construction is clearly an inversion, when an introductory phrase contains a verbal (examples 1, 3, 5), and when the subordinate and main clauses have different subjects (example 4). The comma should always be used if it makes the sentence pattern clearer and the reader's job easier.

▶ *In the following sentences insert commas to set off inversions and introductory constructions where desirable.*

1. Dissatisfied with our blocking the coach announced an extra session on defense.
2. In a last desperate effort to score the team went into a spread formation.
3. If you want it take it.
4. On learning that his wife had never formally renounced her share of the property and could still block its sale we told the real estate agent that we were no longer interested.
5. As far as I know that is the answer.
6. Just the other day I saw his mother.
7. Whoever he is he should be punished.
8. If he objects tell him to talk with me.
9. Knowing that he had a tendency to make a ten-minute speech in five minutes Hugh timed his delivery with a stop watch.
10. Angry my roommate threw the tickets in the fireplace.

P 2 *Misuse of the Comma*

Too many commas are often more annoying than too few. The following "don't's" should be carefully observed.

a. Do not use a comma instead of a period between independent sentences.

The use of a comma instead of a period between independent sentences may cause serious misinterpretation. (See "Comma Splice," **S 7**; see also **P 3a.**)

Comma Splice	*Conventional Punctuation*
He spoke very quietly, as I listened, I had the impression that he was speaking to himself.	He spoke very quietly. As I listened, I had the impression that he was speaking to himself.
There was nothing more to be said, when they took that attitude, further negotiation was impossible.	There was nothing more to be said. When they took that attitude, further negotiation was impossible.

b. Do not use a comma between closely related elements except to mark an interrupting construction.

The comma should reveal the structure of a sentence, not disguise it. Closely related elements (subject-verb, verb-object, verb or noun and modifier) are unnecessarily separated if a single comma is placed between them. If, however, these elements are interrupted, a pair of commas to enclose the interrupting construction helps to bridge the interruption.

Misuse of Comma Between Related Elements	*Correct Use of Comma Between Related Elements*
My car, is at the service station.	My car, which is at the service station, needs a thorough overhauling.
He said, that he would try.	He said, when I asked him, that he would try.
The student who lost this money, may need it badly.	The student, who had lost money on other occasions, was reprimanded for his carelessness.

The last illustration contrasts a restrictive with a nonrestrictive clause (see page 434). The comma is misused in the version at the left because the subordinate clause is not an interruption but a necessary part of the whole subject. It is a restrictive modifier.

c. Do not use commas excessively.

It should not be assumed that a comma *must* be used in a particular sentence because convention recommends its use in sentences of that type. The conventions are statements about general practice. There are times when slavishly following the rules will chop a sentence to pieces by commas. In such cases, either revise the sentence or ignore the strict letter of the convention. The following examples illustrate excessive and adequate punctuation:

Excessive	*Adequate*
However, it is not, in my opinion, desirable.	However, it is not in my opinion desirable.
Yesterday, a little, old lady, in a dilapidated, old Ford, picked me up and brought me home.	Yesterday a little old lady in a dilapidated old Ford picked me up and brought me home.
Sometimes, she would appear in an elaborate beach outfit, sometimes, she wore a simple, white suit, and, occasionally, she put on a red, white, and blue bathing suit, with a detachable skirt.	Sometimes she would appear in an elaborate beach outfit, sometimes she wore a simple white suit, and occasionally she put on a red white and blue bathing suit with a detachable skirt.

P 3   *Uses of the Semicolon*

a. Use a semicolon to separate closely related independent clauses not connected by a conjunction.

> Try this one; it seems to be your color.
> His mother won't let him; she is afraid he might get hurt.
> Your car is new; mine is eight years old.

In each of these sentences a period could be used instead of the semicolon. But the clauses, even though grammatically independent, are felt to be so closely related that a period makes too sharp a separation.

The semicolon provides a more emphatic separation than the comma; it affords an easier transition between statements than the period; it is therefore the most appropriate punctuation to balance two contrasted ideas parallel in form:

> Take care of the children; the adults can take care of themselves.
> It was not the hours or the wages that discouraged me; it was the constant monotony of the work.

b. Use a semicolon before a transitional connective (conjunctive adverb) between two main clauses.

Transitional connectives are words like *also, besides, consequently, furthermore, hence, however, likewise, moreover, nevertheless, in addition, then, therefore,* which provide a transition from one sentence to the next.

> His argument has some merit; *however,* he goes too far.
> His eyes went bad; *consequently,* he had to resign his position as a proof-reader.

c. Use a semicolon to separate elements in a series when they contain internal punctuation.

> Among those present were Dr. Holmes, pastor of the First Methodist Church; A. C. Levitt, superintendent of schools; B. L. Rainey, manager of the Benson Hotel; and M. T. Cord, vice-president of Miller and Sons.

Had commas been used between the elements in this series they might be confused with the commas which set off the appositives.

P 4   *Misuse of the Semicolon*

a. Do not use a semicolon as the equivalent of a colon.

Although their names suggest a close relationship, semicolons and colons have quite different uses and are not interchangeable. The colon (see **P 7**) is used chiefly to indicate that something is to follow, usually a series of items; the semicolon is never used to introduce a series. In the following examples the faulty semicolon is followed by the correct colon in parentheses.

> My records show that the following students have not handed in the assignment; (:) Mr. Andrews, Mr. Richardson, Mr. Smith, and Miss Wallace.
> Dear Sir; (:) May I call your attention to an error. . . .

b. Do not use a semicolon as the equivalent of a comma.

Except in the special usage illustrated in **P 3c,** a semicolon cannot be substituted for a comma between a main clause and a subordinate construction. In the following examples the faulty semicolon is followed by the correct comma in parentheses.

> Although I seldom have trouble with grammar or spelling; (,) I never seem to use the right punctuation.
> We stayed up until two o'clock in the morning; (,) hoping that they would arrive.

P 5 *The Period*

a. A period is used to mark the end of a declarative sentence.

Unless a sentence is intended as a question, a command, or an exclamation, it is declarative and is closed by a period.

> Today is Tuesday.
> We have three days to go.

b. A period is used to mark an accepted abbreviation.

> *Titles:* Col., Dr., Hon., Mrs., Rev.
> *Degrees:* B.A., B.S., M.D., Ph.D.
> *Names:* John A. Jones; Chas. W. Brown
> *Months:* Jan., Feb., Aug., Nov.
> *States:* Ala., Ga., Me., Ill., Wash.
> *Miscellaneous:* Ave., St., vol., p., U.S.A., B.C., A.D.

Notice, however, that periods are not used in such shortened forms as *exam, gym, prom, per cent, 1st, 2nd, 3rd.* Periods are usually omitted in abbreviations of government agencies — *USNR, TVA, AEC, FBI, CIA, UNESCO.*

c. A period is used before a decimal and between dollars and cents.

The error is less than .01 inch.
The correct answer is 57.39.
The price tag read $11.98.

P 6   *Question and Exclamation Marks*

a. The question mark is used almost entirely to indicate that a sentence is to be understood as a question.

Whose is this?
You mean he's ill?

But if the question is a courteous way of stating a request, the end punctuation is a period, not a question mark:

Will you please hand in your papers now.

The question mark is sometimes used in parentheses to query the accuracy of the preceding word:

These amateurs (?) make a comfortable living out of sports.

As a device for irony, however, it is generally weak.

Notice that a question reported in indirect discourse does not have a question mark:

They asked where we were going.

b. The exclamation mark is used to show that a statement is imperative or that it is spoken with strong emotion.

Be quiet!
Buckle your seat-belts!
Don't just stand there! Do something!
Oh, what a mess!
God help us!

P 7   *The Colon*

The main uses of the colon are:

a. To indicate that something is to follow, especially a formal series.

Here are the facts: The money was there five minutes before he entered the room; it was missing immediately after he left; the next day he bought a new suit, although he had previously spent all of this month's allowance.

The slogan goes like this: Look sharp! Feel sharp! Be sharp!

b. In place of a comma before long or formal direct quotations.

In that speech Bryan said: "You shall not press down upon the brow of labor a crown of thorns; you shall not crucify mankind upon a cross of gold."

This is his statement as reported in the papers: "I have never advocated such ideas; I do not advocate them now; I do not approve of them; and I have no reason for believing that I ever will approve of them."

c. Before a clause which is intended to restate in different form the idea of the preceding clause.

Henry V is one of the great experiences in the history of motion pictures. It is not, to be sure, the greatest: the creation of new dramatic poetry is more important than the re-creation of the old.

Except for differences of subject matter, the rules of grammar are exactly like the laws of physics and chemistry: they are scientific generalizations about the facts.

In such uses the clause following the colon says, in another way, what was already said in the clause preceding the colon. The restatement, however, is not needless repetition: it serves to illustrate or amplify the content of the preceding clause.

P 8 *Quotation Marks*

This section is limited to the use of quotation marks. The troublesome question of the position of other punctuation with respect to quotation marks is treated separately in the next section.

Quotation marks may be double (" ") or single (' ').

Double Quotation Marks

Double quotation marks have the following uses:

a. To enclose the actual words of a speaker (direct discourse).

I said, "That's your worry."
"Bob," he said, "you can't do that!"
"What is the matter?" she asked.

Notice that since all the words of a speaker are enclosed in quotation marks an interrupting *he said, she replied,* etc., requires two sets of quotation marks in the sentence. Notice also that when direct discourse is reported as indirect discourse the quotation marks are not used.

She asked what was the matter.

b. To identify words which are being discussed as words.

> The word "garage" comes from the French; the word "piano" comes from the Italian.
>
> "Buxom" originally came from the Old English verb meaning "to bend."

This use is sometimes extended to include technical terms (*A "field" in mathematics is not what it is in agriculture*) and slang terms (*Her brother "socked" her in the eye and "beaned" her with a ruler*). Though occasionally acceptable, this usage is often overdone in student writing. Quotation marks do not make a term appropriate. If a word is appropriate in context, it can usually stand without quotation marks; if it is not appropriate, it should not be used.

An alternative method, and one preferred by some writers, is to underline or italicize the word being cited (see page 464):

> *To be* is the trickiest verb in the language.

c. To enclose the titles of short stories, poems, paintings, songs, etc. (but not books).

> I think Kipling's best short story is "Without Benefit of Clergy."
>
> It was Cole Porter who wrote "Begin the Beguine."
>
> Tennyson asked to have "Crossing the Bar" placed at the end of every edition of his poems.
>
> He says that Da Vinci's "Mona Lisa" is a portrait of an Italian noblewoman.

d. In bibliography, to distinguish the title of a selection from that of the whole book in which the selection is printed.

> Faulkner, William. "Two Soldiers," *Collected Stories of William Faulkner*. New York: Random House, 1950.

For additional examples of this use, see pages 259–260. Notice that titles of books are set in italics rather than in quotation marks.

Single Quotation Marks

Single quotation marks are used:

a. To mark quotations within quotations.

When it is necessary to include one set of quotation marks within another, the internal quotation is placed in single quotation marks, the longer quotation in double quotation marks:

> Here is an excerpt from my brother's letter: "Today in class Mr. Blair quoted Wordsworth's line 'A three-months darling of a pigmy size,' and said it appeared in one edition as 'A three-months darling of a pig my size.'"

When the director said, "Let's try that passage again, beginning with 'Once more into the breach,' and remember that this is a battle, not a declamation contest," there was an audible bronx cheer from one of the soldiers.

b. In print, as a substitute for double quotation marks to improve the appearance of the page.

When in a printed work it is necessary to place quotation marks around a great many single words, an editor will sometimes attempt to improve the appearance of the page by substituting single marks for double marks. The need for this substitution almost never exists in college writing.

P 9 *Punctuation with Quotation Marks*

Whether punctuation should be placed *inside* or *outside* quotation marks is often a problem. Practice is not uniform, but the following excerpt from *The MLA Style Sheet* — a respected authority among English instructors — states the prevailing procedure succinctly:

> For the sake of appearance put all commas or periods *inside* quotation marks. . . . Other punctuation goes inside quotation marks only when it is actually part of the quoted matter.[1]

This convention may be stated in detail as follows:

a. When the quoted words are followed by a comma, put the comma inside the quotation marks.

"If you insist," I said, "I'll do it."
The word "skirt," for example, has both standard and slang meanings.

Notice that this convention applies only to quoted material. It does not mean that a comma after *he said, she replied,* etc., should be placed inside the quotation marks.

b. The period, like the comma, always goes inside the quotation marks.

That is not the way to spell "eclectic."
He said, "You can always count on Tom to muddle the issue."

c. If the quotation is a question, the question mark goes inside the quotation marks; otherwise, it goes outside.

Somebody yelled, "Why don't you go home?" (What was yelled was a question.)

[1] From *The MLA Style Sheet*, Revised Edition, compiled by W. R. Parker, for the Modern Language Association of America. The omitted material indicated by the ellipsis refers to exceptions which almost never occur in freshman writing.

Did he actually say, "Let Williams do it"? (The quotation is not a question, but the whole sentence is; therefore the question mark goes outside the quotation marks, and no other punctuation is used at the end of the sentence.)

Well, how *do* you spell "eclectic"? (The whole sentence is a question, not the word "eclectic.")

d. The exclamation mark, like the question mark, goes inside if the quoted part is an exclamation; otherwise it goes outside.

"Get out of my sight!" he yelled. (The quoted part is an exclamation.)
I did, too, say "Friday"! (The whole sentence is an exclamation; "Friday" is not.)
His only answer was "Nonsense!" (Only the quoted word is an exclamation.)

e. Since the semicolon and the colon almost never occur as part of quoted material in terminal position, the practice is always to place them outside the quotation marks.

He said, "You can be confident that I'll do it"; but I was by no means confident.

If the sentence ended with the quotation, there would be a period inside the quotation marks. The semicolon is used to provide contrast between the two main clauses, not to end the first one.

"There are three parts," she said; "we have two of them."

Although the semicolon would be included in the quotation if it were written — She said, "There are three parts; we have two of them." — the semicolon is always placed after *she* (*he,* etc.) *said* when it interrupts such quotations.

f. When the dash is used to stand for an omitted part of a quotation, it is included within the quotation marks.

Occasionally a speaker is interrupted or for some reason fails to finish what he has begun to say. When this happens, a dash is used to show that the quotation is not finished.

"But Mary said — " she began, then stopped suddenly.
Nicholson said loudly, "In my opinion, our instructor is — " Just then the instructor walked into the room.

Notice that a concluding period is not used after the dash.

P 10   *The Apostrophe*

The apostrophe (') has three general uses:

a. Use an apostrophe to indicate the possessive case of a noun.

An apostrophe followed by *s* is added to the common case of the following types of nouns:

Both singular and plural nouns which do not end in s:

> boy's, girl's, ox's, mouse's, tooth's, antenna's
> men's, women's, oxen's, mice's, teeth's, antennae's

Singular nouns ending in s:

> James's, Charles's, Keats's, Burns's, Dickens's

Usage for the latter group varies. Some writers omit the final *s* (James', Charles', etc.). When a noun already contains two *s* sounds, there is a greater reluctance to add a third one (Massachusetts', mistress', Jesus'), but since most written communications are not read aloud the repetition of *s* sounds is usually not so objectionable as it might seem to be. With such nouns, follow your own preference. Notice that an apostrophe without an *s* is added to plural nouns ending in *s* — *babies' clothing.*

Indefinite pronouns:

> anybody's, anyone's, everybody's, one's, nobody's, someone's

b. Use an apostrophe to indicate the omission of letters or figures.

> I've, can't, hasn't, isn't, '48 (1948), the class of '39

c. Use an apostrophe to indicate the plural of letters or figures.

> Let's begin with the A's; look under the K's; the S's look like 8's.

P 11   *Ellipsis and Dash*

Ellipsis (. . .)

The basic use of the ellipsis (three periods) is to mark an incomplete construction.

Usually the ellipsis indicates that one or more words have been omitted from a quotation. It is also used to indicate that a progression of numbers continues beyond the last figure given (1,4,7,10,13,16 . . .). If an ellipsis occurs at the end of a sentence, a fourth period is usually added:

Original Quotation	*Elliptical Quotation*
Death is at all times solemn, but never so much as at sea. A man dies on shore, his body remains with his friends, and "the mourners go about the streets," but when a man falls overboard at sea and is lost, there is a sadness in the event, and a difficulty in realizing it, which gives it an air of awful mystery.	Death is at all times solemn, but never so much as at sea. A man dies on shore, his body remains with his friends, . . . but when a man falls overboard at sea and is lost, there is a sadness in the event, and a difficulty in realizing it. . . .

Dash

The dash should not be used as a general utility mark to substitute for a comma, period, semicolon, or colon. It is a specialized punctuation mark which serves the following purposes:

a. To stress a word or phrase at the end of a sentence.

In the whole world there is only one person he really admires — himself.

And now it is my pleasure to present a man whom we all know and admire and to whom we are all deeply indebted — the Reverend Dr. Mason.

Absence makes the heart grow fonder — of somebody else.

b. To sum up or complete an involved sentence.

To live as free men in a free country; to enjoy, even to abuse, the right to think and speak as we like; to feel that the state is the servant of its people; to be, even in a literal sense, a trustee and a partner in the conduct of a nation — all this is what democracy means to us.

c. To mark an interrupted or unfinished quotation.

"I'd like to," he said, "but I'm — "
"You're what?" I asked.
"Well, I'm — I — you see, I've never done anything like that before."

d. When used in pairs, to set off a pronounced interruption.

There will never again be — you may be sure of this — so glorious an opportunity.

This answer — if we can call it an answer — is completely meaningless.

447

P 12 *Parentheses and Brackets*

Parentheses

The three most common uses of parentheses are:

a. To enclose an explanation, qualification, or example.

His wife (he married about a year ago) is a member of a very fine New England family.

Nice (in the old sense of *discriminating*) has almost fallen out of use.

Foreign words (*data,* for example) slowly become naturalized and lose their foreign characteristics.

b. To enclose cross-references.

(*See* Appendix A), (See page 271)

(Consult *Webster's Biographical Dictionary.*)

George Bellows transcribed the world of sports in vivid oil paintings like "Dempsey and Firpo" (see Plate VI).

c. In formal business transactions, to repeat a sum previously stated in words.

I enclose three hundred dollars ($300.00) to cover my share of the costs.

Brackets

Brackets are used chiefly to enclose an editorial explanation or comment within a passage being edited or reported. The words within the brackets are supplied by the editor or reporter.

According to the Associated Press, Mrs. Henry Thall [the former June Wexler of this city] was a passenger on the missing plane.

I have written to [name of correspondent illegible] that I will not be a party to that transaction.

Brackets are occasionally used to enclose symbols which cannot conventionally be left without some enclosing device. The identification of the various punctuation marks on page 429 is an example of this use.

Review Exercises

A. Rewrite the following sentences, inserting as you write any punctuation clearly required by the conventions. If no punctuation is necessary, do not copy the sentence. To make your insertions obvious, use red ink or red pencil for punctuation which you add.

1. He said I propose to transfer at the end of the semester.
2. He said he would transfer at the end of the semester.
3. I expect he said to transfer at the end of the semester.
4. Dr J A Frazer was born on March 18 1901.
5. Dr Koch a German scientist discovered the tuberculosis bacillus.
6. The lecturer was the Rev Nelson Laird D D
7. Have you read his latest book
8. The cars in that series were as follows Aerosedan Fleetline Fleetmaster and Stylemaster.
9. The manuscript was dirty blotched and unevenly typed.
10. I have not seen him since his wife left he has been keeping to himself.
11. Mr. Reynolds the insurance man called.
12. She is quite inexperienced and has never worked in an office before.
13. See the new revolutionary car of the year the Ford.
14. She said, When I asked his opinion, he answered, I don't give advice on such questions.
15. I am enclosing eighty-five dollars $85.00 for the semiannual premium.
16. This meaning see *The American College Dictionary* is now established usage.
17. He looked at it enviously. Its a beauty he exclaimed
18. However I still have five payments to make.
19. That she wont like it may be taken for granted.
20. Do you think he will accept she asked

B. Distinguish between restrictive and nonrestrictive modifiers by inserting commas around the nonrestrictive modifiers in the following sentences. Use red ink or red pencil for inserted commas.

1. Girls who hate cooking are poor matrimonial risks.
2. Girls who are physically less rugged than boys should not be subjected to strenuous athletic programs.
3. The man driving the Ford is Clark.
4. Clark driving a Ford won easily.
5. Salesmen who don't argue with customers make more money.
6. Salesmen most of whom are young men lead an unsettled life.
7. The pilot realizing his plight radioed for instructions.
8. The pilot who radioed for instructions does not answer.
9. His wife satisfied with these concessions wisely kept quiet.
10. His wife resentful of his extravagance asked for an increased allowance.
11. They questioned the man who reported the robbery.
12. The man who reported the robbery cannot be found.
13. The man at the back of the room was told to leave.
14. The man evidently seriously hurt was taken to the hospital.
15. The fighters who were quite obviously stalling were disqualified.
16. Their wives who needed the money were indignant.

C. The best way to develop a confident knowledge of the conventions of punctuation is to observe how punctuation marks are actually used in modern writing. In the following selection particular punctuation marks have been numbered. Write down each number and describe the purpose for which the punctuation is being used.

Turning to the more modern theories,[1] which agree at least that language is of human rather than divine origin,[1] we encounter first what is best known by its nickname,[2] the "bow-wow" theory. This asserts that primitive language was exclusively *"echoic";*[3] that is,[3] that its words were directly imitative of the sounds of nature or of animals. All the wordstock is thought to have originated in a way parallel to the child's calling a dog "bow-wow"[4] or a duck "quack-quack."[4] The great objection to this theory is that it has not been demonstrated that early or primitive languages are composed exclusively or in great part of onomatopoetic words; on the contrary,[5] it is clear that the primitive languages of savage tribes are largely made up of words that are quite as conventional as those of civilized peoples. At best,[6] the "bow-wow" theory can explain the origin of but a part,[7] and not the largest part,[7] of language. Yet it seems fair to add that the theory has in the past been somewhat unjustly derided. Words that are imitative or at least partly so —[8] for there are many gradations between the purely imitative and the purely conventional —[8] do form an appreciable part of the vocabulary of most languages. There are many words that we instinctively feel to be symbolic, or semi-echoic. Thus,[9] such English words as *battle*,[10] *roar*,[10] and *thunder* have not perhaps a completely imitative quality, certainly not as compared with *hiss*,[11] *whistle*,[11] *bang*,[11] and *crash;* yet they approach echoism in a way that the conventional words of language do not. If,[12] then,[12] the "bow-wow" theory does not solve the riddle of the origin of language,[13] it does at least help to account for the sounds of many words.*

D. In the following selection all punctuation has been omitted, except the periods at the ends of the sentences. Copy the selection, adding all necessary punctuation in red.

The Bible is written in very poor English isnt it remarked a grade school child to his father as they walked home from church.

What makes you say that inquired the astonished parent for whose ears the musical dignity of the King James Version approached the perfection of English prose.

Well our teacher said it was bad English to begin sentences with and. But almost every sentence the minister read this morning began with and replied the child.

The father smiled as he recognized the accuracy of the childs observation. The reading had been from the eighth chapter of the Gospel according to St Matthew it was true enough that almost every sentence began with and. He thought a moment longer before he spoke. Your teacher has made a natural mistake he began. In trying to give good advice to boys and girls just learning to write she has made a rule about and. The rule is too big. People who know how to write well use and correctly and effectively at the beginning of sentences. On the other hand boys and girls in schools use and too much. Your teachers purpose in trying to help you was good but the rule she stated is untrue.

In this trifling episode may be found the epitome of the problem of correctness in English. It lies in the recurrent conflict between rule and practice. Rules of usage are usually made to cover specific situations to govern the use of language at a certain time for a certain purpose. Gradually as the rule is taught and applied the specific purpose for which it was created is forgotten and the rule is applied universally often in defiance of a language custom centuries old. Take for example the much taught but erroneous rule that a sentence must not end with a preposition. Or as one grammar is supposed to have stated it A preposition is a bad thing to end a sentence with. In certain types of formal literary English the terminal preposition is considered undesirable because of the rhetorical looseness it gives to the style. Because certain formalists disliked the construction the rule was created. It was repeated copied placed in school books. Teachers unaware of the reason behind the origin of the rule taught that a sentence must never end with a preposition. Teachers are still teaching this rule. Yet English for centuries has been idiomatically and correctly expressed in such sentences as Where are you from I didnt know whom to give it to. John will go but I dont expect to. What city has he lived in To apply the rule to such sentences as these which are characteristic of informal or colloquial English is to make an absurdity of a caution. Many such absurdities have been created and are being perpetuated through honest but misguided zeal.*

* From Robert C. Pooley, *Teaching English Usage.* Copyright, 1946, by the National Council of Teachers of English. Reprinted by permission of Appleton-Century-Crofts, Inc.

Mechanics

sp *Spelling*

One requirement of standard English is that words be spelled as they are spelled by educated writers and recorded in dictionaries. Colleges and universities are held responsible by society for ensuring that their graduates have a reasonable mastery of standard English. It is for this reason that college instructors insist that all college writing — even the most informal — show a decent regard for accepted spelling. The real purpose of this insistence is to protect the student; for conspicuously bad spelling is generally considered a clear sign of illiteracy. Socially and professionally, a student who cannot spell is at a disadvantage. It is easier to judge a man's spelling than most other things about him; and, whether rightly or not, people do jump to conclusions about a person's education and intelligence on the evidence of his spelling. A student who refuses to make a serious and sustained effort to cure major spelling deficiencies penalizes himself in college and out of it.

Students who spell poorly usually act on one of three assumptions: (*a*) that spelling is not important, (*b*) that nothing much can be done to improve one's spelling, or (*c*) that the only way to learn is to spend hours memorizing spelling lists. None of these assumptions is sound. Spelling *is* important. Provided that misspelling is not a result of an organic or psychological disorder, there is no reason why any student cannot train himself to be a reasonably good speller within a single semester. And an uncritical memorizing of spelling lists is not conspicuously effective.

How to Improve Your Spelling

The first step in improving your spelling is to take an inventory of your errors. Keep a record of those words *which you actually misspell in your writing*. This is your basic list. It should be reviewed periodically and kept up to date by dropping those words you have mastered and by adding new spelling errors.

In studying your list, concentrate on the *part* of the word which you misspell. Generally we do not misspell words but syllables. For example, most students who misspell *secretary* interchange the second and third vowels; most misspellings of *tragedy* are a result of placing an extra *d* before the *g;* and misspellings of such words as *receive, belief,* and *friend* come from reversing the *i* and *e*. Identifying your specific errors allows you to concentrate on the syllable in which the error occurs.

For words which prove unusually troublesome it is often helpful to learn or invent some memorizing device: a rule, a slogan, a jingle — anything, no matter how absurd, which will remind you of the correct spelling of a particular syllable. The rule of *i* before *e* except after *c,* which is stated as a jingle on page 456, and the rules for prefixes and suffixes, are generally useful memorizing devices. Unfortunately some rules have so many exceptions that they are hardly worth learning. It is therefore often wise to invent your own memorizing device. Some students find it extremely helpful to remember statements like *A good secretary keeps a secret, Remember the gum in argument,* and *Every cemetery has a "meter" in the middle.* Other students are helped by capitalizing the danger spots during spelling practice — tRAGedy, mainTENance, desPERate. If these devices help you, use them; if not, invent your own.

Finally, a concern with spelling during composition should, so far as is practicable, be postponed until revision. If you break off the writing of a paragraph to consult a dictionary, you may lose a thought you cannot recapture. If you keep a record of your misspellings, you will be conscious of troublesome words, so that when you are uncertain of a spelling, you can place a check in the margin and go on. Then, when the first draft is finished, look up the correct spelling of all checked words. Indeed, a student with severe spelling troubles will be wise to proofread his whole paper at least once for spelling alone.

In short, then: (1) Keep a spelling record, (2) study it at regular periods, (3) identify the trouble spot in the word, (4) devise a means of remembering the correct spelling, and (5) check your spelling when proofreading. If this procedure is followed conscientiously, spelling will soon cease to be a major problem.

The Most Common Traps in Spelling

Although any word which is not spelled phonetically (as it sounds) may give trouble, six types of words are especially likely to cause errors. These are:

1. **Words containing a "colorless" vowel.** Vowels in unstressed positions (*ago, agent,* awkw*a*rd, maint*e*nance, incred*i*ble, bachel*o*r) are likely to be pronounced as a very weak *uh.* This sound is called the colorless or neutral vowel.[1] Because it is quite common in English and because its sound gives no indication of its spelling, the colorless vowel is responsible for many spelling errors. There is nothing to guide one in spelling this sound. The only solution is to memorize the vowel in any word which repeatedly causes trouble. The best help is a memorizing device, such as magnifying

---

[1] Most dictionaries represent the colorless vowel by the phonetic symbol called the *schwa,* and written ə, like an inverted e.

the syllable in question — *baLANCE, indepenDENT, eligIBLE, sponSOR, foREIGN, chauffEUR.*

2. Words with *ie* or *ei*. Words like *niece, receive,* and *friend* are frequently misspelled through the interchanging of the *e* and the *i*. Most of these errors may be easily removed by following Rule 4 on page 456 and memorizing the eleven exceptions.

3. Words with similar sounds but different meanings. Such words as *altar, alter; peace, piece; weak, week; weather, whether* are easily confused. A list of troublesome contrasted pairs is given on pages 457–458. You should study that list and copy into your personal spelling record any pairs which you tend to confuse.

4. Words with irregular plural forms. Since most English nouns take *s* plurals, all plurals formed in any other way may be considered irregular. The most troublesome plurals to spell are those of nouns ending in *o* or *y*. Such nouns have regular *s* plurals when the *o* or *y* immediately follows a vowel (*cameo, cameos; key, keys; studio, studios*), but are generally irregular when the *o* or *y* follows a consonant (*cargo, veto, lady, torpedo*). See Rules 6 and 7 on page 456.

5. Words which double the final consonant before a suffix beginning with a vowel. Some words double a final consonant before adding a suffix beginning with a vowel (*refer, referred*), while others (*benefit, benefited*) do not. This lack of consistency causes many spelling errors, and the "rule" is so cumbersome and has so many exceptions that students often prefer to study the individual words which cause them trouble. The more useful part of the rule concerning doubled consonants is given as Rule 9 on page 457.

6. Common exceptions to general rules. Any exceptional spelling is likely to be difficult because of the tendency to make it conform to the regular pattern. For example, a student who is not sure how to spell *seize* is likely to interchange the *e* and *i* because of the *i*-before-*e* rule. Similarly the rule that a silent *e* at the end of a word is retained in adding a suffix beginning with a consonant leads many students to misspell *argument*. Words like these are exceptions to general rules and cause many spelling errors. The only safe procedure is to *memorize the exceptions along with the rule.* Whenever a rule is given in the following pages, the common exceptions are also noted. Study these as carefully as you study the rule itself.

Rules of Spelling

The rules given here are those which are most generally useful.

1. The prefixes *un-, dis-, mis-* do not affect the spelling of the root.

Thus, *unafraid* but *unnecessary; disappoint* but *dissatisfy; misrepresent* but *misspell.*

unable	disable	misbehave
unknown	disorder	misconduct
unopened	disregard	misguided
but	*but*	*but*
unnatural	disservice	misshapen
unnerved	dissimilar	misspent
unnoticed	dissolve	misstatement

2. When a suffix beginning with a consonant is added to a word ending in silent e, the e is retained.

Examples: *absolutely, achievement, extremely, indefinitely, sincerely.*

Exceptions: *argument, awful, duly, ninth, probably, truly, wholly.*

Three common words have alternative spellings:

abridgment, abridgement; acknowledgment, acknowledgement; judgment, judgement.

3. When a suffix beginning with a vowel is added to a word ending in silent e, the e is dropped unless it is required to indicate pronunciation or to avoid confusion with a similar word.

Examples: *accumulating, achieving, boring, coming, grievance, icy.*

Exceptions:

To Keep *a c or g Soft*	*To Prevent* *Mispronunciation*
advantageous	canoeist
changeable	eyeing
courageous	hoeing
manageable	mileage
noticeable	shoeing
outrageous	
peaceable	*To Prevent Confusion*
serviceable	*with Other Words*
singeing	
tingeing	dyeing
vengeance	

4. The order of the vowels in the *ie* combination (*ceiling, niece*) is explained in the jingle:

> Write *i* before *e*
> Except after *c*
> Or when sounded like *ay*
> As in *neighbor* and *weigh.*

Exceptions: *counterfeit, either, foreign, forfeit, height, leisure, neither, seize, seizure, sovereign, weird.*

5. Words ending with the sound *seed* are usually spelled -*cede.*

Examples: *accede, concede, intercede, precede, recede, secede.*

Exceptions: There are only four exceptions. Three of them end in -*ceed* (*exceed, proceed, succeed*); the fourth is the only word that ends in -*sede* (*supersede*).

6. Singular nouns ending in a consonant plus *y* form their plurals by changing the *y* to *i* before adding -*es.*

This rule also applies to the third person singular of verbs.

Examples: *ally, allies; baby, babies; city, cities; cry, cries; try, tries.*

Exceptions: The plurals of proper names often add *s* immediately after the *y: the Kellys, the Marys, the Sallys.*

Notice that singular nouns ending in a vowel plus *y* are regular and simply add -*s* to form the plural:

> *attorneys, donkeys, valleys.*

7. Singular nouns ending in a consonant plus *o* generally form their plurals by adding -*es.*

There are, however, so many exceptions that it may be safer to dispense with the rule and learn troublesome words individually.

Examples: *buffaloes, cargoes, echoes, heroes, potatoes, torpedoes, vetoes.*

Exceptions: The chief exceptions are musical terms: *altos, bassos, oratorios, pianos, solos, sopranos.* Others are *autos, cantos, dynamos, Eskimos, halos, mementos, provisos, quartos.*

Notice that singular nouns ending in a vowel plus *o* are regular and simply add -*s* to form the plural:

> *cameos, folios, radios, studios.*

456

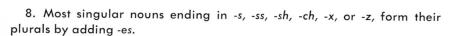

8. Most singular nouns ending in *-s, -ss, -sh, -ch, -x,* or *-z,* form their plurals by adding *-es.*

Examples: *Jameses, Joneses, ashes, bushes, matches, pitches, foxes, taxes, buzzes.*

Exceptions: *bass, fish, perch, six's, Swiss,* and borrowed Greek nouns ending in *-is* (*ellipsis — ellipses, thesis — theses,* etc.).

9. Words of one syllable double the final consonant before adding a suffix beginning with a vowel if (1) they end in a single consonant, and (2) they contain a single vowel.

Notice that the rule holds only if both conditions are satisfied. Thus a word of one syllable ending in two consonants does not double the final consonant before a suffix beginning with a vowel (ac*t*ing, as*k*ed, par*t*ing, si*ft*ed, etc.). And a one-syllable word containing two vowels does not double the final consonant (bea*r*ing, cree*p*ing, dea*l*ing, ree*l*ing, soa*r*ing, etc.).

This rule is extended to words of more than one syllable, provided that the accent falls on the last syllable (thus prefér — preferred, but bénefit — benefited; confér — conferring, but cónference). This part of the rule, however, has so many exceptions that students sometimes find the rule more confusing than helpful.

Review Exercises

A. Errors in the following words may be classified as errors in spelling or errors in diction, since both meaning and spelling are involved in the correct usage. Study these words carefully. Check those which you have confused in the past or of which you are uncertain and look them up in your dictionary.

accept, except	cite, sight, site
access, excess	coarse, course
adapt, adopt	complement, compliment
adaptation, adoption	conscience, conscious
affect, effect	council, counsel
all together, altogether	dairy, diary
altar, alter	decent, descend, descent
angel, angle	desert, dessert
berth, birth	dining, dinning
born, borne	dying, dyeing
canvas, canvass	elicit, illicit
capital, capitol	emigrant, immigrant
censor, censure	euphemism, euphuism

fare, fair	presence, presents
formally, formerly	principal, principle
forth, fourth	prophecy, prophesy
hear, here	quiet, quite
holy, wholly	respectively, respectfully
instance, instants	right, rite
irrelevant, irreverent	shone, shown
its, it's	sleight, slight
knew, new	speak, speech
know, no	staid, stayed
later, latter	stationary, stationery
lead, led	straight, strait
loath, loathe	suit, suite
loose, lose	threw, through
luxuriant, luxurious	to, too, two
moral, morale	troop, troupe
past, passed	vain, vein, vane
peace, piece	weak, week
plain, plane	weather, whether
precede, proceed	who's, whose

B. Some of the following words form their plurals by adding *-s* to the singular form, some by adding *-es*. Write out the plurals which take *-es:*

alto, analysis, auto, ditch, dynamo, echo, Eskimo, fox, hero, piano, radio, solo, synopsis, tobacco, tomato, veto.

C. Write the plural forms of the following nouns:

alley, alumna, alumnus, attorney, axis, baby, basis, belief, category, crisis, half, key, lady, loaf, major general, mother-in-law, ox, quantity, study, tax, taxi, try, 5, 7, A.

D. Write the simple past tense form of the following verbs:

act, annul, benefit, confer, crop, defer, develop, drip, drop, equip, excel, gas, kidnap, occur, propel, quiz, reap, rebel, refer, regret, rip, rob, scar, slip, stop, strap, worship, wrap.

abr *Abbreviations*

In general, abbreviations should be used in college writing only if they satisfy two conditions: they must be standard abbreviations recognized by dictionaries, and they must be appropriate to the context. The first condition rules out such slang abbreviations as *b.f.* (boy friend) and *n.g.* (no good). The second requires students to recognize that many standard abbreviations (*advt., Ave., Feb., Xmas*) are inappropriate in a formal style and that abbreviations of certain titles (*Col., Dr., Mr., Rev.*) are used only when followed by the name of the person to whom the title applies.

The following is a summary of the most common standard abbreviations. For the correct form of abbreviations not included in this list, consult your dictionary.

Bibliographical terms: *cf., ibid., vol., pp.* (For these and others, see pages 275–278.)

Names of days: *Sun., Mon., Tues., Wed., Thurs., Fri., Sat.* (Used only in dates.)

Names of months: *Jan., Feb., Aug., Sept., Oct., Nov., Dec.* (Used only in dates.)

Names of organizations: *A.F.L., C.I.O., D.A.R., U.S. Steel, W.C.T.U.*

Names of government agencies: *AAA, CIA, FBI, SEC, TVA.* (Notice that abbreviations of government agencies generally do not require periods.)

Names of states: *Calif., Del., Mass., N.Y., Ill.* (Used chiefly in addresses.)

Signs: When the context permits, the following signs are used as abbreviations: & (ampersand: see Glossary), $ (dollar), £ (British pound sterling), % (per cent), *" "* (ditto marks, used in tabulations to repeat the item immediately above the marks).

caps *Use of Capital Letters*

a. Capitalize the first word of each sentence and of each line of regular poetry.

Ask for Mr. Lane. He is in charge of service.
Too bad! Better luck next time.

> Earth has not anything to show more fair;
> Dull would he be of soul who could pass by
> A sight so touching in its majesty: . . .
> — Wordsworth, "Composed Upon Westminster Bridge"

b. Capitalize the first word of a direct quotation.

The President's answer was, "No comment."
"If you will give me a receipt," I said, "you can have the money now."

c. Capitalize proper nouns.

Sergeant York was one of the great heroes of World War I.
She works for the National Broadcasting Company.
Laurence Olivier was knighted after his production of *Henry V*.
I find French easier than German.
The *Saratoga* was sunk at Bikini.
The Amazon is longer than the Mississippi.

Note: Words which were originally proper nouns but have taken on more general meanings are regarded as common nouns and are not capitalized: *boycott, calico, china* (dishes), *port* (wine), *tweed*.

d. Capitalize adjectives formed from proper nouns.

> They seem to be ignorant of the *American* point of view.
> There is a *Miltonic* quality in this verse.
> The *Renaissance* period was Italy's second hour of glory.
> The inductive method has been called the *Baconian* method.
> He is studying the *Pauline* doctrines.

Note: Words originally derived from proper nouns cease to be capitalized when they are used as allusions rather than as direct references to the original noun. For example, *colossus, gargantuan, herculean, meandering,* and *panic* do not take capitals. *Philippic* is capitalized when it refers directly to the orations made by Demosthenes, but not when it is used to describe some other denunciatory speech.

e. Capitalize nouns or pronouns referring to the deity:

> *God, Lord, our Father, Saviour, Messiah, Trinity, Holy Ghost, He, His, Him.*

f. Capitalize names of offices only when they are used as titles:[1]

Capitalized	*Not Capitalized*
District Attorney Johnson	Tell it to the district attorney.
Prime Minister Wilson.	Eden is a former prime minister.
Dr. A. L. Street, Chairman of the Civic Betterment Committee.	He was made chairman of the committee.
Professor Swanson	He is a college professor.

Note: President, Presidential, and *Presidency* are capitalized when they refer to the office of President of the United States: *One of these men will be our next President; the Presidency is at stake.*

g. Capitalize *north, south, east,* and *west* and their derivatives only when they refer to geographical areas.

Capitalized	*Not Capitalized*
We found the South charming.	Next year we are going south.
Her parents live in the East.	New York is east of Chicago.
They live on the West Side.	The west side of the field is wet.
The Southern armies fought gallantly.	The house has a fine southern exposure.

[1] The convention stated here is a simplification of actual practice. The usage of newspapers varies: some capitalize important offices when they are not used as titles; others omit capitals even in titles.

h. Capitalize titles of books, magazines, plays and the headings of chapters or sections of a work.

The preferred practice is to capitalize all significant words in a title, including the first word:

> *A Child's History of the United States*
> *The Return of the Native*
> *Mourning Becomes Electra*

Some publishers, however, capitalize every word in the title:

> *A Child's History Of The United States*

Either form is acceptable in college writing, but be consistent.

i. Capitalize the names of days, months, and holidays.

> New Year's Day will fall on Tuesday.
> Next Sunday is Mother's Day.
> The favorite vacation months are July and August.

j. Avoid unnecessary capitalization.

In general, do not use capitals unless they are required by one of the conventions stated above. The modern tendency is to use a small letter whenever the conventions permit. Especially avoid unnecessary capitalization of the names of the seasons, of family relationships (*father, mother, sister, uncle*), and of such words as *army, college, freshman, navy, sophomore, university,* unless they are being considered as proper nouns.

Capitalized	*Not Capitalized*
He is a captain in the Army of the United States.	In foreign affairs an army is a political instrument.
Whom do you pick in the Army-Navy game?	The senator said we must have an army and a navy second to none.
Uncle Bill and Aunt Martha are here.	All the uncles and aunts were present.
Where is Sanford Junior College?	He wants a college education.
The University will have a strong team next year.	He is a university professor.
Are you going to the Freshman Hop?	Are you a freshman or a sophomore?
The Summer Festival starts next week.	I like summer best and winter least.
He belonged to The Society for the Prevention of Cruelty to Animals.	He belonged to a society for the prevention of cruelty to animals.

hyph *Hyphenation*

Hyphens are used for two purposes: to divide a word at the end of a line, and to join two or more words of a compound which is not written solid.

a. Use a hyphen to break a word at the end of a line.

The use of a hyphen to break a word at the end of a line is less frequently necessary in manuscript copy than it is in print. In student writing, words should be broken at the ends of lines only when failure to hyphenate would result in obviously awkward spacing. If hyphenation seems necessary, the following conditions should be observed:

1. Do not break words of one syllable.

If there is not room at the end of a line for such words as *burst, change, drink, through,* carry the whole word over to the next line.

2. Do not separate a suffix of less than three letters from the rest of the word, or break on a one-letter prefix.

An *-ing* may be separated, but single letters or *-al, -le, -ly,* and *-ed* endings should not. Words like *about, against,* and *open* should not be broken.

3. Break words only between syllables.

When in doubt about syllables, consult your dictionary.

4. Break compound words between the elements of the compound.

Compound Word	*Hyphenation*
armchair	arm-chair
blackbird	black-bird
sailboat	sail-boat

5. Subject to the limitations stated in (2), hyphenate between prefix and root or between root and suffix.

Between Prefix and Root	*Between Root and Suffix*
ante-cedent	adapt-able
be-loved	back-ward
com-mit	depend-ent
con-tagious	ego-ism
dis-appear	kitchen-ette
inter-rupt	lemon-ade

Between Prefix and Root	*Between Root and Suffix*
intro-duce	mile-age
per-suade	racket-eer
trans-late	trouble-some

b. Use a hyphen between elements of a compound when usage calls for it.

Hyphenation of compounds varies so much that college students should keep two points in mind: (1) for any particular word, the only safe authority is a reliable, up-to-date dictionary; (2) whenever usage is uncertain, a writer is allowed a choice between competing usages.

Some compounds (*applesauce, blackboard, steamship*) are written solid; others (*dirt cheap, place kick, wedding ring*) are nearly always written as separate words; still others (*father-in-law, ready-made, up-to-date*) are hyphenated. A hyphen is required in the following types.

1. Hyphenate a compound modifier preceding a noun.

A self-made man	An off-the-cuff judgment
A well-dressed woman	A tear-jerking movie
A pay-as-you-go tax	A Sunday-morning golf game
A round-by-round report	A dog-in-the-manger attitude

Notice that compound numerical modifiers fall into this class: *Twenty-seven dollars, one hundred and twenty-five pounds, a two-thirds majority.* However, whole numbers below twenty-one are not hyphenated: *Their nineteenth anniversary; the sixteenth of May.* Notice also that a compound modifier following a noun is usually not hyphenated: *The woman was well dressed; the machine is worn out.*

2. Hyphenate a compound consisting of a prefix and a proper noun.

pro-Russian, un-American, anti-Castro.

3. Hyphenate compounds of ex ("former") and a noun.

ex-wife, ex-sweetheart, ex-President.

4. Hyphenate to avoid confusion with another word.

re-cover to prevent confusion with *recover*.
re-creation to prevent confusion with *recreation*.

5. Hyphenate most compounds beginning with *self*.

self-satisfied, self-government, self-conceit. (But *selfless* and *selfsame* are written solid.)

463

ital *Use of Italics*

Words in print are made to stand out by using a special kind of slanting type called *italic;* they are similarly set off in manuscript by underlining. Italics or underlining is used for the following purposes:

a. To indicate that a word is still considered a foreign element in the language.

> *en rapport, in absentia.*

b. To mark titles of publications, movie and stage productions, musical compositions, etc., and the names of airplanes, ships, and trains.

> Mencken's *The American Language*
> the *Saturday Review*
> Beethoven's *Eroica*
> Da Vinci's *Last Supper*
> the New York Central's *Twentieth Century Limited*
> Lindbergh's *Spirit of Saint Louis*

c. To call attention to a word being named. (See also page 443.)

> The word *judgment* has two spellings.
> What does *discriminate* mean?
> A good example is the phrase *to go scot free.*

d. To emphasize a word.

> Not *Angles* but *angels.*
> That is *precisely* the point.

This last device should be used sparingly. Overused, it becomes a poor substitute for emphatic diction.

no *Forms of Numbers*

Whether numbers should be written in words or figures depends partly on the nature of the writing. Scientific, statistical, and technical writing uses figures whenever possible. In essays and literary publications numbers are more frequently written out, and the more formal the style, the less figures are used. The following advice holds for the kind of writing you will do in a composition class.

a. Figures are used in writing dates, hours, and street numbers.

January 22, 1967	5:00 A.M.	17 Main Street
January 1	6:15 P.M.	417 Fifth Avenue
the year 1860	0430 (military style)	1021 Third Street

Notice that figures are used for street numbers but that street names, even when they are numbers, are usually written out to avoid confusion with house numbers.

b. Figures are used in recording sums of money other than round sums.

$2.75; 98 cents; *but* a hundred dollars; thirty cents.

If the style is informal, even round sums may be expressed as figures.

$40 million; 100 dollars; 30 cents; 40,000 spectators.

c. Use figures for large numbers that would be awkward to write out.

365 days; 1760 yards; 14,320 students.

d. Use figures in citing volume, chapter, and page references.

This whole question is discussed in Volume 2 of Brand's work. Our topic is discussed in Chapter 5; turn to page 37.

e. Do not use figures at the beginning of a sentence.

Sixty per cent is a passing grade. *Not:* 60% is a passing grade.

f. Generally avoid figures when a number can be conveniently expressed in one word.

one, five, third, quarter, twelve.

But in an informal style and in scientific writing, numbers over ten are frequently expressed in figures.

g. Do not use figures in a formal invitation or reply.

on Saturday the twenty-third of June
at seven-thirty o'clock in the evening

This most formal usage is an exception to the practice recommended in **a** above.

465

h. Roman numerals are used chiefly as volume and chapter numbers in some books and as page numbers in the front matter of books.

Because Roman numerals are so little used, they are often confusing to students. Most of this confusion can be eliminated by first recognizing the key numerals and then understanding the principle by which these are combined.

The key numerals are i (1), v (5), x (10), l (50), c (100), d (500), m (1000), which may be written in capitals: I, V, X, L, C, D, M. The basic principle is that higher numbers are created by adding another unit to a lower number — i, ii, iii, vi, xi — or by subtracting a unit from a higher number — iv, ix, xl, xc.

	Units	*Tens*	*Hundreds*
1	i	x	c
2	ii	xx	cc
3	iii	xxx	ccc
4	iv	xl	cd
5	v	l	d
6	vi	lx	dc
7	vii	lxx	dcc
8	viii	lxxx	dccc
9	ix	xc	cm

Review Exercises

A. Rewrite the following sentences to substitute abbreviations and figures where permissible in college composition:

1. Have you seen the new professor? He has a Doctor of Philosophy degree from Cornell.
2. Mister Thompson is not here, but you can telephone him at three-nine-seven–five-seven-five-two.
3. My sister graduated from the University of Illinois with a Bachelor of Arts degree in June nineteen hundred and sixty-one.
4. She was married on the twentieth of January, nineteen hundred and sixty-two.
5. Her husband is Doctor William Reid, a research economist with the American Federation of Labor.
6. Look on page one thousand four hundred and seventy.
7. He was born on January thirty-one at five minutes after eleven post meridiem.
8. The date of the battle of Hastings is anno Domini 1066.
9. Send this letter to Colonel Donald Andrews, care of the Thirty-third Division at Fort Sam Houston.
10. Fifty-four people were hurt in the wreck, including the three top executives of the Columbia Broadcasting System.

B. Rewrite the following sentences to remove any abbreviations or figures which would be undesirable in college composition:

    1. The speaker was a prof. from the U. of Indiana.
    2. I saw her downtown this A.M.
    3. 10 days later, the man died.
    4. The candidate spoke as often as 8 times in a single day.
    5. Somebody said to me, "Mr., this man needs a Dr."
    6. The party consisted of Brig. Gen. T. A. Smith, a Col., and two Lt. Cols.
    7. The math exam will be held in Rm. 511 at 2:00 P.M.
    8. He paid $20; he could have bought a good second-hand one for $5.

C. In the following sentences, change lower case letters to capitals wherever the conventions require such a change:

    1. She asked, "what makes it spin?"
    2. it is one of the best of the english movies.
    3. Some of his activities are alleged to be unamerican.
    4. The words are, "our father which art in heaven, hallowed be thy name."
    5. The greeks called their chief god *zeus;* the romans called him *jupiter.*
    6. The king James bible is called the authorized version. It was translated by a committee of biblical scholars.
    7. The title is *20,000 leagues under the sea.*
    8. F. D. Roosevelt is the only president who won the presidency four times.
    9. What did you get your mother for mother's day?
    10. The bowl games are played chiefly in the west and south. The winter weather in the north and east is not suitable for post-season football.

D. In the following sentences remove unnecessary capitalization:

    1. He is a Four-Star General in the U.S. Army.
    2. Our Navy is twice as large as that of the British.
    3. This course is required for all Freshmen. Sophomores who are transfers from another University may also be required to take it.
    4. My Father wants me to be a University Professor, but I prefer a better-paying Profession.
    5. Spring may be the most beautiful Season, but I prefer Fall.
    6. Go East for three blocks and then turn North.
    7. It will soon be time for the birds to start their Southern migrations.
    8. Her Uncle is a Rear Admiral in the Navy and an authority on Naval strategy.
    9. He studied for the Ministry before going to Law School.
    10. "I will do it," She said, "If you will help me."

▶ Glossary

This is a reference section. Its main purpose is to list those words and constructions which frequently cause trouble in composition and to advise you whether particular usages are acceptable in college writing and, if they are, under what conditions. A secondary purpose is to explain some grammatical and rhetorical terms not discussed elsewhere in the text. Since this book has a separate index giving page references for all subjects discussed in the text, the Glossary usually does not duplicate these references.

The judgments about usage recorded here have been made after consulting the following sources: *The American College Dictionary, The Oxford English Dictionary, Webster's Third New International Dictionary, Webster's New World Dictionary,* Theodore M. Bernstein's *The Careful Writer,* Margaret M. Bryant's *Current American Usage,* Bergen and Cornelia Evans's *A Dictionary of Contemporary American Usage,* and H. W. Fowler's *A Dictionary of Modern English* (Second Edition); but because these sources do not always agree, the judgments made here are the author's conclusions. Since dictionaries do not distinguish between formal and informal standard usage, except by the label "Colloquial,"[1] it has seemed wise to indicate whether particular usages would be more appropriate to a formal than to an informal style, and whether certain colloquialisms would be generally acceptable in college writing. The usefulness of this advice, however, depends on your understanding its limitations. In any choice of usage, the decision depends less on what dictionaries or textbooks say than on what is consistent with the purpose and style of the writing. The student and his instructor are the best judges of that question. All that this Glossary can do is report what is generally acceptable. You yourself must decide whether a specific usage is appropriate in the particular paper which you are writing. The general assumption in the Glossary is that college writing is predominantly informal rather than either colloquial or formal. That assumption implies that the classification of a usage as *informal* in no way suggests that it is less desirable than a *formal* usage.

access — excess The second syllable of both words comes from a Latin root meaning "to go." Etymologically, *access* means "a going toward," hence "approach" or "admission" [The auditor has access to the records]. *Excess* originally meant "going out or beyond," hence its present meaning of "beyond what is necessary or desirable" [He worries to excess; a tax on excess profits].

---

[1] *Webster's Third International Dictionary* has dropped the "Colloquial" label used in previous editions of *Webster's New International Dictionary* and no longer identifies usages which are more appropriate in conversation than in writing.

accusative case   In modern English, the objective case.

acronym   An abbreviation which is pronounced as a word and is made up of the first letters of the title or phrase being abbreviated [CORE (Congress of Racial Equality); snafu (situation normal, all fouled up)].

ad   Clipped form of *advertisement*. Colloquial. Appropriate in informal styles, but the full form, *advertisement,* is preferred in formal writing, especially in letters applying for a position.

A.D.   Abbreviation for Latin *Anno Domini* (in the year of our Lord). Opposite of B.C. (before Christ). Used to distinguish dates before and after the beginning of the Christian era [He lived from 31 B.C. to A.D. 12; from 100 B.C. to A.D. 100 is 200 years]. A.D. is properly written before the figure; B.C., after it.

adapt — adept — adopt   *Adapt* means "adjust to meet requirements" [The human body can adapt itself to all sorts of environments]. *Adept* means "skilled" or "proficient" [He is adept at various sports]. *Adopt* means "to take as one's own" [He immediately adopted the idea] or — in parliamentary procedure — "to accept as a law" [The motion was adopted].

advice — advise   The first form is a noun, the second a verb [I was advised to ignore your advice].

affect — effect   Words often confused because of similarity of sound. Both may be used as nouns, but *effect,* meaning "result," is almost invariably the word wanted [His speech had an unfortunate effect; the treatments had no effect on me]. The noun *affect* is a technical term in psychology. Though both words may be used as verbs, *affect* is the more common. As a verb, *affect* means "impress," "influence," or "disturb" [His advice affected my decision; does music affect you that way?]. As a verb, *effect* is rarely required in student writing, but may be used to mean "carry out" or "accomplish" [The aviator effected his mission; the lawyer effected a settlement]. For students who have chronic difficulty with these words, a useful rule is to use *affect* only as a verb, and *effect* only as a noun.

affective — effective   See **affect — effect**. The common adjective is *effective* [an effective argument], meaning "having an effect." The use of *affective* is largely confined to technical discussions of psychology and semantics, in which it is roughly equivalent to "emotional."

aggravate   Distinguish between the formal meaning, "to make worse" [His remarks aggravated the dispute], and the informal meaning, "to annoy or exasperate" [Her manners aggravate me]. Dictionaries classify the second meaning as colloquial. It is appropriate in very informal writing, but in some contexts *exasperate, irritate, annoy,* or *provoke* will be more precise.

ain't   Unless a student is attempting to record nonstandard speech, the use of *ain't* is not acceptable in college speech or writing.

alibi   In formal English the word is a legal term used to indicate that a defendant was *elsewhere* when the crime was committed. Colloquially *alibi* is used to mean excuse [I'm not worried about being late, I have a good alibi]. This usage is common in informal writing.

all the farther, further, quicker Colloquial in some areas but generally unacceptable in college writing. Use "as far as," "as quick as."

all together — altogether Distinguish between the phrase [They were all together at last] and the adverb [He is altogether to blame]. *All together* means "all in one place"; *altogether* means "entirely" or "wholly."

alliteration Repetition of the same consonant, especially an initial consonant, in several words within the same sentence or line of poetry [The *m*urmuring of *imm*emorial el*m*s; *T*ippecanoe and *T*yler *t*oo]. Alliteration is a common device in poetry and in slogans, but it should be used with restraint in ordinary prose since its overuse or inappropriate use may seem affected.

allow When used to mean "permit" [No smoking allowed on the premises] *allow* is acceptable. Its use to mean "think" [He allowed it could be done] is nonstandard and is not acceptable in college writing.

allude — elude — refer When we *allude* to something we make an indirect or casual reference to it [He never actually identified himself as an officer, but he frequently alluded to details of army life as though he knew what it was to command troops in the field]. *Elude* means "to escape or avoid detection" [By these means he eluded the police for years]. *Refer* means "to direct attention" to something [The instructor referred us to the *Oxford Dictionary*].

allusion — illusion Words sometimes confused because of similarity of sound. An *allusion* is a reference [The poem contains several allusions to Greek mythology]. An *illusion* is an erroneous mental image [Rouge on pallid skin gives an illusion of health].

alot Although *a lot* is idiomatic and is appropriate in informal writing, it must be written as two words.

alright An established variant spelling of *all right,* but there is still considerable objection to it. *All right* is the preferred spelling.

altho Now accepted as a variant spelling of *although,* but the longer form is preferred in English classes.

A.M., P.M., a.m., p.m. Abbreviations for the Latin phrases *ante meridiem* (before noon), *post meridiem* (after noon). A.M. is used to indicate the period from midnight to noon; P.M., from noon to midnight. These abbreviations are used only when a specific hour is named [The first watch on a ship is from 12 P.M. to 4 A.M.]. The use of these abbreviations to stand for *morning* and *afternoon* when no hour is named [He gets up late in the a.m. and goes back to bed early in the p.m.] is a slang use not acceptable in college writing. Notice that either capital or small letters may be used in these abbreviations.

amount — number The occasional confusion of these words in college writing creates awkwardness. *Amount* suggests bulk or weight. [We collected a considerable amount of scrap iron]. *Number* is used for groups, the individual members of which may be counted [He has a large number of friends; there is a number of letters to be answered].

ampersand   The sign &, an abbreviation for *and,* is used in some company names [G. & C. Merriam Co.] and in various types of notations. Except in statistical tabulation it is not acceptable in college writing.

an   Variant of indefinite article *a.* Used instead of *a* when the following word begins with a vowel sound [an apple, an easy victory, an honest opinion, an hour]. When the following word begins with a consonant sound, or with *y, u,* or a pronounced *h,* the article should be *a* [a yell, a unit, a history, a house]. Such constructions as *a apple, a hour* are nonstandard. The use of *an* before *historical* and *humble* is an older usage which is dying out.

angle   The use of *angle* to mean "point of view" [Let's look at it from a new angle] is acceptable, but the word is so overused in college writing — and so often used inaccurately — that many instructors object to it. Use it sparingly.

antonym   A word opposite in meaning to a given word. Thus, *love* is the antonym for *hate.*

anybody's else   An old form of *anybody else's.* It is no longer conventional.

anywheres   A nonstandard variant of *anywhere.*

apposition   In grammar, two constructions are in apposition when the second follows and identifies the first, as in "Mr. Botts, *the chemistry instructor,* has resigned." Most frequently the appositive is treated as a nonrestrictive modifier (see pages 433–435) and is therefore set off by commas, as above. When, however, the appositive word or phrase is felt to be so closely related to the construction with which it is in apposition that the two cannot be separated, it is treated as a restrictive modifier and written without commas [*Secretary of State* Rusk, *Commander-in-Chief* Lyndon B. Johnson].

apt   See **liable.**

Arabic numerals   The numbers 1, 2, 3, etc., as contrasted with Roman numerals [I, II, III; i, ii, iii].

around   The uses of *around* to mean "about" [He arrived around four o'clock], "near" [That is how they pronounce it around Brooklyn], and "throughout" [We traveled around the country] are colloquial. They are generally acceptable in college writing.

as . . . as   The use of *as . . . as* in a negative statement [I am not as old as she is] is sometimes censured on the assumption that this construction should be used only for affirmative statements and that the correct negative form is "not *so* old as." In a very formal style the "not so . . . as" form may be preferable; but both forms are educated usage, and either is appropriate in college writing. In an affirmative statement, use *as . . . as.*

as = because   Although it is accepted standard English, *as* is weaker than *because* to show causal relation between main and subordinate clauses. Since *as* has other meanings, it may in certain contexts be confusing [As I was going home, I decided to telephone]. Here *as* may mean *when* or *because*. If there is any possibility of confusion, it is wise to use *because* or *while* — whichever is appropriate to the meaning.

as = that   The use of *as* to introduce a noun clause [I don't know as I would agree to that] is colloquial. This usage would be hopelessly inappropriate at a formal level and would be rejected by most college instructors at an informal level. Unless you are deliberately aiming at a colloquial style, use *that*.

as if = as though   Synonymous constructions. The first is slightly less formal, but either is appropriate in college writing.

as to = with respect to   Although *as to* is unquestionably standard usage, many instructors object to it on the ground that it is jargon (see page 486). Certainly its overuse should be avoided, and in an informal style *about* would be more appropriate than either *as to* or *with respect to*. For example, "I am not concerned as to your father's reaction" sounds stilted. It would be more natural to say, "I am not concerned [*or* I do not care] about your father's reaction."

assonance   The similarity of vowel sounds in words which do not rhyme [we — weep, fine — white].

asterisk   The sign *. A single asterisk is sometimes used as a footnote marker or to indicate items in a list which deserve special attention. A row of asterisks is sometimes used to indicate that the action of a story has been broken off or to suggest an interval of time.

at   Avoid the use of the redundant *at* in such sentences as "Where were you at?" "Where do you live at?"

auxiliary verb   A "helping" verb which combines with another to form a verb phrase [I *am* going; he *has been* talking]. The most common auxiliaries are *be, can, do, may, must, ought, shall, will*.

awful, awfully   The real objection to *awful* is not that it is colloquial but that it is worked to death. It is inappropriate in a formal style unless used to mean "awe-inspiring." As a utility word it has become almost indispensable in informal speech, but the more deliberate nature of writing and the opportunities it allows for revision make the overuse of this word objectionable.

back of = behind   The latter is the more formal usage, but both are generally acceptable in college writing.

bad   The ordinary uses of *bad* as an adjective cause no difficulty. As a predicate adjective [An hour after dinner I began to feel bad] it is sometimes confused with the adverb *badly*. After the verbs *look, feel, seem*, the adjective is preferred. Say, "It looks bad for our team," "I feel bad about that quarrel," "She seemed bad this morning." But do not use *bad* when an adverb is required, as in "He played badly," "A badly torn suit."

badly = very much   *Badly* is used in informal and colloquial writing as an intensifying word [I wanted badly to be asked; he was badly in need of a shave]. When it is used in this way, care should be taken to avoid misleading word order. In "I wanted to play very badly" the adverb may be interpreted as a modifier of *to play,* which the writer did not intend. In college writing it would be safer to avoid this use of *badly* and to use one of various possible synonyms. For example, "He was obviously in need of a shave," "I was eager to play."

balance = rest of, remainder   Now accepted as established usage in all dictionaries, though *rest of* or *remainder* would be preferred in a formal style.

bank on = rely on   In college writing the more formal *rely on* is generally preferred.

because   See **reason is because.**

being as   The use of *being as* for "because" or "since" in such sentences as "Being as I am an American, I believe in democracy," is nonstandard and is not acceptable in college speech or writing. Say, "Because I am an American, I believe in democracy."

between, among   In general, *between* is used of two people or objects and *among* for more than two [We had less than a dollar between the two of us; *but* We had only a dollar among the three of us].

The general distinction, however, should be modified when insistence on it would be unidiomatic. For example, *between* is the accepted form in the following examples:

He is in the difficult position of having to choose between three equally
   attractive girls.
A settlement was arranged between the four partners.
Just between us girls . . . (Any number of girls)

Bible   When used to refer to the Scriptures, "Bible" is always capitalized, but not italicized. When used metaphorically [*Das Kapital* is the bible of the Communists], the word is not capitalized.

blame on   This usage [He blamed it on his brother] is accepted without reservation by some dictionaries but labeled colloquial by others. The more formal usage would be "He blamed his brother for it," but either would be generally acceptable in college writing.

blond — blonde   In French the first is the masculine form, the second the feminine. This distinction is largely, but not always, preserved in English when the sex of the person is clearly known, but when the adjective refers to groups of persons of both sexes, use *blond* [All the children are blonds].

broke   When used as an adjective, *broke* is a slang synonym for "bankrupt" or "out of funds." This usage is common in informal, educated speech, but in college writing it should be restricted to papers clearly colloquial in style. The use of such circumlocutions as "financially embarrassed" is generally more objectionable than the slang itself. Simply say, "I had no money."

When used as a verb, *broke* is the simple past tense of *break* (past participle, *broken*). Do not confuse the past tense with the past participle. Say, "He has broken his leg," not "He has broke his leg."

business letters   All business letters follow a relatively standardized form which is illustrated by the example given below. For convenience, the various parts of the letter have been numbered.

115 Ohio Street *1*
Galesburg, Illinois
December 28, 1966   *2*

3 Fisher Paint Company
    212 West Madison Street
    Chicago 7, Illinois

4 Gentlemen:

5 In your advertisement of Colopake in recent issues of <u>Time</u> you say that the superiority of Colopake over other paint products is achieved by reducing the size of the pigment particles. Since I am making a comparative study of various paints I should like to have more information on this point. Would it be possible for me to obtain a copy of the comparative data which were the basis of your advertising statement?

6   Yours truly,

                 John A. Baker

7   John A. Baker

As the example shows, a business letter consists of at least seven parts:

1. The Return Address. This part will be omitted, of course, if stationery containing a printed letterhead is used, since the letterhead itself is the return address. The form used in the example is called a *block* heading with *open* punctuation. In a block heading the lines are not indented; each line begins flush with the one preceding. In open punctuation no marks are used at the ends of lines, but elements within the lines are separated in accordance with the usual conventions.

2. The Date Line. The date line is written as part of the first heading.

3. The Inside Address. This heading consists of three or more lines and follows the form established in the first heading. Abbreviations such as *Co.* and *Inc.* are used only if these terms are abbreviated in the letterheads of the companies being addressed. When the title of the addressee is given, it is usually placed after his name on the first line [Dr. David D. Henry, President]; but if this practice would result in an awkwardly long line, the title may be given as a separate line.

4. *The Salutation.* When an individual is being addressed, the salutation usually takes one of the following forms: *Dear Mr.* (or *Mrs.*) *Blank, Dear Sir* (or *Madam.*) Such an informal salutation as *Dear Bob* is acceptable only in writing to a personal friend. The form, *My dear Mr.* (or *Mrs.*) *Blank* may be used in distinctly formal letters. When the letter is addressed to a company, rather than to an individual, the accepted salutation is *Gentlemen;* the form *Dear Sirs* is seldom used in modern business letters. If the company is known to consist of women, the salutation may be either *Mesdames* or *Ladies.* A colon follows the salutation.

5. *The Body.* The body of the letter usually consists of one or more paragraphs of single-spaced text, with double spacing between paragraphs. There is a marked preference for starting all paragraphs in a business letter at the left margin, with no indention to mark the opening of a paragraph. However, the older style of starting the first paragraph under the colon of the salutation and thereafter indenting the first line of each paragraph seven spaces from the margin is still common.

6. *The Complimentary Close.* The most common endings are *Yours truly, Yours very truly, Very truly yours, Yours sincerely,* or *Sincerely yours.* Such closes as *Cordially,* or *Cordially yours,* are used only when the writer is on familiar terms with his addressee. *Respectfully* is a formal close used chiefly in submitting a formal report to a superior. A comma is used at the end of the complimentary close.

7. *The Signature.* The signature consists of two parts: the written signature, and below this the writer's name and official position, if any, typed in. Both parts are necessary. The written signature is the legal identification of the writer; the typed name is a safeguard against misreading of the signature. Since it is conventional in business to address a woman as *Miss* unless she signifies that she is married, married women enclose *Mrs.* in parentheses before their typed signatures:

Helen White

(Mrs.) Helen White

Helen White

(Mrs. John White)

When a letter is typed by someone other than the author, the typist puts first the author's initials, then her own (with a colon between them) flush with the left margin and below the author's signature.

can = may The distinction that *can* is used to indicate ability and *may* to indicate permission [If I can do the work, may I have the job?] is a stylistic distinction. It is not generally observed in informal usage. Either form is acceptable in college writing.

can but A formal variant of *can only* [I can but hope you are mistaken].

cannot but A formal variant of *cannot help* or *must* [We cannot but accept the verdict]. In most college writing "We must accept the verdict" would be preferred.

cannot (can't) help but   While this construction is accepted in informal usage, it represents a confusion between the formal *cannot but* and the informal *can't help*. In college writing, the form without *but* is preferred.

can't hardly   A confusion between *cannot* and *can hardly*. The construction is unacceptable in college writing. Use *cannot, can't,* or *can hardly*.

can't seem   A colloquial short cut for "I seem to be unable." Acceptable at informal levels.

caret   The symbol (∧) used to identify the place in a printed, typed, or written line at which something is to be inserted.

case = instance, example   There is no question that this usage [In the case of John Jones . . .] is established, but a widely read essay labeling it jargon has created some objection to it. Like most utility words, *case* (meaning *instance*) may be overused, but its restrained use in college writing should be acceptable.

censor — censure   Both words come from a Latin verb meaning to "set a value on" or "tax." *Censor* is used to mean "appraise" in the sense of appraising a book or a letter to see if it may be made public [All outgoing mail had to be censored] and is often used as a synonym for "delete" or "cut out" [That part of the message was censored].

Censure means "to evaluate adversely," "to find fault with" or "rebuke" [The editorial writers censured the speech; such an attitude will invoke public censure].

circumlocution   Literally, "round-about speech." An attempt to avoid a direct statement by a circuitous reference, as in "She is expecting a little stranger" for "She is pregnant."

cite — sight — site   *Cite* means "to refer to" [He cited chapter and verse]. *Sight* means spectacle or view [The garden was a beautiful sight]. *Site* means "location" [This is the site of the new plant].

claim = assert *or* maintain   All dictionaries accept this usage [I claim that the assignment was never announced] as established. Despite continuing protests by Fowler, Bernstein, and others, there would seem to be no valid objection to the construction in most college writing.

cliché   A synonym for "trite expression": an overused or threadbare expression, or an observation which lacks originality.

clipped words   Shortened forms [auto, exam, gym, plane] which are considered whole words rather than abbreviations of the longer form. Clipped words do not require a period to mark abbreviation and are more appropriate to informal than to formal styles.

coherence   The quality of being logically integrated. In composition, chiefly used to refer to the integration of sentences within a paragraph. See page 120.

collective noun   A noun which refers to a group or class of individuals: *army, audience, committee, team,* etc. For the agreement of a collective noun and its verb, see page 418.

combine = combination   This use of *combine* [Several fraternities have formed a combine which will present its own slate of candidates] is colloquial. It is acceptable at informal levels of college writing. The more formal statement would be "Several fraternities have combined to present a common slate of candidates."

common case   In Modern English, nouns have the same form for nominative, dative, and accusative cases. This form is called the common case. Modern nouns, therefore, have a common case and a possessive or genitive case.

compare, contrast   *Contrast* always implies differences; *compare* may imply either differences or similarities. When followed by a preposition, both verbs usually take *with* [Contrast the part of the lawn that has been fertilized with the part that has not; the handwriting on the lease compares with this signature; if you compare the old leaves with the new you will see that the old leaves are darker]. However, the past participial form, *compared,* usually takes *to* as its preposition [Compared to her mother, she's a beauty].

comparison   In grammar, the system of inflection used to indicate positive, comparative, and superlative degrees of an adjective or adverb: *good–better– best, tall–taller–tallest, beautiful–more beautiful–most beautiful.*

complected   Nonstandard form of *complexioned.* Not acceptable in college writing.

complement   Literally, a completing construction. Used in grammar chiefly to refer to the construction which completes a linking verb. See next entry.

complement of "to be"   In formal usage, the complement of the verb *to be* takes the subjective case (It is *I.* Was it *she?*). In colloquial usage the objective is more common in the first person (It's *me*). The choice, therefore, between *It is I* and *It's me* is not a choice between standard and nonstandard usage but between formal and colloquial styles. This choice seldom has to be made in college writing, since the expression, in whatever form it is used, is essentially a spoken rather than a written sentence. Its use in writing occurs chiefly in dialogue, and then the form chosen should be appropriate to the speaker.

  The use of the objective case in the third person (That was *her*) is less common and should probably be avoided in college writing except when dialogue requires it. The use of the objective case in a clause containing a subjunctive form of *to be* is especially to be avoided, because the subjunctive is a fairly formal construction, and the contrast between formal and colloquial usage points up the inappropriateness of the pronoun form:

Inappropriate	*Appropriate*
If I were *him,* I should resign.	If I were *he,* I should resign.
Would you do it, if you were *her?*	Would you do it, if you were *she?*

But notice that when the infinitive form of *to be* is used, its subject and complement both take the objective case:

> She wants *me* to be there. (Pronoun is subject of infinitive.)
> I wouldn't want to be *her*. (Pronoun is complement of infinitive.)

complex, compound sentences   Sentences are usually classified as follows:
simple: containing only one clause, and that a main clause.
compound: containing two or more main clauses but no subordinate clauses.
complex: containing a main clause and one or more subordinate clauses.
compound-complex: containing two or more main clauses and at least one subordinate clause.

compound words   Combinations of two or more words into a combined form, the parts of which may be written solid [blindfold], hyphenated [father-in-law], or separately [blood bank]. When in doubt about the spelling, consult your dictionary.

considerable   The use of *considerable* as a noun [I have spent considerable on this enterprise] is acceptable at a colloquial level. In a formal style, the preferred usage would require a noun after *considerable* [I have spent considerable money on this enterprise].

context   The environment — usually the verbal environment — in which a word occurs. Thus the other words in a sentence, paragraph, or page provide a context for a particular word. The context may also include the whole situation in which the word is used — the time, place, and attendant circumstances. For the influence of context on meaning, see page 165.

contractions   The use of contractions [I'll, can't, couldn't, didn't, he's, shouldn't] is appropriate in informal and colloquial styles but not in a formal style.

copula   See **linking verb.**

could of = could have   Although these two constructions have almost the same sound in informal speech, *of* for *have* is not acceptable in college writing. In writing, *could of, should of, would of* are nonstandard.

counter words   Utility words. See page 180.

cute   A word used colloquially to indicate the general notion of "attractive" or "pleasing." Its overuse in writing shows haste or lack of discrimination. A more specific term will generally improve communication.

> His girl is cute. [lovely? petite? pleasant? charming?]
> That is a cute trick. [clever? surprising?]
> She has a cute accent. [pleasant? refreshingly unusual?]
> She is a little too cute for me. [affected? juvenile? demonstrative? clever?]

data   Since *data* is the Latin plural of *datum* (given or admitted as a fact) it has long taken a plural verb or pronoun [These data have been double-checked]. This requirement is now often ignored, so that in informal English "This data has been double-checked" is acceptable. *Data* is thus losing its foreign characteristics and being made to fit the general pattern of English nouns. The requirement of a plural verb is still observed, however, in scientific writing and in a formal style. For alternative pronunciations, see dictionary.

dative case   In Old English and in some other languages, generally the case of the indirect object.

demonstrative   *This, that, these, those* are called demonstratives when they are used as pointing words [This is the man; that coat is mine].

dialect   A pattern of speech habits shared by members of the same geographic area or social level [New England dialect; the standard dialect].

didn't ought   Nonstandard for "ought not" [You didn't ought to have told her] and not acceptable in college writing or speech. Say, "You ought not to have told her" or "You should not have told her."

dieresis   A diacritical (distinguishing) mark consisting of two dots placed over the second of two like vowels to show that they are to be pronounced separately — *reëntry, coöperation, coördination.* In Modern English the dieresis is so little used that it is not included among the characters on a standard typewriter keyboard. Such vowels are often separated by a hyphen without a dieresis — *re-entry. Cooperation* and *coordination* are now commonly written without either a dieresis or a hyphen.

different than   The preferred idiom is *different from,* although all dictionaries recognize *different than* as established usage. *Different to* is British usage.

digraph   Two letters pronounced as a single sound, as in bl*ee*d, b*ea*t, *th*in, sti*ck, p*sychology, gra*ph*.

diphthong   A combination of two vowel sounds run together to sound like a single vowel. Examples are the *ah-ee* sounds combining to form the vowel of *hide, ride, wide* and the *aw-ee* sounds combining in *boy, joy, toy.*

disinterested — uninterested   The distinction between these words is that the first is a synonym for *unbiased,* the second for *apathetic* or *not interested.* A disinterested critic is one who comes to a book with no prejudices or prior judgments of its worth; an uninterested critic is one who cannot get interested in the book. In recent years this distinction has lost ground, and so many speakers and writers have used *disinterested* to mean *uninterested* that the dictionaries have accepted this usage. The distinction, however, is strongly maintained in the schools, and you will probably be expected to observe it.

don't   As a contraction for "do not" it is appropriate in informal and colloquial styles, but not acceptable in college speech or writing as a contraction for "does not."

double negative   The use of two negative words or particles within the same construction. In certain forms [I am not unwilling to go] the double negative is educated usage for an affirmative statement; in other forms [I ain't got no money] the double negative is uneducated (nonstandard) usage for a negative statement. The fact that the latter usage is an obvious violation of the conventions of standard English justifies its censure in high school and college speech and writing, but the objection that "two negatives make an affirmative" in English usage is a half-truth based on a false analogy with mathematics.

dove = dived Both forms are established usage. *Dived* would be preferred in a formal style.

due to The use of *due to* to mean "because of" in an introductory adverbial phrase [Due to the icy roads, we were unable to proceed] is an established usage to which some people object. The objection reflects personal preference rather than the facts of usage.

economic — economical *Economic* refers to the science of economics or to business in general [This is an economic law; economic conditions are improving]. *Economical* means "inexpensive" or "thrifty" [That is the economical thing to do; he is economical to the point of miserliness].

editorial "we" A practice employed by editors and authors of referring to themselves as *we*, even when the reference is to only one writer.

effect See **affect.**

e.g. An abbreviation for the Latin phrase *exempli gratia* (for the sake of example; for example). Used to introduce an example in publications, such as dictionaries, in which space must be conserved. Seldom used in freshman writing.

either Used to designate one of two things [Both hats are becoming; I would be perfectly satisfied with either]. The use of *either* when more than two things are involved [There are three ways of working the problem; either way will give the right answer] is not generally accepted. When more than two things are involved, use *any* or *any one* instead of *either* [There are three ways of working the problem, any one of which will give the right answer].

elicit — illicit The first word means to "draw out" [We could elicit no further information from them]; the second means "not permitted" [an illicit love affair].

elliptical constructions A construction which is literally incomplete but in which the missing terms are understood [*I am taller than he* (is tall); Who told him? (It was) *Not I* (who told him)].

emigrant — immigrant An emigrant is a person who moves *out* of a country; an immigrant one who moves *into* a country. Thus, refugees from Europe who settled in the United States were emigrants from their native countries and immigrants here. A similar distinction holds for the verbs *emigrate* and *immigrate.*

enormous — enormousness — enormity *Enormous* refers to unusual size or measure — *huge, vast, immense* [an enormous fish, an enormous effort]. *Enormousness* is a noun with the same connotations of size and can be applied to either good or bad effects [The enormousness of their contribution is only beginning to be recognized; the enormousness of the lie almost made it believable]. But *enormity* is used only for evil acts of great dimension [The enormity of Hitler's crimes against the Jews shows what can happen when power, passion, and prejudice are all united in one man].

enthuse   Colloquial for "to be (become) enthusiastic." The more formal phrase is preferred in college writing.

epigram   A short, pithy statement, usually witty or cynical, in either prose or poetry:

Yes, the meek shall inherit the earth — six feet of it.

> Here lies our sovereign lord, the King,
> Whose word no man relies on,
> Who never said a foolish thing,
> And never did a wise one.

equally as   In such sentences as "He was equally as good as his brother," the *equally as* is a confusion of *equally* and *as good as*. Write, "He was his brother's equal," "He was as good as his brother," or "Both brothers were equally good."

etc.   An abbreviation for *et cetera* (and so forth). Should be used only when the style justifies abbreviations and then only after several items in a series have been identified [The data sheet required the usual personal information: age, height, weight, marital status, etc.]. Avoid the redundant *and* before *etc*.

etymology   The study of the derivations of words.

euphemism — euphuism   A *euphemism* is a word or phrase used as a substitute for an expression which is felt to be crude, improper, or vulgar. Examples are "a lady dog" for "a bitch," "pass away" for "die." *Euphuism* is a name given to an ornate and affected literary style which was popular in England at the end of the sixteenth century and to any modern style which shows similar characteristics.

exam   A clipped form of *examination*. Although classified as colloquial by some dictionaries, it is accepted at all but the most formal levels of college writing.

expect = suppose *or* suspect   This is a colloquial usage. In college writing, use *suppose* or *suspect* [I suppose you have written to him? I suspect that we have made a mistake].

expletive   In such sentences as "There are two answers to the question" and "It seems to me that you are mistaken," the words *There* and *It* are called *expletives*. In such sentences the order is expletive, verb, and real subject, the expletive occupying the normal position of the subject.

fact   Distinguish between facts and statements of fact. A fact is something which exists or existed. It is neither true nor false; it just *is*. A statement of fact, or factual statement, may be true or false, depending on whether it does or does not report the facts accurately. But there are no true or false facts. Also, avoid padding a sentence with unnecessary use of "The fact that" as in "It is a fact that all the public opinion polls predicted Truman's defeat in the 1948 election." The first five words of that sentence add no meaning.

Similarly, "His guilt is admitted" says all, in fewer words, that is said by "The fact of his guilt is admitted."

famous, notorious *Famous* is a complimentary and *notorious* an uncomplimentary adjective. Well-known people of good repute are famous; those of bad repute are notorious (or infamous).

fare — fair *Fare* comes from the Old English verb *faran* (to travel) and is related to the expression *fare you well*. It is most commonly used today to indicate the cost of transportation [The fare to Chicago is $10.40]. *Fair* has a variety of meanings [a fair decision, a fair copy, a fair skin, just fair, fair weather, a fair profit, a county fair].

farther, further The distinction that *farther* indicates distance and *further* degree is now less widely observed than it used to be. All dictionaries consulted recognize the two words as interchangeable. But to mean "in addition," only *further* is used [Further assistance will be required; we need further information on that point].

feature (verb) The use of *feature* to mean "give prominence to" [This issue of the magazine features an article on juvenile delinquency] is established standard usage and is appropriate in college writing. But this acceptance does not justify the slang use of *feature* in such expressions as "Can you feature that?" "Feature me in a dress suit," "I can't feature her as a nurse."

fellow As a noun, *fellow* for "man" or "person" is appropriate only in colloquial and informal styles. As an adjective [fellow students, a fellow traveler] *fellow* is acceptable at all levels.

figures of speech Metaphors, similes, personifications, allusions, and similar devices are grouped under the general name *figures of speech*. See page 183.

fine writing In college, often used as an uncomplimentary term for writing which, because of its attempts to be "literary," is artificial, pretentious, or wordy.

fix As a noun, *fix* is colloquial for "predicament" [Now we *are* in a fix!]. As a verb, it is colloquial for "repair" or "adjust" [My pen is broken and I can't fix it; will you help me fix this desk?]. Both uses are appropriate in an informal style. The verb *fix*, meaning "to make fast," is acceptable at all levels.

flaunt — flout *Flaunt* means "to display conspicuously" [Here comes the Easter Parade, with the women flaunting their new dresses]. *Flout* means "to scoff at" or "to treat with scorn." It is used chiefly for open rejection of social or moral conventions [They seem to want to flout every decent custom which the community respects].

flunk = fail Colloquial. Not suited to a formal style, but so commonly used in college that there would seldom be objection to its use in an informal paper.

foreword — forward Despite similar spelling, these two words have quite different meanings. A *foreword* is a prefatory statement at the fore or front of a book — a preface. The common use of *forward* is well known; it is also used with unfavorable connotations to mean *bold* or *presumptuous* [a forward girl, a forward manner].

formally — formerly   *Formally* means "in a formal manner" [They dressed formally]. *Formerly* means "previously" [He was formerly with A. C. Smith and Company].

funny   The use of *funny* as a utility word [She gave me a funny look; it was a funny observation to make] is greatly overdone in college writing. Although appropriate at informal and colloquial levels, its constant use makes for vague diction. Select a more exact synonym:

> She gave me a funny look. [hostile? alarmed? annoyed? scathing? perplexed? baffled?]
> It was a funny observation to make. [comical? humorous? astounding? puzzling? unusual?]

gender   A grammatical division of words into masculine, feminine, and neuter categories, which is important in highly inflected languages and is only partly related to differences in sex — for example, *nauta* (sailor) in Latin is a feminine noun, *das Kind* (child) in German is neuter. Except for personal pronouns (he, she, it) and a few feminine forms of nouns (actress, niece, etc.), English makes little use of grammatical gender.

genitive case   The possessive case.

gentleman, lady   These are good words, but avoid their use as synonyms for "man" or "woman" in expressions in which the latter terms are normal [manservant, man of the house, women's building, woman's point of view]. Also avoid their euphemistic use to designate the sex of animals [bull, tomcat, mare, ewe].

get   The use of *get,* either as a single verb or in combination with infinitives, adjectives, or adverbs, is extremely popular and varied in colloquial and informal styles. It should be used discreetly in a formal style, but the student should also guard against overuse of more formal synonyms such as *acquire* or *obtain.*

good   The use of *good* as an adverb [He talks good; he played pretty good] is not acceptable in college writing. Even though it is recognized as established by *Webster's Third International,* this usage is discouraged in college speech. In both writing and speaking, the accepted adverbial form is *well.*

This discussion does not apply to the use of *good* as an adjective after verbs of hearing, feeling, seeing, smelling, tasting, etc. See **bad.**

good and   Used colloquially as an intensive in such expressions as "good and late," "good and sleepy," "good and ready," "good and tired." The more formal the style, the less appropriate these intensives are.

got   See **get.**

gotten   Leading dictionaries now accept *gotten* without comment as one of two past participles of *get.* The other one is *got.*

guess The use of *guess* to mean "believe," "suppose," "think" [I guess I can be there on time] is accepted by all dictionaries on which this glossary is based. There is still objection to its use in formal college writing, but it should be acceptable in an informal style.

hackneyed diction See **cliché.**

had have, had of Neither form is appropriate in college writing. Use *had.*

had (hadn't) ought Nonstandard for *ought (ought not)*. Not acceptable in college writing or speech.

hanged, hung Alternative past participles of *hang*. When referring to an execution, *hanged* is preferred; in other senses, *hung* is preferred.

hardly See **can't hardly.**

headword The chief word in a phrase: a noun modified by adjectives, or a verb modified by one or more adverbs, or the noun in a prepositional phrase [a very tall *tale;* they *danced* mechanically and routinely; at the *beginning*].

height — heighth The form *heighth* is nonstandard and probably reflects a confusion with the final *th* in *breadth* and *width.*

historical present Also called *dramatic present*. The use of the present tense in narrative style to record action in the past [His friends try to persuade him to escape, but Socrates reasons with them and shows them he must die].

home Used colloquially and informally for "at home" [We have been home all afternoon; if you arrive too late, we will not be home]. In a formal style "at home" would be preferred.

homonyms Words which are pronounced alike [air, heir; blew, blue; plain, plane; sail, sale].

hopefully This adverb is misused when attached loosely to a sentence to mean "I hope" [Hopefully, the plane will arrive on schedule].

idea In addition to its formal meaning of "conception," *idea* has acquired so many supplementary meanings that it must be recognized as a utility word. Some of its meanings are illustrated in the following sentences:

The idea [thesis] of the book is simple.
The idea [proposal] he suggested is a radical one.
I got the idea [impression] that she is unhappy.
It is my idea [belief, opinion] that they are both wrong.
My idea [intention] is to leave early.

The overuse of *idea,* like the overuse of any utility word, makes for vagueness. Whenever possible, use a more precise synonym.

i.e. An abbreviation of the Latin phrase, *id est* (that is), used to introduce a restatement or an explanation of a preceding word or phrase. Its use is generally confined to publications in which space must be conserved; it is rarely used in freshman writing.

illusion   See **allusion.**

immigrant   See **emigrant.**

imply — infer   These two words are so often confused that the Merriam dictionaries now recognize *infer* as one meaning of *imply*. The difference between the two words is that *imply* refers to what a statement means, usually to a meaning not specifically stated but included in the original statement, whereas *infer* is used for a listener's or reader's judgment or inference based on the statement. The difference is illustrated by the following dialogue:

> Reporter: Senator, you have stated that you are opposed to the present policy of maintaining large concentrations of American troops in Europe. Does that imply that you favor a significant reduction of our NATO forces?
>
> Senator: Yes, my criticism of the present policy implies that I would like to see a reduction of American NATO troops in Europe.
>
> Reporter: May we infer, Senator, that you think NATO is no longer necessary?
>
> Senator: No, that inference goes too far. I would like to see NATO continue, and I think we should support it with men and materiel, but not to the extent that we are now doing.

in back of   See **back of.**

individual   Although the use of *individual* to mean *person* [He is a fascinating individual] is accepted by the dictionaries, college instructors frequently disapprove of this use, probably because it is overdone in college writing. In its formal uses *individual* signifies "single" or "separate" [We are all Americans but we are also individuals; the instructor tries to give us individual attention].

Indo-European   The ancestral language of most of the modern languages in India and Europe. Of the nine main branches of Indo-European, two are of special interest to us: the Germanic, from which modern English, Dutch, German, Icelandic, Norwegian, and Swedish are descended; and the Italic, from which, through Latin, modern French, Italian, Portuguese, Romanian, and Spanish have come.

inferior than   Possibly a confusion between *inferior to* and *worse than*. Say "inferior to" [Today's workmanship is inferior to that of a few years ago].

in regards to   The only acceptable form is *in regard to*. The *-s* ending is not uncommon in speech, but it is not acceptable in college writing.

inside of   The use of *inside of* to mean "in less than" [I'll be there inside of an hour] is accepted as established usage. There should be no objection to it in college writing.

intensives   Such modifiers as *much, so, too, very* merely add emphasis to the words they modify [much obliged, so tired, too bad, very good], but the overuse of intensives (especially *very*) is more likely to result in wordiness than in emphasis. The pronouns *myself, yourself, himself, herself, themselves* may also be used as intensives [You yourself are the best judge; he built the cabin himself].

irony   A mode of statement in which the writer implies almost the opposite of what he explicitly states. The writing proceeds on two levels at the same time. Ostensibly, the writer is developing the literal meaning of his message, but he counts on the reader to see the implications of each statement in the total context and so to respond at the implied level. The most famous example in English is Jonathan Swift's *A Modest Proposal,* which under the guise of suggesting a workable plan for improving the economy of Ireland, makes an incisive criticism of England's exploitation of the Irish. Irony is difficult to handle, and for that reason many teachers of freshman English prefer that students read it rather than write it. But as the essay "Why We Need More Westerns on TV" (page 13) shows, it can sometimes be handled effectively by an able student.

irregardless   A nonstandard variant of *regardless.*

irrelevant — irreverent   *Irrelevant* means "having no relation to" or "lacking pertinence" [That may be true, but it is quite irrelevant]. *Irreverent* means "without reverence" [Such conduct in a church is irreverent].

its — it's   The confusion of these two forms causes frequent misspelling in college writing. *It's* always means "it is" or "it has." The apostrophe is a sign of contraction, not of possession [The dog wagged its tail; it's (it is) too difficult a problem; it's (it has) been raining all night].

it's me   This construction is essentially a spoken one. Except in dialogue, it rarely occurs in writing. Its use in educated speech is thoroughly established. The formal expression is *It is I.*

jargon   A name applied to diction which is wordy and unnecessarily abstract. The name is also applied to the technical vocabulary and usages of special groups — the jargon of the medical profession, legal jargon.

kid   Colloquial for "child," but often applied to young people of any age, even by parents to their married sons and daughters. Appropriate in informal but not in formal writing.

kind of, sort of   Use a singular modifier and a singular verb with these phrases [That kind of person is always troublesome; this sort of attitude will get us nowhere]. The use of *a* or *an* after *of,* in this construction, is colloquial and is avoided by most careful writers.

kind (sort) of = somewhat   This usage [I feel kind of tired; he looked sort of foolish] is colloquial. It would be inappropriate in a formal style and should be used sparingly in an informal style.

learn = teach   The use of *learn* to mean "teach" [He learned us arithmetic] is nonstandard and is not acceptable in college speech or writing. Say, "He taught us arithmetic."

leave = let   The use of *leave* for *let* [Leave us face it] is slang and is not acceptable in college speech or writing. Say, "Let us face it," "Let (*not* leave) us be friends."

let's A contraction of *let us*. The expression *let's us* is redundant and not acceptable in college writing.

liable, likely, apt *Liable* to mean "likely" or "apt" [It is liable to rain; he is liable to hit you] is a colloquial usage to which instructors sometimes object. *Liable* means "subject to" or "exposed to" or "answerable for" [He is liable to arrest; you will be liable for damages]. In formal usage *apt* means "has an aptitude for" [He is an apt pupil]. The use of *apt* to mean "likely" is accepted colloquially [She is apt to leave you; he is apt to resent it].

like = as, as though The use of *like* as a conjunction [He talks like you do; it looks like it will be my turn next] is colloquial. It is not appropriate in a formal style and many people object to it in an informal style. The safest procedure is to avoid using *like* as a conjunction in college writing.

likely See **liable**.

line The use of *line* to indicate a type of activity or business [What's your line? His line is dry goods] is accepted as established usage; its use to indicate a course of action or thought [He follows the party line] is also accepted. However, the overuse of *line* in these senses often provokes objection to the word.

linking verb (copula) A verb which is neither transitive nor intransitive, but is followed by a complement, usually a noun, a pronoun, or an adjective [That man is her father; they seem happy; we became ill]. In such sentences the complement both completes the verb and modifies the subject.

loan, lend Both forms of the verb are accepted in educated American usage.

loath — loathe The form without -*e* is an adjective meaning "reluctant," "unwilling" [I am loath to do that; he is loath to risk so great an investment] and is pronounced to rhyme with "both." The form with -*e* is a verb meaning "dislike strongly" [I loathe teas; she loathes an unkempt man], and is pronounced to rhyme with "clothe."

locate = find This usage [I cannot locate that quotation] is established, but its extension to mean *remember* [Your name sounds familiar, but I cannot locate your face] is not acceptable.

locate = settle This usage [He and his family have located in San Francisco] is colloquial. In college writing *settled* would be preferred.

loose, lose The confusion of these words causes frequent misspelling. *Loose* is most common as an adjective [a loose button, a loose nut, a dog that has broken loose]. *Lose* is always used as a verb [You are going to lose your money; don't lose your head].

loose sentence A technical term used to describe a sentence in which the main thought is completed before the end. The opposite of a *periodic sentence*. Loose sentences are common sentences and should not be thought of as faulty.

lot(s) of The use of *lot(s)* to mean a considerable amount or number [I have lots of friends; they gave us a lot of excuses] is colloquial. This usage is common in informal writing.

lower case (l. c.) Printer's terminology for small letters as contrasted with capitals. Frequently used by college instructors in marking student papers.

luxuriant — luxurious These words come from the same root but have quite different connotations. *Luxuriant* means "abundant" and is used principally of growing things [luxuriant vegetation, a luxuriant head of hair]. *Luxurious* means "luxury-loving" or "catering to luxury" [He finds it difficult to support so luxurious a wife on so modest an income; the appointments of the clubhouse were luxurious].

mad = angry or annoyed This usage is colloquial [My girl is mad at me; his insinuations make me mad]. In formal and informal styles, use *angry, annoyed, irritated, provoked,* or *vexed,* which are more precise.

majority — plurality Candidates are elected by a *majority* when they get more than half the votes cast. A *plurality* is the margin of victory that the winning candidate has over his leading opponent, whether the winner has a majority or not.

malapropism A humorous, though unintentional, confusion of words similar in form and sound [Henry VIII died of an *abbess* on his knee; one of the most momentous events in early English history was the invasion of the *Dames*]. The error is named for Mrs. Malaprop, a character in Sheridan's play *The Rivals,* whose speech often illustrated this kind of confusion.

math A clipped form of *mathematics.* Appropriate in a colloquial or informal style but not in formal writing.

may See **can.**

mean = unkind, disagreeable, bad-tempered These uses of *mean* [It was mean of me to do that; please don't be mean to me; that dog looks mean] are colloquial. They are appropriate in most college writing, but their overuse sometimes results in vagueness. Consider using one of the suggested alternatives to provide a sharper statement.

might of See **could of.**

moral —- morale Roughly, *moral* refers to conduct and *morale* refers to state of mind. A *moral* man is one who conducts himself according to the conventions of society or religion. People are said to have good *morale* when they are cheerful, cooperative, and not too much concerned with their own worries.

most = almost This usage [I am most always hungry an hour before mealtime] is colloquial. In college writing *almost* would be preferred in such a sentence.

must (adjective and noun) The use of *must* as an adjective [This book is must reading for anyone who wants to understand Russia] and as a noun [It is reported that the President will classify this proposal as a must] is accepted as established usage by the dictionaries.

must of See **could of.**

myself = I This usage [John and myself will go] is not generally acceptable. Say, "John and I will go." *Myself* is acceptably used: (1) as an intensifier [I saw it myself; I myself will go with you]; (2) as a reflexive object [I hate myself; I can't convince myself that he is right].

myself = me The use of *myself* as the equivalent of *me* [He divided it between John and myself] is not generally accepted, and is not even recognized by some dictionaries. The preferred usage is "He divided it between John and me."

neither See **either.**

nice A utility word much overused in college writing. Avoid excessive use of it and, whenever possible, choose a more precise synonym.

It was a nice dance. [enjoyable? exciting? genteel? well-organized?]
That's a nice dress. [attractive? becoming? fashionable? well-made?]
She's a nice girl. [agreeable? beautiful? charming? virtuous? friendly? well-mannered?]

nice and See **good and.**

nominative absolute An introductory participial phrase which is grammatically independent of the rest of the sentence [*All things being considered,* the decision is a fair one; *the interview having been ended,* the reporters rushed to the phones]. This construction is common in Latin but should be used sparingly in college writing, partly because it is sometimes unidiomatic, and partly because it may result in a dangling modifier. The first example given above is idiomatic English; the second would normally be written, "When the interview was ended, the reporters rushed to the phones."

nominative case Another name for the subjective case.

not . . . as, not . . . so See **as . . . as.**

notorious See **famous.**

noun clause A subordinate clause serving usually as the subject, object, or complement in a sentence — that is, used in the positions in which a noun is normally used:

(What he needs) is more exercise. [Noun clause as subject]
He predicted (that it would happen). [Noun clause as object]
His actions were (what you would expect). [Noun clause as complement]

nowhere near = not nearly Established usage, but *not nearly* is often preferred.

nowheres Nonstandard variant of *nowhere.*

object An object is a noun or pronoun which completes the action of a transitive verb [We bought the *car;* I asked *her*] or completes a preposition [She smiled at *me;* it is lying on the *table*]. An *indirect object* identifies the recipient of the action indicated by a verb-object combination [We bought *Dad* a car; the children gave *her* a party].

off of In such sentences as "Keep off of the grass," "He took it off of the table," the *of* is unnecessary and undesirable. Omit it in college speech and writing.

OK, O.K. Its use in business to mean "endorse" is generally accepted [The manager OK'd the request]. Otherwise, it is colloquial. It is a utility word and is subject to the general precaution concerning all such words: do not overuse it, especially in contexts in which a more specific term would give more efficient communication. For example, contrast the vagueness of OK at the left with the discriminated meanings at the right.

The garagemen said the tires were OK.	The garagemen said the tread on the tires was still good.
	The garagemen said the pressure in the tires was satisfactory.

one . . . he, his The feeling that the repetition of *one . . . one's* [One must do what one can to ensure one's family a decent standard of living] makes for a stilted style has led to the permissible shift from *one, one's* to *he, his* [One must do what he can to ensure his family a decent standard of living]. In general a shift in the number or nature of pronouns is undesirable, but this particular shift is established usage.

only The position of *only* in such sentences as "I only need three dollars" and "If only Mother would write!" is sometimes condemned on the grounds of possible ambiguity. In practice, the context usually rules out ambiguous interpretation, but a change in the word order would often result in more appropriate emphasis [I need only three dollars; if Mother would only write].

out loud = aloud Generally acceptable in college writing. In a formal style, prefer *aloud*.

outside of = aside from, except This usage [Outside of his family, no one respects him; outside of that, I have no objection] is colloquial. It would be inappropriate in a formal style, but not objectionable in an informal one.

over with = completed, ended This usage [Let's get this job over with; she is all over with that romance] is informal. It should be generally acceptable in college writing unless the style is quite formal.

part, on the part of This usage [There will be some objection on the part of the students; on the part of businessmen, there will be some concern about taxes] often makes for a wordy and flabby style. Simply say, "The students will object," "Businessmen will be concerned about taxes."

party = person Colloquial, and generally to be avoided in college writing. In telephone usage, however, party is the accepted word [Your party does not answer].

past — passed Although both forms may be used as past participles of the verb *to pass*, *past* is primarily used as an adjective or a noun [in days past, the past tense, she is a woman with a past]. *Passed* is a past tense or past participle form [They have passed the half-way mark; he passed all his examinations].

per = a This usage [You will be remunerated at the rate of five dollars per diem; this material costs $1.50 per yard] is established. As the second illustration shows, the *per* need not be followed by a Latin noun. This use of *per* is most common in legal and business phraseology. For most purposes, "five dollars a day" and "$1.50 a yard" would be more natural expressions.

per = according to, concerning This usage [The order will be delivered as per your instructions; per your inquiry of the 17th, we wish to report] is business slang which is unacceptable in both college and business writing. Use "according to" or "concerning," whichever is appropriate.

per cent, percent Originally an abbreviation of the Latin *per centum,* this term has been Anglicized and is no longer considered a foreign word. It may be written as one or two words and no longer requires a period to indicate abbreviation [There is a ten percent markup; interest is at three per cent].

periodic sentence A sentence in which the main thought is not completed until the end. See page 148.

personification A figure of speech in which animals, inanimate objects, and qualities are given human characteristics [Death cometh like a thief in the night; the breeze caressed her hair].

phonetics The science dealing with the sounds of language. These sounds are represented by phonetic symbols which ignore the appearance of a word and record only its pronunciation [Phonetically, *schism* is transcribed *sɪzəm*]. When words are spelled as they are pronounced, the spelling is said to be phonetic; thus, *tho* is a phonetic spelling, *colonel* is not.

photo Colloquial clipped form of *photograph.* In a formal style, use the full form.

plagiarism The offense of representing as one's own writing the work of another. The use of unacknowledged quotations.

plan on When *plan* is used in the sense of "arrange" [I plan to be in Columbus on the seventh], the accepted idiom is *plan to.* When, however, *plan* means "intend" or "hope" [I plan to see that picture whenever it comes to town; they are planning on saving enough money to buy a new car], either *plan to* or *plan on* is acceptable. The safer usage is *plan to.*

plenty The use of *plenty* as a noun [There is plenty of room] is acceptable at all levels. Its use as an adverb [It was plenty good] is colloquial and would not be appropriate in college writing.

plurality See **majority.**

précis A summary which preserves the organization and principal content of the original.

predicate That part of a sentence which makes a statement about the subject. The predicate may consist of an intransitive verb, with or without modifiers; or of a transitive verb and its object, with or without modifiers; or of a linking verb and its complement, with or without modifiers.

predicate adjective An adjective completing a linking verb [His mother is *sick;* oh, it is *beautiful!*].

predicate noun Same function as *predicate adjective* above [His mother is a *writer;* her brother became a successful *lawyer*].

prefix A word or syllable placed before the root of another word to form a new word [*anti*bodies, *mono*syllabic, *un*natural].

proven Alternative past participle of *prove.* The preferred form is *proved,* but *proven* is permissible.

providing = provided This usage [I will go, providing you accompany me] is established. Either form is acceptable in college writing, though *provided* is more common and more widely accepted.

real = really (very) Unless the style is intentionally colloquial, use *really* [It was a really (*not* real) difficult assignment; she can be really (*not* real) annoying when she talks that way].

reason is because Although Bryant offers impressive evidence (*Current American usage,* pp. 170–171) to show that this is an established idiom, there is still some objection to it. In a formal style, "The reason is that" would be preferred.

redundancy Repetitious wording. For an example, see the next entry.

refer back A confusion between *look back* and *refer.* This usage is objected to in college writing on the ground that since the *re* of refer means "back," *refer back* is redundant. *Refer back* is acceptable when it means "refer again" [The bill was referred back to the committee]; otherwise, say *refer* [Let me refer you to page 17; from time to time he referred to his notes].

referent The *thing* as contrasted with the symbol which refers to it. The person, object, event, or idea to which a word refers. The word is pronounced with the stress on the first syllable.

respectfully — respectively *Respectfully* means "with respect" [He spoke respectfully; Respectfully submitted]. *Respectively* means roughly "each in turn" [These three papers were graded respectively A, C, and B].

Reverend *Reverend* is used before the name of a clergyman and in formal usage is preceded by *the* [I met the Reverend Alexander White]. It is not used immediately preceding the surname [the Reverend White], but must be followed by Dr., Mr., or a Christian name or initials [Rev. Dr. White, Rev. Mr. White, Rev. A. L. White]. In informal written usage, the *the* is often omitted and the word *Reverend* abbreviated.

Formal	*Informal*
The Reverend Alexander L. White	Rev. A. L. White
2472 Bancroft Street	2472 Bancroft Street
Toledo, Ohio	Toledo, Ohio

right — rite A *rite* is a ceremony or ritual. This word should not be confused with the various uses of *right.*

right (adv.)   The use of *right* as an adverb is established in such sentences as "He went right home," "It served him right," "Please try to act right," "I will go right away." Its use to mean *very* [I was right glad to meet him; that's a right pretty girl] is colloquial and should be used in college writing only when the style is colloquial.

run-on sentence   A sentence which consists of a number of main clauses loosely joined together by *and*'s and *so*'s. The ideas in the sentence lack organization. See page 389.

said (adj.)   The use of *said* as an adjective [said documents, said offense] is restricted to legal phraseology. Do not use it in college writing.

same as = just as   The preferred idiom is *just as* [He acted just as I thought he would].

same, such   Avoid the use of *same* or *such* as a substitute for *it, this, that, them* [I am returning the book, since I do not care for same; most people are fond of athletics of all sorts, but I have no use for such]. Say, "I am returning the book because I do not care for it," "Unlike most people, I am not fond of athletics."

scarcely   In such sentences as "There wasn't scarcely enough," "We haven't scarcely time," the use of *scarcely* plus a negative creates an unacceptable double negative. Say, "There was scarcely enough," "We scarcely have time."

scarcely than   The use of *scarcely than* [I had scarcely met her than she began to denounce her husband] is a confusion between *no sooner . . . than* and *scarcely . . . when*. Say, "I had no sooner met her than she began to denounce her husband," or "I had scarcely met her when she began to denounce her husband."

seldom ever   The *ever* is redundant. Instead of saying, "He is seldom ever late," "She is seldom ever angry," say, "He is seldom late," "She is seldom angry."

-selfs   The plural of *self* is *selves*. Such usages as "They hurt themselfs," "They hate theirselfs," are nonstandard and are not acceptable in college speech or writing.

semantics   The science of the meanings of words as contrasted with phonetics (pronunciation), morphology (form), and syntax (function).

sensual — sensuous   Avoid confusion of these words. *Sensual* has unfavorable connotations and means "catering to the gratification of the senses" [He leads a sensual existence]. *Sensuous* has generally favorable connotations and refers to pleasures experienced through the senses [The sensuous peace of a warm bath; the sensuous imagery of the poem].

series   Parallel constructions arranged in succession [He was *tall, tanned,* and *lean*]. The elements of a series may be single words, phrases, subordinate clauses, or main clauses, but all elements must be in the same grammatical form. See page 392.

493

shall — will For a long time the schools have attempted to enforce the distinction that *shall* is used in the first person and *will* in the other two when the verb is expressing future action, but *will* in the first person and *shall* in the other two when the verb is expressing determination rather than futurity. This distinction has little support in American usage, except in northeastern New England. In all other areas of the country, *will* is the preferred form for all persons, whether the verb is expressing futurity or determination.[2] This *shall-will* distinction cannot be accepted as an accurate description of educated usage in America, Scotland, or Ireland. It is primarily a description of the usage of educated Englishmen, but the following quotation from a celebrated speech by Winston Churchill shows that the distinction is not consistently observed even in England. Churchill was speaking on a very formal occasion (an address to the House of Commons after the evacuation of Dunkirk in World War II). There can be no doubt that he was expressing determination rather than simple futurity, yet he consistently uses *shall* in the first person:

> . . . we shall not flag or fail. We shall go on to the end, we shall fight in France, we shall fight in the seas and oceans, we shall fight with growing confidence and growing strength in the air, we shall defend our island, whatever the cost may be, we shall fight on the beaches, we shall fight on the landing-grounds, we shall fight in the fields and in the streets, we shall fight in the hills; we shall never surrender . . .

In view of this ·diversity of usage, any concise statement is bound to over-simplify, but the following summary should meet most of the needs of American college students:

1. To express simple futurity only, *will* is used in the second and third persons and either *will* or *shall* in the first person, *shall* being the more formal. *Shall* is not used in the second and third persons when the sentence implies futurity only.

2. To express determination, resolve, or compulsion, *shall* is used in the second and third persons and either *shall* or *will* in the first person. But if the context clearly implies determination rather than futurity only, either *shall* or *will* may be used for all persons.

3. Shall is predominantly used in statements of laws [Congress *shall* have the power . . .], in military commands [The regiment *shall* proceed as directed], and in formal directives [All branch offices *shall* report weekly to the home office].

4. In questions, *shall* is often used in the third person as well as in the first [Where *shall* he be tomorrow? *But also:* Where *will* he be tomorrow]?

should — would These words are used as the past forms of *shall* and *will* respectively and follow the same pattern [I *would* (*should*) be glad to see him tomorrow; he *would* welcome your ideas on the subject; we *would* (*should*) never consent to such an arrangement]. They are also used to convert a *shall* or *will* in direct discourse into indirect discourse.

[2] See Margaret M. Bryant, *Current American Usage* (New York: Funk and Wagnalls, 1962), p. 183.

494

Direct Discourse	*Indirect Discourse*
"*Shall* I try to arrange it?" he asked.	He asked if he *should* try to arrange it.
I said, "They *will* need money."	I said that they *would* need money.

In addition, *should* and *would* have specialized uses:

Should is used:

1. To express obligation, necessity, or duty [I really *should* go to her tea; the two sides of the equation *should* balance].

2. To express probability [She *should* be home by then; these tires *should* be good for another 5000 miles].

3. In a subordinate clause, to express a supposition [If I *should* be late, will you hold dinner for me?].

Would is used:

1. To express a customary action in the past [During those years he *would* write once or twice a year and send a card at Christmas].

2. As a synonym for "were willing" in conditional clauses [He could do it, if he *would*].

3. As a polite form in requests or commands [*Would* you mind making three copies of this letter?].

Avoid the overuse of the auxiliary *would*. Repeating *would* in a compound sentence is often awkward or wordy.

Awkward	*Revised*
If they *would have done* that earlier, there *would have been* no trouble.	If they *had done* or (*Had* they *done*) that earlier, there *would have been* no trouble.
We *would want* some assurance that they *would accept* before we *would make* such a proposal.	We *would want* some assurance of their acceptance before we *made* such a proposal.
If I *would be* in your place, I *would apologize*.	If I *were* in your place, I *would apologize*.

should of See **could of.**

show = chance This usage [Give him a fair show] would be appropriate only in a colloquial style. In formal and informal style use *chance* or *opportunity*.

show = play, motion picture Generally acceptable in college writing, but the other terms may be more precise.

show up The uses of *show up* to mean "expose" or "appear" [This test will show up any weaknesses in the machine; I waited for an hour, but he didn't show up] are established. The use of *show up* to mean "prove much superior to" [The girls showed up the boys in the spelling bee] is colloquial but would not be objectionable in college writing.

sic The Latin word *sic,* pronounced *sick,* is used in brackets to indicate that an error in a quotation appeared in the original source and was not made by the person copying the quotation. Example: "The significant words in the paragraph are these: 'No person will be allowed on the premises unless he is duely [*sic*] authorized.' "

sick = disgusted This usage [All these pious platitudes make me sick] is now recognized by the dictionaries. It should be acceptable in most college writing, but not in formal style.

so (conj.) The use of *so* as a connective [She refused to exchange the merchandise, so we went to the manager] is thoroughly respectable, but its overuse in college writing is objectionable. There are other good transitional connectives — *accordingly, for that reason, on that account, therefore, for example* — which could be used to relieve the monotony of a series of *so's*. Occasional use of subordination [When she refused to exchange the merchandise, we went to the manager] would lend variety to the style.

some The use of *some* as an adjective of indeterminate number [Some friends of yours were here; there are some questions I'd like to ask] is acceptable in all levels of writing. Its use as an intensive [That was some meal] or as an adverb [She cried some after you left] is slang and should be avoided in college writing.

somebody's else Say, "somebody else's." See **anybody's else.**

somewheres Nonstandard variant of *somewhere*. Not acceptable in college speech or writing.

sort (of) See **kind (of).**

strong verb A verb which uses a change in the vowel rather than inflectional endings to distinguish between present and past tenses [sing, sang, sung]. Weak verbs [walk, walked, walked] are regular, strong verbs irregular.

suffix A syllable added at the end of a word to make a derived word, as in *like + ly = likely, child + hood = childhood.*

suit — suite The common word is *suit* [a suit of clothes, follow suit (in cards), suit yourself, this doesn't suit me]. *Suite* means "retinue" [The President and his suite arrived late], "set" or "collection" [a dining room suite, a suite of rooms]. Check the pronunciation of these words in your dictionary.

sure = certainly This usage [I sure am annoyed; sure, I will go with you] is colloquial. Unless the style justifies colloquial usage, say *certainly* or *surely.*

swell = good, fine This usage [It was a swell show; we had a swell time] is slang. It is generally unacceptable in college writing.

symbol A word, signal, or sign. The word as contrasted with what it stands for. See **referent.**

synonym A word having the same meaning as a given word. Thus, *patio* is often a synonym for *courtyard.*

syntax The relationships of words within a sentence. The chief units of syntax are the subject, verb, object, and modifiers.

take and   This usage [In a fit of anger he took and smashed the bowl] is not acceptable in college writing. Simply say *smashed* [In a fit of anger he smashed the bowl].

take sick   This usage [He took sick and died] is disputed. Authorities differ in classifying it as established, dialectal, or regional. It would generally be safer to avoid it in college writing.

terrible, terribly   An overused colloquialism for *very* [She was terribly nice about it]. Its restrained use in informal papers is not objectionable.

terrific   Used at a formal level to mean "terrifying" and at a colloquial level as an intensive. The overuse of the colloquialism has rendered the word almost useless in formal writing. For most students the best thing to do with this word is to forget it.

theme   Used in two ways in college composition courses: (1) the dominant idea of an essay [The theme of this essay is that self-deception is the commonest of vices]; (2) a general name for a composition assignment [Write a 500-word theme for Monday]. The first meaning is synonymous with *thesis* as it is used in this book.

thesis   As used in this book, the dominant idea or purpose of an essay.

tho   A variant spelling of *though*. The longer form is preferred in formal usage.

through = finished   This usage [Aren't you through with that story yet?] is now accepted by all dictionaries consulted. "Finished" would be preferable in a formal style [Haven't you finished (*not* finished with) that story?].

tough   The uses of *tough* to mean "difficult" [a tough assignment], "hard fought" [It was a tough game], "hard to bear" [It was a tough blow for all of us] are accepted without qualification by reputable dictionaries.

toward, towards   Both forms are acceptable. *Toward* is more common in America, *towards* in Britain.

troop — troupe   Both words come from the same root and share the original meaning, "herd." In modern usage *troop* is used of soldiers and *troupe* of actors [a troop of cavalry, a troop of scouts; a troupe of circus performers, a troupe of entertainers].

try and   *Try to* is the preferred idiom. *Try and* would generally be acceptable in informal and colloquial styles.

understatement   The opposite of exaggeration. The device of deliberately saying less than one means, as in Winston Churchill's comment, "My life so far has not been entirely uneventful." Understatement is often used for ironic or humorous effect.

unique   The formal meaning of *unique* is "sole" or "only" [Adam had the unique distinction of being the only man who never had a mother]. The use of *unique* to mean "rare" or "unusual" [Spinal anesthetics allow the patient the unique experience of being a witness to his own appendectomy] has long been popular and is now accepted. But *unique* in the loose sense of uncommon [a very unique sweater] is generally frowned upon, especially when modified by an intensive adverb.

up   The adverb *up* is idiomatically used in many verb-adverb combinations which act as a single verb [break up, clean up, fill up, get up, tear up]. Often *up* adds a note of thoroughness to the action of the verb. Compare "They ate everything on their plates" with "They ate up everything on their plates." Avoid unnecessary or awkward separation of *up* from the verb with which it is combined, since this will have the effect of making *up* seem to be a single adverb modifying the verb rather than combining with it. For example, "They held the cashier up" is subject to misinterpretation; "She made her face up" is simply awkward. Say, "They held up the cashier," "She made up her face," "They filled up the front rows first."

used to   Notice the final *d* in *used*. We do not pronounce it in informal speech because it is elided before the *t* of *to*. But the phrase is written *used to,* not *use to.*

used to could   Nonstandard for *used to be able.* Not acceptable in college speech or writing.

very   A common and useful intensive, but avoid its overuse in any one paper.

vulgate   Synonymous with *nonstandard.* Any usage characteristic of uneducated speech.

wait on   *Wait on* means "serve" [A clerk will be here in a moment to wait on you]. The use of *wait on* to mean "wait for" [I'll wait on you if you won't be long] is a colloquialism to which there is some objection. Say *wait for* [I'll wait for you if you won't be long].

want for   The use of *for* or *should* after *want* in such sentences as "I want for you to come," "I want you should come," is not acceptable in college speech or writing. After *want* in this sense use the objective case plus an infinitive [I want you to come; I want them to go at once]. When the sentence does not require an object, the infinitive is used immediately after *want* [I want to go home; he wants to return next week].

want in, out, off   This usage [The dog wants in; I want out of there; I want off now] is colloquial. In college writing it would be safer to supply an infinitive after *wants:* "The dog wants to come in," etc.

want = ought   This usage [You want to save something every month; they want to be careful or they will be in trouble] is colloquial. *Ought* is the preferred idiom in college writing.

ways   Colloquial for *way* in such sentences as "You must have come a long ways from home," "They walked a long ways this morning." Except in a colloquial style the accepted form in college writing is *way* [You must have come a long way; they walked a long way].

when (in definitions)   In college writing avoid the use of a *when*-clause in defining a term [A comma splice is when you put a comma between two separate sentences]. Instead of *when* use a noun phrase or clause (A comma splice is the use of a comma between two separate sentences].

where (in definitions)   Same comment as for **when** above.

where . . . at, to   The use of *at* or *to* after *where* [Where was he at? Where are you going to?] is redundant. Simply say, "Where was he?" "Where are you going?"

where = that   The use of *where* in such sentences as "I heard on the radio where there was a violent storm in Chicago," "I see in the paper where the sniper was caught," may be occasionally acceptable in a colloquial style, but it is inappropriate in formal or informal writing. Use *that* [I heard on the radio that there was a violent storm in Chicago; I see in the paper that the sniper was caught].

which   *Which* is not used to refer to persons. It is used to refer to things [The house which he built]. When referring to persons use *who, whom,* or *that* [The man who is talking, the girl whom I love, the doctor that I called].

who — whom   In informal and colloquial writing *who* is often used instead of *whom* when the pronoun is in subject territory — that is, when it comes at the beginning of the sentence [Who is she marrying? Who are you look-ing for?]. This is the colloquial and informal usage of educated people, but in a formal style *whom* would be required [Whom is she marrying? For whom are you looking?].

-wise   Avoid adding the suffix *-wise,* meaning "concerning," to nouns to form such combinations as *budgetwise, jobwise, tastewise.* Some combined forms with *-wise* are thoroughly established [*clockwise, otherwise, sidewise, weather-wise*], but the fad of coining new compounds with this suffix is generally objectionable in English classes.

Xmas   Pronounced "Christmas." An informal abbreviation much used in busi-ness and advertising, but generally not appropriate in college writing.

you = one   The use of *you* as an indefinite pronoun instead of the formal *one* is characteristic of an informal style, but be sure that this impersonal use will be recognized by the reader; otherwise he is likely to interpret a general statement as a personal remark addressed to him. Generally avoid shifting from "one" to "you" within a sentence.

INDEX

Abbreviations, 458–459; in footnotes, 275–276, 278; punctuation of, 440

Absolute construction, 379–380, 381; as interrupting element, 401; as parenthetical clause, 412, 413

Accusative case. *See* Objective case

Acronym, 469

Active voice, 156–157, 373

Actor-action sequence, 375, 376

Address: punctuation of, 431; in business letters, 474

Adjective-adverb, confusion of, 427–428

Adjective clause, position of, 400

Adjective phrase, position of, 400

Adjectives, 373–374, 380; attributive, 374; predicate, 374; comparison of, 374, 477; position of, 400; complements of sensory verbs, 426; confusion with adverbs, 427–428

Adverbial clause, position of, 400

Adverbs, 373–374, 380; interrogative, 374; as sentence modifiers, 374; conjunctive, 374; comparison of, 374, 477; position of, 400; confusion with adjectives, 427–428

Agreement (pronoun-antecedent), 414, 420–423

Agreement (subject-verb), 414–415; with compound subject, 415; with indefinite pronouns, 417; with relative pronouns, 417; with introductory expletive, 417–418; with collective noun, 418–419; with titles, 419; with plural numbers, 419; with nouns plural in form only, 419–420

Agreement (tenses). *See* Sequence of tenses

Agreement, method of (in argument), 338

Alliteration, 470

Allusions, 184–185

Almanacs, 243

Alternative syllogism, 350–351

Ambiguous order (in sentences), 401–402

Ambiguous terms (in syllogism), 347

Ampersand, 471

Analogy (in argument), 340–342; false, 341; trivial, 358–359; (in exposition), 41–43, 50, 62. *See also* Comparison

Analysis: as tool of thought, 38; causal, 74–76, 82; of sentence structure, 150; of words, 193–195; of examination questions, 205–207; technical, 219, 223–224

Analytical pattern of organization, 67–75

Antecedent: in hypothetical syllogism, 349; agreement of pronoun with, 414, 420–423

Antonym, 471

Apostrophe, 446

Apposition, 471

Appositives, punctuation of, 433–434

Argument: defined, 76; basic structure (premise-conclusion relationship), 76–79, 333; conclusion, 76, 82–83, 333, 344; premise, 76, 82–83, 98–99, 333–334; inference, 77, 333, 334, 343–344; persuasiveness of, 333; reliability in, 333, 343–344; induction, 334–342; deduction, 342–352; combined induction and deduction, 353–354; fallacies, 354–359

Argumentative pattern of organization, 76–82

Argumentum ad hominem, 356

Arts, reference material on, 244

As . . . as construction, 471

Assonance, 472

Asterisk, 472

Attributive adjective, 374

Author card, 237

Autobiographical essay, elements of, 7–10

Auxiliary verb, 472

Balanced sentence, 147–148

Begging the question, 354–355

Bibliography: preliminary in research procedure, 253, 255–256; defined, 255; use of cards for, 256; form of, 256–261; final, 262, 272–273

Biography, reference material on, 244–245

Correction Symbols

adj	Use adjective instead of adverb (p. 426)
adv	Use adverb instead of adjective (p. 427)
agr	Make circled words agree (subject-verb, pp. 414-419; pronoun-antecedent, pp. 420-422; tenses, pp. 407-410)
apos	Use apostrophe (p. 446)
bib	Check form of bibliography (pp. 256-262)
cap	Use capital letter(s) (pp. 459-461)
case	Incorrect case form (pp. 411-413)
chop	Choppy sentences (pp. 142-144)
cs	Comma splice (pp. 390-391)
d	Indicated diction needs revision
det	Provide details (pp. 110-113)
det?	Details not pertinent (pp. 113-114)
dg	Dangling modifier (pp. 394-395)
fn	Check form of footnote(s) (pp. 274-278)
frag	Sentence fragment (pp. 386-387)
gen	Diction or statement too general (pp. 179-181)
id	Incorrect idiom (p. 172)
lc	No capital. Use small letter(s) (pp. 459-461)
lev	Confusion of stylistic levels (pp. 178-179)
log	Faulty logic
no	Use numbers (pp. 464-466)
ns	Nonstandard usage (p. 170)
¶	Begin new paragraph
no ¶	No paragraph
p	Punctuation needed
no p	No punctuation needed
ref	Clarify reference of pronoun (pp. 423-424) or modifier (pp. 401-402)
rep	Undesirable repetition
sep	Undesirable separation (pp. 403-404)
sp	Consult dictionary for correct spelling
t	Use correct tense form (pp. 407-410)
wo	Revise word order
wordy	Reduce wordiness (pp. 152-155)
wr	Write out: do not use abbreviations (p. 458) or numbers (pp. 464-466)
ww	Wrong word
?	Illegible word
∧	Something omitted
/	Remove word, letter, or punctuation so slashed
x	Careless error
,/;/	Provide punctuation indicated